Doing Quantitative Research
in the
Social Sciences

Doing Quantitative Research in the Social Sciences

An Integrated Approach to Research Design, Measurement and Statistics

Thomas R. Black

Los Angeles | London | New Delhi
Singapore | Washington DC

First published 1999

Reprinted 2003, 2005, 2009

SAGE Publications Ltd
1 Oliver's Yard
55 City Road
London EC1Y 1SP

SAGE Publications Inc.
2455 Teller Road
Thousand Oaks, California 91320

SAGE Publications India Pvt Ltd
B 1/I 1 Mohan Cooperative Industrial Area
Mathura Road
New Delhi 110 044

SAGE Publications Asia-Pacific Pte Ltd
33 Pekin Street #02-01
Far East Square
Singapore 048763

British Library Cataloguing in Publication data

A catalogue record for this book is available from the British Library

ISBN   978-0-7619-5352-4 (hbk)
ISBN   978-0-7619-5353-1 (pbk)

Library of Congress catalog card number 98-61330

Typeset by Alden Bookset
Printed and bound in Great Britain by
Antony Rowe, Chippenham, Wiltshire
Printed on paper from sustainable resources

FSC
Mixed Sources
Product group from well-managed
forests and other controlled sources
Cert no. SGS-COC-2953
www.fsc.org
© 1996 Forest Stewardship Council

CONTENTS

Preface   vii

PART I INTRODUCTION TO RESEARCH DESIGN

1   The Nature of Enquiry   2

2   Beginning the Design Process   27

3   Initial Sources of Invalidity and Confounding   59

4   Basic Designs   87

5   Identifying Populations and Samples   110

6   Additional Sources of Confounding by the Measurement Process
    and Interactions   140

7   Refining the Designs   157

PART II MEASUREMENT DESIGN

8   Principles of Measurement and Collecting Factual Data   188

9   Measuring Attitudes, Opinions and Views   215

10 Measuring Achievement   242

11 Evaluating Data Quality: Determining Instrument Reliability and
    Validity   272

PART III TURNING DATA INTO INFORMATION USING STATISTICS

12 Descriptive Statistics Using a Spreadsheet   304

13 Probability and Statistical Significance   337

14 Power, Errors and Choosing α 372

PART IV EX POST FACTO, EXPERIMENTAL AND QUASI-EXPERIMENTAL DESIGNS: PARAMETRIC TESTS

15	Comparing Two Groups: t-test	402
16	One-way Analysis of Variance	441
17	Factorial Designs	484
18	Randomized Block Designs and Analysis of Covariance	514

PART V NONPARAMETRIC TESTS: NOMINAL AND ORDINAL VARIABLES

19	Nonparametric Tests: One and Two Samples	550
20	Nonparametric Tests: Multiple and Related Samples	584

PART VI DESCRIBING NON-CAUSAL RELATIONSHIPS

21	Correlation and Association	618
22	Regression	659
	Postscript	695
	Appendices	
A	An Introduction to Spreadsheets	699
B	Statistical tables	716
	Glossary of Mathematical Symbols, Equations and Excel Functions	731
	Bibliography	741
	Index	746

PREFACE

This book is aimed at students in the social sciences, education and related subjects who have only a basic background in statistics and quantitative research design. It builds on the assumption that the reader has mastered the content of (i.e., has acquired the concepts and fundamental interpretative skills presented in) *Evaluating Social Science Research: An Introduction* (Black, 1993) or a comparable introductory text on research that introduces basic research design, measurement, and descriptive and inferential statistical concepts.

The emphasis of this book is on the *design and execution* of research projects, and includes issues of planning and sampling, measurement, choice of statistical model, and interpretation of results. Frequently, the topics of research design, measurement and statistics tend to be covered in three separate texts and any links are left to the struggling student or novice researcher, who too often finds it difficult to integrate these. The aim of this book is to encourage researchers to consider all the assumptions and their interactions when making decisions. They need to take into account the interrelationships between 'technologies' when designing the structure of the study, creating measuring instruments, collecting data, selecting statistical tools, and interpreting the results. As others have said, it is not just a matter of adopting a quantitative emphasis. What is important is to apply a scientific approach with sufficient rigour to produce valid conclusions, one that usually requires the collection of quantitative data and the use of statistical tools. This obliges us not only to acquire specific analytic skills but also to become social *scientists* in more than just name. To keep the emphasis on research in general, the variables in examples have been kept simple and restricted to everyday occurrences and basic concepts from sociology, psychology, education and commerce. This leaves the instructor or tutor with the freedom to supplement the activities in the book with problems more idiosyncratic to his or her discipline.

Designing research is a combination of creativity and techniques like many endeavours in life, including oil painting. History tells us that seventeenth-century artists, such as Rembrandt, regularly had 'schools' where apprentices came to learn the skills of the master. Sometimes they duplicated his work in an endeavour to practise a technique – for example, presenting the drapery qualities of the dress, facial details, or a sense of depth in landscapes. The seventeenth-century Dutch artists painted for accuracy and could almost be thought of as the photographers of their day, and, as such, observed and recorded much about society then. As a result, we have greater insights into dress, the countryside, housing, status and social events, as illustrated by such artists as Vermeer, van Ruisdael, de Hoogh, Verspronck and Steen. Yet a considerable part of the creativity in their painting was manifest in the choice of the scene, not just the application of techniques, just as the quality of research is dependent on asking the right questions as much as on collecting, interpreting and presenting data.

One important difference exists between these seventeenth-century social recorders and contemporary social scientists: unlike them, we endeavour to be objective. Rembrandt almost did not receive payment for one of his better-known pictures, *The Night Watch* (1642), a massive portrait of 20 or more local worthies, because he employed artistic licence in arranging their portraits on the canvas. Many of the 'subjects' were upset about their placement since they felt the arrangement did not properly represent their real status in local society. While artistic licence is not an option in research and unbiased objectivity is a goal to strive for, this does not eliminate the need for great creativity in the design and execution of a study. As with 'schools' everywhere, your teacher can provide you with skills and techniques using this book as a resource, encouraging you not just to copy but to make your own decisions. Teaching is still much the same after several centuries: you learn from existing practice and step off from there, but you must practise making decisions as well as mastering techniques.

STRUCTURE

This is a 'how to' book in the sense that it guides the researcher, but it is *not* a cookbook in the sense that it tells you the *only* way to do it. It does have some recipes, but you are the caterer or chef and consequently must make all the decisions. It provides assistance by raising issues to be addressed and questions to be answered, accompanied by guidelines and criteria for decisions to be made during the processes of designing a study, collecting and processing the data and drawing conclusions. There is practice in decision-making in the form of numbered activities placed throughout each chapter. These allow you to consider critically research designs, the development of measurement instruments and the choice of statistical tests, as well as an opportunity to learn how to use computer-based tools. In the chapters on statistics, these activities are a planned part of the process of understanding of what underlies tests rather than just practice exercises at the end of a chapter. Throughout, each one is an endeavour to make you an active rather than a passive learner. The book also refers to other texts that take specific approaches, skills or techniques to even greater depths. As complex as research design, measurement and statistics are, it is not surprising to find whole books that will elaborate on what is presented in one or two chapters here.

In the sections on statistics, the emphasis is on using statistical tests as decision support tools, rather than having the tests make the decisions for you. The book avoids the task of carrying out long calculations on paper or calculators and instead focuses on using a readily available software package, the Excel spreadsheet and occasionally SPSS-PC. Excel worksheets also offer a medium for modelling the statistical tests in such a way as to allow the user to ask 'What if . . .?' questions. Using these, you will be able not only to explore the factors that influence the outcomes of statistical tests, but also to make predictions on likely sample sizes required for a study. When carrying out statistical tests, the emphasis will be on deciding why a particular technique or test is the most appropriate, what assumptions underlie its use, what the results actually tell the researcher, how to enter data to obtain results and how to interpret them. It is a little easier to enter data for processing on a spreadsheet than it is to use more sophisticated statistical packages, and the test mechanisms can be more transparent. Graphical output is easy to achieve using spreadsheets, though users must protect themselves against poor choice of 'default' settings. If it is necessary to use a more powerful package, such as SPSS, it is possible to bring in raw data from worksheets easily.

The examples have been contrived to be conceptually simple and not restricted to any one discipline. This leaves the tutor or instructor free to choose additional subject-based examples for use in class or as additional activities.

TIME

Ideally, the teaching of all the material in the book would result in dividing it into *two* 15-credit (CATS) postgraduate modules in the UK, equivalent to two 3-semester-hour courses in the USA, presented over two academic terms or semesters. Each should engage the learner in about 130 hours of class work and self-study, though this is an estimated mean. Individual differences in background, basic mathematical ability and learning rate will influence the actual time spent. While the original aim was to make each chapter about a week's work, they are not all equally demanding in terms of time since the material did not naturally lend itself to clean divisions. None of the statistical sections will require more than secondary or high school level sophistication in mathematics. If the whole text were used, the first module or course would focus on quantitative studies in general, including basic research designs and sampling, measurement issues, and descriptive statistics (Chapters 1–12). The second would continue with quantitative analysis, including the statistical tools needed for experimental and quasi-experimental designs, and correlations, covering both parametric and nonparametric tests (Chapters 13–22). Throughout, the emphasis is on the integration of the three skill areas – design, measurement and statistics – to assist the learner in understanding the interrelationships and interdependency of these.

A SUMMARY OF THE CONTENT

Part I: Introduction to Research Design

Chapter 1 introduces the idea of a scientific approach to social science research, showing its relationship to the development of theories as well as its role in solving more practical problems. The complementary association with qualitative studies provides an eclectic view of research. It is suggested that understanding is cyclic in nature and that all answers should be considered tentative. While quantitative data are important, they should be considered as an artefact of scientific enquiry. The true nature of this approach lies in the analytic and design skills that researchers must develop.

Chapter 2 presents an overview of the design process, the choice of a research question and the development of hypotheses is presented. This approach treats the design of research as an iterative process (systems approach model), needing continual analysis of intent, evaluation of processes and procedures, rigour, and awareness of assumptions behind any statistical tests employed. The main stages are outlined, and readers encouraged to keep records of all decisions to allow the analysis and evaluation of their own research process and procedures. The overall validity of the outcomes of a study will depend on various component validities: internal, external, construct and statistical.

Problems of stating a question of sufficient, but not too ambitious, scope will be considered, with an emphasis on research projects. The research should be one whose variables can be operationally defined in the form of potentially reliable and valid instruments, with some anticipation of potential data collection problems. Any design will be refined in conjunction with the choice of statistical tests and reality of data collection. Since these are covered in later chapters, the designs at this stage will be tentative. Activities on stating hypotheses for given exemplar questions are provided.

Eight sources of threats to internal, external, construct and statistical validity are introduced in Chapter 3, based upon Campbell and Stanley's (1963) schema, elaborated in Cook and Campbell (1979). In this and the next chapter, a brief survey of basic models for design of quantitative research are presented as a basis for translating hypotheses into an action plan. These first-level designs are revised and refined as additional issues are covered in subsequent chapters. In this chapter, three pre-experimental designs are used to illustrate the possible sources of invalidity in research. Each design is presented with an example that includes a statistical test employed to illustrate the links between design, sampling, measurement and statistics.

The coverage of possible designs continues in Chapter 4, with two experimental, one quasi-experimental and two ex post facto models, each considered in light of the eight potential sources of invalidity and confounding introduced in Chapter 3.

Initial implications for even tentative designs require a careful definition of population(s). Decisions will have to be made on anticipated level of generalizability of the results, which will determine sampling needs (external validity). In Chapter 5 various techniques serving experimental, quasi-experimental and ex post facto designs, as well as survey sampling approaches, will be described with examples provided, with an activity on devising sampling techniques for given exemplar populations. Ways of avoiding being left with 'volunteers' through care in the initial design and chasing subjects will be considered. With a general aim to ensure the highest possible representativeness and avoiding confounding (threatening internal validity), there will be a need to ensure that criticism of non-responses can be defended by justifying that non-response has nothing to do with the research or the instruments. An introduction to ethical issues is provided, since it relates closely to sampling.

In Chapter 6, seven more potential extraneous confounding variables related to measurement issues are introduced and interactions among the various sources discussed. To illustrate the consequences, the three pre-experimental designs introduced in Chapter 3 will be used as examples.

Chapter 7 continues the coverage of basic designs, revisiting the two experimental, the quasi-experimental and two ex post facto designs in Chapter 4. In addition, two more designs (one experimental and one quasi-experimental) are introduced to show how to overcome some limitations of the other designs. These sources introduce limitations due, in particular, to measurement, thus it is appropriate to pause and digress into this area before considering statistical tests.

Part II: Measurement Design

Basic concepts and criteria for the design of measuring instruments are introduced in Chapter 8 to ensure that the resulting operational definitions are valid, reliable and objective. The definition of construct validity is elaborated and other related validities defined. Starting with the most straightforward form of data collection, factual information is used to illustrate how these concepts are manifested in real situations.

Chapter 9 is an introduction to the design of questionnaires and observation schedules that will serve as operational definitions of constructs defining attitudes, opinions, perceptions and views of subjects.

Chapter 10 discusses techniques for establishing validity, enhancing reliability, and ensuring objectivity of instruments in the cognitive domain, such as content tests, class examinations and aptitude tests related to skills. A variety of testing techniques is introduced, including paper based objective and free response, as well as oral and observation.

Part II concludes by considering, in Chapter 11, trials of measuring instruments and selection of the most appropriate items by carrying out an item analysis and reliability calculations. The process provides techniques for identifying questions needing improvement based upon a trial of the instrument. The numbered activities provide guidance on setting out the different types of item analysis on spreadsheets to facilitate calculation and to illustrate relationships among factors that influence reliability.

Part III: Turning Data into Information Using Statistics

The presentation of quantitative results graphically can greatly enhance communication. Chapter 12 introduces the advantages and limitations of software-generated graphs and tables, with an emphasis on what appropriate practice is and how to override software defaults that produce deceptive graphs. Calculating means, standard deviations, medians and quartiles is demonstrated. There are several activities that involve using spreadsheet software to generate frequency tables, measures of central tendency, variability, and various types of graphs for given data.

Chapter 13 presents the notion of probability, the Gaussian curve, normal distributions, statistical significance and hypothesis testing, with underlying assumptions. The z-test for determining whether a sample belongs to a known population is also introduced. There are spreadsheet activities to allow one to see the interrelations among design factors and their impact on test outcomes.

The choices of statistical test, the level of significance and the interpretation of results are often misunderstood. Chapter 14 allows the exploration of Type I and II errors and power, plus how they influence the choice of test and level of significance. Spreadsheet-based activities allow one to see the effect of changing sample size, level of significance, instrument reliability and magnitude of difference between groups, on the potential for a test to support conclusions. In subsequent chapters, power will be employed as one factor to consider when planning the details of a design in anticipation of statistical analysis.

Part IV: Experimental, Quasi-experimental and Ex Post Facto Designs: Parametric Tests

Using previous research, one can plan experimental, quasi-experimental and ex post facto designs that involve two groups. Chapter 15 includes a review of statistical significance between/among groups. Several forms of the t-test will be introduced, along with criteria for choice and underlying assumptions of each. Risks of Type I and II errors will be considered with reference to types of data, measurement issues, power and potential degradation. Activities on proposing variables to control and investigate for exemplar situations are provided.

Chapter 16 considers how to identify when ANOVA is most appropriate for answering research questions. Basic underlying assumptions are introduced and corrections for violating homogeneity of variance provided. Resolving design issues with reference to power using spreadsheet models allows the investigation of interactions among sample size, magnitude of differences across means, and standard deviations. Problems of control of variables and interaction of variables will be addressed with reference to sources of confounding discussed in earlier chapters. The interpretation of ANOVA results, including interactions, will be complemented by activities using sample data. This includes post hoc analysis and addresses the question of how to decide which one is most appropriate, based on relative conservatism of tests: Tukey, Scheffé, Duncan, Neumann–Keuls, etc.

Factorial designs, the subject of Chapter 17, provide the opportunity to investigate more interesting combinations and interactions of variables, but also provide a challenge for interpretation of results. There are activities on interpreting outcomes of factorial designs plus several using the spreadsheet model of the statistical test. These include post hoc analysis and power calculations, allowing the investigation of consequences of design decisions.

There will be situations where analysis of variance is not sufficient to control all the extraneous variables and results of such a test would be misleading. The two approaches considered in Chapter 18, randomized block designs and analysis of covariance (ANCOVA), allow for the control of variables that are often entry characteristics of subjects that would influence the outcomes. Randomized block designs include both matched samples and repeated measures; there is a spreadsheet model for this test. For ANCOVA, the emphasis is on considering when it is appropriate to use this test and the interpretation of the results from SPSS output.

Part V: Nonparametric Tests: Nominal and Ordinal Variables

Our treatment of nonparametric tests is divided into two chapters, the first covering one- and two-sample cases and the second dealing with multiple and related samples. Chapter 19 provides a set of nonparametric analogues to the z- and t-tests. This includes an introduction to the chi-square test for one- and two-sample situations. The chi-square distribution will be considered and activities on a worksheet will be carried out to illustrate its role in resolving hypotheses, with power calculations. Kolmogorov–Smirnov and Wilcoxon tests are introduced for situations where the dependent variable is at least ordinal.

Other selected tests will be introduced in Chapter 20; exemplar data are processed in spreadsheet activities to illustrate the use of these. The choice of tests based upon error analysis and power considerations is discussed and links with measurement issues are raised. The tests covered include chi-square for $m \times k$ tables and the Kruskal–Wallis one-way analysis of variance for independent groups. For matched or related groups, the McNemar change, Wilcoxon for two matched groups, Cochran Q and Friedman two-way analysis of variance tests are provided. A major activity at the end focuses on the choice of parametric and nonparametric tests for a variety of cases.

Part VI: Describing Non-causal Relationships

The type of research questions that can be answered and the limitations of correlational results are reviewed in Chapter 21. Activities are provided on the interpretation of correlations and on the selection of variables to correlate, using cases describing data collected. Various parametric and nonparametric coefficients, their calculations, and how they are interpreted are considered, with activities that use a spreadsheet as a data-processing tool for sample data. These include Pearson's product moment, Spearman's rho, Cramér's C, phi and point biserial coefficients.

Chapter 22 introduces regression equations, drawing regression lines, and their use as prediction tools. Many packages now have this functionality built in, thus the focus is on how to employ the approach. Activities will include data analysis on a spreadsheet and the interpretation of both linear and multiple regression equations.

ACKNOWLEDGEMENTS

Finally, I would like to thank all the students who have used these materials in various courses for providing comments on their content, structure and learning potential. In particular, I would like to thank George Dines, Maizam Alias and Brian Wilson for their detailed comments and recommendations on each chapter. Not only were these sources of feedback students at the time, but teachers, thus their insight has been particularly valuable. Recognition must go to Richard Leigh who not only carefully copy-edited the entire book, but also made valuable comments on wording that added clarity where it was needed. The reviews on the content provided by Professor Richard Pugh of Indiana University and Daniel Wright of the University of Bristol were of particular benefit. Simon Ross of Sage provided needed support and arranged reviews by others at various stages that also contributed significantly to the development of the book. Rosemary Campbell of Sage ensured that the final product is well-presented, including my occasional novel page layout requirements. I would also like to thank the University of Surrey for providing funding for half-time for a year to work on the material, with special thanks to Faith Butt for convincing them it was worthwhile. Without their support, it would still be interred in the word processor. I would also like to thank my wife, Sandy, for her patience while I worked on what seemed like a never-ending task, and for reading and providing valuable comments on all the chapters. As always, the responsibility for the final product is mine.

Thomas R. Black
University of Surrey

Teaching support materials prepared by the author can be downloaded from:

http://www.sagepub.co.uk/books/details/b005869.html

Part I
Introduction to
Research Design

The Nature of Enquiry

1

Ways of viewing the world

It is human nature to try to explain what we observe occurring around us, a process that people engaged in long before physical, biological or social sciences were established as disciplines. The difference between 'common sense' explanations and scientific ones lies in the way the two originate. Everyday observations are haphazard, careless and not systematic, whereas those carried out by scientists endeavour to be specific, objective, well focused and systematic, to the extent that they could be replicated by someone else. So what difference does it make in the long term? If we were just to sit around passively and contemplate life, it might not matter on what basis explanations were derived. In reality, however, decisions are made about people, objects and events, often on the basis of explanations of why things happen, and extrapolations as to what would happen under certain circumstances. Incomplete or even incorrect explanations lead to poor if not disastrous decisions, whether they be about bridge construction, social conditions in high-rise apartment blocks or the effects of stress on individuals. While there are few true guarantees, the more systematic and organized the studies we conduct, the more likely they will produce valid explanations that can be used to support decisions.

In the social sciences, achieving a thorough understanding of a situation often requires constructing a model of events and how people interact. The acquisition of information to support such a model may come from a number of sources, some of which will be more organized and systematic than others. In some situations what is needed is sufficient understanding to make a sound decision, while in others the goal is more academic, the refinement of an elaborate model. Figure 1.1 outlines a simplistic way of considering the processes employed for understanding the world around us. In reality, final choices, decisions, judgements and model building are usually based on the simultaneous or collective employment of more than one of these, though there may not be a conscious effort to include more than one.

This view of building understanding and decision-making introduces a variety of concepts, some of which will be more familiar than others. All of them, though, are in need of defining if an appreciation of how this book proposes to contribute to the realm of developing an ordered view of the world is to be achieved. The first division, if you like, is between empirical and non-empirical approaches – basically a difference between directly collecting information from outside ourselves, and using indirect sources, vicarious experiences and introspection. As will be seen, there are situations where all of these unavoidably come into play when decisions are made, and entire courses of study cover individual approaches. This book is no exception in that it can only focus on a limited area and enhance the development of appropriate skills.

Empirical approaches

To lay a foundation for considering primarily the branches on the far right of Figure 1.1, empirical systematic, we need to have a common understanding of terminology. *Empirical* indicates that the information, knowledge and understanding are gathered through experience and direct data collection. Daily we gather information just through contact with others and our environment, but it is not necessarily intentional or conscious, and usually not very systematic. Thus it is not difficult to miss events or to observe them in an inappropriate context. The police have a difficult time finding reliable witnesses to crimes or other events, since people just do not know what to look for and are not trained to do so in stressful situations. Systematic observation implies that we know what type of event we are expecting to see, though not necessarily the actual outcome. Identifying a 20-year-old actor dressed as a 70-year-old woman in a shopping mall is not as easy as it may seem, particularly if you do not expect to encounter such a person. A trained observer might succeed where the casual

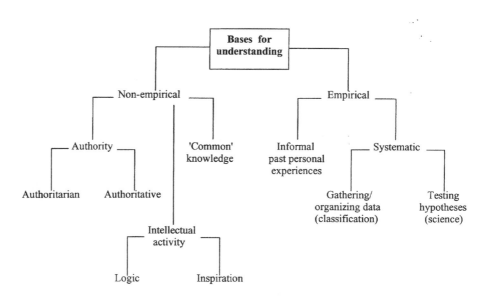

FIGURE 1.1
Foundations for
understanding

encounter would result in a perfect deception. Yet as will be seen, there is more to it than just observation and classification when the issues become more complex. The emphasis in this text will be on techniques that enhance one's ability to make systematic observations and use these as part of the process of testing guesses (hypotheses) about how events can be described. Such an approach is usually described as *scientific* because of its systematic approach and goal of producing replicable studies, but this does not necessarily divorce it from humanity nor simply reduce people to the status of numbers on a computer file.

Non-empirical approaches

Non-empirical sources of information include forms of introspection, vicarious experiences and other people's analysis of events. Like empirical sources, some of these are more valid as a basis for understanding and decision-making than others. For example, when we refer to an *authority*, the source may be someone who issues instructions that must be followed regardless of the reason why (*authoritarian*) or someone who expresses a position on the basis of vicarious and systematic first-hand experiences (*authoritative*). You may consider the university to be authoritarian for dictating that you must take a particular course for your degree, but the teacher to be authoritative because of his or her knowledge and experience in the subject. You accept what is presented in a course as truth, even if it is based upon someone else's experiences. Vicarious learning is necessary if for no other reason than there is not time to learn everything first-hand. We may accept that wholewheat bread is 'better' for us (even if we do not eat it) because someone else has taken the time and effort to demonstrate its benefits.

It is well recognized that '*common*' *knowledge* is a significant part of any culture. We all 'know' that all lawyers are just interested in making money, politicians lie only when their lips move, and that Scotch is better than rye whiskey. Some statements such as these are more easily verifiable than others, and others are not worth the effort (except possibly to the advertising industry). For example, European cultures tend to value the nuclear family, while in most parts of Africa the extended family is paramount. The issue of an indisputable universal 'best' simply does not arise in many situations, since traditions, values and beliefs have evolved over time and are part of that culture. What becomes of interest to the social scientist is the relative truth of some of these – for example, stereotypes of ethnic groups. If it were not for the fact that these have been exploited to the extreme of inciting genocide more than once in the history of humankind, it might be a topic only of academic interest.

The third major source of non-empirical understanding is *intellectual*, what goes on between our ears. Whole courses are taught about *logic*, and the world would be quite chaotic without it. Rarely, though, is logic capable of providing complete understanding on its own. As history has shown, in isolation or with limited information some rather bizarre explanations have arisen, such as the flat-earth model. This is not to belittle logic as a way of knowing, but, like all of these, alone it is limited.

At the other extreme are the experiences that fall in the category of *inspiration*, which could originate from a mystical or religious experience, but could also include others where we gain some sort of insight that governs or changes the course of our lives. What inspires us to choose a career? Is it logic, collecting information, having work experience, or reading about job descriptions and then weighing up all the alternatives? Or how many of us *decide* in the dark of night because of some inspiration? Most likely it is a combination of information gathering, logic, listening to authorities, and personal inspiration. Religion, political and philosophical commitments, and even choice of spouse, probably result also from this sort of event. The computer dating agency may seem scientific and encourage a logical approach, but in the end why pick one person over another? People have gained insight or altered their views through mysticism or inspiration triggered by such varying experiences as listening to music, reading religious tracts, viewing scenery or talking to someone. While such experiences provide personal insight, they are difficult to share and are limited in their value as a common source of understanding that can be shared across a wider audience.

Integrated thinking

Let us return to an integrated view of thinking in social sciences for a moment, having dissected the basis for understanding and classified the parts. Consider, for example, cultural values and their interaction with government policy, and recall from recent history a rather extreme but real case. We all have relatives, regardless of which our society values more, the extended family or the nuclear family. In recent years, China has tried to contend with an exploding population by having a policy (*authority*) of one child per family. An interesting *logical* consequence of this will be that after two generations, there could be no aunts or uncles. What will be the long-term impact on family, society and culture? To answer this question, does one depend only on

- logic (if no uncles, then . . .),
- 'common' knowledge or informal past personal experience (I know someone whose parents were only children, and they . . .) or
- a more systematic *gathering* of experiences and *testing of hypotheses*?

One would hope that policies imposed as a consequence of economic, political and environmental needs would have been researched in terms of potential outcomes, based on comprehensive models of society, social interaction and personal development. Sources of understanding in such situations could be based on empirical systematic studies of contemporary societies, combined with the consideration of past parallel situations (vicarious learning), and perceived values of those whose culture will be changed. Yet history is littered with cases where this has not been done, or the flawed models on which decisions are made have been untested, poorly tested, or in some cases based solely upon one source of understanding alone. The consequences have frequently been unfortunate for the targets of actions based on such representations of reality.

One corner of the chart

As noted earlier, this book will focus on one corner of Figure 1.1, on empirical systematic approaches, with some concern for gathering, but primarily with the aim of testing hypotheses in situations where there are quantitative data. In light of everyday experience with people and the study of human activity, one other goal of this text should be expressed at this point. While it is human nature to want to be 'right', the rather grand aim here is to provide the skills with which one is better equipped to pursue the 'truth'. This has the disconcerting consequence that sometimes when resolving issues, our preferred view of the world may not be shown to be the best or most accurate. As human beings, it hurts to admit that we are somehow wrong. The story is told of a physics professor who commented to a class that he regretted doing his Ph.D. at a certain university because the research team pursued the 'wrong' model of the nucleus. He believed that had he gone elsewhere and worked on the 'right' model, his efforts might have been recognized. The unfortunate aspect of models is that they are rarely right or wrong, but dynamic (ever changing) and often have a limited life (until a better one comes along).

It is no different in the social sciences. The pursuit of the truth is desirable, but often this constitutes trying to develop a *model* of reality, an explanation of events employing abstract and intangible concepts. Have you ever seen poverty? Not likely, but you may have seen the consequences: poor health, inadequate housing, etc. Have you ever seen an electron? Neither has any physicist, though we all use electric lights to read by. Even with such well-established models for describing why electric light bulbs give off light, the physics community would be willing to consider alternatives were they to be presented. Human nature being what it is, though, it is usually easier to achieve acceptance of new models after the originator (and his or her disciples) have passed on to the big research room in the sky. To assume such a position, ideally one must be more like a judge in a court looking for the truth, rather than a lawyer trying to prove he or she is right.

While focusing on the systematic pursuit of truth, we will obviously draw upon other sources of understanding in Figure 1.1. 'Common' knowledge provides us with views of the world to test for accuracy which will be combined with the expectation that any study is logically consistent throughout. Since time is limited, other authorities will be consulted for vicarious experiences and previous developments. Now let us consider a more formal way of describing the nature of explanations and how their validity can be enhanced.

THEORIES, LAWS AND INFORMATION

At the foundation of the process of trying to understand events and their causes are observations, which necessarily must be distinguished from inferences. From a distance, we see a man walking erratically down the street and could infer that he is drunk or on drugs, is ill with a nasty virus, or has had a stroke and lost some of his co-ordination. If we approach the man, additional observations will allow us to decide which inference is the most accurate. In more systematic research, we often wish to infer the existence of a mental state based on observations. For example, is seeing a smile sufficient evidence for inferring the existence of a state of pleasure? It might be in very small children, but in adults, who are much more sophisticated in their social interactions, the smile and 'Have a nice day!' greeting may be more of a wish than an existing state of mind.

As part of understanding the world around us, we engage in classification of people and events, sometimes with the intent of judging, other times just for the sake of knowing where they fit in our personal scheme of things. That was a good film, a handsome lad, an attractive blonde, a poor person, a tedious lecture. These often constitute potential *variables*, non-constant traits, which allow us to consider the possibility of relationships. Is there any relationship between the clothes worn and the perception of 'handsomeness'? Do blondes have more fun? What contributes to poverty? Data gathered as a result of such questions might result in verifiable relationships – for example, people who live in poverty tend to have parents who also lived in poverty. Fashionable clothes may tend to make men appear more handsome than they would in less stylish apparel. From such results, *laws* may be formed that describe relationships among variables, but these may not describe causality. Also, since they describe isolated variables, they do not give a very complete picture, which is not surprising since rarely are events so simple as to be completely explained by one simple law.

To provide a more complete explanation of events in ours lives, *theories* – models and explanations that elaborate on why events have occurred – are devised to describe causal relationships between actions and/or events. These may involve a number of laws – relationships among variables – that appear to influence events. The value of a theory is in its ability to allow us to explain and predict outcomes, though often it can be found to be incomplete. Gathering supporting evidence to extend the applicability of a theory to *all* possible situations is not feasible for many reasons. The main limitation is simply one of scale: it is unlikely that a single study could cover all the relationships in all the situations described by a theory of any consequence. Many research studies, therefore, are tests of limited subsets of relationships to allow for maximum control over unwanted variables, to avoid ethical problems, and/or simply to contend with the difficulties of using human subjects. One challenge to the researcher is to ensure that the study of a component of a theory fits like a puzzle piece in order to enhance its impact on the theory as a whole.

As our understanding of a given situation improves, so the theory may change. But if the observations that underpin a theory are not systematic and replicable, the theory will develop in an erratic manner. Thus, based on observations, some people have elaborate theories to explain the existence of flying saucers, the inferiority of minority groups, and basic suspicions about the honesty of politicians. We all have pet theories developed from reading the newspapers (digested data), personal first-hand observations (not necessarily representative), and beliefs (religious, political, ethical). The building of theories in the physical and biological sciences usually results from carefully managed, manipulated and restricted observations and measurements. Unfortunately, in the social sciences the attempts at understanding human actions and interactions are often based on observations and data collection in relatively less well-controlled conditions. Human beings are notoriously uncooperative subjects. Thus sufficiently rigorous research to support theories tends to be very demanding intellectually, requiring great ingenuity, deep insight into the problem, and imaginative ways of controlling the numerous variables that will ultimately impinge on the situation being investigated. Scientists need numerous skills if they are going to achieve their goal of building theories that can withstand scrutiny and continual testing. This will be achieved through new studies as well as the replication of those that may have been the original basis for the theory.

Such a dynamic approach to describing the world has led to the explanation of science as being a process, rather than a set of products, static ideas or answers. The view is that science is the ongoing process of refining models and consequently any explanation is the *best* possible at the time, based on available information, understanding and models. This does not mean that anyone's theory is acceptable, but that no matter how well a theory is substantiated, it can always be improved. Theories include models of the world but do *not* constitute reality. No theory is perfect and yet in the spirit of contemporary science would strive for the unachievable, the perfect theory. To be honest, the aim is to provide a *better* rather than the perfect theory. Such a theory should be able to withstand inspection, but no matter how good it is, it will eventually be improved upon. This is somewhat contrary to human nature, which seems to find security in absolutes and definitive answers, which for our own sanity in our personal lives may be essential. We all harbour beliefs such as the family is most important, there is a God, and honesty is the best policy. On the other hand, the theories that academics and researchers study tend to encompass more global issues. Since social science theories are occasionally used as the rationale for policy decisions, then, unlike most of our personal theories, there is a need for these to be as sound as possible and produce reasonably accurate predictions.

Theories are the basis of research studies and can be thought of as formal statements or explanations of events, expressed in such a way as to allow their investigation, confirmation and verification. They are dynamic and not static, which means they are expected to change and improve. This is because they usually have been developed through *induction*, a process through which observations are made (possibly casually at first), data are collected, general patterns are recognized and relationships are proposed. Social science theories are no exception and, in describing this process, Gilbert (1993) maintains that a good theory should not be too restrictive. To be of value to a discipline, it needs to cover a variety of situations and conditions. A theory restricted to attempting to explaining why vandals damage just the digital displays on public telephones in Tooting may have some validity, but will not be very valuable in explaining the causes of vandalism in general. In addition to the shortcomings of such confined theories as this, there are some severe limitations to the role of social science in decision-making.

One could be asked: of what value is a theory except that it can be used to explain or predict other events? Starting with a theory that frustration is the basis for such action and having discovered a group of vandals in Tooting who have devised ingenious ways of destroying digital displays on public telephones, we look for additional information. It is suggested that their action is the result of their physics teacher in school never letting them use the expensive equipment with digital displays. Thus when young Johnny is caught with his screwdriver poking and prodding at one, could this be the explanation? Unfortunately, the explanation could be wrong and yet the theory could still possess some validity, since the process known as deduction was applied. *Deduction* assumes that one can explain, or deduce an explanation, by matching a specific situation to a more general one – in other words, the circumstances fit the theory.

Hempel (1966) has offered an alternative type of explanation that is more suitable to the types of theory that have been developed in the social sciences, *probabilistic explanations*. This assumes that generalizations that have universal application are rare, and that it is only possible to provide explanations in terms of trends. Figure 1.2 summarizes the source of this dilemma: support for any theory is based on evidence-gathering approaches, quantitative and/or qualitative. Ideally these processes will complement each other, quantitative research being based on the collection of considerable data from representative samples of a larger population for a few variables, while qualitative research pursues fewer subjects but investigating in much greater depth. In any case, it is often only possible to make logical deductions about *tendencies* in groups, rather than to predict accurately individual conduct or behaviours.

So why is it that all that remains is a potentially inadequate explanation for an individual's actions? One way of considering the problem is to realize that both of these sets of supporting evidence are based upon carefully controlled observations or measurements on selected representatives of the whole population. Thus quantitative research describes group tendencies: what members of a group tend to do. If a group is examined, there will be a variety of responses or reasons for some action, but the conclusions usually employ a single characteristic to describe what most commonly happens or how the group most comm-

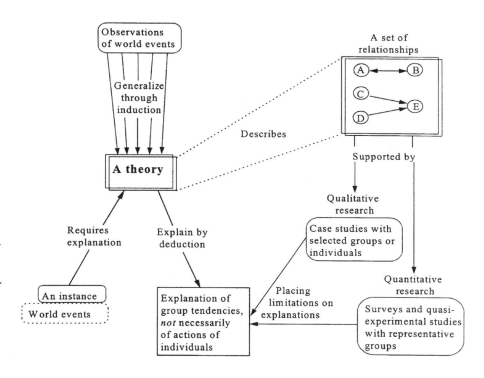

FIGURE 1.2
Theory building through induction, confirmed by research, and used by deduction to try to explain instances, but limited by the nature of the research support for the theory (developed from an idea presented in figures in Gilbert, 1993)

only or typically responds (sometimes represented by mean or median scores). Thus the individual becomes lost.

Even if we were to observe an action carried out by an individual or individuals, one that has all the traits covered by the theory, of what use is the theory in explaining these actions? For example, using the theory above to explain Tooting digital display vandalism, it becomes necessary to consider some supporting evidence. Imagine that there is a study that shows a group engaged in vandalism from the physics class has a higher mean score on Bloggs' Frustration Test than those in the same class who do not engage in vandalism. But even within these two groups, the scores will vary and maybe the distribution of scores may overlap, as shown in Figure 1.3. While people who vandalize *tend* to have higher Bloggs' Frustration Test scores than those who do not, there are individual exceptions. So when Johnny is arrested, it is still not known for sure whether he would fit at point A (very frustrated), point B (typically frustrated) or point C (not as frustrated as most in his group). Even if he is subsequently found to be at point C, it does not mean that the theory is 'wrong', but that it cannot unequivocally be applied to individuals. Johnny simply confirms the view that there is probably more than one cause for this phenomenon and the theory needs refining if it is to describe even group characteristics more comprehensively.

While frustration may contribute to vandalism, it may not necessarily be due to the physics teacher's unwillingness to let his students use equipment; it could be coincidence that they are in his class. The frustration could have its sources elsewhere (social class, unemployed parents, etc.) and the digital display destruction tendency could be enhanced by the availability of cheap screwdrivers at the local hardware store, combined with teenage ingenuity and boredom. This is an example of a theory looking for too fine a reason. Consequently, it would be unwise to get rid of the physics teacher, which might constitute an experiment, if the lack of ethics were ignored. It would still be difficult to control all the variables to determine if he were the only cause. Yet this study could *contribute* to understanding of frustration in general, a much more valuable basis for theory building.

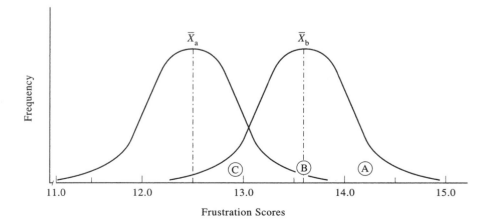

FIGURE 1.3
Comparing the distributions of Bloggs' Frustration Test scores for two groups, with scores of three individual respondents, A, B and C identified

MORE PRACTICAL PROBLEMS

In addition to providing support for theories, research can assist in the evaluation and validation of sound practices in the 'real world' of organizations, institutions and policy decisions (Cook *et al.*, 1990; Hedrick *et al.*, 1993; Robson, 1993). Thus the outcomes of a study can have immediate practical implications for procedures or processes in an institution, company, school or whole nation. While these would not be without a foundation in theories and understanding of why, they would more than likely focus on optimizing an outcome rather than refining a model or explanation. Such an approach is often aimed at enhancing a service, such as improving the well-being of patients, the effectiveness of teaching, or even the efficiency of production. Generalizability may be limited, but value will still be there for the organization.

As a consequence, one might be tempted to draw a line between 'theory' and 'practice'. This is hardly feasible. We need theories in order better to understand why people behave or react the way they do, if improvement in practice is to progress. Modelling the world based upon theories provides a basis from which to extrapolate to different situations. Research methods provide the tools with which we can decide upon the validity of the application to specific situations. Without the careful and methodical collection of data on outcomes, poor practices can go unnoticed as easily as good ones. Care in evaluating procedures that are a consequence of policy decisions can prevent unnecessary discomfort or unpleasant outcomes, even for a minority. Such a process can also identify beneficial processes that may have the potential to be extended to other situations. As we will see, it is reasonable for a researcher to extend generalizations of outcomes to groups, but only to those for which the research procedure provides reasonable justification. While limitations of generalizability may be a consequence of more practical research, it is one that is not always recognized. There are occasions where the results of studies on unrepresentative groups are inappropriately applied to others. We will return to this issue in later chapters as research procedures are considered in depth.

One area of focus at the applied end of the spectrum of research is the evaluation of innovations, new procedures or changes in policy. Even these should have a sound basis in more encompassing, wide-ranging theories, which would allow them to build upon the work and understanding of similar situations by others. Too many 'bandwagons' have flared up momentarily only to die because they offer excessively simplistic solutions to complex problems, weakly based on earlier research or on unsubstantiated theories or models. This is not to say there are not good ideas that constitute progress, but that they need evaluating, and that evolution rather than revolution will be more likely to provide long-lasting positive change.

Take, for example, the concern over increasing world population. As a 'solution', imagine a benevolent body that gives an unlimited supply of condoms to anyone, anywhere in the world. This would not be cheap, nor necessarily an effective way to limit population growth, since it only contends with one aspect (an important one, mind you) of population control. People would have to be convinced of the need for smaller families. How many of us in the affluent part of the world have more than one sibling, parents with many siblings, or grandparents who might have had a dozen siblings in the days when a farm needed many hands? In many parts of the world, convincing parents of the desirability of smaller families would entail proving to them that the medical care available would prevent the deaths of half their children before they were 5 years old. Also, it may be that many children are needed to ensure that parents will be taken care of in their old age, since their society lacks pensions, old people's homes, meals-on-wheels services, etc. Children are their security in old age. These are only a few of the possible reasons that might contribute to the success of any programme to reduce the rate of population growth. Flooding the world with a mechanism to reduce the number of children would make an impact, but not nearly as great as that which could be made if the other issues were addressed as well. Not every country is willing to take the approach of China where families with more than one child may be financially penalized through taxes or fines. It is necessary to understand all the reasons why families have many children *before* a solution is implemented and evaluated if lost time, wasted money and even human discomfort are not to be the consequences. Researchers must be aware of the limitations of radical policy decisions based upon poorly researched theories.

Some writers will maintain that there is a distinct difference between 'applied' research where one is involved in real-life problems, and theoretical or 'basic' research aimed solely at testing theories and models. The former is supposedly carried out in the 'real' world and the latter in a laboratory. This would be a nice distinction if it were accurate, but considering the wide range of research topics and conditions necessary to resolve research questions, a more credible description would seem to be based on two continuums: applied to basic, and real world to laboratory, as shown in Figure 1.4. While some researchers feel that their studies might be best described as fitting in either the upper left or lower right quadrants, it is not difficult to think of situations that exemplify positions elsewhere, even midway along one or both of the axes. For example, if we consider a study of the sitting positions of those of us who use word processors (ergonomics), are our offices the real world, or is there sufficient control over the situation to consider them to be laboratories? As applied research, it would probably fit somewhere in the lower left, maybe on the border between real world and laboratory. The study of social class and basic research derived from theories describing the impact of economics on personal well-being could hardly be conducted in a laboratory and would appear somewhere in the upper right quadrant. As we will see, the more we venture into the real world, the greater the problems will be in preventing other unwanted factors from influencing the results. When in the more controllable environment of something like a laboratory, we have more difficulty justifying to our colleagues that the results generalize to real situations. Where on the playing field we find ourselves presents different advantages and problems, but each piece of research will have its own unique challenges.

CAUSALITY

There has been an assumption up to this point that we are dealing with identifiable *causal* relationships, but causal links are not that easy to identify and prove.

FIGURE 1.4
Considering the nature of research, its purpose and environment – two continuums, with five examples: A, ergonomic study involving posture of typists; B, consequences for pensioners of increased inflation; C, short-term memory; D, variables influencing learning by hearing-impaired children; E, curative potential of a new antibiotic. Where on the playing field does your study reside?

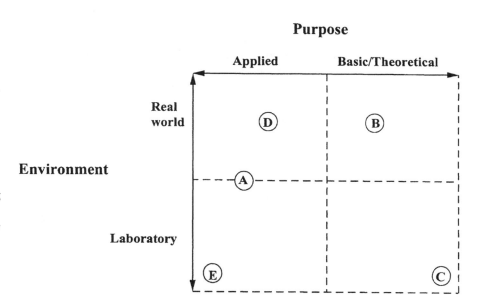

Often when reading journal articles, one feels that the authors speak with such confidence that the relationships found must describe cause and effect, but we may have nagging doubts. Frequently it is not the structure of the study, but the nature of the actual variables employed and their hypothesized relationships that stimulate the uncertainty.

Identifying *meaningful* potential variables that fit in *sensible* causal chains in the social sciences and education can be a difficult task. To assist in this, Cook and Campbell (1979) have devised a way of considering causality that involves two levels of classification: molar and micromediation. 'Molar' refers to variables which, while not the direct cause, do have a place as apparent identifiable contributors in the causal chain – examples might be frustration, social class or racism. These variables will be referred to as *macrovariables*, since they are the ones we contend with on a macroscopic level, in everyday situations (also sometimes referred to as *manifest* variables). 'Micromediation' on the other hand, refers to the actual causal connections that make up the molar level of causality. Variables at this level will be referred to as *microvariables* as they tend to function at the microscopic or unseen level (sometimes referred to as *latent* variables). In social science research and the building of theories, we often do not work at this level, partly because it may not be understood (brain scans can just about tell which part of the brain is working for certain types of tasks, but we cannot 'see' what is happening), and partly because it would not be functional in terms of the theory or model in question. Even in medicine, it is frequently profitable from a public health point of view to work with macrovariables. In epidemiology, for example, initial studies of the spread of a disease may be facilitated by simply labelling occurrences on the basis of diagnosis using recognized symptoms. This allows the monitoring of the social patterns related to the spread of a disease and will complement the understanding of the transmission by the microbiological mechanism.

As Cook and Campbell (1979) argue, events at the molar level result in macrovariables that can be inferred from direct observations of human activity. Also, these often accurately represent reality in a way that is intuitively or obviously meaningful. On the other hand, because the outcome variables are usually contingent on other conditions, they tend to be best described in probabilistic terms. For example:

- If you *come in contact with* (potential cause) someone with measles there is a finite probability that you will *get the disease* (possible effect), but it is not certain even if you have not had it before.
- If a random selection of 18-year-olds is provided with two weeks of *tennis lessons* (cause), their relative *proficiency* (effect) at the end will vary and not all will be equally good at the game or improved by the same amount.
- We would expect that if individuals are provided with *university education* then they will achieve a higher *income* than those without this opportunity, but any prediction would be within a range and not exact.

When considering social science variables, there is an added problem of how subjects arrived at the state in question. Our definitions of such variables as social class, intelligence, frustration and level of education are all classifications that depend on not only how they are defined, but also how subjects have come to be in their level within a category. Also, most molar causal relations are the result of multiple causes, thus making almost impossible the task of identifying a single relationship absolutely. While it may seem best to devise research situations involving molar relationships that are highly controlled and contrived, this rarely is possible. Therefore, most research is carried out in the 'field', in real live environments or 'open systems'. This impediment to control will make the identification of causal relationships among macrovariables even more problematic.

While this may seem to be an argument for considering microvariables, let us step back from the brink and not carry this too far. A recent book by Crick (1994) hypothesizes that the human character is simply the coming together of atoms, molecules and neurones. This *reductionist* view of the world presents an interesting view, though even if it were true it would have little influence on research in most areas. Yes, we can explain why people suffer from Down's Syndrome (a rather massive malfunction not of a few genes, but a whole chromosome full of genes), and we may eventually be able to identify genetic contributions to less extreme mental states. Yet the understanding of most human behaviour and interaction of interest to social scientists is much more difficult since the causes are usually multiple and the result of environmental macrovariables. We are more akin to the epidemiologist looking for the types of human interaction that spread disease than the microbiologist who is trying to isolate the virus. Now carry out Activity 1.1.

> ## Activity 1.1
>
> Select at least three macrovariables from your area of interest, variables that are commonly used in research. For each one, identify as many potential microvariables as you can. Are these ever considered? Are they useful, relevant to decision-making or even understanding of human behaviour, at least with respect to present theories? Are there any which might be of greater interest in the future?

A second consideration when trying to propose causal links or establish their validity is the identification of the time sequence of events. In order to establish a logically consistent system of order, Davis (1985) proposes four possible basic relationships between specified variables X and Y:

(a) $X \rightarrow Y$ X could possibly influence Y, but Y cannot influence X.
(b) $X \leftarrow Y$ Y could possibly influence X, but X cannot influence Y.
(c) $X \leftrightarrows Y$ X and Y could influence each other.
(d) $X \leftrightarrow Y$ X and Y could possibly have a correlational relationship (no assumptions are made about which influences the other).

Consistent with the understanding of probabilistic nature of outcomes, these relationships are all interpreted as possible, rather than absolute, influences. Cases (a) and (b) are dependent on the impossibility of the opposite. For example, the following macrovariables exemplify X and Y in the order they are presented ($X \rightarrow Y$):

- parents' educational level before children are born and children's educational achievements;
- gender and income;
- the recession of 1992 and election results in 1993.

In none of these situations could the second be considered to cause the first, as there are definite time sequences. On the other hand, how the variables are defined may result in considering situation (c) where X and Y might influence each other ($X \leftrightarrows Y$). For example, if the first relationship were expressed simply as

- parents' educational level and children's educational achievements

it might be possible that children's success in education could motivate parents to return to education or participate in non-credit adult education. This forewarns of the problem of variable definition, one that we will return to later in this chapter. Situation (c) is possible when there is not a rigid time sequence and events leap-frog each other. Consequently, knowledge of surrounding events is extremely important in identifying potential relationships. For example, the arrow between the number of hours per week women work and number of children women have could be in either direction. There is (at least) one other variable, Z, the woman's choice as to whether she has more children and spends more time with them, *or* she works more and defers having more children:

Macrovariables that bypass intervening variables may result in indeterminate direction for a relationship. Knowledge (and careful definition) of the situation or conditions is necessary if the relationships are to be logically consistent even at the planning stage.

As Davis (1985) notes, relationship (d) could be all or none of the above, since correlational relationships are not expressions of causality nor do they constitute proof of causality. They may be indicators of the possibility, but it would require a different type of study to provide more substantive support for such a supposition, as will be seen in Chapter 2.

Finally, Cook and Campbell (1979) maintain that causality implies that by intentionally varying one variable, the other will change. In the real world of social science research, rarely do we as researchers have sufficient control to be able to manipulate a variable. This limitation is the basis for creating conditions whereby we are able to *observe* the putative cause by sampling subjects who have experienced the variable (education, gender, social class, political commitment) rather than actually expecting to have sufficient control to allow us to be able to expose them to varying situations. Now carry out Activity 1.2.

Activity 1.2

For each of the pairs of variables below, pencil in arrow(s) indicating the possible direction of causality (if any) using the scheme above, and be prepared to defend your choice. If you do not like the variables as stated, improve them as you see fit or elaborate on the conditions.

(a)   unemployment   crime rate
(b)   truancy   expenditure per pupil in schools
(c)   xenophobia   ethnic cleansing
(d)   technological development   urbanisation of society
(e)   self-esteem   occupational attainment

For those which you specify a single-direction arrow, can you describe conditions under which the direction might be reversed?

LIMITS OF THEORIES

Applying a theory to explain individual actions fails for another reason, which is related more to the collection of qualitative than of quantitative data. It is difficult to confirm *why* actions are taken even when asking people in an interview: they probably do not know why. If they do, their reason may reflect their personal theory, not the interviewer's more academic one. The interviewer must *infer* reasons from the personal responses to questions and there is always the possibility of alternative inferences. Even assuming that some common set of explanations could be identified among selected interviewees, are they representative of the whole population? This takes the problem back to the distribution of frustration scores and multiple causation. Thus, to explain why a specific youngster, Freddie Smith, drifts into crime, steals cars and joyrides, is not the role of a theory, though theories might well guide the social worker in asking Freddie relevant questions that may eventually determine the reason(s). This might be useful in helping Freddie out of his situation, but it will be the *indirect* result of a theory, not a direct result of the theory explaining the actions of this individual. Establishing why Freddie steals cars by questioning him (assuming he will answer truthfully) may also help to understand more about the validity of a theory, rather than the theory explaining what motivates Freddie to steal.

So theories have a role in the social sciences, but not usually as the sole source of explanation of individual events as they often do in the physical sciences or sometimes occasionally do in certain areas of the biological sciences. Human actions and interactions are rarely so simple that a single source of causality can be identified. Social science theories do help to provide possible explanations of tendencies or actions of groups with common characteristics. Even when the evidence supports a multiple-causality theory, one may have to draw upon a number of overlapping theories to arrive at a comprehensive explanation. There are exceptions to this, but these are just that – exceptions rather than common practice. For example, Canter (1994) was asked to predict the characteristics of a serial killer to provide a profile to assist in his capture by the police, based upon evidence from the crime. When caught, the perpetrator actually had characteristics and traits very *close* to those predicted. What must be recognized is that the evidence and the theories applied were contending with *exceptional* behaviour, not common characteristics, traits and events. In many respects, such situations are like that of the social worker working with individuals when attempting to diagnose the source of problems. The predictions of future behaviour, or the extrapolations back in time to possible causes, are analogous to the questions (based on theories which generated hypotheses) put forward by the social science researcher. Not until more evidence is collected will the validity of these be established. In many cases, it is either not possible to verify them, or even if it is, the predictions or extrapolations are not generalizable to a larger population. To establish the types of 'criminal profile' that make the newspaper headlines requires the systematic collection of data and testing of hypothesized relationships with subjects that are very elusive.

If the theories were so precise as to allow the deduction of explanations of behaviour, then, for example, they would be applied on a grander scale and most criminals would be apprehended, economists would provide perfect economies, and politicians would devise more equitable systems. Phrenologists (those who tried to explain behaviour by the shapes of skulls) thought they had a versatile theory, but can you imagine being compelled to queue up with your head shaved as part of a screening process? Maybe society is fortunate that there is an understanding of the proper role of theories, one that says that they do *not* provide all the answers all the time, but only some of the answers some of the time, and that more frequently they are the basis for asking good questions.

There are individuals who do attempt an oversimplified description of events based upon social science theories, but they tend to be politicians rather than social scientists. The aim of the former often is to control or manipulate people, while that of the latter is to understand them.

This does not mean that theories are not useful in their own right; their ability to provide probabilistic explanations of group actions and characteristics is of value. Those that acquire support having been recognized as valid by the academic community, may form the basis for policy decisions in governments. Research that has shown no significant difference in physical and mental traits of different racial groups has contributed to improving attitudes towards and promoting laws on racial equality. Social science research has shown that while most unemployed people do not really enjoy not working, there is a minority who actually prefer to sit around just collecting the dole. Educational research has shown that positive reinforcement (praise) for success at learning has a more favourable impact on motivation to learn in most children than the application of negative reinforcement for failure to do work (punishment). None of these results, however, came from a single study and quite frequently they supported explanations that were counter to common culturally based belief: beating children made them learn, other ethnic groups were considered inferior, and the unemployed poor on the dole enjoyed being unemployed. Yes, there are individual exceptions: some children do learn having been continually punished (but what are the other effects?), there are some people in most ethnic groups who are not very smart, and some people on the dole do enjoy being idle, at least for a while. Keep in mind, though, that research explains *group tendencies*, and can at best only provide probabilities for individual behaviour or traits.

As noted earlier, theories can supply practitioners with the starting points for asking questions to determine the sources of problems in individuals, whether these are social (origins of poverty), psychological (difficulty in adjustment to grief) or educational (problems in learning). Thus there are potential links between contemporary research and practice, though it has been argued that this is not frequently in evidence (Kerlinger, 1986). It could be suggested (an interesting hypothesis for someone's research) that many practitioners simply use the theories and models acquired as undergraduates, treating them as unchanging truths rather than as the more tenuous suppositions that they are. They have not grasped the true meaning of a theory: a working model that should be continually checked against reality and refined in light of new evidence. But then, it could be said that we are products of a culture that feels more secure with certainty than uncertainty, and will not only strive for it, but sometimes muster irrational arguments to establish it. Science is still almost a counter-culture in that it assumes no absolute answers or theories. What we have today is the best possible, accepting that theories are not perfect and better theories that provide improved explanations may become apparent tomorrow. As one conducts research and reads of others, it is worthwhile keeping this in mind when encountering strongly held beliefs.

Finally, not everything in life has to have an immediate pragmatic function. Among academics, there often exists a simple desire to understand. This is moderated with the assumption that the understanding is not perfect, but as a theory is refined, the understanding becomes increasingly complete. Among researchers, there is considerable satisfaction in contributing to the better understanding of human events. This is true even when we are driven by a hope of making the world better, but our zeal must be tempered with a realization that few of us will succeed in a spectacular fashion. There are unlikely to be comparable discoveries in social sciences to the cure for and elimination of smallpox, the discovery of the atom, or the development of Teflon. When you consider how many biologists, chemists and physicists there are doing research, even these advances begin to look like flukes or serendipitous discoveries.

A SCIENTIFIC APPROACH

The acceptance of the imperfectness of any model or theory underlies all scientific endeavour. A car company may have the perfect car, a baker the perfect loaf of bread, but science is more like knowing where you want to go, never expecting to get there, yet enjoying getting closer. No matter how complete a model or theory is, it can always be extended or improved. The challenge is to provide sufficient evidence of a nature that other social scientists will accept as proof (objectivity). Frankfort-Nachmias and Nachmias (1992) maintain that 'empirical objectivity depends on verification so much that the scientist cannot make claims for objectivity until verification has been carried out'. This does not mean having the same opinion, and scientists are not always as objective as we might expect, but this is the goal towards which the community strives. The acceptability of a theory is based upon its ability to withstand continual tests, though it is usually not the entire theory that is tested at once. Since theories tend to attempt to describe complex events, such 'tests' are usually conducted on limited parts and the validity of those parts (set of relationships) is put forward as suspect. To challenge a key part of a theory potentially challenges the validity of the whole. A similar state of affairs exists when trying to extend a theory into new realms or refine it. The proposed relationship is stated as something to be subjected to a test, and is commonly referred to as a *hypothesis*. Such a formalized way of stating the problem helps to maintain the logic of any argument for or against the truth of a proposed relationship. It is a communication tool within the scientific community.

Difficulty arises with hypothesized relationships among macrovariables primarily because hypothesized causality cannot be established directly using statistical tests (Cook and Campbell, 1979; Popper, 1972). Instead, the aim of this approach is to eliminate plausible rivals, which provides support for the credibility of a hypothesized relationship until the next contender appears. For individual studies that endeavour to provide support for an explanation, this is not as daunting as it may first seem. One can identify possible alternative causes and include them in the design as potential competing variables for the cause, in addition to the one of interest. Other possible variables can be controlled so their potential effects are distributed evenly across all groups receiving the planned treatments. Thus, if gender is not of interest as a key variable, then every group has equal proportions of males and females. This just increases the demand on designers of social science research to be as analytic, perceptive and rigorous as (if not more so than) their physical and biological counterparts.

Such striving towards objectivity often manifests itself in the standard of acceptability for any experimental or observational evidence: can the process be *replicated* by someone else such that the same results are produced? Even in the physical sciences, confirmation of hypothesized relationships is occasionally made by one group but the proof of existence turns out to be impossible to replicate by others. Recent examples include cold fusion as a phenomenon to support a model of containable nuclear reactions, and numerous 'cures' for cancer which would support various biochemical or genetic theories for explaining the cause of this disease. Even without studies that replicate the original results, each may still have an existence as an unsupported hypothesis, but that is all.

Applying a philosophy of science to the extension of understanding of societies and of people's actions requires some adjustments. Using a scientific approach to resolve the validity of hypotheses suggests a need not only to understand relationships among variables, but also to be able to extend that understanding to larger populations. Physical and biological scientists have a similar problem: do all animals behave this way, does this chemical reaction occur in the same manner out of as it does in the laboratory? Usually, though, they have greater control over all the variables than can be achieved by social scientists. For example, physicists can control the physical conditions surrounding the events being investigated, chemists can restrict the elements and compounds that are involved in a reaction, and biologists can select their animal or plant subjects carefully so as to be representative of larger groups. Social scientists rarely have such absolute control and therefore if they are to succeed in confirming the existence of any relationships, they have a much more difficult task. Success is potentially enhanced by a number of technical and statistical tools, but because of the nature of the questions and the subjects being studied, the complexity of selecting the best combination of tools can seem daunting.

Kerlinger (1986) speaks with the conviction of a true scientist when he notes that the difference between common sense and science lies in the methods of knowing. Primarily, scientific research strives to be *systematic* in:

(a)   the use of conceptual schemes and the building of theories while being rigorous and methodical, with concepts being carefully defined and theoretical structures checked for logical consistency;

(b)   testing these and the resulting hypotheses empirically – in other words, structuring a study to collect data that will, by design, provide supporting or refuting evidence for proposed relationships;

(c)   restricting itself to descriptions of relationships among isolatable variables, controlling all other possible variables that might influence an outcome through representative sampling;

(d)   devising self-checking mechanisms to ensure replicatability of a study, avoiding the use of fortuitous evidence in favour of representative phenomena that can be reproduced;

(e)   avoiding metaphysical explanations, those that cannot be tested, including those based on religious belief – which does not mean they are rejected, only that they are not sufficient explanations, equivalent to untested hypotheses.

While this set of characteristics does not guarantee good research, it does encourage approaches that are assumed to be available for scrutiny with respect to soundness of logic and process. The ultimate test is that a comparable study should be able to produce comparable results, showing that this was not just a one-off occurrence. This emphasis on a systematic approach to the design of research does provide the researcher with criteria by which his or her procedures can be checked as the project progresses.

The above also forms the basis of arguments by those who would question the value of a scientific approach. Some would criticise the apparently reductionist approach of (c), which compels researchers to consider a few variables at a time, maintaining that human activity and actions cannot be simplified in such a way. Most social scientists would dispute that they take an extreme reductionist view that all human behaviour can be reduced to biochemical reactions. This does demand that the intellectual skills of the researcher prevent studies from focusing on trivial variables, or variables out of context and divorced from reality. In fact, one goal of sampling is to recognize the complexity of human activity, but to allow only selected variables to influence outcomes of interest, keeping all others under 'control'. This does not suggest that they are suppressed, but indicates a need to ensure that all outcomes that represent variables of interest are equally influenced by those variables not of interest.

For example, if the aim of a study were to compare several possible methods for introducing new information technology in an organization in order to select one for overall implementation, then a study comparing them would be in order. It might already be recognized that several variables other than the nature of the implementation programme could influence the introduction – for example, age, gender and educational background of employees. Consequently, the induction programmes to be compared could be tested by conducting trials on groups that were typical of all employees – for example, equivalent in distribution of age groups, balance of gender, number of years employed in the company, and educational background. Thus any influence that these potential variables might have would be applied equally to all the trial programmes, leaving any differences in effectiveness attributable to the programmes themselves. It would be beneficial to consider a number of outcomes in addition to achievement of skills, which could be quantified. While this text does focus on quantitative approaches, it is well recognized that qualitative, phenomenological, ethnographic approaches can provide valuable insights and deeper understanding that would complement quantitative studies. As a consequence, identification of desirable aspects of programmes could be best achieved through interviews.

Alternatively, a study could be conducted under similar conditions to investigate the suggestion that encouragement (positive reinforcement) is just as effective at enhancing learning in adults as it is in children. In this situation, the researcher would organize the presentation of two identical induction programmes to matched groups, with the only difference being in the use of encouragement during discussions and activities in one of the groups. If the outcome did show a greater level of achievement for the group receiving encouragement, it would potentially provide support for a more encompassing 'theory' relating to the use of positive reinforcement in teaching and learning. The question asked would determine which approach would be used.

All of these components can be put together in a diagram that illustrates the cyclic, ongoing nature of scientific enquiry. Figure 1.5 provides such a view, one that highlights the tenuous existence over time of a given theory and its susceptibility to examination and verification. A theory may begin life from informal observations that result in a loose set of laws, but thereafter, if it is to acquire any acceptance, it will have to sustain the rigour of being 'tested'. Any worthwhile theory will have consequences that can be put forward as generating potential (hypothetical) outcomes, which should be observable and therefore verifiable. If these are what are predicted, then the relationships tested will have acquired support and this in turn provides some support for the overall theory. If not, then the results may provide the basis for revising and improving the laws and consequently the theory. Negative results from a piece of research do not necessarily negate an entire theory since they are usually concerned with some limited aspect, but they will at least necessitate adjustments in the theory, which in turn must be tested. Thus the cycle continues.

Having made the point that theories grow and evolve, there is an interesting phenomenon in the social sciences that appears almost to defy this. All too frequently articles, theses and dissertations report 'new' and outstanding theories which, under closer scrutiny, are only modifications of older, more established ones, using new terminology. This does not deny the possibility of the development of new and radical theories, but part of this phenomenon may be attributable to the so-called need for originality in research. This seems to be interpreted as a need for a whole new theory, when most existing ones have not been adequately tested to establish their limits. Considerable original thinking is required (and will be demonstrated by the successful researcher) when testing various aspects of existing theories, finding their limits and modifying them in light of research. It is simply not necessary to start from scratch to be original!

RESEARCH SKILLS

As has been implied up to this point, designing and carrying out research is demanding, requiring the application of a number of skills rather than the simple ability to follow a set of instructions. Presented below is a set of skills that build on the definition of science as a process. Many of these have been mentioned earlier, and they are most likely employed (though usually not consciously by researchers) as part of carrying out any study (Black, 1993). You will recognize that you possess most if not all of these to some degree, though it will probably be necessary to enhance your proficiency in some or develop tools to ensure a more systematic use of others.

To employ a number of these successfully in systematic research will require the development of new skills, such as the design of measuring instruments and the ability to select and use statistical tools.

1 *Observation*. Events occur around us all the time, some of which we notice and others we do not. Observation during research must be selective in that we need to focus on a limited number of events, otherwise our senses would

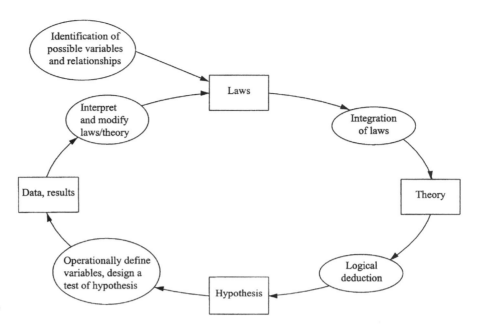

FIGURE 1.5
Cyclic life and
evolution of a theory

be overwhelmed. In social science research, there is often the necessity to be trained as an observer, since some of the actions that need to be observed and recorded are so common that they would not seem significant to the untrained. For example, to study the use of positive reinforcement in a classroom may require a researcher to count how often it is used within a lesson. This may require knowing what the learners perceive as reinforcement and watching the classroom interaction carefully. Whether the reinforcement is effective may be a separate question.

2 *Event/time relations.* This involves investigations that are time-dependent – for example, where frequency of an event may be important. This may result in considering rates of occurrence, sometimes over relatively short periods (minutes) and for other studies over relatively long periods (months, years). For example, if one were investigating alcoholism, there is a considerable difference between subjects who consume a half-litre of whisky in an evening and those who take a month to consume the same amount. The *rate* of consumption would be of more interest than the amount.

3 *Communication.* It is often assumed that educated adults can communicate, at least in writing. But there is a considerable difference in writing a letter to a friend, an essay, a research report or a novel. Many studies fail to communicate essential aspects of the process, leaving the reader wondering if the conclusions were really justified.

4 *Prediction.* An intelligent guess, extrapolation, or interpolation ultimately may be the source of a question that will be the basis of a research project. A 'What if . . .?' question can stimulate speculation on the truth of the outcome that will only be resolved if followed by an investigation.

5   *Classification*. We all classify objects and events as a way of bringing order to observations. Some schemes have relatively wide acceptance (such as physical characteristics, professions, cognitive level of questions on a test) while others generate considerable discussion (such as social class). Devising a classification scheme can be a very complex task that may involve creating new concepts, isolating characteristics into which persons or events can be categorized, and/or operationally defining (see 9 below) abstract concepts. In any case, the defining of mutually exclusive categories that can be used effectively by researchers is not a trivial task.

6   *Inference*. Distinguishing between observation and inference is not always easy. An inference is a subjective explanation of an observation. One may observe the wick sticking out of each end of a candle and infer that it is a single string through the candle, but this is not the only possible inference. Further investigations would be necessary to be sure. Upon observing a teacher praise a child for an answer in class and the child subsequently smiling, you may infer that the child is encouraged. Alternatively, the child could be smiling for other reasons (relief, embarrassment, self-satisfaction, because another child has suddenly started giggling). Resolving conflicting inferences in human situations is much more difficult than deciding which is most accurate in material ones, like the candle. This makes the choice of what to observe even more difficult, since to resolve conflicting inferences may require multiple observations.

7   *Number relations*. Quantified data can be more meaningfully presented and analysed in tabular and graphical form. Some statistical tests will help to resolve issues after the data have been collected, in a way which would not otherwise be possible. For example, a correlation coefficient may not mean as much to some people as the scatter diagram from which it is derived. Selecting the most appropriate mathematical tool will often help in conveying one's results.

8   *Measurement*. In a physical sense, measurement means using instruments such as rulers and balances. Here we shall take it to mean designing and using measuring instruments such as tests, questionnaires, and interview or observation schedules. There is a considerable technology associated with the design of these and some of the more common approaches will be covered in later chapters.

9   *Making operational definitions*. As noted earlier, most concepts that tend to be investigated in the social sciences are abstract. This means that there is a necessity to select or devise an observable activity that is indicative of the concept. The relative validity of an operational definition may well be dependent upon the possession of measurement skills (see 8 above) and/or the ability to make sound inferences (see 6 above).

10 *Formulating hypotheses*. A hypothesis is an educated guess, an expectation, stemming from observations and either existing or new models or theories. It may suggest a causal relationship, but not necessarily. Whatever the hypothesis, the aim is to test it in some way to see if it is supported or not. Formulating a hypothesis is not an easy skill and one too often neglected by researchers who leap into a study without the adequately defined reason that every investigation needs. A formal statement often

compels a researcher to resolve issues that a more woolly statement or question can hide. The whole design of a research study will be affected by a hypothesis, thus it is better to establish one early before too much intellectual effort is invested in a dead end. This process will highlight the need for clear operational definitions and sound definition of concepts, as well as the need to clarify how variables will be identified and controlled (see 12 below).

11 *Interpreting data.* Data appear in many forms – for example, some components may be numerical, while others may be in the form of transcripts of interviews. Raw data have little meaning and must be turned into understandable information. Numbers and statistical results by themselves are of little interest and difficult to interpret. What does it mean to have a correlation of 0.45? It is not easy for a reader to understand the significance of a graph on its own. For example, does the shape of a histogram of scores make any difference in a study? Some results can be statistically significant without, for example, being educationally significant. What does a statistical significance level of 0.05 tell us in a specific case? A researcher's ability to interpret the data collected in a logically consistent manner without making unwarranted claims or underrating the strength of the findings is an essential skill.

12 *Identifying and controlling variables.* This is a difficult enough task in the physical and biological sciences, where the experimenter has a reasonable amount of control of the environment. In the social sciences, it is even more difficult. Just being able to identify variables in a social interaction requires considerable perception, and is related to other earlier skills. For example, what are possible factors that might contribute to a 'discipline problem' in a classroom? The pupil's behaviour? Provocation by the teacher? Domestic (home) problems on either side leaving one party short-tempered? To control variables can be even harder. For example, an investigation into the effectiveness of a set of learning materials has little or no control over what the children do outside class or what they see on television at home. On a truly practical level, consider the efforts of judicial systems to prevent jurors from being influenced by information other than that which is presented in court. When carrying out research, if some effect is observed, it is up to the researcher to justify that this was the result of a specific variable, which is only going to be achieved through the careful design of the investigation. Subsequent chapters will consider ways of achieving control of variables through the design of the study and its execution (see 13 below).

13 *Designing an investigation.* This is the integration of all the above skills in the design of an investigation that will collect data and ultimately provide meaningful information. The design will take into account problems of determining the question and hypothesis, of defining, controlling and measuring/observing variables, and of interpreting and communicating results. A well-planned study is conducted with considerable foresight, so that in the final report few excuses are made for flaws and the results are justifiable *and* educationally or socially significant.

Having considered these skills, carry out Activity 1.3.

Activity 1.3

1 What skills do you already have? Go back through the list of 13 process skills and indicate next to each your assessment of your own proficiency using the following scale:

A – very proficient
B – quite proficient
C – having some proficiency
D – not very proficient
E – in need of help!

You can look back on this list and see how you feel you have progressed later in the course.

2 Did you spot the potential measurement problem? This has left you, the respondent, with the responsibility for defining 'proficient' – thus if used as part of a study, the results would have to be interpreted as the subject's perception of proficiency, and not proficiency itself. Would actual proficiency at such skills be easy to measure? Choose one or two and suggest what you would accept as evidence of proficiency, in other words, what observations you could make that would allow you to infer levels of proficiency.

Beginning the Design Process

2

The process of designing a research project cannot be likened to slavishly following a manual for assembling a model aeroplane. On the other hand, there are issues that must be addressed and criteria of sound practice to be heeded if the ensuing investigation is to be carried out in a sufficiently rigorous manner. The results of a study should provide evidence to help resolve the validity of the hypotheses stated, and at the same time, the process should be replicable by another independent researcher. Without intending to be prescriptive, a set of procedures is presented in Figure 2.1 to guide further discussion and to provide some milestones in the process. This simply unrolls and expands the cyclic view of research described in Figure 1.5 to provide guidance on the design of a single specific project. The sequence of events presented here simply serves as a set of contemplation points for the researcher. As with any systematic approach, the aim is to entice the participant in the process to *ask the right questions at the right time*.

Note that this approach has been divided into two stages, planning and execution. Often studies fail to produce defensible results due to incomplete

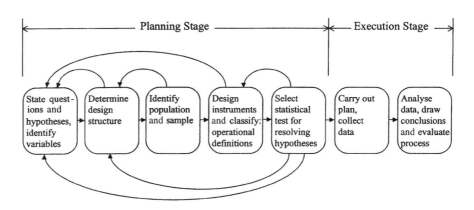

FIGURE 2.1
Stages of designing and carrying out a study, including iterations for modifications and improvements during planning

27

planning before taking irreversible action: in other words, not all the issues were addressed and resolved before proceeding to collect the data. For example, it is more than likely that researchers who materialize in the computing unit with a pile of data, asking how to process them statistically, have failed not only to carry out the fifth step, 'Select statistical test', but also to consider the implications of any statistical tests on the other stages of the research. That is to say, they have missed the opportunity to ensure systematically that there is continuity across the component parts, checking that

- the hypotheses logically follow the question,
- the sample is the most representative and consistent with the hypotheses,
- the measuring instruments are the most appropriate for the variables identified in the hypotheses and
- all are consistent with the intended statistical tests of the relationships.

The caveat provided here is that it is possible to have jumps back, reconsiderations, and modifications. No 'procedure' is a recipe, but rather a skeleton outline. This proviso is an important reminder that the research process is very complex and the human mind does not work totally in a strict sequential fashion.

The main stages outlined in Figure 2.1 can also be considered to be points where major decisions must be made by the researcher. Each of these can be expanded further and as we progress through the rest of the book, that is exactly what will happen. Greater detail will be added in the form of specific issues to be addressed, skills to be developed, and criteria against which the appropriateness of the answers to questions of quality can be judged. Figure 2.2 shows which chapters address the skills implied by each stage. While three chapters are devoted to the design of measurement and ten to statistics, this does not imply greater importance but simply indicates the extensive variety of tools available at these stages.

Based on the assumption that all researchers can improve their practice, it is a good idea that *all* decisions should be documented so as to allow the analysis and evaluation of the research process and procedures. A research project is a complex process and the events therein should not be preserved in one's memory alone. The practice of keeping a log of events followed by captains of ships and by many biological and physical scientists working on laboratory experiments is one that could be profitably employed by the social science

FIGURE 2.2
Chapters in which skills for the various stages of research are presented

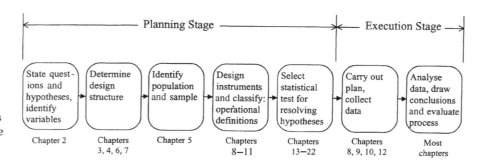

researcher. One major part of the purpose of a dissertation is to evaluate the process, not just to find an 'answer'.

A second word of caution should be heeded before actually considering the numerous skills and techniques that will be developed in detail as part of carrying out research. There is a view that all activities should be shown to be performed at a high standard and that teachers, researchers and academics should be accountable for the quality of their activities. This minefield has resulted in an approach incompletely borrowed from the manufacturing and engineering world: if all the components are of high quality, then the assembled end-product must be of high quality. This over-simplification has resulted in an emphasis on the various component processes of academic activities, with buzzwords such as total quality management. There is a demand for indicators of success and quality, which usually focus on the more easily measured products of a task. These include examination results, the presence of clearly stated objectives for courses, good feedback from students on course presentation, etc. While none of these is undesirable, they will not ensure quality if considered alone. If the process is not carried out in the spirit intended, continually referring to the overall task at hand, then the end-results may be ridiculous (Figure 2.3). Thus, as you consider the techniques and processes covered in the rest of this book, remember that even if each were carried out perfectly, you could still end up with less than perfect results. To plan and carry out research you require not only the separate skills, but also the ability to integrate them and apply them to a specific problem, which is the part that is *most* difficult to teach! Individual skills are isolated and presented separately to make them easier to learn, but their integration can be even more demanding on the intellect. Activities presented at appropriate places in the text will provide you with

FIGURE 2.3
Planning requires
the integration of all
skills

opportunities to carry out such integration and consider the interrelations and implications of decisions. Having said that, let us look at beginning the process.

CHOOSING A RESEARCH QUESTION

The next part of this chapter will address the key issues implied by the first box in Figure 2.1, though not without the occasional reference to later issues (boxes) that need resolving as part of the process. The problems related to stating a question of sufficient scope, but not too ambitious, are the focus here, with some reference to postgraduate research projects. The research should be devised such that the operational definition of the variables will result in potentially reliable and valid instruments, and with some anticipation of potential quantitative data collection problems. Any design will be refined in conjunction with trials of the resulting measuring instruments, the choice of statistical tests and reality of data collection. Since these are covered in later chapters, any designs at this stage will be a working draft, subject to improvement.

Questions and hypotheses describe potential relationships between and among variables that are to be tested. Usually research questions arise from personal professional experience and the 'better' ones will be based upon not only observations but also links made between those observations in real life and existing theories. Even those that are the consequence of a research contract that specifies a very practical question may require refinement in the light of contemporary knowledge, previous research and existing theories. Personally motivated research is most likely to arise from a combination of experience and reading, where a question arises that is of sufficient immediate or long-term interest to compel one to find an answer.

A research question should in general be potentially testable. In other words, the question should be of sufficient scope as to be resolvable with the resources available, *not* involved in proving right or wrong, and stated in such a way as to define clearly the problem to be investigated. With criteria that compel the researcher to state a question that is neither trivial nor excessively ambitious, one is left with a certain amount of uncertainty: how much specificity is enough? The complex and multivariate nature of many situations can make it difficult even to identify isolatable phenomena. It is then difficult to investigate a reasonable number of variables while, at the same time, eliminating others that might contribute to the outcomes of interest. An initial statement may be imprecise and subsequently refined with time, based on one's personal knowledge of the area.

Other criteria are a little less vague. Research results may contribute to discussions in the areas of values (politics, philosophy and religion), but do not in their own right have the capability of resolution of disputes or formulation of policy. Research studies can provide clarification of relationships between variables, but they cannot tell whether the outcome is good or bad: the world of values is separate from answering questions about relationships. These may guide a researcher in what sorts of questions to attempt to resolve, but the actual questions cannot be answered.

For example, the question of whether one racial group is superior to another and therefore has the right to better facilities and opportunities through segregation, apartheid, or simple job discrimination, is a political issue founded primarily on *belief* with as few well-defined variables as possible. Thus if one definition of 'superior' (say, difference in intelligence as indicated by IQ tests) is proven non-existent or of dubious validity because of the nature of the instruments, then the definition will simply change (say, to assertiveness, cultural proclivity, and so on *ad nauseam*). This does not mean that the researcher should not contribute to the discussion by providing objective and replicable research, but it does mean that it is unlikely that the overall question will be answered in such a way as to satisfy decision-makers, unless it agrees with their value system. This also presents an ethical problem for researchers who hold strong beliefs themselves: do they report all their findings, or only the ones that support their views and values? History has its fair share of situations where, if not actually proven, there is evidence that suggests researchers have ignored unwanted results because they were part of 'experimental error'.

Having a general idea for a research question, how should it be stated? Research questions can be categorized based on the nature and purpose of the resulting study. The scheme used here is a synthesis of several others (e.g., Hedrick *et al.*, 1993; Polit and Hungler, 1991). The categories that follow provide a wide range based primarily on the purpose of the study:

1. *Descriptive*. What events or outcomes are occurring? What are the characteristics of a category of persons or organizations? How prevalent or widespread are the events or phenomena? For example:
   - What is the frequency of the use of different training methods in industry?
   - How prevalent is the use of drugs among prison inmates?
   - What are the reasons given for absences from work among information technology workers?
   - What is the distribution of members of each social class in a geographic area?
   - How prevalent are sleep disorders among middle management personnel?
   - What do customers use as criteria for choosing which supermarket to patronize?
   - What is the range of support available to unemployed young people in the community?
   - What is the nature of counselling support provided for overseas students?

2. *Explorative*. Which characteristics or details relate to observed events, phenomena or reasoning? For example:
   - Do assembly-line workers suffer more or less from sleep disorders than the general population of employed persons?
   - How do the voting patterns of a given community compare to the results of the most recent election?
   - Is there any relationship between age and perception of quality of music?
   - Do employers have the same perception of aims for schools as does the general population?
   - What is the nature of preferences for specific religions among members of social classes?

3. *Evaluative*. How well did a process or procedure work? Such questions tend to be more applied than basic, but still ought to be founded on an established model or theory, or form the basis for a new one. For example:

- Which of several possible programmes had the greatest impact on reducing long-term unemployment?
- Do the subjects young people study at school differentially increase the probability of subsequent employment?
- Which assembly-line procedure has the greatest effect on productivity?
- Which of several counselling approaches had the greatest success on reducing the return to drinking among alcoholics?
- Which teaching approach had the greatest appeal to the learners?

4) *Predictive.* What will happen if one variable changes? We do not always have control over variables: things happen and we are observers. There is not necessarily the intent to determine causality, but to identify the existence and strength of relationships between variables. For example:

- If family size (number of children) increases, is there necessarily any increase or decrease in family income?
- Are there any relationships across social class, educational achievement, and drug use among 18–24-year-olds?
- What relationships exists across marriage stability, family income, job stability, and educational level of partners?
- At which times of the year do people of different age groups prefer to take overseas holidays?
- Do people who are good at mathematics, science or technical subjects tend to be poor at English?
- Is there any relationship between household income and home do-it-yourself (DIY) activities, and is there a link to the decline in usage of professionals?

5) *Explanatory.* What are the causes of an observed outcome? Here we are interested in testing proposed causal relationships, identifying one or more potential independent variables and their effect on the dependent variable. For example:

- Which side of the brain is predominantly responsible for computer mouse manipulation?
- During periods of high unemployment, does the perceived threat of unemployment reduce spending among those employed?
- Do genetic traits or environmental conditions have the greatest impact on the tendency for male children of alcoholics to become alcoholics themselves?

6   *Control.* What will happen to a second proposed dependent variable if the suspected independent variable is changed? Are there any side-effects to the independent variable of interest? We could test the application of a relationship described in a theory to a new situation, or replicate another study that has tested a causal relationship. For example:

- Is stress in patients about to undergo surgery reducible by specific types of nurse intervention?
- If the organization changes to flexitime (flexible starting and finishing times for employees), will productivity increase over present levels?
- Would raising the minimum income level for qualifying for food stamps (or income support), an increase in tax allowances for low-income families or separate payment for day-care for children or retired parents have the greatest impact on reducing unemployment?

- What night-time medication regime (where prescriptions allow) would enhance quality of sleep for hospital patients?
- Will tranquillizers enhance examination performance of highly stressed students?

All the above, including the most practical sounding questions, have potential links to existing research and theories. For example, the regime for night-time medication could build on understanding of sleep patterns identified by psychologists. Many of these will be satisfactorily resolved if the variables implied are more restrictively defined and the measuring instruments or category systems carefully developed. Yet these are the types of general questions that arise in our minds as we start a research project.

In addition, any given research project may well involve more than one of these types of questions. One interesting misuse of research is that of using the results of studies that were designed to be descriptive in order to make predictions – for example, assuming that just because a set of schools has certain learning outcomes (achievement levels) this year they will necessarily have the same next year. A study that intends to find out what will happen in the future will necessarily have a different focus than one that is looking at the past. Descriptive studies may be forming the baseline for change rather than intending to be valid predictors of the future. Now carry out Activity 2.1.

Activity 2.1

(a)   Print out a statement of your research question in letters at least 1.2 cm (½ inch) high and put this on the wall over your desk. Refer back to this not only as you read this book, but also as you conduct your literature review. Changing it is not undesirable, but should occur intentionally, with some thought and reason.

(b)   In which of the six categories above would your question best fit? Why do you think its intended outcomes support this classification?

SPECIFYING VARIABLES

A major concern facing social scientists is what will be acceptable as evidence. As noted earlier, watching individuals and groups is a common means of gathering data. This focus on behaviour does not mean that all social scientists are behaviourists in the traditional sense, where the behaviour is of interest in itself. Kerlinger (1986), for example, notes that many psychologists make observations of human behaviour but use these as a basis for making inferences about what occurs in the mind. Figure 2.4 illustrates the process, which is essentially what any researcher is trying to do when making different types of observations (through watching, having subjects complete a questionnaire, etc.). It is not the behaviour on its own that is of interest, but what can be *inferred* from it. Such a model is used by psychologists, educationalists and even market researchers investigating potential demand for a product. In some cases, the bottom box may contain a prediction (whom people will vote for, what they will buy), or may ultimately be used to classify individuals (social class, mental state, relative aptitude). Inferences about social structures are also made from observing interactions within or among groups, as illustrated in Figure 2.5. Social scientists use more than just their eyes to observe, there are many other procedures for collecting data as well.

The devising of hypotheses raises the issue of which variables to employ, requiring that careful consideration be given to macrovariables (closer to reality and experience) and intervening variables, including microvariables (sometimes not even understood). The hypothesis not only defines the variables, at least in

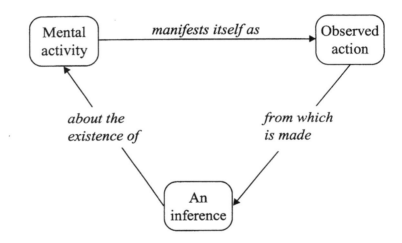

FIGURE 2.4
Making inferences about mental activity from observations

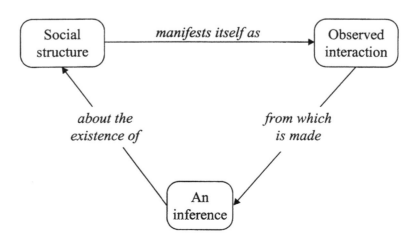

FIGURE 2.5
Observations and inferences in social contexts

general terms, but also, and even more important, puts forward a relationship to be investigated. Any statement expressing or implying causality must be logically consistent with time sequences of events and reflect the possibility of multiple causation or a chain of causal events. Even variables that are not of interest must be identified and defined if they are not going to interfere with the results.

Concepts, constructs and operational definitions

In most cases, social science research involves the investigation of events that reflect aspects of complex theories and models. Consequently, these involve *constructs*, ways of elaborating on abstract concepts, created (or accepted ones enhanced) in order to facilitate making observations that will support the theory under investigation. Often such theories define actions or interrelations among constructs that have an intuitive basis. For example, everyone has some personal meaning for the concept of intelligence, based upon informal observation of the behaviours of individuals in everyday situations.

Theories, however, tend to go a step further in that they attempt to describe relationships between intelligence and ability to learn, or environment and the development of intelligence. Thus the definition of intelligence grows in specificity, necessitating a more limited meaning and the generation of constructs. A similar development of the concept of social class could be described. We all have an intuitive feel as to where we fit in a social class structure or as members of a social group. Sociologists attempt to improve on this common sense definition of this concept. Therefore, they will bring in characteristics that they rationalize as contributing to class identification: income, education, home ownership, type of occupation, accumulated wealth, etc.

Both of these examples need to be taken yet one more step further since most research that will be dealt with here will have a quantitative nature. Consequently, a definition that produces quantitative indicators of degree is required. In other words, how can the level of intelligence of individuals be measured and quantified, how can the social class (rank) of an individual or group be determined? What is needed are rulers, instruments that will produce an acceptable way of measuring constructs, usually referred to as *operational definitions*. To establish these requires not just another level of greater specificity, but one that achieves agreement among fellow experts, and, for quantitative research, one that results in a numerical value (ordinal or interval). This is not a trivial problem and the two examples presented illustrated just how difficult it can be. One cynic has suggested that there are as many operational definitions of social class as there are sociologists. There are many intelligence tests, some of which are commercially available to purchase and others generated by research projects. Both constructs are highly contentious and it is difficult to achieve total agreement on how they should be defined, either at the construct level or operationally. This is best referred to as the problem of establishing *construct validity* – making sure the instrument measures what it is supposed to measure.

As suggested, sometimes the problem is not so much with the instrument, but with how the underlying construct has been defined. Figure 2.6 summarizes the

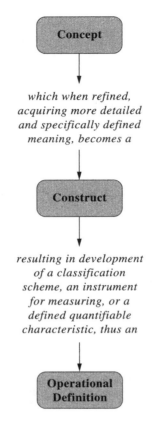

FIGURE 2.6
Ensuring construct
validity of an
operational
definition by
maintaining logical
continuity in
development: does it
measure what it is
supposed to
measure?

levels of increasing specificity and highlights the difficulty of ensuring the validity of the resulting operational definition.

Is this not jumping ahead in the model in Figure 2.1? A little bit, but the issue
of operational definitions is raised now simply to warn of the interrelationships
that exist between the stages. Initially, to define a research question and ultimately a hypothesis will require clearly defined concepts and constructs.
These tend to be based upon, or to build upon, existing theories and models,
but can still provide uncertain foundations for research considering the contentious nature of some constructs. It is best to consider these as early as possible,
particularly if the use of existing instruments is planned. It must be established
that these really do constitute a valid operational definition of the concept(s)
being considered, as defined by the research questions.

For example, there have been numerous errors committed when attempting
to define concepts operationally using responses to questionnaires. This again
has its origins in the sequence of events described in Figure 2.6. Concepts
have arisen – such as administrative effectiveness, usefulness of computers,
and quality of teaching using a specific medium (to name just a few) – which
researchers have tried to measure by asking subjects who are on the receiving
end of the process to rank various aspects of these. What is *not* being measured
is the concept described, but the subjects' *perceptions of that concept* (recall

Activity 1.3). The questionnaires will at best measure perceptions of administrative effectiveness, of usefulness of computers or of quality of teaching. This is entirely different from the concept itself and seems to be primarily a problem of progressing from concept to construct. Going back to the examples, by and large the criteria for administrative effectiveness, usefulness of computers and quality of teaching using a medium will be most validly determined by establishing performance criteria and checking to see how well the results of the given situation meet these criteria.

This is not to say that measuring the subjects' perception of effectiveness is not worthwhile. Personal perception of the three concepts above might be related to the morale of an individual and how well the administration is able to maintain a high level, attitudes towards computers, and the personality of the teacher. But personnel do not tend to be experts on administration, computer users are not necessarily knowledgeable on the potential of computers in a given situation, and determining the quality of teaching requires more than the subjective evaluation by students. Questionnaires are 'fashionable', deceptively easy to create (though not necessarily good ones) and commonly used in research. This introduction to a problem that will be discussed in greater detail in later chapters is just to forewarn at the stage of devising a hypothesis, of a potential pitfall.

Kerlinger (1986) identifies two types of operational definitions, measured and experimental, which will be given what are considered to be slightly more meaningful names related to their roles as variables: *observed* and *manipulated*. Observed operational definitions are concerned with characteristics of subjects that are measured (such as intelligence), observed behaviour (such as frequency of smiling as an indicator of being pleased), achievement (as measured by a test), or such attributes as social class, gender, age, attitudes and long-term memory. The term 'manipulated' will be used for things that happen to subjects that are operational definitions of the construct (hypothesized dependent variables), such as reinforcement in the classroom (positive, neutral or negative), frequency of interruption of sleep, amount of background noise. In experimental studies, researchers may want subjects to experience different levels of a construct, and, as a consequence, they will manipulate conditions to generate these. Later the problems of deciding how variables are to be measured will be considered in greater depth, but an operational definition cannot be comprehensive in its measurement of a concept or construct. At best, it will be an indicator from which the researcher will be able to infer the level of its existence. A questionnaire cannot ask all the possible questions, so a sample of possible statements is used. Observations cover a sample of events, again not all that are possible.

The term *validity* is one that is frequently used in the world of research and measurement. There will be several types of validity to consider as the details of the various skills of research are revealed, and it will be worthwhile keeping them in perspective. If all the decisions have high validity, then the results of the research will have strong support. Recalling the problem implied by Figure 2.3, the value of considering issues of validity is that the questions raised usually transcend more than one step in the diagram of stages of carrying out a research project. Therefore, as shown in Figure 2.7, the consideration of the first type that has been introduced, *construct validity* of the variables to be measured, occurs at least three points in the procedure, and probably others: when devising

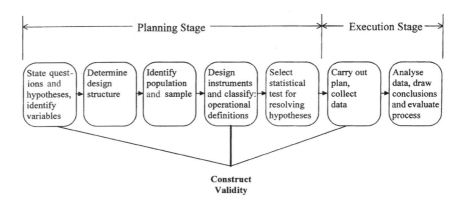

FIGURE 2.7
Impact of construct validity on the research design process and the overall quality of the results

a hypothesis; when designing instruments (of prime interest); and when collecting data (including administering the instruments). Obviously, we will return to the issue of construct validity in subsequent chapters, and the other three types of validity will be introduced by the end of this chapter.

A further problem faces the researcher: not all concepts lend themselves to measurement and consequently will not be good variables to try to quantify – for example, effective teaching, quality of life, and good research. This is primarily because these are not really individual variables but rubrics that subsume a variety of characteristics. This does not prevent someone from trying, but because of the complexity of such variables, it will be extremely difficult, if not impossible in some situations, to arrive at a reliable and valid operational definition. Carry out Activity 2.2 now.

Activity 2.2

List and define in as much detail as possible each of the concepts and constructs that you intend to investigate in your research. Are any of them contentious? On what theory or theories are they based? How do you think you will measure these and/or how do you think you will classify outcomes or subjects?

Set these aside for now, they will be referred to and used later.

Ways of classifying variables

When considering how a construct is to be defined operationally, it is necessary to decide how it will be quantified and how it will be used in a study. There are a number of ways of describing these, but the most common place to start is to consider them to be *variables*, which implies that they are not constant and have more than one value, level or aspect. Even the gender of the subjects has two physiological categories. Other constructs will be operationally defined in such a way as to provide a larger number of possible categories or values. In fact there may even be a choice of how one quantifies a variable or how many levels are used. First it is necessary to address an issue of semantics, one that has come across from other science areas and often contributes to misunderstanding of the relationships between variables.

The language of social science research has inherited some interesting terminology from the physical and biological sciences, some of which can be misleading when used inappropriately. It is frequently assumed that all research only aims at establishing cause and effect relationships between variables: if A is changed it will cause B to change accordingly. Causality is extremely difficult to establish in the multivariate world of human activity and there are many non-causal relationships among variables, such as correlations, that are of great interest. These may provide clues to the eventual establishment of causal relationships. Consequently, there is a need to be somewhat cautious in the use of terminology to ensure that the desired meaning is conveyed, keeping in mind the statistical tools that have been adopted.

For example, in assuming the existence of causal relationships, variables are often expressed as being either independent or dependent variables. A *dependent variable*, such as the optimum time between feedings for animals in a zoo, depends on one or more *independent variables,* such as the type of activity or amount of exercise. Time between feedings, for example, implies that the longer an animal goes without eating, the hungrier it will get, though the relationship may not be a linear one. In other words, an animal may not gradually get hungrier and hungrier as time goes on, but may reach a maximum, as illustrated in Figure 2.8(b). While this seems fairly obvious, in reality at a physiological level, the sensation of hunger (a difficult construct to define operationally) depends upon the lowering of blood sugar, as shown in Figure 2.8(a). Yet 'hunger' is possibly a better indicator for determining the independent variable in this situation, since it may be easier to detect, as shown roughly by the lettered points on Figure 2.8b:

- not interested in food up to and around N, creature just lies about;
- a little hungry at O, it starts to look around;
- paces back and forth to food bowl at P;
- very restless in cage, salivating and making noises, close to point R.

The time for interval B is expected to vary with the type and/or amount of exercise the animals undertake.

Just what *are* the independent and dependent variables in situations that involve a chain of events? If we choose to measure as Y the type or amount of activity since last feed (independent) versus time T, the interval B until maximum hunger and it is necessary to feed (dependent), using the indicators described, then we are assuming the presence of the two intervening variables, blood sugar drop and increased hunger:

Y				$\rightarrow T$
amount of $\rightarrow$ activity	enhances blood sugar drop	$\rightarrow$ sensed as increased hunger	$\rightarrow$ demonstrated as restlessness in cage	$\rightarrow$ used to delimit time until next feed

To a certain extent, the classification depends on what the research question is and what is to be measured. Time intervals are considerably easier to measure

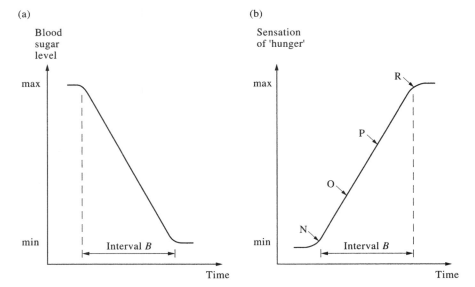

FIGURE 2.8
Changes in (a) blood
sugar and (b)
sensation of hunger
in animals over time

using hunger as an indicator than blood sugar levels in an animal (this assumes a lack of nice modern microtechnological components relaying sugar levels to the researcher, ones that could be innocuously attached to the animal). It is recognized that possibly neither graph is linear, but what is important is that the time interval *B* is the same for both. This means that one would have to test the operational definition of *maximum sensation of hunger at R*, when the animal becomes most restless, to see how well it corresponds to minimum blood sugar (not necessarily an easy task). But the real issue is to clarify what the research question is: how long should it be between feedings in the zoo, or how much exercise should the animals receive? Or, what is the relationship between activity and level of blood sugar? If it is the zoo personnel who initiate the study, then they are interested in preventing stress in animals. Who wants a grumpy gorilla or an irritable aardvark?

Though the variable of time until hungry is not the most direct macrovariable, for this study of feeding of animals, it is an acceptable observed dependent variable for the research question asked. The level of blood sugar would be considered in this case to be the microvariable, or in some texts, the intervening variable. The researcher could vary the activity, an experimental, manipulated independent variable, which should affect the rate of decline of available blood sugar, which in turn should increase the sensation of hunger (macrovariable), and the restlessness of the animal, resulting in a time interval between feedings that could be recorded.

This kind of thinking has carried over into social science research, though the intervening (or micro) variables are often less well understood and frequently not even directly measurable in such a way as to confirm the relationships. For example, as Kerlinger (1986) points out, intelligence is one of the better-known latent variables: it is an underlying construct that contributes to subjects' performance on verbal and mathematical ability tests. Unfortunately it is not possible to measure intelligence physiologically like blood sugar levels, at least not yet. Consequently, this leaves such a construct on a weak foundation, so it is not surprising that its measurement through an IQ test (operational definition) is contentious. At the same time, it is also not surprising that scores on such tests are considered to be a convenient macrovariable for research studies.

Social class is even more difficult to employ since it is often difficult to tell whether it is an independent or a dependent variable. Is a person middle class because he or she read certain types of books and specific newspapers, owns a car of a specific type, and has an income within a certain range, or does being middle class compel one to buy books and specific newspapers, drive certain cars and be assured of having a good income? What *is* the intervening or latent variable? Is the problem that there is not just one but *many*? With such a tenuous grip on tangibility, it is not surprising that much research based on such constructs is less concerned with cause and effect and more with non-causal associations, such as correlations and associations between variables. Some constructs may be like a good cheese, they need time to mature to see whether they become acceptable or just go off and smell bad.

On a more practical level, studies on people – for example, travellers passing through a train station, somewhat analogous to the one described above on animals in a zoo – are much harder to conduct. Yes, people tend to eat breakfast, lunch and dinner, but there are seemingly constantly grazing young people, travellers who missed breakfast to catch the early train, etc. Put yourself in the position of a consultant and consider the problem presented in Activity 2.3 now.

Activity 2.3

Albert McDougal, hamburger entrepreneur at Waterloo Station in London, wants to know how best to staff his stand to cope with hungry commuters from the trains. Albert wishes to commission a piece of research to help him determine *optimal* staffing of his stand to provide McDougal Burgers and McDougal Scones to a hungry clientele rushing through Waterloo, which, for those who have not passed through this station, has 41 tracks and thousands of travellers per day. He could do it by trial and error, but over-staffing wastes money and under-staffing deters impatient customers. The first question is: Are there any eating patterns?

(a) What would be a possible dependent variable? Note that Albert may not be getting sufficient customers for a number of reasons – for example, the McDougal Burgers may be awful, staff uniforms may be unattractive, his stand may not be optimally sited, etc. – so just the number or rate of customers might be poor dependent variables. In other words, is it possible to find an indicator of hunger easily recognizable in people in order to see if there is a pattern in potential customers? This is more difficult since most people do not drool (at least not noticeably) in public when hungry while walking through a train station. Restlessness or irritability may be due to hunger or just the stress of travel. So what may work for animals may not be good variables for people.

> (b)   What are some of the independent variables that might influence the
>   dependent variable? Are they measurable or detectable, and could
>   they be influenced by Mr McDougal?
> (c)   Propose a chain of causality that includes intervening variables. This
>   may prompt you to reconsider or revise your answers to (a) and (b).
>
> After any eating pattern is identified, Albert still has other independent
> variables to consider that would influence eating at his stand, but let us
> keep this simple for now. Obviously, there are any number of acceptable
> answers to the above questions and these might make a productive start-
> ing-point for a class discussion.

Non-causal relationships

While causal relationships are the most satisfying to find, not all relationships
that are identified by researchers are necessarily causal. There are situations
where both variables increase together or as one increases the other decreases
because both are effects caused by a third variable. These relationships are
usually described as linear correlational, and they are best illustrated as scatter
diagrams of data points, such as in Figure 2.9, with one variable along the horizontal axis and the other along the vertical axis. Thus if one variable is related
to another for a well-defined group, then a known value of one can be used to
provide a corresponding predicted value for the other. The precision of such a
prediction will be governed by how tight the scatterplot is, which is quantified
by the correlation coefficient. The more the data points group around a straight
line, the closer the correlation will be to 1.0. If the plot were to form a circular
cloud of points, the correlation would be zero and it would be impossible to predict one variable from the other. The scatter diagram in Figure 2.9 would result
in a correlation of about 0.80. Finding the two regression equations and plotting
the lines as shown would allow one to predict a value for variable A given a
value for variable B from one line, or B from A using the other line. Even
with these data, care should be taken not to imply that one causes the other
simply by virtue of choice of axes. Such studies are considering the interrelation-
ship between two variables for a *single* group. Traditionally in the physical
sciences, the dependent variable is plotted along the vertical axis (usually
referred to as the Y-axis) and the independent variable is plotted along the horizontal axis (referred to as the X-axis).

With some uncertainty facing the researcher as to the nature of the relationship between variables, a certain amount of caution needs to be exercised when
describing a research question and hypotheses. Questions are usually stated in
terms of concepts, and hypotheses tend to be more specific statements describing relationships among constructs and possibly operational definitions. The
difficulty in wording is exacerbated by the amount of control over the variables
that can be exercised by the researcher. Kerlinger (1986) describes those that can
be manipulated as *active variables* – examples are time until being fed, type of
learning materials encountered, and nature of rewards and punishments for
actions. Variables over which researchers do not have control and which are

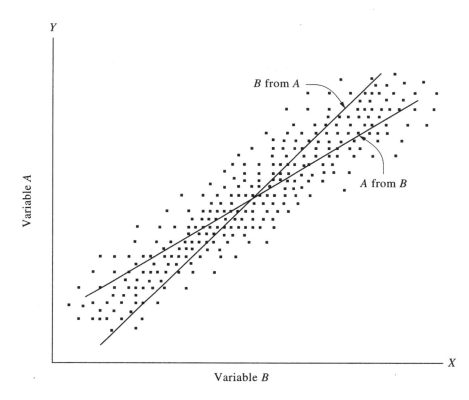

FIGURE 2.9
Scatter diagram
showing a
correlational
relationship with
regression lines
provided

basically characteristics of subjects are *attribute variables*, – examples are age, sex and aptitude of subjects. Sometimes intelligence is included in the latter group, which would raise the blood pressure of some researchers who maintain that it is a manipulable variable: changeable with experience and learning. So even these categories need to be treated with care due to implied meanings associated with their use.

The nature of the relationship between variables will influence the subsequent design of the research, thus the statement must be unambiguous. The choice of variables and their relationship needs to be based upon reasonable expectations, particularly if the hypothesis is to establish support for a causal one. The situation of a chain of events was presented earlier, but it is possible to choose variables that are related, where the direction is of causality is ambiguous, possibly because there is a third variable:

$$Z$$
$$\swarrow \quad \searrow$$
$$A \quad \leftrightarrows \quad B$$

Thus choosing to describe the relationship as *A causing B* ($A \rightarrow B$) could result in a situation that would adversely affect the possibility of achieving any support for the hypothesis. Recall the example of animals and feeding times: stress might be a good example of Z, which would potentially have an impact on both A, the type of activity an animal might engage in, and B, the time it took to grow hungry. If there is such a degree of uncertainty, then a causal relationship ought not even to be hypothesized. More appropriately, a correlational study would help to understand the relationships among the three (or in some cases, more) variables.

Controlling variables

Having soundly established the nature of a potential causal relationship, the subsequent design will focus on ensuring that if an effect, *B*, is observed then only *A* will have been able to cause it. Preventing other extraneous variables from interfering is a difficult task and the focus of following chapters, but this can be expressed as follows: a design that includes a proposal for a clear causal relationship, and allows for the control of all other possible contributing variables, is said to possess a high level of *internal validity*.

The threats to internal validity are many. The list that follows was started by Campbell and Stanley (1963) and has subsequently been modified and expanded. The relative importance of each will vary with academic discipline and specific study, and these will be further sub-divided in later chapters:

1   Choice of variables and any uncertainty of direction of causality have already been discussed above.
2   The number of groups of subjects may influence one's ability to ensure that unwanted variables do not influence the proposed dependent variable. The extreme situation, a study having no internal validity (no support for causality), is the one conducted with a single group. This approach lacks a similar comparison group that was not subjected to the variable in question (a control group).
3   Time is often a potential problem: if too much goes by there is an increased chance that other events or even internal changes of subjects may influence outcomes.
4   The nature of the sample(s) themselves and whether or not any members are lost before the study is completed may well affect the overall results for a group.
5   The actual measuring instruments used and how they are administered can introduce unwanted variables. For example, in situations where more than one measurement is taken of a group, subjects may actually learn from the first administration, or be influenced in some other way by the instrument.

As might be guessed, there may even be reactions between these, such as an inappropriate time-scale for a specific sample group: time may potentially introduce other variables that would influence some samples more than others. To protect the outcomes of a study from the influence of these unwanted potential variables, a number of established designs will be introduced as starting-points in Chapters 3 and 5. At this stage in the process, we need to provide a sound statement of a hypothesis. It should be noted that the appropriateness of the statement of the relationship among the variables will have a bearing on the design of the test of this relationship. Figure 2.10 shows the main points within the design process where decisions will be made to ensure that internal validity will be maintained. This involves making certain that only the variables we want will be possible causes.

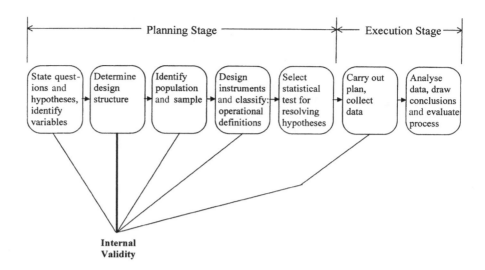

FIGURE 2.10
Ensuring internal
validity during a
research study

DEVELOPING HYPOTHESES

Few of us would even engage in research if the outcomes were not of interest to us. In reality, this means we have expected outcomes in mind, but these do not have to prejudice the results of the study. On the contrary, they can, and should, be expressed as *hypotheses*, statements of expected outcome which can be subsequently tested. Such expressions of outcomes usually refer to expected relationships between variables, though not necessarily causal ones. Such relationships, expressed in unambiguous terms, assist in determining the direction the study will take. This does not mean that once the hypotheses have been stated you cannot change your mind in light of additional reading or planning, but by stating specific hypotheses you have set a direction. It is possible intentionally to change it, but it should not be allowed to drift and change unintentionally. Such a statement should allow you to stand back from your research and examine what the nature of the outcome of the research will be. If you find that the hypotheses are too general or vague, then it will be difficult to make decisions on constructs and operational definitions. In fact the realization of just how weak a hypothesis is may not become apparent until you try to devise operational definitions for the variables indicated. If this occurs, a jump backwards to the first box in Figure 2.10 would be appropriate.

Too specific a hypothesis may imply relationships among trivial variables. While it is necessary to keep a project down to a manageable size, there is always the danger that one will focus too finely. Kerlinger (1986) provides the example of a study on the relationship between reading speed and size or type of font. While this may be valid and interesting, it would not be of sufficient consequence to constitute a viable study on its own. On the other hand, it may be a valid component of a larger study on media, presentation and communication, which might be exploring various variables related to enhancing understanding of written materials. A balance must be found between too great a specificity and vague generality that tries to encompass too many variables at once.

Earlier a scheme was presented for classifying different types of research questions based upon the purpose of the study. Now let us consider the problem of just how such questions may be resolved, since the design approach should be a consequence of refining the research question and producing specific hypotheses about expected outcomes. While there is notable lack of consensus on the meanings of the following, the definitions given should provide a basis for considering the nature of approaches. In any case, most studies employ more than one approach and the intent is to reflect on what are likely to be the most profitable tools to employ in resolving the research question at hand. The six types of approaches are defined as follows:

1   *Qualitative description.* There is always the necessity to describe processes and relationships verbally. Many studies involve interviews and observations that do not result in quantitative data, but written descriptions of results and impressions of events. Through such approaches, it is sometimes possible to determine chains of causality that could not be ascertained any other way. The techniques employed in such qualitative approaches are not part of this text and are presented in other volumes as large as this one. To carry out such approaches properly is not an easier option than employing more quantitative approaches as they are subject to equivalent demands for rigour. The limitation to qualitative studies is often one of lack of generalizability. It is usually not feasible to include representative samples of sufficiently large groups, either because of practical problems of scale, or the nature of the observations or situations.

2   *Descriptive statistics.* This involves collecting quantitative data, but presenting them only descriptively, often in the form of graphs and charts. Simply collecting and collating data about groups can be quite revealing, providing insights that would not otherwise be apparent. Such an approach, though, does not provide evidence to support the existence of relationships. Neither correlational nor causal links can be established from the clever juxtapositioning of graphs and charts.

3   *Normative.* Such an approach implies that one is comparing the results of group traits or performance to a known population. These can provide the support for further studies, allowing the investigation of whether a group deviates sufficiently from the 'norm' to merit further study. Such an approach can also be used to evaluate the effectiveness or impact of change, or test the representativeness of a sample. The difficulty with such an approach lies in the fact there are few traits for which we have population data. IQ tests are designed to produce a mean of 100 and a standard deviation of 15 for populations of age groups. It may be possible to obtain population data for comparison from demographic data or complete databases, but often these are not available.

4   *Correlative.* This refers to quantitative approaches that investigate relationships as pairs of variables, to see how they vary with respect to each other. Though unable to establish much support for causality, such studies can provide the rationale for more structured experimental or quasi-experimental studies when population parameters are known. Correlative studies can also be considered ex post facto (see 6 below).

5 *Experimental/quasi-experimental.* In such approaches, there is an endeavour carefully to control variables other than the ones under consideration through highly structured designs, as will be seen in subsequent chapters. These approaches have the greatest potential for acquiring substantive support for causality, but are often extremely difficult to conduct in real-life situations. When the samples are not completely random and subject to practical considerations that possibly reduce the generalizability of the results, such designs are referred to as quasi-experimental.

6 *Ex post facto.* This term literally means 'after the fact' and refers to what one might call real-life studies that employ some of the same measurement and statistical tools as used in experimental and quasi-experimental studies. The difference is in the lack of direct control over the independent variables: life experiences (amount of education, IQ, occupation) replace researcher-determined treatments that would have been possible in a more structured situation. The validity of possible independent variables is ensured through the quality of sampling from groups that have undergone the live experiences that constitute those variables. While it may be possible to establish causality in some situations, the results may only support associations. The nature of the variables and conditions will help the researcher to decide which is the most appropriate description of the outcomes.

How do these categories compare to those described earlier in the chapter for classifying research questions? Some of them have greater potential than others for providing the mechanism by which these questions can be resolved. Also, as seen above, the nature of the question may determine whether one employs a representative sample, employs a quasi-experimental design, or carries out a *case study* using an existing limited group or purposively selected subjects and employing a combination of quantitative and qualitative approaches. Case studies allow the researcher the opportunity to pursue issues to a greater depth in more realistic situations (assuming the researcher does not become a variable through his or her actions). Thus it is probably not surprising that when the two classification schemes are compared in a matrix such as shown in Table 2.1, each category of questions does not profitably employ potentially every approach. This is indicated by the fact that not all the boxes have ticks (✓) in them to indicate appropriate combinations.

TABLE 2.1
Types of research questions and corresponding appropriate design approaches

	Design approaches					
	Case Study		**Representative Samples**			
Questions:	**Qualitative description**	**Descriptive statistics**	**Normative**	**Correlative**	**Experimental, quasi-experimental**	**Ex post facto**
Descriptive	✓	✓	✓			
Explorative	✓		✓	✓		
Evaluative	✓		✓	✓	✓	✓
Predictive				✓	✓	✓
Explanatory	✓			✓	✓	✓
Control					✓	✓

Going across the top of Table 2.1, there is an overlap of approaches employed by case studies and by those involving representative samples: both can use descriptive statistics. There is a slight problem with the terminology since, to be pedantic, the term *statistics* describes the numbers that represent the quantitative characteristics of a sample of a larger population. *Parameters*, on the other hand, are the values for the population. It could be argued, that since case studies do not use representative samples, the groups investigated are really populations and any quantitative data are not statistics but parameters. In any case, this does not prevent one from plotting graphs to facilitate understanding of quantitative data collected during a case study.

More important to notice is that none of the four approaches that result in inferences about larger populations (normative, correlative, experimental/ quasi-experimental, ex post facto) is included under case studies. The term *inferential statistics* indicates that on the basis of the statistics collected on representative samples, inferences will be made about characteristics, traits or performances of populations. Thus the distinction is based upon sampling and issues will arise later on just how representative a sample is. For example, can a study employing a convenience sample (e.g., the neighbours, the school down the road, your friends in class) be considered capable of finding outcomes representative of a larger population, or is the group to be considered a population in its own right and the research to be classified as a case study? The outcome of such a decision would be the basis for determining the validity of the choice of statistical tools employed. As we proceed, we will return to this issue again.

This is not to belittle case studies, but let us call a car a car and not mistake it for a donkey: there are places you cannot get to in a car and only on a donkey (for example, down the cliff paths of the Grand Canyon) and places you do not belong on a donkey (on a motorway, autobahn or interstate highway). In reality, case studies and those employing representative samples of populations complement each other, adding another dimension to the evolution of a theory or resolving a practical (applied) problem. Case studies enhance the investigation of subjects in real situations where interaction is of paramount interest and they encourage greater depth of study of chains of events. On the other hand, they do not allow one to generalize either to larger populations or general situations. Studies with representative samples justify greater generalizability but tend to involve fewer variables and may be in a context somewhat less than ideal for relating the results to real situations. Case studies tend to allow one to answer 'why' and 'how' questions more thoroughly than those with representative samples, whereas the latter allow one to see how widespread the phenomena are.

Many projects, not surprisingly, have a bit of both, or investigations of one type build upon the findings of research employing the other. A case study on establishing successful counselling practices employed by a selected group of counsellors with a small number of alcoholics (evaluative) may be followed by an investigation involving the observation of a more representative sample of counsellors contending with a more diverse group of alcoholics to determine whether or not such techniques can be successfully implemented by others (evaluative). A survey that finds support for a tendency for availability of methods of birth control to be linked to a decline in the number of children per family (explorative) would be profitably followed by in-depth interviews of a few sub-jects (case study) to try to determine *why* this has happened (explanatory). This in turn might be followed by a survey to determine whether the reasons ascer-tained in the case-study interviews are widely held in a larger population, or were idiosyncratic to the group contacted (explanatory). Figure 2.11 emphasizes some of the benefits of this symbiotic relationship between approaches, one that is too often missed by texts that try to take sides, choosing one to the exclusion of the other.

So what makes a statement of a hypothesis different from that of a research question? First, it will be more specific and indicate the variables involved. Second, it is not unusual to find one question generates a number of hypotheses. Third, it would indicate the population and situation to which the study's results could be extended. Table 2.2 takes a few of the research questions presented as examples earlier and provides corresponding possible hypotheses. As will be seen later, many of the designs implied are not as strong as they could be, but stating the hypotheses explicitly allows one to evaluate them with time and further consideration.

For the majority of this text, we will focus on those studies that employ as representative a sample as possible, and recommend that those wishing to pursue a non-quantitative case-study approach seek guidance from alternative resources. Thus for the hypotheses to be described in subsequent chapters, one component will be a statement (or implication) of the population to which and in what situations and times the relationship will apply. Acquiring a sample and ensuring that the conditions under which the study is carried out are represen-tative of the situations and time to which the results are to apply ensures what is referred to as *external validity*.

External validity can be adversely affected by failing to ensure that pro-cedures listed below are carried out appropriately:

1   The sample must obviously be representative and stable over the period of the study in order to ensure generalizability to the larger population(s).
2   The sample must not be influenced by time, allowing other events to inter-fere.
3   When the independent variable is an observed trait (such as gender, occupa-tion, educational background) instead of one that can be manipulated, the representativeness of the sample influences the validity of that variable. In other words, having specified the characteristics of four different occupa-tional groups (construct validity), it is necessary to obtain representative samples of each if the results will generalize to them.

FIGURE 2.11
The relationship between case studies and studies involving representative samples of larger populations

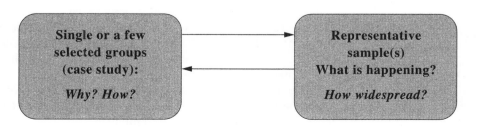

TABLE 2.2
Sample hypotheses
derived from
exemplar questions

Questions	Hypotheses
Do assembly-line workers suffer more or less from sleep disorders than the general population of employed persons?	A random sample of assembly-line workers in factories in Birmingham will be found to suffer a greater frequency of sleep interruptions, and a longer amount of time awake after going to bed, than the population as a whole.
Which of several counselling approaches had the greatest success on reducing the return to drinking among alcoholics?	One of three counselling approaches, A, B or C, will produce a larger reduction in frequency of return to drinking among alcoholics.
Are there any relationships across social class, educational achievement, and drug use among 18–24-year-olds?	It is expected that there will be a negative correlation between social class and drug use, and a negative correlation between educational achievement and drug use, for a representative selection of 18–24-year-olds.
Do genetic traits or environmental conditions have the greater impact on the tendency for male children of alcoholics to become alcoholics themselves?	For a sample of identical twin boys who are the sons of alcoholic fathers and fostered or adopted from infancy separately from each other, one to a family with at least one alcoholic parent, one group will show a greater tendency towards alcoholism than the other.
What night-time medication regime (where prescriptions allow) would enhance quality of sleep for hospital patients?	In a given hospital, patients on 24-hour prescriptions will be expected to feel more rested if they are awakened for medicines at times that follow rapid eye movement (REM) rather than just at equal time intervals.

4 For experimental studies where a sample group has an experience or 'treatment', it should not be out of context or unnatural if the results are to be generalizable to 'real-world' situations. This also includes studies involving multiple treatments.

5 The measuring instrument should not interact with any one sample group that represents an observed trait differently from others. For example, it has been suggested that any differences in IQ scores between ethnic groups could be attributed to cultural bias in the wording of the test questions.

To ensure that the results validly apply to the groups and situations specified, the researcher will address issues of design, planning and execution at each of the points indicated in Figure 2.12. This starts with specifying a well-defined population in the hypothesis or hypotheses from which it is feasible to take representative sample(s).

While trying to devise a statement of your hypotheses (or after you have made an attempt at writing one), consider the following which summarize the criteria for a sound statement of research intent:

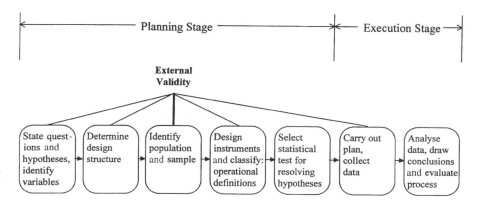

FIGURE 2.12
Ensuring external
validity of a study at
the various stages

1   The hypothesis is based on accepted theory or personal well-justified theory,
    and other research including case studies and descriptive accounts, specify-
    ing some relationship among variables.
2   A limited number of variables are included, all of which are measurable or
    classifiable as potentially valid operational definitions of concepts in the
    theory.
3   The direction of potential causality is not questionable.
4   Representativeness of the conditions in which the study will be conducted
    and of the sample(s) are both potentially achievable.
5   Any treatment necessary could be designed to be sufficiently natural as to
    allow extrapolation of results to the relevant real-world situation.
6   By implication, the time-scale over which the study will necessarily be con-
    ducted will not introduce other variables (e.g., outside influences, matura-
    tion of subjects).

Now carry out Activity 2.4.

Activity 2.4

(a)   Choose at least one research question from each of the six purpose
      groups presented earlier (or use one of your own from each group)
      and generate a possible hypothesis.
(b)   Based on your research question (see Activity 2.1), print out a state-
      ment of your research hypothesis or hypotheses in letters at least
      1.2 cm (½ inch) high and put it on the wall over your desk. Is it
      (are they) consistent with your research question(s)? There is no
      reason why these cannot change with time before the data are
      collected.
(c)   What approaches are implied by your questions/hypotheses?
(d)   Check your hypothesis or hypotheses against the six criteria above,
      and revise your statements if necessary.

IDENTIFYING MEASURABLE VARIABLES

Variables by definition are constructs, traits or characteristics that vary. For example, within a group of subjects, it is possible to find both males and females having a range of ages. This example illustrates that for a variable to vary may result in different categories (sex) or a difference in magnitude (age). Operational definitions of constructs that vary will result in data which will fall into one of four categories:

1   *Nominal.* Variables of this type have name value only and there are at least two categories, as with sex, profession, school attended, county of residence, race, religion. No order or ranking is implied or intended, and inclusion in a category is binary: a subject either belongs or does not.
2   *Ordinal.* In this category some order or rank is intended: examples are social class, opinions solicited on a questionnaire, or job position in a hierarchy. The intervals between ranks are not assumed to be equal, thus the difference between first and second is not necessarily the same as the difference between second and third.
3   *Interval.* Data of this type could have a value on a continuous scale but there is no zero point where the trait does not exist. This differs significantly from ordinal data in that the intervals between each number are the same and, more important, the magnitude of what is measured and represented by numbers has equal intervals. This includes IQ scores, for which zero would have no meaning.
4   *Ratio.* In this case the scale is continuous, but there is an absolute zero and it has meaning: there is nothing there. For example, scores on an achievement test (how many points out of 10 possible) can have a score of zero, indicating a total lack of skills and knowledge of that topic.

Classifying individual subjects into nominal and ordinal categories based upon personal characteristics can be complicated and not without difficulty: which social class, what level in school (age, year, courses), which political affiliation (and at what time). The process can be alleviated by defining rigorously, and in considerable detail, what constitutes the category or level, that is, operationally defining the construct in sufficient detail to remove all ambiguity. This may also make the researcher a target for criticism, but you should be able to defend the operational definition's construct validity. In other words, are the levels defined in sufficient detail to delineate identifiable characteristics clearly?

The differences between interval and ratio data are subtle, since both generate a continuous scale of numbers. These include the fact that a trait represented by a ratio value describes the actual amount of that trait. Thus on an achievement test, a person having a score of 26 has correctly answered twice as many questions as a person having 13, and someone who is 42 has lived twice as long as someone who is 21. But on an IQ test (interval data) having an IQ of 140 does *not* mean the person is twice as intelligent as the person with an IQ score of 70. The raw score may be interval data (number of correct answers) but the actual traditional IQ score was the raw score converted into a mental age divided by chronological age, thus zero had no meaning. On a questionnaire of 10 items with five choices each, it would be possible to award each choice one to five points. Then the range of scores would be 10 to 50 and zero would have no meaning with respect to the operational definition, assuming a subject answered all the questions.

One must be a bit careful about some continuous variables as they do not necessarily result in being interval variables. For example, while time is a continuous variable (it is on a scale that can have any value), in some circumstances it may not be an interval variable. For example, if one were considering an event in schools, it might be that class contact time across different courses or institutions varied. The length of a period or class may differ in increments of five minutes: 30, 35, 40, 45, 50 or 55 minutes. Thus observations of frequency of use of positive reinforcement would be best expressed as a rate: number per unit time (e.g., number of reinforcements per minute), rather than the number of times reinforcement was used in a class. Then the time duration of the class would not matter.

Measurement of a human characteristic as such is just a means by which an *indicator* of the relative level of a trait is ascertained. Often we cannot 'see' the trait or how much of it is possessed; we must infer the level of its existence and therefore the numerical results are one level away from reality. Again, the issue of construct validity arises: is it possible to infer validly the relative level of possession of a trait (e.g., intelligence) by someone based upon their score on the designed test (e.g., IQ score)? Typically, the most interesting variables tend to be the ones for which it is most difficult to find or design a good indicator.

With several ways of classifying variables, it is useful to see how they can combine into categories that assist in the design of a hypothesis. Figure 2.13 shows how the three schemes actually overlap, providing 12 separate possible categories for variables that might be part of a study. Deciding in which of the 12 cells each variable would reside will eventually assist in deciding which statistical tests will be available for resolving the hypotheses.

Null hypotheses

The rather convoluted thinking of null hypotheses is necessary if we are going to set the scene for testing hypotheses using statistical tools. As noted in Chapter 1, theories survive and gain support as a result of not being disproved, rather than being proven conclusively. For sound theories, this does not imply a ticking bomb waiting to explode in the form of some researcher in the future proving it wrong. What it does suggest is that researchers are usually trying out components of a theory in different situations or with different groups; they are looking for the *limits* of applicability or refinements in detail. Hypotheses, as described above, express anticipated outcomes as predicted by a given theory or the expected consequence of an application of principles to a situation, stated in more specific terms than those of a general research question.

When it comes to testing hypotheses, all that statistics can tell us is whether the outcomes we ultimately see could have happened due to some causal relationship *or* simply by chance alone. In other words, the effect has to be big enough, whether it is the difference in average scores on some performance task for two groups, or the size of a correlation coefficient. The null hypothesis

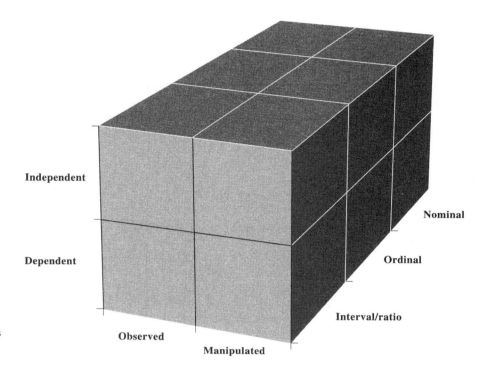

FIGURE 2.13
A scheme for
classifying variables
in hypotheses

simply states that 'no significant difference' is expected between what we obtain
and what would happen by chance alone. If the difference observed is greater
than some minimum, then it is considered significant and whatever has happened (probably) did not occur by chance alone. It is still up to the researcher
to prove through sound design and data collection that nothing could have
caused the observed effect other than what is described in the hypothesis.

So the next stage in refining our statement of hypotheses would be to try to
express them as null hypotheses related to the data that will be collected. As
a consequence of a given study, several types of null hypothesis could be generated – for example, describing differences in scores or frequencies of events
between the sample and the population (normative), *or* between two groups
or among three or more groups – i.e., they actually belong to the same population, not to separate populations (experimental, quasi-experimental or ex post
facto). The statements simply anticipate that any difference(s) will be too
small to be attributable to anything but chance.

Alternatively, if one were carrying out a correlational study, the null hypothesis of 'no significant correlation' anticipates correlations that will be so small
that they could have happened by chance alone. To illustrate this, the hypotheses of Table 2.2 above are provided in Table 2.3 with corresponding possible
null hypotheses.

The process of specifying a null hypothesis is one that focuses the attention on
what will happen next, stating the implications of the proposed relationship
among variables in terms that can be resolved by statistical instruments (see
Figure 2.14). At this stage, it is sometimes possible to identify potential difficulties in carrying out the research. For example, where are we going to find the

TABLE 2.3
Hypotheses from
Table 2.2 and
potential
corresponding null
hypotheses

Hypotheses	Null hypotheses
A random sample of assembly-line workers in factories in Birmingham will be found to suffer a greater frequency of sleep interruptions, and a longer amount of time awake after going to bed, than the population as a whole.	(Both of the hypotheses assume that population data exist.) There will be no significant difference between the mean number of times per night that assembly-line workers in Birmingham awaken and the mean for the population of employed adults as a whole, or between the mean number of minutes that these workers are awake per night and that for the population of employed adults.
One of three counselling approaches, A, B or C, will produce a greater reduction in frequency of return to drinking among alcoholics.	There will be no significant difference frequencies of 'dry' and return drinkers across three equivalent sets of alcoholics participating in the three counselling approaches, A, B, C.
It is expected that there will be a negative correlation between social class and drug use, and a negative correlation between educational achievement and drug use for a representative selection of 18–24-year-olds.	There will be no significant correlation between social class and frequency of drug use, or between educational achievement and frequency of drug use for a random selection of 18–24-year-olds (i.e., any correlation will not differ from that which could be expected by chance alone).
For a sample of identical twin boys who are the sons of alcoholic fathers *and* fostered or adopted from infancy separately from each other, one to a family with at least one alcoholic parent, one group will show a greater tendency towards alcoholism than the other.	There will be no significant difference in frequency of alcoholism between groups of separated twins, all sons of alcoholics, when one twin goes to a family with at least one alcoholic parent and the other goes to a family with no alcoholic parents.
In a given hospital, patients on 24-hour prescriptions will be expected to feel more rested if they are awakened for medicines at times that follow REM rather than just at equal time intervals.	There will be no significant difference in the perception of feeling rested, as measured by the Bloggs Restedness Scale completed by patients, between two groups: those whose medication was administered at regular time intervals and those whose medication was administered at times close to times prescribed but following a period of REM.

sample of twins implied by the fourth proposal in Table 2.3? Some of the more interesting questions generate very difficult scenarios for resolving them, compelling researchers to rethink the hypotheses resulting from a question. Obviously, it is better to consider such issues early in the research process before too much is invested in an impossible task.

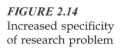

FIGURE 2.14
Increased specificity
of research problem

A word of caution is in order, one that will be reiterated later: finding statistical significance is neither the only nor the most important goal of quantitative research. It is possible to find statistically significant differences that are very small and not necessarily academically or practically significant. In other words, you could find a difference across the three counselling approaches described in the second example of Table 2.3, but the success levels of all three processes could be so low as to make *none* of them worth adopting. This does not make the research useless, but while the outcomes may not result in change in practice, they may provide clues for further research. Finding the equivalent to penicillin through social science research is unlikely, but that does not mean research results are insignificant. We must simply recognize that the pace of discovery is slow and that while we build on the results of others, we also contribute to future research. Now would be an appropriate time to carry out Activity 2.5.

Activity 2.5

Write one or more possible null hypotheses for some of the following statements of research hypotheses. For some of them, you will have to decide just what is to be measured.

(a) One of Albert McDougal's consultants (recall Activity 2.3) has suggested that as a week progresses, people are less willing to spend money, thus the volume at any one 'session' (morning, around noon, or evening) will drop off during the week. Another consultant on the team suggests that Friday is the exception since people 'celebrate' the end of the week and treat themselves before getting on the train.

(b) Flexitime has been suggested as one way of making the most of employees' creative ability in an organization that designs plastic components for the computer industry (plugs, sockets, mice, keyboards, keys, etc.).

(c) Observations by a group of social workers suggest that there is a relationship between drug use and social amenities for young people. As a consequence, they want to introduce a new idea for a social centre. (There are two projects here; one should precede the other.)

SUMMARY

Theories are the foundation of most research, though there are limitations in their functionality in the social sciences. While ultimately useful to practitioners as a basis for asking questions about individuals and their behaviour or activities, they rarely have the same capability as in the physical and biological sciences of being able completely to explain individual actions. Social science theories provide models related to group tendencies, primarily because of the multivariate nature of causality in human activity. In common with all theories, they are of value until their limitations or deficiencies are proven and a new or revised theory does a better job of explaining. Most research tends to test limited aspects of theories or their application to new situations, by setting up hypotheses describing the interaction or interrelations between variables.

A systematic approach to research design has been described, one that aims to ensure all the appropriate issues are considered and provides the mechanism by which research processes and practices can be evaluated. If the results of a study are to be valid, then one must consider the validity of the components of the study: four constituent types of validity have been introduced. Laying a proper foundation for a research project consists of a sound hypothesis describing relationship(s) between/among variables, based upon a theory, established or new, providing the researcher with a baseline from which to work. There is no reason why hypotheses should not be modified before collecting the data, as long as this can be justified. Carefully defining concepts and consequential constructs helps to eliminate ambiguity and establishes a basis for ensuring *construct validity* and reliable operational definitions of the variables.

The actual design of the research process will contribute to ensuring that no other variables than the ones of interest can differentially affect the studied outcomes, thus enhancing *internal validity*. Procedures at later stages of the research will also influence how well unwanted variables are controlled, as will be seen in subsequent chapters. To achieve the goal that a study tests the desired range of populations and situations as indicated by the underlying theory, it is necessary to choose the subjects so that they are representative of the population(s) and that the conditions under which the study is carried out are typical. This is all part of enhancing the *external validity* of the results. Clearly stating hypotheses stimulates researchers to consider these conditions early in the planning, if for no other reason than to evaluate the feasibility of carrying out the study.

Finally, mentioned before only in passing, there is the appropriate choice of statistical test, which is necessary if a study is to have *statistical validity*. This is also dependent on decisions made about measuring instruments and influenced by data collection processes. Statistical validity is included in Figure 2.15, which illustrates how the various stages of the planning and execution of a research study influence the various types of validity and consequently the overall validity of the results.

Subsequent chapters will provide guidance on how to maintain the highest level of each of these through intellectual skill development, the provision of criteria for good practice, and the raising of issues to be addressed at each stage. In order to give you an opportunity to consolidate the skills presented in this chapter, carry out Activity 2.6 now.

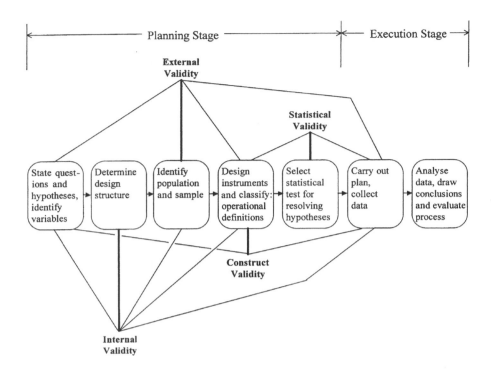

FIGURE 2.15
Validity
considerations as
part of research
design

Activity 2.6

Prepare, and duplicate sufficient copies for the class, responses to the following, describing your own research (no more than two pages):

(a) Very briefly identify the theory on which your research is to be based and state the questions to be answered.

(b) Turn your research question(s) into more specific hypotheses and finally into possible null hypotheses. These will focus your study, though one must be careful to not focus it on trivial aspects.

(c) List all the variables that you intend to consider in your research, classifying each as independent or dependent, and each as nominal, ordinal, interval or ratio, and stating whether each is observed or manipulated (i.e., where each one fits in Figure 2.13).

(d) Briefly justify each variable's relevance and appropriateness to your research question and hypotheses.

(e) Describe any difficulties you anticipate or have already encountered in establishing operational definitions for these variables.

Alternatively, you could take a report of a research project or a journal article and evaluate its hypotheses and choice of variables, applying the criteria described in this chapter, using questions (a)–(e) above.

Initial Sources of Invalidity and Confounding

3

After deciding upon a research question and specifying a set of hypotheses, the next step is to consider possible strategies to resolve the adequacy of these. In the real world of limited resources, there is often a need to balance the choice of design against the potential sample size, which will result in selecting the 'best' plan as opposed to the ideal. Consequently, this chapter and the next will introduce fundamental options for an overall design for testing hypotheses and some of the criteria needed for making a decision as to which would be 'best'. They will include the start of a survey of statistically testable designs, both correlational and experimental/quasi-experimental (Campbell and Stanley, 1963), initiating the process of turning hypotheses into a planned design. This first step will be tentative since subsequent chapters will introduce ways of overcoming limitations of these basic designs and will provide more refined ones. Statistical tests will be included in the examples, to illustrate their role in testing hypotheses. Some of these may be new to you, but at this stage all you have to remember is that such tests only determine whether the outcome could have occurred by chance alone or not.

Finally, this chapter will lead into the next four, the first of which will complete the survey of basic designs, the next will cover sampling techniques and the final two more complex designs that are based on measurement considerations. With a foundation of possible designs provided, Chapter 8 will follow with the process of developing measuring instruments. This assumes that some idea has been formed as to how the hypotheses will be tested. Chapters 8–11 will provide guidance on what sort of instrument or operational definition will be best, the nature of the data (nominal, ordinal, interval or ratio), and the range of constructs to be investigated. On the one hand, there is little value in collecting data that will not be used; and on the other, there is nothing worse than getting to the data-processing stage and finding that there are data that are desperately needed but have not been collected. Obviously, these are almost parallel decisions, so it will be necessary to reconsider the details of the chosen design in light of decisions made about the operational definition, and vice versa. This is why the systems approach of Figure 2.1 can only provide guidance and not definite stages for a linear process.

TRANSFORMING HYPOTHESES INTO A BASIC DESIGN

While hypotheses tend to develop from personal interest in testing or extending a theory, those that will be the focus of the designs here will describe potential relationships between or among distinct and definite variables. The previous chapter provided an initial opportunity to convert general hypotheses into *null* hypotheses, ones that purport *no* relationships. This is followed by asking what sorts of tests and situations can be devised to see whether these actually do exist. From reading the literature, one might gain the impression that there might be an infinite number of designs for resolving hypotheses, considering the variety and range of designs and statistical tests. In reality, there are a limited number, though there can be a large number of variations on these basic themes. In order to present the alternatives in an organized manner, a series of ideal structures for designs will be presented, preceded by some designs which are flawed. By the end of this and the next chapter, a few acceptable ones will remain, and these will be built upon in two later chapters as more issues related to design structure are raised and criteria for solutions provided. It should be kept in mind that the illustrative statistical tests are not the only ones possible for the designs, but they are presented to show how such tests are used. This approach allows the gradual introduction of necessary concepts and skills for implementing these.

Other variables

When planning research to resolve hypotheses, it is necessary to take into account variables other than those of interest. One must devise a test that unequivocally would show that the chosen variables were *the only* possible causes or precursors (in other words, somewhere in the causal chain) of the effects. If, in the end, the predicted outcomes do not occur, then the structure of the test should also be such that nothing else could have prevented their occurrence. Remember that statistical tests can only resolve whether two or more groups (probably) belong to a common group or not for a given set of traits, characteristics or qualities. Thus it is up to the researcher to construct the study in such a way as to take into account all the other possible *extraneous variables* – those that could be competing independent variables, influencing the dependent variable, but are *not* of interest to the research.

Ensuring that the study has been designed in such a way that all these extraneous variables would not have had an effect on the final results means that they have been *controlled*. These unwanted variables fall roughly into three categories, based on how they will ultimately be controlled:

1   *Identified variables*. These do have recognizable consequences or at least are strongly suspected of having an impact on the dependent variable (they will include the variables of primary interest to the study).

2   *Unanticipated variables*. These have not yet been recognized, but one assumes they are possibly there.

3   *Variables influenced by the study itself*. Even after identifying the independent and dependent variables, there is the problem of measuring them. If the independent variables are nominal or ordinal, how does one ensure that the characteristics of the categories are mutually exclusive and provide groups with distinguishable characteristics? Also, one of the problems all researchers have is how to conduct a study without directly influencing the results (the dependent variable) through their actions when data are collected, thus inadvertently introducing extraneous variables.

The consequence of not controlling these extraneous variables is that they will possibly affect the dependent variable, and *confound* the results. Thus, when a study is properly designed, they are still there but their impact is nullified or equally distributed and they are just *controlled extraneous variables*. But if they are not controlled and they influence the dependent variable, then they become a source of corruption and are considered *confounding variables*. Extraneous variables are always present in social science research since studies invariably involve events or effects that have multiple causation. The researcher is usually interested in only a few of the possible variables, therefore the challenge is to isolate the others and make them harmless, controlled extraneous variables, not allowing them to become confounding ones.

Extraneous variables can be best controlled when they have been identified. One technique to facilitate this has been adapted from concept maps (Novak and Gowin, 1984) and involves making a *variable map*. This consists of recording all the variables that might influence the outcome (dependent variable) using different-shaped containers: rectangles for independent variables, rounded boxes for dependent variables, and ovals for extraneous variables. Figure 3.1 provides an example for the first question/hypothesis in Tables 2.2 and 2.3: which of three counselling approaches will produce the greatest reduction in frequency of return to drinking among alcoholics.

The first two types of variable, identified and unanticipated, will have the greatest contribution to the structure of the basic designs that follow. They are the ones that will influence how many and which variables are chosen as independent variables, and how samples of subjects will be selected. To a certain extent, the final choice of design will determine whether these variables are even potentially controllable. Choosing a weak design, as we will see, can leave one with no potential control over unanticipated extraneous variables. Many of the variables introduced when the study is carried out will be covered in the chapters on measurement and their potential impact on design structure. Necessary modifications and refined designs will be considered in that context.

Identified and unanticipated variables

Each of the potential independent variables identified in the original hypotheses to be tested will obviously constitute one of the identifiable variables. Then one

FIGURE 3.1
A variable map, consisting of proposed independent variables (boxes), the operational definition of the dependent variable (box with rounded corners), the dependent variable (heavy box with rounded corners) and identified extraneous variables (ovals). Can you add other extraneous variables?

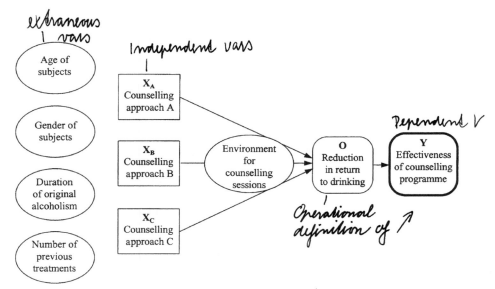

has to consider whether to include others that either the underlying theory or other research has shown to influence the dependent variable. The original hypotheses may not include such variables as age or sex of the subjects, but these could be recognized variables from previous research that need to be controlled. Either they have to be considered as variables in their own right or they must be distributed evenly across the identified groups (observed variables).

Kerlinger (1986) notes that a potential extraneous variable can be controlled by including it as another attribute, an observed variable, in the study. Most studies investigate multivariate situations – in other words, more that one possible independent variable. What often makes these studies particularly interesting is how the various variables *interact* with each other – that is to say, one variable by itself may not appear to cause a difference, but combined with another it does. For example, the comparison of the effectiveness of two learning media might find an overall difference in learner achievement between two balanced groups of boys and girls using them. A more interesting study might reveal whether or not the difference could be attributable to some gender bias. This could be achieved by having four groups instead of two, as shown in Table 3.1. Each group (matched on ability) would use the assigned media and their achievement compared afterwards. This would allow the detection of the possible situation where there was no overall difference between the boys and girls or across media, but there was between the various combinations. In other words, there was some sort of interaction between gender and media. The comparison would not identify the source, but it would confirm that an interaction existed.

TABLE 3.1
Imaginary results for comparing achievement using different media

	Boys	Girls
Medium A	High	Low
Medium B	Low	High

In order to obtain sample groups, researchers use random selection techniques, which serve two purposes: to ensure representativeness of the subjects of the study and to control unwanted variables in the study. To be able to generalize to a larger population, it is necessary to acquire a sample that is as representative of that population as possible. This is usually achieved by *random sampling*, selecting subjects as randomly from the original population as is possible. A number of alternative techniques will be considered in Chapter 5 that allow the representative selection of subjects when, as is usually the case for large populations, it is not possible to have a complete list from which to select randomly.

There may also exist <u>unanticipated extraneous variables</u>, ones not previously identified. These can be controlled (that is, made so as not to affect the outcomes unequally) by <u>random selection and random assignment</u>. As a result, each independent variable group has an equal chance of having these variables influence them. *Random assignment* simply involves randomly assigning individuals to the groups that will receive different treatments or have different experiences. This can be used to control both identified and unanticipated variables. In the example in Figure 3.1, not only would random sampling ensure a representative sample, but also random assignment would ensure that the four potential extraneous variables on the left (age, gender, duration of original alcoholism and number of previous treatments) would be equally distributed across the groups. The environment in which the counselling sessions are held is related to how the experiment is conducted: all should be similar, equally conducive to helping clients be at ease. How long one waits to see if a subject returns is related to the actual definition of the dependent variable and therefore would have to be defined as a fixed time limit for all groups. Now try Activity 3.1.

Activity 3.1

Consider the final question/hypothesis in Tables 2.2 and 2.3: What night-time medication regime (where prescriptions allow) would enhance the quality of sleep for hospital patients? Devise a variable map and identify potential extraneous variables. How would you control them?

TYPES OF DESIGNS

When there is a definite hypothesized independent–dependent variable relationship, then there are definite advantages to a design that employs experimental techniques. For example, consider the situation where it is suspected that the variable *capacity of short-term memory* is dependent upon the *age* of the subject. The reverse is not possible, age cannot be dependent upon short-term memory, even if some of us wish to forget how old we are. A correlational study involving a single random sample of people of all ages would establish whether the relationship existed and whether it was linear or not. A more experimental approach would involve taking several random samples, each from an age range, to establish whether or not there is any difference across different age groups in short-term memory. Put simply, the two approaches are asking different questions:

- *Correlational* studies are asking about the nature of relationship and whether it exists, with no pretence to establishing causality.
- *Experimental* approaches are asking whether there is a difference. *If* extraneous variables are adequately controlled *and* the variables in question are appropriate, then it may be possible to provide support for a causal relationship.

As with most things in life, there is a continuum of quality even when considering possible designs. Selecting a structure for a study is complicated by the numerous potential sources of problems, events that could make the outcomes and conclusions of a study invalid. Consequently, there is the possibility that while the resulting study is not a total disaster, it is also not perfect. This is roughly equivalent to judging apple pies: few are terrible and few are perfect, but there is considerable good eating in the process. In an attempt to try systematically to identify pitfalls, a rather simple category system for classifying designs will be employed. The designs that will be considered (not all that are possible) will be grouped into five categories:

A *Pre-experimental.* These designs provide the least amount of control; consequently they are the ones most unlikely to provide any justification for causality or support for associational relationships. Descriptions of these are provided so that you know what to avoid.

B *Experimental.* These are at the other extreme, carried out with the greatest amount of control in (near) laboratory conditions, though even these have pitfalls when it comes to resolving some social science issues. Traditionally, these are thought of as being carried out in a laboratory, but sometimes such designs are quite suitable for studies in the real world.

C *Quasi-experimental.* These endeavour to control extraneous variables, but lack all the rigour of an experimental design – for example, they employ intact groups rather than pure random samples. Sometimes there are advantages to these designs since they can reflect real-life situations more closely than investigations conducted under more clinical conditions.

D *Ex post facto.* Such studies have limited control over possible independent variables, since they tend to be life events or experiences. The variables tend to be macrovariables and consequently establishing causal links is more difficult. Often the results provide strong support for associational relationships, identifying where one variable is associated with a difference in another. Though many of the same statistical tools are used, they do not necessarily meet all the conditions of experimental designs since they tend to occur in the 'field'. If conducted rigorously, they can justifiably resolve issues, sometimes better than experimental designs. These tend to be a greater challenge, as will be seen, since there are so many more possible extraneous variables to consider.

E *Correlational.* These are also ex post facto, but, as noted above, the intent is to determine the nature of a relationship and not whether there is a difference, therefore these will be treated separately.

As a start, Table 3.3 summarizes five common designs that would purport to test various numbers of independent variables for a dependent variable, with Table 3.2 providing a key for the symbols used. The dependent variable, Y, is operationally defined and observed through the measurable outcomes, O. The independent variable, X, tends to be what happens to the subjects, either as part of a treatment in experimental designs, or life events (education, social class, gender). It is assumed that good practice has subjects randomly selected, RS, and/or randomly assigned, RA, to treatment and control groups. Thus, the schematic description of a randomly selected group to receive a treatment, followed by a measure of the outcome (*not* a good design) would be displayed symbolically showing a time sequence of events as follows:

RS	$\rightarrow$	X	$\rightarrow$	O
random selection		treatment (independent variable)		observed outcome (operational definition of dependent variable, Y)

Subscripts in this notation allow the identification of multiple independent variables (groups), multiple outcomes and multiple sources for selection or assignment of subjects to groups.

TABLE 3.2
Notation key for describing research designs

Notation	Meaning
$X_a, X_b, X_c, \ldots$ X_0	Potential independent variables (treatments/experiences), and a 'control' experience/treatment where nothing happens (includes placebo).
O	Observation made on subjects before/after treatment
$O_1, O_2, \ldots$	with more than one observation made on the group of subjects, variable over time, with the number in the subscript indicating the order, or
$O_{a1}, O_{a2}, O_{a3}, \ldots$	with the subscript indicating multiple observations of subjects related to the independent variable X_a, i.e., group a (see above).
Y	Potential dependent variable, which could be operationally defined as O or some combination of $O_1, O_2, \ldots$, such as gain scores $(O_2 - O_1)$
$Y_a, Y_b, Y_c, \ldots, Y_0$	with the subscript indicating the value of Y corresponding to the category of the independent variable (e.g., $X_a, X_b, \ldots$; see above).
RS	Random *selection* of a single sample from a larger population, followed by
$RA_a, RA_b, \ldots, RA_0$	random *assignment* of subjects to groups to experience treatments as the independent variables $X_a, X_b, \ldots$, control (manipulated), or
$RS_a, RS_b, \ldots, RS_0$	random *selection* of several samples from larger groups where 'life experiences' are the independent variables, $X_a, X_b, \ldots$, control (observed).
(RS)	In a design, this indicates that random selection is optional and is unlikely to make any difference.

	Design description	Design structure (time sequence of events)	Sources of problems (general)
TABLE 3.3 Summary of basic pre-experimental and experimental designs (see Table 3.2 for the key to symbols)	**A. Pre-experimental:** A1 *One group post-test/ observation only:* one group tested or observed for a dependent variable for one instance of the independent variable, observed or manipulated.	$(RS) \rightarrow X \rightarrow O_1$	A single group, nothing equivalent with which to compare, even if the group were randomly selected; results only descriptive, no causality established.
	A2 *One group pre- and post-test/observations* for some single event or treatment.	$(RS) \rightarrow O_1 \rightarrow X \rightarrow O_2$	Where $Y = O_2 - O_1$: many possible confounding variables, even if the group were randomly selected; weak support for causality: $X \rightarrow Y$.
	A3 *Two available groups,* one subjected to event or treatment, the other not, both are tested/observed post-event/experience only.	$X_a \rightarrow O_a$ $X_0 \rightarrow O_0$	Where $Y_a = O_a$, $Y_0 = O_0$ and compare Y_a to Y_0. Were the two groups the same initially? Other possible confounding variables, weak support for causality: $X_a \rightarrow Y$.
	B. Experimental: B2 *Pre- and post-test/ observation* of proposed dependent variable with single event of possible independent variable with a control.	$RS \rightarrow \begin{cases} RA_a \rightarrow O_{a1} \rightarrow X_a \rightarrow O_{a2} \\ RA_0 \rightarrow O_{01} \rightarrow X_0 \rightarrow O_{02} \end{cases}$	Where $Y_a = O_{a2} - O_{a1}$ $Y_0 = O_{02} - O_{01}$ and compare Y_a to Y_0. Some improvement on design A2, ensuring that there is a control group with which to compare; stronger support for causality: $X_a \rightarrow Y$.
	B3 *Post-test/observation only, with a control group.* Original sample randomly selected, groups randomly assigned, including control.	$RS \rightarrow \begin{cases} RA_a \rightarrow X_a \rightarrow O_a \\ RA_0 \rightarrow X_0 \rightarrow O_0 \end{cases}$	Where $Y_a = O_a$, $Y_0 = O_0$ and compare Y_a to Y_0. Some improvement on design A3, ensuring comparability of groups through randomization; stronger support for causality: $X_a \rightarrow Y$.

This scheme is presented as a means for comparing various structures, and the number of designs will be expanded as the sources of problems become better defined. The tables should be referred to while reading the following paragraphs describing each in detail. Many of these designs have advantages and limitations inherent to the designs themselves, including how well or poorly they potentially enhance the control of unanticipated extraneous variables that might cause confounding. More refined designs will be presented in later chapters, after considering how the development of instruments and collection of data can eliminate or at least reduce the likelihood of introducing confounding variables due to the study itself. While choosing an appropriate design is important, just how it is executed is equally critical if the results are to be considered valid and the process able to withstand scrutiny.

Each of the designs will be described briefly, then a set of criteria for evaluating them will be introduced. This will be followed by a re-examination of each design in light of the criteria to identify strengths and weaknesses.

Pre-experimental designs

These are not truly experimental designs, simply because the studies are conducted in such a way that there is no comparison made to another comparable group. In addition to the three that Campbell and Stanley (1963) identified, correlational studies will be included later, since no causal relationships can be established. Comparisons are an essential aspect of research since, with a single group, it is not possible to manipulate the independent variable and guarantee that this is the only cause. Also, there is a tendency to depend on memory, attempting to recall the effects of the independent variable in other situations. Thus it is not possible to establish causality, no matter how good the measuring instruments are. These are presented because examples of such studies still appear in the literature, and they are useful for illustrating many of the sources of limitations of poorly designed research.

Design A1: One group post-test/observation only

In this design a group of subjects are tested or observed to see if one treatment (manipulated) or an event in their lives (observed variable), X_a, affects the dependent variable, Y. For example, a class is given a new textbook and learns the topic, with a resulting high mean score on a test. Even if the group itself is randomly selected, this type of study does not confirm or refute the hypothesis that the book was responsible, since any number of possible extraneous variables could have caused the results. Campbell and Stanley (1963) maintain that inferences are often made (wrongly) based on a comparison with an imaginary group (in this example, possibly the previous test scores) that did not have the treatment or experience and did not show any influence on Y. One should not be mislead by the care taken in designing the measuring instrument (whose results are O), since it is applied to only one group. This does not negate the value of trying out a new textbook on a group for purposes of obtaining feedback on various components and improving it, but as a design to 'prove' its value in facilitating achievement on the basis of a single measure, it is grossly deficient. At the risk of being repetitive, just what was the research question?

Design A2: One group pre- and post-test/observations

Here the group is initially observed, O_1, then subjected to an experience or treatment, X, and observed again, O_2. The dependent variable is the change from O_1 to O_2 and the question most often asked is whether the experience made a significant difference. Equally, one could ask, if something did happen, how we know it would not have happened anyway. Without a comparable group with which to compare, there is no answer to the second question and consequently this provides no evidence to resolve the question. For example, the teacher gives a pre-test to a class, provides them with a new textbook for learning and, after a chapter of work, gives a post-test. Yes, the students' scores increased, but perhaps they would have done so anyway, since they may have learned what was required through some other medium (television, other classes, reading, etc.), another example of possible uncontrolled extraneous variables.

Design A3: Two available groups

In this design one of the groups is subjected to an experience, X_a, and the other to nothing as a control, X_0, and both observed, O_a and O_0 for the potential independent variable, Y. The question to be resolved tends to be whether the two groups were different after one had had the experience. Even if the answer is 'yes', unfortunately, it is not known whether they were both the same before the experience, since these tend to be convenience groups and not representative samples. Any outcome could be the result of the independent variable, but it could also be the result of some extraneous variable. As an improvement consider, for example, a comparable situation to that in A2: one class gets the new textbook and another class uses the old textbook; both take the same pre- and post-learning tests. This leads us to better-structured designs.

Experimental designs

These meet the criteria for being truly experimental since each provides a comparison group, one that can be observed and measured in the same way as the experimental group. These parallel observations provide essential data rather than having the researcher depend on unsubstantiated experience or past data that are probably not comparable. With the experimental group receiving the treatment (potential independent variable) and the comparison group not under identical conditions, it is easier to justify that extraneous variables are controlled. Such studies do require the facility directly to *manipulate* the proposed independent variable, which is often not possible in social science research. Thus, while these designs may be the 'ideal' way of resolving hypotheses, it is not possible or ethical to impose the necessary constraints on subjects to achieve them. They are achievable in laboratory conditions and sometimes with human subjects, but even then they may have to be volunteers, which would make the samples questionable. Having said that, there are comparable situations where the proposed independent variable is observed and the situation is 'real life', which will be considered in the next section. Two initial types of structure will be considered, building on and improving those presented in the subsection on pre-experimental designs above, simply because they do allow the types of questions posed to be answered. The numbers following the letter in the designation, therefore, are the same as for the pre-experimental designs to assist in making comparisons.

The following two designs are highly desirable as they provide the opportunity to control both anticipated and unanticipated variables, and consequently these are the structures around which most of the inferential statistical tests are based.

Design B2: Pre- and post-test/observations with a control

Here two groups are measured for the proposed dependent variable before and after the event. One group experiences the manipulated independent variable (treatment) and a comparable control group does not. The dependent variable is defined by the *gain scores*, the difference in scores between the two times measured for a group. The comparison is between the gain score $(O_2 - O_1)$ for group X_{a1} and the gain scores for group X_{a0}. As will be seen below, this structure potentially offers control over all possible extraneous variables since each group, control and treatment, consists of subjects randomly assigned from a randomly selected group. This is a direct improvement on design A2 above. According to Stanley and Campbell (1963), such a structure is the basis for the ideal study. This is not surprising as it forms the basis for most tried and proven experimental designs in biological, medical and pharmaceutical research. The difficulty is that in the social sciences, the potential for control over sampling and experimentation often does not exist.

Design B3: Post-test/observation only, with a control group

In this design, measurement for the proposed dependent variable takes place only after the event, having ensured that the groups are comparable through sampling from a larger population and randomly assigning subjects to the two groups. This offers some improvement on design A3 above, providing comparable groups through randomization, both in the selection from the original population and in subsequent assignment to groups. The difference with respect to A2 of not having a pre-test has advantages and disadvantages. The advantage is that the pre-test will not inadvertently become a variable by influencing subjects ahead of the treatment. The disadvantage is that one does not have a measure beforehand with which to compare. This is not a problem in situations where it is known that the two groups are comparable – for example, if teaching an entirely new subject or skill. Even so, this is often hard to achieve in social science research in the field since random assignment to experimental and control groups is usually difficult if not impossible to accomplish.

Quasi-experimental and <u>ex post facto designs</u>

Quasi-experimental designs employ strategies that have a similar structure to experimental designs such as B2, but lack much of the control of a true experimental design. Comparisons tend to be made between (among) non-equivalent groups (Campbell and Stanley, 1963; Cook and Campbell, 1979). The best description appears in Cook *et al.* (1990), '*quasi-experiments* primarily depend on self-selection or administrative decisions to determine who is to be exposed to a treatment'. The researcher still controls the nature of the treatment, but the subjects tend not to be randomly selected or randomly assigned, nor do they necessarily constitute equivalent groups for all characteristics.

Alternatively, there are situations when the independent variables tend to be natural or life experiences, such as social class, gender, amount of education, type of school attended, where residing, etc. These are referred to as <u>ex post facto</u> designs. Kerlinger (1973) provides the clearest description: '*Ex post facto* research is systematic empirical inquiry in which the scientist does not have direct control of independent variables because their manifestations have already occurred or because they are inherently not manipulable.'

For reasons unstated, in a later edition of his text Kerlinger (1986) refers to such studies as non-experimental, but the term 'ex post facto' will be kept simply because it is more descriptive, intuitive and still used (e.g., Coolican, 1994; Cohen and Manion, 1989; Lehmann and Mehrens, 1979) – though be warned, other writers have used the term to mean something else.

As a consequence of using natural or life experiences, random selection is extremely important since the validity of each variable is dependent on how representative the sample is of the larger populations having the characteristic or experiences. For these types of studies, the independent variables are *not* manipulated, but observed (recall Figure 2.13). There are limitations to such designs, but where true experimental designs are not feasible, these can offer opportunities to explore potential relationships among variables. Correlational studies will fall in the ex post facto category, but since there is neither a control group nor comparisons and causality cannot be substantiated, these are also considered to be pre-experimental.

Obviously, it will be necessary to recognize potential confounding introduced by such designs, but, interestingly enough, it will be shown that an appropriately executed design can eliminate some potential confounding characteristics of even true experimental designs (e.g., the possible unnatural situation of the laboratory). Two basic designs are provided initially and others will be introduced in later chapters.

Design C2: Non-equivalent control group design with pre-tests

Cook *et al.* (1990) maintained that this is the most common quasi-experimental design employed. In spite of its limitations, it has considerable value. It differs from the true experimental design B2 in that the subjects are in existing groups, often classrooms of learners or established work groups within an organization. Which group becomes the treatment group and which the control may be a matter of random assignment. This is shown schematically in Table 3.4. As will be seen in Chapter 5, such a sampling technique weakens the generalizability of the sample, particularly if the groups are simply used because they are convenient. The case can be strengthened if the groups are shown to be representative with respect to general characteristics and are purposively chosen for this reason. The pre-test may help to ensure equivalence of groups and the measure would be of gain scores, which overcomes some of the criticism of lack of control of extraneous variables.

Design D3: Post-test/observation only, with a control group

Here the independent variable is observed, not manipulated. This ex post facto design is a variation on experimental design B3, and an improvement on pre-experimental design A3. It allows the investigation of real-life variables in natural settings, but the control of most possible confounding variables depends on the sampling technique to provide a group homogeneous for a single trait (life

	Design description	Design structure (time sequence of events)	Sources of problems (general)
TABLE 3.4 Summary of basic quasi-experimental, ex post facto and correlational designs (see Table 3.2 for the key to symbols)	**C. Quasi-experimental:** C2 *Non-equivalent control group design with pre-tests.* Original sample is not random, but already there, as with work groups, classrooms. Treatment group may be randomly determined.	$(RA_a) \rightarrow O_{a1} \rightarrow X_a \rightarrow O_{a2}$ $(RA_0) \rightarrow O_{01} \rightarrow X_0 \rightarrow O_{02}$	Where $Y_a = O_{a2} - O_{a1}$ $Y_0 = O_{02} - O_{01}$ and compare Y_a to Y_0. Allows investigation of real-life variables, but control of most possible extraneous variables depends on sampling; possible support for causality: $X_a \rightarrow Y$.
	D. Ex post facto: D3 *Post-test/observation only, with a control group,* but independent variable, (life event) is observed not manipulated.	$RS_a \rightarrow \underline{X_a} \rightarrow O_a$ $RS_0 \rightarrow \underline{X_0} \rightarrow O_0$	Where $Y_a = O_a$ $Y_0 = O_0$ and compare Y_a to Y_0. Allows investigation of real-life variables, but control of most possible extraneous variables contingent on sampling; possible support for causality: $\underline{X_a} \rightarrow Y$.
	E. Correlational: E1 *One group observed* for a number of traits to see if any relationships exist.	$RS \rightarrow O_a, O_b, O_c, \ldots$	Descriptive studies, surveys, correlational studies; no causality can be considered.

event or experience). In these situations, the symbolic schema should be interpreted as follows:

$$RS_a \qquad \rightarrow \qquad \underline{X_a} \qquad \rightarrow \qquad O_a$$

random selection from population a observed trait a (independent variable)   observed outcome (operational definition of dependent variable Y)

From the above time-sequence notation, the validity of the independent variable, $\underline{X_a}$ (note the underline), obviously relies on the quality of the sample, RS_a. In such situations, the so-called control group is often a group with a different set of experiences rather than one with no experiences at all. Employing such a design implies it would also have to be possible to assume that the source of any differences could be attributed to these different experiences. The design including the two groups is shown schematically in Table 3.4.

Design E1: One group observed

Here one group is observed for a number of traits O_a, O_b, O_c, etc., to see if they are related and if any might be possible candidates for future research as Y (see Table 3.4). Either the results are presented descriptively, or correlations are found to determine the strength of possible relationships. This type of study can be considered ex post facto and not without value. It will be covered in considerable detail in Chapter 21, but it is still pre-experimental since it is not possible to explore causal relationships.

Specific sources of invalidity and confounding of results

In order systematically to plan studies that avoid designs which will encourage unjustifiable conclusions, 15 basic sources of invalidity have been identified as commonly found in educational and social science research. These threaten one or more of the various forms of validity described earlier and could invalidate the conclusions of a study. Focusing on minimizing these sources, criteria for the design of studies that should have the greatest potential for resolving hypotheses are provided. The criteria have been adapted from those originally proposed by Campbell and Stanley (1963) with modifications subsequently suggested by various writers on research (e.g., Cook and Campbell, 1979; Kerlinger, 1986; Cohen and Manion, 1989; Cook *et al.*, 1990). Ten of the 15 sources owe their origins to the original papers, but the total scheme reflects additional analysis. The sources will be used in enhanced versions of Tables 3.3 and 3.4 to pinpoint specific sources of errors characteristic of the selection of designs presented.

The scheme used in this text is somewhat more practical and consequently less academic and philosophically orientated than the originals. The emphasis here is on providing guidance criteria to be considered when *designing* a study, recognizing that for relatively new researchers a more pragmatic approach is needed. The original papers are recommended reading for those who wish to delve into the issues more deeply, as their emphasis is on evaluation of studies. In order to maintain some consistency with the originally identified stages of research in Chapter 2 (Figure 2.1), the 15 sources will be clustered according to stages of research. This will reflect the combined concerns for the choice of design and how component tasks are executed. Each of the 15 sources is described in detail below, but these groups are shown in Table 3.5. These sources of invalidity can each be linked individually to the four types of validity introduced in Chapter 2, which are also shown in Table 3.5. As you read about each of the sources, refer to the table and note which of the types of validity are affected and how:

- construct validity – making sure that the instrument (operational definition) measures or can measure what it is supposed to measure;
- internal validity – ensuring that the design takes into account a clear causal relationship and allows for the control of all other possible contributing extraneous variables;
- external validity – ensuring that both the samples and the conditions under which the study is carried out are representative of the populations and situations to which the results are to apply;
- statistical validity – the appropriate choice of statistical test, which is dependent on decisions made about measuring instruments and influenced by data collection processes.

The first eight potential sources of problems that could result in invalid conclusions are described in detail below and will be used in activities in this chapter

TABLE 3.5
Summary of sources of invalidity, with types of validity affected

		Types of validity affected			
Sources of invalidity (Stage of study)	**Description**	**Construct**	**Internal**	**External**	**Statistical**
Primarily design choice:					
1 No comparison across groups	Just one group		✓		
2 Time: other events	Additional to treatment		✓		
3 Time: maturation	Internal change of subjects		✓		
Sampling and assignment to groups:					
4 Selection: sample (and assignment)	Poor original sample and/or non-random assignment to groups	✓	✓	✓	✓
5 Selection: regression	When classifying extreme groups	✓	✓	✓	
6 Selection: sample stability			✓	✓	
7 Interaction of time with sample	Time delay reduces sample quality		✓	✓	
8 Interaction of independent variable with sample	Often due to poorly defined population		✓	✓	
Externally imposed treatment:					
9 Direction/nature of causality uncertain	For example, time sequence not established		✓		✓
10 Unnatural/invalid experiment/ treatment	Difficult to generalize to reality			✓	
Instrument design:					
11 Invalid measurement of variables	Weak instrument/classification	✓			
12 Instrument reliability	Low reliability		✓		
Data collection:					
13 Learning from instrument	Instrument influences dependent variable	✓	✓		
14 Instrument reacts with independent variable/treatment	Often during data collection	✓	✓	✓	✓
15 Other interactions	Idiosyncratic to designs				✓

and the next. After considering sampling techniques in Chapter 5, the remaining seven will be covered in Chapter 6.

1. No comparison across groups

An investigation of a single group offers no comparison and thus there is no way of proving that the independent variable was the only possible cause of the observed effect. Having a control group, one that does not receive the treatment or undergo the experience of interest to the study (independent variable), enhances the argument for causality by that variable. Assuming that extraneous variables have been controlled, any difference between groups can be attributable to the specified variable. Traditionally this has meant *nothing* happens to the control group, but in many situations it is much more reasonable to have a group with which to compare that is receiving the 'usual' treatment or is experiencing what usually happens to the subjects, such as the existing classroom procedure. It is often impossible to have nothing happen to a control group and the common way medical research contends with this is to issue a placebo, a pill that looks like the experimental one but has no medicinal properties. Ensuring that the subjects do not know to which group they belong results in a *single-blind* experiment. Since observers (or those administering the treatment) might behave differently towards subjects if they knew which group they were in, this is kept from them, resulting in a *double-blind* experiment. Due to the nature of the treatments, keeping such information from research staff is often not possible in social science research. Without any control group, the alternative argument can be put forward that any number of extraneous variables could have caused the outcomes observed equally well. Thus studies without a control group have very little internal validity. This is an obvious limitation to designs A1 and A2, as shown in Table 3.3.

2. Time: other events

This is what Campbell and Stanley (1963) refer to as history, events that could occur, experiences the subjects could have had *in addition to* the treatment or experience that constitutes the independent variable. It is quite conceivable that the longer the time between a first measurement of the dependent variable and a second, the more likely something else will influence the second measurement. Such a situation would not allow the researcher to determine which event caused any differences in the measurements of the dependent variable in a design such as A2, unless the subjects could be completely isolated from outside events. This is virtually impossible in social science research, and, even if it were, the isolation itself might constitute an extraneous confounding variable. This reduces the internal validity of such designs considerably.

If there were a control or comparison group as in design B2 (Table 3.3) and any extraneous variables influenced both groups equally over the time interval of the study, then it would be possible to maintain that any difference in results, i.e., measures of the dependent variable, could be attributable to the independent variable alone. On the interpretative side, though, one could not necessarily attribute all the increase in gain scores for the experimental group to the independent variable if the control also had an increase in gain scores in such an experimental design as B2. The intent of such a design is to show that the experimental variable does cause an increase through establishing a statistically significant difference. Just how much of an increase occurred (relating to social science significance) might still be difficult to establish in design B3, which has no pre-test for comparison across time.

3. Time: maturation

Much of the discussion for the previous potential source of confounding applies to the situation where the changes are external to the subjects. It is also necessary to consider the possibility of change *internal* to the subjects, where biological or psychological changes occur over time. This is particularly relevant in studies where children are involved in long-term studies since they are undergoing both physiological and psychological maturation independent of external events. It could also apply to situations where the passage of time affects the mental state of subjects – for example, when, over time, people are able to come to terms with grief, trauma or some similar event in their lives. Again, the internal validity of such a study is reduced because of possible extraneous variables influencing the dependent variable during the time interval of the investigation.

4. Selection: sample (and assignment)

This has an impact on the external validity of studies, in other words, the representativeness of the sample group and subsequent generalizability of results to an appropriate larger population. As a consequence, all the questions related to the appropriate selection of sample groups are of interest. Even so, it should be noted that a sound selection procedure alone, one that produces a representative sample, is no guarantee of a valid structure or results. This can be seen in designs A1, A2 and E1, each of which could have a representative sample and still not produce unambiguous findings.

Selection of samples does become an essential component of establishing independent variables in ex post facto designs such as design D3, where the variables are observed as opposed to manipulated. The actual characteristic of the group (education, sex, age, social class) is the proposed cause of differential results in the dependent variable. Therefore defining and randomly selecting from larger populations is the major consideration in maintaining the construct validity of the independent variable. Chapter 5 will introduce sampling techniques and strategies.

Experimental designs ensure representativeness not only through selection from a larger population, but also through the control of extraneous variables by randomly assigning the subjects to two (or more) groups. The groups will usually experience experimental treatments or experiences, plus one that has no (new) treatment/experience (the 'control' group). This is an endeavour to distribute any extraneous variables, identified or unanticipated, equally across all groups. Thus any effects such variables might have would be felt equally by all groups, enhancing internal validity. There is a complete lack of random selection and random assignment for design A3, which uses existing intact groups. Thus not only will the results not be generalizable, but also there is little control of any hidden extraneous variables. For experimental designs such as B2 and B3, there is always a specific concern for selection bias. Design C2 would also depend on available groups, but there is an endeavour to ensure they are equivalent and groups randomly assigned to treatement. These are typical of situations where the process by which individual subjects arrive in groups is a consequence of their belonging to existing units (classrooms, housing areas, volunteers, etc.). Methods of random assignment are also described in Chapter 5.

Finally, the use of *inferential* statistics to resolve the truth of hypotheses assumes that all samples are representative since any inferences are to be extended to the populations. Therefore, the quality of the sample will influence the appropriateness of the choice of statistical test, and consequently statistical validity.

5. Selection: regression

This is a tendency for groups with extreme scores to have scores closer to the overall mean on subsequent tests, and not necessarily because of the effect of the independent variable. Simply put, this can be attributed to imperfect relationships between variables and the difference in the *true* score (what the subject would receive if the measuring instrument were perfect) and the *observed* score on the measure, best described as measurement error. These concepts will be considered in greater detail in Chapters 8 and 11 since they are the basis for the formal definition of reliability of measuring instruments, and in Chapter 22 on regression. In some cases, it is a function of the correlation between the two test–retest measures, and therefore the reliability of the instrument. The lower the reliability, the greater the error and the greater the probability that scores will *regress* towards the mean in multiple measures. Consequently, later measures will tend to be closer to the mean. Thus the potential confounding does not arise directly from the measuring instrument used for the dependent variable, which should determine any effects of the independent variable. Instead, confounding is a result of using a measuring instrument to classify extreme groups selected for study (such as 'low achievers'). Alternatively, confounding can arise as a result of selecting members of a group for the independent variable using an instrument when it is an observed characteristic in an ex post facto study. Consequently, such a procedure would reduce the construct validity of the classification, as well as the internal validity of the study and to whom the results could be extended (external validity).

6. Selection: sample stability

There is the continual problem of keeping the members of randomly selected (and assigned) groups together, preventing differential and unattributable attrition. It is possible that either the experimental or control groups will experience a loss of subjects, essentially resulting in a study with volunteers. This will be brought up again under source 14, which includes data collection (see Chapter 6), and in greater detail in Chapter 5 when considering sampling problems, and in other chapters when looking at issues surrounding data collection. This has an impact on both the external validity, ability to generalize, and internal validity, preventing other variables from causing the outcome, since the reason for dropping out could have been an extraneous variable.

7. Interaction of time with samples

Time delays can reduce the sample quality or appropriateness of the assignment of subjects to groups through loss of subjects due to the possibility of other events or maturation increasing sample attrition. Alternatively, time could even change the category to which they should belong as they undergo changes. In other words, the sample has changed either in content or characteristics. The threats to internal and external validity are much the same as for source 6: are these samples *still* representative of the population(s) for the traits identified, and has time consequently allowed any extraneous variables to enter and influence outcomes?

8. Interaction of independent variable and samples

This can be a problem particularly when no comparison group is selected or the population is poorly defined. Also, the sample groups' characteristics could interfere with the experimental variable if there were a loss of subjects, through volunteers leaving, or the study could have started with available groups or volunteers. Non-representative samples could result in subgroups that react or respond to the treatment (independent variable) overall as a group differently than a truly representative group would, thus reducing the internal validity.

It is useful to consider how these eight sources potentially impinge on the validity of conclusions, both individually and as a group. Figure 3.2 provides a concept map, one that you may wish to alter and improve with additional thought. An updated version of this figure will be presented in Chapter 6, and the final seven potential sources will be considered in detail then.

THE BASIC PRE-EXPERIMENTAL DESIGNS IN DETAIL

Now that an initial set of specific potential sources of invalidity and confounding has been identified, there is a basis for systematically evaluating potential designs. In this section, you will consider examples of each of the three pre-experimental designs to see how these sources manifest themselves in real situations. In every case, Table 3.6 should be used as reference as individual examples of the reasons for the various symbols are identified. The following symbols are used to indicate the ability of designs to control the influence of the potential sources:

+	The design controls for this.
(+)	It depends on procedure.
−	It is not controlled by the design, thus it could be a source of confounding.
?	It is a possible source of confounding, depending on other actions.
< blank >	The factor is not relevant to this design.

For these first three designs, you will be provided with examples of typical (contrived) studies with explanations. Each example will provide you with an opportunity to suggest additional extraneous variables to the ones provided.

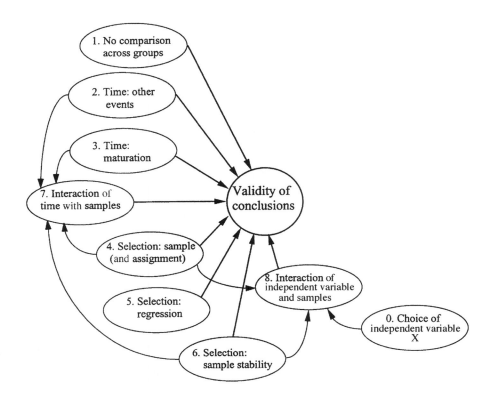

FIGURE 3.2
A concept map
showing the
relationships of the
first eight potential
sources of
confounding and
invalidity

Recall that designs A1, A2 and A3 are not recommended, but they are useful as examples to highlight why not to pursue such approaches, if at all possible. It was decided to make up fictional studies, based upon common approaches seen in research, in order to ensure that as many good and bad practices as possible could be illustrated. Statistical tests and their results are provided when this enhances the understanding of the approach. The details of these calculations will be presented in the appropriate chapters in the second half of the text.

Design A1: One group post-test/observation only

In this situation, a group is observed or measured after being subjected to some treatment or experience. This is the situation most teachers are placed in when they wish to implement an innovation in a class. For example, Professor Jones wanted to know if a computer-based learning (CBL) simulation package on statistics (X) would help his psychology students (not RS). He had found that classes in the past seemed to have a difficult time with the concepts and their applications. The package was installed on a set of computers in the Computing Centre and the class was informed that it was there and what its purpose was. His hypothesis was that students would benefit from this package (Y). All 40 students tried it and all of them passed the examination (O_1) in statistics that year, with a mean score greater than that of the previous year. He asked each person who used the package to fill out a questionnaire (O_2), which was intended to measure how the class perceived the package's utility and ease of

TABLE 3.6
Summary of basic pre-experimental designs with potential sources of invalidity and confounding of results (symbols explained in the text); 'best' ratings are given, some of which could be worse for individual studies, depending on how they are carried out

A. Pre-experimental designs	Design structure (time sequence of events)	Potential sources of invalidity and confounding														
Design description		1 No comparison across groups	2 Time: other events	3 Time: maturation	4 Selection: sample (and assignment)	5 Selection: regression	6 Selection: sample stability	7 Interaction of time with sample	8 Interaction of ind. var. with sample	9 Direction/nature of causality uncertain	10 Unnatural/invalid exper./treatment	11 Invalid measurement of variables	12 Instrument reliability	13 Learning from instrument	14 Instrument reacts with ind. variable	15 Other interactions
A1 *One group post-test/obs. only:* one group observed or tested for one possible dependent variable for one instance of independent variable, observed or manipulated.	$(RS \rightarrow)X \rightarrow O_1$	—	—	—	(+) —		?		—							
A2 *One group pre- and post-test/observations* for some single event or treatment.	$(RS \rightarrow)O_1 \rightarrow X \rightarrow O_2$	—	—	—	(+) —	?	+	—	—							
A3 *Two available groups,* one subjected to event or treatment, the other not, both are tested/observed post-event/experience only.	$X_a \rightarrow O_a$ $X_0 \rightarrow O_0$	+	?	?	—		—	—	—							

use. The questionnaire responses indicated that the students found the package useful and enjoyed going through it. On the basis of these results, Professor Jones has decided to integrate the package into his course next year. For those of us who have a teaching role, this is not an unusual situation, but does it provide us with any conclusive evidence that the package facilitated learning any more than previous approaches?

First, let us consider a variable map for this situation. Figure 3.3 outlines some extraneous variables (some more will be added in Chapter 6) that would possibly influence the quality of learning of statistics. In no particular order:

- Its earlier exposure to statistics means that this class could be better than previous ones.
- The fear of failure means students work harder in order to avoid repeating the course.
- They have used other learning resources, including the usual class sessions, since the simulation was a supplement.
- The class was the Professor's and not typical of all classes of psychology students.
- They were 'sold' the CBL which simply provided more practice.

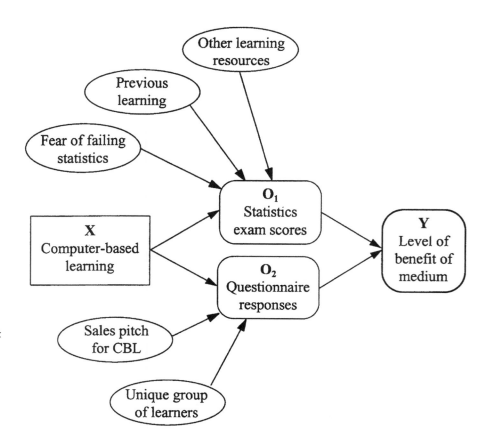

FIGURE 3.3
A variable map for Professor Jones' test of the effectiveness of computer-based learning materials. Can you add other extraneous variables?

The difficulty is that there is no way of knowing which of these would be actively influencing the learning. Considering each of the eight potential sources of invalidity and confounding will help to see how the lack of control can have an impact on the outcomes of the study:

1   *No comparison across groups* [−]. There was no group that received comparable traditional learning materials that omitted the CBL simulation, allowing a group with which to compare. The previous year's results are not a valid comparison group as they did not do the same examination.

2   *Time: events* [−]. The outcome of learning (shown by the final examination) could have been influenced by any number of variables – for example, the use of other learning resources during the course.

3   *Time: maturation* [   ]. A possibility if, as the class progresses, panic or fear of failure influences motivation to learn, which will depend on the subjects.

4   *Selection: sample (and assignment)* [−]. Here the professor had only his class.

5   *Selection: regression towards the mean* [   ]. Not an issue here: a single measure.

6   *Selection: sample stability* [+]. Fortunately, every one in class tried the package, took the test and completed the questionnaire, but this is not enough to redeem the study.

7   *Interaction of time with sample* [   ]. Not relevant here with one group.

8   *Interaction of independent variable with sample* [−]. Due to the nature of the class selected to be the sample, Professor Jones' own, their response to the new learning materials could be specific to them and not typical of all students (they like him, he sold the package very well, etc.).

There is no dispute about their learning, but the only real support Professor Jones has for causality is that the package apparently did not interfere with that learning. He lacks any real evidence that they learned any more than they would have without it. As Cook *et al.* (1990) note, the group may be perceived to behave the same as another group in the past, one that was already proven to demonstrate causality (learned as a result of materials). Thus, it is assumed that the causality link must be the same for this group, an example of the concept of a *modus operandi*. In this situation, since the students learned it is assumed that the CBL package had something to do with it. Such a conclusion was justified by the fact that other innovative learning materials had been successful in facilitating learning in other situations. If this were to be proven instead of being based upon circumstantial evidence, it would require a more rigorous procedure than just looking at the pass rate on the final examination. Additional evidence would be required, such as observing students interacting with the learning materials in the computer laboratory, tests at various stages, etc. The need is particularly compelling since there was no comparison group learning at the same time under comparable conditions, using alternative materials, and taking the same examination. Altogether, there is little support for either internal or external validity, with neither causality nor generalizability being justified. We would have to know more about the questionnaire and examination to know whether there is adequate construct validity, and since no statistical tests were used, statistical validity is not even an issue. We will examine some possible improvements for this study later.

Design A2: One group pre- and post-test/observation

Super Catflap Ltd is a small company that makes the little doors that permit cats to enter and leave their home by themselves. These novel, high-technology flaps are designed to allow only the owner's cats to enter since only they will have the transmitter code on their collars that will release the catch on the door. It was felt that the average productivity level for the doors was insufficient (O_1) and, with rising demand, there was a desire to increase productivity rather than hire more staff, since the production site was full to capacity with employees. It was decided to provided an immediate bonus in the form of shares in the company (X) to encourage increased motivation to produce more per shift. Consequently, it was expected that overall productivity would rise (production cost per completed unit would drop). The hypothesis was that the incentive plan would lead to a reduction in staff hours (cost) per unit produced. The null hypothesis was that there would be no significant difference between the average staff-hours per unit before and after the incentive plan was introduced.

After three months, sufficient time for the effects of the plan to be felt, the average productivity level (O_2) was then compared with that before the share plan was introduced. It was found that the difference in output per day over a 30-day period before and after was an improvement from a mean of 5.4 staff-hours per unit (standard deviation 0.80; 35 workers) to 5.1 staff-hours per unit (standard deviation 0.75; 38 workers). A t-test proves non-significant: $t = 1.65$, $p > 0.05$. As a consequence, the board of directors decided to phase out the plan. Was this a reasonable action to take?

Let us look at the variable map for this situation in Figure 3.4. The variables of interest are the production cost per unit (dependent variable) and the incentive plan (proposed independent variable). Since there was, for comparison purposes, no group that did not receive the incentive at the same time, it was not possible to control for unrecognized extraneous variables. Potential candidates that can be identified include the possible consequences of the time between the incentive and the second measure. The effect of the bonus could have worn off or inflation could have simply made the bonus equivalent to a cost-of-living rise in pay.

Now consider the first eight standard sources of invalidity to see how they relate to the study structure and the variable map, keeping in mind that we will come back to this study later to see if it can be improved.

1 *No comparison across groups* [−]. Without a group with which to compare over the same period of time, how would the researchers know whether or not production would have changed without the incentive plan? This lack of comparison group will manifest itself in a number of the other sources.
2 *Time: events* [−]. In three months, many things could influence worker productivity, as suggested in Figure 3.4, including a perceived loss in apparent value of the bonus because of inflation.
3 *Time: maturation* [−]. This might have occurred in the form of the impact of a bonus declining over time.
4 *Selection: sample (and assignment)* [−]. In this case, the whole factory was the sample, so that it would not be possible to generalize to a larger population as it *was* the population.

FIGURE 3.4
A variable map for Super Catflap Ltd's study on increasing productivity ($Y = O_2 - O_1$). Can you add other extraneous variables?

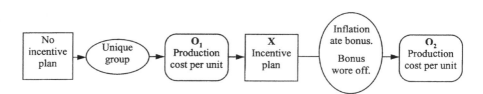

5   *Selection: regression towards the mean* [?]. It is possible that another set of events could have an impact, such as inflation combined with an announcement that income tax allowances would not be increased. Thus the share plan would only provide for compensation, leaving effective salaries unchanged. These other events could introduce error in the chosen 'measure' of motivation (individual productivity), with the result that the overall productivity among workers would regress towards the usual mean.

6   *Selection: sample stability* [+]. With company records, individual productivity could be monitored for the two times, thus taking into account those who left or joined in the intervening period.

7   *Interaction of time with sample* [−]. Having a single group, it is not possible to determine if the change (or lack) would have occurred only with this sample over time (maturation, see 3 above) and not another. The idiosyncratic nature of the sample might result in it reacting uniquely over time.

8   *Interaction of independent variable with sample* [−]. Unless there were a control group, it would not be possible to determine whether the repercussions of the incentive plan (or lack) on motivation were idiosyncratic to the group. In other words, another group might have reacted differently.

There are a number of possible contributions to lack of internal validity (which of the above? See Table 3.5.) There is little external validity unless it could be proven that this factory and these employees were somehow typical. The indicator of productivity seems appropriate and the average over time allows for natural variance, thus there is a reasonable level of construct validity. If there were a number of distinct assembly lines, then productivity could have been averaged over these. There may be some statistical validity since the data were interval in nature, but since there are so many possible sources of change (or even lack of change), the source of any difference or lack of difference would be virtually impossible to identify.

Decisions are frequently made on negative results as well as positive ones. In this situation, considering all the possible sources that could influence the validity of the conclusions, it would be wise for the company to investigate further before withdrawing the share plan. We will consider some other threats to the validity of the results in Chapter 6 and suggest an improved study design.

Design A3: Two available groups

In this situation, there is the opportunity to compare the outcome of an experimental treatment, but the choice of groups is one of convenience so that they may not be equivalent at the beginning. As an example, let us consider two free health centres for pre-school children that were to be established in inner-city low-income areas. The question was whether it would be possible to encourage mothers to bring their children for more frequent check-ups and inoculations? The hypothesis was that a site with a playroom (X_a) with toys and games for the children as part of the waiting area would be more effective in encouraging mothers to bring their children for regular check-ups than one without (X_0). The null hypothesis was that the frequency of visits would not be different for the two sites.

Two locations were chosen whose catchment areas contained families occupying roughly equivalent housing and two free clinics for pre-school children established: one with and one without a playroom. After a year, the database of records was interrogated and the visiting patterns determined, as shown in Table 3.7. It was found that the number of parents registering children in each clinic was roughly the same but that the frequency of visits tended to be higher in the centre with the playroom (O_a) than the one without the playroom (O_0) ($\chi^2 = 31.01, p < 0.05$). This was taken as evidence of different attitudes towards child health care (Y), one group showing a higher interest than the other. On the basis of these results, it was decided to implement playrooms in all the pre-school health centres in inner-city areas.

Some of the possible extraneous variables are included in the variable map in Figure 3.5. The most important ones here are those that arise as a consequence of sampling. The process employed raises the question of whether these are equivalent groups which would influence the generalizability of the study. It also prompts one to question the possible reaction of non-typical groups and their impact on the results. In other words, two non-equivalent groups might react quite differently to the same situation, here because of preconceived views, traditions, or past experiences. Having non-equivalent groups in different situations simply makes it difficult, if not impossible, to guarantee that the desired independent variable is the only cause of the effect observed.

So was the evidence sufficient to justify such an expenditure? Let us consider each of the first eight potential sources of invalidity in light of the variable map.

1   *No comparison across groups* [+]. In this case there is a group with which to compare, though it should be asked whether the groups were equivalent at the beginning.

2   *Time: events* [?]. With no pre-treatment observations, interviews or questionnaire, one does not know what other events might influence attendance

TABLE 3.7
Visits to two clinics by parents with pre-school children over a one-year period

Number of visits/year	Number of parents bringing children	
	Playroom	No playroom
1	40	80
2	45	60
3	66	50
4 or more	80	40
Totals	231	230

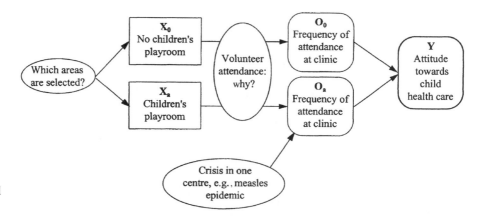

FIGURE 3.5
A variable map for
the problem of
clinics for pre-school
children

during the time, particularly with this study over such a long period (e.g., a measles epidemic in the playroom area).

3 *Time: maturation* [?]. In this situation, it is not likely to be an issue, though the novelty of the toys and games might wear off with time.

4 *Selection: sample (and assignment)* [−]. Obviously, since the study used available groups, it would not be possible to extend inferences to a larger group, unless it could be shown these were representative of other inner-city low income areas. It also means that it is not possible to justify that the groups were equivalent initially and no process for refuting the supposition that any difference was due to traits in the original groups (ethnic background, income, etc.). While they were matched on the basis of some criteria (inner city, equivalent housing), such a measure can be extremely unreliable as an indicator of attitudes.

5 *Selection: regression towards the mean* [ ]. As there was no grouping based upon a measure nor a second measure, this would not apply.

6 *Selection: sample stability* [−]. Even if a group were identified, there is no way of knowing why non-participants did not participate or how many did not return, and of those who did not, why.

7 *Interaction of time with sample* [−]. With the group basically being volunteers and the observation extended over time, there is the possibility of other events influencing one group more than another.

8 *Interaction of independent variable with sample* [−]. There is the possibility that the bias in selection reduced attendance. For example, even though the two centres were in an inner-city area, there could be differences in, say, social class, ethnic background or religion that would enhance or deter a group from attending. This could have a strong influence on the results if the area were fairly homogeneous for such a trait.

Internal and external validity have not been maintained, leaving some doubt as to not only justification of the causal link but also generalizability. The construct validity of the measure, frequency of attendance, as being a valid operational definition of 'positive attitude towards health care' is suspect, since the centre could be seen as a nice day out. While this still achieves the desired end, it should not be stated as an indicator of attitude towards health care unless there is some corroborative evidence (e.g., questionnaire or interview) from parents attending. Statistical validity has been maintained through the choice of a nonparametric test for an ordinal variable. With so many doubts raised, other data would be needed to determine the wisdom and true potential effectiveness of spending money on such a scheme. In Activity 3.2, you will be asked to consider another study and analyse it. Carry this out now.

Activity 3.2

(a) For the study described, classify the structure as being equivalent to A1, A2 or A3, identifying each of the components (e.g., *RS, X, O, Y*) and sketch out a variable map.

Albert Farmical, a researcher, wanted to test the possible influence of vitamins on children's intelligence. He hypothesized that a regular dose of multiple vitamins would positively enhance children's IQ scores. His null hypothesis was that after the trial, there would be no significant difference between two groups: one taking vitamins and one not.

For the trial, 100 children in a school district (local education authority) were randomly selected to participate. They were all given an IQ test both before the trial and again after six months on a strict regime of vitamins. The results showed the mean IQ of the group increasing from 105 (s.d. = 14.5) to 110 (s.d. = 15.5), a statistically significant difference ($t = 2.36, p < 0.05$), thus it was maintained that the vitamins enhanced intelligence.

(b) Sketch a variable map, and for each of the eight potential sources of invalidity and confounding listed below, enter a −, +, ? or < blank > in the [ ], and say why.

1 *No comparison across groups* [ ]
2 *Time: events* [ ]
3 *Time: maturation* [ ]
4 *Selection: sample (and assignment)* [ ]
5 *Selection: regression* [ ]
6 *Selection: sample stability* [ ]
7 *Interaction of time with sample* [ ]
8 *Interaction of independent variable with sample* [ ]

(c) Were the conclusions justifiable? Why or why not?

Basic Designs 4

This chapter will continue the survey of designs with examples of the experimental, quasi-experimental and ex post facto designs introduced in Tables 3.3 and 3.4. Though these illustrate acceptable designs, they are not without faults, limitations and potential pitfalls.

Experimental designs

As noted earlier, these are the 'ideal' structures, though when it comes to studying human activity in real situations, they either may not be possible or would introduce problems intrinsic to their configuration. Consequently, modified alternatives will be considered in following sections.

Design B2: Pre- and post-test/observation

This is sometimes considered the 'best' design, the one that epitomizes quantitative studies. The approach is often based on the comparison of gain scores: how much difference in gain (or loss) is there between groups using measures before and after the treatment. A second characteristic is the random selection of the sample and the random assignment of this group to two (or more) subgroups, one of which should be the control group and not receive the treatment. Thus, if there is a difference in gain scores between the two groups, there is justification for attributing this to the treatment alone, since any potential extraneous variables would be experienced by both groups equally. This is not as easy as it first seems, and as we will see here and in Chapter 5, there are pitfalls even to this design.

Let us start with Martha Proughit, a business studies teacher, who observed that girls at the secondary school level were less inclined to use computers in classes than boys, and consequently learned less about applications. Considering the importance of information technology skills in many jobs, she felt that this could have a detrimental effect on career prospects of women in the future. It was hypothesized that appropriate learning experiences for girls would overcome this reluctance. Consequently, a set of materials was designed aimed specifically at girls to encourage their use of computer application packages by illustrating their relevance in jobs, how they facilitated work, and the satisfaction that one could get from using them as tools. The null hypothesis for the study was that there would be no difference in gain scores in attitude towards use of computers between two groups, one using the materials and one not. A random sample of 100 girls (RS) aged 14 were chosen from the 2000 in the city's schools, with half randomly assigned to each of two groups (RA). Both groups were assembled at their schools (about 20 per school) and told they had been selected to participate in a new computer survey. All were asked to complete a questionnaire on computers and their uses, which was the attitude instrument devised for the study (O_{a1} and O_{01}). Then one group of girls were given the package, which included a videotape on careers and jobs, a computer simulation demonstrating word-processing, spreadsheets, data bases and graphics, and some written materials (X_a). They were asked to complete this package over five half-hour sessions at lunch, followed by a parallel form of the attitude instrument (O_{a2}). The girls in the control group were asked to return and complete another questionnaire (O_{02}) in two weeks' time. The results of the attitude instruments showed a statistically significant greater gain score ($O_2 - O_1$) for the treatment group than for the control, as shown in Table 4.1 and illustrated in Figure 4.1 (one of several possible outcomes of such a study). The two groups are not exactly the same to start with, but there was very little difference and the gain scores were the important indicators of improvement in attitudes. It was decided that the package would be reproduced and distributed to schools.

Before considering possible sources of invalidity, let us look at the variable map for this study, shown in Figure 4.2. If there are two groups to be compared, they need to be as alike as possible before the study, otherwise group differences, such as prevailing attitudes in one group, could affect the outcomes. Also, the two groups need to be kept separate, otherwise the interaction could result in an influence on the results. For example, the control group could feel left out or have their attitudes changed by new enthusiasm by the treatment group. Another possible extraneous variable difficult to control would be other events or learning experiences, such as a television programme on computers and information technology. Again, this would have no net effect as long as both groups saw the same programme.

TABLE 4.1
Summary of gain scores for test of attitudes towards computers

	Control	Treatment
Mean	0	3.1
s.d.	1.2	1.1
n	50	50
$t = 13.47^*$		

* $p < 0.05$.

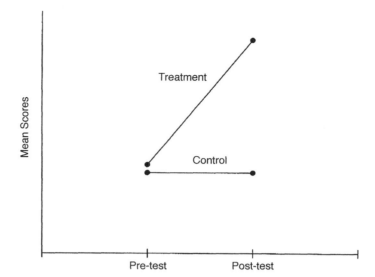

FIGURE 4.1
Results of a pre- and
post-test/
observation
experimental study

FIGURE 4.2
A variable map for
the trial of learning
materials aimed at
attitude change in
girls towards
computers and
careers in
information
technology (the
dependent variable
Y is change in
attitudes between,
before and after).
Are there other
extraneous
variables?

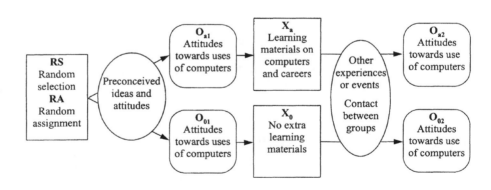

Now let us consider each of the first eight sources of invalidity to see how well
such a study can control extraneous variables:

1 *No comparison across groups* [+]. There were two groups.
2 *Time: events* [+]. Using two groups over the same period of time, what
   happened to the one outside the study should have happened to the other
   so that such an extraneous variable (such as a television programme)
   should exert no differential influence on gain scores.
3 *Time: maturation* [+]. Since the groups start the same, any tendency to overcome anxiety just with time should be much the same.

4 *Selection: sample (and assignment)* [+]. The group was randomly selected, thus the results should be generalizable to the larger population of girls. Also, they were divided into two groups randomly, distributing any extraneous variables (such as attitudes, or even unknown ones) equally across both groups.

5 *Selection: Regression towards the mean* [+]. Since the group is randomly divided, it is less important how extreme they were in the first place for the trait. The control group would regress the same as the treatment group. In any case, random selection and assignment should ensure that both groups are equivalent for the variable of interest.

6 *Selection: sample stability* [+]. By measuring the groups before and after, the structure of the study has the opportunity to monitor and control drop-out. This provides an opportunity to determine whether the reason anyone withdrew had anything to do with the treatment or instruments.

7 *Interaction of time with sample* [+]. This should be controlled for by the random selection and random assignment ensuring equality of groups, time alone not having any possible differential effect on one or the other. If the researcher stopped group contact, it would prevent the possibility that the control group would change so as not to appear foolish, gain access to the materials, or have contact between the two groups, since the control group could simply change through contact with the treatment group. This is where the execution of the design is as important as the design choice.

8 *Interaction of independent variable with sample* [?]. This does not necessarily control for the possibility that the topic of computers would deter some girls from participating in the first place, or from responding truthfully.

While most of these potential sources provided no problems (except possibly 7 and 8), some may arise in the second set, which will be considered when we return to this study in Chapter 6. At this point, it appears that the study results support the decision.

Design B3: Post-test/observation only, with a control group

While this design does not appear to have the same potential for controlling extraneous variables as the previous one since it lacks a pre-test, there are situations where such an approach is more appropriate. Primarily this occurs when both groups are starting off on an equal footing for the trait or attribute being investigated and both could be expected to change. Take, for example, Widget-Digit Microchips Inc., which wanted to start production of a new line of microchips for a company that was making 'intelligent' toasters. These would actually monitor the bread colour and pop up the toast when it was browned to the desired level *and* speak to tell the user it was ready. The design engineers could not agree on the most efficient and effective production procedure between two entirely new ones, process A (X_a) and process B (X_b instead of X_0). It was decided to resolve the issue by taking a randomly selected group of production personnel (*RS*), divide them randomly into two groups (*RA*) of 20 workers each and have them produce the chips in both ways. The measure of success would be through the Quality Control Laboratory which would monitor chip failure rates (O_a and O_b) for both groups as the indicator of success of the process (Y). The null hypothesis was that there would be no significant difference between the failure rates for the two groups. After the three-month trial period, the results showed that the process A group produced chips with a mean of $\bar{x}_a = 5.6$ failures per day, with a standard deviation of 1.3. Over the same period of time, the process B group had a mean of $\bar{x}_b = 7.4$ failures per day, with a standard deviation of 1.4. Using a *t*-test, the results showed statistically significantly fewer failures for process A than for process B, $t = 4.21$, $p < 0.05$. It was decided that all production would follow process A.

The variable map in Figure 4.3 highlights some possible extraneous variables, the first being previous experience on production work of a similar nature. Training for each process would need to be of comparable quality and delivered with the same enthusiasm if the test is to be fair. Relationships between the two groups could influence failure rates if the groups became competitive in terms of output rates, but this had a detrimental influence on quality. On the other hand, knowledge of failure rates could also influence quality and it would have to be decided whether or not this would be revealed during the trials.

How well does this design control such variables? Let us go through the first eight sources of invalidity for this study:

1   *No comparison across groups* [+]. This design obviously provides two groups for comparison. In this case, there is not the traditional 'control' group to whom nothing is done, but instead it is one of comparison across two different processes.

2   *Time: events* [?]. Was the difference found due to the implementation process or the training given to personnel? What other events could have occurred that could affect production differentially? Such a study is not very effective in identifying extraneous variables that might contribute to one being better than the other, unless other observations are made.

3   *Time: maturation* [?]. This is possible if one considers maturation to include how time affects one's performance. For example, one task may be more boring than the other. While this could be considered part of the process itself, the study does not allow the possibility of pinpointing this as a contributing variable.

FIGURE 4.3
A variable map for Widget-Digit microchip production process tests. Are there other extraneous variables?

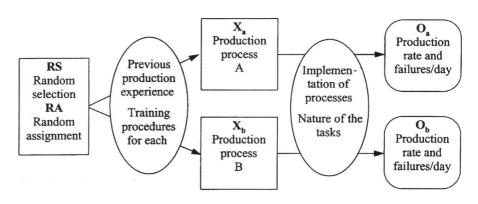

4 *Selection: sample (and assignment)* [+]. The group was randomly selected and divided randomly, thus overall previous experience of both groups should have been much the same.

5 *Selection: regression* [+]. Since the group was randomly divided, there should not be extreme differences in the groups.

6 *Selection: sample stability* [?]. In this situation, where the subjects are monitored employees, it would have been possible to determine losses, resulting in a [+] assessment here, instead of a more general assessment of [?] because the design does not have any implicit control over sample loss.

7 *Interaction of time with sample* [+]. As the sample is random and the groups determined by random assignment, what will affect one should affect the other.

8 *Interaction of independent variable with sample* [?]. This approach does not necessarily help to control *differential* mortality in the two groups, as a result of one process, for example, boring subjects badly. This is a possibility unless a special effort is made to prevent mortality being increased by one process or the other. It also does not control for the effect of changing jobs abruptly or any radical change in the nature of the job.

In addition to these research design issues, there is also the question whether either process had an *acceptable* failure rate, one of engineering and production significance. In other words, even if process A had a lower failure rate than process B, it would still be up to the engineers to decide whether to refine the processes or look for another. It does point out the fact that such designs can sometimes answer only *part* of the question.

Table 4.2 summarizes the characteristics of the two experimental designs for comparison. Now try Activity 4.1, where you are given another experimental design that you can analyse.

QUASI-EXPERIMENTAL AND EX POST FACTO DESIGNS

Having considered designs that ought to be avoided and some designs that seem to contain all the desirable characteristics (with some limitations), let us consider the domain in between these extremes. The following are the first two of a number of designs that reflect the problems of conducting research in the real world, trying to answer academically or practically significant questions. They bring with them some of the problems of the first set of pre-experimental designs, but avoid some of the criticisms associated with true experimental studies. Quasi-experimental designs have been defined as those having all the characteristics of experimental designs, but 'primarily depend on self-selection or administrative decisions to determine who is to be exposed to a treatment' (Cook *et al.*, 1990). As will be seen in Chapter 5, purposive sampling can result in more representative groups that just convenience sampling. Therefore the validity of any generalization will vary depending on how much control one exercises over such sampling. Ex post facto designs, on the other hand, often involve life experiences as the treatment rather than ones that are experimenter-contrived. Thus, the sampling technique becomes all important since it has a strong influence over the validity of the independent variable.

TABLE 4.2
Summary of basic experimental designs with potential sources of invalidity and confounding of results; *'best'* ratings are given, some of which could be worse for individual studies depending on how they are carried out

B. Experimental designs		Design structure (time sequence of events)	Potential sources of invalidity and confounding															
	Design description		1 No comparison across groups	2 Time: other events	3 Time: maturation	4 Selection: sample (and assignment)	5 Selection: regression	6 Selection: sample stability	7 Interaction of time with sample	8 Interaction of ind. var. with sample	9 Direction/nature of causality uncertain	10 Unnatural/invalid exper./treatment	11 Invalid measurement of variables	12 Instrument reliability	13 Learning from instrument	14 Instrument reacts with ind. variable	15 Other interactions
B2	Pre- and post-test/ observation of proposed dependent variable with single event of possible independent variable with a control	$RS \rightarrow \begin{cases} RA_a \rightarrow O_{a1} \rightarrow X_a \rightarrow O_{a2} \\ RA_0 \rightarrow O_{01} \rightarrow X_0 \rightarrow O_{02} \end{cases}$	+	+	+	+	+	+	+	?							
B3	Post-test/observation only with a control group	$RS \rightarrow \begin{cases} RA_a \rightarrow X_a \rightarrow O_a \\ RA_0 \rightarrow X_0 \rightarrow O_0 \end{cases}$	+	?	?	+	+	?	?	?							

*Key: + compensated for by design; − not compensated; ? compensation uncertain; <blank> not relevant or covered in this chapter.

Activity 4.1

In an endeavour to confirm that positive reinforcement is applicable to classroom practice, Professor Bloggs set up a study. Ten classes of 10-year-old children were randomly selected from the education authority's list of 100. These were randomly assigned to two groups, group A to be taught with the teacher consciously using positive reinforcement and group B with the teacher avoiding it.

The teachers involved agreed upon a common topic, verb tenses in grammar, using the same learning materials for a series of five lessons over a week. The children were given a standardized test on verb tenses before the experiment and a parallel version after it. The teachers were observed before the experimental sessions and during to record the relative frequency of the use of positive reinforcement in class. In the pre-experimental situation there was little difference among the teachers, but during the experimental period those teaching group A pupils used more positive reinforcement than usual and those teaching group B used less than usual. The post-experience test showed no significant difference between the groups in use of grammar. It was concluded that positive reinforcement seemed to make no difference in classroom learning.

(a) For the study described, classify it as to whether it has a structure like design B2 or B3, identifying each of the components (e.g., *RS*, *X*, *O*, *Y*).

(b) Devise a variable map for this study, indicating possible extraneous variables.

(c) For each of the eight potential sources of invalidity and confounding listed below, enter a −, +, ? or < blank > in the [ ], and say why.

1 *No comparison across groups* [ ]
2 *Time: events* [ ]
3 *Time: maturation* [ ]
4 *Selection: sample (and assignment)* [ ]
5 *Selection: regression towards the mean* [ ]
6 *Selection: sample stability* [ ]
7 *Interaction of time with sample* [ ]
8 *Interaction of independent variable with sample* [ ]

(d) Based on this analysis, were the conclusions justifiable? Why or why not? (We will re-examine this study in Chapter 7).

Design C2: Non-equivalent control group design with pre-tests (quasi-experimental)

We will consider two cases here, simply because one will be resolved using parametric statistics and the other a nonparametric test. First let us return to the example of Super Catflap Ltd, used as an example for design A2 in the previous chapter: demand grew so much that the company expanded and doubled the size of its premises and hired new staff. Realizing the inconclusive nature of the outcome of its earlier study, the company decided to try the experiment on the share bonus plan again, but with two groups. This time, the consultant researcher selected ten existing employees to monitor as a control and ten new employees who had just been trained and knew nothing of the previous experiment. When they were up to the average production rate, they were offered a bonus of shares as an incentive if they worked more efficiently. Every week that their production was 10% above the norm for the past year, they received a share bonus. A revised variable map is shown in Figure 4.4.

After three months, the production rates were monitored again, with the results shown graphically in Figure 4.5. While the treatment group of newer employees had gone up in production rate, the control group of older employees had also gone up, though not as much. The original measure of hours per unit produced was changed to units per hour produced, the inverse, as any improvements would be more intuitively obvious. Thus the base line of 5.4 staff-hours per unit was equivalent to a production rate norm of 0.185 units per hour per person for existing employees. The new employees rose to a rate of 0.190 units per hour per person when the study began. After the three-month trial period, the mean rates were 0.191 units per hour per person for the established employees and 0.208 units per hour per person for the new employees. The difference in improvement in mean rates was 0.006 units per hour per person (s.d. = 0.0018) for the existing employees and 0.018 units per hour per person (s.d. = 0.0020) for the new employees, which was statistically significant ($t = 14.2, p < 0.001$). This indicated that the difference was not due to chance alone, but left the management with another issue to resolve. Was the difference large enough production-wise, in other words did it cover the cost of the share bonus? Not all questions can be resolved by statistics alone!

While the variable map looks much the same as in Figure 3.4, with the addition of a comparison group and a better reinforcement schedule, there is still one other design issue that remains. Was it better to test the two distinct groups as

FIGURE 4.4
Revised variable map for a quasi-experimental design for the Super Catflap problem.
($Y = O_2 - O_1; PS$ indicates purposive selection for samples)

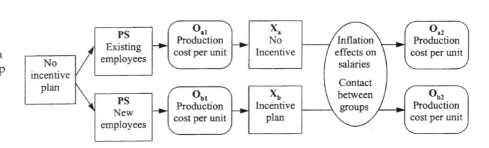

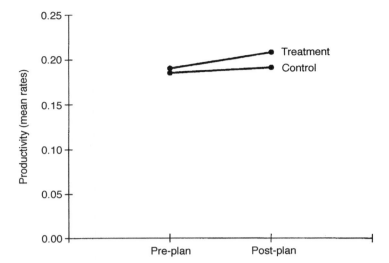

FIGURE 4.5
Productivity changes
for two groups in
Super Catflap Ltd

they were to prevent the influence of a previous programme, or would it have been better to randomly select the two groups from the whole workforce, having some existing and some new in each group? What are the advantages of each of these alternatives?

Let us consider the first eight sources of invalidity:

1   *No comparison across groups* [+]. Two groups.
2   *Time: events* [+]. With pre- and post-treatment observation, one can see that the control group changed as well, thus it would be worthwhile asking why: were there any events that could have differentially contributed? Or was there an event that affected both groups?
3   *Time: maturation* [+]. Though less likely, there might be some aspect that contributed as suggested in 2.
4   *Selection: sample (and assignment)* [−]. By choosing members for each group, the representativeness is doubtful, limiting to whom the results can be generalized. This is particularly true since the origins of the two groups were different, which in itself could introduce an extraneous variable: different attitudes towards work.
5   *Selection: regression towards the mean* [?]. Because the groups were not necessarily equal to begin with, there is the potential for differential regression towards their true means of productivity. This might contribute to some of the increase by the more experienced control group.
6   *Selection: sample stability* [+]. Having pre- and post-treatment observation means that stability can be monitored.
7   *Interaction of time with sample* [−]. Because of the basic difference in the groups, it is quite possible that over time the two groups reacted differently to events, either enhancing or decreasing any influence due to the share plan (recall the extraneous variables in Figure 3.4).

8   *Interaction of independent variable with sample* [−]. For example, if the control group found out about the scheme, some members might work harder so as to qualify for shares. Also, it may be that new employees might respond better to the scheme than existing employees, possibly being less cynical or mistrusting of the management. Had the groups been reversed, and the old employees received the treatment instead of the new, the results could have been more like Figure 4.6. What would be the conclusion then?

We will return to the problems of Super Catflap Ltd later and see how the design could be improved further. We will also consider some additional variations in the possible outcomes of test and retest designs, to complement the three seen so far.

The second study employing this design is an improved version of the one carried out to determine the desirability of incorporating playrooms in clinics for pre-school children to increase attendance and overall understanding of child health care. This was presented in Chapter 3 to illustrate design A3 (two available groups). While the problem of finding exact equivalents may be very difficult, incorporating pre- and post-implementation observations goes a long way towards overcoming criticisms. The study was replicated using two new areas that were in the same city and reasonably close to each other. Attendance records for parents in the two area clinics were consulted for a period before the plan was implemented in one of the areas. The attendances in both areas during the implementation period were then used to determine changes in attendance patterns, as shown in the variable map in Figure 4.7, producing the results shown in Table 4.3. This time any *change* in attendance would be considered as an indication of change in attitude, *Y*.

To determine whether or not the differences were statistically significant, the Kolmogorov–Smirnov two-sample (one-tailed) test was used since the data

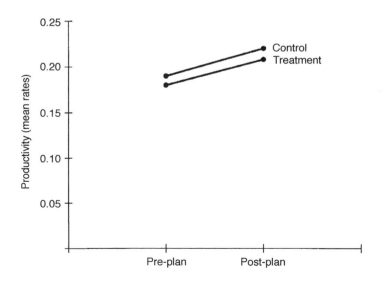

FIGURE 4.6
Possible outcome if the groups had been reversed in the Super Catflap study

FIGURE 4.7
A variable map for the revised plan to evaluate the effectiveness of playrooms in clinics to attract mothers and their pre-school children (the dependent variable, $Y = O_2 - O_1$, is the change in attitude over time)

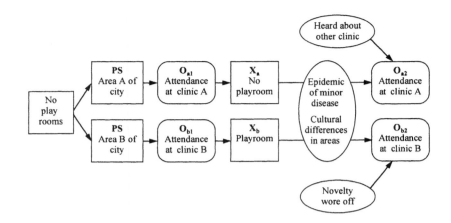

TABLE 4.3
Results of the study to evaluate the effectiveness of playrooms in clinics to improve attendance for pre-school children

Change in no. visits/year	Playroom	No playroom
1 fewer	5	10
No change	5	20
1 more	20	20
2 more	25	15
3 more	20	8
4 more	8	3

were ordinal and not interval. A one-tailed test was used since it was expected that the change would occur in one direction only: the playroom clinics would have an overall improved attendance. The test was significant (Goodman approximation (Siegel and Castellan, 1988), $\chi^2 = 13.95, df = 2$), supporting the hypothesis that the playroom would increase attendance. The justification for implementing such an innovation is now sounder, though the process would need to be monitored over time to see that it continues to work as expected. Considering the first eight sources of problems:

1   *No comparison across groups* [+]. Two groups.
2   *Time: events* [+]. With pre- and post-treatment observations, one can see how much the control group changed as well, thus it would be worthwhile asking why: were there any events that could have differentially contributed? Or was there an event that affected both groups, such as chicken-pox?
3   *Time: maturation* [+]. Though less likely, there might be some aspect that contributed as suggested in 2. If it were to occur in the children, it could be expected that it would influence both groups.
4   *Selection: sample (and assignment)* [−]. By choosing just the two clinics for the study, the representativeness could be considered doubtful, limiting to whom the results can be generalized, unless they can be shown to be typical of a larger population of clinics. A larger study involving two *sets* of clinics

would provide greater generalizability. There is an advantage of using whole clinics of subjects rather than individuals tempted away from their usual clinic or area, since they are more natural and less likely to introduce additional extraneous variables.

5 *Selection: regression towards the mean* [?]. Because the groups were not necessarily equal to begin with, there is the potential for differential regression towards their true pattern of attendance.

6 *Selection: sample stability* [+]. Having pre- and post-treatment observation means that stability can be monitored.

7 *Interaction of time with sample* [−]. Because of any basic differences in the groups, it is quite possible that over time the members of the two would react differently to other events, either enhancing or decreasing any influence due to the playroom (recall the extraneous variables in Figure 3.5). Monitoring local events would be of value as a process by which any potentially confounding events could be identified.

8 *Interaction of independent variable with sample* [−]. For example, if the control group found out about the scheme, some parents might try to change clinics or be discouraged because they were being deprived of this inducement. If there had been no difference between the two groups, then becoming bored with the playroom over time could have contributed and the study design would not have controlled for it. To identify this source would require more than counting numbers attending.

This study has a higher level of internal validity than the earlier one, but still may not have high external validity. Construct validity is acceptable if attendance and not necessarily an attitude change towards the need for check-ups for children were the concept. The choice of test is appropriate for the nature of the independent variable data (ordinal), thus enhancing statistical validity. We will return to this study in Chapter 7 to see what other extraneous variables might influence the outcome.

Design D3: Post-test/observation only with a control group (ex post facto)

Here life events provide the independent variable and such studies endeavour to observe or measure some dependent variable. They also reflect the near-impossibility of carrying out pre-treatment observations, though there may be possibilities if a national event, such as an election, were pending, and this was the 'treatment'. There are many situations where it would not be possible to control an identifiable independent variable (amount of education, social class, profession) and most of these tend to be macrovariables. As a consequence, the sampling of subpopulations becomes the means by which the levels of the independent variable are operationally defined.

Let us consider the example of Professor Boffin, who was interested in science teaching. It has often been maintained that it is equally desirable and intellectually honest to teach science as a process (in other words, enquiry skills) as well as a product (concepts and facts specific to a discipline: chemistry, biology, physics). In an attempt to determine whether the subject one taught had any influence on the emphasis placed on problem-solving in the classroom, he carried out a study which compared three types of teachers in schools in an education authority (school district). The samples consisted of 16 randomly selected teachers from each register: (RS_a) physics teachers $(\underline{X}_a)$, (RS_b) biology teachers $(\underline{X}_b)$, and (RS_c) chemistry teachers $(\underline{X}_c)$. Everyone was asked to submit a sample test on a topic of his or her choice. Each question on the test was classified as to whether it demanded recalling factual information, concept understanding, or problem-solving. The three groups were compared on the basis of percentage problem-solving questions (O), as it was maintained these reflected a demand for enquiry. The hypothesis was that there would be a difference in demand for enquiry in the classroom (Y) across the subjects. The null hypothesis assumed that there would be no statistical difference across the groups.

Using one-way analysis of variance (ANOVA) across the results for the three groups, Professor Boffin found a significant difference, a summary of the results being shown in Table 4.4. A Scheffé test was subsequently used to make pairwise comparisons to find the source of the difference. This indicated that the physics and chemistry teachers had a statistically significantly greater proportion of higher-level questions than the biology teachers, but that there was no significant difference between the physics and chemistry teachers. It was concluded that there was something in the nature of the disciplines that resulted in physics teachers demanding more problem-solving and enquiry than biology teachers.

Figure 4.8 provides a variable map, which illustrates the difficulty of determining the actual source of causality in such an ex post facto study. Just which factor or set of factors influences teachers' question-asking propensities is not easy to determine and such results may be best described as associational: we can expect a higher level of problem-solving questions from physics and chemistry teachers than biology teachers. Thus the best that can be done here is to indicate the difference without necessarily proposing a specific cause.

Let us consider the first eight potential sources of confounding and invalidity for this study:

1   *No comparison across groups* [+]. There were three groups.
2   *Time: events* [−]. This is the most serious source of difficulty, since there are so many possible contributing (intervening) variables other than just what

TABLE 4.4		Physics	Chemistry	Biology	All teachers
Summary of the results of a one-way ANOVA for Professor Boffin's study of proportions of higher-level test questions on science teachers' tests	Means	0.50	0.47	0.39	0.46
	s.d.	0.092	0.085	0.074	
	n	15	16	14	45
	ANOVA	*df*	**MS**	**F**	**p**
	Subjects	2	0.0466	6.56	<0.05
	Error	42	0.0071		
	Scheffé test	**Phys–Chem**	**Phys–Bio**	**Chem–Bio**	**C–statistic min**
		0.99	3.51*	2.59*	2.54

*$p < 0.05$.

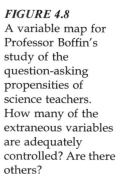

FIGURE 4.8
A variable map for
Professor Boffin's
study of the
question-asking
propensities of
science teachers.
How many of the
extraneous variables
are adequately
controlled? Are there
others?

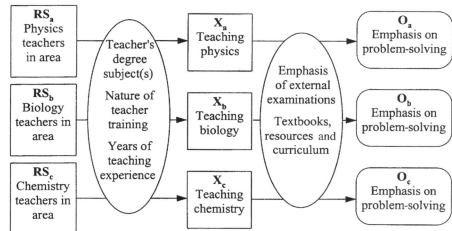

subject is taught. These include the background of the teachers (were all groups educated to the same level?), the nature of the textbooks and curriculum they were to follow, the type of teacher training they may have undergone, and in countries with external examinations for students, the emphasis of those examinations.

3 *Time: maturation* [−]. Without knowing the age distribution of both groups, it would be difficult to know whether or not this would have any effect, but if one group were older and more experienced, then this might influence the outcome.

4 *Selection: sample (and assignment)* [+]. All groups were randomly selected from their respective populations of subject teachers.

5 *Selection: regression towards the mean* [+]. Not likely to be a problem since selection for groups was based on nominal categories and not ranked data.

6 *Selection: sample stability* [?]. While the sample was randomly selected from those who were in post at the time, this does not sample teachers who may have recently started or dropped out of teaching.

7 *Interaction of time with sample* [−]. It would be virtually impossible with a study of this type to discount the interaction of time since, for example, there is no control for possible differential length of service of teachers across groups.

8 *Interaction of independent variable with sample* [−]. This does not take into account the actual backgrounds of the teachers: what subject their degree was in – physics, chemistry, physics and chemistry, physical science, etc.? It also does not take into account that these people chose to teach the subject, thus the other traits that might contribute to self-selection may also contribute to a group's use of higher-level questions.

With such lack of control of extraneous variables, the evidence for causality here is less convincing than for a true experimental design. On the other hand, such a design makes it possible to explore variables that one could not possibly explore in a true experimental design. This does not detract from the value of the study in identifying a difference in practice, but more sophisticated studies would be needed to identify the true cause(s). To substantiate any claims that might be made would require additional supporting data or information. These might include determining correlations and considering the impact of more variables, such as length of service, age, number of years as a university student, type of degree, and time in industry or research, that the teachers had. The study highlights the problem of employing macrovariables, which are potentially subject to influences from more constricted variables that are better defined.

Internal validity is not well maintained from the viewpoint of determining causality. External validity is acceptable for the variables chosen in that it would be possible to generalize to larger groups of teachers. Construct validity may be questionable in the case of the choice of independent variable: subject taught. The validity of using types of test questions as an operational definition of degree of enquiry in the classroom could be questioned. The mere fact that they test it does not mean they teach it. Statistical validity has been maintained as the choice of test was appropriate.

As a footnote, it should be realized that there will be situations where these last two designs could be combined to produce a hybrid, one that would take advantage of opportunity events in a community. It is possible that changes in legislation could provide an experimental 'treatment' that might differentially affect two groups with different characteristics. For example, would a change in income tax that gave 'spouse allowances' to people living together as well as those legally married influence marriage rates or divorce rates differentially for different age groups? There is, even in this study, as Cook and Campbell (1979) point out, a problem of distinguishing between forecasting and identifying causal relations in real situations. It is not as difficult to establish predictive relationships based upon correlations as it is to provide support for causality. In forecasting, it does not matter whether the true path of causality has been identified and that the true cause may be found in intervening variables. When describing such associations between variables, what does matter is that the claim is not made for causality when it cannot be justifiably established even though forecasts and predictions can be accurately made.

Design E1: One group observed

This results in collecting data on characteristics of a single group, which at best will be presented using descriptive statistics complemented by relevant correlations between pairs of traits. It is possible to investigate potential relationships, but it must be recognized that causality cannot be determined. Surveys often fall into this category and can and should be conducted using representative samples if inferences about relationships are to be extended to larger populations.

Take the example of Pete Boggs, admissions tutor for the undergraduate course in the Department of Tourism, who wanted to find out the best way to select potential students. Traditionally, A-level results are used in English universities, but he had read a number of articles that indicated that A levels were not very accurate predictors of university success. So, believing that motivation was as important as academic ability, he and several colleagues created an instrument to measure *career commitment*. They wanted to test the effectiveness of using responses as information that could be used as part of selection.

His hypothesis was that his team's instrument would be a better predictor than those traditionally used. Since he was conducting a survey and expected to generate correlations, a more refined hypothesis was that he would find a higher correlation between the careers test and first-year university success than between other measures and first-year success. His null hypothesis was that the correlations would not be different from those one would achieve by chance alone.

Pete carried out a survey of 1000 randomly selected beginning university students in England. This included asking basic factual questions about public examination results, the respondents' six best grades in GCSEs (General Certificate in Secondary Education, taken at age 16+) and their best two GCE A-level examination grades (taken at age 18+). These results were combined with their score on the instrument to measure how definite their career plans were. At the end of their first year in university (usually 19+), the results for those that had survived the year were acquired. The results were presented as a set of correlations, shown in Table 4.5. It was concluded that A-level results were not very good predictors of success, while GCSE results were better, and the score on the career planning instrument was the best. All of these correlations were found to be statistically significant, thus not just a chance occurrence, and consequently the null hypothesis was rejected for these. The correlations between the career plans test and GCSEs and A levels were not statistically significant and could have occurred by chance, thus it was assumed no relationship existed across these pairs of variables.

Figure 4.9 provides a variable map that includes the four variables in the study linked with solid lines where correlations were significant. It also includes some possible extraneous and intervening variables that might influence outcomes linked with dashed lines (can you identify others?). First, note that the figure portrays the four measured variables as observations with no implication of treatments that might be considered causal. While time sequences might seem to imply causality, when each pair is considered in detail, little evidence arises to support more than related indicators of outcomes. Time order may well determine which predictions are sensible and which would be silly. Observe that each of the four potentially has multiple overlapping influences, as suggested in the

	Best 6 GCSEs	Best 2 A levels	First-year university grades
Best two A levels	.78[*]		
First-year university grades	.45[*]	.28[*]	
Definiteness of career plan score	.14	.18	.43[*]

TABLE 4.5 Correlations for the Boggs career commitment study

[*]$p < 0.05$.

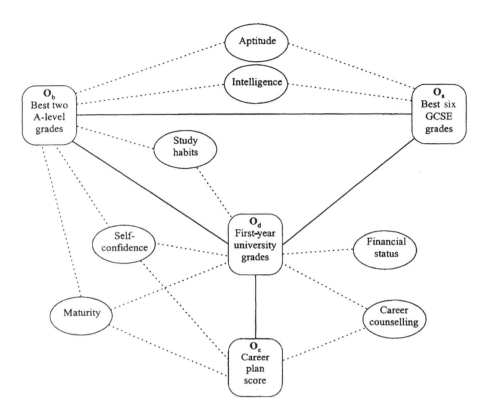

FIGURE 4.9
A variable map
showing extraneous
and intervening
variables for the
correlational study
to determine
predictors of
university success

variable map. For example, aptitude influences what subjects one chooses at
GCSE and A level (there is a tendency to choose subjects in which one can succeed) which in turn limits choices at university. Study habits become most
important when the pressure increases at A level and university. Finally, self-
confidence will influence perseverance and certainty in aspirations, etc. It just
so happens that the variables measured were considerably easier to measure
than some of the others indicated, a not uncommon situation in research.
This does not mean they were the most appropriate.

As was expected, there are no grounds for proof of causality, though the
potential for predicting university success based upon public examinations
and the instrument has been evaluated. The lack of support for causality is
mainly due to having only a single group, but it is also a result of employing
macrovariables (see Chapter 1) which all have intervening variables as causes.
Some of these have been potentially identified or proposed, others are unknown
(for example, intelligence, motivation, maturity, all of which have contentious
definitions). The comments that follow pertain to the issue of establishing causality. Employing the categories described above, the following potential sources
of invalidity and confounding are considered:

1   *No comparison across groups* [−]. There is a single group with no control
    group, thus it was not possible to ensure that other extraneous variables
    were responsible for the relationships, as will be seen in the following.

2   *Time: events* [−]. There is too much time between paired observations (e.g., GCSEs and first year at university: 3 years), allowing for other events.

3   *Time: maturation* [−]. There is too much time between paired observations allowing for subjects to mature, particularly for this age group.

4   *Selection: sample (and assignment)* [+]. This receives a plus only because surveys tend to randomly select their samples. This may allow the results to be generalized to a larger population, university students who have completed one year successfully, but does not include those not admitted or those who were, but were not successful in their first year. It does not enhance any argument for causality.

5   *Selection: regression towards the mean* [ ]. This is not relevant as no groups were classified and there is only one measure of each variable.

6   *Selection: sample stability* [?]. This would be an issue only if not all those contacted responded. If there was an incomplete response but with justification for why this occurred, showing that the reasons had nothing to do with the study, it would receive a [+].

7   *Interaction of time with sample* [−]. Since the group was selected from those who went to university, the time prevented selecting any who could have gone to university but did not.

8   *Interaction of independent variable with sample* [−]. The sample was randomly selected for a trait related to only one of the variables (university attendance) and thus by implication the sample determines the validity of the independent variable. Whether this is a valid indicator of the true independent variable could be questioned since there are so many possible intervening variables.

This analysis does not negate the value of the study as one that explores the construct (predictive) validity of employing various measures to forecast future success. What it does question is the validity of using these results to determine causality – for example, to say that having definite career plans *causes* a high level of university success. Those who failed to enter or succeed could have had equally high commitments. While the correlation was statistically significant, Pete should also ask if it is educationally significant, since the correlation is not very high. We will consider the issue of size of correlations in a later chapter, but at this point it should be noted that it is relatively small, thus indicating a weak connection between the variables. Also, while it does provide some justification for using the careers commitment test as another (but not the only) piece of information for selection, as we will see later, the content of this test would need to be checked to ensure that it measures what was intended.

In summary, Pete has established external validity (he can generalize to a larger population), but has little or no support for internal validity that would support a causal relationship. The construct validity of the instrument would need to be established. It does appear for the data collected that correlations are an appropriate choice of statistics, thus he seems to have maintained statistical validity.

Table 4.6 summarizes these last three designs, allowing you to compare them. Carry out Activity 4.2 at this time.

TABLE 4.6
Summary of quasi-experimental and ex post facto designs with potential sources of invalidity and confounding of results; 'best' ratings are given, some of which could be worse for individual studies depending on how they are carried out

Quasi-experimental and ex post facto designs:	Design / diagram	Potential sources of invalidity and confounding														
		1 No comparison across groups	2 Time: other events	3 Time: maturation	4 Selection: sample (and assignment)	5 Selection: regression	6 Selection: sample stability	7 Interaction of time with sample	8 Interaction of ind. var. with sample	9 Direction/nature of causality uncertain	10 Unnatural/invalid exper./treatment	11 Invalid measurement of variables	12 Instrument reliability	13 Learning from instrument	14 Instrument reacts with ind. variable	15 Other interactions
C2 Non-equivalent control group design with pre-tests. Original sample is not random, but already there, as with work groups, classrooms. Treatment group may be randomly determined.	$(RA_a) \rightarrow O_{a1} \rightarrow X_a \rightarrow O_{a2}$ $(RA_0) \rightarrow O_{01} \rightarrow X_0 \rightarrow O_{02}$	+	+	+	−	?	+	−	?							
D3 Post-test/observation only, with a control group, but independent variable is observed, not manipulated.	$RS_a \rightarrow \underline{X_a} \rightarrow O_a$ $RS_0 \rightarrow \underline{X_0} \rightarrow O_0$	+	?	?	+	+	?	?	?							
E1 One group observed for a number of traits to see if any relationships exist.	$RS \rightarrow O_a, O_b, O_c, \ldots$	−	−	−	+		?		−							

* Key: see Table 4.2.

Activity 4.2

Professor Blooper wished to investigate the hypothesis that watching aggression on television will encourage aggressive behaviour in children. Through the school psychological service, he was able randomly to select 20 children aged 8–10 who were undergoing counselling for aggression in the classroom. He then selected 20 children who matched the first ones on IQ, parental income, sex and race, but were considered well behaved. He had each child keep a diary of programmes watched on television for two weeks. These were also watched by researchers and the amount of time each child was exposed to aggressive action was tallied for the two weeks. It was found that the aggressive children were exposed to statistically significantly more violent scenes than the non-aggressive children. He concluded that exposure to violence on television encourages aggressiveness in children.

(a)   Classify this study as to whether it has a structure like design C2, C3, or some combination, identifying each of the components (e.g., *RS*, *X*, *O*, *Y*).

(b)   Create a variable map for this study that includes as many extraneous variables as you can identify.

(c)   For each of the eight potential sources of invalidity and confounding listed below, enter a −, +, ? or < blank > in the [ ], and say why.

   1   *No comparison across groups* [   ]
   2   *Time: events* [   ]
   3   *Time: maturation* [   ]
   4   *Selection: sample (and assignment)* [   ]
   5   *Selection: regression towards the mean* [   ]
   6   *Selection: sample stability* [   ]
   7   *Interaction of time with sample* [   ]
   8   *Interaction of independent variable with sample* [   ]

(d)   Describe how well each of the four varieties of validity was maintained. Were the conclusions justifiable? Why or why not?

SUMMARY

This chapter has introduced a considerable number of new ideas and concepts, and compelled you to consider their interactions. Five more designs falling in one of four categories (experimental, quasi-experimental, ex post facto, correlational) have been provided. To evaluate these, eight potential sources of invalidity of conclusions and confounding of variables related to design structure and sampling were used. Having considered a number of examples to see how these potential sources can be used as guidelines for designing experiments, you have had an opportunity to evaluate some additional designs. In Chapter 5 you will be introduced to sampling techniques, and in Chapter 6 you will encounter seven more potential sources related primarily to measurement and treatment design. Facing 15 potential sources of confounding and invalidity, one student asked: 'Do we have to make sure *all* of these are under control if we are going to have a good study?' The answer, unfortunately is not simple and you could have a few minor transgressions or imperfections and provide reasonably defensible results, while one major oversight could totally invalidate a study. Being aware of the potential pitfalls when planning will probably prevent you from making such a blunder, thought creating a 'perfect' study is unlikely. You are using human beings as your subjects and they have a tendency to do the unexpected. To engage in some planning practice that will allow you to apply these new concepts and ideas, carry out Activity 4.3 for discussion in class.

Activity 4.3

In preparation for class discussion, briefly outline your proposed research design, or that of a research report you have analysed, completing Table 4.7 at the end of this chapter, using only columns 1–8 now (9–15 will be completed in Chapter 7). Add a variable map and a brief written justification with a description of anticipated problems and solutions, also including a description of population(s). Present this on one page for distribution with the completed Table 4.7 and be prepared to defend your design.

Potential sources of Invalidity and Confounding

Quasi-experimental and ex post facto designs:	Design structure (time sequence of events)	1 No comparison across groups	2 Time: other events	3 Time: maturation	4 Selection: sample (and assignment)	5 Selection: regression	6 Selection: sample stability	7 Interaction of time with sample	8 Interaction of ind. var. with sample	9 Direction/nature of causality uncertain	10 Unnatural/invalid exper./treatment	11 Invalid measurement of variables	12 Instrument reliability	13 Learning from instrument	14 Instrument reacts with ind. variable	15 Other interactions
Design description																

TABLE 4.7
Summary of –
design, with
potential sources of
invalidity and
confounding of
results

IDENTIFYING POPULATIONS AND SAMPLES

5

All the research design models that have been and will be considered depend to some extent upon appropriate identification of populations, the selection of representative sample(s), and sometimes suitable assignment of subjects to groups. Such procedures are necessary to avoid the potential confounding by extraneous variables described in Chapter 3, confounding that would invalidate any conclusions purporting to have established causal links among identified variables (internal validity). As was suggested, this is particularly important for ex post facto designs where the actual selection of samples is the primary means of isolating independent variables. The selection of samples will also determine whether the results are legitimately generalizable to a larger population (external validity). Consequently, the details of population identification and sampling techniques will be considered before progressing to more complex designs. These procedures will influence the execution of the chosen design, through the definition of the sample and how subjects are acquired. Since this challenge has been around for a long time, there is a well-established set of procedures from which to choose.

The problems of sampling are most commonly associated in people's minds with large surveys. One must be careful not to assume that a survey is the solution to the research question, as this often assumes a large sample, questionnaires and computer data-processing. It is a classic case of a tool looking for a job. Sampling is an essential consideration when carrying out most designs. What will constitute an appropriate sample of adequate size, and ultimately how difficult it will be to contact and collect data from subjects, will depend upon the original research question and the design chosen. As more quasi-experimental and ex post facto designs are considered, it will become increasingly apparent that the size of the sample may be less of a problem than ensuring and justifying the representativeness of the subject groups selected. A relatively small sample carefully selected may provide a more valid result than a large sample poorly chosen.

It should be noted that the techniques, diversity of situations and ensuing problems associated with acquiring an appropriate sample cannot be entirely covered in a single chapter. Whole books have been devoted to the topic and entire courses or modules are provided in some universities. Therefore, this chapter will consider common approaches and provide guidance on the practical problems of selecting a sample, but will refer the reader to even more advanced texts as sources of detailed procedures. Once you have decided upon a course of action, it would be wise to pursue the procedure in even greater depth.

IDENTIFYING THE POPULATION(S)

People are the primary interest in the social sciences, and even if a study focuses on an organization (school, political party, company, country), it is the people who belong that usually are of interest to the researcher (students, teachers, party members, employees, citizens). Often it is the characteristics of these subjects that draw attention to them, how life events have affected their status, relative success, attitudes and opinions. Consequently, a *population* is considered to be any group that shares a set of common traits, such as all mathematics teachers in Wales, all drivers of Fords, or all persons in the state of Indiana whose parents or grandparents were farmers of at least 200 acres between 1900 and 1930. Why a researcher would specify a population will depend on to whom he or she wishes to extend his or her results. By defining the population, the researcher is saying: 'This is the group from which I will select a representative sample for my study.'

This might be all that was needed if one were carrying out a truly experimental study, since then it would be a matter of taking a random sample from the group and randomly allocating these subjects to separate groups for the subsequent experiment. For example, one might assign the Welsh teachers to different in-service training programmes and compare how these affected teaching in the classroom; contact the sample of Ford drivers to provide them with different information on driving economies and insert a device to monitor their fuel consumption for a year; or contact the sample of Indiana farmers and subject them to different advertising campaigns on safety with farm machinery and monitor their accident rates. These are rather obvious approaches where experiments are to be performed, but not all questions we wish to ask can be answered this way.

Many research questions ask about the effects of various aspects of life on people's behaviour or attitudes. In essence, life is the experimenter, the life experience is the treatment, and the researcher is only the observer. For example, are Scottish teachers' attitudes towards corporal punishment dependent on their age? Do urban-resident drivers have fewer accidents than suburban or rural residents? Do Iowa crop farmers have fewer or more accidents than pig or cattle farmers? In each of these situations, the comparisons are actually across populations and the researchers will have to sample each as randomly as possible. The independent variables are not under the control of the researcher, they are the experiences of life. What the researcher does have control over is how he or she selects samples from each population. For such ex post facto studies, the quality of sampling becomes extremely important and random assignment may not even enter the discussion.

In experimental, quasi-experimental and ex post facto studies, it is necessary to define the populations carefully if the conclusions are going to be justifiably extended to them. To say loosely that the population is human beings for a study on the effect of (say) the type of music one listens to while studying or learning, and then use volunteers from the first-year psychology class, may open one to some criticism. Are first-year psychology students typical human beings? Are they even the same as, say, first-year physics students? Older students? Younger learners? Need I say more? Thus, one could say that the statement of the question was excessively ambitious and that maybe it would be more honest to say that the population was first-year psychology students, then try to obtain the co-operation of other universities and try to avoid ending up with volunteers from just one institution. Now that does sound a bit more difficult, but it is necessary if one is going to avoid having to endure the criticism that the sample is not representative of the specified population.

Where do you start in identifying the populations from which the samples will be taken? One must return to the original research question. It may be at this stage that it becomes compelling to refine the research question, listing all the possible related specific questions, setting aside many of them because to answer all of them would require several lifetimes, or at least several Ph.D.s. Large numbers of questions may result in a survey that is so expansive as to result in correlational data showing possible relationships among a large number of variables. A more selective study building on earlier large surveys may be able to isolate a few of these variables in order to resolve the nature of the relationships employing an ex post facto design.

To illustrate the role of the research question in determining the population, Jaeger (1984) presents two questions related to school drop-outs that are the basis for a survey study, resulting in nine factors related to possible reasons for deciding to leave school. First:

I.   What social pressures are associated with dropping out of school?

For this question he suggests five possible factors to investigate, the occurrence of: closest friends who have dropped out; closest friends who underrate education; families that underrate education; parents who have not completed high school; and parents who wanted their children to quit school. Second:

II.   What perceived economic pressures are associated with dropping out of school?

Here he suggests four specific factors that should be investigated, related to a feeling that: young people must work to support their families; they must work to support themselves; school will not equip them for employment; and the job market will be worse if they wait. The implication is there would be a single population to survey: school drop-outs of a specified age range.

Keeping this potential investigation in mind, let us also consider a variation on the question, one that will result in a different approach:

Does educational background really influence immediate employment prospects?

This intentionally challenges the popular wisdom that finishing high school in the USA or passing a minimum number of GCSE examinations in England provides one with a better opportunity for employment. Also, such a question begs the issue of the need for a generally well-educated populace, but we tend to emphasize the former since young people tend be more receptive to more practical arguments for staying in school.

Let us refine the new general question to express it in research terms so that the populations from which samples might be taken can be identified:

Are unqualified school leavers (e.g., those with few or no GCSE passes in England or lacking a full high school diploma in the USA) as likely to become employed as those with qualifications?

First, whom are we talking about, who would be in the population? Would there be more than one population? Are we considering all school leavers, or just those who will try to find employment but not those continuing with their education? What of those not looking for jobs for other reasons? Do we want equal numbers of each or to see what the distribution is? Even the research question needs to be further refined, with concepts such as 'unqualified' and 'employed' expanded in detail to the level of constructs. Are there other potentially confounding variables that might be of interest, ones that might contribute to employment or unemployment, such as social class (which might result in job contacts), race and gender? Are all of those unemployed actively seeking employment (for example, those young women who marry and are fully employed raising children)? In answering such questions, the researcher should arrive at an unequivocal definition of the populations from which samples will be taken.

Jaeger's proposed study would investigate factors related to young people dropping out, with a long-term aim of contributing to identifying why, while the above alternative would investigate whether leaving school without qualifications makes any difference in employment prospects. Both questions are valid, but will result in different designs and different populations from which samples will be drawn. It should be noted that while Jaeger's proposed study implies that the factors described might cause a young person to drop out, the structure of the study would only allow the identification of factors that are *associated with* dropping out (see Tables 3.4 and 4.6, design E1). For example, finding a high frequency of respondents who do not believe that school will equip them for employment does not prove that this attitude causes them to drop out. The same attitude may be held by those who continue with education well after the minimum school-leaving age. With no other group with which to compare, such a survey can only identify associations, not causes.

Using the alternative proposed question on the relationship between education and employment, a multidimensional extension of ex post facto design D3 (Tables 3.4 and 4.6) is employed. We define below 12 possible populations for purposes of comparing employment or unemployment levels (dependent variable) among identifiable groups that would correspond to the three chosen independent variables: colour, gender and educational background. While it would be quite reasonable to ignore colour and gender by selecting sub-groups for only educational background, a three-dimensional design allows relevant possible variables to be tested as well as interactions at the same time. This is one of the advantages of multidimensional studies. Obviously, a different researcher might wish to consider a different set of variables, based upon other research that indicates the potential existence of other relationships (for example, social class of parents, geographical location in the country). To illustrate the problem showing parallels in two education systems, comparable groups will be described: with at least 80% of students in England leaving school at 16+ years with five or more GCSE passes, one could consider this roughly comparable to US high school graduates, though the latter tend to be about 17 years old. Both will have undergone 12 years of education. The possible populations are as follows:

(a)   white, male, high school diploma or at least 5 GCSE passes;
(b)   black, male, high school diploma or at least 5 GCSE passes;
(c)   white, female, high school diploma or at least 5 GCSE passes;
(d)   black, female, high school diploma or at least 5 GCSE passes;
(e)   white, male, 10–12 years of school but no high school diploma or 1–4 GCSE passes;
(f)   black, male, 10–12 years of school but no high school diploma or 1–4 GCSE passes;
(g)   white, female, 10–12 years of school but no high school diploma or 1–4 GCSE passes;
(h)   black, female, 10–12 years of school but no high school diploma or 1–4 GCSE passes;
(i)   white, male, less than 10 years of school or no GCSE passes;
(j)   black, male, less than 10 years of school or no GCSE passes;
(k)   white, female, less than 10 years of school or no GCSE passes;
(l)   black, female, less than 10 years of school or no GCSE passes.

Here, 'drop-out' could be defined as someone who does not have a high school diploma, or has less than five GCSE passes, but rather than use such gross terminology, an intermediate group will be considered (finished at least 10 years of school but no diploma or obtained one to four GCSE passes), in addition to the person who has nothing (less than 10 years of school or no GCSE passes). The groups of characteristics in our 12 populations might imply a multidimensional structure such as shown in Figure 5.1. If significant differences are found across each of the three major variables (number of GCSEs, gender and colour), with significant interactions, then significant differences between pairs of cells can be tested. There are $(12 \times 11)/2 = 66$ possible pairwise comparisons for this study! In many studies, though, not all major variables will be statistically significant. The actual mechanism for such tests will be explored later.

There is no right or wrong population for a study, but a population must be consistent with the variables being investigated and must be defined in sufficient detail that it is possible to place a potential member in it or a competing one, not leaving him or her or it on the fence. Populations do not have to consist of

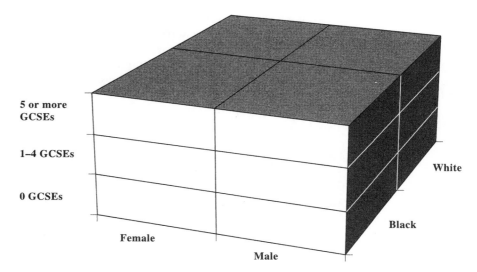

FIGURE 5.1
A possible structure
for the study and
populations
described

persons but could be made up of institutions such as schools, churches or hospitals. The best test of the quality of the definition of a set of parallel populations is to try to place individuals in one of them: if they do not fit without doubt, then this may be an indication that the definitions need to be refined. Activity 5.1 provides an opportunity to try this, which you should do now.

Activity 5.1

(a)   First let us consider some potential unemployed young people to see how they will fit into the above populations as a test of the definitions. Decide to which category each *best* belongs (if any), noting any difficulties you have in deciding:

- Johnny Bloggs: male, black (Jamaican parents), school leaver aged 19 with two GCSE passes (English and home economics).
- Mary Smith: white, female, school leaver aged 18 with three GCSE passes, from single-parent family (raised by mother), eight months pregnant; she has never had a job.
- Henry Jones: white, male, school leaver aged 17 with no GCSE passes, parental income over £50 000; he is in jail for burglary.
- Albert Singh: of Asian descent though born in Birmingham, three GCSE passes; he is enrolled in local technical college studying for three more GCSEs.

(b)   Modify the population definitions in light of any difficulties you had with placing any of the above young people, and any other ambiguities you have identified.

Going back to Jaeger's study, in order potentially to offer any proof as to why students dropped out would require matched groups with which to compare. In other words, just to consider the possibility of one variable (families that under-rated education) being a contributing cause of dropping out, one would need a sample of young people who dropped out and who had families that underrated education matched against a sample of young people who had not dropped out and who had families that underrated education. An ex post facto design that would cover all nine proposed variables would include *at least* 18 populations to sample ($5 \times 2 + 4 \times 2$). If interactions among these variables were to be investigated, there could be three dimensions, with $2 \times 4 \times 5 = 40$ cells (that is, 40 populations to sample). Just from this discussion, it is possible to see potential practical limitations to such designs when considering the number of variables one could hope to investigate in a single study. It is not unreasonable for a researcher at this point to go back and ask whether it is feasible to answer the research question in its present form, whether perhaps it needs revising.

As we have seen, identifying and specifying the populations from which samples will be taken will essentially be the same as defining the independent variables for an ex post facto design. The process will also provide control over identified potential extraneous variables, either by including them as independent variables or by defining the population so that if a representative sample is selected, the characteristics will be evenly spread over all parallel populations (variables). For example, as noted in the study to determine possible causes of unemployment, one could either include colour as a variable, or define the population on a non-colour basis and sample accordingly, assuming that each subgroup would be proportionally represented by various colour/ethnic groups consistent with the proportion in the population. In this way, the extraneous variable would be evenly distributed across all groups and would not affect any one of them, thus avoiding confounding.

SAMPLING

There are two important consequences of taking samples from populations. First, one of the aims of experimental, quasi-experimental and ex post facto studies is to draw conclusions based upon samples that will extend to populations, ensuring external validity. These usually relate to quantifiable traits and characteristics, so while the population parameters (e.g., mean, standard deviation) may often remain unknown, it is assumed that the sample statistics will be accurate estimations of these. The only way that this can be achieved is by securing a representative sample. Second, having defined populations consistent with the design, how does one obtain a sample that will not introduce new, previously unidentified, potentially confounding variables? Hidden extraneous variables could corrupt the independent variables in a study, reducing the internal validity and making the final conclusions invalid and the research unreplicable.

Entire texts have been produced providing the statistical rationale for random sampling (e.g., Jaeger, 1984). For purposes of the approach taken here, let it suffice to say that it is recognized that a *random* sample from a well-defined population would be the most likely (unfortunately, there are no guarantees) to be representative and to prevent the introduction of new extraneous confounding variables. This does present a problem of what is meant by 'random'. Of the many definitions available, the following discussion will assume Kerlinger's (1986) functional one as the main criteria when considering sampling procedures: '*Random sampling* is that method of drawing a portion (sample) of a population so that all possible samples of fixed size *n* have the same probability of being selected.'

This definition is sufficiently flexible to allow the consideration of alternatives to sampling a population list directly, ones that will still provide representative samples. There are a number of techniques that employ randomness at some point and are referred to as *probability sampling*. In the following subsections, eight methods for selecting samples will be described, with advantages and disadvantages, all summarized in Table 5.1 to facilitate comparison now and for quick reference later. There are alternative ways of classifying sampling procedures, but the one used here should cover all the important aspects and problems. These should provide criteria for evaluating whatever technique is employed so that you are aware of the limitations, since not all procedures provide equally representative samples. Figure 5.2 should trigger some suspicion, since the outcome there is dependent on where in a line of children the teacher starts. If where she starts is not truly random, then the outcome is predictable and the results will not produce a true random sample, and consequently it will be subject to the criticism that it is not representative. In the end, it is often very difficult to get the 'perfect' sample, but one simply tries to get the most representative possible with the resources available and knowledge of the populations.

FIGURE 5.2
Not all sampling techniques are truly random

TABLE 5.1
A summary of
common sampling
techniques with key
issues to take into
consideration when
choosing one

	Description	Advantages	Disadvantages/limitations
Simple random	Random sample from whole population	Highly representative if all subjects participate; the ideal	Not possible without complete list of population members; potentially uneconomical to achieve; can be disruptive to isolate members from a group; time-scale may be too long, data/sample could change
Stratified random	Random sample from identifiable groups (strata), subgroups, etc.	Can ensure that specific groups are represented, even proportionally, in the sample(s) (e.g., by gender), by selecting individuals from strata list	More complex, requires greater effort than simple random; strata must be carefully defined
Cluster	Random samples of successive clusters of subjects (e.g., by institution) until small groups are chosen as units	Possible to select randomly when no single list of population members exists, but local lists do; data collected on groups may avoid introduction of confounding by isolating members	Clusters in a level must be equivalent and some natural ones are not for essential characteristics (e.g., geographic: numbers equal, but unemployment rates differ)
Stage	Combination of cluster (randomly selecting clusters) and random or stratified random sampling of individuals	Can make up probability sample by random at stages and within groups; possible to select random sample when population lists are very localized	Complex, combines limitations of cluster and stratified random sampling
Purposive	Hand-pick subjects on the basis of specific characteristics	Ensures balance of group sizes when multiple groups are to be selected	Samples are not easily defensible as being representative of populations due to potential subjectivity of researcher
Quota	Select individuals as they come to fill a quota by characteristics proportional to populations	Ensures selection of adequate numbers of subjects with appropriate characteristics	Not possible to prove that the sample is representative of designated population
Snowball	Subjects with desired traits or characteristics give names of further appropriate subjects	Possible to include members of groups where no lists or identifiable clusters even exist (e.g., drug abusers, criminals)	No way of knowing whether the sample is representative of the population
Volunteer, accidental, convenience	Either asking for volunteers, or the consequence of not all those selected finally participating, or a set of subjects who just happen to be available	Inexpensive way of ensuring sufficient numbers for a study	Can be highly unrepresentative

Simple random sampling

Life for the researcher would be pleasant and relaxed if achieving a random sample from the whole designated population were a simple process, or in some cases, even possible. The main difficulty is often one of obtaining a list of all the members of the population, sometimes referred to as a *sampling frame,* from which to select a sample. As we have seen, definition of the population from which a sample will be selected is essentially the operational definition of the life experience variable to be investigated in ex post facto studies. For example, if one of the independent variables to be investigated were a person's educational background, then each of the levels or qualifications would need to be carefully defined. Next, it would be necessary to find lists. If a study were to be conducted among teachers in a school district or local education authority, then it might well be possible to obtain a list of all teachers with their qualifications, allowing population lists to be organized with all non-graduates, graduates and those having masters' degrees or doctorates. These lists would be the sampling frames for the populations defined.

Why is it necessary to make the distinction between the sampling frame and the population? Assume you receive the list of teachers on the first day of the month, break it down into subgroups, select samples, stuff the envelopes and post them out, taking (optimistically) two weeks. How many new teachers have come in and how many have left by the time the letters hit the postbox? It may well be that in two weeks, little change has occurred, but how old was the list, did it contain names of teachers who had submitted resignations and did it omit new teachers that had just joined? Even in the era of the computer database, obtaining an up-to-date list is not always straightforward, thus it could be weeks old when the researcher receives it. Therefore one might have to define the population as those teachers in post *on a certain date.* This is just another practical consideration that one must take into account when planning a study.

Having obtained a sampling frame for a population, it is a matter of employing a random numbers table, such as the one in Appendix B (Table B.10), to select a sample. A variety of strategies are possible, depending on the nature of the list. If it is already numbered, say 1 to 2345, then it would be straightforward to consult a four-digit table, starting randomly (close eyes, point finger) and selecting subjects with numbers that correspond to those that follow in the table. Alternatively, one could use a succession of two or three digits to decide how far down the table to skip each time to select someone, making sure that it would be possible to select a person at the end of the list. For example, using two-digit jumps (01 to 99) to select ten names from a list of 10 000 would definitely exclude those beyond the first 1000. Also, it would not be possible to select adjacent pairs on a single pass through a list, or even near-neighbours. This could eliminate selecting related people in an alphabetic list. The approach of randomly selecting a starting-point and jumping down the table the same number each time is limited by the fact that the only randomness is the starting-point (recall Figure 5.2).

If, on the other hand, one reaches the end of the list before acquiring a sufficiently large sample, it is a simple matter of starting over at the beginning of the list, since everyone has an equal probability of being selected. In the situation where someone selected cannot subsequently participate, *sampling with replacement* by another randomly selected individual is a possibility. This does not cause any difficulty unless there is a high probability of individuals being selected twice, as for small populations or a large proportion of a population being selected (Jolliffe, 1986). It is necessary, though, to consider just who would keep such lists and how sure can you be that they are reasonably up to date.

What does one do about *overregistration*, where it is necessary to use a list of population members that contains more members than actually belong on the designated date? For example, the sampling frame might contain names of those who have already departed, one way or another. This could include such situations as enlisted personnel who trained and became officers, workers who used to not belong to a union but recently joined, ward nurses who became full-time administrators, as well as those who simply left the hospital or even the profession. Updating the sampling frame is the obvious solution, since it is not desirable just to toss out misfits when they are discovered later during the study, or wait for non-returns of questionnaires, particularly when it is not possible to replace them. If sample loss does happen (and the reason for the loss has nothing to do with variables in the study), then one consequence might be unequal cell size in the design. Most statistical tests can tolerate differences that are not too radical.

Underregistration is the opposite situation where the sampling frame does not contain all the members of the population. For example, based on a September class list, October voter registration list, etc., the researcher selects 100 names in December. Inevitably, some new people will have moved into the area or joined the teaching force. The time delay between the formulation of the sampling frame and taking the sample is the biggest factor, but unless there has been a radical change in housing, or hiring policy in the schools, then the changes should not influence the representativeness of the original sample. A little investigative work can check on such possibilities, since some sampling frames will be updated only once a year.

There are some situations where a single population list does not even exist or would be too expensive to assemble from scattered local lists. Considering the time and human resources required to carry out a national census, and the fact that the data are virtually out of date as soon as they are collected (people die, are born, change jobs, get married, get divorced, leave town, arrive, etc.), to even obtain a perfect list of all Scottish or Welsh teachers, all Ford drivers, or all Indiana or Iowa farmers would not be possible. Being practical, what can the typical researcher with a restricted budget realistically do to obtain a representative sample of his or her designated population? The next three strategies are some alternative probability sampling approaches that employ random selection at some stage to provide a reasonable level of representativeness.

Stratified random sampling

This approach involves taking a random sample from identifiable groups (*strata*) that are homogeneous for the desired characteristics, such as people living in a geographical areas or belonging to organizations. Therefore, choosing from separate lists of males and females would give proportions equivalent to the combined population, for example in a factory, multinational organization, voting ward, or university system. While gender may be a relatively easy division (though not without some contention, witness the gender tests in the Olympics a few years ago), other strata may require some careful defining. Stratified samples will be particularly important when endeavouring to secure comparative groups for life experiences that constitute variables in ex post facto designs. A desire to compare pupil performance in different types of schools for an age cohort could lead the researcher first to select schools on the basis of type – for example, tax-funded or private, single-sex or mixed – and then randomly to select pupils from each. Alternatively, to obtain a random selection of pupils across a school system or education authority the same procedure could be followed, and then the children could be randomly assigned to treatment groups for an experimental study.

The advantage to such an approach is that one can be sure that specific groups are represented in proportion to their appearance in the population, particularly when subpopulation characteristics are the variables. It also avoids the possibility of selecting from a combined population in the hope that the appropriate proportions will appear in a single population sample. There will be situations, though, where the strata are not identifiable from lists before sampling and *stratification after sampling* becomes necessary. For example, it may be that only through interviews or questionnaires from a sample from a larger population could one assign individuals to strata on the basis of voting intentions. Jolliffe (1986) suggests that this is potentially no less representative than the reverse.

There are disadvantages in that the procedure is more complex than simple random sampling and requires greater effort in defining strata and identifying population components of each. Strata must be carefully defined to avoid unintended imbalances as a result of selection, since there is a need to acquire homogeneity of some factors across strata to minimize variability among other variables. Stratification after sampling should provide samples in proportion to the population if the sample is randomly selected, but without knowledge of the population there is no way of knowing. This will be of concern primarily for surveys resulting in correlational results, whereas experimentally structured designs tend to require equal cell size and are not as dependent upon population proportions.

Cluster sampling

This involves random samples of identified smaller groups – clusters of subjects, for example, by institution or location. It is quite appropriate when the alternative of taking subjects individually from their groups would be disruptive and possibly distort the results. For example, to test spelling skills of 8-year-olds in a school district or local education authority, it might be possible randomly to select 125 children from the total roll of 2450, but less distracting and less likely to upset the subjects if five whole classes of 25 were randomly selected. Removing small children individually from class to test their spelling ability might affect their performance. Cluster sampling here provides an interesting example of how taking into account the link between measurement and sampling could prevent unnecessary confounding.

Cluster sampling makes it possible to select randomly when no single list of population members exists, but local lists do. Many groups provide data collected on members – for example, school rolls, voter registration lists and hospital employee rosters – that would allow one to choose a representative sample. Selecting several smaller identifiable clusters such as these would provide a more representative sample than drawing from a few counties or larger entities.

Such an approach is not without some disadvantages. There is a need for clusters that constitute a sample to be equivalent and some natural ones may not be for essential characteristics. For example, if one wanted to examine secondary school truancy rates and select schools on the basis of location, even by similar-sized cities, the numbers might be equal, but other factors would possibly influence the results. There could be different employment levels and opportunities for jobs, differentially tempting young people from school. If this were not an identified variable, the process might introduce a potentially confounding variable. Also, it is possible that clusters would result in subjects being too homogeneous for the variables being investigated. For example, a study on the influence of teaching approaches on reading levels that tested only few classes would have the potential of incurring confounding since an individual teacher could reduce potential variability in performance due to the approach itself as a result of his or her interpretation or presentation. More representative variability might be found across a selection of pupils subjected to different teachers since teacher interpretation may be part of the approach. Data collected from all members of a household on the consequences of an advertising campaign on social issues could be confounded by the interactions among members of households. This highlights the need for a sound definition of the population characteristics if these are to be valid operational definitions of the proposed independent variables for designs having an ex post facto component. The definitions will be needed to determine the most appropriate sampling techniques.

Stage sampling

This involves combining aspects of cluster sampling with random or stratified random sampling. The researcher can take successive samples from levels or clusters until it is possible to take a random sample of individuals. It is an obvious choice for situations where lists are held only on a very local level and combing them would be an inordinate task. Also, for many quasi-experimental studies where a number of related populations are to be selected, this may provide the most valid approach to obtaining a probability sample. The disadvantages are the same as indicated above: it is complex and demands equality of clusters and careful definition of strata, since this approach combines the limitations of cluster and stratified random sampling.

To illustrate the process, consider the study described above and illustrated in Figure 5.1 which would require 12 groups of (ideally) at least 20 persons each. Since this is to be a national survey, the group size will be expanded to 40. One approach would be to divide the country initially into four distinct equal-population areas (strata). Then one could randomly select five local education authorities or school districts (clusters) from each stratum with number of leavers in each category in each authority or district the same (or as near as possible) so that there would be equal probability of individuals being selected. From the authority or district lists of school leavers, the final step would be randomly to select two young persons for each of the 12 categories (strata), a total of 480 subjects.

There are other possible combinations of sampling that would provide a representative probability sample. However it is done, it would be necessary to employ randomness at every stage, even within specified well-defined strata. To conform to the working definition of randomness put forward at the beginning of this section, the goal must be that there is equal probability of subjects ultimately being selected from a population. Such a demand may present challenges to the researcher and may make necessary some adjustments in sampling approach. In the example above, if one authority has *twice* as many (say) leavers with no GCSEs as any of the other four, then the probability of an individual being selected from the first would be half that of any of the others! One way to compensate would be to treat the double-sized authority as two and select twice as many subjects from it.

The names of the above approaches are less important than the underlying principle of randomization whenever there is a choice (among groups or individuals) to be made. Additional examples of multi-stage sampling can be found in several other books (e.g., Jaeger, 1984; Jolliffe, 1986; Kish, 1965). You should now carry out Activity 5.2, where you will be asked to consider these techniques in light of the proposed study (not necessarily a well-structured one) and decide on possible sampling procedures.

Activity 5.2

Using the following research proposal, devise three alternative sampling techniques for the indicated population(s). Justify each approach with respect to its representativeness, avoidance of confounding and practicality, and rank-order them, being prepared to defend your order. Also identify any sources of confounding inherent in the design.

In 1993, the tax base for local taxation in Britain changed to a banded system with seven ranges of house value as the basis: the higher the band the greater the household tax (equivalent to local property taxes in the USA). It is proposed that a study be conducted to determine whether this has had any influence on political preferences of voters. This tax was introduced by the Conservative Party, the party in power, after a considerable amount of public objection to its 'poll tax', a flat-rate tax on each adult (with some exceptions) in a household. Voting patterns before and after the change are to be elicited from subjects.

Identify independent and dependent variables and suggest how probability samples could be drawn. Postal codes (each code includes up to 40 households) for all parts are available and voter registration lists exist in each ward or parish.

The four approaches that follow do *not* employ randomization and are considered to be non-probability sampling. Each may suffer lack of representativeness and has the potential to incur confounding. In some cases, this may be unavoidable because of the nature of the population, but most studies in the literature employing such techniques seem to do so for reasons related to limited resources or lack of resourcefulness.

Purposive sampling

The researcher hand-picks subjects on the basis of specific characteristics, building up a sample of sufficient size having the desired traits. This can provide balanced group sizes when multiple groups are to be selected, but it is difficult to justify the representativeness of the resulting sample(s). Criticism is usually levelled at the potential subjectivity of the researcher and the available group from which the sample is drawn. Though a tight definition could go a long way towards overcoming the problem of subjectivity and the reliability (consistency of classification) could be statistically tested, the second criticism is more difficult to overcome. One could, for example, choose classes of children for a study on the basis that the mean IQ scores were about 100 with a standard deviation of about 15. Whether they were representative with respect to other traits could be missed, leaving some doubt as to whether the sample is representative of all children.

Quota sampling

This often involves selecting individuals as they come, for example standing in a shopping mall with a questionnaire, choosing a neighbourhood and going door to door and contacting enough respondents. The objective is to contact a numerical quota of persons with specific characteristics, usually resulting in numbers that are proportional to the identified population. This approach is an inexpensive way of providing adequate numbers of subjects with appropriate characteristics, but it is not possible to prove that the samples are representative of designated populations. One may interview 56 shoppers in a mall, but are they representative of all shoppers? This is difficult to answer since no comprehensive list of 'shoppers' exists and this may be the best sample possible, for the time of day. Door-to-door contacts present the researcher with the potentially subjective choice of who is to respond from among those at home and what to do if no one is at home. Market research for new products seems to use this technique, but it is very difficult to tell whether or not the responses are representative of potential consumers. On the other hand, any feedback on products may be better than none. Even when combined with some form of random sampling, particularly with large surveys, there can be difficulties associated with contacting subjects. This has to be faced when conducting a telephone survey which employs a computer program that randomly selects telephone numbers. When there is no response, does one go on to the next subject to fill the quota of contacts, or try the non-answering one again later?

Snowball sampling

This is an interesting approach where subjects with desired traits or characteristics give names of further appropriate subjects to be contacted. It is of value when there are *no* lists of population members anywhere, not even identifiable clusters. For example, this could include drug abusers or joyriders (not in jail), political dissidents, illegal residents in a country, or skill areas where there are no comprehensive lists (quilt makers, wood turners, amateur artists). The disadvantage is that there is no way of knowing whether the samples are representative of the populations.

Volunteer, accidental, convenience

As a Boy Scout, one learned never to volunteer, but somehow this rule does not seem to be followed by subjects. Notices are frequently placed on the bulletin boards in universities asking for volunteers for psychological or medical experiments. In some cases, because of the consequences or just the demands on time, this appears to be the only way to obtain subjects. The term 'volunteers' is also applied to the remaining group of randomly selected subjects after a sizeable number have dropped out (this problem is considered in greater detail below).

One student of research visiting London who saw a sign pointing to 'Public Conveniences' (toilets) in a train station came away with a false impression of convenience sampling. It simply means selecting groups that are convenient, such as the youth club down the road, the pub around the corner, or the children in the class of a friend who is a teacher in a local school. It is a relatively inexpensive way of obtaining sufficient numbers for a study, but the approach can produce a highly unrepresentative sample. The extreme approach of selecting just any group that is there can severely limit to whom the results can be extended, and can be wholly inappropriate. The latter may be acceptable for research training, but not serious research. Alternatively, convenience samples are often the basis for quasi-experimental designs, providing homogeneous groups. In such cases there is usually an endeavour to justify representativeness through the characteristics of the subjects and/or groups. These purposive samples may be more representative because of their group structure than randomly selected individuals, but the defence is up to the researcher.

Then there is that grey area . . .

There also exists what Fowler (1993) calls *modified probability sampling*, which usually involves stratified random or cluster sampling up to the point of selecting individuals, which is then left to the interviewer or questionnaire administrator. For example, groups of houses (streets, apartments) are randomly selected, but the instrument administrator decides which house or apartment to contact, not returning if no one is there. A set of schools is randomly selected in each district or education authority and classes randomly selected in each, but students are chosen by the instrument administrator (for example, the teacher). Just how much discretion should be left to instrument administrators in the field is a point of discussion, but it can lead to bias in the sample that may influence the results.

SAMPLING ERRORS

Errors in this domain are not mistakes, but inaccuracies in resulting data. *Sampling errors* occur simply because data are being collected on a sample and not on the population. The first four sampling techniques considered in the previous section were devised to enhance the probability that any sample would be representative of a population, thus endeavouring to minimize these errors. To illustrate this, consider the distribution of IQ scores for a small population of 3000 shown in curve (a) of Figure 5.3. Beneath this is the distribution for a single sample of 40 subjects, curve (b). Note that its mean, $\bar{x}_A$, is not exactly that of the population, μ, nor would we necessarily expect it to be, due to natural random variability. One way to quantify the collective errors attributable to sampling for interval or ratio data is to consider what would happen if we were to take sample after sample from a population. For each sample, the mean could be found and plotted on a graph, providing us with a *distribution of sample means*. It is expected that for representative samples, though, these means would be very close to that of the population mean. It is also assumed that since this sampling error would be random, the distribution of sampling means would be normal with the mean of the sample means being the population mean, as in the narrow peak shown in curve (c) of Figure 5.3. This natural variability in a set of sample means of scores/measures around the population mean provides an opportunity to describe the outcome mathematically.

Hays (1994) provides a rigorous discussion of the calculation of sampling errors, probabilities and the variance of this distribution, with respect to sampling for surveys, for those who are interested. The derivations given, as well as justification for them, do generate a commonly used and conceptually useful estimation. We use an estimate of the distribution standard deviation simply because it is not reasonable to take all the possible samples from a population and plot a graph of the means. Usually described as the *standard error of the mean* (the square root of this variance), it is estimated from the population standard deviation and the sample size as follows:

$$\sigma_{\bar{x}} = \frac{\sigma}{\sqrt{n}} \tag{5.1}$$

where σ is the standard deviation of the population and n is the size of the samples. Its dependence on the size of the samples can be seen from the equation: note that the larger the samples, the smaller the variability of the set of sample means. This estimate is based on the assumption that these are simple random samples. Other approaches can produce greater error and consequently a higher value for the standard error of the mean than the one provided by equation (5.1).

Using this value, we can consider some interesting issues. In situations where the population mean is known, it would be possible to determine whether, on the basis of the mean of a sample of size n, it is likely that a particular sample is representative of the population, in other words, whether its mean is within

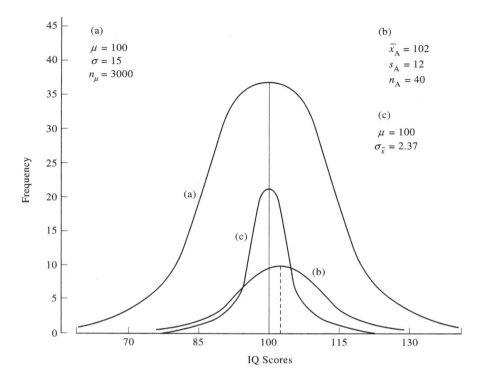

FIGURE 5.3
(a) A population
distribution of IQ
test scores for all
3000 11-year-olds in
a local authority; (b)
a single sample
distribution for 40
children; (c) the
distribution of
sampling means for
samples size 40

acceptable limits. Obviously, what is 'acceptable' could be an arguable point, but usually it is assumed (as with many statistical tests) that a mean which falls within the range of 95% of all possible means in the normal distribution is representative. When we look at a normal distribution, it is necessary to remember that the area under the curve represents the number of samples. Assuming that the total area represents 100% of all possible samples, then we can identify various percentages. The easiest way to do this is to use the number of standard deviations away from the mean as the x-axis, referred to as a z-score. Thus for a given mean score for a sample and the population mean, we can find a corresponding z-score,

$$z = \frac{\bar{x} - \sigma}{\sigma_{\bar{x}}}$$

where $\bar{x}$ is the sample mean and $\sigma_{\bar{x}}$ is standard error of the mean. Looking at the table showing the areas beyond any given z-score (Table B.1 in Appendix B), we find that 2.5% of the area is beyond 1.96 standard deviations from the mean. Thus, any mean producing a z-score greater than 1.96, is unlikely to be part of the population, as shown in Figure 5.4. This would allow us to reject any null hypothesis that there was no significant difference between the population and sample means. Therefore, there is a difference between the sample and population means greater than what could be attributed to natural variability. The natural expectation is that not all samples will be exactly the same (some possible sources of the extra difference will be considered in the next section). If the difference is too great, it is said to be *statistically* significantly different, because the probability that it belongs to the population is so small. Even if the probability is finite (less than 5%), it is considered to be *so* unlikely that the sample is labelled unrepresentative.

How does one determine this mathematically for a given sample? Let us consider the example of Harry Teacher, who wished to conduct a study on the effectiveness of a new reading programme in primary school. He wanted two equivalent classes of children; he randomly selected two local schools and randomly selected a class in each. In order to try to justify some generalizability of the study based on these two classes of Year 4 children, he decided to see what their mean IQs were and whether they were typical. He found from the teacher that one class of 30 had a mean IQ of $\bar{x}_A = 104$, and the other $\bar{x}_B = 99$. First he had to find the standard error of the mean. Knowing that the population mean for IQ scores was 100 with a standard deviation of 15,

$$\sigma_{\bar{x}} = \frac{\sigma}{\sqrt{n}}$$
$$= \frac{15}{\sqrt{30}}$$
$$\sigma_{\bar{x}} = 2.74$$

This provides a value for the standard error of the mean for simple random samples of 30 children. Thus the z-score for the two means would be

$$z_A = \frac{99 - 100}{2.74} = \frac{-1}{2.74} = -0.36$$
$$z_B = \frac{104 - 100}{2.74} = \frac{4}{2.74} = 1.46$$

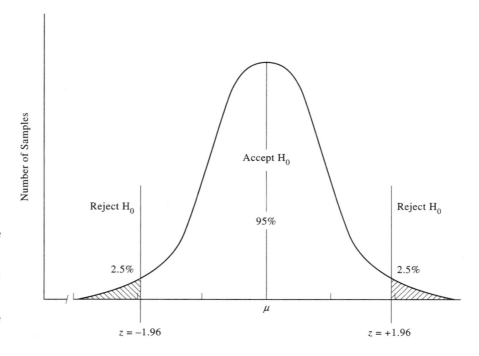

FIGURE 5.4
Normal distribution of sample means with 5% significance levels, where m is the population mean and the z-scores are the means expressed as number of standard deviations above and below the mean

Since neither of these means was more than 1.96 standard deviations from the population mean, he could assume that the samples were representative of the population, at least for IQ scores. This does not protect him against other traits and experiences for which the two classes might not be typical, but it does provide some support.

Fowler (1993) points out that this estimate of the standard error of the mean is only valid if one has taken a simple random sample. Stratified random samples tend to produce lower values for the standard error of the mean, while cluster samples tend to have higher values than for simple random samples. Thus, Harry Teacher's analysis may produce an underestimate of the standard error of the mean, since his selection of clusters of students may produce a more homogeneous grouping for the trait than that for the population. In some situations, this may be an important factor and may actually influence the results, but here the aim is to test the relative representativeness of the sample.

If population parameters are not available, the standard error of the mean can be estimated using sample statistics,

$$s_{\bar{x}} = \frac{s_A}{\sqrt{n_A}} \tag{5.2}$$

where s_A is the standard deviation of sample group A and n_A is the sample size of sample group A. It does give one some indication of the error, though strictly it also applies just to simple random sampling. This situation allows us to make a different type of statement about the results: is the sample mean, $\bar{x}_A$, close enough to the population mean, μ? Using the estimate of the standard error of the mean in equation (5.2), it is possible to establish a *confidence interval*, an interval of scores in which we can be reasonably confident that the population mean will fall. For example, if we wish to establish an interval in which we are 95% confident that the population mean occurs, then it will be

$$\bar{x}_A \pm 1.96 \, s_{\bar{x}} \tag{5.3}$$

For example, if a simple random sample of 25 children had a mean score on a school-based test in mathematics, $\bar{x}_A = 71.60$, with a standard deviation, $s_A = 12.20$, then

$$s_{\bar{x}} = \frac{12.20}{\sqrt{25}} = 2.44$$

and therefore the 95% confidence interval for the population mean, μ, would be

$$71.60 \pm 1.96 \times 2.44$$

or

$$71.60 \pm 4.78$$

Alternatively, it could be expressed as

$$66.82 < \mu < 76.38$$

This means that for 19 out of 20 samples, we could expect the true population mean to be within the interval. This is illustrated in Figure 5.5 as mean scores with their corresponding confidence intervals for 20 samples with 19 of them overlapping with the population mean, μ, while one does not.

Obviously it would also be possible to calculate 99% confidence intervals as well, if needed. Examining the equation, it becomes apparent that the best way

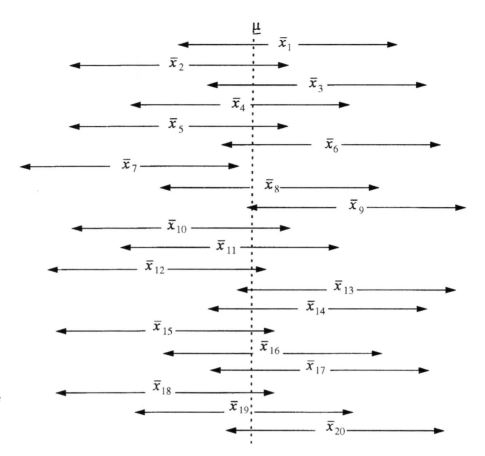

FIGURE 5.5
Twenty samples
with 95% confidence
intervals and true
mean: which one
does not include *m*?

to reduce the confidence interval would be to increase the sample size (increase the denominator and the overall value increases). This is not the only consideration of importance and again one must remember that the sampling technique may have a considerable influence on population estimates. More accurate estimates of the standard error of the mean may be lower for stratified samples and higher for cluster samples, thus altering the confidence interval. The importance of this, though, is dependent on the nature of the inferences to be made about the populations.

This is all satisfactory as long as we are considering interval data, I hear you say. So let us consider another example, one where the trait under consideration is nominal (a set of categories) rather than interval or ratio. In a recent study in Uganda in which the author participated (Black *et al.*, 1998), it was necessary to employ a sampling technique that had to be seen as representing secondary schools from each of the 39 districts in the country. The sampling frame consisted of a list of 550 government-supported secondary schools grouped by district. A simple random sample of all schools could have left some sparsely populated districts out of the study, so it was decided there would be at least one school randomly selected from each district (stratum) and districts with over three schools would be proportionally more randomly selected. Thus each district was represented by at least one school and larger districts had a larger representation, providing a sample of 77 schools (14% of the total). Having agreed on this, it was necessary to justify that the sample was still representative of schools in the country for other important traits: day versus boarding, separate sex versus mixed, and foundation body (parents, religious group, etc.). To test the hypotheses that the sample was representative of the whole population of schools for each of these three traits required the use of a non-parametric test: chi-square, χ^2. This involves comparing the observed frequencies of occurrence in each category of the sample with what one would expect from national frequencies. Analogous to normal distributions of interval data for samples which did not match exactly with the population, we would not expect samples to have exactly the same proportions of categories as the population. Again, the question must be asked, how much is too much of a deviation?

Table 5.2 provides the data, with the observed frequencies, O_i, for each type of school foundation body in the first column. The second column has the national percentages and the third contains the frequencies based on what would be expected if the 77 schools were *exactly* like the national distribution, the expected frequency, E_i. Visual inspection of the data does not show much difference, but the χ^2-test provided an indication of the probability that the sample was one that was representative of the whole population. (We will come back to this test later in Chapter 19, and investigate it in greater depth then.)

Roughly speaking, the test sums the absolute differences in frequencies between the two groups for all the characteristics, then determining whether the total is more, or less, than what would be expected by chance. Since the differences between observed and expected frequencies could be either positive or negative, the differences are squared before being added together. Otherwise, the total could approach zero even when there were large differences, the negative cancelling the positive values. The formula for the χ^2-statistic is quite simple, the sum of all the differences squared, each divided by the appropriate expected frequency,

$$\chi^2 = \sum_{i=1}^{m} \frac{(O_i - E_i)^2}{E_i} \tag{5.4}$$

where the O_i are the observed frequencies in the sample, the E_i are the expected frequencies based upon population percentages, and i represents the categories

TABLE 5.2
Distributions of Ugandan secondary schools by foundation body: a sample and as expected from national data

Foundation body	Observed O_i (sample)	National percentage	Expected E_i
Church of Uganda	35	42.1	32.4
Catholic Church	15	21.2	16.3
Parents	13	16.4	12.6
Muslim Schools Council	1	1.1	0.8
Government	6	7.7	5.9
United Muslim Schools	3	5.2	4.0
Other	4	6.3	4.9
Totals	77	100.0%	77.0

ranging from 1 to m. Note, when consulting tables for this statistic (see, for example, Table B.9 in Appendix B), that it has $df = m - 1$ degrees of freedom.

The easiest way to process such data is to add another column to the table, in which the differences squared divided by the expected frequency are placed. As we will see later, this is conveniently done on a spreadsheet, but for small amounts of data, the calculation is easily carried out on a calculator. The column values are added as shown in Table 5.3, and the sum compared to the standard table for χ^2. Which value one uses depends on the number of categories minus one: in the example, there are seven foundation bodies, thus six *degrees of freedom*, since six frequencies could vary, but then the seventh would be fixed. Table B.9 in Appendix B provides a value of 14.07, thus a χ^2-ratio greater than this would indicate a significant difference between the sample and the population. In the example in Table 5.3, the final value is 0.74, nowhere near significant ($p \gg 0.05$): thus, at least for this trait, the sample of secondary schools could be said to reflect the national pattern.

Sampling errors are unavoidable, though hopefully minimized through sound sampling procedures. On the other hand, *non-sampling errors* can be attributed to such processes as incorrect sampling frame, poor measuring instruments, incorrect data processing and non-response by subjects in the sample. The definition of sampling frames was considered earlier, and incorrect ones are equivalent to defining the population to be all voters and using a telephone number list as the sampling frame. The skills related to the design of measuring instruments and data collection are the subjects of Chapters 8–11, and the choice of statistical test is covered in Chapters 13–22. This leaves non-response, which is to be considered in the next section with suggestions as how to minimize it and any effects that it may have on the validity of the results. Before going on, carry out Activity 5.3.

AVOIDING SUBJECT LOSS

Unfortunately, it is not enough just to select a representative sample using random sampling techniques, ideally one must also ensure that all those who were selected do participate. If there is a loss of subjects then one is in danger of having the samples described as 'volunteers', unless the researcher can provide evidence that the drop-outs did not drop out for any reason associated with the research procedure or the variables. Subjects do not participate in surveys and ex post facto studies for a wide range of reasons, some of them quite unrelated to the research itself. On the other hand, it has been known for either the process of collecting data or even how subjects are grouped to cause offence and non-participation. Irritating subjects by telephoning in the middle of a meal or their favourite television programme may not be related to a political preference survey, but such action might be to a study enquiring about preferred television channels or family eating habits. Long questionnaires (any over four pages is too long in my estimation) can put people off, as can poorly worded questions. For example, telling subjects that they have been selected to be part of a study on obese golfers, inebriated pub patrons or non-churchgoing heathens may not display sufficient tact, even if that was what the study aimed to consider.

TABLE 5.3
Chi-square calculations added to the example in Table 5.2

Foundation body	Observed O_i (sample)	National percentage	Expected E_i	$\dfrac{(O_i - E_i)^2}{E_i}$
Church of Uganda	35	42.1	32.4	0.20
Catholic Church	15	21.2	16.3	0.11
Parents	13	16.4	12.7	0.01
Muslim Schools Council	1	1.1	0.8	0.04
Government	6	7.7	5.9	0.00
United Muslim Schools	3	5.2	4.0	0.24
Other	4	6.3	4.8	0.14
Totals	77	100.0%	77.0	$\chi^2 = 0.74$

Activity 5.3

1   Calculate the 95% confidence interval for ages of children in the fourth year of primary school using simple random samples of 16, if the population mean is 125 months with a standard deviation of 8 months.

2   The Psychology Department at Dandelion University asked for volunteers for a study on reaction time under the influence of alcohol (no shortage there!). To make sure that their normal reaction time was typical, they tested a random selection of 20 volunteers and found for a series of standard tests that their mean was 0.78 seconds with a standard deviation of 0.05 seconds. The accepted population norm for the age group is a mean of 0.70 s with a standard deviation of 0.04 s. Could the group be considered typical of the population? Why or why not?

3   In the sample of secondary schools in Uganda, the following distribution of boys-only, girls-only and mixed schools was found, along with the national distribution. Was the sample representative for this trait?

	Sample	National %
Boys	4	5.7
Girls	8	10.0
Mixed	64	84.3

Answers: 1. 121.1 to 128.9.   2. Not really, since $z = 8.94$, and the 95% confidence interval was $0.682 - 0.718$. A random sample from volunteers is not the same as a random sample from a population.   3. More than likely yes, since $\chi^2 = 0.047$, considering that the critical value at 5% for $df = 2$ is 6.99.

One must convince subjects of the worthwhileness of participating and describe the purpose of the study, orally or in any introductory letter accompanying a questionnaire. They should be assured that the data collected will not be used for any other purpose unless permission is sought. Anonymity must be ensured and maintained as well as respect for the privacy of subjects, taking care that the wording of questions does not give offence. Careless descriptions of results can allow readers to infer who the subjects were, particularly when there is only a small sample. Even the timing of a postal survey can be critical. For example, one researcher unfortunately sent out a questionnaire to a sample of general practitioners (family doctors) a week after the British Medical Association had conducted a rather extensive survey itself. It is suspected that the timing may have contributed to the meagre 20% return. But how can researchers identify the source of non-participation? How can they determine whether the reason is an extraneous variable that causes confounding, or whether it is random or unrelated to the study (lost in the post, eaten by the dog)?

Contending with non-responses

To justify external validity, there will be a need to counter criticism of non-responses by providing evidence that any non-response has nothing to do with the research or the instruments. In the case of underregistration of the sampling frame, assuming the reason also has nothing to do with the study, this should be minimal and sampling with replacement should correct for any non-response. One must be aware of the possibility that underregistration could be related to the study. For example, it would be unfortunate to carry out a study on the effects of a change in social policy and to have apparent underregistration occur because subjects left town as a consequence of that change.

Whether the contact with subjects is face to face, over the telephone, by post or even by electronic mail, it is essential to find out why those subjects decided not to respond. There tends to be a lower rate of return from postal and telephone surveys than from studies that involve direct contact with subjects, thus there has been considerable discussion on the problems associated with non-response survey research (Fowler, 1993). Following up non-responses because of a need to acquire additional responses or just to find out why there was no response will depend on the nature of the study and the subjects. It is conceivable that the window of opportunity could be very small, since a study may be time- or event-related (close to an election or some other particular event). Thus the only recourse is to determine why there was no response for future reference. Any enquiry into 'why' could be carried out by a second visit, telephone or post, but in any case it would be desirable to include a self-addressed, stamped envelope or postcard so that subjects can respond in writing. Trying to contact subjects from transient populations (students who are away at university part of the year, migrant workers, military personnel, oil-rig workers) is particularly difficult. This may require considerable ingenuity and incur extra cost of sending questionnaires to more than one address in order to obtain an adequate response or to determine the cause of any non-responses. When contacting subjects about why they did not reply, any questions (written or verbal) should be brief and solely to determine why they chose not to participate, and should have nothing to do with gathering data. If it turns out that they were never contacted in the first place (telephone disconnected, questionnaire lost in the post) then a new questionnaire could be sent.

Subjects' failure to answer all the questions in an interview or written questionnaire presents another problem to the researcher. It essentially represents lost data, though it is necessary to determine whether it is a matter of the question being inapplicable to the respondent or whether it was not answered for another reason. Interviewers can note the reason, but questionnaires should be structured so that optionally answered questions do not constitute data loss. Such questions can complement those that constitute the operational definition of the variable of interest, but not necessarily be part of it. Such questions may potentially apply to only part of the sample.

This still leaves the problem of what to do about no responses on individual questions. If it is not possible to elicit an answer or determine why a question was not answered, one solution is to leave those subjects' scores out (resulting in non-respondents). Alternatively, it is possible to omit those questions from the study (a not unreasonable approach if a large number refuse to answer a question), though this could have an affect on the reliability and validity of the question set (see Chapter 11). Even when a questionnaire or measuring instrument has been completed, it is possible to identify subjects who have not taken the task seriously, just making the same choice straight through, not uncommon among young people in a classroom compelled to participate as part of a cluster sample. This can be the fault of not providing a sufficiently convincing reason for participating, an aspect of instrument design that will be reiterated later. If such responses still occur, then these may have to be treated as non-respondents. Other more elaborate approaches are suggested by Jolliffe (1986) for specific types of data loss. In the end, the researcher has to weigh up the consequences of non-responses in order to determine a course of action: chase subjects, replace subjects, find out why they failed to respond, etc. At least some of these will be necessary if the representativeness of the sample is to remain justifiable. Some statistical techniques do exist for reducing the error in data due to non-response (Fowler, 1993; Kalton, 1983), though minimizing non-response should be the priority. Now try Activity 5.4, putting all these factors together.

Activity 5.4

1 For each of the following descriptions of sampling, identify the sampling approach, describe the population(s) to which inferences could be extended and what appears to be the variable each represents, any potential sources of confounding (describe the extraneous variables), and identify at least one potential pitfall in achieving the sample:

(a) One of Professor Bloggs' psychology students has decided to investigate the effects of sleep loss on memory. He obtains a list of students in the university and randomly selects from four groups that overlap: men and women, science and humanities students.

(b)   Researcher Jones intends to determine the cause of abuse of the unemployment benefits system. He randomly selects ten areas of the city and plans to use his contacts to find at least one claimant who is illegally working and use him or her to lead to others. These persons will be categorized as to social class, five age groups and political affiliation.

2   For each of the sampling approaches proposed above, describe an optimum way of organizing data collection to ensure maximum return for the samples described.

3   For each of the sampling approaches proposed in Question 1 above, describe at least one way of determining why non-participants did not participate.

How sampling techniques and size influence design

Proponents of pre-experimental designs, including surveys, tend to emphasize the need to predict optimum sample sizes in order to achieve the minimum amount of error in the sample means. Techniques for predicting sample size based on acceptable tolerances of errors in the means are provided in numerous texts on survey design (e.g., Jaeger, 1984; Jolliffe, 1986; Kalton, 1983; Kish, 1965). Basically, these calculations take into account the fraction of the population that a sample will constitute, being determined by what error can be allowed. This can mean that it would require a large sample to result in a very 'accurate' statistic. Fowler (1993), on the other hand, emphasizes the need to consider the absolute size of the sample rather than the proportion of the population. Unless a sample constitutes a larger proportion of the population (over 10%), the fraction has less of an impact on the standard error of the mean than the actual sample size. He maintains that for surveys, the nature and quality of the sample, and the techniques employed, have a greater impact on the relative error when making inferences about the population – for example, when describing the confidence interval in which the population mean is likely to occur.

When the design is experimental, quasi-experimental or ex post facto, the aim is to compare groups to see if they (probably) belong to a common population. Parametric statistical tests (e.g., t-tests, analysis of variance) that test comparisons across groups are able to compensate for sample size by making it more difficult to claim statistical significance the smaller the number of subjects in each cell. Thus the prime concern of the researcher is to ensure that cell sample size is as high as can be afforded, considering one's resources. The smaller the sample, the greater the risk that one will commit a Type II error, accepting the null hypothesis that there is no difference when in reality there is. Thus the risk of committing a Type II error can be reduced by increasing the sample size. There is a tendency to strive for more than 30 subjects per cell, but it is possible to see that even in relatively simple multidimensional designs (see Figures 2.13 and 5.1), the total number of subjects can escalate if this is the goal. One must also consider the problem of non-responses, which will become particularly important and have a considerable impact when cell sizes are small. In such cases, sampling with replacement may need to be included as part of the sampling strategy in order to maintain as homogeneous a set of cell sample sizes as possible.

Though it is less obvious from the calculations of nonparametric tests such as χ^2 that they are dependent on sample size, the same risk of making a Type II error exists and is dependent on subject numbers. Due to the nature of the probability distributions that underlie these tests, there are minimum frequencies below which inferences may not be justified. Since achieving a balance between available resources and desired sample size is not a trivial problem, this topic will be considered again in later chapters. A mathematical treatment of the consequences of sample size and techniques for determining optimum numbers will be presented in Chapters 14–20 when considering the power of specific statistical tests.

Random assignment in experimental designs

True experimental designs need to employ two levels of randomization: first there needs to be a (sizeable) random selection of subjects from as homogeneous a population as possible. Second, these subjects must in turn be allocated to different levels of treatment (including any control groups). As was seen with quasi-experimental designs, which borrow the statistical tests of experimental designs, sample size is important in the same way and the sum of the cell sizes can escalate.

ETHICS IN SAMPLING AND DATA COLLECTION

This seems to be the most appropriate point at which to introduce the issue of ethics in research, since at this stage the researcher will be trying to gain access to either a sampling frame (population list) from which to select a sample, or individuals for complementary case-study work. Even if a sampling frame exists, there can be difficulties in acquiring lists, securing permission to contact subjects, and acquiring the co-operation of the subjects themselves. These problems can tempt researchers into questionable actions, and it is worthwhile consulting existing codes of ethics and legislation for guidance. The issue of the legality of holding databases of personal details may vary from country to country, but with huge computer databases being passed from organization to organization, the laws relating to personal privacy are being tightened. For example, in the UK, the Data Protection Act requires that persons on any such database know what is on it and that they can ask to be removed. Professional organizations are a sound source of codes of ethics and will specify unacceptable practices (e.g., British Psychological Society, 1993) as will the professional writings in journals and books (Frankfort-Nachmias and Nachmias, 1992).

On a more practical level, advice is available and case studies are cited as examples on problems specific to the area of research. Hornsby-Smith (1993) encourages persistence in penetrating closed groups, providing some interesting examples, but these relate more to small groups for case studies. The examples bring to mind the possibility of the sampling technique actually distorting the outcomes of the study, particularly when one has to go to extremes of enticing subjects or when there is a need for the appropriate gender, religion or ethnic group. Would it be appropriate to lie about your lack of commitment to the Nazi cause to gain access to an organization? This raises the age-old question about whether the ends really do justify the means.

Unobtrusive observations, where subjects are not informed of observations being made on them, may seem an alternative in such situations, but what about the rights of the subjects? Even if the researcher were to guarantee that the identity of subjects would not be revealed – for example, in studies of sexual deviance or criminal behaviour – the ethics of not telling subjects could become an issue.

For intrusive studies, the issue of the right to *not* to participate must be considered, whether one ends up with volunteers or not. This may seem obvious, but there are situations where the subjects are not even asked, such as school children who might be the major subjects in research on teaching and learning. The teachers may be asked, but are their charges? Children may not recognize such insensitivity, but some parents surely will.

In his discussion of the British Sociological Association's *Statement of Ethical Practice*, Hornsby-Smith (1993) notes the requirement for 'informed consent' of subjects, where they are told not only that they will be participating, but also what the research is about, who is conducting it and how the results will be disseminated. This is also covered by the British Psychological Society (1993), which addresses the issue of children by stating that consent should be obtained from 'parents or from those "in loco parentis" '. This brief summary does not do justice to the details presented in such documents and these (plus the organization's advisers, if you are in doubt) should be consulted. Confidentiality of results and anonymity of individual subjects, or even of whole organizations, must be maintained. The consequences may be more than just personal offence: in some countries it can mean loss of employment, freedom or even life. If, for some reason, a researcher cannot maintain confidentiality and the subjects would be put at risk, the study simply should not be conducted.

It is not possible in a textbook to cover all the possibilities, and many issues will not become apparent until one is engaged in research. You will begin the process by carrying out Activity 5.5 at the end of this chapter, which will engage you in reflecting on your study or project.

SUMMARY

This chapter has introduced a variety of techniques for sampling. Surveys may draw upon one sample and try to identify links between factors based upon questionnaires or interviews. Experimental designs also need representative samples to ensure external validity. Alternatively, ex post facto designs use life experiences as variables and consequently will often have to draw from a number of populations that are in essence the operational definition of these variables (age, gender, type of education, experiences). Additional considerations will be raised in later chapters that cover the specific statistical tests, but at this stage it becomes clear why there is a compelling need to identify the structure and design of the research *before* selecting the sample and to be clear what characteristics will constitute the definition of a population. In addition, selecting samples from some populations will require innovative procedures if randomness and a high level of representativeness are to be maintained. Appropriate sampling also provides the backbone to many studies, protecting against possible confounding by extraneous variables, enhancing internal validity.

The decisions to be made on anticipated level of generalizability of the results will determine the ideal sampling needs. Limitations on resources and availability of subjects will often compel the researcher to consider what would be the optimum among a number of choices. While this may reduce the strength of the argument for generalizability, a rational choice should prevent reducing the strength to zero.

The ultimate size and type of sample will have an impact on the choice of design, so these two issues are closely related. In addition, researchers must be aware of ethical issues related to subjects, which must start when the sample is identified and first contacted. In the end, the choice of sampling strategy will be primarily determined by resources available and the relative benefits of alternatives. Many of the decisions will be based upon the research design employed, the nature of the data to be collected, and the statistical tests to be used in resolving the truth of hypotheses.

Activity 5.5

(a) For your own research, outline briefly how you plan to establish a frame and how you intend to identify the sample. What will you do to minimize attrition, that is, loss of subjects from your sample?

(b) Consult the code of ethics or guidelines appropriate for your discipline. What issues need to be resolved with respect to your own research? How might these affect your sample or how you conduct your study?

ADDITIONAL SOURCES
OF CONFOUNDING BY
THE MEASUREMENT
PROCESS AND
INTERACTIONS   6

As seen in Chapters 3 and 4, a successful design is one that is unassailable from the viewpoint that the observed effects on the dependent variable could *only* be attributable to the independent variable(s). Thus the aim is to control all other possible extraneous variables in such a way that they will not confound the results. In other words, the aim is to prevent extraneous variables influencing the dependent variable, or reducing the generalizability of the results. Chapter 5 provided sampling techniques to enhance the probability that samples for experiments will be representative of larger populations, and consequently to improve the external validity. The same approaches will also provide representative samples for each life-event macrovariable (education, social class, gender, etc.) so as to enhance construct validity and internal validity for ex post facto studies.

In this chapter, seven more unwanted potential sources of extraneous variables will be considered. Five of these could possibly be introduced through the design and implementation of any treatment, the measuring instruments and/or the data-collection process itself. The seven sources will be used to demonstrate further why the pre-experimental designs considered in Chapter 3 are so weak. In Chapter 7 the experimental, quasi-experimental and ex post facto designs will be considered in light of these potential sources, illustrating their greater desirability.

The seven new sources have the potential of reducing construct, internal, external and statistical validity, as indicated in Table 3.5, which would reduce the validity of any conclusions drawn from a study. It is also worth emphasizing that while sound designs go a long way towards controlling the influence of extraneous variables, avoidance of introducing new unwanted variables can be achieved only through sound sampling, careful execution of any treatment, the appropriate design of measuring instruments and care in collecting the data. To complement the design process, guidelines for development and procedures for checking the quality of instruments and data collection processes will be provided in Chapters 8–11. These will include general techniques for establishing construct validity, enhancing reliability of instruments and ensuring objectivity during data collection.

Seven more sources of extraneous variables

Four of the seven new potential sources of invalidity and confounding introduced in this section are related to measurement and the actual collecting of data. Few experimental designs can compensate for failure to define clearly and unambiguously the basic variables. Assuming sound variables, it is possible to devise procedures that either avoid or allow one to determine the relative effects of the following, thus preventing confounding. Recall that those sources in the tables that have a question mark against a design have the potential to prevent confounding, but that this will be achieved only through the employment of appropriate sampling techniques, instrument design and data collection. Consideration of the possibility of other sources of confounding based upon the interactions of two or more sources is also encouraged. After completing the descriptions of all of these, the examples in Chapter 3 will be reconsidered to see the implications. Finally, Table 6.1 at the end of the chapter will provide summaries of the effects these potential sources of confounding and invalidity variable may or may not have on the pre-experimental designs considered. Continuing with the numbering system started in Chapter 3 (it may be useful to refer to Table 3.5):

9. Direction/nature of causality uncertain

The greater the time interval or social distance between the proposed independent variable and the dependent variable, the more difficult it will be in some cases to determine the direction of causality. In other words, it may be ambiguous whether X caused Y or they simply influenced each other ($X \leftrightarrows Y$). This can be particularly true in correlational studies, which might also be subject to the situation where the actual causal source is a third (possibly unknown) variable, as shown in Figure 6.1 (a).

Alternatively, when considering macrovariables in ex post facto studies, it is quite possible to find that while an apparent causal link can be established, the true causal relationship is more accurately described as a chain of events. It may even be that while the chain may begin with the variable of interest, there may even be more than one possible true causal chain, as shown in Figure 6.1 (b).

This raises the issue of how one phrases conclusions, when it is obvious that true causal source (a microvariable) is on a different level from that investigated (a macrovariable). For example, studies claimed to have shown that cigarette smoking 'caused' cancer, when in reality it was certain carcinogenic compounds

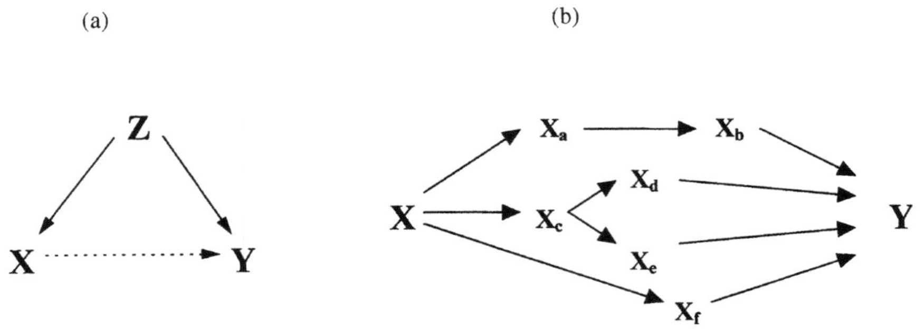

(a)   (b)

FIGURE 6.1
Alternative causality
chains for the
dependent variable
Y: (a) third variable;
(b) multiple routes

in cigarette smoke that were the true cause. Therefore, while the correlational evidence was damning, it was not conclusive and not until the biochemists could show the full mechanism was all doubt removed. While this may seem pedantic, it does have implications for considering variables in multi-variable situations. Using the above example, studies are now under way to investigate the effects on people who do not personally smoke cigarettes, but are exposed to cigarette smoke – referred to as 'passive smoking'. We are all exposed to numerous potential carcinogens that potentially could either be the cause or enhance the effect of passive smoking. Untangling the web of events is not a simple task. In social science research the webs are even more complex, and any uncertainties need to be recognized so subsequent studies can focus on resolving these. Failure to establish the direction or sequence of causality will jeopardize the internal validity of any study trying to establish causal links. It will also result in an inappropriate choice of statistical test to resolve hypotheses related to causality, damaging statistical validity. Thus, in some studies – for example, correlational and some ex post facto – it may be best not even to suggest causal links, but to express relationships as tendencies for variables to change in tandem.

10. Unnatural/invalid experiment/treatment

This can influence the outcome (dependent variable) and is always a potential problem when employing true experimental designs that have experimental or treatment group(s). Planning the experiences of these groups so that they are as close to reality as possible is necessary if extending the outcomes to larger populations in real situations is going to be valid. Ensuring external validity requires not only representative samples but also representative situations. Psychology experiments performed in university laboratories or education studies conducted where learning environments are artificial can seriously jeopardize external validity. Momentarily ignoring the sampling problem (can undergraduate volunteers be considered typical of any larger population?), the justification of extending the results of an experiment that involves, say, memorization of nonsense syllables to memory in general have been frequently criticized. Yet there is the conflicting problem of how to establish control over known extraneous variables if one does not conduct such a study under these conditions.

In addition, the effects of participating in an experiment can change the outcomes (dependent variable) directly. The classic example of a situation where just the subjecting of people to an experiment can influence the outcome is the study that originated the term *Hawthorne effect*. This was named after an investigation carried out in the 1930s in the Hawthorne works of the Western Electric Company in Chicago (Haralambos and Holborn, 1991). The purpose of the study was to determine the possible effects on productivity of such variables as lighting levels, room temperature, etc. Researchers became aware of the fact that ultimately it did not matter what they did (raise or lower light levels, etc.), productivity went up. The subjects were apparently responding to the fact the experiment was taking place rather than the intended experimental variables. On the other hand, the questionable ethics of conducting an experiment on subjects without them knowing it tends to discourage the alternative. This means there is a necessity of identifying designs that allow the researcher to determine whether or not the actual act of putting subjects through an experiment is a variable. This problem has resulted in the practice of the control group receiving a placebo, so that they think they are being experimented on as well as the experimental group. In medicine, everyone receives some tablets; in social science research, all groups would have to be under the impression they were receiving the experimental treatment. This becomes extremely difficult in quasi-experimental designs, as will be seen.

Control over this potential source of confounding is not possible in pre-experimental designs since there is neither a pre- and post-test situation nor an equivalent control group. Question marks appear against all experimental and quasi-experimental designs simply because it is up to the researcher to prevent confounding through appropriate techniques applied when devising experiments and collecting data, even though these designs offer the opportunity to monitor this form of confounding by employing control groups.

11. Invalid measurement of variables

No design can overcome the handicap of a measuring instrument or classification that is not valid. Construct validity is simply how well a measure represents a concept or how appropriately something or someone is classified. Do the numbers in a quantitative measure accurately represent levels of that concept? Construct validity relates to the representation of both independent and dependent variables, as will be seen in the second half of the text when considering statistical tests. The appropriateness of classification of subjects will determine the validity of variables often resulting in ordinal or nominal scales (e.g., social class, education, type of mental illness). On the other hand, the construct validity of the measuring instrument will be determined by its representativeness of levels of variables resulting in interval or ratio scales. Three types of situations will occur:

- The independent variables are ordinal or nominal (gender, social class, etc.) and the dependent variable is measurable, ordinal or interval/ratio, such as scores on a test, totals from a questionnaire or scores from an observation schedule.

- Both independent and dependent variables are classifications: which social class tends to vote for what political party?
- Both independent and dependent variables are measured as interval/ratio data: age versus income.

Low validity of measurement or classification of any variables in a study can invalidate the results and any conclusions since one will simply not be discussing accurate indicators of the variables. No design can compensate for low construct validity, but processes for enhancing this will be discussed in Chapters 8–11 for a variety of types of instruments.

12. Instrument reliability

The design of measuring instruments themselves can introduce a potentially confounding variable, not least through reduction of instrument reliability for measuring the dependent variable. For simplicity, consider a basic definition of reliability to be the degree of consistency in producing the same results for the two measures of same thing. This could include two different instruments, one measure used on two occasions, or even two parts of a single instrument (see Black, 1993, for an introduction to reliability). This means that a highly reliable test or set of observations conducted today will produce the same data tomorrow (obviously assuming nothing has changed), or two observers using the same observation schedule will report the same data.

Reliability has several forms, depending on the nature of the data collected, though all of them are concerned with consistency:

- *Within the instrument.* How uniform are the responses to questions that make up an operational definition? Lack of consistent answers due to misinterpretation can introduce error in the measurement, as will be seen in later chapters.
- *Across time.* For example, when there are multiple observations using an observation schedule, is there consistency in applying criteria between pre-treatment and post-treatment observations? Alternatively, with many observations over a long period of time, were the observations at the beginning consistent with those at the end?
- *Across observers.* In studies that involve a team of observers, are all the observers 'seeing' the same things, agreeing in their classifications? Is there consistency across observers?

Sound designs need to employ techniques for the development and administration of measuring instruments that protect against low reliability, rather than finding out after the fact that considerable error has been introduced. As Campbell and Stanley (1963) noted in particular, studies using observers, raters or markers over a period of time are particularly prone to loss of consistency (reliability) when there is a gap between the two measures, as in designs employing both a pre-test and a post-test. If there are two groups being measured by the same instrument, then there should not be a difference in the reliability, unless some characteristic of one group influences responses or ratings.

There are a number of coefficients of reliability that can provide the researcher with a check on the quality of an instrument, as we will see in Chapter

11, but as Cronbach (1990) notes, 'Excellent reliability cannot compensate for unacceptable validity.' An instrument that is reliable but not valid is of no use to the researcher as it would only measure reliably something other than what was intended.

Designs B2 and B3 potentially compensate for limitations in instrument reliability since there is equal probability of these influencing the outcomes of experimental and control groups as subjects were randomly assigned. This assumes good practices to minimize technical problems, such as random assignment of observers, trials of instruments, and revisions of written tests. Designs A3, C2 and D3 could introduce different levels of reliability since the groups are not necessarily equivalent. Without the comparison, designs E1 (assuming some variables are measured), A1 and A2 offer no compensation for confounding from limitations in validity or reliability of the instrument(s), thus internal validity can be jeopardized. On the other hand, low reliability can introduce sufficiently large error in measurement that statistical tests will not be able to detect true differences when they occur. This can reduce statistical validity as well, which will be demonstrated through a more mathematical rationale later.

13. Learning from instrument

Just applying a measuring instrument can have a detrimental impact on the outcomes of a study. Subjects can inadvertently learn from taking a test or change their attitudes as a result of completing a questionnaire. They can simply become more proficient at answering a certain type of question used in an achievement test, which is particularly prevalent in test–retest designs where an instrument is used more than once, or a parallel version used the second time. Even the time between tests can be used by respondents to learn specific tasks they felt they were unable to perform on a test, a real problem since most people do not like to feel as if they have failed. By completing it the first time a questionnaire is administered, respondents can become aware of what is wanted, expected, or socially acceptable, which could bias responses on subsequent administrations.

Even assurance of anonymity can influence respondents' perception of what range of responses would be acceptable. For example, asking young people about drug-taking may result in more honest answers if they know they cannot be identified. On the other hand, responses may be exaggerated, though there are ways of checking the possibility of this. Intelligence tests, because of their questioning style, might initially be unfamiliar, and the first application may become a learning experience on how to respond. The subjects can become test-wise and therefore subsequent results could be distorted, reducing the construct validity of IQ as a measure of intelligence, particularly with multiple applications where change is the variable of interest.

Alternatively, there is the possibility that an instrument may contribute directly to the dependent variable. For example, if the experiment were to try to measure any effects of a treatment (independent variable) on short-term memory (dependent variable), the process of testing subjects' short-term memory might cause theirs to improve, reducing the internal validity of the design. To some extent, even the wording of questions on a questionnaire or those used in an interview can contribute to outcomes, and therefore can be related to the overall validity of the instrument.

These issues have no relevance for design A1 since there are no pre-tests. Design A2 would be susceptible to confounding since there is a pre-test with no comparison group. Designs A3, B3 and D3 have no pre-tests, thus avoiding the problem, whereas designs B2 and C2 have pre-tests for both groups, thus both receive the same experience and therefore any impact would be felt by both groups. It might increase the total gain scores but not whether there was a difference between the two groups, which is what the design would be attempting to determine.

14. Instrument reacts with independent variable(s)

There can be situations where the actual measuring instrument reacts or interacts with the treatment or independent variable(s), making the subjects more or less sensitive to the treatment. For example, just knowing that they will be asked questions on political issues could raise the subjects' awareness of the need to read the newspaper more carefully. How often do people try to lose a little weight before they go for their annual medical check-up? As Stanley and Campbell (1963) suggest, encountering the high concentration of provocative statements found on a test of prejudice is unlikely to be matched in real life and may well have a sensitizing influence. Thus the sample would no longer be representative of the population from which it had been selected, reducing the external validity.

This can also be a problem in studies investigating attitude change, where the pre-test actually makes the subjects aware of their own attitudes before the treatment. This may differentially harden existing attitudes and strengthen resistance to any attempt to persuade one group to change, thus reducing the construct validity of the classification of subjects.

A classic example that demonstrated the potential of such a confounding variable was demonstrated in a study conducted by Rosenthal and Jacobson (1968; described in Haralambos and Holborn, 1991). The researchers informed new teachers of a group of primary children that a randomly selected subgroup should be expected to show rapid intellectual growth. At the end of the year, this subgroup was reported to have performed exceptionally well, even though one would not have expected this of a randomly selected group. Again, the issue of ethics has been raised, but it did illustrate the potential of self-fulfilling prophecy in studies. Haralambos and Holborn (1991) present evidence that the opposite can happen: labelled groups perform in contradiction to what is expected because of their knowledge of the expectations of that label. For example, Fuller (1984) found that a small group of black girls in a London comprehensive school resented the stereotype of subordinate women restricted to domestic work and tried to prove it wrong through acquiring academic qualifications while maintaining an air of independence of adult authority. Thus it should be recognized that self-fulfilling prophecy (labelling subjects) could work either way: magnifying the outcome or opposite to expectation. The point to keep in mind is that when labelling becomes known to subjects, it could introduce a confounding variable by changing the independent variable (treatment) in a study by either enhancing or reducing its effect.

On a more subtle level, it is possible for the measuring process itself to interfere with the experimental variable by becoming a cause of change. For example, an observer in a classroom or in proximity to some social situation may influence the behaviour of the participants in that situation. Even an audio- or videotape recorder in an interview can change the types of responses subjects will make. The more the measuring process creates a situation that is out of the ordinary, the greater its effect can be. This is why researchers are sometimes encouraged to devise unobtrusive instruments/techniques in situations relating to social interaction, such as two-way mirrors, though even these can influence behaviour when the subjects become aware of being observed. This does raise the ethical issue of watching people without their consent, which some might consider offensive since it is at least 'being nosy' if not downright spying. If avoidance of such techniques is impossible, then it becomes necessary to alter the design to take into account this potentially confounding variable.

In summary, it is the unique nature of any stimulus provided by a measuring instrument that will require the researcher to be aware of the potential interaction with the independent variable. As Campbell and Stanley (1963) note: 'Where highly unusual test procedures are used, or where the testing procedure involves deception, perceptual or cognitive restructuring, surprise, stress, etc., designs having unpretested groups remain highly desirable if not essential.' This would provide a way of either avoiding the problem, as in design B3, or determining the level of any influence, as will be seen in designs introduced later. Designs A1, A3, B3 or D3 do not have pre-test, therefore it is not an issue. Designs A2, B2 and C2 do have pre-tests and therefore are susceptible to confounding. Design E1 (correlational) is not experimental in structure, therefore this is not relevant.

15. Other interactions

In some cases, the interaction (as seen in sources 7, 8 and 14) is the source of confounding rather than the individual sources alone. Others may occur that are more idiosyncratic to the study, and the researcher should always be aware of the possibility. Some such interactions may be between the personal characteristics of the actual subjects (selection) and the treatment or its setting, or the instruments. Problems of the control groups *not* receiving treatment or even suspicion of receiving a placebo, combined with a misunderstanding of what is being measured, can occur. It is not possible to predict all the possibilities of sources and this one is left as an incentive for you, the researcher, to be aware of the possibility of the unexpected and unpredictable. The other 14 sources could be considered to be the obvious ones: you may find that your task is to identify (and control) the less obvious as well! Figure 6.2 provides a conceptual summary of all 15 potential sources of confounding and invalidity of conclusions. To this can be added the warning that the subject groups may bring their own characteristics to bear on the study.

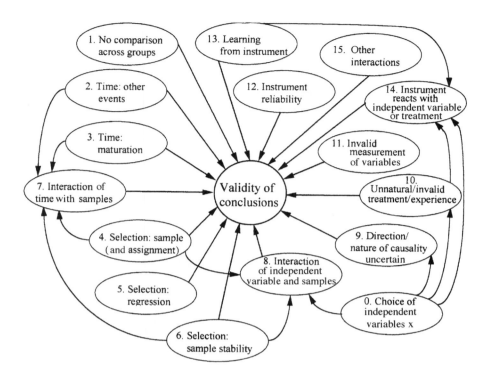

FIGURE 6.2
Potential sources of
invalidity and
confounding

RECONSIDERING THE BASIC PRE-EXPERIMENTAL DESIGNS IN LIGHT OF THE NEW POTENTIAL SOURCES

In this section, each of the examples of the pre-experimental designs presented in Chapter 3 will be considered again to see how the additional seven potential sources of invalidity and confounding will manifest themselves. A summary is given in Table 6.1. Experimental, quasi-experimental and ex post facto designs are considered in Chapter 7 (see also the summaries in Tables 7.1–7.3).

As the limitations of each of the three pre-experimental designs for establishing causality are reconsidered with reference to the above sources, some new information on each study may be added. You will want to revisit the original descriptions in each case. Also note that the rating of the individual studies (+ , − , ?) may differ from that in Table 3.6 in that the table only indicates tendencies. Individual studies may be better or worse than might be expected.

Design A1: One group post-test/observation only

Recall that Professor Jones' psychology class was enticed to use a computer-based learning package in statistics, with the intention of seeing if it improved learning of what was perceived as a difficult subject for his students. Two separate outcomes were used, allowing the investigation of perceived utility of the package (a questionnaire) and the learning value (end-of-year examinations).

An initial set of potential extraneous variables was presented in Figure 3.3. Let us consider some additional possibilities, this time related to three aspects of the study: the 'treatment'; the evidence he was willing to accept as indicating success (both the test and the questionnaire); and the way he collected his data. Figure 6.3 shows the variable chart with some new sources to consider:

• The novelty of computer-based learning could have influenced the outcome, and if so, would it still have the same effect next year if those students had encountered such packages in other courses? In other words, would the novelty have worn off?
• There is no assurance that the measuring instrument is valid. Does the questionnaire measure what it is purported to measure and is the statistics test valid (and new enough so as to not have been seen before)?
• The reliability of the measuring instruments: they were project devised and probably not tested, thus it may be low.

Using existing instruments intended for other purposes (here, a test for grades) does not guarantee that they are appropriate for resolving research hypotheses. Considering each of the seven new categories of sources of invalidity in turn:

9   *Direction/nature of causality uncertain* [?]. The control of the time sequence of discrete events had the potential to establish a direction of causality, but with no comparison group it would be difficult to tell whether any improvement of outcome was due to the package or extraneous variables.

10   *Unnatural/invalid experiment/treatment* [−]. If there were an outcome, would it be the novelty of a new medium or the intrinsic value of the struc-

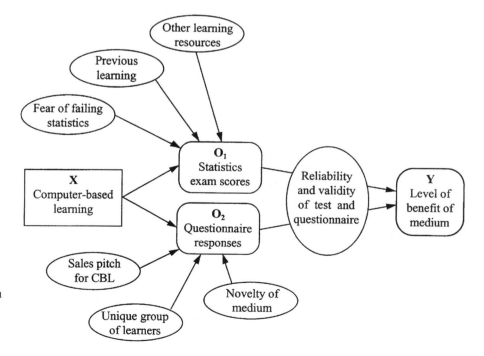

FIGURE 6.3
An enhanced variable map for Professor Jones' test of effectiveness of computer-based learning materials (design A1). Can you identify any other extraneous variables?

ture of the content, or some combination? It is not even clear which of these would be of interest, but considering the value of looking for sustainable change rather than a 'flash in the pan' (one-off success), a more sophisticated study would be necessary.

11 *Invalid measurement of variables* [−]. The lack of control group in the design structure does not allow one to see if the measure reflected any differential outcome as a result of the new learning experience. Thus the passing of the examination could have had nothing to do with the courseware and one would never know to look. On the other hand, the study could have been better structured with a control group. If the outcome had arisen where there was no difference in performance (both learned equally well), reasons for this could possibly be identified. For example, if personal contact with or observations of students indicated they did learn more, then one possible reason that could be investigated would be the validity of the outcome measure. Existing instruments rather than custom-designed ones for testing specific outcomes tend to have poor validity for research purposes and should be suspect in their own right.

12 *Instrument reliability* [−]. As with the previous source, in this situation there is the suspicion that the existing (rather than a custom-made) instrument has unknown reliability anyway.

13 *Learning from instrument* [   ]. As there is only a single measure, it is unlikely to be an issue in such studies.

14 *Instrument reacts with independent variable/treatment* [−]. Without a control group, it is difficult to distinguish improved motivation and performance due to the nature of the instruments (were they disproportionately sensitive to computer-based learning outcomes?).

15 *Other interactions* [?]. Whether Professor Jones' enthusiasm for the package or his personal charisma falls under the heading of source 10 above (Hawthorne effect) or is an interaction between treatment and subjects that could be idiosyncratic for that subject group needs to be considered. The possibility that any media would have succeeded simply indicates the difficulty in carrying out replicable classroom studies.

Usually such studies provide little valid support for investing additional resources, as they tend to be simplistic and try to employ raw numbers to support a view. If only one class or group is available, then a more carefully planned case study would be more appropriate. In that situation, a study could involve watching students use the package, interviewing them to determine the scope for improvement, and assessing the achievement of specific learning outcomes that the package was intended to enhance (and not the whole course).

Design A2: One group pre- and post-test/observation

Recall the original plan of Super Catflap Ltd to determine the effectiveness of the scheme to increase the motivation of staff to produce more per shift by an award of bonus shares in the company. This was based on establishing productivity levels before the bonus and then checking productivity levels three months after the award had been made. In addition to the extraneous variables indicated on the map in Figure 3.4, the following potential extraneous variables related to the treatment and measures may have influenced outcomes, as shown in Figure 6.4:

- Since there was no change in productivity, there is the possibility that the employees did not understand the plan and did not even perceive of the incentive as an incentive.
- This is not the most effective way of employing positive reinforcement as a means for encouraging behaviour and could be perceived of as negative reinforcement: work harder or the money will be removed.
- The link between motivation to produce more and the realization of this motivation could be hampered by other factors (delay in receipt of parts, machinery breakdown), thus productivity may not be the most valid measure of increased motivation. In other words, they may have been motivated, but something else prevented the realization of that motivation.
- High reliability is of no value if the measure is not valid.
- There is the possibility that monitoring productivity was an implied threat to their integrity and sense of pride, a feeling that they were not to be trusted.

Taking into account these factors in the variable map, let us consider them in light of the seven new categories of sources of invalidity,

9   *Direction/nature of causality uncertain* [?]. With command over the sequence of events, even with this design the potential nature of the direction of potential causality would seem clear. Yet what if the way this was presented resulted in the employees not perceiving this as something that was to be an incentive to be more productive?

10 *Unnatural/invalid experiment/treatment* [?]. Without a comparison group, it is not clear whether the lack of increased productivity was due to *how* the share plan was introduced, or for some perverse reason the staff chose not to consider it an incentive. Reinforcement theories and supporting research suggest the researchers did it backwards anyway, providing the reward *before* the staff increased production, contradicting basic understanding in psychology: reinforcement is most effective *after* a desired behaviour.

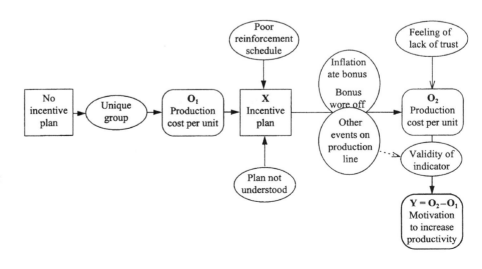

FIGURE 6.4
An enhanced variable map for Super Catflap's study on increasing productivity, single group (design A2 version). Are there other extraneous variables?

Was it perceived by employees that if production did not increase the incentive would be removed (threat), or implemented in such a way that such a threat was imagined? If so, they do not seem to realize that negative reinforcement is not a very effective way of encouraging people.

11   *Invalid measurement of variables* [−]. If productivity is the measure of motivation to produce more, then it is susceptible to other factors, such as supply of raw materials. This would make the validity of the measure questionable. There is no way of taking this into account in this study, nor is it possible here to check the impact by comparing results with a control group.

12   *Instrument reliability* [−]. If the content validity is questionable, then it makes little difference how reliable the measure is. As with source 11, the lack of a control group prevents identifying any impact on reliability.

13   *Learning from instrument* [?]. In this situation, unless the staff were informed that their productivity before the bonus had been recorded, any unobtrusive recording of it could result in a [+]. Usually one could expect a [?] because of the potential for introducing extraneous variables with this design, but it depends on the nature of the instrument. For example, do the subjects even know it is being used?

14   *Instrument reacts with independent variable/treatment* [−]. Could knowledge of being watched result in defiance? Also, as noted above, without a control group, it is not possible to know which way production would have gone without the share plan. With only a single measure of productivity, it could have gone up and down again by the third month.

15   *Other interactions* [?]. With so many potential sources of extraneous variables, other interactions are likely to exist.

Remember that a revised plan was contrived, and we will reconsider it in Chapter 7.

Design A3: Two available groups

Recall the study that compared two free health centres for pre-school children, where it was decided to take the opportunity to see if attendance could be encouraged by establishing a playroom in one of them. The original variable map is in Figure 3.5. On the basis of a difference in the patterns of number of visits per year (Table 3.7), it was decided that the playroom did encourage attendance and that it was worthwhile. Several sources of invalidity were initially identified.

The enhanced variable map in Figure 6.5 shows the additional variables that need to be considered when evaluating the structure of the study. While the playrooms did not seem to 'cause' a greater awareness of the value of clinic visits or change parental attitudes towards them, it did entice them to come more frequently. The construct validity of the measure, frequency of attendance, is suspect since it is not a valid operational definition of 'positive attitude towards health care for children'. The centre could have been no more than a nice day out. While this does achieve the original stated end, it may not produce a sustainable change. Later, we will see how some corroborating evidence could be collected through a questionnaire for parents. While there is some question

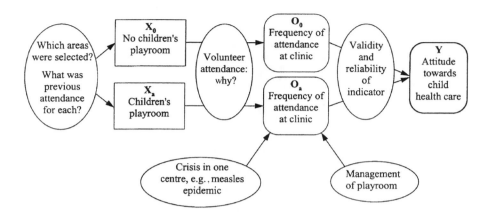

FIGURE 6.5
Enhanced variable map for the clinics for pre-school children (design A3 version)

about the generalizability of the results to other areas, the following categories of other potential sources of extraneous variables provide a mechanism for evaluating the study:

9 *Direction/nature of causality uncertain* [?]. Even with a control group with which to compare, the identification of direction and the nature of any causality are limited since there was no pre-implementation observation. This did not allow one to see the role of the playroom in enhancing attendance, as previous attendance was not known. This design is more appropriate for studies where nothing has happened before and one knows that the groups are on equal footing concerning the dependent variable.

10 *Unnatural/invalid experiment/treatment* [?]. While attendance at the clinic was the stated intent, obviously more than attendance is required if the clinic is to be successful, in other words to enhance child health. There is reason to believe that mere attendance alone would not change attitudes, since medical personnel tended to explain why they carried out tests and gave immunizations. In general, there will frequently be a question about control of this potential source in social science research.

11 *Invalid measurement of variables* [?]. Uptake may seem the obvious measure of success, but without the questionnaire to determine whether the reason for attendance had something to do with the playroom, it is difficult to say attendance alone was valid. Attendance may confirm *what* has happened but not *why*. As it was, the playgroup attendance increase could not be considered a valid indicator of changed attitude towards child care, thus this study would receive a [−] for controlling for an invalid indicator. Choice of instrument becomes very important in a study without justifiably equivalent groups, since differences could easily be the result of specific traits or characteristics. On the other hand, no design will automatically protect a study from poor construct validity.

12 *Instrument reliability* [+]. Any lack of reliability in the indicator of success could influence the conclusions, since the measured outcomes could vary due to such practices as time of day used or who records attendance. With no mechanism in the design to monitor administration or detect variations, reliability could be doubtful, increasing the variability of the

TABLE 6.1
Summary of basic pre-experimental designs with potential sources of invalidity and confounding of results;* 'best' ratings are given, some of which could be worse for individual studies depending on how they are carried out

A. Pre-experimental designs

Potential sources of invalidity and confounding

Design description	Design structure (time sequence of events)	1 No comparison across groups	2 Time: other events	3 Time: maturation	4 Selection: sample (and assignment)	5 Selection: regression	6 Selection: sample stability	7 Interaction of time with sample	8 Interaction of ind. var. with sample	9 Direction/nature of causality uncertain	10 Unnatural/invalid exper./treatment	11 Invalid measurement of variables	12 Instrument reliability	13 Learning from instrument	14 Instrument reacts with ind. variable	15 Other interactions
A1 *One group post-test/ observation only:* one group observed or tested for one possible dependent variable for one instance of independent variable, observed or manipulated.	$(RS \to)X \to O_1$	–	–	–	(+) / –		?		–	? ?	? ?	–	–		–	?
A2 *One group pre- and post-test/observations* for some single event or treatment.	$(RS \to)O_1 \to X \to O_2$	–	–	–	(+) / –	?	+	–	–	? ?	? ?	–	?	?	–	?
A3 *Two available groups,* one subjected to event or treatment, the other not, both are tested/observed post-event/experience only.	$X_a \to O_a$ $X_0 \to O_0$	+	?	?	–		–	–	–	+	? ?	?	?	+	–	?

*Key: + compensated for by design; – not compensated; ? compensation uncertain; <blank> not relevant or covered in this chapter.

results. Assuming both groups employed the same practices, then the results of both would be equally affected, essentially controlling this as a variable, but increasing variances would make it harder to detect true significant differences. This will be considered mathematically in the chapters on statistics, showing the link between statistical validity and reliability.

13   *Learning from instrument* [+]. As there was no pre-test to influence the outcomes, this does not occur.

14   *Instrument reacts with independent variable/treatment* [+]. Since the data collection process was observational, it is unlikely that it would interact.

15   *Other interactions* [?]. With such a causal chain, other variables such as how the centres were managed could interact with treatment, including the administration and supervision of the playroom.

This study has highlighted the difficulty of evaluating designs as they become more complex, since there are so many possible sources of problems even though there is greater protection against invalidity. Without a questionnaire, the conclusion that the playroom was a good way of enhancing attitudes towards child care would not be valid. While this last study is an improvement on the first two, it still has limitations in its external validity. Replication in other areas with different pairs of clinics would help to resolve the issue. We will return to this study once more later, employing an improved quasi-experimental design.

Table 6.1 summarizes the three designs just considered. It is a useful way of comparing the potential for controlling extraneous variables across designs.

SUMMARY

The 15 sources of invalidity and confounding provide a set of criteria that can be used to evaluate not only existing studies, but also the new ones that will be encountered in Chapter 7 and any 'hybrids'. They are not prescriptions, but general pitfalls that one must avoid when planning and executing a research project. The list is a prompt to ask probing questions early in the planning. Now try Activity 6.1 before proceeding.

Activity 6.1

(a)   Recall the study described in Activity 3.2 on intelligence enhancement by vitamins: IQ tests traditionally have high reliability. The vitamins were administered at school each day free of charge, and the purpose of the study was explained to students and their parents. The teachers were unaware of who was receiving vitamins. Sketch a variable map.

(b)   For each of the seven new potential sources of invalidity and confounding listed below, enter a − if not controlled, + if controlled, ? if control is uncertain, or < blank > if not applicable in the [ ], and say why.

     9   *Direction/nature of causality uncertain* [ ]
   10 *Unnatural/invalid experiment/treatment* [ ]
   11 *Invalid measurement of variables* [ ]
   12 *Instrument reliability* [ ]
   13 *Learning from instrument* [ ]
   14 *Instrument reacts with independent variable/treatment* [ ]
   15 *Other interactions* [ ]

(c)   How have these affected your evaluation of the justifiability of the conclusions and why? What improvements to the study would you recommend?

REFINING THE DESIGNS

7

T his chapter continues the survey of designs, in each case applying the second set of seven sources of invalidity and confounding of results. Experimental, quasi-experimental and ex post facto models will be considered. As a consequence of limitations identified during this process for even the best designs, some new designs will be introduced. While these are not exhaustive of all those possible, they provide a basic set on which one can build when planning a study.

EXPERIMENTAL DESIGNS

The two designs presented in Chapter 4 will be reconsidered in light of the new potential sources of confounding and invalidity. This will allow us to see why they are an improvement over the pre-experimental designs, and subsequently to see the limitations of quasi-experimental and ex post facto designs.

Design B2: Pre- and post-test/observation

Recall the study to determine whether girls' attitudes towards computers and information technology could be improved through a set of specifically designed learning materials and activities. Upon completion of the study, it was found that the two parallel forms of the attitude survey given before and after had high internal consistency (reliability was determined to be high for both, about 0.80 each). The validity of the questionnaire was established by including both questions on the perceived relevance of computers and a semantic differential to determine basic feelings towards them.

Design structures using pre- and post-treatment observations are commonly and successfully used in biological sciences, where variables are usually well defined and observable. In the social sciences, there are potential sources of

157

extraneous variables associated with the measured dependent variables, since they tend to be more abstract and difficult to define operationally. Treatments may limit the validity of conclusions as they can either be artificial or out of context. It is possible that such pitfalls will contribute to a less valid result than for a study employing even the 'best' design. Let us use this example to illustrate the problem; several sources of invalidity exist:

- What constitutes a chain of causality may be difficult to ascertain in this situation since the study involves attitudes and a choice of independent variables.
- The fact that there was any treatment at all could contribute to the outcome. In other words, someone took an interest in the careers of girls (Hawthorne effect).
- The construct validity of the instrument may be questionable since the attitudes could be considered short-term and not influencing long-term career decisions. Obviously, it is more difficult to wait several years to see what the outcomes would be, and that would allow time (events) to become a possible extraneous variable.
- The actual measuring instruments could influence the groups perceptions of careers in computing and information technology through increased awareness.

These sources are illustrated in the variable map in Figure 7.1, which is an enhanced version of Figure 4.2. Using the classification scheme, these influence the categories as follows:

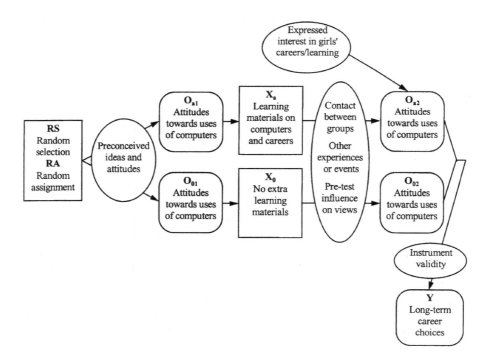

FIGURE 7.1
Martha Proughit's study on girls' attitudes towards computers: enhanced variable map

9   *Direction/nature of causality uncertain* [+]. With two groups and pre-/post-test/observation, it should be possible to determine and justify the direction of causality. The difficulty arises in the nature of causal relations which are dependent on the choice of variables. Here the investigation is contending with a macrovariable (attitude towards computers) which would have multiple causes and uncertain direction. For example, does poor attitude towards computers stop girls from using them, or does using computers instil the poor attitude? Thus it might be more realistic to rate this particular study as [?].

10 *Unnatural/invalid experiment/treatment* [?]. While it is difficult to imagine a subtle way of testing such a hypothesis, in the study described there could be some suspicion that just the interest expressed in the girls learning about computers would be sufficient to improve their attitudes towards computers and information technology. This design has the potential to protect against the Hawthorne effect, if the second group were also given the same impression that interest was being expressed in them (equivalent to a placebo). Thus how the study is carried out will determine whether this source is of consequence.

11 *Invalid measurement of variables* [?]. While no design can guarantee perfect validity, a radically unexpected outcome would be highly noticeable and might be due to an invalid instrument. The control group in the design would help to identify low validity since one would expect there to be little difference in performance on the pre-tests for randomly selected and assigned groups, though this is no guarantee even with randomly selected and randomly assigned groups. Figure 4.1 shows little difference between the pre-test scores, supporting the validity of the instruments. On the other hand, the conclusion implies that the differential attitude towards computers and information technology would result in improved *commitment toward learning* in the classroom by the treatment group. It could be suggested that there is no support for this from the instruments used nor that the effect would last and influence career choice (Y). If this was the case, the study should receive a [?] for control of instrument validity.

12 *Instrument reliability* [+]. As noted earlier, there is the danger of reduced reliability for observers because of the time gap between pre-test and post-test, though if it happens to both groups then there is no differential loss of reliability. Both groups would be assumed to have suffered the same effect, so the design does provide some protection. On the other hand, as we will see later, an overall loss of reliability could increase the potential for making a Type II error, missing rejecting the null hypothesis when it is really false. In the present example, reliability is potentially higher primarily because of the use of a paper-based fixed answer measure, though administration bias could reduce this if care were not taken. Since groups were formed from random selection and random assignment, there should be no differential influence on the reliability.

13 *Learning from instrument* [+]. It is assumed that any influence the pre-test had on learning would affect both groups equally, since both groups and instruments are equivalent.

14   *Instrument reacts with independent variable/treatment* [−]. As the focus is on changing attitudes, it could be argued that such an attitude instrument would raise expectations that might not be realized by the control group, thus their second test would reflect a confirmation of disappointment in computers. Alternatively, the treatment group could be primed to be more sensitive to the learning materials. This is a danger in using participant-completed pre-tests.

15   *Other interactions* [?]. Though there are fewer opportunities for interactions not already mentioned, one should always be aware of less obvious effects. For example, few studies of this scale could control for how teachers might influence attitudes as part of the study, by simply increasing their enthusiasm in class because something is being done. Totally isolating a single variable in such a situation is very difficult.

Studies with groups are always fraught with potential extraneous variables, not the least of which are the interactions between the groups. The difficulty in guaranteeing that the treatment is the only possible cause is one argument for replication of such studies.

Design B3: Post-test/observation only, with control group

Recall the Widget-Digit Microchips Inc. problem: the company wanted to determine which of two production techniques would be the most effective in order to implement one on a larger scale. Since the microchip was new and both the alternative production techniques were new, no pre-test/observation seemed necessary. Chip failure rates for each line of production were monitored by Quality Control, providing an indicator of relative success of the processes. Both had roughly the same output volume but process A had a lower failure rate than B. Considering this design, would the choice of procedures be valid? Even at this stage there is the possibility of extraneous variables creeping in to the study, such as the following:

• Being asked to test a new procedure could influence ones motivation and concentration (again, the old Hawthorne effect), but it might be that the influence would be the same for both groups.
• Are output rate and quality the only important outcomes, particularly when one is looking to the future for sustained output?
• The groups are unlikely to be separate, and therefore a competition could be established, influencing output rates and/or quality.

Even if the Hawthorne effect were the same for both groups, there is the problem of whether either process would have the same high output and low failure rate if it were adopted on a larger scale and the novelty wore off. This is where the actual execution of a design is very important, so as not to introduce unwanted variables. These could influence outcomes and adversely affect the construct (including predictive) and external validities of such a study. These sources are illustrated in the revised variable map in Figure 7.2.

Placed in the context of the second set of seven categories of sources of extraneous variables and invalidity, the following list highlights the problems.

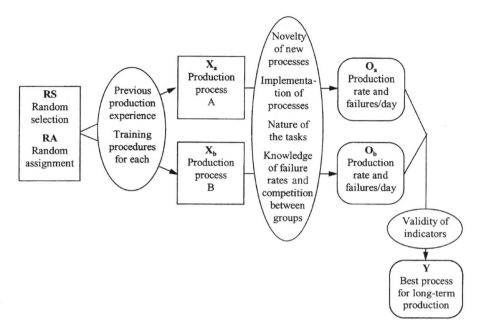

FIGURE 7.2
Enhanced variable
map for the Widget-
Digit production line
processes test

9 *Direction/nature of causality uncertain* [+]. The time sequence of events
   and the use of two groups ensures that this is fairly certain. Even though
   macrovariables are being employed, the groups were randomly formed
   and the outcome of interest is productivity and not necessarily why one
   would be better than another.

10 *Unnatural/invalid experiment/treatment* [?]. Organizing a special group to
    test a procedure could influence the effectiveness of either that group or
    the control, considering the number of intervening variables that would
    be involved. Just having an experiment could influence productivity
    (Hawthorne again).

11 *Invalid measurement of variables* [?]. While there are two groups, there is no
    protection against invalid measures. In this case, one might wish to ask
    whether or not productivity and low rejection are the only things that
    matter. Is either procedure sustainable – in other words, could staff con-
    tinue the pace and quality over a longer period without, say, getting
    bored? Do these results validly predict status quo production output?
    This is a situation that highlights the difference between statistical signifi-
    cance and practical significance.

12 *Instrument reliability* [+]. With two randomly assigned groups from a
    random selection, it would be possible to protect against different levels
    of reliability attributable to the instrument. Here the use of an external
    body (Quality Control Laboratory) ensures high consistency (reliability)
    of analysis.

13 *Learning from instrument* [+]. With no pre-test or intrusive observation,
    this would not occur.

14   *Instrument reacts with independent variable/treatment* [?]. Though there is
      not the potential influence of the pre-test as in the previous design, there
      is the possibility that the post-test/observation could constitute a differen-
      tial influence. For example, in this study, knowing (or even suspecting)
      what individual chip rejection rates were could influence efficiency,
      though one would expect that it would affect both groups equally here as
      this involves the comparison of two potentially equal processes, resulting
      in a [+]. On the other hand, competition could enhance the treatment
      effect of both, giving exaggerated outcomes.

15   *Other interactions* [?]. As noted before, contending with macrovariables can
      result in other possible contributing variables that could interact, such as
      who is team leader or supporting engineer?

While the study may confirm that one process has immediate advantages over
the other, sustainable productivity and low rejection rates are something that
would be of equal interest to the company. Potential problems arise when the
more obvious indicators are taken as the only ones necessary, since they may
not be the most valid predictors of success in long-term implementation. This
harks back to the necessity to ask the right question first. No matter what the
quality of the design may be, it cannot make up for other errors in judgement.

Table 7.1 allows you to compare the potential of these two designs to control
extraneous variables and enhance validity. Now consider the example in Activity 7.1.

Activity 7.1

Recall that in Activity 4.1, a study was conducted to test the effect of the
use of positive reinforcement in the classroom. The standardized test was
considered to be highly valid and had a published reliability of 0.84.

(a)   Complete the variable map you started for Activity 4.1(b) so as to
      include any potential sources of extraneous variables related to cate-
      gories 9–15.

(b)   For each of the seven new potential sources of invalidity and con-
      founding listed below, enter a − if not controlled, + if controlled,
      ? if control is uncertain, or < blank > if not applicable in the [ ],
      and say why.

      9   *Direction/nature of causality uncertain* [ ]
      10   *Unnatural/invalid experiment/treatment* [ ]
      11   *Invalid measurement of variables* [ ]
      12   *Instrument reliability* [ ]
      13   *Learning from instrument* [ ]
      14   *Instrument reacts with independent variable/treatment* [ ]
      15   *Other interactions* [ ]

(c)   How have these influenced your evaluation of the justifiability of the
      conclusions and why? What could have been done that would have
      improved the study?

TABLE 7.1
Summary of basic experimental designs with potential sources of invalidity and confounding of results* 'best' ratings are given, some of which could be worse for individual studies depending on how they are carried out

B. Experimental designs

Potential sources of invalidity and confounding

Design description	Design structure (time sequence of events)	1 No comparison across groups	2 Time: other events	3 Time: maturation	4 Selection: sample (and assignment)	5 Selection: regression	6 Selection: sample stability	7 Interaction of time with sample	8 Interaction of ind. var. with sample	9 Direction/nature of causality uncertain	10 Unnatural/invalid exper./treatment	11 Invalid measurement of variables	12 Instrument reliability	13 Learning from instrument	14 Instrument reacts with ind. variable	15 Other interactions
B2 *Pre- and post-test/ observation of proposed dependent variable with single event of possible independent variable with a control.*	$RS \rightarrow \begin{cases} RA_a \rightarrow O_{a1} \rightarrow X_a \rightarrow O_{a2} \\ RA_0 \rightarrow O_{01} \rightarrow X_0 \rightarrow O_{02} \end{cases}$	+	+	+	+	+	+	+	?	+	?	?	+	+	−	?
B3 *Post-test/observation only with a control group.*	$RS \rightarrow \begin{cases} RA_a \rightarrow X_a \rightarrow O_a \\ RA_0 \rightarrow X_0 \rightarrow O_0 \end{cases}$	+	?	?	+	+	?	?	?	+	?	?	+	+	?	?

*Key: + compensated for by design; − not compensated; ? compensation uncertain, < blank > not relevant or covered in this chapter.

Quasi-experimental, ex post facto and correlational designs

Recall that these designs tend to lack some of the controls traditionally associated with true experimental designs, often taking place in 'field' conditions rather than a laboratory. Revisiting the exemplar studies provided earlier, we will introduce some new considerations to be taken into account when planning to employ such designs.

Design C2: Non-equivalent control group design with pre-tests (quasi-experimental)

In Chapter 4, we considered a revised evaluation of the Super Catflap Ltd plan for increasing productivity by offering a bonus of shares as an incentive if staff worked more efficiently. The outcome that was determined to be an indicator of efficiency (or lack thereof) was microchip failures per day. The use of existing non-equivalent groups (established and new employees) to provide treatment and control groups overcame some of the criticisms of the earlier study. There are a number of similarities to the experimental design B2, and, with respect to measuring outcomes, some of the same limitations. The problem of reinforcement psychology was overcome: if productivity increased (the outcome) then the bonus (reinforcement) would be provided, now awarded *after* the action to be reinforced. Several sources of invalidity arise when considering the treatment and measurement of consequences:

- The groups are not equivalent, each bringing with it traits that could influence the outcomes.
- The structure of the study and award of bonuses would be hard to hide from the control group.
- Would the plan effectively transfer to the entire staff as policy?
- Does the monitoring of productivity have as much influence on worker motivation as does the bonus?

While the design is a significant improvement over the initial single group, it is still flawed as a mechanism that would provide maximally valid decision support information. Figure 7.3 shows the sources of potential extraneous variables that might introduce invalidity; compare this with Figure 4.4. The following covers each of the second seven potential sources of invalidity.

9   *Direction/nature of causality uncertain* [?]. While pre- and post-treatment testing/observation should allow one to determine the time sequence of events, and the direction and nature of causality seem defensible here, the fact that the groups are not equivalent brings the nature of the potential causal relationship into doubt. Some intrinsic trait that varies between the two groups could be the cause of the difference in productivity, which could be as simple as new employee enthusiasm versus old employee cynicism.

10   *Unnatural/invalid experiment/treatment* [?]. Since the 'treatment' was a change in income for a selected group and it would be virtually impossible to hide this from other employees (no placebo), it is unlikely that this could

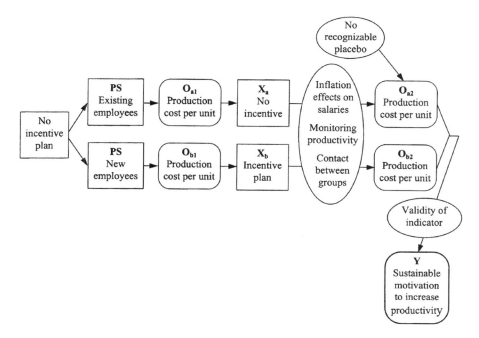

FIGURE 7.3
An enhanced
variable map for the
revised productivity
study at Super
Catflap Ltd

be considered natural. Yet such situations offer a greater opportunity for designs that are more natural than some of the true experimental ones. Here, even if employees productivity monitoring were unobtrusive but known, the nature of the experiment could even influence the control group since they would probably not want to appear to be unproductive.

11   *Invalid measurement of variables* [?]. With pre- and post-treatment observation the design allows one to monitor the dependent variable, and radical unexpected outcomes before and after might provide some indication of a potential problem. The problem in this study is extrapolating the results to the future on the basis of just these observations. The questions still exist whether this would transfer to a more permanent situation, whether the high productivity rate would be sustainable over time. As before, it is not possible to control for invalidity in any design. Convenient measures are not always the most valid, so what would you suggest as additional measures that would enhance the validity of any conclusions?

12   *Instrument reliability* [?]. This is dependent on the nature of the measure, if considering consistency. Here this is dependent on monitoring the number of units produced per hour, a simple counting process. What might influence the reliability would be the period over which the count was made: do workers tend to be more productive on certain days of the week? Were all the counts made on the same day of the week? Would one group be differentially affected by the measuring process and not perform consistently?

13   *Learning from instrument* [−]. Here the instrument could interact differently with the two groups since they are not equivalent. Knowledge that their productivity was being monitored could differentially influence their subsequent performance. For example, new employees might be more afraid of

losing their jobs than established ones, thus monitoring their productivity would potentially have a greater impact than the incentive scheme.

14 *Instrument reacts with independent variable/treatment* [−]. This is a good example of where this could be true. The treatment subjects will probably be more responsive to the bonus (X) because their productivity is being measured (O), but, as noted in 9 above, which is the cause of any increased productivity: the bonus or fear of being identified as under-productive?

15 *Other interactions* [−]. Due to the non-equivalence of groups as well as their non-representativeness, there is the potential for the sample to interact with other events so as to provide extraneous variables.

What would you suggest for improvements in the implementation of this design? It has the potential for resolving the issue, as long as the outcomes are unambiguously defined and they relate to the original question: would an incentive plan increase productivity?

The second study in this category of designs was an improved version of the one carried out to determine the desirability of incorporating playrooms in clinics for pre-school children. The new approach included pre- and post-treatment unobtrusive measures of attendance used to indicate parental attitudes of both groups. While the reliability of the indicator would depend upon the accuracy of the records of attendance, the validity of using changes in frequency of attendance as an indicator of parental attitude could be challenged. One goal appears to have been achieved, that the parents bring their children more frequently, but why is still unknown. Figure 7.4 shows the newly identified potential variables in an enhanced variable map which can be compared to the original in Figure 4.7. In its present form, due to the inadequacy of the indicators, the results do not provide sufficient evidence to resolve the issue.

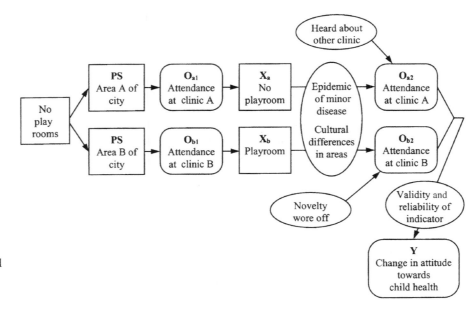

FIGURE 7.4 Enhance variable map for quasi-experimental design for determining value of playrooms in child care clinics (trial group observations, O_b and control group observations, O_a)

9   *Direction/nature of causality uncertain* [?]. While pre- and post-treatment observations were carried out, the non-random sampling would still leave some doubt as to the possible cause(s) of the outcome: could group idiosyncrasies contribute? Matching groups would reduce the possibility of this, allowing a [+].

10   *Unnatural/invalid experiment/treatment* [?]. If the groups have no contact with each other during the study, then there is no need for a placebo. Thus this particular study could receive a [+], as it was conducted under field conditions.

11   *Invalid measurement of variables* [?]. With pre- and post-treatment observation of attendance, resulting in the change in rate of attendance as the dependent variable, it is still not possible to justify that attitudes towards child health care have improved. No design by itself can guarantee construct validity and this study in its present form would probably merit a [−]. If the question were related simply to increased attendance, then there would be evidence to support it though without any enlightenment as to why.

12   *Instrument reliability* [?]. As both groups were subject to the same attendance recording system, any instrument reliability would have been much the same. On the other hand, not being exactly equivalent groups, one does not know whether the scheme of recording attendance is an equivalently reliable indicator of attitude towards child health for both. For example, if one area were predominantly of one religious persuasion and the period of the study included a religious holiday that prevented going out, then frequencies for this area would be unnaturally lower.

13   *Learning from instrument* [−]. Usually this is a minus, but the main part of the study used unobtrusive observation of attendance, so that there would be no learning from the pre-test (initial observations), so this study would receive a [+] this time.

14   *Instrument reacts with independent variable/treatment* [−]. This is often a minus because instruments frequently involve subjects directly (tests, questionnaires), but here the main instrument was observation of attendance, thus this particular study would result in a [+].

15   *Other interactions* [−]. This could be interactions due to the non-equivalence of groups which should have been investigated.

  This is a good example of where it would be worthwhile going back to the original question. Was the aim simply to get parents to bring their children to a pre-school health clinic? Or was there a more ambitious aim of changing attitudes? If it was the first, then the study did seem to succeed and could attribute the cause (at least for these two groups) to the playroom. If the aim was the second, then there is scant evidence to support any success in changing attitudes.

Design D3: Post-test/observation only, with control group (ex post facto)

This design involves observing the potential effects of life events (potential independent variable) on subject characteristics (the dependent variable). In the example in Chapter 4, Professor Boffin wanted to investigate the type of thinking demanded by physics, chemistry, and biology teachers (randomly selected, the subject they taught being the independent variable $\underline{X}$). Each one submitted a sample test for which the questions were classified according to the level of thinking they demanded (O). This was considered to be an indication of the emphasis on problem-solving in their classrooms (dependent variable, **Y**). An inter-judge reliability coefficient of 0.78 on classification of questions in a random selection of six tests using a panel of four experts was reported. The validity of using Bloom's (1956) taxonomy, described in detail in Chapter 10, as a classification tool was justified through reference to a wide selection of research and it is used by examining bodies, plus links drawn between the various levels and generic skills in science needed to solve problems and conduct investigations. Some uncertainty exists as to whether or not the cognitive emphasis of tests could be a valid indicator of the type of teaching. Some teachers devise examinations more difficult than the level of their teaching in order to provide a 'challenge'. Others might give easier questions than the problems or activities set in class. These issues have been added to the variable map in Figure 7.5, which can be compared to the original in Figure 4.8. Using the second set of categories, the potential sources of invalidity are as follows:

9   *Direction/nature of causality uncertain* [−]. The direction and nature of causality as implied here would be very difficult to determine. For example, is it the chemistry or physics background that compels teachers to ask the questions they do, or did they become physics or chemistry teachers because they were drawn to those types of questions typical of the discipline? This would be equivalent to Figure 6.1(a), both hypothesized variables caused by a third. Alternatively, it is possible to suggest that it is not the science discipline that is the cause, but subsequent teacher training, experiences in the classroom, or even national examinations. This would be equivalent to Figure 6.1(b), a complex causality chain. While the use of macrovariables such as these is more relevant to real problems, they introduce considerable difficulty when trying to establish causality. The best that

FIGURE 7.5
Enhanced variable map for Professor Boffin's study of teaching and testing in the sciences

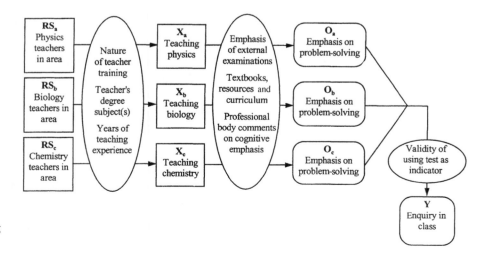

may be concluded in such a study is one of association without suggesting direct causality.

10   *Unnatural/invalid experiment/treatment* [+]. This study is typical, employing the design as a consequence of trying to investigate real-life situations, thus it would be surprising (though not impossible) if it were unnatural.

11   *Invalid measurement of variables* [?]. In particular, there is a potential to apply weak classification systems to subjects as part of the independent variable. This is not the case here (which subject is taught is clear), unlike situations that might use such categories as social class, level of anxiety, or even severity of pain experienced by a patient. On the other hand, the validity of the dependent variable as an indicator of what goes on in the classroom is questionable and validity can not be guaranteed by the design alone.

12   *Instrument reliability* [?]. The classification of questions was a reasonably reliable process, as indicated, so this study might receive a [+]. On the other hand, whether the voluntary submission of tests is a reliable way of obtaining representative questions, or whether tests are equally reliable indicators of classroom activity for the three groups, is questionable. The design itself would not ensure high instrument reliability.

13   *Learning from instrument* [+]. There is only one measure and it occurs after the so-called treatment (life experience), so learning from the instrument should be unlikely. There would be the possibility that which test was selected for submission could be influenced if the teachers' had any knowledge of the purpose of the research. In other words, the teachers could choose ones with atypical emphasis. Existing practice is being investigated and the outcomes were not known until after the study, thus this particular study would seem still to deserve a [+].

14   *Instrument reacts with independent variable/treatment* [?]. Here the independent variable is based upon sampling, random selection from existing populations. Therefore, not unlike the situation in the quasi-experimental design above, there could be a different response between groups to having their test questions investigated. In other words, one population may respond differently to the instrument. For example in this study, if chemistry teachers in general had been admonished for being 'too demanding' or 'too easy' in recent journals, conferences or by politicians, they might be selective in their choices of examinations for submission.

15   *Other interactions* [?]. Considering that this study is typical of those employing such a design in that they tend to involve macrovariables, there is a reasonable possibility that there would be other interactions.

Thus, while it is possible to compare cognitive emphasis on tests, it is more difficult to justify making an inference about teaching in the classroom. Additional observations would need to be carried out if a valid comparison were to be made across subjects.

Design E1: One group observed (correlational)

In Chapter 4, we considered a survey of 1000 randomly selected students in England. The study provided correlations across O-level examination results,

A-level examination results (both of which could be considered highly reliable and possessing content validity), first-year university grades and an instrument for determining how definite career plans were (see Figure 4.9). This last instrument had a published value of 0.78 for reliability (internal consistency) and its validity was corroborated by a team of four psychologists, though there was no information available on the parallel traits of the university grades. To add to the variable map in Figure 4.9 would not provide many new insights into the analysis, considering that this is a correlational study lacking any controls.

From Figure 4.9, it would seem that there is no way of being absolutely sure of the nature of causality, though the study might supply some ideas for more structured studies that could provide information about the more important factors that may contribute to university success. Also, it could be argued that 'success' in university is not just a matter of grades or grade point averages (GPAs). The young person coming in with a poor pre-university academic record and completes the first year with a B average would, by one definition, be a greater success than the one who enters with an excellent record and also finishes with a B average. In addition, while national examination boards in the UK tend to go to great lengths to ensure validity and reliability, the timing of end-of-term/semester/year examinations in universities simply does not allow similar efforts to be made, thus their reliability and validity will not be as high (including consistency across universities). Also, it is essential that students learn how to take examinations through experience, so instruments may partially measure how 'test-wise' they are as well as the subject matter. Finally, questionnaires on careers cannot help but raise awareness, thus this instrument may influence outcomes, though it is difficult to imagine a questionnaire of this sort that would not. This may call for a longer-term study using less interactive measures when devising more structure studies. Let us consider the second set of seven categories:

9   *Direction/nature of causality uncertain* [−]. A study of this type covering a long time-span has little hope of establishing causality, considering that there are probably other variables (perseverance, self-regulation, self-confidence, aptitude, intelligence, social class, etc.) that could quite conceivably influence all the variables measured. While some of these are very interesting from the viewpoint of identifying predictors, the results do not constitute evidence for causal links.

10   *Unnatural/invalid experiment/treatment* [+]. As a survey of existing conditions, this has the advantage of enquiring about reality.

11   *Invalid measurement of variables* [?]. The validity of the implied dependent variable, university success, is questionable since it is doubtful that first-year grades are a necessarily valid measure of success. Some consistency may be maintained across institutions through the external examiner system, where degree course examinations are monitored annually by academics from other institutions, but this would only check that a minimum level of consistency of content and severity of grading exists across institutions.

12 *Instrument reliability* [−]. Unlike national examinations, which tend to have a high level of reliability and comparable validity, no two universities, or even departments of the same subject, have the same examinations. Also, few, if any, endeavour even to check the reliability of the examinations that make up year grades. Such lack of reliability would not be compensated for by comparison to another group.

13 *Learning from instrument* [−]. It is almost assumed that university students get better at examinations and assessment, or they do not survive, though this is a situation that is somewhat unique. Many correlational studies would be one-off and not involve the repeated use of an instrument.

14 *Instrument reacts with independent variable/treatment* [?]. Such instruments themselves can raise awareness of the need to make decisions about a career and can increase motivation. Even the *time* when such a test is administered in this type of study might determine its potential impact as a variable. Also, considering the time-scale and nature of the influences on the subjects, examinations could be considered to be part of a treatment, as they get them frequently.

15 *Other interactions* [?]. As noted earlier, studies over time that are really looking to establish predictive instruments rather than causality are likely to have other interactions, even between the sample and the instruments or experiences encountered.

The best such a study could hope to establish would be the predictive validity of instruments or past performances. Whether any of these, such as the propensity to plan a career, had a causal link with university performance (intuitively one might suspect that it does) would need to be established through a more experimental or a better ex post facto structure.

Table 7.2 provides a summary of the characteristics of the three studies described above. While there are more pitfalls than for true experimental designs (see Table 7.1), some of these provide the distinct advantage of studies in real situations rather than the laboratory. Now try Activity 7.2.

ADDITIONAL DESIGNS

It is fairly obvious that a perfect design has not been described and that even the better ones are sometimes fraught with potential pitfalls. At this point it is worthwhile introducing two more designs, again not perfect (as there is no such thing), which offer new structures that avoid problems in certain situations. The first is a true experimental design that combines the best traits of the two considered earlier, B2 (pre- and post-test/observation) and B3 (post-test/observation only). Referred to as the Solomon four, it includes pre- and post-tests but the design compensates for potential confounding from potential interaction between the measuring instrument and the independent variable. The second is a quasi-experimental design that involves multiple observations/tests over time, before and after treatment, on a single group: a time series design.

TABLE 7.2
Summary of quasi-experimental and ex post facto designs with potential sources of invalidity and confounding of results; *'best' ratings are given, some of which could be worse for individual studies depending on how they are carried out

Quasi-experimental and ex post facto designs: Design description	Design structure (time sequence of events)	Potential sources of invalidity and confounding														
		1. No comparison across groups	2. Time: other events	3. Time: maturation	4. Selection: sample (and assignment)	5. Selection: regression	6. Selection: sample stability	7. Interaction of time with sample	8. Interaction of ind. var. with sample	9. Direction/nature of causality uncertain	10. Unnatural/invalid exper./treatment	11. Invalid measurement of variables	12. Instrument reliability	13. Learning from instrument	14. Instrument reacts with ind. variable	15. Other interactions
C2 Non-equivalent control group design with pre-tests. Original sample is not random, but already there, as with work groups, classrooms. Treatment group may be randomly determined.	$(RA_a) \to O_{a1} \to X_a \to O_{a2}$ $(RA_0) \to O_{01} \to X_0 \to O_{02}$	+	+	+	—	?	+	—	?	?	?	+	?	—	—	—
D3 Post-test/observation only with a control group, but independent variable is observed, not manipulated.	$RS_a \to \underline{X_a} \to O_a$ $RS_0 \to \underline{X_0} \to O_0$	+	?	?	+	+	?	?	?	—	+	?	?	+	?	?
E1 One group observed for a number of traits to see if any relationships exist.	$RS \to O_a, O_b, O_c \cdots$	—	—	—	+		?			—	+	?	—	?	?	?

*Key: see Table 7.1.

Activity 7.2

Recall Professor Blooper's study, described in Activity 4.2, that investigated a possible link between aggressive behaviour in children and watching aggression on television. The amount of aggression in a specific programme was quantified by counting the number of three-second intervals that contained aggressive actions by characters. The reliability across a panel of researchers in classifying a set of six programmes was 0.67.

(a)   Draw an enhanced version of the variable map you drew for this study in Activity 4.2.

(b)   For each of the eight new potential sources of invalidity and confounding listed below, enter a − if not controlled, + if controlled, ? if control is uncertain, or < blank > if not applicable in the [ ], and say why.

    9   *Direction/nature of causality uncertain* [ ]
  10 *Unnatural/invalid experiment/treatment* [ ]
  11 *Invalid measurement of variables* [ ]
  12 *Instrument reliability* [ ]
  13 *Learning from instrument* [ ]
  14 *Instrument reacts with independent variable/treatment* [ ]
  15 *Other interactions* [ ]

(c)   How have these affected your evaluation of the justifiability of the conclusions, and why?

Design B5: Solomon four

This design divides the randomly selected set of subjects into four groups: two which will receive the treatment (RA_a and RA'_a) and two which will not (Ra_0 and RA'_0), two which will undergo a pre-test (RA_a and Ra_0) and two which will not (RA'_a and RA'_0):

$$RS \rightarrow \begin{cases} RA_a \rightarrow O_{a1} \rightarrow X_a \rightarrow O_{a2} \\ RA_0 \rightarrow O_{01} \rightarrow X_0 \rightarrow O_{02} \\ RA'_a \rightarrow \phantom{O_{01}} X_a \rightarrow O'_{a2} \\ RA'_0 \rightarrow \phantom{O_{01}} X_0 \rightarrow O'_{02} \end{cases}$$

Such a design would allow the detection of any influence from other events, maturation and pre-tests, thus the major improvements over B2 or B3 are as follows (Campbell and Stanley, 1963):

2 *Time: other events* [+]. The possible effects of this would be indicated by differences between the pre-treatment tests/observations (O_{a1} and O_{01}) and the final observation on the group that received neither the pre-treatment tests/observations nor even the treatment (O'_{02}). If there were no effects (as one would hope) there would be little difference among the three observations.

3 *Time: maturation* [+]. This is improved for the same reasons as 2 above.

13 *Learning from instrument* [+]. This design allows one to check this possible outcome by multiple comparisons. For example, if this design were used instead of B2 for the exemplar study on girls' attitudes towards computers above, the expectation would be that those experiencing the learning materials would have a higher score on the attitude test than those not. This assumes that the following relationships would be found in terms of scores: O_{a2} greater than O_{a1}; O_{a2} greater than O_{02}; O'_{a2} greater than O'_{02}; and O'_{a2} greater than O_{01}. In other words, the two post-treatment groups would have scores greater than the scores for the two control groups *and* greater than the two pre-treatment scores (see Figure 7.6).

14 *Instrument reacts with independent variable/treatment* [+]. This design avoids the potential confounding that is part of design B3, by allowing the researcher to use pre-tests where necessary but comparing the final results to an equivalent group that did not have a pre-test. Differences here with the treatment group but not the control group would indicate a reaction between the pre-test and the independent variable/treatment, something that could go unnoticed in design B3.

All other potential sources are the same as for B3. Such a design would require a sample twice the size of the other two experimental designs. This may seem like a heavy price to pay just to check that the pre-test does not interfere with the study, but this is potentially a major source of confounding when the instrument is more than unobtrusive observation. One should also remember that ethical issues can be raised about whether or not one should even carry out observations or tests on subjects without their knowledge of the process and/or understanding of why the study is being conducted.

FIGURE 7.6
Anticipated relationships between pairs of observations: the first of each pair is expected to be greater than the second (the one pointed to)

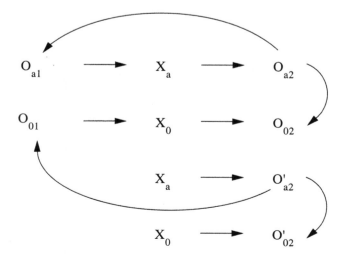

An alternative way of considering this design is to think of it as a two-dimensional study, with treatment/control on one dimension and pre-test/no pre-test on the other, as shown in Figure 7.7. Assuming interval data, this would be evaluated using analysis of variance. Now carry out Activity 7.3.

Activity 7.3

Which of the studies described earlier in this chapter and in Chapter 4 would have been greatly improved by employing a Solomon four design? Would the added cost and effort have been justified?

Design C6: Time series

Time series designs are characterized by periodic measurement or observations, both before and after any treatment. Only the simplest design will be considered here, though obviously this could be combined with earlier designs to provide some complex combinations (see, for example, Campbell and Stanley, 1963). A simple time series design involves making regular periodic observations on a group for some time, providing some treatment, then continuing the observations:

$$(RS) \rightarrow O_1 \rightarrow O_2 \rightarrow O_3 \rightarrow X \rightarrow O_4 \rightarrow O_5 \rightarrow O_6$$

Six observations are shown here, but obviously more could be introduced. There are several sound reasons for employing such a design in the social sciences, not least of all to see if any change persists. Figure 7.8 shows some possible measurable quantitative outcomes, each point being a mean score for a group at the indicated periodic observation. The explanations are as follows:

(a) *A lasting effect:* the scores are consistently low before treatment and high after treatment, staying high. This is what one would hope to see.

	No Treatment	Treatment
Pre-test	O_{02}	O_{a2}
No Pre-test	O'_{02}	O'_{a2}

FIGURE 7.7
Solomon four design shown as two-dimensional

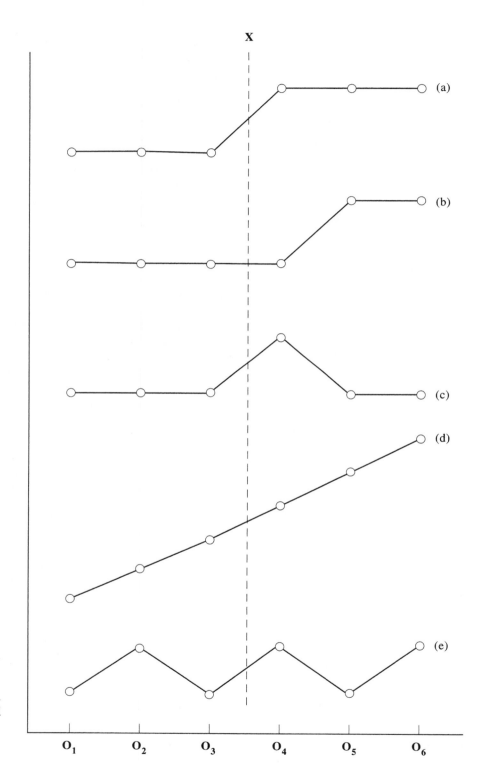

X

FIGURE 7.8
Five potential
observation/test
result patterns for a
time series design
(single group)
around a treatment,
X; each is explained
in the text (after
Campbell and
Stanley, 1963)

(b) *A delayed influence:* the effect is not seen until the second observation after the treatment, and persists. Even design B2 with a control group would not detect this, thus the effect could go unnoticed.

(c) *A spurious effect* or one that does not last: the score rises but then falls, thus this is possibly a short-term effect or, alternatively, it is uncertain that there was an effect. Again, even design B2 would not detect this, and any claim of an effect could be dubious in some circumstances.

(d) *An extraneous variable:* there is gentle continuous rise. Other two-measure designs might detect this trend, particularly with a control group. On its own, this could be the result of maturation.

(e) *Erratic results:* the scores rise and fall, possibly due to an invalid or unreliable measuring instrument. Alternatively some traits have time-dependent or seasonal variations and any net change would be observed only with a time series design.

Other patterns could exist that would provide evidence for a more valid conclusion where a single observation/test before and after treatment (even with a control group) might not reveal the true pattern. Such a design would be optimized by having two groups, one being the control.

For the purpose of exploring the basic design, consider the problem of Ms Magillicutty, headmistress of a secondary school. As in most schools, there were absences that were not excusable, thought it was felt that they were not always detected (forged notes, good acting on student's part, etc.). Being concerned that this might be occurring, Ms Magillicutty decided to monitor the situation over several weeks, then introduce an attendance incentive. It was important that students with legitimate reasons for absences would not be or feel punished, nor should the incentive be so great as to encourage students with diseases to come to school anyway and spread them around. In consultation with students, it seemed that the most popular out-of-school activity at that time might provide a starting-point, so it was decided to pave over a section of the playground for a skateboard/rollerblade obstacle course. Monitoring would then continue to see not only if it worked, but also if the impact persevered. Figure 7.9 graphs the results of the study, which seem to have confirmed Ms Magillicutty's suspicions, though there were several sources of doubt:

• This is only one school and one group; could some other event have influenced the students in parallel with the study?
• Were all students financially able to participate?
• Was there already a downward trend due to impending examinations?
• Other events: new jobs in the area for qualified school leavers.
• Students caught cutting classes are suspended for two weeks.
• Is tackling attendance this way going to improve the quality of education?

Figure 7.10 provides a variable map for this study. There are a number of potential sources of invalidity, extraneous variables not controlled by a design with one sample group. On the other hand, some issues would not be resolved without multiple observations. Due to the uniqueness of this design, all 15 potential sources of invalidity will be considered:

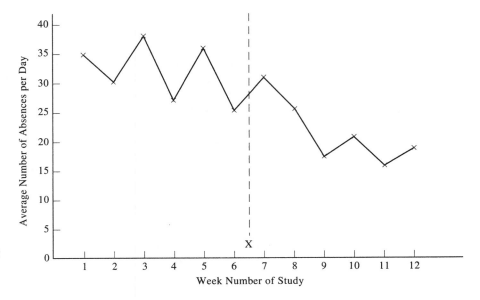

FIGURE 7.9
Absences over time as monitored in Ms Magillicutty's school, with X indicating the time at which the incentive was introduced

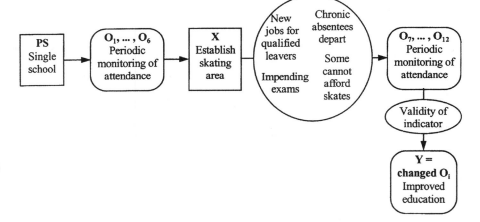

FIGURE 7.10
Variable map for Ms Magillicutty's initiative to reduce voluntary absences

1 *No comparison across groups* [−]. In the basic design there is only one group, but it could be extended to two groups if it were combined with a more experimental design.

2 *Time: events* [−]. Without a second group, it is not possible to control for the possibility that other events caused any change, even if the pattern were analogous to (a) or (b) in Figure 7.8. To overcome this would require a careful observation of external events to identify any that could impinge on the results, which is extremely difficult in real situations outside laboratory conditions. This is potentially the greatest weakness of the design. In Ms Magillicutty's study, students are subjected to a wide variety of external influences (for example, an increase in jobs in the area for qualified secondary school leavers).

3   *Time: maturation* [?]. A steady rise over an appropriated period, as shown
    in pattern (d) in Figure 7.8 (or decline, depending on the variable), might
    indicate maturation. This design would possibly allow its detection,
    though one can never guarantee that maturation would cause an increase
    in such a smooth and regular fashion. It is conceivable that a result such
    as pattern (a) in Figure 7.8 could be the result of maturation if the time-
    scale were too long. Thus this design does provide the potential for identi-
    fying maturation effects, assuming an appropriate time-scale. In Ms Magil-
    licutty's case, the time of year and pending examinations could
    progressively focus the minds of students, encouraging them to attend
    more regularly, thus resulting in a steady decline, and this would need to
    be investigated. A control group would allow a comparison.

4   *Selection: sample (and assignment)* [+]. The group could be randomly
    selected, thus the results should be generalizable to a larger population.
    This does assume that it is one cohort (the same group) being observed
    over the period of the study. In the above example, it is a whole school,
    thus not a representative sample and resulting in a [−] with respect to
    external validity.

5   *Selection: regression* [?]. Regression effects usually result in a change in
    scores towards a mean over time and would be an unlikely explanation
    of a continued increase across the treatment line, but with only one
    group it would not be possible to rule this out when there are multiple mea-
    sures.

6   *Selection: sample stability* [+]. By measuring/observing the group(s) con-
    tinuously, the structure of the study has the opportunity to monitor and
    control drop-out, thus providing an opportunity to determine whether
    the reason anyone withdrew had anything to do with the treatment or
    instruments. For example, were some chronic absentees leaving the
    school permanently?

7   *Interaction of time with sample* [?]. This would not necessarily be controlled,
    and will depend on the nature of the sample group. For example, the age
    range of some groups may make them more susceptible to maturation
    than others. Some groups might be more sensitive to external events over
    the time of the study than others, and without a comparison group any
    extraneous time dependent variables could be difficult to detect.

8   *Interaction of independent variable with sample* [?]. This refers to the possi-
    bility that any effect the treatment might produce could be idiosyncratic to
    the sample, here a specific school.

9   *Direction/nature of causality uncertain* [+]. With multiple observations a
    time sequence should be much easier to establish. The difficulty arises in
    the nature of causal relations which are dependent on the choice of vari-
    ables. There is some uncertainty in this case, so it might be prudent to
    assign it a [?].

10 *Unnatural/invalid experiment/treatment* [?]. In this situation, the study is
    carried out in a school, a natural setting, and not in a laboratory, thus it
    would receive a [+].

11 *Invalid measurement of variables* [?]. While no design can contend totally
    with lack of validity, a radically erratic outcome would be highly noticeable

due to multiple testing and might indicate an invalid measure (like pattern (e) in Figure 7.8). In this case, one threat to construct validity could be the practice of suspending those caught cutting classes: would they appear as absent or not? Either way, it is not their decision. Also, this study does not address the issue of why the students do not attend. Is simple attendance the aim of the school or is learning the goal? Students need to be there in mind as well as body, attendance alone is not sufficient for good education.

12 *Instrument reliability* [?]. This can be a distinct problem when using archival data, as the data may not be recorded consistently (Cook *et al.*, 1990). For example, using hospital records over a period of time for frequency of type of injury could depend on who classified the injury. Recording pain levels in patients could depend upon which nurse was on duty at the time. Low instrument reliability could account for changes such as seen in patterns (a), (b), (c) and (e) in Figure 7.8, if the data were based upon observations of researchers with expectations. This is not a problem for Ms Magillicutty as there was no attempt to distinguish legitimate from non-legitimate absences, so her study would get a [+].

13 *Learning from instrument* [?]. It would seem unlikely that testing at O_3 would influence the results of O_4 alone: any effects would have shown up in earlier results (for example, between O_1 and O_2). In this study, the observations were carried out for purposes of the study without the knowledge of the subjects.

14 *Instrument reacts with independent variable/treatment* [?]. With the continuous testing/observation, there could be a distinct interaction of the treatment and the testing/observation, either positive or negative, and it would not necessarily be detectable with this design. Stanley and Campbell (1963) maintain that, in schools where testing goes on all the time, repeated testing might not have any effect, but schools are not the only situation where such a design could be used. This is also an argument for unobtrusive measurement, an approach taken in the above study, which would merit a [+].

15 *Other interactions* [?]. With a single group and frequent observations, there may be fewer opportunities for these to go undetected, but there are still possibilities with single groups such as classes where the teacher in charge could interact with the treatment or even the testing.

Try Activity 7.4 before continuing.

Activity 7.4

Put yourself in the shoes of a local education authority which hears of Ms Magillicutty's study, and has money to spend on innovative projects: you plan to replicate the study. How would you improve it so that the new results would be sufficiently valid that they could be used to support a decision?

In other situations, there might be a temptation to apply such a design to ex post facto situations – for example, where the X was an event not controlled by the researcher like a national election, natural disaster, etc. A major threat to validity would be the choice of instrument or indicators: their construct validity and reliability could be questioned if they had not been originally designed to be operational definitions of the variables to be considered. Is family expenditure on household appliances a valid indicator of the feel-good factor in the economy? In other words, does a change in spending on appliances, such as might be illustrated in pattern (a) or (b) in Figure 7.8, indicate an improvement in the health of the economy? This one is left to the politicians and economists to battle over.

Also, as Campbell and Stanley (1963) note, using an observed change and then looking for a possible X is highly inappropriate (data snooping) as there is no justification for causality based upon opportunistic association. Such an approach would provide no greater support for causality than a correlational study, but could be a starting point for a more rigorous investigation. Table 7.3 summarizes the potential sources of invalidity for the time series design and a number of examples can be found in Cook and Campbell (1979) and Cook *et al.* (1990).

There are many possible variations on this theme, such as introducing multiple treatments, say before O_2, O_3, O_4, O_5 and O_6. In some situations, this would be advantageous, though not without the possibility of introducing new difficulties. A sequence of treatment, measurement, treatment, measurement, etc., would raise the issues as to whether it would be (externally) valid to extend generalizations to real-life situations where only one application of the treatment would be administered. For example, would it be reasonable to expect the same pattern of voluntary return for treatment to exist among non-institutionalized persons dependent on drugs as for those in a clinic? To maintain high external validity, there would be a necessity for explicit instructions as to time sequence and intervals for treatment. Alternatively, it may not be possible to ignore the effects of earlier treatments on later ones, thus multiple treatment may be essential. There is also the danger that multiple treatment would interact with the sample for example, an advertising campaign may be effective only for the already committed and multiple presentation might alienate others.

Now try Activity 7.5 before continuing with the next section.

MULTIVARIATE AND MULTIDIMENSIONAL STUDIES

Up to this point, we have considered basic designs that potentially test only one independent variable. The first clue as to how designs could be constructed to consider more than one variable at a time was provided by the Solomon four where the pre-test was considered to be a potential variable. There are obviously any number of situations where it would be advantageous to consider more than one variable at a time. The value of such studies is that the causal potential of more than one variable can be investigated, as can the possibility that the influence of one variable is most strongly felt when it is in combination with another (interaction effects).

TABLE 7.3 Summary of another experimental design and another quasi-experimental design, with potential sources of invalidity and confounding of results;* 'best' ratings are given, some of which could be worse for individual studies depending on how they are carried out

Design description	Design structure (time sequence of events)	Potential sources of invalidity and confounding														
		1. No comparison across groups	2. Time: other events	3. Time: maturation	4. Selection: sample (and assignment)	5. Selection: regression	6. Selection: sample stability	7. Interaction of time with sample	8. Interaction of ind. var. with sample	9. Direction/nature of causality uncertain	10. Unnatural/invalid exper./treatment	11. Invalid measurement of variables	12. Instrument reliability	13. Learning from instrument	14. Instrument reacts with ind. variable	15. Other interactions
B5 *Solomon four:* combining designs B3 and B4, avoiding confounding by potential source 13.	$RS \rightarrow \begin{cases} RA_a \rightarrow O_{a1} \rightarrow X_a \rightarrow O_{a2} \\ RA_0 \rightarrow O_{01} \rightarrow X_0 \rightarrow O_{02} \\ RA'_a \rightarrow \phantom{O_{01}} X_a \rightarrow O'_{a2} \\ RA'_0 \rightarrow \phantom{O_{01}} X_0 \rightarrow O'_{02} \end{cases}$	+	+	+	+	+	+	+	?	+	?	?	?	+	+	?
C6 *Time series:* a number of observations/tests carried out over time before and after the treatment.	$(RS) \rightarrow O_1 \rightarrow O_2 \rightarrow O_3 \rightarrow X \rightarrow O_4 \rightarrow O_5 \rightarrow O_6$	−	−	?	+	+	+	?	?	+	?	?	?	?	?	?

Activity 7.5

(a)   Freddie Constable wishes to conduct a study to determine the possible effect of a new range of youth centre activities on vandalism among young people using a modified time series design with a control group:

$$(RS) \rightarrow \begin{cases} (RA_a) \rightarrow O_{a1} \rightarrow O_{a2} \rightarrow O_{a3} \rightarrow X_a \rightarrow O_{a4} \rightarrow O_{a5} \rightarrow O_{a6} \\ (RA_0) \rightarrow O_{01} \rightarrow O_{02} \rightarrow O_{03} \rightarrow X_0 \rightarrow O_{04} \rightarrow O_{05} \rightarrow O_{06} \end{cases}$$

One of Freddie's options was to use existing groups (no RS or RA), since the youth centres already exist in his city, in other words, a quasi-experimental design. Suggest what will be observed for the Os, construct a variable map to assist in identifying possible extraneous variables and sources of confounding, and complete a copy of the blank chart (Table 4.7) for this study.

(b)   The second option was a time series design with control group, using random selection (RS) from all the youth centres in the city and random assignment (RA) to the two groups, an experimental design.

Briefly describe why and how each of these designs is an improvement over the basic time series design, whether one has any advantages over the other, and what the limitations of each would be.

The choice of variables and consequential design is frequently a matter of how well the theory is established, how many variables are to be investigated and the nature of intervening variables, including whether they have even been identified. In other words, a lack of understanding of the intervening variables may eliminate experimental or quasi-experimental designs, particularly when the purpose of the study is to explore the possibility of relationships among variables. Without some basis for strongly suspecting that there is a causal relationship between variables, there is a greater chance that the results will produce no support for that relationship. This is particularly true when the relationships obviously consist of multiple independent variables, though the support is weak.

For example, if the research question were to investigate the relationships among women's ability to pursue a career, their educational background, their age and having children, this could be done from two divergent viewpoints. First, it could be hypothesized that there would be significant correlations between career level and age, and between career level and number of children (expected to be negative), which could be repeated for several different levels of education. Note that for the second pair, it is not obvious which variable would cause which: does having children potentially limit one's career aspirations and achievement, or do career women by and large choose not to have many children? This study would produce some interesting, though limited results and would possibly show how closely education and careers are linked, as well as how the number of children and careers are linked.

Alternatively, a second approach might be more informative, proposing a more ambitious hypothesis: that women with specific traits were more disadvantaged in pursuing a career or holding down a job than those without, thus looking for a difference. Therefore, it would be of interest to investigate the impact of amount of education and number of children on women's careers, and it would be desirable (and not difficult) to control for age by including it as a third variable. This second approach assumes a potentially causal relationship: years of education (X_a), age (X_b) and the number of children (X_c), and may influence relative career success (Y), which suggests an ex post facto design. It would be desirable not only to investigate the relationship between each of the potential independent variables and the dependent variable, but also whether various combinations would have any effect. The design will be experimental in structure, but since life will be the laboratory, sampling will be of critical significance, as will be seen.

Pursuing the second approach further, the three independent variables constitute fairly obvious constructs which require minimal effort to define operationally (age ranges, number of children and qualifications), whereas the dependent variable may cause some problems. Career is a concept, but this needs to be refined to become a construct. Success in a career must be defined in terms of levels or degrees (a variable) which in turn would need to take into account a characteristic that can be quantified or at least ranked as part of the operational definition. One possibility is income (ratio data: easy to quantify, but not the only measure of success), another is level on a pay scale (ordinal) or level of responsibility (ordinal). A fourth that is independent of extrinsic reward (salary or position in an organization) but dependent upon intrinsic satisfaction would be the person's own perception of relative success or sense of achievement. All three ordinal measures present problems when defining what constitutes a quantifiable level of career success, but let us leave that issue until later.

Possible hypotheses could be the following:

- Women's career success is dependent on the number of children.
- Women's career success is dependent on their age.
- Women's career success is dependent on their education.
- Women's career success is dependent on interactions of number of children, age and/or educational background.

The last hypothesis allows us to consider issues such as: while women might be initially disadvantaged (i.e., younger women just returning to work), older women might have been able to make up for the time out. Educational background may combine with number of children to increase the disadvantage for better-educated women, because the effect of their being absent from the job scene would have a greater detrimental affect on aspired careers than for the less well educated.

The resulting design could look something like that shown in Figure 7.11, which treats each of the independent variables as a dimension of the matrix. Each cell in the matrix will contain a measure of career success for a group having that combination of three characteristics. Other designs considered so far could also be expanded to include multidimensional studies, and these possibilities will be considered in greater detail in the chapters on statistical tests. When presenting the structure of designs, it has been simplest to describe them in their most basic form as one-dimensional with the minimal number of groups. Do note that many designs can be expanded as illustrated above to include a number of potentially interacting independent variables. As suggested, these designs are often the most interesting, as it can be the interactions that are of the greatest importance. There will be consequences for the selection of statistical tests, required sample sizes, and the likelihood of finding significant differences, as will be seen later.

Earlier, situations were described where there appeared to be the potential for considering interactions which were not included in the experimental design – for example, between the sample and the treatment. If, for example, a differential response to a teaching style (treatment) between boys and girls, then gender could profitably become another variable (dimension) in the study. Which extraneous variables are promoted to becoming variables of interest in a multi-dimensional study will depend on the research question, but this approach is one to keep in mind when planning a study.

SUMMARY

In this chapter and Chapter 4, ten basic designs have been considered using 15 potential sources of confounding and invalidity as a mechanism for systematically identifying potential problems when designing research. One student did ask: 'Is it essential to make sure all 15 are covered?' One could consider presenting the results of one's research for public scrutiny as being equivalent to standing in front of a firing squad. Even if some of the squad are a bit near-sighted, what counts is not so much how many times you are hit, but where. In other words, a number of minor limitations or imperfections may not reduce the validity of your conclusions disastrously and may only limit the quality of

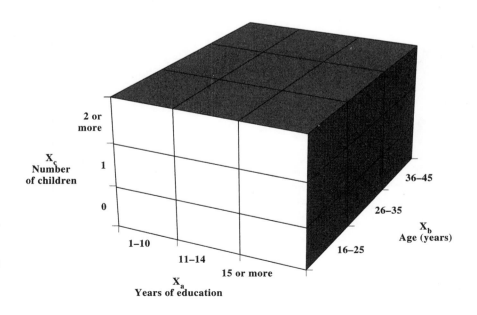

FIGURE 7.11
A model showing the quasi-experimental design for resolving the hypotheses stated (dependent variable: women's career success)

your research slightly, but that one major oversight could be fatal. The point of systematically analysing the research process as one progresses is to minimize problems. Few research designs will be perfect, but by simply being aware of and compensating for or avoiding common pitfalls, you are unlikely to end up with a total disaster. How astute one is at identifying problems before they manifest themselves will more than likely improve with time and experience, and these chapters only present you with a basic outline.

It should be recognized that the rating of designs in Chapters 3, 4, 6 and 7 is that of the author and could vary with individual studies. The ratings are not absolute, they are meant to be guidelines and deviations will likely occur. Thus one should not treat a [+] with complacency, nor should one reject a design with a [−] in several places – there may be ways around these. They are there to flag up potential pitfalls and to help prepare you to survive the firing squad; Activity 7.6 should give you some useful experience. Whether you start with the 15 potential sources or variable maps, or use them together, is up to you. They are intellectual tools to help you plan research while minimizing sources of invalidity.

Activity 7.6

In Activity 4.3 you wrote a brief outline of the design for your research or for a piece of research you had read about. Return to Table 4.7 and complete columns 9–15. Place a +, −, ? or leave a blank in each column according to your evaluation. Duplicate it with a brief description of the study (and perhaps a revised variable map) for distribution in class and be prepared to defend your evaluations as indicated in the columns.

PART II
MEASUREMENT DESIGN

PRINCIPLES OF
MEASUREMENT AND
COLLECTING FACTUAL
DATA

8

The various designs considered in earlier chapters depended on operationally defining variables through some form of classification or measurement. In many, it was even necessary to establish a rigorous definition of populations so that representative samples could be acquired for experimental and quasi-experimental studies. This process required placing people into categories dependent on descriptive attributes (occupation, gender, education) or quantitative traits (age, income, number of children, IQ), in order to delimit to whom generalizations could be made. Random assignment ideally follows to ensure distribution of other traits equally across treatment groups, or treatment and control groups, to test the impact of the purported independent variable, X.

Taking a different view for the ex post facto designs described, subjects had to be selected according to the trait(s) associated with the proposed independent variable ($\underline{X}$), as life events were the treatment. Such categorization results in nominal or ordinal groupings of subjects, often as part of defining the independent variable. Categorization may also be necessary for the dependent variable (Y), such as for which party subjects voted, what type of product was selected, which person was selected for a trait by subjects. Frequently the hypothesized dependent variable will be an outcome that is measured (achievement on a test, income). This occasionally can result in confusion as some traits or characteristics will be the independent variable in one study and the dependent variable in another, depending on the nature of causality being hypothesized. For example, in one study it may be suggested that the amount learned is *enhanced by* a certain teaching approach, whereas in another the amount learned may *determine* the potential to get a job. The examples shown in Table 8.1 illustrate the range of possible combinations, each the result of the statement of the research hypotheses. The choice of statistical tests available to resolve a study

	Independent variable (X)		
Dependent variable (Y):	**Nominal**	**Ordinal**	**Interval/ratio**
Nominal	If investigating voting practices of various groups, then does the organization to which they belong (*X*) seem to determine the party for which they vote (*Y*)?	Does religious preference (*Y*) vary with different age groups: young, middle-aged, retired (*X*)?	To test the tee-shirt hypothesis 'Insanity: you get it from your children' investigate the relationship between the frequency of four major mental illnesses (*Y*) among parents with different numbers of children (*X*).
Ordinal	Does the annual number of attendances at a clinic (*Y*) depend on whether it has a playroom for children (*X*)?	Does level of political conservatism (*Y*), high, medium or low, as determined by score ranges on Bloggs' Test of Conservatism, depend on social class (*X*)?	Does the level of educational qualification achieved (*Y*) depend on parental income (*X*)?
Interval/ ratio	Does the production rate in a factory (*Y*) depend on which production process (X_1, X_2 or X_3) is being used, as seen in Chapter 4 with the Widget-Digit microchip production process?	Does general mathematical ability, as measured by a standardized test (*Y*), depend on the Piagetian developmental stage of children of a given chronological age (*X*)?	What is the relationship between IQ (*X*) at age 16 and income at age 40 (*Y*)?

TABLE 8.1
Examples of studies with combinations of types of scales for proposed independent and dependent variables

will be limited by the type of variables involved – in other words, in which cell the study belongs.

As we have seen, sometimes the variables are simply a matter of classification, or rank ordering, while others require some form of measurement resulting in quantification. All three of these processes involve establishing an operational definition for some concept or construct: classifying, rank ordering and devising quantified measures. Just how these are carried out will depend on the variables, but the range of tools and possible instruments available is extensive. To explore the possibilities, we will first place data into one of two broad categories:

- classification or ranking (nominal or ordinal) data, requiring non-measurement-based judgements (though measurements may underlie some judgements); or
- data from measurement instruments that are operational definitions of quantifiable traits (interval or ratio), requiring measurement and instruments.

Then we will group the methods of acquiring the corresponding data into one of four types of instrument or techniques commonly used to define them operationally:

- direct factual data collection;
- questions – scales, choices, open-ended with keys;
- observations/structured interviews;
- tests.

This will allow us to keep sight of the forest while examining the trees. These categories will also allow an overview of how this chapter and the next three will cover the realm of measurement in particular.

First, consider the sources of data to be collected:

1   *Classification traits*, data resulting in categories (nominal) or ranks (ordinal), typical of independent variables (but not exclusively), such as:

- demographic or background – age, sex, marital status, number of children, income, number of rooms in home, education, ethnicity, occupation, etc.;
- social class, based on several indicators;
- preferences – political, religion, membership in organizations;
- intentions, expectations or aspirations;
- social and economic indicators – crime rate, quality of housing, gross enrolment ratio in schools, gross national product, unemployment, infant mortality, etc.;
- personality, abnormality, mental illness, etc.;
- type of organization or institution – schools, businesses, establishments, etc.

2   *Quantification of other personal traits* that result in continuous data (typically dependent variables, though not exclusively), such as:

- attitudes, beliefs, perceptions, opinions, degree of commitment;
- personal traits, such as honesty, perseverance, or citizenship;
- aptitude;
- achievement;
- intelligence, creativity, etc.

While this is not to be exhaustive, it does provide a wide range of applications that can form the basis of further discussion.

Table 8.2 indicates common uses of each of the four types of instruments or techniques, with some types of variables being operationally defined by alternative types of instruments, and others by combinations. Thus the four chapters in this part of the book address the issues and skills as follows. This chapter is an introduction to the general principles of measurement and ways of collecting factual information from respondents. Chapter 9 covers questions and scales, including structured interviews and observation schedules, for quantifying the strength of attitudes, views and perceptions held by subjects. Chapter 10 will consider the design of tests and observation schedules related to measurement of achievement; the creation of standardized tests of aptitude, intelligence and creativity is somewhat beyond the scope of this book, though their basic char-

TABLE 8.2
Summary of
instrument types
and purposes, with
chapter coverage
indicated

Purpose	Instrument type			
	Direct factual data collection	**Questions: choices, scales**	**Observations/ structured interviews**	**Tests**
Classification/ranking based on quantitative data:				
Background, personal and demographic data	8			
Social, economic and performance indicators	8			
Social class (possibly using several indicators)	8	9	9	
Type of organization or institution	8	9	9	
Preferences		9	9	
Personality traits		9	9	
Quantification of other personal traits that result in continuous data:				
Attitudes, perceptions		9	9	
Values and motives		9	9	
Achievement			10	10
Aptitude			10	10
Intelligence, creativity, etc.			10	10

acteristics will be considered. Chapter 11 provides some statistical instruments to assist in evaluating reliability based upon trials, and ways of identifying sources of low reliability, assuming that the validity and objectivity of the instruments have been established by applying the principles introduced in Chapters 8–10. Whole books have been written on specific aspects of what will be covered. Here, basic principles of instrument design common to all will be presented with reference to additional sources idiosyncratic to sociology, psychology and education for greater depth and additional specific examples. The focus will be on the design of instruments that generate quantitative data and the interpretation of the results, commensurate with the theme of this book. This does not diminish the value of non-quantitative results from interviews, observations, essays, etc., but these approaches are simply beyond the scope of this text.

Before looking at the collection of factual data, some basic criteria for the use of data need to be established. There are three fundamental principles of measurement design that will provide overall guidance through the process regardless of instrument type: validity, reliability and objectivity.

VALIDITY

It has been maintained that if any one of the four forms of validity that have been discussed in Chapter 2 were low, then the overall validity of the conclusions of a study would be suspect. The validity of measurement, *construct validity*, has been described as an aim to maximize the consistency between concept, construct and operational definition. To what extent can the scores be interpreted as indicative of the magnitude of specific traits or constructs? To answer this requires both logical analysis of consistency and justification through empirical data. Traditionally, much of the discussion has focused on links with psychological theories, but it will be used in a more generic form here for all social science research. Such a simplistic definition is difficult to use as a guide for evaluating the instruments and processes that may be used to supply data for research. Thus not only should the construct validity of an IQ test (how well does it really measure intelligence?) be considered, but also the validity of using various indicators as the basis for placing people in different social classes.

The use of the term 'construct validity' is not wholly consistent across the literature; measurement textbooks, in particular, tend to focus on different areas and uses of instruments. Up to this point, the term has been used as a general designation of the overall validity of a measuring instrument (or homogeneous subsections), observation technique, or classification scheme to represent a construct in research. Cronbach (1990) suggests that it is not really separable from the other forms of validity commonly discussed, such as criterion and content validity.

Following this thinking, construct validity as loosely defined above will continue to be considered as concerned with measurement validity in general, and in particular with the logical consistency arguments, though this is not without its own problems, as Cronbach (1990: 185–6) notes when discussing validation as persuasive argument:

> Many sentences are required to defend an inference from a score. Some of these sentences are value judgements, some are appeals to common sense or prior evidence, and some are logical or legal premises. If the relevant audience finds the sentences plausible and the chain of argument coherent, it accepts the conclusion. A critic, replacing a sentence with a plausible alternative, can reach a contradictory conclusion. When discussion is confined within the profession, it is fellow experts whom the interpreter must persuade. Other interpretations reach a public forum; the psychologists view is adopted only if nonspecialists find her argument more reasonable than competing arguments.

Here the various other related types of validity associated with instruments will be considered as complementary, enhancing the argument, and reflecting their specific usage and process of justification.

The term *criterion validity* reflects the use of an instrument as a method for classifying subjects based upon a quantifiable trait – for example, by the descriptive characteristics or the cut-off scores on a test used for including them in a group. One way to validate a quantitative instrument would be to consider the scores of subjects who are deemed to possess the characteristic, as specified by a separate technique. This can be accomplished in one of two ways, depending on the purpose of the instrument. One way is to evaluate its *concurrent validity* by checking against a parallel measure or classification. For example, an instrument to identify subjects with a personality disorder could be administered to two groups of persons, those known not to have the disorder and those known to have it. If the scores show a definite cut-off point distinguishing the groups, then this test would be valid. Alternatively, do the scores on the instrument correlate highly with another instrument with high validity for the construct? The other way is to focus on its *predictive validity* by comparing the score on the test with a predicted outcome. For example, how well do the scores on an academic aptitude test in mathematics for secondary school students correlate with performance in an undergraduate mathematics degree programme? Will a young offender scoring high on an instrument tend to reoffend?

In other situations, one may wish to consider the *content validity* of a test: does it adequately represent the subject matter and skills for a subject or set of topics? For example, how well does the end of semester examination in English literature reflect the facts about the literature considered plus the interpretative and analytic skills presented? Specific processes for enhancing content validity through test design techniques will be considered in Chapter 10. Content validity is of primary relevance to those instruments indicated in the 'Tests' column of Table 8.2.

This brief discussion highlights the problem: where is the line drawn between one form of validity and another, and which does one use? The answer should be found in the intended purpose or application of the instrument. A single instrument may be used for more than one purpose, and therefore demand more than one type of validity check. Table 8.3 provides an outline of possible uses of the results of a public examination, but specific applications in different types of research show the nature of the problem. For example, grades from A-level examinations given at age 18 + in England and Wales are considered by potential employers as indicators of level of possession of knowledge and skills in specific subjects. Also, university admissions tutors will use them as predictors of university success and select students accordingly. The examination boards that produce these tests will defend the content validity of such examinations by describing the origin of the content tested. On the other hand, numerous research studies have shown that these examinations are poor predictors of university success, with very low correlations between A-level grades and final university results. The difficulty is that here is a case of an instrument created specifically for one purpose (testing achievement) which does not have as high a validity for other purposes (construct validity for research or predictive validity for academic performance).

Murphy and Davidshofer (1991) reinforce this view in maintaining that the four types of validity are widely accepted as representing four strategies for establishing the validity of making inferences from scores. While referring to the aspect of validity related to instruments as construct validity in the overall discussion of sources of validity and invalidity of research, it should be recognized that the original restrictive definition based on logical argument may not be sufficient alone to guarantee maximum validity. It is up to the researcher to employ all the tools available to develop the instruments so that they are the appropriate ones for the task.

This does highlight the practical problem of how one decides which criteria to use if designing a new test, or what evidence of validity should be accepted if selecting an existing instrument to use. It is not always possible to develop an

TABLE 8.3
Examples of how to establish each of the four types of instrument validity for a given instrument: an A-level examination in pure and applied mathematics (after Anastasi, 1990)

Purpose of test results: research or decision support	Exemplar methods for ensuring validity	Required validity
A study to determine whether those students with a high general quantitative reasoning ability have a greater capability to work in three dimensions than those without	An analysis of the skills tested in the A-level examination to see how well they reflect *quantitative reasoning ability* as defined by the study	Construct
One criterion for determining selection for university entrance into psychology, sociology or education programmes: a minimum grade on this examination	A check is made to show that students who have done well in A-level mathematics subsequently achieve high grades in social science subjects at university	Criterion – predictive
A study to investigate any relationships between general mathematical ability and performance in various subjects taken at A level	Students who do well in the A-level examination will also tend to do well in a battery of standardized tests of general mathematical ability	Criterion – concurrent
An employer needs to be assured that applicants have the mathematical skills indicated in the A-level mathematics syllabus	The content and skills tested on the examination are shown to test a representative sample of skills and knowledge specified by the examination syllabus	Content

original instrument, or existing ones may be too cumbersome. It might seem desirable to use an existing instrument, but validity for that particular application would have to be checked. In some instances, it may be possible to justify the validity of one instrument which is easier to use by correlating performance on it with that of another which is more difficult to administer (concurrent validity). For example, a research project on spatial skills of schizophrenics would first need an instrument to classify their condition. Since many instruments already exist, it would be desirable to ask for evidence of concurrent validity. In other words, do the score ranges of persons institutionalized as schizophrenics reflect the severity of their problem? Such an instrument (for example, the Minnesota Multiphasic Personality Inventory; see Anastasi, 1990), if valid, would be much easier to administer on a large scale than a series of interviews.

Predictive validity is often established by finding the correlation between the instrument or measure of interest and a measure of the predicted performance. For example, do scores on an aptitude test used in counselling the unemployed validly reflect their potential to succeed in the areas specified?

No instrument is going to be perfectly valid and one could imagine that the outcome of defending validity will be an assessment of the instruments validity on some scale – say, between 1 and 10. What is more important than where on such a scale the instrument might fall, is how well the validity has been justified and how well this justification has been documented for further consideration and scrutiny. One of the intended outcomes of research can be to change or modify the concept or construct, rather than the instrument. In other words, it does not measure what we thought it did, but it does measure something of interest. For example, over time there has been an evolution of thinking on the nature of intelligence, based upon the application and development of intelligence measures. Personal observation concurs with the view that high intelligence is exemplified by an ability to learn and contend with novel problems, and is more than an ability to remember facts and understand concepts. This is reflected in Kline's (1991) view that most intelligence measures now include a combination of two types of ability: crystallized (verbal, mechanical, numerical and social skills) and fluid (reasoning necessary for problem-solving). Early tests tended to measure mainly crystallized ability, which often reflects cultural values. The arguments still rage as to the balance between these (and others), what proportion of these are inherited, and how much can be enhanced through learning, either formally or informally. The endeavours to measure intelligence are interesting to follow if for no other reason than accessibility to the ongoing debate and the range of arguments presented, which vividly illustrate the nature of the problem of justifying the validity of abstract concepts.

Finally, *face validity* is a term occasionally used that is not related to construct validity, but should none the less raise concerns with the instrument designer. It asks whether the *subjects* will perceive the instrument as being valid. If they do not they may not respond, or may respond dishonestly or not take it seriously and provide misleading responses.

RELIABILITY

In its broadest sense, *reliability* is an indication of consistency between *two* measures of the same thing. The two measures could be (with sources of error in parentheses):

- two separate instruments (lack of equivalence);
- two like halves of one instrument (inconsistency across matched items);
- the same instrument applied on two occasions (instability over time);
- the same instrument administered by two different persons (inconsistency across observers/scorers).

To understand the relationship between the two measures and reliability, it is necessary to consider how reliability is quantified. When a series of measurements is carried out on a group of subjects, it is highly unlikely that everyone will respond in the same way and end up with the same score, even if they were all the same for that trait. Therefore, there will be variability in scores, which is mathematically described as the *variance* (standard deviation squared). Where does this variability originate? Some of it will be attributable to the natural variability in the trait or characteristic across the population and some to error in the instrument used to measure it. This is true to varying degrees no matter what is used for an instrument, whether it is a ruler or an attitude measure (see Black, 1993, for an example). If we were to measure the heights of 100 randomly selected 11-year-old boys all born on the same day, there would be a mean height and a spread of scores fitting a normal distribution. Most of the variability would be due to natural variation in height, but a small amount may be due to the instruments or how the measurer used them, or what kind of haircut the boys had. On the other hand, if we were to give the same boys a test of mathematical ability, then (hopefully) most of the variability would be due to differences in the boys ability. In this case, however, the amount due to the instrument, how the questions are interpreted by the boys, choice of questions, etc., may be considerable. The actual test scores are referred to as *observed scores*, which include any errors in the instrument. There are also the unmeasurable *true scores*, which would be the perfect scores without any error. While we can only imagine that these exist, they do prove useful in understanding reliability.

Mathematically, the relationship among sources of variability is expressed as follows:

$$S_x^2 = S_t^2 + S_e^2 \tag{8.1}$$

where S_x^2 is the variance in the observed scores of subjects (what is actually measured) S_t^2 is the natural variance in the true scores of subjects (the perfect scores) and S_e^2 is the variance due to error in the instrument.

Conceptually, reliability can be thought of as indicating what proportion of the variability in a score is due to the trait itself. From this, reliability is defined as a ratio of variances

$$r_{xx} \equiv \frac{\text{variance in the true scores}}{\text{variance in the observed scores}}$$

which when written mathematically is

$$r_{xx} \equiv \frac{S_t^2}{S_x^2} \tag{8.2}$$

This is all very elegant, except that it has already been stated that the true score cannot be determined. A bit of manipulation is required so that there is an equation that relates to reality. If equation (8.2) is rearranged to solve for the unattainable true score variance, we have an expression in terms of variances that can at least be estimated:

$$S_t^2 = S_x^2 - S_e^2 \tag{8.3}$$

In other words, the variance in the true scores is just the variance in the observed scores less the error variance. Substituting this into equation (8.2) provides a new expression for reliability:

$$r_{xx} = \frac{S_x^2 - S_e^2}{S_x^2} \tag{8.4}$$

and dividing through by S_x^2 simplifies the expression to:

$$r_{xx} = 1 - \frac{S_e^2}{S_x^2} \tag{8.5}$$

Now S_x^2 is nothing more than the square of the standard deviation of the raw scores, thus it is easily found. The second term, S_e^2, is a bit more difficult to ascertain, as it depends on what is the source of variability due to error. The method of determination (estimation) will depend on the nature of the instrument – whether it is

- a set of questions or attitude survey (thus do all the questions in the survey consistently measure aspects of the construct?);
- a set of observations or measures over time (thus do respondents' answers remain the same over the time interval?);
- a set of observations or classifications made by several observers/scorers (thus is there consistency across observers/scorers?).

Once this has been decided, then an estimate of the error variance can be made, which is the focus of Chapter 11. In the meantime, this highlights the fact that there is likely to be more than one type of reliability, depending on the source of the error variance: consistency in content and its interpretation; stability over time; or consistency among scorers. Table 8.4 brings all this together and presents a picture of the range of possible ways of expressing reliability. Each of the rows will result in one or more coefficients, which can be calculated only *after* the instrument is used, which could be a trial rather than the full application. It will not provide any information on why an instrument has a high or low reliability, which will require some careful scrutiny of the instrument. So for now, let us consider what can be done to keep the error variance low and the reliability of instruments high through planning and the design of the questions.

There are several factors that influence instrument reliability, some of them directly reflected in the way that error variances are estimated. Other factors seem almost common sense, but their existence is supported by research:

- *Sufficient numbers of questions or identifiable components of responses* for sets of questions that constitute the operational definition of a construct. Single questions may be a reliable means of acquiring factual information, but, as we will see in Chapters 9 and 10, attitudes, views, opinions, skills and knowl-

TABLE 8.4
Types of reliability, sources of variance and ways of determining coefficients

Which two measures?	Source of variability	Type of reliability
Two separate instruments with a time delay	Time	Stability
Two separate instruments, no time delay	Content, interpretation	Consistency
Two like halves of one instrument	Content, interpretation	Consistency
Same instrument given twice with a time delay	Time	Stability
Same instrument administered by one person with time delay	Time	Consistency
Same instrument administered by two different persons	Scorers	Consistency

edge all require sets of questions or observations. Even open-ended questions benefit from having a number of identifiable components to rate or assess. Longer instruments are more reliable since the random errors have a better chance of cancelling each other, reducing variability due to error, though this does not enhance reliability of two measures over time.

- *Quality of wording* of questions, including both single factual questions and individual questions in a set constituting an operational definition. If the wording is ambiguous to the subjects, then answers will not be consistent on two occasions, much less when read twice in one sitting. This also applies to achievement tests, not only from the view of understandability, but also difficulty. Tests for which it is expected that the scores will be normally distributed have the highest reliability when the items are neither too hard nor too easy.

- *Time* allowed and time needed. If instruments eliciting factual information or surveying opinions or views are too long, subjects will rush through them, not answering questions with the thought required. Timed achievement (speed) tests can suffer the same fate, and some examinees may not even finish. If these are really justified, then special steps must be taken to determine a meaningful reliability coefficient.

- *Group homogeneity* for the trait being measured can reduce the reliability, since the true score variance will be lower. When piloting an instrument, it is advisable to use the same range of subjects as expected in the full study.

As you consider the various techniques for operationally defining variables, keep these in mind as they tend to relate to the overall instrument or homogeneous subsections (Mehrens and Lehmann, 1984; Anastasi, 1990; Traub, 1994).

There is one further consideration related to instrument construction, and that is the *objectivity* of question statements: the wording or nature of presentation should avoid encouraging one type of answer. Lack of objectivity of questions would reduce the overall validity of an instrument by biasing responses and consequently influencing consistency between concept and instrument outcomes. It could also reduce its reliability by eliciting different responses at different times, or, if only some items lacked objectivity, eliciting inconsistent responses within the instrument. This is not as easy as it may seem and care must be taken in the use of adjectives and adverbs, as well as tone of voice in an interview. We will return to this issue in the next two chapters as the construction of questions is covered.

In general, it is worth remembering that an instrument without reliability cannot be valid, but one that is reliable can lack validity for the desired construct. In other words, an instrument could be reliably measuring something other than what you intended, but it cannot be validly measuring anything if it is not reliable.

Whole research projects have been devoted to the development of instruments and the enhancement of their validity and reliability. While there are coefficients that are accepted as reasonable estimates of reliability, the process of validation of a new instrument can be thought of as equivalent to testing a hypothesis, fraught with many of the same difficulties. As you progress through the four chapters in this part of the book, you will be introduced to some of the practical problems of instrument design that will enhance validity, reliability and objectivity. It is recommended that if you decide to develop your own instrument that you consult one of the many specialized texts on instrument design in your area as well.

PRACTICAL ISSUES: PREVENTING THE INTRODUCTION OF NEW EXTRANEOUS VARIABLES

As part of controlling extraneous variables and preventing new ones from being introduced as a consequence of instrument design or administration, several tasks need to be carried out at the development, administration and data-recording stages.

- *Validate the instrument(s)*: have other experts in the field consider the instrument from the viewpoint of evaluating its consistency with the desired constructs. As the developer, it is possible to be so close to the instrument as to miss the obvious.
- *Pilot* with a small group representative of the population. Are the questions interpreted by subjects in the way intended? Sit down with individuals and go through the questions one by one to determine what they think the questions are asking. The guidelines for good practice in question construction provided here and elsewhere will help to prevent the worst sins, but there is no substitute for a trial run (see Oppenheim, 1992: Chapter 4). If the pilot sample is representative of the population, then a reliability coefficient can be calculated, and, as will be seen in Chapter 11, individual item quality indicators can be calculated. If these turn out to be low, then there is still time to find the source of the problem and repair it *before* carrying out the full study.
- *Coding* of the data involves translating entries on questionnaires or interview schedules to letters or numbers. It is necessary to establish guides for translating responses and it may be necessary to teach colleagues working as a team on a large project. Having a written coding guide with explanations (essential for open-ended or free-response questions) prevents inconsistencies in the results. Some enlightening examples are provided in Oppenheim (1992: Chapter 14).
- *Data recording* involves transferring information from questionnaires, interview schedules or code sheets to computer files for processing. This can often be done more quickly and more accurately if two people work together: one reading while the other types.
- *Data cleansing* involves double-checking the data entries on the computer files, particularly if there are large numbers of respondents. At the most basic level, just look for outlandish responses – for example, an age of 501 years (a typing error). Any computer program processing such data is unlikely to find such errors for you.

These basic tasks all help to maintain the quality and accuracy of the data, and need to be planned as part of the research project procedure. Carry out Activity 8.1 now.

> ### Activity 8.1
>
> (a) How do you plan to justify the validity of your instruments? Which forms of validity do you propose to invoke and why?
> (b) Which form of reliability is most relevant to your instrument? What do you plan to do to enhance its reliability during construction?
> (c) Discuss planned procedures for validating, piloting, data coding and data cleansing of your instrument(s). What additional problems would arise if you were working with a team?

COLLECTING FACTUAL DATA: BACKGROUND AND DEMOGRAPHIC DATA

Factual information would appear to produce less contentious data than do tests, scales or observation, though when information is used collectively to provide the criteria for classification, agreement may be harder to achieve. Data may be collected either as part of a written questionnaire or during an interview. How such data can be used directly as variables will be considered first, and the practical problems associated with the collection of factual data will follow. The use of these data in generating classifications or their use as indicators will be discussed separately below. It is not suggested that this is an exhaustive coverage, but the applications presented ought to provide sufficient breadth for you to extrapolate to new situations.

One potential problem with factual information on a questionnaire is that it is so easy to collect. The researcher needs to give some thought very early on to whether *all* of this is essential. You might ask what is the harm of too much information? Three primary problems can erupt out of excessive demand for factual data:

1 Subjects will potentially be offended or feel that you are prying, particularly when asking about antisocial behaviours, income, etc., and will simply not bother to reply. This can leave you with volunteers (a potentially harmful interaction between instrument and sample mortality).
2 The inclusion of such data in computer analysis may provide nonsensical correlations or tests that are simply distracting. This is true for all data, but numerical responses from factual questions can be very tempting.
3 As noted earlier, it can result in an overly long instrument that respondents rush through without due care, thus lowering the reliability of the results.

The first question to ask is what each piece of information has to do with the variables of interest in the study. It is essential that one refers back to the hypotheses *before* any instruments are designed. It is a waste of resources (and subjects' patience) to ask unnecessary questions and a potential disaster to find too late that questions one should have asked were not included and essential data are lacking or inadequate.

Some factual questions relate directly to variables that are of interest in a study, such as gender, amount of education, age, residence, occupation, etc. These may even be independent variables in an ex post facto or correlational designs. It is not unreasonable to want to consider the influence of any of the following on specific variables: age; size of home; gender; educational qualifications; income (range); membership of organizations; number of children; location of home; marital status; place of birth; religion; how often the local library is used; number of traffic tickets or motoring offences; amount and frequency of alcohol intake; number of cigarettes smoked per day. This is by no means an exhaustive list.

Such personal questions can be considered as prying, consequently a statement of the rationale for the study in the introduction of the questionnaire, survey instrument or interview saying why this information is needed would potentially enhance co-operation. Other factual questions may relate to activities or actions, such as brand of soap purchased, times for meals, or which candidate/party the subject voted for in the last election.

In terms of construct validity, there is little about which to argue. Often such questions result in variables that are correlated with others, or respondents are grouped according to one or more traits as part of an ex post facto study. Assuming the respondents answer truthfully about these, the reliability should be reasonably high, though some questions may produce less than perfect answers if the events were in the distant past or required remembering exact times or dates or of low importance. As Oppenheim (1992) notes, though it is not reasonable to ask the same question twice, it is possible to ask related questions that would help to identify weak questions or questions out of context that mislead the respondents.

Having established what factual information is essential to the definition of concepts or to constitute variables (gender, income, age, etc.), one practical source of difficulty is whether or not the subjects answer truthfully, a problem especially with questionnaires which are sent out on a large scale. Whether it is worse to have mischievous answers or no answers at all is difficult to say, but the only preventive steps that can be taken are to ensure that the instrument appears to be as professional as possible, and to build in checks on the data. The latter can be difficult if the subjects feel that the checks appear to invade their privacy.

The need to ensure clear and inoffensive communication is as important to the acquisition of factual information as it is to attitude, opinion and perception questions, so the principles discussed below, included as part of question-asking structure and the wording of the questions, will apply to them as well.

WORDING OF QUESTIONS

The task of planning and assessing the quality of all the questions in any questionnaire requires some systematic scheme to assist in covering all the important issues. This will need to take into account the potential sources of problems generally associated with how questions are phrased. The scheme that will be used here (obviously not the only one possible) will consider four aspects and guidelines for each, to provide:

(a)　enhanced uniformity in the nature of expected responses from subjects;

(b)　assistance in choosing the vocabulary used and maintaining consistency of meaning to all subjects;

(c)　sentence structure suitable to the subjects and sentences of appropriate length;

(d)　reduction of inaccurate answers due to social desirability bias and/or sensitive issues.

Considering each of these during the question design phase will help prevent the introduction of undesirable extraneous variables or loss of subjects.

Uniformity in expected responses

The first issue to settle is the nature of the answers to questions: all respondents need to answer in a way that generates meaningful data. One scheme for considering the potentially different types of questions that could be asked is to consider whether they encourage a long response or just a simple answer. *Open* questions allow for a free, unpredictable response by subjects such as used in interviews, while *closed* questions result in only a limited range of possible responses, such as multiple-choice questions or rating scales, or factual questions requiring a predictable range of responses (Fowler, 1993; Oppenheim, 1992). Guilford (1956) further divided these questions into four categories which, when slightly modified, are quite appropriate for considering the types of questions to ask either on paper or during an interview, based upon the demands made on the respondents. For Guilford there are two types of closed question:

- *Recall* of facts, experiences, names, dates, etc.
- *Convergent*, demanding predictable answers or restricting the respondent to a limited number of choices – for example, responding to a multiple-choice question on an achievement test or rating scale on an attitude survey.

There are also two types of open question:

- *Divergent*, generating unpredictable (but sensible) answers, allowing and encouraging expression of creative thinking, exploration of a new solution or extrapolation to a new situation.
- *Evaluative*, which is more than expressing an opinion or making judgements, it ought to involve the defence or justification of a choice or judgement through free expression, either orally or written. The rationale is more important than the choice.

This highlights one of the major differences between interviews and essays, which can exploit the opportunity to ask open questions and record responses, and questionnaires and multiple-choice questions, which require closed, standard responses. There are advantages to both and the choice of the type to be used will be dependent on the nature of the research. Interviews can exploit the opportunity to elicit more open-ended responses, determining why events occur or attitudes are held through divergent and evaluative questions. The difficulty comes in contending with all the responses. On the other hand, closed questions (often part of a survey) in research are preferred for testing the generalizability of traits, actions, abilities, views and attitudes to larger populations. While the responses to these are easier to collate into quantifiable data, the range of variables addressed is much more limited since sets of questions often constitute the operational definitions, not individual questions (except for factual data). The focus of this text is on variables that can be quantified; consequently, one would expect questions that result in reliable and valid quantifiable variables to be closed. This is not essential, though, as there have been studies that asked respondents to answer open questions and the frequencies of certain types of responses have constituted the variable. The value of considering such a scheme as presented above is to help you become aware of the need to word questions carefully so as not to elicit divergent responses when recall was required, or vice versa when designing interviews.

For example, the question:

What traits determined why you chose the candidate you voted for in the last election?

is a *divergent* question since the answer is quite unpredictable, but a more directed and focused *convergent* version might be:

Which of the following best describes your reason for voting for the candidate of your choice in the last election?

(a)   International policy
(b)   Domestic policy
(c)   Style of clothes worn
(d)   Sincerity and caring attitude
(e)   Honesty and integrity

The second would be more appropriate as one of a set of questions to determine whether voters focused more on personality or issues when voting.
　　Even factual questions can suffer from unintentionally divergent answers if not worded carefully. For example,

When did you first become aware of the differences in political parties?

could result in responses such as 'When I was in secondary school' or 'After I got my first job'. If the intent were to ascertain a time, then asking the question such that the time-scale is obvious enhances the probability of getting an appropriate answer:

How old were you when you first became aware of the differences in the political parties?

Obviously, having a variety of people serve as a trial group would assist in identifying questions that elicit non-uniform or unpredictable and undesirable answers before the questionnaire were used as part of the full study.

Consistency of meaning across respondents

It seems reasonable that if an instrument (whether a test, an attitude questionnaire or even a set of factual questions) is going to be highly reliable, it will be necessary for all respondents to interpret the questions in the same way. How questions are phrased, the use of appropriate vocabulary and even the length of sentences can have an impact on understanding and subjects' subsequent responses. Drawing on suggestions from Oppenheim (1992), Fowler (1993) and encounters with a number of questionnaires, the following list highlights some of the frequent sources of misunderstanding of questions:

1   *Ambiguous terms or phrases* can leave the respondent not understanding what is wanted. For example, the question

Do you have a telephone?

is unclear, since it could be interpreted to mean access to a telephone at a neighbour's apartment, possession of a telephone in the home, use of mother's when at home, ownership of a portable (cell or mobile) telephone, use of a telephone at work, or simply access to the common or pay telephone in the hallway outside one's room in a residence hall. Thus a reasonable answer by the person with a home telephone but not a portable telephone, would be 'No, not on me', leaving the researcher wrongly informed.

Another example comes from asking how many bedrooms there are in a subject's home: what if the sewing room or study is a room that under other ownership would be used as a bedroom? Is the intent to find out how many rooms are used as bedrooms or to find out how big the house is?

2   *Time* can present problems of understanding. The question

Have you bathed in the past week?

could be interpreted as the past seven days, thus if asked on Wednesday, the person would answer 'Yes' since Saturday night is bath night. But if he or she were to interpret past week as this week starting on Monday, then Saturday is not here yet, so the answer would be 'No'. Confusion can arise over time periods or blocks of time and how far in the past (or future) an event occurred (or will occur): does 'in the next week' mean in the next seven days *or* in the next block of Sunday to Saturday, *or* in the next block of Monday to Sunday?

3   *Inappropriate vocabulary* must be avoided. There are different interpretations of words used in everyday communication that can lead to misleading answers. For example, a person asked the question in 2 above might answer 'no' if he or she had had a shower, or, since most people in the world lack a bathtub, used a two-gallon bucket. If the intent were to determine cleanliness, this question would be a failure.

Researchers must be sensitive to alternative meanings for words. In the past, 'having tea' meant taking a light meal in England (though even that is changing among some age groups, social classes and localities), whereas in America you are lucky to get a cup with hot water and a tea bag in it. What constitutes supper and how does it differ from dinner, who are members of the 'family', and what makes up a neighbourhood? These will vary from locality to locality, across ethnic groups, and even across generations of related persons (nuclear family or extended family?). This may result in questions that sound a bit pedantic, but they will avoid misunderstanding in the end. Imagine that you have asked the question

How many persons are there in your family? and got the answer '23'. In an interview you could ask, say, whether all 23 lived together under one roof, but what would you make of such an answer if it were given in a questionnaire? Consider the question

How many rooms are there in your house?

Now, do you count just the main rooms (living room, kitchen, bedrooms) or do you include the bathroom and the toilet under the stairs as well?

4   *Use of clichés, colloquialisms or jargon* should be avoided simply because meanings can change and not everyone is necessarily familiar with the latest additions to the English (or any other) language. While we may all think we know what it means to 'get ripped off', some will not know what it means to 'sus out the situation'. It is desirable to keep the language simple, but do not inadvertently introduce new problems.

Jargon that we as academics and researchers use may not be understood at all, or some words may have different meanings. English is a wonderful language in the hands of academics: take a nice common everyday word and they will give it a technical meaning – for example, intelligence, efficiency, productivity and ability. Other words are simplifications of technically complex issues, such as ozone depletion, common European currency and sexual harassment. Then, there is the use of acronyms. What, for example, do the following mean: HIV, UNESCO, FTSE, USAID, ODA, DFID and BMW? It has already been recommended that the name of a concept being measured should never appear as part of a question in the questionnaire, since it could be interpreted differently by respondents. The use of clichés, colloquialisms and jargon can inflict the same sort of consequences on a study: low reliability of responses.

5   *Use of emotive words* should also be avoided – for example, adjectives that might bias responses such as democratic, natural, holistic, attractive, modern, alien. It is not uncommon for persons selling an idea or position to use such adjectives, but if you are truly trying to design questions that elicit as objective and reliable a response as possible, avoidance is desirable. One does not want to lead the respondent into answering in a certain way. For example, how would *you* respond to the following question:

Which type of research approach do you plan to employ?

(a)   A holistic, naturalistic case study involving humanistic interviews.

(b) A rigid scientific survey, assigning numbers to subjects and numerical values to their views.

Those of you choosing (b) *must* be part of the evil empire!

This does not mean that one avoids emotive issues, but it will be necessary to define what is meant by certain terminology that may not be fully understood. For example, the issue of 'gun control' in America can polarize people quite quickly, with positions changing when it is explained what it means. In Europe, the issue of 'open borders' has a similar impact on those expecting mass immigration. Exploration of such emotive issues may be better carried out through endeavouring to elicit why they are held, rather than how widely they exist. In either situation, it is necessary that there is a common understanding of the issue, if there are to be meaningful results.

Suitable sentence structure

The level of English used will obviously have to match the reading ability of your subjects, but there are several considerations that will simply make questions easier to understand.

1   Sentences which are too long make it possible to forget what was asked by the end. For example, try breaking the following into two sentences to enhance its understandability:

Since this study is interested in finding out how much leisure time a person has during each week, would you please indicate how many hours per week you spend on recreational activities such as sport, relaxing at your local pub, cinema, etc.

2   Sentences which are too short and terse are a source of ambiguity, as exemplified by the following:

Age? _____

As of when? To what degree of accuracy? A better question might be

How old are you? _____ years _____ months

3   Double-barrelled questions can provide inexact data, as the following example illustrates:

Do you own a car or a motorcycle? (Y/N) _____

If answered yes, does that mean a car, a motorcycle or both?

Impact of bias and sensitive issues

Asking questions about personal facts in their lives can threaten the self-image of respondents, which can result in less than fully accurate answers. Who wants to admit that their spouse collects garbage? He or she is a sanitation engineer.

One could argue that subjects are more willing to indicate their income, age, etc., as being in a range than to give a more exact value. The risk taken here is that if you ask for a person's exact age or income, they will take offence and not complete the question or even the whole questionnaire. On the other hand, choosing age or income ranges automatically reduces your data to ordinal rather than interval. This can leave you with less powerful statistical tests from which to choose. Knowledge of the subjects and their proclivities is one factor to consider, but the wording of questions and assurances of confidentiality will also assist in collecting data of the highest order.

Stating questions in such a way as to imply the subject has erred or done something foolish, for example:

How many video nasties have your children watched this month?
List five examples of junk food that you have bought in the past week.

is not likely to elicit the most honest answer, if any at all. If these represent truly important issues for research, then a much more subtle approach needs to be taken.

Questions on time or frequency of events can present unique problems due to memory and perception as well as wording: people do not always remember accurately, or they misinterpret the question. Also, answers can be distorted by an unconscious desire to appear better or more proficient than in reality. For example:

How many sexual partners have you had in the past year?
How often in the past six months have you drunk so much alcohol that you could not stand?

Men might inflate the numbers while women might reduce them, depending upon the cultural context and even the age group. Now carry out Activity 8.2.

> ## Activity 8.2
>
> (a) List the factual data you intend to collect, describe why they are essential and how they relate to variables in the study.
> (b) Describe what aspects of design of instruments you have included to enhance the quality of questions, their appeal and the likelihood that they will be answered.

SOCIAL INDICATORS

A single value, such as age or income, can provide a basis for classifying subjects into age or income groups, but if we wish to explore more complex concepts, then such isolated single values have to be compared with others. As a simple example, inflation indices do not just consider prices and incomes at one time, but reflect several observations over a period of time. The total number of teachers in a school means little when considering workloads, while a teacher to student ratio is more useful. Indicators tend to involve comparisons, and Horn (1993) provides a schema for classifying them:

- *time series*, comparing characteristics across time periods;
- *structural series*, comparing within internal components or characteristics;
- *corresponding series*, comparing across external organizations or entities.

For the sake of comparing and contrasting these, Table 8.5 illustrates how individual quantities used in different contexts could generate each of these three types of indicator. If you consider the housing situation in 1980, it is possible to compare across the two regions of the country (corresponding series), and at the same time between income groups (social structural series). Alternatively, it is possible to review how housing has changed between the two census surveys (time series).

If there had been a specific policy implementation or economic change during this time, it would be possible to investigate the impact on housing conditions. It should be obvious that any one cell on its own provides little meaningful information on housing conditions. Such numbers do not provide much insight on their own and some comparison would need to be made relative to other regions, countries, geographic locations, etc.

Also, think back to the earlier section on the wording of questions: on an international basis, many homes in the tropics do not have a kitchen as such, the cooking being done outside over a wood or charcoal fire, possibly under a pavilion. Consequently, most houses automatically would have one room less – not necessarily a 'bad' thing if you live in a climate that allows year-round barbecues!

Such indicators are neutral tools, though their interpretation may reflect value judgements. The *social indicator movement* began in the 1960s with an attempt to employ analogues of economic indicators to assist in social planning (Carley, 1981; Horn, 1993). It was felt that economic indicators, such as gross national product, alone did not reflect the true well-being of societies and that planning would benefit from more eclectic indicators. Endeavours to adapt economic indicators and develop complementary but more meaningful social indicators proceeded until the end of the 1970s. By then, it became apparent that the task was not as simple as first expected, essentially because the development of social theories was at a very early stage. Over-ambitious use of social indicators led to inappropriate utilization and reduced enthusiasm

TABLE 8.5
Indicators of housing conditions in Serendip

Regions (corresponding series) and income groups (structural series)		Number of rooms per person in household		
		1980 Census	1990 Census	Increase, % (time series)
Northern region:	Upper income	4.6	5.2	13
	Lower income	1.5	2.0	33
Southern region:	Upper income	4.4	5.3	20
	Lower income	1.4	1.8	29

for their application in policy-making, though the resulting debate has provided considerable insight into measurement issues for researchers.

To illustrate the link between issue and indicator, a list of social concerns and corresponding social indicators developed by the Organization for Economic Co-operation and Development (OECD) is provided in Table 8.6. Indicators can be much more modest than these. On the other hand, the ones here illustrate not only the policy-making base but also the potential obstacles in devising measures and justifying their validity. Some of the indicators would be very difficult to quantify.

It could be argued that weak theories are a good reason to try to find social indicators, since these could be tested as well as the evolving theories. This would shift the emphasis away from social policy and towards social research, which has the potential for greater objectivity due to the more open and intellectually honest debate that occurs in academia as opposed to politics. A view of indicators more consistent with research has been provided by Carlisle (1972), who notes:

TABLE 8.6
Social concerns and corresponding social indicators

Social concern	Indicators
Health	
Length of life	Life expectancy, perinatal mortality rate
Healthiness of life	Short- and long-term disability
Education and learning	
Use of educational facilities	Regular and adult education experience
Employment and quality of working life	
Availability of employment	Unemployment (incl. part-time working)
Quality of working life	Work hours, travel to work, atypical work, leave, earnings, injury, environmental nuisances
Time and leisure	
Use of time	Free time, free-time activities
Command of goods and services	
Income	Distribution, low income, deprivation
Wealth	Distribution
Physical environment	
Housing conditions	Indoor and access to outdoor space, amenities
Services accessibility	Proximity of selected services
Environmental nuisance	Exposure to air pollution and noise
Social environment	
Sense of belonging	Social attachment, suicide rate
Personal safety	
Exposure to risk	Fatal and serious injuries
Perceived threat	Fear for personal safety

Source: Horn (1993), adapted from the work of the OECD.

A social indicator is defined as the operational definition or part of the operational definition of any one of the concepts central to the generation of an information system descriptive of the social system.

She then considers the use of such indicators as

- *informative*: operationalized system components and goals to describe the system and changes taking place over time.
- *predictive*: those fitting explicit models or theories, involving relationships among informative indicators.
- *problem orientated*: describing social problem areas and enhancing the understanding of the process of change.
- *programme evaluation*: representing targets to allow evaluation of policy effectiveness.

These are not mutually exclusive, but do have the benefit of compelling one to think about what the purpose of the research is. As one way to view performance indicators, it is not difficult to link these with potential use in the different categories of research: experimental, quasi-experimental and ex post facto.

Cazes (1972) suggests three sources of errors in social indicators:

- A lack of logical continuity between the social concept and the resulting operational definition. For example, the use of patient numbers in mental hospitals as an indication of mental illness ignores out-patients.
- Data compiled for other purposes are enlisted as operational definitions of concepts for a study.
- Collective attributes may depend on units that are not really sociologically meaningful. For example, it is not justified to consider a correlation between a mental health indicator and local income as indicative of a correlation between mental health and social status.

With the origins of social indicators in social policy there is an assumption of causality: why else spend the money? The pressure for accountability can, unfortunately, force changes in the definitions of indicators that make it difficult to justify the use of some. For example, how does one define who is 'unemployed' and consequently unemployment rates? Are they those who are looking for work, or just those who qualify to collect unemployment benefits? In some countries, the latter leaves out the one without a job in a two-earner family, people over a certain age, and even those who have planned for unemployment and have saved too much.

There are major drawbacks to employing social indicators such as those in Table 8.6 in research. They represent macrovariables on such a large scale that in reality they tend to be a rubric for sets of variables; consequently, isolating potential cause and effect relationships to explore systematically would be extremely difficult. Not all of them are easily quantifiable as a single ratio, difference or percentage variable. Finally, on this scale of investigation, replication would be unlikely, thus making any findings difficult to defend as constituting worthwhile support for theories (Carley, 1981). All of these provide considerable threats to both internal and external validity, though while this should not stop researchers from trying, it does forewarn them of design and implementation difficulties.

Finally, the use of social indicators tends to be value-laden. While it is quite reasonable to have values related to social issues and for governments to develop policy decisions based upon these values, there are pitfalls for research. With many social indicators being linked to economics, or having a considerable economic component, the implications of employing a set of values that may be in conflict with the subjects of a study present some interesting philosophical issues. Organizations dominated by Western economic perceptions view pre-industrial societies with some disdain, attempt to cajole traditional agricultural societies into market economies, and rationalize the consequential change on the societies as 'for the better'. An interesting field for research would be the analysis of the impact of new cultural and economic systems on traditional societies, including the sense of well-being and happiness of the members.

Latent variables

Social class can be considered an example of a rather special type of variable, one that is based on several individual characteristics such as occupation, education and income. It is typical of what Kerlinger (1986) calls *latent variables*. These tend to be of greater importance in the social sciences than the single constituent variables because they are seen to be better suited for explaining phenomena and their relationships on a larger scale. Another latent variable whose origins are not found in straight factual information, but in more elaborate instruments, is IQ, tests for which are commonly based on three components: verbal, numerical and spatial ability.

Other sources of data

There is also a considerable amount of data available on various aspects of society in addition to what a researcher will collect directly, often compiled by government bodies. These 'statistics', as they are referred to, are useful sources of information, but need to be considered with great care. It may be reasonable to consider factual information collected on a census survey at face value and as indicative of the state of society, but not all surveys produce unambiguous data. Census data that describe income, size of houses, number of children, etc., are usually reliable. Surveys that ask for opinion or interpretation may operationally define a variable in a way not consistent with others; the difficulty in arriving at a consensus on what constitutes different social classes is a prime example. While it may be unwarranted to test hypotheses using someone else's data, such numbers may be of value at other stages of research. Kerlinger (1986) suggests four other roles for other researchers' data:

- to provide background information and provide insight into organizations and institutions;
- to suggest hypotheses;
- to check sample data – for example, to check that the sample is representative of a community by looking at census records on race, income, education, etc.;
- to help select samples, using such survey data as voter registration lists.

Schonfield and Shaw (1972) warn about the use of public statistics as indicators for research studies, since they were not collected with research in mind. On the other hand, Cazes (1972) points out that such secondary analysis has the advantage of providing access to data that would be otherwise difficult if not impossible for an individual to collect. A serious difficulty comes when making comparisons, as there can be variations in definitions of the basic measures. What the FBI uses to determine crime rate is probably not going to be the same as what is used by New Scotland Yard. What constitutes secondary education when comparing across nations?

Since the way public statistics are compiled not only varies, but the underlying systems themselves differ, valid international comparisons become difficult. Institutions with the same names have different structures. For example, in the USA, students typically go to university for four years after high school, starting at about age 17. In Britain, they typically go for three years after A levels, starting at age 18. The first degrees have the same names and often cover the main subjects to much the same depth, but there are numerous other differences. How does one compare expenditure per student, class sizes and even degrees? Medical care is another area presenting difficulties in comparison across countries. Thus, while it may be possible to compare gross outcomes such as life expectancy, the underlying institutions present greater difficulties when trying to identify contributing factors. Carry out Activity 8.3 now.

Activity 8.3

1   Judge how valid the following indicators are, giving reasons in each case:
    (a)   The average number of books checked out of a local library per card holder as a relative indicator of literacy in the area.
    (b)   Which newspaper someone reads as an indicator of political party preference.
    (c)   Average attendance rate for lectures as an indicator of the quality of a course.
    (d)   The number of subscribers to a wildlife magazine in a group as an indicator of their commitment to environmental care.
2   The following are nationally published statistics, each with a possible concept for which it could be an indicator. Evaluate their validity and give reasons for your answer:
    (a)   Inflation at 3.5% as an indicator of how much the cost of living has increased since a year ago.
    (b)   Percentage of age cohort earning university first degrees as an indicator of how well educated a country is.
    (c)   Number of public libraries per 100 000 population as an indicator of general literacy.
3   If you have used any one else's 'statistics', describe for what and how they were used in your research. What assurances do you have that these data are reliable and valid?

Collecting the Data

A major challenge with surveys is to succeed in getting the subjects to return the questionnaire. There are few guidelines for the design of questionnaires that will enhance return rates that have not already been mentioned: careful wording of questions; restraining one's temptation to produce too long a questionnaire; and ensuring the appearance of the document is as professional as possible.

Covering letters need to appeal to subjects as well as assure them that any information will be kept strictly confidential. This is essential even when no names are requested, since in many situations it would not take a great detective to trace back to individuals specific responses. On the other hand, if you do not know who has responded, you also do not know who has *not* responded so that a reminder can be sent.

Having done one's best in designing a questionnaire, what else can be done to avoid the research being labelled as using 'volunteers' for subjects and consequently dismissed as involving an unrepresentative sample? One of the most important issues is to ensure that non-response was not due to some aspect of the questionnaire itself, in other words, that the instrument did not offend or for some other reason prevent the person from responding. For example, a questionnaire about the perceived qualities of Conservative Party politicians may not result in a sizeable response from Labour Party members if there were no opportunity to criticize. Questionnaires that are seen to be too personal or prying, to have a political or religious bias, or even to be just too long will be ignored. It is essential to follow up when questionnaires are not returned in order to try to find out why. All sorts of irrelevant and virtually random reasons that would not affect the validity of a study may contribute to non-returns. It may be that the questionnaire was lost in the post, it arrived while the subjects were away and they felt it was not worth returning it late, subjects had personal problems or pressures that prevented responding (death in the family, divorce, etc.), or the subjects moved. It is important to remember simple things such as having a return address on the envelope so that undelivered postal questionnaires can be returned. In the case of those who do not respond (one reason for knowing who has returned and who has not) it is worthwhile trying to contact them to find out why, providing return postage on this enquiry as well. All of these efforts take resources, but the value of knowing why or getting a greater percentage to respond is important when trying to defend the validity of conclusions.

There does seem to be a tacit assumption that a 60% return is 'acceptable' – but why did the other 40% not respond? Professional survey organizations strive very hard to get much higher response rates often because the accuracy of any predictions or conclusions reflects on their reputation. Recent poor predictions about voting intentions, for example, have prompted some companies to consider providing opportunities for written 'secret' ballots as opposed to asking subjects to respond verbally in person or over the telephone. This is not only to enhance return rates, but also to try to increase the validity of the response and remove any possibility of a reluctance of subjects to give a verbal answer to another person. Companies that survey purchasing tendencies for market research have been known to go to extremes to get high return rates, including interviewing each subject and completing the questionnaire there on the doorstep. This is expensive and time consuming, but a smaller complete random sample may be more representative than a larger set of volunteers.

Activity 8.4

Describe how you plan to ensure that your subjects will participate and respond.

SUMMARY

This chapter has introduced some basic principles of measurement to provide a basis for instrument design. There has been an elaboration on the original definition of construct validity to focus on the source of the validity and to indicate how it can be justified and enhanced. A formal definition of reliability was provided to show how this relates to the calculation of a coefficient. Again, there are different types of reliability, depending on the nature of the instrument and how the data are collected. On a practical level, suggestions were provided on ways of increasing instrument reliability.

Building on these general principles, the collection of factual data was considered. This aspect of data collection requires a clear definition of terminology and variables if the wording of questions is to provide valid and reliable responses. Finally, combining factual data and making comparisons can provide social indicators, though their definitions and relationships with original concepts do provide some challenges to the researcher.

The following chapters will continue the application of measurement principles to the design of questions for instruments to determine attitudes and views, as well as achievement and learning. In both chapters, issues related to reliability and validity will again be raised.

MEASURING ATTITUDES, OPINIONS AND VIEWS

9

Questionnaires for quantitative research in the social sciences are usually designed with the intention of being operational definitions of concepts, instruments that reflect strength of attitudes, perceptions, views and opinions. This involves trying to measure and quantify how intensely people *feel* about issues, as opposed to what they know or can do. With respect to social science research, it should be asked, why bother to investigate people's attitudes, opinions and beliefs? They will all be different and everyone is entitled to an opinion, or so common knowledge has it. While this may not be far from the truth, there are usually similar sets of views held by groups homogeneous for some traits. Investigating what attitudes, beliefs and opinions groups of subjects with common traits hold is of value simply because it is assumed that these attitudes will influence behaviour. The political views people have can be indicative of whom they will vote for in the next election and help us understand why. While expressed prejudice towards racial minority groups may not be a predictor of violence by one group against members of a community, it may be the starting-point for research to see if it is indicative of present and future social interaction or tendencies on the part of employees not to hire members of the community. Endeavouring to understand why groups of people tend to act as they do or possess certain views is a common aim of social science research.

Some inferred potential causality links based upon views of subjects have greater possibilities for being valid than others. Researchers must be careful about drawing unwarranted conclusions, making extreme generalizations or stereotyping respondents. For example, just because a group of men expresses chauvinistic attitudes (or a group of women think men are unfeeling and insensitive) does not mean the group would not work with members of the opposite sex. Such discoveries might be the basis for further investigations of the nature of relationships, but sweeping predictions of future behaviour on the basis of expressed opinions are often inaccurate for no other reason than other variables enter into decisions about actions. Most women abhor men who exhibit chauvinistic behaviour and will avoid working for them. The quality of their work under them might suffer, but the need of a job and individual ability to work in adverse conditions may intercede, resulting in action that defies predictions. Most societies have a healthy suspicion of politicians (author's suspicion), but still accept them and relatively rarely execute them.

When conducting quantitative research, what *individuals* do is of little interest in such situations, since predicting individual behaviour is, as noted earlier, unlikely to be very successful. What research into attitudes, opinions and beliefs can help us to understand is *tendencies*: how do these *tend* to influence decisions and actions in groups of people who have some characteristic(s) in common? There will always be exceptions, but one aim is to see if there are any traits or characteristics of specific identifiable groups. For example, learner attitudes (as a specific group) towards a teaching approach can be as important as how thoroughly they learned what they were supposed to learn (effectiveness). Unappealing, tedious learning materials or media can adversely affect the efficiency of learning, reducing the overall amount learned in the time available, and have a negative impact on wanting to learn more. Since teaching tends to be delivered to groups (even if individualized), one is trying to satisfy most of the learners most of the time. Thus instruments administered to trial groups provide more valid information on group tendencies than interviews with a few outspoken individuals. One wants to avoid only the squeaky wheel getting all the grease.

Also, this chapter will focus on quantifiable data in order to be able to see how far such measurable attitudes are generalizable to larger populations. It is recognized that there are a number of techniques and approaches for acquiring qualitative information about attitudes, values and beliefs that can be of considerable relevance to a study. Such an approach may be either the precursor to questionnaires for a representative sample, or part of a follow-up to investigate findings in greater depth.

Collecting valid and reliable data on attitudes, opinions and beliefs is not trivial and requires careful planning. The problem is still there: it is necessary to get subjects to respond or take action, then we can *infer* what they are thinking (recall Figure 2.4). Responses are indirect evidence, so it is necessary to ensure that these are a sound basis for inferring specific attitudes, opinions, perceptions or beliefs. Thus the design of written questionnaires, interview questions, and observation schedules requires as much planning and consideration as the design of tests of achievement, if not more.

What do instruments tell us?

Attitude surveys are frequently used for decision-making by organizations – examples are market research on new products, polls of political views in different areas to determine canvassing emphasis, instruments to assist in counselling students or employees, and job interest profiles to help provide guidance on career choices. In this book, the focus is on research and the aim is to create valid and reliable operational definitions for variables for which we wish to investigate interrelationships. Some texts on measurement focus on consumers or customers rather than research issues; while many of the principles of design are the same, some caution must be exercised in heeding all the guidance in such texts.

Also, there is always the possibility that instrument design may be the prime interest of a study, where the aim would be to improve on the validity of an existing one or replace it or substitute a more tedious or time-consuming established method with a more efficient one. Such instruments may be *standardized*, designed in such a way that the mean for the population is fixed and known – for example, career interest profiles. This is based upon applying the instrument to a number of carefully selected representative samples, which then allows the administrator to compare the results of individuals to that of a population. By comparing individuals' scores with population parameters, information on the likelihood of succeeding in specific career choices can be conveyed to clients to help them decide. Creating a standardized instrument is a complex task; if one is needed for a research project as a measure of a variable or a means for classifying subjects, then using an existing one may be more efficient and effective than creating one from scratch. There is insufficient space here to provide guidance for generating a standardized instrument, though the chapter does provide criteria for choosing an existing one to maximize construct validity for the variables of interest in research. Its main function is to provide some basic guidelines for creating your own instruments for immediate use on a research project.

How do we decide what sort of instrument is needed? Going back several chapters, it was suggested that to enhance construct validity, it would be necessary to maintain logical links across research questions, concepts, constructs, hypotheses and instruments. Table 9.1 outlines this process for four examples of research questions addressing issues related to views or attitudes, providing and highlighting some of the main planning stages. The purposes of the four studies are based on the following statements of research intent:

1   The aim is to determine whether one news programme is more appealing than another, based on what the researcher thinks constitutes 'appealing'. The researcher has decided that, for this population (viewers) and corresponding samples, this will consist of a combination of personal traits of the broadcaster and how the programme is presented, as well as the content of the news broadcasts. The total score on a set of questions will be the quantitative indicator of appeal.

2   What are young people's attitudes towards drug use, as indicated by the total score on the instrument (the higher the score the more positive the attitude), and does social class or educational achievement have any bearing on these attitudes?

3   Would a specially planned regime of personal attention and teaching/coaching by a trained teaching assistant result in a lasting improvement in classroom behaviour among disruptive children?

4   The outcome of interest here is how well rested patients are after a night's sleep. This is based on the assumption that speed of recovery is enhanced by high-quality rest and sleep. Two regimes for drug administration during night-time periods of sleep are to be compared. The challenge is to devise an instrument to quantify 'restedness'.

TABLE 9.1
Exemplar research questions with hypotheses, designs, samples, constructs and possible instruments

Research question	Hypothesis	Design	Sample*	Concept/construct	Instrument(s)
1 Which television news programme is the most appealing and effective to the viewing audiences?	One news programme will be perceived by the public as more appealing and effective than another.	D3 (ex post facto) $RS \to \underline{X}_a \to O_a$ $RS \to \underline{X}_b \to O_b$ (Table 3.3, modified)	A random sample of viewers, in the broadcast area of both programmes, who watch both programmes.	*Concept*: appealing and effective news broadcast. *Construct*: traits of broadcasters, style of presentation, and content of programmes.	Self-report attitude questionnaire on various aspects of presentation, style, appearance, etc. Measure: total score.
2 Are there any relationships across social class, educational achievement, and attitudes towards drug use among 14–17-year-olds? (Modified from Table 2.2)	It is expected that there will be a negative correlation between social class and attitude towards drug use, and a negative correlation between educational achievement and attitude towards drug use for a representative selection of 14–17-year-olds.	E1 (correlational) $RS \to O_a, O_b, O_c, \ldots$ (Table 3.3)	A random sample of students at local schools.	*Classification*: by social class. *Construct*: family characteristics. *Classification*: academic achievement. *Construct*: grade point average, expected GCSE grades. *Concept*: attitude towards drug use. *Construct*: views on use by self and friends, benefits, harm, etc.	Factual information to establish categories, questionnaire to determine attitudes. Attitude measure: total score on questionnaire.
3 Would a regime of personal attention and teaching have a lasting effect on behaviour of disruptive children in primary classrooms?	Changes in behaviour of disruptive children will be long lasting if there is a period of personal attention to improve self-image through success in work.	C5 (time series) $(RS) \to O_1 \to O_2 \to O_3$ $\to X \to O_4 \to O_5 \to O_6$ (Table 7.3)	A sample of children in a school that have been classified as highly disruptive.	*Concept*: disruptiveness in the classroom. *Construct*: specific behaviours that are initiated by the child to draw attention and/or disrupt the class.	Observational ratings to determine the degree of disruptive behaviour over a one-hour period. Measure: number of incidents per hour.
4 What night-time medication regime (where prescriptions allow) would enhance quality of sleep for hospital patients? (Table 2.2)	In a given hospital, patients on 24-hour prescriptions will be expected to feel more rested if they are awakened for medicines at times that follow REM (X_a) than equal time intervals (X_0).	C2 (quasi-experimental) $RA_a \to O_{a1} \to X_a \to O_{a2}$ $RA_0 \to O_{01} \to X_0 \to O_{02}$ (Table 3.3)	Random assignment of patients in an available hospital ward to one regime or the other.	*Concept*: degree of 'restedness'. *Construct*: (a) perception of having a good night's sleep, feeling rested; (b) inverse of irritability next day.	(a) Self-report questionnaire asking respondent's perception of restedness; (b) nurse's rating of patient based on perceived restedness. Measures: total scores.

* Not all of these are as good as they could be.

Developing an appropriate instrument requires not only maintaining construct validity through appropriate choice of questions linked to the concept and construct, but also taking into consideration the population and sample and their idiosyncrasies. Each row takes one research question through the major decision-making stages, summarizing the results leading to the instruments. Questions 1 and 4 will be used as examples in the subsequent sections, while 2 and 3 will be used as the bases for Activities 9.1–9.3. The process of making decisions for the last column – in other words, what instruments seem most appropriate – will be discussed as each type of question or process is considered below.

Another way of thinking about which instrument(s) would be appropriate is to consider the design and execution process backwards: what data do you expect to obtain that will resolve your hypotheses and answer your question? Will the quantitative data provide what is needed for the statistical tests? As a final check, Oppenheim (1992) suggests that one use the pilot results: does the instrument potentially produce the necessary data? Can you resolve your research question with these kinds of results? If you don't face this issue until the last questionnaire is coded or the last interview is conducted you may find yourself in trouble. We will come back to this approach later as various statistical tests are considered in relation to the different research designs proposed earlier. In reality, both processes should be carried out in parallel, but here we will focus on the consistency with the research question and variables described in the hypotheses. This will involve developing some criteria for choices, a few useful tools and approaches for organizing thinking to make the process more systematic, and guidelines for the development of different types of questions and instruments. Working systematically and documenting what one does will maintain consistency and make it possible to change your mind in a justifiable manner. It is easier to review what has been done and check the consistency of decisions when they are written down, than when keeping them in your head. Obviously, the 'tools' and techniques presented are not the only ones possible, but they should help to organize your thinking and keep track of progress and decisions.

CONSTRUCT VALIDITY: THREE APPROACHES

It is appropriate to note that the process of instrument design that will be covered here is not the only one possible, though it is probably the most appropriate for researcher-developed instruments. How one ensures that an instrument measures what it is supposed to measure tends to be achieved in one of three ways (Mehrens and Lehmann, 1984; Murphy and Davidshofer, 1991).

- The *logical* or rational approach. Based upon a theory, each concept to be measured with an instrument results in construct elaboration and in turn a set of questions or observations. Trial sets of questions are piloted on subjects and those that contribute the most to high reliability are used in the final instrument. This is common in academic research and the construction of questions will be described below; the process of quantifying reliability will be presented in Chapter 11.

- The *factor-analytic* or homogeneous approach. Starting with a concept (for example, intelligence), a set of questions is generated that is given to a trial group of subjects. Using factor analysis on the results, groups of questions are identified with sufficient commonality to determine constructs that make up the concept. For example, Kline (1991) maintains that fluid intelligence (reasoning ability) and crystallized ability (the set of skills valued by a culture, exemplified by vocabulary tests) account for a considerable part of the variability in scores on intelligence tests. Construct sets are then used to make up the final test. See also McKennell (1978) and Traub (1994) for more information on this process.

- The *empirical* approach. Using the characteristics or behaviours of recognized, independently classified subjects for a reasonably well-defined trait (for example, schizophrenia), a set of questions is generated. These are administered to the group possessing the trait and to a control group lacking the trait. Those questions that best discriminate between the two are subsequently used in the final instrument. For example, the Minnesota Multiphasic Personality Inventory has been designed this way to identify the presence of a number of recognized personality disorders. The process of developing such instruments is highly specialized and beyond the scope of this book, though more information can be found in Anastasi (1990) and Nunnally and Bernstein (1994).

These three approaches are summarized for comparison in Figure 9.1; and this chapter will concentrate on the first.

Rational or logical approach

As noted, the main focus in this chapter is on researcher-designed instruments, so the following guidelines will provide ways of enhancing the validity and reliability of these. Ideally, in order to obtain the highest reliability, a set of questions should be developed for trial, using a greater number than what will be necessary on the final instrument. Correlations between each item and the total score on trials can then be calculated and those with the highest would be included in the instrument (McKennell, 1978; Traub, 1994). We will consider an example of this in Chapter 11 after introducing reliability coefficients.

To provide an instrument with a high construct validity, it is necessary to proceed systematically through the stages of development. The need to maintain

FIGURE 9.1
Three approaches to question set construction for a concept/variable

Logical:	Theory → concept → constructs → question set
Factor-analytic:	Concept → questions → factor analysis of trial data → question set → constructs
Empirical:	Observations → questions → group scores → constructs → question set

logical consistency may seem obvious, but it is not trivial and one must be careful about semantics. Consider for example, the intention of a researcher to investigate the efficiency of an organization. A questionnaire to a sample of employees would, at best, measure their *perception* of efficiency and not organizational efficiency. Efficiency can be defined to be a quantifiable concept based on indicators such as productivity per employee, lack of down time, good use of time, etc. Most employees would not have direct access to these data; therefore, the most appropriate concept to measure would be what they perceive to be the level of efficiency. As with many concepts, there can be a distinct difference between the concept and the subjects' perception of the concept, a difference the researcher must make clear from the beginning.

One way of approaching the task of elaborating on a concept is to list methodically all the contributing components of the construct for that concept. This process may result in changing the nature or number of variables to be investigated. For example, using case 1 in Table 9.1, it was decided by the researcher that two concepts were potentially involved, as shown in Table 9.2. When the list was initially made, it was felt that 'appeal of news broadcasts' had two distinct contributing factors worth considering: the announcers' traits and presentation style (how the news was presented) as well as the broadcast content (what was presented). When all the components are listed in this way, they may naturally divide into constructs supporting more than one concept.

As a second example, consider case 4 from Table 9.1. The researcher decided that there were two groups of observations (what hospital patients do and their perceptions), as shown in Table 9.3. Rather than constituting two variables, it was decided that these simply contributed to a single concept and the difference would be in how the data would be collected, not in the construct. In other words, to get a complete view of their state of restedness, it was worthwhile not only asking the subjects, but also observing them.

These two exemplar lists provide a starting-point that will be built upon as the instruments develop in subsequent sections. Carry out Activity 9.1 now.

TABLE 9.2
Table of constructs for the concept 'appeal of news broadcasts' (to be used for questionnaire construction)

Components	Announcers' traits/ presentation	Programme content
Use of vocabulary and terminology in news reports		✓
Clarity of speech, enunciation of words, rate of speaking	✓	
Facial expressions and their effective use	✓	
Sense of fairness, objectivity in reporting		✓
Lack of obvious political bias		✓
Projected image of self-confidence and authority	✓	
Taste in clothes	✓	
General personality	✓	
Balance of gender of broadcasters	✓	
Effective use of pictures and video		✓
Relevance of topics to viewers		✓
Provides background for less well-known issues		✓
Are not condescending when presenting complex issues	✓	

TABLE 9.3
Table of constructs
for the concept 'level
of restedness', for
study 4 in Table 9.1
(to be used for
observation schedule
and interview)

Components	Patients' perception	What patients do
Frequency of dozing off during day		✓
Clarity of thought, logic, forgetfulness		✓
Demands on nursing staff		✓
What patients think their sleep quality was	✓	
Disorientation level, lost wandering about		✓
Irritability, crabbiness		✓
Appetite at breakfast		✓
How much time patients think they slept	✓	
How often patients think they were awakened	✓	
How fresh and rested patients think they are	✓	
How often patients think they awakened themselves	✓	

Activity 9.1

(a) Consider the components in Tables 9.2 and 9.3: would you add, delete or change any of these? Why?

(b) Using studies 2 and/or 3 in Table 9.1, set out a table of constructs for the elaboration of the concepts/variables to be measured. Keep this for use in later activities.

(c) If you are intending to use a questionnaire in your own research, make up a list of contributing factors that would elaborate on the concept to be measured. Discuss this with colleagues to determine the comprehensiveness of coverage.

(d) Acquire a questionnaire or interview schedule and list what you think are the factors being measured and ultimately what the original concept is. How effective and comprehensive do you think the researcher was in elaborating on the original concept? Try to improve on the list.

INSTRUMENT VALIDITY: GENERAL CONSIDERATIONS

It is much more difficult to devise instruments that measure attitudes, views and opinions reliably and validly than it is to measure achievement of intellectual (cognitive) skills. Attitudes can change over short periods of time, under different stimuli, and with the feeling at the moment, whereas skills and knowledge are much more stable. We are continually assaulted by images, other people's views, news, and discussions that influence our opinions and attitudes, consequently predictive validity will tend to be very low. The concern here is for construct validity with the emphasis on maintaining logical consistency between the concept, construct and instrument content to provide a measure at that moment. This may be verified by checking against another measure (concurrent validity) – for example, comparing recent voting patterns against a set of questions on political views. This example does point up the problem of distinguishing between attitudes and understanding. Does someone vote for Conservative (or Liberal) candidates because they have a grasp of the issues or because they would agree with anything that is said by members of that party or faction? Some 'attitudes' can be a replacement for rational thinking, a product of intellectual inability or laziness; it can be easier just to succumb to pressure and agree. Other attitudes are so strongly held as to prevent a person from even considering the logic and reasoning of alternative perspectives. 'Technophobia' has purportedly hindered people learning about computers, though it could be argued that it is a fear of failure which is frequently the real problem.

As noted earlier, attitudes are of interest because of their potential to influence actions, but causal links are very difficult to establish since most overt actions are the product of numerous variables. Even though we might infer from an instrument that someone is prejudiced towards an ethnic group, how this is manifest in behaviour could range from simple avoidance of interaction to fire-bombing. A Ghanaian colleague once said, when he was a student, that he preferred landlords in Germany who would tell him 'we do not rent to black people!' rather than those in England who would very politely say when he appeared at the door 'Oh, sorry, I've just rented it to someone else', he having just called from the phone box across the street.

In recent years, the impact of attitudes towards learning on learner motivation has prompted interest in affective measures. A teacher does not always have control over the causes of attitude problems, but being able to identify some of them is a start. Most techniques involve either observation or self-report forms (questionnaires) that learners complete. Specific applications, such as course evaluation schemes, tend to be a mixture of learners recording observations and attitudes on various rating scales, which have contributed to evaluation studies. As with any data-collecting situation, the validity of these will depend on identifying what concepts are to be measured and avoiding the temptation just to sit down and producing a quick questionnaire.

How accurately we can infer attitudes from responses to questions is limited by a number of personal traits of respondents (some of these are referred to as *response sets*), which include the following (Cronbach, 1990; Mehrens and Lehmann, 1984; Murphy and Davidshofer, 1991):

- *Faking* results in the respondent answering in a way that he or she thinks will make a good or bad overall impression. This is a serious problem with personality tests when the intent of items is rather transparent. This may be more of a challenge for clinicians than researchers, unless the instrument is being used either to classify subjects for treatment or to assess the success of a treatment. Communicating the purpose of the study and convincing subjects that the results will have no personal consequences for them or yourself may alleviate this. Alternatively, it has been suggested that the purpose of the instrument should be disguised, though the ethics of this is questionable. Faking is sometimes referred to as *dissimulation*.
- *Social desirability* results in answers that are commensurate with what the subjects think they should say, rather than what they feel. Middle-class, middle-aged men are not expected to like hard acid rock. Getting people

who are prejudiced to admit it may be difficult in some countries, or to admit that they think positive discrimination is a good idea in others. Preceding the 1992 general election in the United Kingdom, opinion polls (telephone or face to face) predicted the Conservative Party would lose, but they were wrong. Subsequent investigations suggested that many people did not want to be seen to vote for the party that advocated greed, so they said they would not vote Conservative, but did. It has been suggested that letting subjects answer on paper (like a ballot), thus giving them a greater sense of anonymity, would reduce false answers. On the other hand, questionnaires administered to colleagues can elicit the response 'What do you *really* want for answers?'. Unfortunately, such an intention to be helpful can generate invalid results.

- *Bias* towards either end, or the middle, of a rating or Likert scale may indicate an inability to make a decision or take a stand. Choosing mostly in the middle could also be due to poorly worded questions that do not stimulate subjects to take a stand.
- *Misinterpretation* of questions, due to vocabulary, local use of words, or limited vocabulary of respondents can adversely affect the validity of results. Careful piloting should minimize this.
- *Random* responding on scales or multiple choice can happen with an audience that is captive, as when one's respondents are students in a class 'volunteered' by the teacher.
- *Uncommon*, intentionally misleading responses, can also distort results. Again, if subjects are not convinced of the value of responding, this can occur.

Sometimes there is a need for separate external or internal verification of responses, particularly if there is a tendency in trials towards any of the above. Without careful question construction, you may end up measuring personality traits rather than attitudes! In the following sections, suggestions for writing different types of questions, and ways of avoiding distorted responses as a result of these, will be considered.

MEASURING INSTRUMENTS FOR ATTITUDES, OPINIONS AND VIEWS

It has long been recognized that paper-based instruments cannot validly and reliably measure all the abilities that are relevant to an individual's personal development or state of mind. Some tasks can be performed adequately through the integration of cognitive and psychomotor skills, while others require cognitive skills that are effective only if the person has the appropriate attitude. For example, the insurance salesperson must not only understand different types of policies and be able to advise a client appropriately, but also bring to his job a caring and concerned approach. To assess the effectiveness of an interaction would require an observer to watch an actual sales situation or possibly a role-play activity, and systematically record all observations.

Opinions and beliefs unrelated to someone's job may be even more difficult to ascertain, simply because the target group may not be in one place or in a single job role. Researchers conducting surveys of attitudes, opinions and beliefs of groups have a notoriously difficult task in getting all subjects to respond. Some organizations have resorted to personal interviews and enticements (prizes, coupons for goods, etc.) instead of depending on just the voluntary return of a questionnaire. They still have volunteers, though they may be happier ones. If a sample is going to be of any size, this will more than likely require resources beyond those available to the typical postgraduate student or academic researcher. Thus, one's instrument must not only elicit the desired information, but also sell itself. Criteria for using different types of instruments will be provided as each is introduced, along with some guidelines for their construction.

To provide a reasonably comprehensive coverage of the types of instruments commonly used, the following types of instruments will be considered:

- written question sets in self-report questionnaires;
- open-ended or free-response questions;
- observation schedules;
- structured interviews.

As each is presented, guidelines for writing questions and schedules will be given. Further details and additional examples can be found in the numerous specialist texts on measurement.

Questionnaires: Written question sets for completion by subjects

The design of attitude surveys in the form of questionnaires is not a trivial task and entire books have been written on this topic, one of the best being that by Oppenheim (1992). What is presented here serves only as an introduction, and the actual construction of any questionnaire should be preceded by additional reading. The format of questionnaires can vary considerably, employing free-response questions, checklists, or rating scales, with all the intrinsic problems of validity and reliability associated with each discussed in earlier sections.

The design of written instruments requires the same degree of planning as that of observation schedules and cognitive achievement tests. It is worthwhile elaborating on the attitude, value, belief or feeling (concept) that is to be measured through the process of devising a table of constructs. Writing statements of general observable indicators of these (construct) before attempting to write an actual set of questions (operational definition) for a questionnaire will help to ensure the validity of the final instrument. For example, consider the survey problem facing organizations whose task it is to determine the popularity of programmes on television channels. Take the specific case of research question 1 in Table 9.1, concerning the comparison of the news broadcasts of two channels: to ensure the validity of the resulting survey instrument, an endeavour must be made to elaborate on just what might contribute to the appeal (or lack of appeal) of such programmes. Among others, a number of factors that make up the construct arise with respect to the perceived conciseness, understandability and effectiveness that could contribute to appeal (concept) of news broadcasts. One way of organizing these was shown in Table 9.2, where it was decided to consider two sources of appeal (concepts): personal and content delivery.

As can be seen, there are a number of attitudes that will be potentially difficult to measure, and what may make the problem more complex is the necessity to ensure that the actual questions are understood by the subjects. Thus, words used in the list of contributing attitudes may have to be presented in simpler terms if respondents are going to be from a broad range of viewers. Words such as 'condescending' and 'objectivity' may have to be replaced by more basic terminology to ensure that persons with a limited vocabulary can respond without having to reach for the dictionary. In such cases, it may be of value to employ a test of readability – for example, the Flesch Reading Ease Scale described in Singer and Donlan (1980) and included as part of some word-processing packages – to help ensure that subjects find the resulting questionnaire understandable.

In many cases, it will also be necessary to adjust the vocabulary to prevent leaving the definition of key terms to the subjects. For example, the concept above relates to the perceived conciseness, understandability and effectiveness of news broadcasts; consequently, *none* of these three adjectives should appear in the questionnaire. It is up to the researcher to define what is meant by understandable, concise and effective. To ask subjects if a broadcast was effective would leave *them* to define what is effective. The English language is littered with words having imprecise meanings, prone to various interpretations. Therefore, it is up to the designer of instruments to ensure that terminology used is unambiguous and not liable to multiple interpretation. This applies not only to words that potentially have multiple meanings or interpretations, but also to colloquial terms, which should be avoided altogether. The wording of questions and statements in a questionnaire is the key to its validity as a measuring instrument, and can contribute significantly to its reliability or lack thereof.

Only a few types of questions will be presented here, and the reader is encouraged to consult various texts for additional information and ideas. The key issue for a designer is to ensure that:

- the resulting questionnaire is comprehensive in its coverage of contributing factors for the concept to be measured;
- the subjects can understand the questions or statements;
- the terms that are used that are unambiguous and do not require the subject to define them.

A more extensive list of guidelines follows the examples of selected types of questions and statements provided below. We will consider binary questions with a yes/no choice, rating scales where respondents choose among alternatives, and Likert scales where the respondents indicate level of agreement or disagreement with statements presented.

Binary questions versus rating scales

Sets of questions that can be answered by a 'yes' or 'no' response should be restricted to truly binary situations. If additional information can be acquired by asking for a rating of an event, perception or attitude, then information would be lost by asking simply whether it existed or not. For example, a questionnaire item asking whether or not a lecturer used the overhead projector effectively, offering only two choices, possibly forces an unreliable answer. In other words, if the same question were asked about the same event later, it might elicit the opposite response. On the other hand, asking for a relative rating of the use of the overhead in a lecture allows a range of answers, but the various levels of a rating scale must be unambiguous to the subject, or again there will be the danger that the answer would be unreliable. In such situations, a binary question could be used as a filter, the rating questions only answered if the binary question were answered affirmatively. Figure 9.2 illustrates the use of both types of questions, building on the analysis in Table 9.2 for the study on news broadcasting. There is a difficulty in designing rating questions in this format in that all those in a set must be answerable using the same scale.

Alternatively, one could have a different scale for each question, as illustrated in Figure 9.3. The advantage of this format is that it is possible to be more explicit about what the extremes indicate, enhancing the reliability and validity of the instrument. The disadvantage is that they take up more space and can make the questionnaire appear longer, possibly discouraging respondents and adversely affecting the representativeness of the sample.

Likert scales

Attitudes can also be ascertained by presenting a list of declarative statements and asking respondents to rate them in terms of agreement or disagreement. Figure 9.4 provides a sample set of statements intended to query the same issues as used in Figures 9.2 and 9.3. Note that not all the statements would require a 'strongly agree' to be positive, thus scoring would require the point value of some to be the opposite of the rest. In other words, 'strongly agree' would be 5 points for (a) but 1 point for (c). Again, it is the total score that would be the quantified indicator of the trait or attitude, in order to achieve maximum reliability and validity. Creating meaningful statements that are unambiguous, but not so strongly worded as to bias responses, requires

1. Do you watch news broadcasts on Channel 3 on the television? .... yes ☐ no ☐

If you responded 'no', please go on to question 2.

If you responded 'yes', please indicate the quality of each of the following by placing an X in the appropriate box concerning the news announcers:

	very poor	poor	acceptable	good	very good
(a) clarity of speech	☐	☐	☐	☐	☐
(b) use of appropriate vocabulary	☐	☐	☐	☐	☐
(c) their taste in clothes	☐	☐	☐	☐	☐

FIGURE 9.2
Sample binary and rating questions of the 'tick the box' format

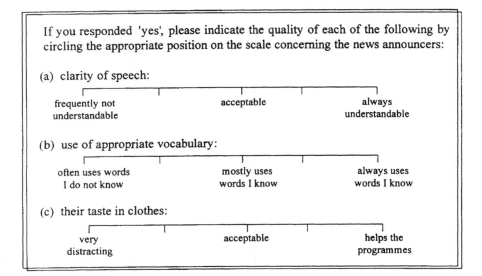

FIGURE 9.3
Alternative rating
scale structure for
the same traits as in
Figure 9.2

FIGURE 9.4
Sample Likert scales
for the same issues
used in Figures 9.2
and 9.3

trying sets of questions with persons typical of research subjects. Scales can have a seven-point spread as opposed to five points, if it is felt that this better represents the range of attitudes or views.

On all of these, there can be some ambiguity as to what the middle choice means to respondents: 'uncertain', 'acceptable', etc. There has been some discussion in the literature as to the desirability of having a neutral point on a scale, with the suggestion that respondents will tend to choose the centre. While this might be true in some situations, each concept must be evaluated individually to see whether or not the central point has meaning and would be valued. Remember that it will be the total score for a set of questions that will constitute the operational definition; therefore, it may not be unreasonable for respondents to have a neutral view on some components of the construct.

The following guidelines for constructing questions and statements for ratings and scales summarize the major points a designer must consider, taking into account the various common response problems suggested earlier. These have been gleaned from a number of texts on measurement (e.g., Mehrens and Lehmann, 1984; Oppenheim, 1992):

1   Use the list of specific attitudes, perceptions, opinions that you want to measure which elaborate on the concept to make it a construct, as illustrated in Tables 9.2 and 9.3.
2   Several statements should be used to measure aspects of each concept (set of attitudes) to ensure reliability and validity.
3   Refer to the present rather than the past; remember that attitudes are transient.
4   Statements should be simply worded using short sentences (less than 20 words), to avoid misinterpretation.
5   Avoid statements that sound like facts.
6   Avoid global terms like 'always', 'never', 'only', etc.
7   Statements should be unambiguous to prevent misinterpretation; for example, terms like 'a fair price' and 'equal opportunities' can have more than one interpretation.
8   Avoid the use of clichés, colloquial terms, jargon, technical terms and acronyms.
9   Do not use the terminology for the concept you are investigating, as it may have multiple interpretations. For example, if you were enquiring about 'administrative efficiency', the construct component list should define what you mean by this and the questions should ask about these components. The words 'administrative efficiency' should not appear in any of the questions.
10   Avoid statements that encourage a specific response or bias; for example, starting a statement with 'Research has shown that . . .' lends undue authority to the claim which this qualifies.
11   Restrict statements to a single issue or component of the construct list.
12   Avoid statements with which everyone would tend to agree or disagree. If everyone agrees, this will reduce natural variability (true score variance) and ultimately lower the reliability of the set of questions (see equations (8.1) to (8.5)).
13   Aim for half positive and half negative statements, randomly distributing them in the questionnaire. This should help to minimize the temptation just to mark all of them the same, reducing bias.
14   Sensitive questions should be towards the middle of a set, but interspersed with less sensitive ones. Care in wording is needed to prevent faking.
15   Use a three- to seven-point scale.
16   Use extremes other than 'agree–disagree' (except Likert scales).
17   Generate more items than ultimately needed to allow for some rejections after trials.

18   Underline or italicize negative components, such as *not, unwanted, irrele-vant*.

19   Try the instrument out on a representative group of persons before using it as part of the actual data collection.

You may find that with experience and further reading this list will grow. The better the questions, the lower the error variance and consequently the higher the reliability (recall equation (8.5)). Such lists will help avoid the worst pitfalls, but piloting is still essential, followed by rewriting and outright rejection of some individual items.

From where do we get the wording of the statements for these? Obviously some will come logically from the elaboration of the concept to its components as in Table 9.2. Others may well derive from interviews, other research, or personal experience and contact with the target group. In any case, the focus should be on how well the subjects will understand and how they will react. While there has been an emphasis on piloting sets of questions, there is nothing wrong with sitting down with a few people typical of respondents and going through the questions one at a time before piloting. Let them tell you what they think they mean.

Making up a questionnaire

When designing a questionnaire, there is a need to decide how many questions to include. Table 9.4 is simply an extension of Table 9.2 with the number and type of each question corresponding to the construct component. Here, two items for each component have been designated since this allows for a split-half reliability coefficient to be calculated. Thus for the trial, the researcher might wish to make up at least three for each so that the weak can be eliminated and the best can be kept.

The total number of items in a set that constitute an operational definition will influence the reliability: the more questions the higher the reliability. As McKennell (1978) notes:

Unreliability at the item level is of course the main justification for scaling [using sets of questions]. Since the errors on a particular item are random they tend to cancel out; and the total score obtained by adding scores on successive items tends increasingly to be determined by the common factor running through the items.

Thus the more items, the higher the reliability will tend to be. The upper limit is determined by how many the respondents can tolerate without tossing the questionnaire in the rubbish bin. More than one overly long questionnaire arriving in the post has decayed slowly on my desk. As a rule of thumb, four pages is the maximum, unless you have the resources to have someone stand over the respondents while they complete the instrument.

As you may have noted, another column has been added to Table 9.4, one that includes the factual questions to be asked. As noted earlier, while one does not wish to pry unnecessarily, sufficient information is needed if you

TABLE 9.4
Table of constructs for the concept 'appeal of news broadcasts', with an indication of number and types of questions for each construct

Components	Announcers' traits/ presentation	Programme content	Classify: Subjects' traits
Use of vocabulary and terminology in news reports		2 rating	
Clarity of speech, enunciation of words, rate of speaking	2 Likert		
Facial expressions and their effective use	2 Likert		
Sense of fairness, objectivity in reporting		2 rating	
Lack of obvious political bias		2 rating	
Projected image of self-confidence and authority	2 Likert		
Taste in clothes	2 Likert		
General personality	2 Likert		
Balance of gender of broadcasters	2 Likert		
Effective use of pictures and video		2 rating	
Relevance of topics to viewers		2 rating	
Provision of background for less well-known issues		2 rating	
Lack of condescension when presenting complex issues	2 Likert		
Age			Factual
Watching time			Factual
Gender			Factual

wish to identify groups, subgroups or traits within a sample. These need to be included in the planning as well, particularly for ex post facto designs, where the responses may contribute to the classification of subjects, or correlational studies, where they may constitute other variables.

While the trial questionnaire may be longer than the final version, it should be produced as professionally as possible, if for no other reason than to try out the page layout. Instruments that appear to be professionally prepared will have a greater probability of being completed (greater face validity). With all the desktop publishing capabilities of contemporary word-processors, there is plenty of scope for producing attractive instruments, pleasantly laid out, and easy to complete. Figure 9.5 provides a truncated version of a questionnaire that illustrates factual questions, a Likert scale, a rating scale and a free-response question. Obviously, there should be more questions, but the intention here is to show page layout. If this were to follow the plan outlined in Table 9.4, then the total questionnaire (14 Likert questions and 12 ratings) for both channels might just fit on four pages. The difficulty of balancing length against presentation quality is one that needs careful consideration. If the typeface is too small and the lines are too close together, respondents will find this irritating. If the questionnaire appears to be too long, there is a tendency not to complete it. The questions could be preceded by a page describing the purpose of the study and thanking the respondents for participating.

The Television News Broadcasting Survey

We are conducting a survey among a selected group of television viewers who watch news broadcasts on both Channels 1 and 2. As you are in the unique position to compare the two, would you please complete this questionnaire and the second one about Channel 2? Thank you.

A. Please tell us a little about yourself:

How old are you? _____ years   Male ☐   Female ☐

Approximately how much time do you spend watching television each day?

0–1 hr ☐   1–2 hrs ☐   2–3 hrs ☐   3–4 hrs ☐   4–5 hrs ☐   more than 5 hrs ☐

B. The following questions refer to news broadcasts on Channel 1

Please indicate the quality of each of the following by circling the appropriate position on the line with respect to the news announcers:

(a) clarity of speech:

    frequently not understandable   usually acceptable   always understandable

(b) projects objectivity and fairness in reporting on present political issues:

    often seem biased   usually acceptable   always unbiased

(c) use of video clips and photographs:

    ineffective use of pictures   acceptable use   always helps understanding

(d)

C. These questions refer to the news announcers on Channel 1

Please indicate your agreement or disagreement with the statements about the quality of each characteristic of news announcers. Place an X in the appropriate box in each case:

	Strongly agree	Agree	Uncertain	Disagree	Strongly disagree
(a) The news announcers speak clearly and can be heard easily	☐	☐	☐	☐	☐
(b) Their use of facial expressions contribute to the quality of programmes . .	☐	☐	☐	☐	☐
(c) Their taste in clothes is not very good and is distracting	☐	☐	☐	☐	☐
(d)					

D. Please tell us in your own words what you think would improve news broadcasts

_____

_____

Thank you for completing this questionnaire. Please return it in the self-addressed stamped envelope provided.

FIGURE 9.5
Exemplar page layout for a written questionnaire

Sitting with a few individuals as they complete an instrument, or even getting colleagues to look at the structure, will help to avoid the worst problems of page design. Allow sufficient time between completing trials and when the questionnaires need to go out to subjects, as revisions and reproduction can take longer than one might expect. Carry out Activity 9.2 now.

> **Activity 9.2**
>
> Use a set of constructs either from your own proposed research (Activity 9.1(c)), or those identified in Activity 9.1(b)
> (a) Which type would be most appropriate? Complete a table like Table 9.4.
> (b) Say why each type was chosen.
> (c) Devise some typical questions. Bring them to class for consideration.
> (d) What would you do to improve the questionnaire in Figure 9.5?

Open-ended or free-response questions

In Chapter 8, it was noted that the opposite of closed questions like those illustrated in the previous sections, was open-ended questions. They tend to ask for *divergent* responses, generating unpredictable (for individual respondents) answers, or *evaluative* responses, where the respondent is asked to justify a judgement or opinion. The results of these tend to be difficult to quantify, since not all respondents will include the same issues or justifications in their answers. For example, consider the simple question at the end of the questionnaire in Figure 9.5. The researcher will be left not knowing whether respondents did not mention an issue because they did not think it was important, or because it just never occurred to them. The number of persons mentioning something is not necessarily an indication of its relative importance to the public. This is where a structured question may have greater validity. Results can be tabulated and displayed as descriptive statistics (bar charts), but inferences based upon comparisons can be dubious. Some respondents may mention a half-dozen issues while others only one. Free-response questions can help to confirm that the issues raised in structured questions are the ones of importance, though again respondents may be prompted to comment based upon the items they have just completed.

At the extreme, whole projects have been based upon a few free-response questions. For example, Levine (1966) quantified achievement motivation among secondary school students cross-culturally, by having them write essays describing what they thought it meant to be a successful person and how to become a successful person. Setting questions that asked them to describe what they thought it meant to be a successful person allowed the researchers to tally the frequencies of specific anticipated indicative responses.

The challenge in constructing and wording free-response questions is much the same as for essay questions in an examination (see Chapter 10). If the question is too vague, then the respondents may never get around to the issues you would like addressed and fill the space with unrelated views. For example, which is most likely to elicit responses related to the introduction of computers and information technology in the workplace and which will possibly draw unrelated responses?

(a) Discuss what you think about computers.

(b) What do you see as the role of computers in employment and, in particular, your present job or one you would like to have?

Being specific without being too restrictive or directing the respondents to a single answer is not an easy task. What does help is to outline the range of responses that you would expect. This will be necessary if you are going to quantify the results, and devising a tentative list will help to decide whether or not the question will stimulate the desired range of responses.

Coding written essays/open-ended responses

Carefully worded questions make it somewhat easier to devise a well-planned *coding frame*, a list of responses for which the frequency can be recorded. While some responses may be anticipated, it may be necessary to construct a coding frame after the questionnaires have been administered to the sample. A tentative coding frame based upon trials will tell you whether or not the questions are eliciting a range of responses, but may not be comprehensive. If not updated, the 'other' category may become disproportionately large. Yet if the survey is large, leaving the coding of open-ended questions until the end could delay producing results for a report.

Unfortunately, reading and coding the responses to open-ended questions can be quite time-consuming. Therefore, unless there is a very good reason for the contrary, only a few tend to be used in instruments. In general, such questions are of limited value for the following reasons:

- An absence of responses due to a vague question or lack of prompting statement.
- Some respondents more articulate than others.
- Responses are difficult to quantify: some may provide more than one response.
- It is not easy to get polarized views.

In addition, it is necessary to train readers who will assign points or tally frequencies for answers, if the responses are to be quantified validly and reliably. Open questions are an advantage when one is not sure what sorts of responses are to be anticipated, and they can lead to understanding why some views or opinions are held. Carefully constructed, such questions can provide responses similar to those from structured interviews.

Non-written measurement techniques: observations

The integration of intellectual skills and attitudes is not an easy task. How often have you encountered a salesperson in a store who knew all there was to know about the products being sold, but conveyed the attitude that you, the customer, were an idiot? Have you been in a bank where it was always assumed that the mistake was yours? When did you last come across a receptionist on the other end of the telephone who made you feel guilty about making the call? How were you treated the last time you went to collect unemployment benefit: 'Here for your dole money, are you, dear?' All the actions encountered have underlying attitudes that would not be easy to identify and separate from intellectual skills, if for no other reason than the fact that many people are not aware that they have them or that they affect their interactions with others. Whether the study of such is the realm of sociologists, psychologists, cultural anthropologists, or trainers in the organizations, the phenomena will be difficult to measure validly.

Observation-based techniques are potentially more valid than a paper-based instrument completed away from the situation for determining the existence of specific attitudes, beliefs or values because the data are collected in the context of a real activity. Even so, unless considerable planning is done before the event, the results can have very low reliability. It is necessary to plan what to look for as unambiguous indicators of attitudes if the exercise is to be of value in providing meaningful and valid feedback. Some general suggestions for ensuring reliability, validity and objectivity are, in summary, as follows:

1   Use a list of statements of indicative behaviours as a starting-point.
2   When observing large groups, focus on a few indicative behaviours.
3   Observation schedules should describe behaviours unambiguously, and each should be mutually exclusive.
4   Be aware of errors due to sampling times and the context in which observations are made.
5   Observations for evaluation of an interaction – such as salespersons selling a product, the use of a teaching strategy, or the responses to enquiries on the telephone – should be related to carrying out the strategy, plan or accepted procedure.
6   Extensive observations of subjects with learning difficulties or personal problems should be carried out individually, not as a group.
7   Employ a systematic recording system (several are described in the following sections) and interpret observational data later.
8   Observations should be carried out unobtrusively, preferably unknown to the subjects (but with their permission: see the section on ethics in Chapter 5).

While there are a variety of ways of collecting quantifiable observational data, two specific techniques that can be used are described in detail in this subsection: checklists and rating scales. These are different in significant ways, but they do share the common characteristic of including lists of events or behaviours that are expected to occur. It will be the relative frequency of exhibition across groups that will be of interest. Such careful planning and predetermination of what are the agreed indicators of the state or trait will enhance the reliability of the data-collection process.

Checklists

A checklist is somewhat like a shopping list, but consisting of a set of events or activities that are considered collectively to be the operational definition of the attitude. How many of these that are exhibited would, for example, indicate the strength of the belief, attitude or value. For example, how often did the subject smile or frown while viewing a video? How often do children volunteer answers in a class, as indicated by raising their hands? As actions are carried out or events occur, each is marked on the form. When observing the activities of an individual, a checklist can provide the observer with the guidance required to ensure that the occurrences of all pertinent events are recorded and that irrelevant ones are ignored. An alternative indicator of strength might be based on identifying the frequency over time of the occurrences, for example, how often in a one-hour period.

For example, in some cultures it is quite impolite and insulting to pass someone something with the left hand. Imagine a group of clerks who work in an unemployment benefits office that is visited by persons from an immigrant community. If a researcher were to observe that a number of these persons frequently passed documents only to immigrant clients with the left hand, would this indicate an intent to insult? On its own, such an observation could produce a potentially unreliable and possibly invalid inference that offence was meant and would have to be followed by an enquiry as to whether the staff were aware of such traditions. Other social cues can provide indicators of attitudes in social interchange, but the validity of inferences based upon these need to be verified.

Other examples of recording interactions in different situations have been developed. Participation charts are a specific type of checklist used as a means of recording the occurrence of participation of individuals in a group, meeting or other social encounter. They can be used to document the progress of individuals over a period of time, or to determine the nature of encounters and to infer personal attitudes during social interaction. There are no real right or wrong events on a list, just those that are agreed indicators of attitudes or perceptions. The distinct advantage of data collected in this manner is that they can be collected in a reasonably natural setting, assuming the observer's presence does not interfere with the interactions. Participation charts offer an opportunity to record not only the occurrence of such events, but also their frequency, which may be more important than just a one-off occurrence. Table 9.5 provides an example of such a chart designed to identify the level of restedness (or lack thereof) of patients in a ward after a night's sleep. Such an approach can be confounded by medication, or, with older patients, levels of senility.

Rating scales

These have the appearance of a questionnaire where each statement is rated on a scale, typically from 1 to 5, but in this situation the rater is the observer obser-

TABLE 9.5 Observation of patients in a ward in the morning, to determine their 'level of restedness', based on the analysis in Table 9.1

Activity/action	Patients			
	Mary	John	Mark	Hillary
Dozed off	///	/	////	/
Repeated oneself	//	/	////	/
Called for a nurse	////	//	//	////
Found wandering about	//		///	/
Spoke harshly to nurse or another patient	//		//	
Refused food or drink	/	/	//	
Incoherent conversation	//		///	

ving someone. Not only is the occurrence of an event recorded, but also a judgement is made on the quality of the event. These are potentially the most reliable and valid, assuming that there is agreement among raters as to the meanings of the levels. Rather than marking a checklist on a binary basis, more information is gathered. Consequently, the technology of designing rating scales is more complex than that of checklists or participation charts.

Such a scheme could be used by students in a classroom to evaluate the quality of teaching. While one might expect that the use of such a scheme by students evaluating teachers or lecturers would lack reliability due to individual interpretation of statements, Mehrens and Lehmann (1984) report that the literature describing a wide range of experiences supports their reliability. One could still question whether student *perceptions* of quality of teaching are consistent with the actual teaching quality, an issue of validity related to distinguishing between such teacher traits as personality, speech accent, content, organizational ability, use of visual aids, etc. Recall that it is possible to have an instrument that is reliable, but not valid for what it was intended.

To enhance both the reliability and validity of observational rating scales, a reasonable number of statements are needed for each concept (ten or so). This ensures that the characteristics of the concept are thoroughly covered, enhancing validity. Also, there should be sufficient components to allow some variability in marking without causing great differences in total scores on a section over time or across observers, to enhance reliability.

An important issue must be resolved when using ratings: is the emphasis on agreed-upon criteria or on comparing subjects to other subjects – that is, are the observations norm-referenced or criterion-referenced? For example, will tutors be completing a rating form thinking in terms of agreed-upon criteria, or in terms of how well the observed subject does with reference to his or her peers? The answer to this question depends upon the purpose of the exercise.

One important potential impediment to the reliable collection of data employing ratings by observers is the possibility of the *halo effect*, which is when an observer's overall impression of an event or person tends to shift scores up or down the scales. It is analogous to the problem of handwriting influencing the marking of essay items. There is the danger that, if the observer 'likes' the observed (fashionable clothes, conventional haircut, etc.), then scores on individual items may be higher. On the other hand, if the observer unconsciously does not identify positively with the subject (odd accent, personal mannerisms, choice of clothes), then marking on scales may be lower. This simply points up the need for cross-checking of ratings by other observers on a sample of observational situations to ensure the reliability of the data. A technique for quantifying consistency across observers is provided in Chapter 11, in the section on inter-scorer reliability.

Table 9.6 provides a brief extract from a rating sheet that was designed to quantify personal commitment to learning by students in a class. The observer was to complete this form for each student based upon observations made over a one-week period. The total score was treated as a quantification of relative commitment and the mean scores were found for groups or subgroups as part of an investigation.

In summary, the design of checklists and rating scales should be carried out taking into account the following points, condensed from Anastasi (1990),

TABLE 9.6
Sample set of rating scales designed to measure the level of commitment to learning in a class

Class participation inventory for_____						
Component skills	low				high	
Writing:	1	2	3	4	5	Comments
(a) clarity in presentation of ideas						
(b) seems to take exercise seriously						
(c) uses non-aggressive language						
(d) follows written instructions						
(e) submits a completed assignment						
Speaking:	1	2	3	4	5	Comments
(a) carries on conversation coherently						
(b) organizes thoughts and presents ideas clearly						
(c) projects self with confidence						
(d) follows verbal instructions						
(e) seems eager to participate						
(f) seems to take exercise seriously						
(g) uses non-aggressive language						

Cronbach (1990) and Mehrens and Lehmann (1984), sources that can be consulted for additional guidance in the design and use of such instruments:

1 Checklists are valid only for binary situations: something happens or it does not.
2 Rating scales need agreed-upon criteria for each level for each event.
3 Traits must be clearly specified by being broken down into observable, individually discernible components.
4 If at all possible, use checklists and rating scales to observe only one person at a time, using separate sheets for each.
5 Persons using checklists and rating scales must be trained to use them.

Piloting observational instruments

Observational instruments need to be piloted to ensure not only that the items on the list are appropriate indicators of constructs, but also, if more than one observer is to be involved, that there is agreement on how to mark a schedule. One way to test this is to have two people observe and record for a single session and compare results. Ultimately, it will be desirable to check the reliability of such instruments; the calculation of this is included in Chapter 11.

Structured interviews

Structured interviews use questions like the rating questions in self-response instruments and open-ended questions. These are orally presented, with the advantage that there is the opportunity for the interviewer to interpret questions, clear up misunderstandings, or even gather data from those not fully literate in the designers' language – for example, in cross-cultural studies. The difficulty is that such an approach is labour-intensive, requiring one-to-one interaction between subject and interviewer. Consequently, interviews are often limited to situations where it is absolutely necessary to get a high return rate – for example, pre-election polls or some market research – or where the subjects may lack literacy skills.

Piloting interviews

Limitations are similar in nature to those for observations: different interviewers may interpret questions and responses differently. Inter-interviewer reliability can be checked, but training and guidance are obviously needed for a team. Even individual interviewers can change over a study and confound the results. The greater the detail for question interpretation and coding forms provided, the less difference there will be across researchers and time. Piloting, where one person conducts the interview and a second observes (or videos the session) can enhance consistency of delivery.

Carry out Activity 9.3 now.

Activity 9.3

1   Look again at study 3 in Table 9.1.
   (a) Set out a table of constructs for the elaboration of what is meant by 'disruptive behaviour in the classroom'.
   (b) Devise a set of observations that correspond to this table of constructs for discussion in class, each person contributing a few. Assemble a pilot observation form, with the aim that the total score will reflect a level of disruptiveness. It may be that the behaviour does not disappear, but may subside to some degree, and the instrument must reflect this.
   (c) Devise a set of interview questions for the teacher of a disruptive child, to help to determine the nature of the disruptiveness and what seems to precipitate it in class.
2   Arrange for two friends or colleagues to watch a current events programme on television where a controversial issue is aired. They should view the programme separately and independently, noting occasions when they think opinions have been expressed as opposed to the presentation of straightforward statements of fact. Compare the lists: how much can the differences be attributed to differences in their personal positions on the issue discussed?

QUANTIFYING DATA

As has been noted before, it will be the total scores on homogeneous sections of the questionnaire, observation schedule or interview responses, and *not* individual question scores that will constitute numerical data, since individual questions of the sort discussed above have little validity or reliability on their own. As to whether such scores, on a number of questions, are to be considered ordinal or interval data is an issue the researcher will have to consider. On the one hand, it could be maintained that since the possible score range would be between 10 and 50 for five choices on ten items, then the difference between pairs of scores (say 45 and 46 or 34 and 35) would be approximately the same, thus this could be considered to be an example of interval data. Alternatively, since each response is a ranking, the total score should be a ranking. The outcome of the argument will determine which statistical tests will be available for resolving the hypothesis, particularly if the measured traits are the dependent variables. This issue will be considered in greater depth later when the choice of statistical tests is covered.

OTHER TYPES OF INSTRUMENTS, FREQUENTLY STANDARDIZED

Other formats for questions exist to elicit data from which one could infer attitudes. These range from simple true–false statements and 'fill in one word' statements, to Osgood's semantic differential. The latter consists of a set of pairs of statements at extremes, such as good–bad, kind–cruel, pleasant–unpleasant, with a five- to seven-point scale between them (Mehrens and Lehmann, 1984). Each set is completed with respect to a single well-defined issue and the total score provides a way of quantifying an attitude or view. The following instruments are aimed at more specific tasks and not as relevant to research as they are to counselling individuals, though they might be used to classify subjects in a study.

Interest scales

Mehrens and Lehmann (1984) distinguish between attitudes and interests by describing attitudes as 'a feeling towards an *object*, a *social institution*, or a *group*', while an interest is 'a feeling towards an *activity*'. Interest inventories have been developed to cover a wide range of client groups and their potential career and job preferences. Like attitude instruments, they are susceptible to faking, but they can also produce unrealistic aspirations due to the ignorance of the subjects. How many young people have a realistic idea of what a medical doctor, an engineer or accountant does, beyond making reasonable salaries? Some inventories use general activities associated with a profession or trade (enjoying mathematics, successful at making models, etc.) and extend the aggregate to predications about potential careers to pursue or avoid. In school counselling situations, this information would be used in conjunction with achievement records and interviews to assist young people choose a realistic career path.

Additional information on interest scales and inventories, with examples and guidance on their construction can also be found in Anastasi (1990: Chapter 18), Cronbach (1990: Chapter 12) and Murphy and Davidshofer (1991: Chapter 16).

Personality

While some writers would describe personality as the whole of a person, including intellectual as well as behavioural traits, Anastasi (1990) employs a more restrictive definition when referring to instruments to measure 'emotional, motivational, interpersonal, and attitudinal characteristics, as distinguished from abilities'. Though sometimes used for screening, their main value is in counselling, and it is accepted that they are to be interpreted only by professionals trained to use them. If used as part of a research project, a member of the research team should be qualified in their application and interpretation. Further information on their scope and development can be found in such texts as Anastasi (1990: Chapters 17, 19 and 20), Cronbach (1990: Chapters 13 and 14) and Murphy and Davidshofer (1991: Chapters 19–21).

SUMMARY

A number of measuring procedures for quantifying attitudes, views and perceptions have been introduced. These are presented recognizing that there are a wide variety of important attitudes, perceptions, values and beliefs that are not necessarily measured most validly by paper-and-pencil procedures. In many situations, an action is the focus of attention, rather than some written response. A number of procedures are based upon observation of the subjects in action, with the aid of a checklist or set of ratings to focus attention on relevant activities. The design of such schemes requires agreement among observers as to what is important and how to record observations. Failure to resolve such issues ahead of time can result in low reliability and validity for any results.

Written instruments for attitudes require planning as careful as that required for achievement tests and will probably not have as high reliability and validity, since the (mis)interpretation of statements and questions by subjects can affect the results. Conducting trials of questionnaires with representative groups that can be interviewed can help to ensure that there is no ambiguity or misunderstanding, as well as providing data to establish an estimate of the reliability of the questionnaire. Now carry out Activity 9.4.

Activity 9.4

If your research involves, or you plan for it to involve, the use of a test of attitudes, beliefs, feelings or values, put before your class a copy of the statement of the concept, the definition of the construct to be measured (even a draft of the types of behaviours or responses that you would expect to be valid indicators) and a copy of the instrument, if it has been developed.

Be prepared to identify factors contributing to its validity and reliability, as well as those that might lower these. Justify your choice of types of items or questions used to elicit responses. In other words, be prepared to defend the instrument designed or to be designed as a valid and reliable operational definition of the concepts indicated in your research question or hypothesis.

The use of questionnaires to ascertain subjects' attitudes and opinions is wide in all the social sciences, but, with the exception of education and cognitive psychology, little is done to measure how much people know or what intellectual skills they may have. This could be an oversight in that going beyond the opinion or attitude and investigating their knowledge and understanding of issues, their capacity to follow logical argument, or their ability to distinguish fact from opinion might provide some understanding of the source of these points of view or convictions. While it is quite reasonable to expect that not all belief is necessarily rational, those attitudes that seem to be socially undesirable (racial bigotry, xenophobia, male chauvinism, religious intolerance) may have their roots in ignorance. If this is not considered, then there is little chance of understanding the nature of such beliefs and introducing change. Higher-level commitment of a rational sort is quite closely linked to understanding of issues and an ability to follow arguments. Thus it is suggested that this chapter is of interest not just to those concerned with research in education, approaches and methods of learning, and other variables associated with achievement, but also to anyone needing a better understanding of the potential sources of attitudes, opinions, beliefs and stances.

WHY DESIGN YOUR OWN INSTRUMENTS?

Since standardized tests are not commercially available for testing every subject and topic, researchers are often left to their own resources when it comes to determining how much subjects 'know' or have achieved. Teachers may have collections of past examinations created by other subject experts, books of past public examination papers, or questions from item banks. While it may seem relatively easy just to use an existing examination or paper in its entirety, these rarely suit the situation without some modification or adaptation.

Researchers in other areas may have to devise an instrument to determine the level of understanding of what may be thought of as common concepts (conservatism, equality, legality, safety). Exactly what is needed will depend on the purpose of the test: what is the concept or skill to be measured? The test will be a measuring instrument that will be the operational definition of that subject or topic, elaborated through a process of building a construct (recall Figure 2.6). A problem that arises with using past versions of papers or examinations or existing standardized tests as instruments is that if the researcher can get copies, so could the subjects. Thus, not only do those who have seen the questions ahead of time have an advantage, but also if someone else works the problems for them and they just memorize the answers, the test of cognitive ability becomes one of basic recall. In either case, the resulting marks have little validity, and confounding of the results will occur. Existing tests may not constitute the most valid operational definition of what is being investigated. Finally, not all learning or understanding that might be of interest in research is tested by available examinations.

An additional problem is that many higher-level skills cannot be tested under traditional examination conditions, a limitation that some examination boards tend to recognize, and as a consequence these require 'practical' or laboratory-based exercises where the assessor completes an observation schedule. This chapter will provide the basic skills necessary to design and develop paper-based and observational measuring instruments of subject matter and intellectual capabilities employing a variety of approaches. The techniques covered will enhance validity, ensure as high a reliability as possible, and encourage a high level of objectivity of instrument(s) developed. It will cover the design of tests in the cognitive domain, those requiring mental processes, exemplified by achievement (content) tests. Further information on the design of tests can be found in such standard textbooks as Cronbach (1990), Mehrens and Lehmann (1984) and Wiersma and Jurs (1990).

DEFINING GOALS

The term *validity* has been used in earlier chapters with reference to measuring instruments and could be quite simply considered to be concerned with whether tests actually measure what they are supposed to measure and not something else. In the case of classroom tests and examinations, the teacher's aim is to enhance the consistency between what is taught and what is tested. For the researcher, it may be to achieve the same aim if the object of the study is to test the efficiency or effectiveness of a new or alternative teaching strategy. On the other hand, it may be to determine aptitude to learn or level of possession of existing skills and knowledge. In either case it is desirable to define the intellectual skills and knowledge unambiguously before writing questions to test these. It is generally easier to establish the potential validity of a test of subject matter by considering the skills and knowledge to be included by defining these as general learning outcomes in terms of goals and objectives. This should be considered equivalent to one step towards refining the definition of an abstract concept or general aim of learning and elaborating on its meaning to develop a construct. Such descriptions of abilities as 'understands French', 'grasps political implications of glasnost', or 'analyses a report for logical inconsistencies', are entirely too vague, as we will see.

Sources of goals for tests of subject matter

How does one arrive at a set of goals for a subject-matter test or examination? The answer to this depends on individual situations, but in many cases it will be linked to the overall planning of the teaching of the material or to the research question to be resolved. Thus, goals can be derived from syllabuses and inferred from past exams, or from concepts or intellectual skills related to the research hypothesis. Teaching goals will have been identified through extensive discussions with teachers in the classroom or trainers in industry. Those derived from research may come from a desire to determine whether understanding of concepts or the possession of skills has any bearing on attitudes or opinions. For example, do only politically ignorant people vote for the Monster Raving Loony Party, or is it an expression of frustration with the present political system? What constitutes 'understanding political issues'? Designing measuring instruments will obviously require considering the content and implied concomitant skills. Discussions with colleagues and other experts in the area can also help in identifying goals.

This brings in another aspect of teaching and testing: does everything that is taught (using the term in its broadest sense) need to be tested? Is it even possible? There will be a number of long-term goals that may be difficult to assess fairly in the short term, such as those that demand creativity, that should be encouraged none the less in the classroom. Traditional A-level examinations (taken at 18 + years) are based upon extensive subject syllabuses covering two years of learning, but these have only a small contribution from such goals as designing experiments, writing a short story or designing a town plan. Often assessment schemes at all levels leave out such important goals as the ability to learn independently of the teacher, the ability to decide when one has learned enough, or the ability to know when to go for help. These are abilities any young person should acquire before going on to higher education, an environment where it is often assumed that the student is a self-motivated, independent learner, no longer in need of 'spoon-feeding'. Such skills may be potential extraneous variables in a study, simply because they may be one of the factors that influences the learning outcomes in addition to the planned learning strategy under consideration. Controlling for such variables may be essential if a study is going to be able to defend any conclusions related to the advantages of new approaches.

In the world of the workplace, teaching and testing will be based upon some form of needs analysis (see, for example, Kaufman and Thiagarajan, 1987) that determines which deficiencies can be made up through teaching or training. Here the requirement for consistency across the identified needs, teaching and testing is paramount if the trainee and the organization are going to benefit from any programme. Training organizations that provide services to industry and commerce will determine goals based upon the stated needs or desires of clients. Recent developments in the UK have resulted in the establishment of a scheme whereby common skills are specified, leading to awards of National Vocational Qualifications (NVQs). The skills required here by designers to identify the actual learning needs and consequent tests are not unlike those for any other service that is contracted out to external organizations. The problem often lies in deciding and agreeing on what the actual deficiency is, which takes careful negotiation by the consultant and sometimes requires educating the client purchasing the service. Professional trainers may be more perceptive of training needs than the manager, but the latter signs the cheque.

As a result of increased awareness of the complex nature of designing measuring instruments for testing subject-matter content and skills, a number of analytic tools have been developed over the years. This does not mean that cognitive testing is an 'exact science' (a self-contradictory statement in its own right), but that these tools do help to enhance validity and reliability of instruments, as will be seen in subsequent sections. These techniques are simply a way of elaborating on vague or general descriptions of learning outcomes to develop detailed descriptions (constructs) before developing the instrument (operational definition).

Thinking about thinking

Simply listing content and vaguely describing goals has often led to confusion in test design. In an endeavour to clarify the intent of tests and examinations, B. S. Bloom and others produced a classification scheme describing the varieties of human activity, to facilitate the analysis of individual test items (Bloom, 1956). Although this was devised over 40 years ago, it is still widely used and has provided the basis for a number of subsequent schemes. For the developer of achievement tests, what is more important than the choice of category system is that *some* scheme is used. For convenience, when planning the design of measuring instruments, all human activity will be considered to belong to one or more of three domains:

- *cognitive domain*: mental activities related to thinking, reasoning, remembering, etc.;
- *affective domain*: mental activities relating to attitudes (see Chapter 9);
- *psychomotor domain*: physical activities, ranging from manual skills (such as assembling equipment or using tools) to whole-body skills (such as dancing).

Each of the above has been further divided into subcategories and has been considered in detail over recent years. While the category systems used here are by no means the only ones available, they do provide a useful mechanism for exploring each of the domains in some detail. Any classification scheme is arbitrary in the sense that someone has made a decision as to what is the optimum way of classifying something (Krathwohl *et al.*, 1964). As with the division between biology and chemistry, often there are overlaps and classifying a topic as one or the other is often a matter of simple convenience. In the case of goals and objectives, the important point is that all the possible learning outcomes are recognized and that each is appropriately considered in the planning of learning and valid assessment as part of a course or programme. The design of instruments for measuring cognitive achievement using Bloom's taxonomy will be considered in this chapter, though other equally functional category systems exist (see, for example, Gagné, 1985).

The cognitive domain

Bloom (1956) and colleagues proposed that there are six levels in this domain, hierarchical in nature and ordered in terms of increased complexity of tasks. The first column of Table 10.1 provides summary definitions for each level of what has come to be known as *Bloom's taxonomy*. The second column provides some sample tasks for each level. The ability to classify a learning task into its appropriate level helps both the designer of learning materials and the designer of test items to ensure their goals are unambiguous. For example, there is a considerable difference between being able to recall and state Newton's third law of motion (knowledge), recognizing an example (comprehension) and being able to use it to solve a problem (application). Recalling the main tenet of some aspect of Plato's philosophy (knowledge) is distinct from being able to describe the logic behind it (comprehension) or argue about its validity (evaluation). Being able to recite the definition of the word 'pathological' (knowledge) is not the same as being able to use it correctly in a sentence (comprehension). Knowing how many legs an insect has (knowledge) is less demanding than being able correctly to classify a newly presented creature as an insect (comprehension). Understanding the rules of poker (comprehension) is obviously a part of, but not the same as, being able to play the game and win (application).

The valid classification of test questions and objectives using such a scheme requires an understanding of the context in which they apply (Bloom, 1956). For example, for a problem to be at the application level, it should be new to the examinee. If it has been seen before and the solution memorized, it is no longer testing application level capabilities and is a knowledge level question. Similarly, if the examination question is so close to classroom practice as to require only changing a few numbers in an equation, it may be more valid to consider it to be at the comprehension level. This causes a dilemma for examination boards, teachers, trainers and lecturers: how do they provide enough information in the course syllabus so as to provide sufficient guidance to the learner without providing so much information that the whole process is reduced to a memorization activity? Researchers developing a test of skills must look for questions that test transfer of skills to (reasonably) new situations if they are to test application level thinking. Questions too close to everyday tasks could require such routine thinking as to be considered no more than comprehension. Such issues must be addressed if the test is going to provide a valid measure of the ability to perform at the desired level.

An additional problem arises which will be discussed in detail later: most 'tests' tend to involve paper and pencil, though not all measurement should necessarily occur under traditional examination conditions. In some cases, to ensure validity of measure of stated higher level skills, alternative assessment techniques may be required. For example, it may be necessary to require a piece of work carried out outside the traditional examination room if thinking at the analysis, synthesis or evaluation level is to be tested. Exemplar activities include a report on the design and development of a process, product or system, research in libraries to carry out a critical analysis of positions on a contemporary issue, or evaluation of a process based upon observations, such as law court cases. The classification of objectives with the implied subsequent testing condi-

TABLE 10.1
The six categories of Bloom's taxonomy for the cognitive domain

Level and description	Behavioural examples	Action verbs
Knowledge Remembering facts, definitions, theories, rules, etc. from previous learning. This does not imply any understanding and is the lowest level of learning in the cognitive domain.	Recalls terms, specific facts, principles, definitions, descriptions, events, dates; states rules and regulations; describes procedures and processes.	States, describes, lists, names, identifies, chooses, tells, selects, labels.
Comprehension The lowest level of understanding, including such activities as translating written material from one form to another, interpreting, predicting, identifying examples of concepts.	Interprets a graph; summarizes a passage; uses a concept; extrapolates or interpolates; identifies examples of a concept in a list of items.	Selects, chooses, identifies, infers, predicts, explains, paraphrases, rewrites.
Application Using learned material in new situations, including solving problems using rules, principles, methods, laws and theories. This requires a much higher level of understanding than that required at the comprehension level.	Applies rules or laws to solve a real problem; uses a process or procedure to correct a fault; constructs a graph from a set of data; finds the solution to a mathematical problem.	Solves, predicts, selects procedure, finds errors, sets out page, assembles apparatus, modifies process.
Analysis Showing some creative ability in critical analysis of a situation or written material by such activities as breaking it down to identify implied meanings, distinguishing fact from opinion, identifying relationships among parts, and recognizing the organizational structure of the material.	Recognizes unstated assumptions, logical fallacies and inconsistencies; distinguishes between fact and inference, fact and opinion; analyses organizational structure of literary, musical or art work.	Discriminates, identifies, infers, selects parts, illustrates, differentiates, outlines.
Synthesis Creatively putting ideas, concepts, rules together in a new way to produce such results as a unique communication (for example, an essay), an original process or procedure, or a new classification scheme.	Writes a well-organized essay or report; devises a new process or procedure; integrates learning from different areas to produce a new solution to a problem.	Creates, designs, makes, produces, plans, composes, reorganizes, develops, writes.
Evaluation Judge the value of written material (such as a process, project report, essay, novel) including justifying any judgements using definite criteria, either external (such as relevance) or internal (organizationally based). This is considered the highest level since it contains elements of all the other categories plus value judgements.	Determines logical consistency of arguments presented, adequacy of support for conclusions; judges literary quality of a novel based on aesthetics or external criteria.	Selects, justifies, criticizes, contrasts, assesses, profiles, adjudicates.

Sources: after Bloom (1956); Gronlund (1970)

tions required to ensure a valid measure will demand careful analysis and creativity on the examiner's part in many situations. Otherwise the questions may not measure what was intended, in other words the desired outcomes of a learning experience or possession of a skill. The conditions under which the 'test' is conducted can affect the validity of the quantitative results, the test score.

ROLES FOR GOALS AND OBJECTIVES

Goals and objectives potentially serve a number of functions in the design of learning situations and materials, as well as in the subsequent assessment and evaluation. By simply specifying what will be expected in terms of learning outcomes, teachers and designers provide a reference point for future development. Such a set of specifications also provides a touchstone, a means of communication to establish and justify the content validity of the instrument. This has resulted in curriculum developers levelling the criticism against very specific objectives that they can limit what happens in the classroom by either not encouraging fast learners to extend themselves, penalizing slower learners for not keeping up, or simply trivializing learning tasks. But like many tools, statements of goals and objectives are only as good as their writers.

When determining goals for a programme or course of study, or elaborating on what is meant by a skill, a number of fundamentals must be addressed, including the following:

- How can a representative sample of questions be selected?
- Is it reasonable to expect high-level skills of all examinees?
- How does one determine levels of proficiency for high-level skills?

Specifying learning outcomes ahead of time provides a mechanism by which such issues can be resolved before the questions are actually written. Working with questions alone can provide a distraction in that one becomes concerned with not only the cognitive emphasis, but also the wording and the specific example provided. Taking one step at a time, in this case ensuring that the class of exemplars representative of the level being tested is agreed upon, helps to ensure the validity of the final instrument.

Another issue arises when interpreting the outcomes of cognitive tests: single marks or scores for an examination can be misleading, begging such issues as what skills are required for the highest marks. Past public examinations have produced a total score that could reflect either an ability to memorize or a problem-solving ability, though often it is some combination. In other words, if 50% were the pass mark, on which 50% was the examinee successful? Single-score results do not differentiate, making the validity of any single score questionable. To increase the validity of an instrument, it may be necessary to have scores for subsections that are not only homogeneous for content but also contain questions at a single cognitive level. The issue of ensuring that the instrument measures what was intended manifests itself in a number of ways.

Specifying goals and objectives also allows testing for a variety of skills, some achievable in the short term and others only in the long term. Discussing goals and objectives for a course of study may even reveal some that are not testable, or would be undesirable to use as part of the measuring process. For example, it may be desirable to raise the awareness of a group to political issues, but not desirable to assess what conclusions they have come to, in order to preserve personal privacy of opinion. It may be of greater value to determine how logical their arguments are as analysis level thinking, rather than the conclusion reached.

The final issue is one of how objectives are stated: as teacher-centred activities or as learner-centred. The next section introduces a specific format for writing objectives that has generated some controversy over the years.

Performance or behavioural objectives

Performance or behavioural objectives are statements of observable behaviours that are indicative of achievement of capabilities, primarily cognitive. Since it is not possible to observe intellectual activities directly, it is necessary to infer their existence based upon observations, which is basically what is done when giving a test or observing an activity (recall Figure 2.4). You cannot see into the examinee's mind, so you give a test or examination and, based upon the results, you infer the degree of possession of the desired knowledge, skills and/or attitudes. Behavioural objectives are just a way of specifying unambiguously what will be accepted as evidence for demonstrating acquisition of skills, including component skills that make up a capability.

A number of formats have been proposed over the past 30 years or so (Gagné *et al.*, 1992; Kibler *et al.*, 1970; Mager, 1962; Popham, 1973; Vargas, 1972). Minimally, each objective has a statement of the activity or action that is to be accepted as evidence of achievement. Often, it is necessary to specify the conditions under which the test will occur (for example, orally or written) or with what the examinee will be provided (for example, a calculator, specific information, data, or even a case study). The increased specificity reduces any ambiguity as to what will ultimately be expected and facilitates deciding the relative emphasis of various levels on an instrument.

There have been objections to the use of specific objectives, frequently because those that have been devised have trivialized the task. Also, it has been suggested that writing specific objectives means that the teacher only teaches those things specified. This is a criticism that is not limited to objectives, but also applies to the interpretation of syllabuses listing only content. The problem is not with objectives (or syllabuses); they are only tools. It is the lack of analytic skills on the part of the designers of learning situations and examinations that needs consideration. The researcher, though, does need to be specific about the cognitive skills that are to be assessed if validity is to be maintained. A set of objectives can be considered to be the definition of the construct elaborating on the concept (again, recall Figure 2.6). For example, if the concept (dependent variable) described in a hypothesis were 'knowledge of the plot of Shakespeare's *Merchant of Venice*' or 'understanding of social security benefit regulations', then the resulting set of objectives would clarify exactly what is meant by *knowledge* or *understanding*, and what would be accepted as evidence of achievement.

Another factor contributing to the difficulty in writing good, meaningful and useful objectives is related to the inherent difficulty in measuring higher-level intellectual skills. This is by no means an easy task compared to devising ways of measuring the possession of knowledge (recall of facts, rules, etc.). Writing objectives and corresponding questions for higher-level skills requires knowledge of the content or discipline and some imagination, tempered with a sense of fairness to the subjects. Assessing higher-level process skills is not an easy task and one that should not be avoided simply because it is difficult to do. It may be essential in establishing the validity of the operational definition of the variable in question. For example, 'understanding of social security benefits' could be expanded to mean 'ability to describe in their own words what the rules for receiving benefits mean' (comprehension), or 'ability to determine to what benefits they are entitled' (application). Which is chosen will be determined by what the researcher means by *understand*.

An additional problem arises in writing the objective in such a way as to avoid reducing the whole exercise to one of memorization. For example, consider the need to design a question that would require the examinees to analyse a passage from Shakespeare or the instructions on the annual income tax form, based upon the stated goal that 'the learner/subject should be able to read and understand Shakespeare' or 'the learner should have a sound grasp of the income tax instruction booklet'. If the task is to be at the analysis level, then the actual skill is in the analysis of the passage, not in the fore-knowledge of the passage itself. Therefore, the objectives could be stated as:

Given a passage from one of Shakespeare's plays, the subject should be able to interpret it, identifying any allegory or play on words, and describe what was the intended or implied meaning.

or

Given a section from the instruction booklet for completing the annual income tax form and a set of financial data, the taxpayer should be able to complete that section properly, supplying the appropriate data.

The teaching of Shakespeare could centre on the analysis of passages in one play and the test passage could come from another, thus the validity of the item would not be jeopardized by knowledge of the objective. Also, it would inform the teacher as to the actual intent of that type of question. And finally, the higher-level skill is more likely to remain with learners, be of greater value in terms of future reading, and transfer to other content areas, than one centred on memorizing passages. Problems lie in the choice of passage for the examination. It must be comparable to those used in class, of sufficient length to provide the context, and one whose understanding is not dependent on a broad knowledge of an unfamiliar play. It should be one that is likely to be new and not have been used in previous examinations. This is where the subject-matter expertise of the designer is most important. Similarly, if one were evaluating the appropriateness and understandability of the tax instructions to the general public, then the second objective would have to pertain to representative sections completed by most and *not* an obscure regulation (such as tax on oil revenues or book royalties). Objectives of this sort have been used in an attempt to specify explicitly the skills needed to qualify for NVQs, with varying degrees of success.

The key to any scheme for writing behavioural or performance objectives is the use of verbs that describe observable behaviours, sometimes referred to as behavioural terms or *action verbs*. Unfortunately, the lists of sample verbs, such as those provided in Table 10.1, can be deceiving, as indicated in the next section.

Objectives in the cognitive domain

Column 3 of Table 10.1 gives some typical action verbs for each level. While these will appear in descriptions of behaviours that are indicative of intellectual activity at the level indicated, do note the appearance of the same action verbs in more than one category. This means that there is no guarantee that if you use what appears to be the 'right' action verbs, you will automatically describe an objective at the intended level.

If it were possible to write objectives at each cognitive level by just including specific terms, then writing such objectives would be a comprehension level task. In reality, writing objectives is a synthesis level task, which often follows the analysis level task of analysing the subject matter to determine relevant inclusions in the curriculum or to determine exactly what specific exemplar skills constitute a valid indication of the construct. For school teachers, this may entail inferring specific objectives from the examination board's published syllabus, tempered with inferences based on past examinations and their own understanding of the subject. For researchers, it means establishing unambiguously what the variable is actually going to be measuring (validity). Writing the actual test questions at all the cognitive levels is an equally challenging task, as will be seen later. Bloom's (1956) original book provides some interesting examples for a wide variety of subject areas. Try your hand at classifying objectives by carrying out Activity 10.1 now.

Balancing content and cognitive emphasis

It is not surprising that the process of designing any cognitive test or examination to ensure reliability, validity and objectivity will be complex. As a consequence, it will necessarily involve asking specific questions at a number of stages to enhance meeting the criteria of a good test. To facilitate this process, some checklists and sets of questions are provided, not to be used as rules to be blindly followed, but as criteria to serve as guidelines for the development of high-quality tests. Classification schemes were introduced as a first step to facilitate the identification of the actual objectives of a test in order to enhance its validity. The next stage is to determine the actual weighting of each level to establish the relative cognitive emphasis of the instrument.

To put the problem of balance of content and cognitive emphasis into context, let us take as an example public examinations in the UK. With the publication of syllabuses and the conduct of the examinations on such a large scale, this is possibly a more highly structured situation than the one with which some researchers will be involved. The major difference may well be in the necessity for the researcher to design his or her own syllabus, but that, too, is an

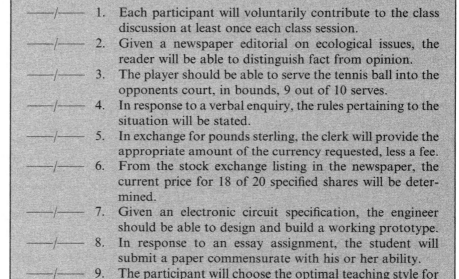

Activity 10.1

Classify each of the following objectives as to domain (C, cognitive; A, affective; P, psychomotor), and the cognitive ones as to level using Bloom's taxonomy (K, knowledge; C, comprehension; Ap, application; An, analysis; S, synthesis; E, evaluation). Compare your answers with those at the end after you finish. Since the objectives are taken out of context, it will not be unexpected for some of your answers to differ from those given. Just make sure that you can defend *your* choice of category.

Domain/cog. level

——/—— 1. Each participant will voluntarily contribute to the class discussion at least once each class session.

——/—— 2. Given a newspaper editorial on ecological issues, the reader will be able to distinguish fact from opinion.

——/—— 3. The player should be able to serve the tennis ball into the opponents court, in bounds, 9 out of 10 serves.

——/—— 4. In response to a verbal enquiry, the rules pertaining to the situation will be stated.

——/—— 5. In exchange for pounds sterling, the clerk will provide the appropriate amount of the currency requested, less a fee.

——/—— 6. From the stock exchange listing in the newspaper, the current price for 18 of 20 specified shares will be determined.

——/—— 7. Given an electronic circuit specification, the engineer should be able to design and build a working prototype.

——/—— 8. In response to an essay assignment, the student will submit a paper commensurate with his or her ability.

——/—— 9. The participant will choose the optimal teaching style for the target class and topic, and rationalize the choice.

——/—— 10. Given a graph of production output, times of low productivity will be identified.

Suggested answers: 1. A. 2. C-An. 3. P. 4. C-K. 5. C-Ap. 6. C-C. 7. C-S & P. 8. A. 9. C-E. 10. C-C.

option available to school teachers. Preparation of students for public examinations is a major component of any secondary school teacher's life in Britain. In the past, all that one had to go on was a syllabus that listed the subject content. More recently, examination boards have become increasingly explicit in describing what will be covered by their examinations, often accompanied by a *summary table of specification*. This provides teachers with some information on which to decide the cognitive emphasis of tests. Though they tend not to use Bloom's taxonomy in its fullest form, its influence is rather apparent and the schemes used are usually somewhat collapsed versions, such as the one seen in Table 10.2. Each of the three categories is described in detail in the published syllabus, though the information typically provided as in this table only gives an overall distribution of levels applied across the subject. In this case, processes include application, analysis and synthesis plus laboratory and data-analysis skills.

CREATING TABLES OF SPECIFICATION

A research instrument measuring achievement may reflect the cognitive emphasis of a final summative examination, a lesser amount of material varying depending on the subject-matter coverage, or a specific skill set of interest in an experiment. A table of specifications providing more detail than the information supplied by examination boards or the general statement of a skill and/or set of knowledge is needed to plan the distribution of questions at all cognitive levels on the instrument. This will have to include an indication of the specific topics to be tested (related to specific objectives) and the relative weighting to be given at each cognitive level. Too often syllabuses provide less specificity than if they had been presented as a set of specific objectives reflecting the anticipated cognitive emphasis for each topic. It would be possible to make some reasonable inferences as to the cognitive levels expected for topics based on past examinations. Also, subject teachers are usually able to decide for specific topics what would be a reasonable level of cognitive emphasis to expect of students of a given age. With some generic skills – for example, the process skills described in Chapter 1 – it is not unreasonable to assume a certain amount of transfer across topics, such as making observations, inferences, and plotting graphs of data. There may also be more general guidelines that provide indications of the level expected. One could assume some difficulty with many new syllabuses or those for professional training programmes, since they can transcend traditional subject areas. These have tended to have varying cognitive emphases

TABLE 10.2
A table of specifications for GCSE physics

Paper	Recall (%)	Understanding (%)	Process (%)
General level			
1	40	30	30
2	30	30	40
3			100
Overall for Papers 1–3	**24**	**21**	**55**
Extended level			
4	10	20	70
Overall for Papers 1–4	**17**	**18**	**65**

on their examinations, and thus one might not expect a homogeneous distribution of higher-level questions across all topics in all areas.

Determining the balance of cognitive levels at which a topic should be tested is not a simple task. For teachers and academics, this is a matter of balancing what the discipline demands with what it is reasonable to expect from learners for a given course. For researchers who might wish to determine depth of understanding (for example, current events), ability to interpret documents (the income tax form), or level of intellectual skill proficiency in a given job (stock control, desktop publishing, interrogation of a database), elaboration of what is meant by the general skill description is essential.

To illustrate the process of building a table of specifications, a basic topic from school learning will be used: energy. Based on a section of an examination syllabus, the first step is to spread out the content topics down the page and the cognitive levels across the top, as shown in Table 10.3. In this case, it was decided for purposes of illustration to use Bloom's taxonomy in full, and add a final column for experiment and data handling. Next, the cognitive levels to be tested for each topic were identified and indicated by placing a × in each appropriate column. This is the point at which it must be decided what is most appropriate for each topic. For example, 'energy concepts' as such can be tested as factual knowledge and for understanding (knowledge and comprehension), whereas identifying transformations from one form to another and using the law of conservation of energy imply the higher-level abilities of application and analysis. Transfer of energy indicates analytic and problem-solving abilities (not necessarily mathematical) as well as an understanding of the concepts, thus four levels are marked. Thermal insulation lends itself to the learner putting all his skills together to evaluate and design well-insulated buildings (evaluation and synthesis), and a number of interesting problems in the physical and biological realm are implied in the syllabus description relating to temperature maintenance and energy loss in objects and living organisms (application and evaluation). Experiment and data-handling abilities would most appropriately contain skills of measuring different forms of energy and data-handling skills for temperature maintenance.

While the resulting table of specifications in Table 10.3 would be reasonably appropriate for secondary school students, a comparable one that delved into the topics to a greater depth and demanded more higher-level thinking might be appropriate for, say, architects. The distinction could be best made by devising a list of objectives to correspond to each of the content topics in the first column.

Having made the decisions reflected in Table 10.3, the final percentages for each cognitive level are included across the bottom as typically specified by an examination board as a guide for determining the relative weightings. This will be reflected in the number of questions and the values assigned to them on the test, if the researcher were to want to make a test comparable to a GCSE examination for this topic. If one were designing a test with comparable cognitive emphasis to that of the examination board, the next step would be to replace the × marks by percentages that add up to be roughly those specified. Note that the sums of questions to be asked at each cognitive level would not necessarily be exactly the same as those indicated in Table 10.3, but would

TABLE 10.3
The first level of analysis in designing a table of specifications for a cognitive test covering 'energy, work and power', typical of part of a GCSE science syllabus

Content	Knowledge	Comprehension	Analysis	Application	Evaluation	Synthesis	Experimental and data handling
Energy concepts							
Kinetic	×	×					×
Potential	×	×					×
Positional	×	×					×
Mechanical	×	×					×
Chemical	×	×					×
Electrical	×	×					×
Heat	×	×					×
Transformations							
Machines			×	×			
Biological			×	×			
Conservation							
Machines			×	×			
Biological			×	×			
Transfer							
Conduction		×	×	×			
Convection	×	×	×	×			
Radiation	×	×	×	×			
Thermal insulation							
Temp. maintenance				×	×	×	×
Environment factors				×	×		
Construction factors				×	×		×
Totals (exam. board specifications):	20%	30%	25%		25%		25%

reflect the researcher's judgement about the relative weightings for those topics based upon syllabus details and what it is reasonable to expect from the learners at that time. Asking questions that are impossible for all learners to answer only lowers the mean score for the instrument and does not provide any meaningful information. If one is investigating the relative effectiveness of learning materials for teaching or training, tables of specification are working tools and should simply be a means of systematically recording content analysis. Thus, as they become more specific, they may well change, as will be illustrated.

The choice of cognitive emphasis on an achievement test will be determined to some extent by whether the test is to measure short-term or long-term learning. Short-term learning tested soon after a learning experience may focus on skills across the entire spectrum, from knowledge to experimental skills, depending on what was included in the experience. On the other hand, the emphasis on tests after a period of time to measure long-term learning may be on higher-level skills, the ones that tend to have the greatest potential for transfer. Obscure bits of information and pedantic definitions of terms may provide a large variance in scores, but at the same time may not accurately reflect the nature of the subject. In the long run, is there greater value in being able to analyse energy transfers in a mechanical system or ecosystem and identify bottlenecks, *or* to recall the definitions of different types of energy? There may be times when principles of traditional psychometrics will conflict with content validity when considering what the aims of teaching the subject are.

The final written test may cover most of the table of specifications, but obviously some of the experimental skills will have to be assessed by observation on the part of the teacher as the student carries out experiments. Designing and using observational schedules for such a purpose provides a means by which the researcher can infer the level of motor skills and any integration of motor and cognitive skills.

In many situations, researchers will design cognitive tests following much the same process, but guided by their own syllabuses instead of someone else's. They will have to specify how they intend to assess at various cognitive levels and, using such a table of specifications as the one in Table 10.3, describe their assessment plans to justify the validity of the instrument as an operational definition of achievement. Such a table provides a comprehensive summary of the content and cognitive emphasis of the topic as seen by the researcher. With such a table, the relative validity of the instrument can be established with other subject-matter experts before actually writing the questions. To finish this section complete Activity 10.2.

Activity 10.2

Obtain an achievement test (for example, one from a professional examination board or one designed by a teacher) and sketch out a table of specifications for it. Do you think it was planned from such a table? Why or why not?

TYPES OF QUESTIONS

A table of specifications such as Table 10.3 provides a definition of the cognitive emphasis of a test or examination, possibly enhanced by a tentative distribution of weightings by topic and level. Next there needs to be an initial selection of question type with an emphasis on an appropriate match between the objective or topic statement and the item or question used to assess the presence of that capability. As the items are written, this may change, but an initial plan should be made. You will have the opportunity to consider the advantages and disadvantages of different types of questions in greater detail later.

Table 10.4 provides a summary of the main issues to consider when deciding what type of items/questions to use. In addition, the purpose of the test will influence choice of type. A test of understanding of basic concepts should be designed to provide the maximum amount of breadth of coverage, and consequently the objective items fulfil this need best. A test of higher-level skills may aim to determine how well the learner can integrate what has been learned, hence requiring the greatest opportunity in responding, thus an essay component or worked problem with rationale for decisions might be preferable.

Table 10.5 gives a final proposed distribution of types of questions in the form of a table of specifications for the topic 'energy, work and power' as an illustration of the process carried to the end. According to this plan, two assessments would be designed: a test consisting of two matching, 24 multiple-choice and 11 short-answer questions, plus a separate report on experiments with two data-analysis questions done as class work. By assessing through essays and project work, there is a greater probability that the task taken on will be more relevant to their own work and situation, and thus more valid for participant. The difficulty for the researcher is to achieve reasonably comparable answers in terms of demonstrating proficiency at skills, a situation not unlike open-book tests. Open-book assessment tends to emphasize higher cognitive tasks, with a reduced need to recall facts and a greater demand for applying concepts to real problems. On the other hand, this may incur a certain risk of lowered reliability, a problem of significant concern for researchers, though one that may be of less concern to classroom teachers designing their own tests for purposes of feedback. Decisions about what aspects of quality are to be put at risk are always part of the design of instruments.

Objective items

As a test is designed, the table of specifications developed in preparation will serve as a guide for the first draft. It will help delimit how many questions and what kind, as well as the cognitive emphasis. It may be that the final version will vary from the original table, but it will be the baseline for any developments.

The term *objective item* has been assigned to such question types as multiple-choice, true–false, matching, etc., as a way of extolling their virtue of having a higher level of objectivity when it comes to marking the answers than free-response questions. There is no doubt that this is true, but it is not achieved without considerable effort, particularly if validity and reliability are to be preserved.

It is often stated that objective items are best for providing information on a broader variety of skills in a short period of time, while essay questions better test higher cognitive skills. When both types of questions are well written this can be true, but there is nothing that automatically guarantees this will be the case. Poorly written essay questions can demand only recall of facts, while extended essay questions can require a breadth of skills as well as depth. On the other hand, it may not be reasonable to expect them to be answered in a limited time – for example, under examination conditions. Similar coverage of content and skills may be achieved through a series of tests using objective items, but three major limitations need to be recognized:

TABLE 10.4
Summary of an evaluation checklist for choosing question types

Factor	Essay	Short answer, completion	Objective
Can measure ability to solve novel problems	+ +	+	+ +
Can measure ability to organize, integrate or synthesize ideas	+ +	+	− −
Can measure originality or innovative approaches to problems	+ +	+	− −
Can isolate specific abilities in subject area from general skills of writing and language usage	− −	−	+ +
Has potential value for diagnosis	− −	+	+ +
Can sample adequately the objectives of instruction	− −	−	+ +
Can sample adequately the content of instruction	− −	−	+ +
Is free from opportunities for guessing answer	+ +	+ +	− −
Discourages bluffing, speculative answers	− −	− −	+ +
Answers cannot be deduced by process of elimination	+ +	+ +	−
Gives consistent scores from scorer to scorer (high reliability)	− −	−	+ +
Is accurate in differentiating levels of competency among examinees	− −	−	+ +
Can be scored by unskilled clerk or machine and quickly	− −	−	+ +
Takes little time for writing individual questions or sets of items	+	+	−

Sources: after Thorndike and Hagen (1977: 257); Mehrens and Lehmann (1984: 78)

TABLE 10.5
The final table of specifications for a class test covering the 'energy, work and power' part of the GCSE science syllabus, including types of questions*

Content	Knowledge	Comprehension	Analysis	Application	Evaluation	Synthesis	Experimental and data handling
Energy concepts							
Kinetic		MC (1)					
Potential		MC (1)					
Positional		MC (1)					
Mechanical	Match(7)	MC (1)					Report (essay) (10)
Chemical		MC (1)					
Electrical		MC (1)					
Heat		MC (1)					
Transformations							
Machines			SA(2)	MC(2)			
Biological			SA(2)	MC(2)			
Conservation							
Machines			SA(2)	MC(2)			
Biological			SA(2)	MC(2)			
Transfer							
Conduction		MC(3)	SA(2)	MC(2)			
Convection	Match(6)	MC(3)	SA(2)	MC(2)			
Radiation		MC(3)	SA(2)	MC(2)			
Thermal insulation	MC(3)	MC(3)		MC(2)	SA(2)	SA(4)	
Temp. maintenance							
Environment factors				MC(2)	SA(2)		DA(7)
Construction factors				MC(2)	SA(2)		DA(7)
Totals from sheet:	15%	19%	24%	18%	6%	4%	24%
Totals (Exam. board specifications):	20%	30%		25%			25%

*Match = matching; MC = multiple-choice; SA = short answer; DA = data analysis (short answer); Essay = essay (number in brackets is percentage value of question).
Source: Southern Examining Group (1988)

- It would be necessary to word items to include examples that all examinees would find relevant, which can be difficult if not impossible for a heterogeneous group – for example adults.
- Such questions may offer little opportunity for creativity, since the responses would have to demonstrate skills that would be equivalent to those exhibited in equivalent essay.
- It may be possible to test evaluation level thinking, but it would require devising case studies with equivalent choices and alternative plausible justifications.

Objective items are often criticized for testing only lower cognitive skills and recall. This is hardly the case when considering some of the more complex and ingenious questions asked on A-level examinations for 18-year-olds. These objective questions often demand abilities at the application and analysis levels. Bloom's (1956) original book provides some imaginative questions that he maintains demand evaluation level thinking, though synthesis level, due to its requirement of creativity, can be demonstrated only through some means of free response on the examinee's part. The only restriction in designing objective questions that demand higher-level thinking lies in the skill and imagination of the question writer and an ability to find relevant examples on which the examinee can operate.

The rest of this section will focus on some of the details of constructing different kinds of objective-type items that can be used on tests and examinations. Additional examples can be found in the various textbooks that are devoted to measurement and assessment, such as Mehrens and Lehmann (1984) and Wiersma and Jurs (1990). There are 11 general guidelines for writing objective items, summarized as follows:

1 Base questions on clearly defined objectives.
2 Follow your table of specifications.
3 Avoid trivia.
4 Design items specifically for the target group.
5 Ensure clarity of wording.
6 Do not quote from texts or lecture notes (unless the quotation is a passage to be analysed).
7 Ensure that all items are independent of others.
8 Ask for only one correct/best answer.
9 Avoid questions with negative statements.
10 Avoid giving clues in wording or other items.
11 Have someone else read your items.

These will be combined with more specific guidelines for writing various types of objective items. Such lists are not for memorizing, but serve rather as checklists to refer to when writing questions.

Short-answer items

Sometimes referred to as 'fill in the blank' questions, short-answer items have considerable value in situations where a word or two, or a numerical answer from a simple calculation, would provide the examiner with sufficient valid information. Giving an example of a concept (either abstract or concrete), providing a definition and then asking for the word it defines, and asking for the best French equivalent of an English word to fit in a sentence are examples that demand more than just recall. There is a limit to the level of thinking that can be demonstrated in such a small space. Also, even though it may be possible to test application level abilities by requiring only the answer to a mathematical problem (in mathematics, science, engineering or economics), it may not be desirable since none of the work or thinking behind the answer is there. The main disadvantage of short-answer questions in this situation arises from the fact that single-number answers will provide few clues for the teacher to use to advise learners on where they went wrong. For a researcher interested in an overall score for a section, this is less of a concern, unless more detail is needed for the study. In that case, either answers that show all the steps in a mathematical problem, or multiple-choice questions for which the wrong answers are indicative of specific errors or misconceptions, would be better.

The following list summarizes the main criteria for short answer items (in addition to the general ones above):

1 For calculations, the questions should include an indication of the number of decimal places and units of measure.
2 Blanks should be filled with only important or key words, formulae, symbols, etc.
3 Too many blanks in an item will cause a loss of meaning.
4 Blanks should be close to the end of the sentence.
5 A direct question is better than an incomplete sentence.
6 Testing for definitions of words or terms should ask for the definition, not the word.
7 Leave sufficient space for the answer.

Matching questions

The matching question provides an opportunity to test such abilities as distinguishing examples from near non-examples of a concept. Such a question would have a list of concepts to be matched with a list of examples. The main problem is to have the lists as homogeneous as possible if the question is to be valid. For example, a question having species names in one list and representatives in the other would be appropriate if they were all animals or plants, but not a mixture, as this would tend to provide unwanted clues. The following is a list of guidelines for writing items, and should be read in addition to the initial list for objective items:

1 The longer question should be on the right and the shorter response on the left.
2 Sets of questions and responses should consist of homogeneous lists.
3 Lists should be short (between 5 and 12 items).
4 The question and response lists should be of different lengths – for example, six questions and seven responses from which to choose.
5 The response list should be in alphabetical or numerical order.
6 Ensure that the rules for matching are clear to examinees.

True–false items

These items can be very versatile but, like short-answer questions, they tend to provide few clues as to why items testing higher cognitive levels are answered incorrectly, thus limiting their value in terms of feedback to the learner or teacher. True–false items can be used to measure a wide range of cognitive abilities, but require considerable care and skill to achieve this. As with other objective-type questions that require only a short time to answer, they can be used to test a large amount of content. On the other hand, the probability of guessing correctly is one in two, where even with five-way multiple-choice questions, the truly unlearned will have only a one in five chance of guessing the answer correctly. This may be a major consideration when constructing achievement or subject-matter content tests where the score on a homogeneous subsection is the desired outcome. New guidelines in addition to those that cover all objective items are summarized as follows:

1 Avoid ambiguity in statements.
2 Statements must be clearly true or false.
3 Avoid using very subtle points as differences.
4 Allow superficial knowledge to mislead.
5 When testing cause and effect relations, the first statement of a pair should be true.
6 Use popular misconceptions that are irrelevant.
7 Avoid the use of qualifiers, such as 'sometimes', 'always', 'never'.
8 Both true and false statements should be about the same length.
9 Have roughly the same number of true and false statements.

Multiple-choice items

These have been widely used in tests and examinations world-wide – for example, in public examinations in the UK and other countries with similar systems, and in the USA in national examinations used for entry into higher education. Thus they present little potential for confounding because of lack of examinee experience, except in very young subjects, and when the questions are novel in wording or structure. Classroom teachers have increasingly used them. However, multiple-choice items have also been subject to considerable criticism. This usually stems from either poorly written items or inappropriate use, resulting in low validity. There is a temptation to use multiple-choice items to test only recall of facts (knowledge), whereas it is quite feasible to obtain a valid measure of higher-level abilities with such questions.

Multiple-choice questions can be used quite effectively in diagnostic situations if wrong answers are designed to identify misconceptions or wrong procedures or processes. The designer must make sure that each alternative is not only reasonable to the uninformed or unskilled (and thus a good distraction), but also indicative of a specific learning problem. Applying an inappropriate concept, using the wrong formula, making a mistake in a calculation, or choosing a poor reason in defence of a judgement can provide valuable feedback to both the teacher and the learner. If most examinees select the same wrong response, then it is possible to look to the learning experience for reasons. On the other hand, individual wrong responses can be used to identify the source of specific individual learning problems on diagnostic and formative tests. The specific role of the test, either for teaching, course evaluation or research, will determine the most appropriate approach to the design of alternative choices.

A summary of guidelines for writing multiple-choice items is as follows:

1   The main part of the question should be in the stem.
2   Avoid repeating the same words or phrases in the choices.
3   Keep the choices short.
4   If the choice is to complete a statement, the gap should be at the end of the statement.
5   Arrange the choices below the stem.
6   Avoid jargon as distracters.
7   Choices should be plausible and homogeneous.
8   All choices should be about the same length.
9   In some situations (such as formative tests), the use of the 'I don't know' option can be appropriate.
10 Have only one correct response (but see the discussion of hybrid items below).
11 Avoid 'All of the above'.
12 Use 'None of the above' infrequently.
13 Use three to five choices.
14 <u>Underline</u> or *italicize* negative statements in the stem if used.

Hybrid items

Up to this point, a variety of objective-type items have been described. In addition, there are a number of ways to create hybrid forms, combining, say, multiple-choice and true–false questions. Figure 10.1 gives an example where three statements are given and the examinee must decide which combination is true. These can be used to test high-level abilities, such as analysis and evaluation, with the statements providing possible rationales.

The disadvantage of such questions is in their complexity, making them difficult to write and to answer. Examinees require some practice in answering such questions before being given the actual test. It would not be fair to present a question with a complex format if subjects have had no experience of it. Variability in scores could come more from a range of ability to cope with the question type rather than possession of the desired skill in the subject.

Another alternative is to have a long stem (several paragraphs or even a case study) and ask a number of questions on this. Such an approach tends to focus on the testing of higher cognitive level objectives. To test objectives validly at analysis and evaluation level will often require the interpretation of a *new* passage to determine whether examinees possess such transferable skills. In such cases, the actual textual material is not as important as eliciting the intellectual skills of analysing and evaluating the materials. The material chosen should be

Answer each item by choosing the appropriate letter:

A	B	C	D	E
1, 2, 3 all correct	1, 2 only correct	2, 3 only correct	1 only correct	3 only correct

A car being driven along a road has the following energy conversions going on:

1. chemical to heat energy

2. mechanical to electrical energy

3. heat to mechanical energy

FIGURE 10.1
A sample hybrid question: multiple choice and true–false, combined

related to the subject studied and new, but not out of context or demand prerequisites that not all subjects would have.

A summary list of guidelines for designing interpretative and hybrid multiple-choice items in general is as follows:

1 Select textual material and design questions to test achievement of the objective at the desired cognitive level.
2 While the material should be brief, it must provide sufficient information.
3 Choose new material, but not out of context.
4 All items should be based upon the material.
5 Pictorial and graphical material should be of high quality.
6 Hybrid items should meet the criteria of all their constituents.

Summary of issues related to objective items

As noted before, objective items take longer to create for a comparable length of examination than essay questions, but they are easier and more objective to mark. Consequently, a set of well-designed items will potentially be more reliable than a comparable essay test. To achieve this, though, they demand considerable design skills if they are to provide a valid measure of abilities, particularly at higher cognitive levels. We have not only provided a set of guidelines for developing and evaluating the quality of items, but also highlighted some of the issues to be considered when deciding what types are most appropriate for a given situation. Now carry out Activity 10.3.

> ## Activity 10.3
>
> Obtain an achievement test that contains objective items, preferably a variety. Use the criteria lists above to evaluate these. How could this test be improved?

Free-response questions: introduction

The appropriateness of the choice of free-response questions will depend upon the individual situation. Numerous factors must be considered, particularly those related to the type of information or skills to be measured. Any testing condition that allows for the examinee freely to express an answer provides a mixed blessing, whether it is in the form of an essay, a worked problem, project work, or an oral response. On the one hand, such conditions for testing cognitive skills may more closely reflect reality and the type of activity that the person will carry out after acquiring the qualification or acquiring a skill, thus the predictive validity is potentially increased. On the other hand, judgements about the quality of performance tend to be subject to a variety of factors that reduce the objectivity and reliability of the assessment. Thus, the designer has to weigh the advantages and disadvantages, and ultimately make a decision. Just *how* essay questions, problems, projects and oral examinations are designed, carried out and marked can also affect objectivity and reliability. Thus once a decision has been made, the designer must consider how to create the best possible questions and most explicit and unambiguous marking scheme for each question.

Over the past 50 years or so, essay questions have come in for a considerable amount of criticism in the examining community, and yet they persist at least as parts of formal examinations. Public examinations in many subjects for 16- and 18-year-olds usually have an essay component. Higher education lecturers in the humanities favour this type of question in final examinations and assessed projects or assignments. The issue that arises is not so much whether they should be used in research, but when and how they can be used appropriately.

Anyone who has had to make up an examination knows that one consisting of free-response questions alone requires a relatively short time to create but a long time to mark. On the other hand, so-called objective tests take a long time to create but little time to mark. Therefore, in terms of total time expended by the examiner, there is little to differentiate between the two types. So why do some express such a dedication to the essay in the humanities or the worked problem in science and mathematics? Is it a lack of resources or skills in writing objective items, a preference for reading student scripts over writing quick-response items, or a belief that this is the only way to measure higher-level abilities? None of these alone constitutes a totally legitimate reason, particularly if the main criterion used in designing a test is content validity. Numerous myths have grown around the design of tests, and for some of these there is evidence that they are not true. Various types of essay questions are described and guidelines for appropriate use are provided below. As you read this, consider how the wording of a question can prompt a response consistent (or inconsistent) with the cognitive level of the underlying objective whose achievement is to be determined.

Designing good essay questions and problems

Having decided to use free-response questions in a test through the process of designing a table of specifications, the designer now has to be concerned with the quality of the individual questions that will make up the instrument. Not all free-response questions are what they appear to be on the surface. For example, a number of years ago, this author discovered a significant anomaly in a past A-level physics examination while adapting it for use as a mock examination. One section gave the examinee a choice of three free-response questions from the five provided. On the surface, all five were problems requiring the learner to demonstrate application-level abilities through working out relatively complex solutions. Upon closer investigation (when trying to write model answers), it was discovered that one was impossibly difficult for A-level students of physics, unless they had memorized the solution as presented in just one of the half-dozen standard texts chosen by teachers! Thus four of the questions were testing at the application level (assuming they were new problems to the examinees) and one was testing at the knowledge level, reducing the validity of the examination since the choices were *not* equivalent in their cognitive demands.

How widespread such a phenomenon might be is not known, but it does point up another reason why the issue of choice should be considered carefully. Examination boards will argue that the reason for giving a choice is based on the fact that an examination of several years' work can cover only a sample of the subject matter covered. Offering a choice to the examinees allows them to excel in topics on which they have spent time or in which they have special interest, providing a certain amount of flexibility for the teacher and learners. The difficulty, as noted by the above example, lies in selecting truly equivalent questions among which the examinees can choose. Also, flexibility in what is 'covered' by a class is already assured by the fact that, at least with public examinations in the UK, it is possible to get the top mark on the basis of a score of around 70%. Thus, examinees having mastered three quarters of a syllabus should be able to achieve top marks, assuming the examination samples the whole syllabus evenly.

Matching the cognitive level of a question to a specific objective or box in a table of specifications is no guarantee of its appropriateness. Individual questions at the same cognitive level can vary widely in difficulty and complexity – for example, requiring the integration of several component skills. Thus it is still up to the designer to determine the appropriate level of difficulty when designing the question and/or determining the standard of the answers. Employing vague questions based upon the 'Discuss . . .' format will probably discriminate between examinees who are clairvoyants and those who are not. How else are they going to determine what aspects of the topic are to be included, except to read the examiner's mind? One should not be reluctant to define the task if a higher-level skill is being tested. The examinee deserves to have sufficient guidance. If all that is required in 'Discuss' questions is regurgitation of facts, then the essay question is not the best mechanism anyway. A wider range of facts could be tested using objective items. Table 10.6 provides a checklist for writing essay questions, one that can also be used to evaluate them after writing the statements of the questions.

TABLE 10.6
Checklist for writing five essay questions: mark each statement with a Y or N or U (undecided)

Individual questions	1	2	3	4	5
1 Is the question restricted to measuring objectives that would not be assessed more effectively by other question formats (i.e., at higher cognitive levels)?					
2 (a) Does the question relate to a course objective?					
(b) Is the cognitive level of thinking demanded by the question consistent with that of the objective and that of the teaching/training?					
(c) Does it require the examinee to demonstrate originality of thought and expression? (not always necessary)					
3 (a) Does the question establish a framework to guide the examinee to the expected answer?					
(b) Is the problem delimited and clearly stated?					
(c) Is the question unambiguous, e.g., are descriptive words such as 'compare', 'contrast' and 'define' used rather than words such as 'discuss' or 'explain'?					
(d) For the restricted-response essay in particular, is the examinee aimed towards the answer by appropriate subdivisions of the main questions?					
4 (a) Is the question novel?					
(b) Does it challenge the examinee?					
5 Is the question realistic and fair in terms of: (a) difficulty?					
(b) time allowed for examinee to respond?					
(c) complexity of the task?					
6 Have a model answer and point scheme for components been prepared for the question?					

Overall examination

7 Are all examinees expected to answer the same questions?	
8 Is there a preponderance of short-answer (restricted-response) questions?	
9 Is the relative value of each question indicated?	

Source: after Mehrens and Lehmann (1984)

Marking essay questions and problems

The lack of reliability (consistency) of marking has been the other damning criticism levelled against essay questions over the years. In considering what this means, two types of reliability can be used as indicators: *inter-scorer* (across examiners or readers of scripts) and *intra-scorer* (across time). The former is concerned with how well the marks given by a number of examiners for a specific set of papers agree, while the latter asks whether a single reader, marking a set of papers, is consistent throughout the process. Reliability coefficients can be calculated for both types as a check after the examination has been given and marked (see Chapter 11).

At the planning stage, there are a number of steps that can be taken to enhance the reliability of marking of answers to free-response questions. Examination boards provide some guidelines for portions of examinations marked in the teaching institution as well. It is still up to the designer of the test to apply these to specific topics, but for essay questions at the comprehension level and above, they at least provide a beginning for creating a marking scheme. Considering that these are criteria for individual items, such a set of guidelines can help to prevent the natural temptation to revert back to comparing examinees with one another when assigning marks (Johnny answered this better than Mary but not as well as Jane, and besides he is a nice lad). If the questions in an examination are to be marked consistently across examinees, then the criteria need to be described clearly and referred to when marking.

Mehrens and Lehmann (1984) describe two types of marking for essays: an analytical method that requires a marking scheme to be written out in detail and agreed upon by all the examiners; and global scoring (sometimes referred to as impression marking), where the criteria are much more general. Second examiners who are engaged to ensure a test and its marking are valid and reliable will enhance the quality of a study. It is essential to have the second examiner mark a sample of papers from examinees independently. This can help him or her to determine whether standards are reasonable and fair, as well as to assess the reliability and objectivity of the researcher's marking.

Mehrens and Lehmann (1984) suggest ten guidelines to assist markers in ensuring a high reliability for their marks. In summary, these are as follows:

1 Before actually marking papers, check your key against a few randomly selected papers to determine its appropriateness. Make any changes then – not later, midway through marking a set of scripts.
2 Strive to maintain consistency in marking over time.
3 Arrange the papers in random order before marking them to minimize the influence of good papers on bad and vice versa.
4 Mark one question on all papers. This will reduce the effect that responses to other questions on an examinee's paper could have on the one being marked.
5 Mark all students' answers to a given question in one sitting. Spreading the marking of a single question over time increases the chance of variation in marking.
6 Students' names should not be on the scripts. This will avoid any prejudices, positive or negative.

7   Strive to distinguish between content and style. Some students are more articulate and/or rigorous with their grammar than others, which can influence marks.

8   Have two independent markers, or mark papers on two occasions. For large groups, this may be possible for only a sample of the class.

9   Give comments on errors to provide feedback.

10 Set standards that are realistic for the learners, avoiding lenient as well as overly hard examinations.

This list should provide the basis for establishing guidelines for marking. Any such list should be understood and agreed upon by all markers concerned.

Projects and coursework for assessment

There is a role in measurement for projects, extended essays done out of class, and other forms of writing not carried out under strict examination conditions, activities that are appropriate indicators of specific abilities. Definite advantages exist in using such work as a source of operational definitions (scores) since it has the potential of providing a valid measure of ability to perform under conditions closely associated with those in real life. Projects usually involve higher-level skills providing problem-solving situations where the synthesis of new ideas and/or processes is required. It is reasonable to expect some level of creativity since the student is not constrained to performing in a short period of time. It has been suggested that it is unreasonable to demand a high level of creativity on formal essay examinations, since creative ability is less likely to be displayed under extreme pressure of time.

On the other hand, similar problems of reliability to those of essay questions potentially exist, both in setting the task and in marking the products. Consequently, the guidance on setting and marking essays applies here as well. Project work where students work together has advantages in providing experience in co-operative effort, very relevant to real-life work situations. The disadvantage lies in assessing it: there can be considerable difficulty in determining individual contributions, though a short oral defence can usually resolve any doubts. Such activities can be used to assess students on co-operative skills (for example, through the examiner observing) rather than using the product for cognitive assessment. Which aspects of project work will be assessed or measured will depend entirely on what the objectives are and the research questions to be resolved.

The oral examination

Some tasks require an oral examination to ensure the validity of the results, such as conversation ability in foreign languages, and the ability to carry out certain interactive skills, such as handling customer enquiries where technique is as important as the information given. An oral examination can also be required in order to provide more or different information (clarification) on a project, justification of approach, or to carry out an in-depth probe of what was done. In some situations, it may be necessary to confirm that the project work was carried out by the person presenting the report, or to find out what the individual contributions were in a group effort. These are formal situations, as opposed to the everyday questioning that will go on in a class as part of learning.

Oral examinations also suffer the disadvantages described earlier for essay questions, as well as some unique to this form of assessment. Thus their design requires the same level of detailed planning to maximize reliability. If they are to reflect the same abilities across a group of examinees, then the same questions have to be asked. Recording scores for responses will require some marking scheme that can be applied as the session is in progress, otherwise a recording will have to be made for review later, adding to an already time-consuming task.

It should be kept in mind that some subjects will find the oral examination situation stressful, while others can cover up ignorance with their ability to talk around the topic. There is a certain amount of danger that the score will reflect the subject's speaking ability more than the intellectual skill being assessed, a problem analogous to handwriting influencing an essay mark. As with any assessment technique, the oral should be used when it enhances the validity of the outcome, but only with careful preparation. Most of the advantages and disadvantages are the same as those identified for essay questions in general. The main basis for deciding whether to use this approach will be the individual situation, which will include the skills and subject matter being examined.

Summary for free-response questions

We have described a variety of assessment techniques that allow the subject a considerable amount of freedom in his or her response. The advantages in enhancing the validity of the results can be offset by low reliability of marks if the examiner does not take extreme care in designing the questions and planning an appropriate marking scheme to enhance objectivity of the marker or scorer, and the consistency of the scores across examiners and time. Now complete Activity 10.4.

Activity 10.4

Obtain an achievement test with essay questions and evaluate them using the above criteria. Can you improve any of the questions? What cognitive level do you think the writer intended to test?

CONCLUSION

This chapter has provided a brief introduction to the design of instruments measuring achievement in the cognitive domain, for researchers wishing to set up operationally defined variables that are indicators of possession of knowledge or skills. Greater detail and additional guidelines for the construction of tests and individual types of questions can be found in any one of a number of textbooks on the subject, some of which are listed in the references. Now carry out Activity 10.5.

Activity 10.5

If your research involves, or you plan for it to involve, the use of an achievement test of cognitive abilities, bring copies of the table of specifications (even a draft) and a copy of the test (if it has been developed) for distribution and discussion.

Be prepared to describe what you have done to enhance the validity and reliability of the test, as well as your choice of types of items or questions used to test the knowledge and skills. In other words, defend the instrument designed or to be designed as a valid and reliable operational definition of the concepts indicated in your research question or hypothesis.

Evaluating Data Quality: Determining Instrument Reliability and Validity

11

Over the last two chapters, you have been introduced to the design of achievement tests and examinations, plus some forms of instruments for measuring attitudes and views. These have included guidelines to assist with the design of such instruments so that they are as reliable, valid and objective as possible. As Nunnally and Bernstein (1994) note, there are potential problems in employing the rational approach for ensuring construct validity emphasized in this text, but these lie not in the way the items are derived and constructed, rather in the tendency for the lack of evaluation after developing them. The next question therefore is what tools are available to evaluate piloted tests or measuring instruments, and, related to this, what tools are of greatest value to help identify deficiencies as a first step in improving the instruments.

There are ways of testing the validity and reliability of instruments that aim to quantify human characteristics and traits, ones that are analogous to testing the design of physical measuring instruments. The process includes conducting a trial run of each measuring instrument, then selecting and carrying out the most appropriate test for determining the quality of individual questions and items, and reliability calculations for the instrument as a whole. On the basis of this information, individual items that need improvement can be identified. Some methods of quantifying validity will be introduced and criteria for appropriate use included. It is necessary to keep in mind that it is possible to have an instrument that is reliable but not valid – in other words, that consistently measures something other than what was intended. On the other hand, it is not possible to have a valid instrument that is not reliable: if it does not produce consistent results (it is unreliable) then those results cannot be measuring what they are supposed to measure (it is not valid).

A number of techniques, some of them statistically based, have been developed over the years to assist in the evaluation of whole instruments and individual questions. Coefficients are calculated that give a relative indication of the quality of the overall test or individual questions. For example, certain reliability coefficients give an indication of how consistently the items in a test contribute to final scores. Like the tests themselves, these tools strive to be reliable, valid and informative to the developer and users of tests and examinations; thus they have to be interpreted as indicating *likelihoods,* rather than absolute judgements. For example, a test with a high reliability coefficient is *likely* to produce very similar results under similar conditions with similar subjects. This chapter covers a number of tools for resolving evaluation issues, in particular:

- several ways of quantifying the reliability of whole instruments or homogeneous subsections, the choice being dependent on the nature of the traits (cognitive or attitudes) and type of questions employed;
- evaluation of individual items in attitude measures using a coefficient as an indicator, having been developed by employing the logical or rational approach and piloted with a small sample of subjects;
- evaluation of individual questions for short-answer tests and components of essay questions using a coefficient;
- evaluation of items in objective achievement tests using coefficients depending on whether they were norm- or criterion-referenced, having been developed from a table of specifications and piloted with a group of learners;
- ways of quantifying some of the several types of validity.

The chapter will start with a definition of reliability, introducing a calculation of an estimate, plus a coefficient for evaluating individual questions. Then several other cases and coefficients will be provided for objective tests, questionnaires and situations involving multiple markers. As you proceed through this chapter, there will be a number of activities that will involve setting up spreadsheet versions of tables. Carefully name and save these, as they will serve as templates for carrying out an analysis of your own instruments later.

RELIABILITY

To begin, recall from Chapter 8 that reliability is defined as

$$\text{reliability} \equiv \frac{\text{variance in true scores}}{\text{variance in observed scores}}$$

which is usually written mathematically as equation (8.2),

$$r_{xx} \equiv \frac{S_t^2}{S_x^2} \tag{11.1}$$

where S_t^2 is the true score variance and S_x^2 is the observed score variance.

Unfortunately, it is usually not possible to know the true score, since we cannot make a perfect measuring instrument, and therefore the true score variance can never be known. The consequence of this is that all reliability coefficients are estimates, depending on what form of reliability one is using. Recall from equation (8.1) that the total variance in instrument scores (observed score variance), S_x^2, is the sum of the true score variance, S_t^2, and the variance due to error in the instrument, S_e^2, which is written symbolically as

$$S_x^2 = S_t^2 + S_e^2 \qquad (11.2)$$

Substituting and rearranging the equations (see Chapter 8) we get an expression for reliability (equation (8.5)) that excludes the never-to-be-known true score variance, but does include error variance and observed score variance, the latter being readily available from subjects' scores:

$$r_{xx} = 1 - \frac{S_e^2}{S_x^2} \qquad (11.3)$$

This will be used as a basis for establishing some of the most common estimates of instrument reliability (internal consistency), which are often based upon some estimate for the error variance, S_e^2. The process of carrying out pilot runs of tests and questionnaires, followed by the type of analysis described in the rest of the chapter, may seem to constitute a rather large effort. Unfortunately, there is no real substitute and the consequences of not doing so can leave you with an unreliable instrument.

Estimates of reliability

Mehrens and Lehmann (1984) describe six major kinds of reliability, and there are any number of coefficients that provide estimations of these. It is worth remembering that since the true score cannot be known, reliability coefficients are always estimates. As a researcher, you may be interested in only a few in detail for evaluating your own instruments, but others may be of interest for interpreting published data on commercial tests. Worked examples are provided below for some of the following, the first six of which assume a normal distribution of scores from the instruments:

1 Measure of stability, for a single instrument administered more than once (test–retest).
2 Measure of equivalence for two different instruments of the same domain (parallel forms).
3 Split-half estimate, dividing a single instrument into two equivalent halves (achievement tests or attitude questionnaires using scales, such as rating and Likert).
4 Cronbach's alpha (α) for internal consistency of essay achievement tests and attitude questionnaires, again using scales such as rating and Likert.
5 Kuder–Richardson estimates of internal consistency, for tests with right/wrong answers (for example, objective achievement tests).
6 Scorer (judge, marker) reliability, for two or more scorers (for example, for essay tests, observer checklists and rating scales), or for a single scorer over time.
7 Estimate of reliability for criterion-referenced tests, allowing for distributions of scores that are not normally distributed, possibly skewed or flat.

At the same time, coefficients for determining the quality of individual questions will be presented. This will allow the identification of those that seem to make a detrimental contribution to reliability. It will still be up to the developer to identify *why* such questions discriminate poorly between those who achieve or have certain attitudes, and those who do not. Like reliability coefficients, these are only indicators of quality and not sources of reasons why – the developer must still be a detective.

Measure of stability (test–retest)

One definition of reliability is concerned with the stability of an instrument over time – in other words, whether it provides much the same score on two different occasions (test–retest). Thus, a simple approach to testing this is to administer the instrument to the same group on two events. The difficulty with this is the probability of incurring confounding when the instrument is completed by subjects, yet in time series designs where measures are repeated over time, stability of the instrument may be essential.

The simplest estimate of reliability is the correlation between two equivalent tests, and the *Pearson product moment correlation* is the most common statistic used for this purpose. It is relatively simple to calculate:

$$r_{12} = \frac{\sum_{i=1}^{n}[(x_{1i} - \bar{x}_1)(x_{2i} - \bar{x}_2)]}{nS_1S_2} \tag{11.4}$$

In this equation x_{1i} is the score of person i on test 1, x_{2i} the score of person i on test 2; $\bar{x}_1$ is the mean score of all subjects on test 1, $\bar{x}_2$ the mean score of all subjects on test 2; S_1 is the standard deviation of test 1, S_2 the standard deviation of test 2; n is the number of subjects taking test 1 and test 2; and $\sum_{i=1}^{n}$ says 'add up everything inside the square brackets as i goes from 1 to n subjects' – in other words, for this equation, for each subject, i, subtract the subject's scores from the means for the first and second tests and multiply them together, adding this to all the others.

Comparing this equation to that of (11.1), it can be seen that

$$\frac{\sum_{i=1}^{n}[(x_{1i} - \bar{x}_1)(x_{2i} - \bar{x}_2)]}{n}$$

is an estimate of the true score variance and that S_1S_2 is an estimate of the observed score variance. The mathematical link between equations (11.1) and (11.4) is beyond this text, but can be found in Traub (1994).

As an example, Figure 11.1 summarizes the data for a test given to a group of $n = 8$ subjects on two occasions. The values would produce a Pearson product moment correlation as follows:

$$r_{12} = \frac{39.38}{(8)(2.83)(2.20)} = 0.79$$

This indicates an instrument which is reasonably reliable (stable over time). Whether it is considered to be sufficiently reliable would be up to the researcher

FIGURE 11.1
Data, for $n = 8$ subjects taking the same test on two occasions, set out in a spreadsheet (raw data in shaded cells), with calculations for finding the correlation between the two test administrations

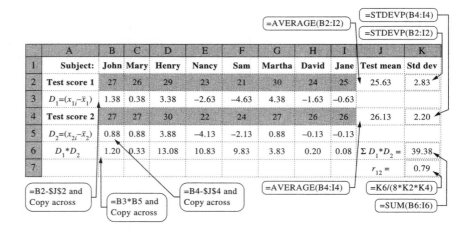

and would depend on the nature of the research. Recalling equation (11.1) though, the implication is that there is some error variance that might be reduced by improving the instrument. The process for determining where, will be covered later in the chapter.

There can be some difficulty in interpreting this estimate of reliability for a number of possible reasons:

- The actual use of the instrument on the first occasion may cause a measurable change in the subjects – recall sources 13 (learning from instrument) and 14 (instrument reacts with independent variable), in Chapter 7.
- In some types of studies – in particular, time series – we would *expect* change in the subjects over time.
- On the other hand, if the time interval between testing is short, the subjects may remember aspects of the instrument from the first administration.

Any of these may lower the estimate of reliability for the instrument below what might be more legitimately found from other estimates, since these could influence the scores on the second administration, increasing the differences from the first. Carry out Activity 11.1 now, in order to see how to set up Figure 11.1 on a spreadsheet.

Activity 11.1

To explore the effects of mathematical data on coefficients and avoid hours of tedious calculations, we will set up tables in a spreadsheet which will do all the number-crunching for you. In order to become familiar with this powerful tool, several activities will initially have you replicate the tables in the text and then make changes. Since this is the first one, the steps below will take you through the process step by step. If you are not familiar with spreadsheets, refer to Appendix A before starting this activity.

1   To implement Figure 11.1 on a spreadsheet:

(a)   Type in the headings in row 1 and column **A**, then enter the eight pairs of test scores in the shaded cells in rows 2 and 4.

(b)   Enter the standard functions to find means and standard deviations in cells **J2**, **J4**, **K2** and **K4**, as shown. Either use the Function Wizard, or type these in as shown. The notation (**B2:I2**) is simply shorthand for 'all the numbers in the cells from **B2** to **I2** inclusive'.

(c)   Insert the equation shown in cell **B3** and **Copy** it across to the others in the row. The column letter **B** in the formula will automatically change to the appropriate column, but **$J$2** will stay the same.

(d)   Repeat this for cell **B6** and **Copy** it across to the other cells on the row.

(e)   Insert the multiplications shown for row **6** by typing the formula in the first cell and **Copy**ing across to the other cells in the row.

(f)   Use the **SUM** function in cell **K6** to add up all the results in row **6**.

(g)   Place the formula in cell **K7** to give you the reliability. This will allow you to do the next question.

2   Change one of the pairs of scores for Sam and Martha, the two with the most divergent pairs of scores, and see the effect on the reliability: make them closer together then further apart.

3   If you have a spreadsheet with full statistical functions, such as Excel 5.0 or later, you will find that there is a built-in correlation function that simply requires you to identify the two sets of data. In Excel, there are two that appear to be the same: **CORREL** and **PEARSON**. To find the correlation here, simply use the function **PEARSON (B2:I2,B4:I4)** in an empty cell and you should again get 0.79 without having to do the calculations in rows **2**, **4** and **6**.

Measure of equivalence

An alternative way of checking the reliability of an instrument is to compare the responses of a set of subjects with those made by the same subjects on another instrument that tests the same concept, preferably on the same day. This would be applicable to achievement tests covering a content area, as well as to questionnaires or other instruments measuring attitudes. Establishing the relative equivalence of two instruments is of value for situations where parallel forms of a test are to be used. On the other hand, it could be used to establish the equivalence of a new test with an established one. The calculation would be the same as above, a correlation between two instruments as shown in Figure 11.1, and the scales and scoring systems would not have to be the same. Again, what is an acceptable level of reliability will need to be determined based upon the purpose of the research.

Measures of internal consistency

Internal consistency is important on any instrument and may be the only measure possible for a single administration of an instrument. The most basic way of estimating the internal consistency of an achievement test or questionnaire is to have a coefficient that takes into account (a) the average correlation among all the questions or identifiable parts, and (b) the number of questions or parts (Nunnally and Bernstein, 1994). Cronbach's alpha (α), does exactly this, with the Kuder–Richardson formulae being special cases for questions with only right or wrong answers (such as multiple-choice items).

Another way of determining internal consistency is appropriate for tests constructed as two matching halves, where each item has an equivalent partner somewhere in the test. The split-half reliability estimate will tend to be higher for such a test than Cronbach's α since the latter is considered to be an estimate of all possible split-half reliabilities. Therefore, there is an advantage to designing split-half instruments, though this is not always possible. To use the split-half reliability coefficient indiscriminately for a test, say by simply dividing it in half by using odd and even questions, could result in a lower estimate than that for Cronbach's α. This may seem odd until it is realized that the number of possible combinations of pairs grows astronomically with the length of the test (Crocker and Algina, 1986):

$$\text{number of possible split-halves} = \frac{N!/2}{[(N/2)!]^2}$$

where N is the number of items or identifiable parts, and $N!$ is the factorial of N – for example, if $N = 3$, then $N! = 3 \times 2 \times 1 = 6$. This relationship is illustrated in Table 11.1. Given the way the number of split-halves increases, it is better to use Cronbach's α if one has not planned a test with matched halves.

SPLIT-HALF ESTIMATES   This process is based on the simple approach of devising an instrument as two equivalent halves: each question has a matching partner that essentially asks the same thing but in different words. The corresponding form of reliability determines how consistently the subjects tend to answer the pairs of questions.

TABLE 11.1
Number of possible split-halves that could be made from a single set of questions on a test

Number of questions	Possible split-halves
2	1
4	3
6	10
8	35
10	126
12	462
14	1 716
16	6 435
18	24 310
20	92 378
30	77 558 760
50	63 205 303 218 876

The test is treated mathematically as two tests with two means and standard deviations. The difficulty is that a correlation coefficient calculated as above in Figure 11.1 would really be an estimate of the reliability of a test *half* the length of the actual test. Since test reliability is quite sensitive to the number of questions, a second calculation must be performed after finding the Pearson product moment correlation, $r_{\frac{1}{2}\frac{1}{2}}$, to provide a better estimate, and is a special form of the *Spearman–Brown prophecy formula* (Mehrens and Lehmann, 1984):

$$r_{xx} = \frac{2r_{\frac{1}{2}\frac{1}{2}}}{1 + r_{\frac{1}{2}\frac{1}{2}}} \tag{11.5}$$

where r_{xx} is the estimated of reliability of whole test and $r_{\frac{1}{2}\frac{1}{2}}$ is the Pearson product moment correlation of the two halves (thus the reliability of half the test). Thus if the data in Figure 11.1 were for the two halves of a single test, then the whole-test reliability would be found as follows:

$$r_{xx} = \frac{2(0.79)}{1 + 0.79} = 0.88$$

Such an approach means that it is only necessary to administer one form of the instrument. It is assumed that not only are the questions matched, but also the variances (thus standard deviations) of the two halves are about the same, otherwise the resulting reliability estimate will be greater than that found by other estimates of internal consistency. This indicator is appropriate for cognitive (achievement) tests as well as affective instruments, such as attitude questionnaires (Oppenheim, 1992). We will return to a more detailed example later to compare the results of the split-half estimate with Cronbach's α for a Likert question set.

CRONBACH'S α

Cronbach's coefficient α is a reasonable indicator of the internal consistency of instruments that do not have right–wrong (binary) marking schemes, thus can be used for both essay questions as well as questionnaires using scales such as rating or Likert (Oppenheim, 1992). It is considered to be the average of all possible split-half coefficients (Murphy and Davidshofer, 1991) and therefore may provide a lower value than that for a specific split-half correlation coefficient based upon matched pairs of items (Traub, 1994). It takes into account both the number of questions (or identifiable parts of an essay question) and the average correlation among questions on a test (Nunnally and Bernstein, 1994). It is calculated as follows:

$$\alpha = \frac{N}{N-1}\left[1 - \frac{\sum_{i=1}^{N} S_i^2}{S_x^2}\right] \tag{11.6}$$

where N is the number of questions (or identifiable parts of an essay question), S_i^2 is the variance of individual questions (or parts) and S_x^2 is the variance of the whole test.

For example, Figure 11.2 provides the marks for a free-response test with five questions (or five distinguishable parts of a single essay), all weighted equally, taken by 10 students. Using equation (11.6),

FIGURE 11.2
Scores for an instrument with five questions, maximum of 10 points each (e.g., five essay questions, five equally weighted parts of a single essay or five responses on a questionnaire) taken by ten students, presented in a spreadsheet to calculate Cronbach's alpha and item–total correlations

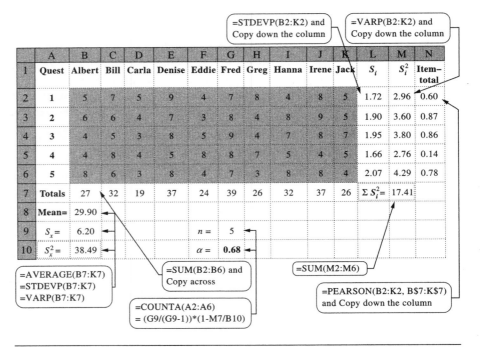

$$\alpha = \frac{5}{5-1}\left[1 - \frac{17.41}{38.49}\right] = 0.68$$

This suggests a moderately reliable test, particularly for such a small number of questions and a small group, but, as we will see in the next activity, this may be deceptive.

Having conducted a trial of an instrument (essay, attitude measure consisting of scales), it is possible to scan the results in a table for items that generate inconsistent responses, such as Figure 11.2. For small samples the results are easily (and disproportionately) influenced by individuals. Also, visual scanning of results is not very likely to identify all the problems. A more systematic approach (Traub, 1994) provides coefficients for each item that serve as relative indicators of quality. These are directly related to the reliability of the whole instrument, therefore improving individual items using them as guidance will tend to improve the overall instrument reliability. A word of warning, though: this coefficient does assume a normal distribution. Therefore, if your test is criterion-referenced and produces a skewed or flat distribution of scores, then you may find that Cronbach's α provides a very low value. An adjustment, to be introduced later, will give a higher value when the cut-off score is not equal to the mean.

The best indicator for evaluating individual items is the *item–total correlation*, which is defined as the correlation between the individual response scores for the item and the total score on the instrument. This reflects how consistently the item is measuring the same thing as the instrument as a whole and therefore it is desirable for this to be high. An item with a low (or even negative) correlation coefficient would indicate that it was not eliciting responses consistent with the instrument (or section of the instrument) as a whole. This is sometimes referred to as the *index of item discrimination*, indicating how well an item discriminates between those subjects who score high and those who score low on the instrument.

These are easily added to the spreadsheet when organizing it to determine Cronbach's α, as you will see in Activity 11.2 which you should do now.

Activity 11.2

1   To set up Figure 11.2:
   (a)   Type in the headings in column **A** and row **1**, then insert the raw data in the shaded cells.
   (b)   Find the totals for each student using the **SUM** function indicated for cell **B7**, then **Copy**ing it across the other cells in row **7**.
   (c)   Use the functions indicated for mean, standard deviation and variance in cells **B8**, **B9**, **B10**, and columns **L** and **M**.
   (d)   Find the column sum for the variances, cell **M7**.
   (e)   Insert the equation shown for coefficient α in cell **G10**.
   (f)   Insert the equation for the item–total correlation in cell **N2**, noting the use of the **$** in the formula, then **Copy** it down the column.
   When you get the values shown, save the worksheet and go to 2.
2   From the item–total correlation for the essay questions evaluated by using Cronbach's α in Figure 11.2, which question is likely to need improvement if the reliability is to be increased?
3   Eddie and Irene each have one question for which the score is radically different from the others they achieved. Try changing the score for question 4 for Eddie from 8 to 5, and also for question 4 for Irene from 4 to 8. What is the effect of making these scores more consistent on item–total correlations and coefficient α?
4   Change the scores for Eddie and Irene back, and now try changing the score for question 3 for Carla from 3 to 8 and for Fred from 9 to 4. How do these influence item–total correlations and coefficient α?

Exercises 3 and 4 illustrate how vulnerable α can be to the performance of one or two subjects on a small part of an instrument when a small group is used in a trial.

Answers: 2.   Question 4 has a very low item–total correlation coefficient compared to the rest and is likely to need investigating. Is its cognitive emphasis and/or content consistent with the rest? Factual essay questions on obscure information can be poor discriminators.
3.   Correlation between item 4 and total is 0.64 (all others except 5 increase slightly) and $\alpha = 0.82$.
4.   Correlation between item 3 and total is 0.30 (all others change slightly) and $\alpha = 0.38$.

KUDER–RICHARDSON ESTIMATES   An achievement test may not have been designed specifically as two matched halves, in which case the split-half reliability would not be appropriate. When the items are either right or wrong (objective items), then the Kuder–Richardson formulae, special forms of Cronbach's α, are appropriate.

The Kuder–Richardson 20 (KR20) estimate is based on equation (11.3) where the observed score variance, S_x^2, is known from the results of the subjects taking the achievement test, and the error variance is estimated, as shown in the numerator inside the brackets:

$$r_{xx} = \frac{N}{N-1}\left[1 - \frac{\sum_{i=1}^{N} p_i q_i}{S_x^2}\right] \tag{11.7}$$

where N is the number of items on the test, S_x^2 is the observed score variance, p_i is the difficulty of each item, i, where i runs from 1 to N, q_i is equal to $1 - p_i$, and $\sum p_i q_i$ is equivalent to $\sum S_i^2$ in Cronbach's α (equation (11.6)).

Along with the reliability coefficient, individual questions on tests can be evaluated with respect to several criteria at once, a process referred to as *item analysis*. For example, Figure 11.3 provides the histogram of scores and Figure 11.4 presents the item analysis for a ten-item multiple-choice test taken by 30 students. This process allows the determination of a *discrimination index*, D, for each item at the same time, indicating the item's tendency to discriminate between those who are in the upper half and those in the lower half.

When the number of examinees is sufficiently large (more than 40), the most appropriate procedure involves using an upper group (those we can be con-

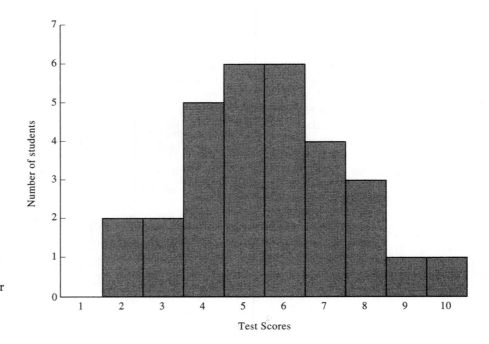

FIGURE 11.3
Distributions of scores for a norm-referenced ten-item multiple-choice achievement test for 30 subjects, where $\bar{x} = 5.57$, $S_x = 1.93$, $S_x^2 = 3.71$

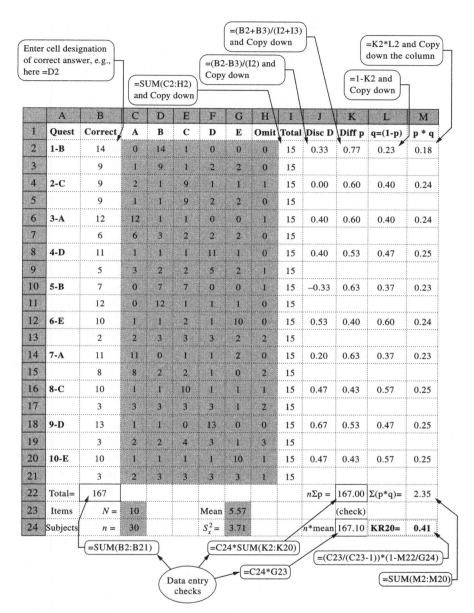

FIGURE 11.4
Item analysis for results of Figure 11.3: 30 subjects answering ten multiple-choice items with raw data in columns **C** to **H** (shaded area) and formulae for calculating Discrimination, Difficulty and KR20

Annotations in figure:

- Enter cell designation of correct answer, e.g., here =D2
- =SUM(C2:H2) and Copy down
- =(B2-B3)/(I2) and Copy down
- =(B2+B3)/(I2+I3) and Copy down
- =1-K2 and Copy down
- =K2*L2 and Copy down the column

	A	B	C	D	E	F	G	H	I	J	K	L	M
1	Quest	Correct	A	B	C	D	E	Omit	Total	Disc D	Diff p	q=(1-p)	p * q
2	1-B	14	0	14	1	0	0	0	15	0.33	0.77	0.23	0.18
3		9	1	9	1	2	2	0	15				
4	2-C	9	2	1	9	1	1	1	15	0.00	0.60	0.40	0.24
5		9	1	1	9	2	2	0	15				
6	3-A	12	12	1	1	0	0	1	15	0.40	0.60	0.40	0.24
7		6	6	3	2	2	2	0	15				
8	4-D	11	1	1	1	11	1	0	15	0.40	0.53	0.47	0.25
9		5	3	2	2	5	2	1	15				
10	5-B	7	0	7	7	0	0	1	15	−0.33	0.63	0.37	0.23
11		12	0	12	1	1	1	0	15				
12	6-E	10	1	1	2	1	10	0	15	0.53	0.40	0.60	0.24
13		2	2	3	3	3	2	2	15				
14	7-A	11	11	0	1	1	2	0	15	0.20	0.63	0.37	0.23
15		8	8	2	2	1	0	2	15				
16	8-C	10	1	1	10	1	1	1	15	0.47	0.43	0.57	0.25
17		3	3	3	3	3	1	2	15				
18	9-D	13	1	1	0	13	0	0	15	0.67	0.53	0.47	0.25
19		3	2	2	4	3	1	3	15				
20	10-E	10	1	1	1	1	10	1	15	0.47	0.43	0.57	0.25
21		3	2	3	3	3	3	1	15				
22	Total=	167								nΣp =	167.00	Σ(p*q)=	2.35
23	Items	N =	10			Mean	5.57				(check)		
24	Subjects	n =	30			$S_x^2=$	3.71			n*mean	167.10	KR20=	0.41

Data entry checks:
- =SUM(B2:B21)
- =SUM(B2:B21)
- =C24*SUM(K2:K20)
- =C24*G23
- =(C23/(C23-1))*(1-M22/G24)
- =SUM(M2:M20)

vinced have learned) and a lower group (those we can be convinced have not learned). For statistical reasons it is advantageous to take the top 27% as the upper group, and the bottom 27% as the lower group (Cureton, 1957). For relatively small groups (less than 40), it is usual to use the upper and lower halves of the whole set of examinees. To calculate the index, D, use the formula below, which will also be used to compare this procedure with that for the criterion-referenced index later:

$$D = \frac{U - L}{n} \qquad (11.8)$$

where U is the number in the upper group getting the item correct (who should), L is the number in the lower group getting the item correct (who should not) and n is the number in each group (27% of total if the examinees number over 40, otherwise half the group if it is a small group).

The value of this index can range from $+1.00$, suggesting the item is a perfect discriminator between those who have learned and those who have not, through 0.00, which indicates it does not discriminate at all, to -1.00, which suggests that all the low-ability examinees answered the item correctly and the high-ability ones got it wrong. Mehrens and Lehmann (1984) suggest that an item with a low or near zero value is either too easy (everyone gets it correct), too hard (everyone misses it), or ambiguous (the correct answer is not clearly identifiable by even the knowledgeable). Which it is in the example and can be determined by examining Figure 11.4, where numbers selecting each alternative for the multiple-choice question are displayed. An item that has little discriminating power does not contribute to the validity or reliability of a test.

What is 'acceptable'? Ideally, the higher the value of the index the better. Some professional examining bodies will reject items that have a value less than 0.60, though Mehrens and Lehmann (1984) suggest that above 0.40 is acceptable for classroom tests. From the view of a researcher, it would be advantageous to produce a first version of a test and try it on a trial group. Using the data from this group, each item could be considered and those with low indices could be either rejected or revised. Such indices are just indicators of a possible problem; unfortunately, they do not say what the problem may be. It is still up to the designer of the test to determine whether it is the wording, the content covered, or some other factor that has resulted in a low index.

The data for each item are recorded in a unique way: for each item, the number of subjects who were in the upper group (in the highest 50% of total scores since $n < 40$) and who chose an option is recorded in the first row and those whose scores were in the lower group in the second row. Thus, for question number 1, of the top 15, none answered A, 14 answered B (correctly), one answered C, and so on. Of the bottom 15, 1 answered A, 9 answered B (correctly), and so forth. Thus the total number answering question 1 correctly was $14 + 9 = 23$.

This table is one way of displaying test results, but it has more information in it than needed just for the calculation of the reliability coefficient and it will be referred to again later when considering individual items. For immediate purposes, it is necessary to calculate the *difficulty* of each item, which requires that one simply divides how many examinees answered correctly by the total number of examinees. Thus this index will range from 0 to 1.00, as recorded in column K, p_i, on Figure 11.4.

$$p_i = \text{Difficulty} = \frac{\text{Number answering correctly}}{\text{Total number of examinees}} \quad (11.9)$$

For example, question 1 had a total of 23 correct answers B, which divided by 30 gives 0.77 for the difficulty index, p_1. To calculate the Kuder–Richardson KR20 coefficient, we also need $q_i = 1 - p_i$, which is in column L of Figure 11.4. Using this information, the Kuder–Richardson 20 estimate is calculated as follows, taking the variance, $S_x^2 = 3.71$, from Figure 11.3:

$$r_{xx} = \frac{10}{10-1} \left[1 - \frac{2.35}{3.71} \right] = 0.41$$

Somewhat contrary to the name, the higher the value of difficulty, the less difficult the question, that is, the greater the proportion who answered it correctly. Consequently, in the literature this coefficient is sometimes referred to as a *facility index*. What is important to note is the fact that difficulty is not distribution-dependent, and is therefore appropriate for norm- and criterion-referenced tests alike.

What is an acceptable level of difficulty for individual items will depend upon the purpose of the test. If a test is norm-referenced (that is, it is expected that the scores for a group will produce a normal distribution, a requirement of a number of statistical tests, as will be seen later), then a medium level of difficulty (around 0.50) would be advantageous. If, on the other hand, the test were criterion-referenced (grades are based upon performance against an established standard or cut-off score) then the distribution of scores may be negatively skewed and the difficulty index quite high.

You should carry out Activity 11.3 now in order to implement Figure 11.4.

Activity 11.3

1 To set up Figure 11.4 in a spreadsheet:
   (a) After typing in the headings in row **1** and column **A** (question number and correct answer), enter the raw data in columns **C–H**.
   (b) In column **B**, type the cell designations for the number answering correctly in the upper and lower groups.
   (c) In column **I**, insert the **SUM** function for all the answers just as a check on data entry, since these numbers should always equal the totals in the upper and lower groups.
   (d) In column **J**, enter the formula for the discrimination index,

   $D = (U - L)/n.$

   (e) In columns **K**, **L** and **M**, use a formula for each of p_i, q_i and $p_i \times q_i$.
   (f) Add three more data entry checks in the cells **B22**, **K22** and **K24**. These will simply help to identify where there are errors.
   (g) Add the equation in **M22** and that for KR20 in cell **M24**.
   When it all works, save the worksheet for future use for your own data.
2 Try changing some of the values in the table to see how they influence the value of KR20.
3 Which item(s) need to be improved? Why?
4 What do the wrong choices suggest might be done to improve them?
Answers: 3. Questions 1, 2, 5 and 7, since D < 0.40. 4. Choice 5C, made by many in the upper group, may indicate that this choice is not distinctly different from the correct answer: check the wording. Others where the upper group did not do distinctly well, such as Question 2, may be due to wording, but could also be due to the question asking for an obscure fact.

The value for KR20 does not seem very high for a multiple-choice test, but the key is in the length of the test. Recall that in Chapter 8 it was suggested that reliability depends upon the number of questions, thus it would be interesting to know what the reliability of a comparable test of greater length would be.

Using the *Spearman–Brown prophecy formula* (Mehrens and Lehmann, 1984), it is possible to estimate the reliability if the test were a more appropriate length:

$$r'_{xx} = \frac{Kr_{xx}}{1 + (K - 1)r_{xx}} \tag{11.8}$$

where r'_{xx} is the predicted reliability for a test K times as long, r_{xx} is the reliability of test as it exists and K is the ratio of number of items on the new test to the number on the existing test. Thus if the test above, which had a reliability of only 0.41 with 10 questions, were expanded to 50 comparable questions (so that $K = 5$), what would its predicted reliability be?

$$r'_{xx} = \frac{5(0.41)}{1 + (5 - 1)0.41} = 0.78$$

Alternatively, if the difficulty, p_i, were constant (or near enough) for all items, then KR21 could be used, but it gives a more conservative (that is, lower) estimate of test reliability:

$$r_{xx} = \frac{N}{N - 1}\left[1 - \frac{\bar{x}(N - \bar{x})}{NS_x^2}\right] \tag{11.9}$$

where N is the number of items on the test, $\bar{x}$ is the mean of the test scores and S_x^2 is the variance of the test scores. Using the item analysis as shown in Figure 11.2, it is not much easier to calculate than KR20:

$$r_{xx} = \frac{10}{10 - 1}\left[1 - \frac{5.57(10 - 5.57)}{10(3.71)}\right] = 0.37$$

For this example, the result produced by KR21 is not very different from that of KR20 above. In either case, as with Cronbach's α, you will find the values may be very low for criterion-referenced tests with cut-off scores different from the mean. In fact for small groups of students in a trial, the value may well be less than zero, and in some cases less than -1.00! While this may seem extraordinary, remember that these values are *estimates* of reliability and the assumptions underlying them will have been violated. Again, a correction that tends to provide a more realistic estimate will be given later.

COMPARING CRONBACH'S α TO SPLIT-HALF RELIABILITY As noted earlier, responses to rating scales, Likert scales and coded free-response questions do not have right or wrong answers, but can be considered comparable to essay questions since the results are quantified. Thus, Cronbach's α can be used to provide a reliability coefficient to indicate the level of internal consistency of the instrument or of a homogeneous section of an instrument. But, as also noted above, this will produce a mean value for all the possible split-half estimates and is likely to be lower than that for a split-half for intentionally matched pairs of items.

Figure 11.5 illustrates the problems: the data are from a set of ten Likert questions administered to ten students. The first set of five was carefully matched in terms of content to the second set of five. When Cronbach's α is

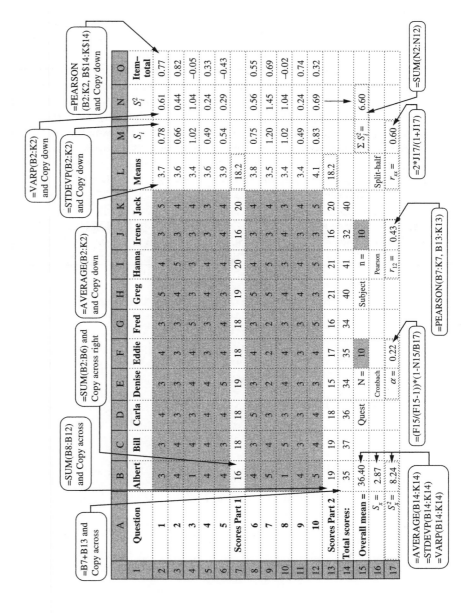

FIGURE 11.5

Analysis of a set of responses on a trial of a set of ten Likert scale (five-point) questions where questions 1–5 were matched to questions 6–10, with two reliability coefficients calculated: coefficient alpha (which would be equal to KR20 for scores of only 0 and 1) and split-half calculated it provides a much lower estimate of reliability than that for the split-half calculation.

Of what importance is this? When conducting a trial of an instrument, you want the most accurate estimate of reliability, since subsequent revisions will be based upon this. Activity 11.4 illustrates the sort of difference that can exist. This activity requires the setting up of an apparently complex worksheet for Figure 11.5, but it is also used when evaluating individual questions.

It could be argued that, since the individual item responses are ranked data, a nonparametric correlation such as Spearman's rho should be used. This will be discussed in Chapter 21, but for this example there is little difference between values for the two correlations, and on Excel version 5.0 there is no function for Spearman's rho.

Carry out Activity 11.4 now.

Activity 11.4

1   Follow the process as outlined below in order to set up Figure 11.5 in a spreadsheet:
    (a)   Insert the raw data in the shaded area for the question responses to correspond to the Likert responses.
    (b)   Insert the formulae in columns **L**, **M**, **N** and **O** and **Copy** them down as shown; cell designations will change automatically.
    (c)   Insert the formulae in **B7**, **B13** and **B14**, and **Copy** them across.
    (d)   In cells **B15**, **B16** and **B17** use the functions **AVERAGE**, **STDEVP** and **VARP** respectively, as shown.
    (e)   Enter $=$**SUM(N2:N13)** in cell **N15**, and the formulae for Cronbach's α, Pearson's correlation and the split-half correction shown.
    Once you have replicated the table, save it in a new file and try question 2.

2   Which four questions are the strongest and which three questions are in greatest need of improvement? Why?

3   Now imagine that the three weakest questions were improved and a new trial produced the same results (the same names will be used even though in a new trial new subjects would be used), with the following exceptions:
    (a)   For question 3, Albert answered such that his score was 4 instead of 1, and Greg 5 instead of 3.
    (b)   For question 5, Denise answered such that her score was 3 instead of 5, Greg answered such that his score was 5 instead of 3.
    (c)   For question 8, Albert answered such that his score was 4 instead of 1, Bill answered such that his score was 3 instead of 5, and Irene answered such that her score was 2 instead of 4.
    What are the new values for the item–total correlations, α and r_{xx}?

4 It is possible to *expand* the number of questions and number of subjects so you can use this spreadsheet for your own data:
   (a) To increase the number of subjects, choose a column like **C** where there are no final calculations at the bottom, click on the **C** and **Insert Columns** from the menu. Repeat as needed. Change cell **J15**, which gives the number of subjects.
   (b) To increase the number of questions, click on row **6** and choose **Insert Rows**, then repeat the process for row **13**. Repeat as needed and then renumber. Change cell **F15**, or its new equivalent, which stores the number of questions.
5 It is possible to *decrease* the number of questions and subjects to suit your own data, but in this case just remove the data and not the row or column:
   (a) To reduce the number of subjects, say by one, highlight all the data for Bill and press the **<Delete>** button on the keyboard. Repeat as necessary. Change cell **J15**. To reinstate them, just **Copy** the equations back into the cells in rows **7, 13** and **14**.
   (b) To reduce the number of questions, block off the data in a row and delete them. To reinstate them, just **Copy** the formulae after adding new data. Change cell **F15**, the number of questions.
Answers: 2. Strongest: 1, 2, 7, 9; weakest: 3, 5, 8.
3. Item–total: Q3 = 0.26, Q5 = 0.60, Q8 = 0.43, others changed slightly;
$\alpha = 0.78, r_{xx} = 0.90.$

Scorer or rater reliability

A second question that a researcher might ask is whether the marking on a free-response (essay) test or the ratings by observers are consistent across markers or observers. For *inter-scorer reliability* (among judges), Ebel (1979) does suggest that Cronbach's α could be used. This would mean replacing the 'questions in Figure 11.2 with raters and marks for questions for each student with raters' overall marks for each student as shown in the example in Figure 11.6, and calculating α as follows using equation (11.6):

$$\alpha = \frac{5}{5-1}\left[1 - \frac{1279}{6022}\right] = 0.98$$

This seems to indicate a very high level of consistency for such a divergent set of scores, but this is not the whole story. When the last column, 'Examiner means', is considered, it becomes obvious that Smith tends to mark severely and Bloggs is more generous overall. A second way of testing consistency would be to find the correlations between each pair of examiners. This has been done in the lower part of Figure 11.6 using the Pearson product moment correlation. The first thing to notice is the pair, Smith and Bloggs, who have the highest correlation! While the first impression is that this is contradictory, one must recall what the correlation tells us: as Smith's scores went up, so did Bloggs'. In other words, they were consistent with each other in both marking high or low, but this correlation does *not* reflect the absolute scores, as can be seen. At the other extreme, we see that while, overall, Jones and Brown gave much the same average number of points, their correlation is the lowest. Looking at the scores, this simply reflects the fact that even though the scores of Jones and Brown tended to rise and fall together, when Jones gave a slightly higher score, Brown gave a slightly lower one, and vice versa. There is not the same high level of consistency between them as for some of the other pairs. Together, the means and correlations provide the designer with information on tendencies to mark high or low, and consistency between examiners. Both situations may be rectified by ensuring that the criteria for marks awarded are clear and unambiguous to the examiners. Thus, while Cronbach's α indicates a high reliability for this situation, a detailed examination of the results indicates there may be a problem that should be addressed by the researcher. Implement this spreadsheet in Activity 11.5 now.

Activity 11.5

1 Enter the titles for rows and columns as shown in Figure 11.6, then enter the scores in the shaded cells. Enter the equations shown, noting that the cell ranges for **PEARSON** in the lower section will be different for each combination.
2 Change some of the scores of one individual to see the effect on the reliability estimate and correlations. How would the interpretation change?

=STDEVP(B3:F3) and Copy down

= VARP(B3:F3) and Copy down

AVERAGE(B3:F3) and Copy down

	A	B	C	D	E	F	G	H	I
1				Students					
2	Examiners	A	B	C	D	E	S_i	S_i^2	Means
3	Jones	63	37	73	76	59	13.8	190.2	61.6
4	Smith	53	33	68	78	60	15.2	230.6	58.4
5	Bloggs	64	46	75	88	68	13.8	189.8	68.2
6	Black	53	45	65	86	61	13.8	191.2	62.0
7	Brown	52	44	67	87	69	14.9	221.4	63.8
8	Totals	285	205	348	415	317	$\Sigma S_i^2 =$	1023.2	
9	Mean =	314							
10	$S_x =$	69.4		Quest =	5				
11	$S_x^2 =$	4818		$\alpha =$	0.98				
12									
13		Smith	Bloggs	Black	Brown				
14	Jones	0.96	0.95	0.83	0.81				
15	Smith		0.99	0.93	0.94				
16	Bloggs			0.96	0.95				
17	Black				0.98				

=SUM(F3:F7) and Copy left across

=SUM(H3:H7)

=(E10/(E10-1))*(1-H8/B11)

=AVERAGE(B8:F8)
=STDEVP(B8:F8)
=VARP(B8:F8)

=PEARSON(B3:F3, B7:F7) and similarly for all the other combinations

FIGURE 11.6 Scores for five students marked by five different examiners, with the resulting Cronbach's α and Pearson product moment correlations for all combinations of the five examiners for the scores presented

The third question that could be asked is related to the consistency of marking free-response questions or ratings on an observation schedule by a single marker over a period of time. In other words, if you are marking a set of essay questions or coding observations from a set of videotaped sessions, for example, are you marking those at the end consistently with those you marked at the beginning? To check *intra-scorer reliability* (over time), the correlation between two sets of marks can be used (Knapp, 1971; Guilford and Fruchter, 1981). The Pearson product moment correlation coefficient can be calculated fairly easily, as shown in equation (11.4) above, but again is best left to a spreadsheet, as done in Figure 11.1.

Criterion-referenced tests: Reliability

Criterion-referenced tests differ from norm-referenced tests in a number of ways that influence how a reliability coefficient should be determined, the main one being that the distribution of scores will not necessarily be normal. Also, the focus of a criterion-referenced test is the criterion score, the cut-off between mastery and non-mastery, or between pass and fail. Mehrens and Lehmann (1984) reference several possible indices and Berk (1978) reviews and compares 13 of these. I suggest that Livingston's (1972) index, k^2, is appropriate and reasonably easy to calculate since it is based upon norm-referenced indices:

$$k^2 = \frac{r_{xx}S_x^2 + (\bar{x} - C)^2}{S_x^2 + (\bar{x} - C)^2} \qquad (11.10)$$

where S_x^2 is the variance of the test scores, $\bar{x}$ is the mean of the test scores, C is the criterion score for the test and r_{xx} is the norm-referenced reliability coefficient (KR20, split-half or Cronbach's α, depending on the type of test).

Looking at the formula, note that when the mean, $\bar{x}$, equals the criterion score, C, indicating a normal distribution, then $k^2 = r_{xx}$. Also, the Spearman–Brown formula for predicting the reliability of a different-sized test also holds (Livingston, 1972). Though there are other possible indices, this one will give a more realistic estimate for a criterion-referenced test than those discussed earlier for norm-referenced tests. Add this to your spreadsheet by carrying out Activity 11.6 now.

Activity 11.6

If Figure 11.2 represented a criterion-referenced test, then Livingston's coefficient, k^2, would be more appropriate than Cronbach's α. Its size would depend on C, the cut-off score, which should be determined as part of defining validity of decisions. Insert the following row into this figure:

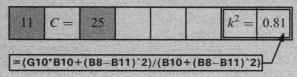

If a value of 25 were chosen, we can see what the effect would be. What would happen if C were equal to the mean, 29.9? A score lower than 25? A higher score? Note how many more would 'pass' or 'fail'.

Answers: If C were equal to the mean, then k^2 would equal α. If C were higher or lower than the mean, then k^2 would be higher than α.

Discrimination index: Criterion-referenced tests

Criterion-referenced tests do not result in any predetermined distribution, and therefore the original index, D, of equation (11.8) is not necessarily appropriate. In fact, many such tests will produce highly skewed results rather than a normal distribution. Alternatively, the discrimination Index, E, does not assume any specific distribution of scores. The user must define a cutting score (for example, mastery/non-mastery, pass/fail) in order to determine an upper and a lower group, but these do not have to be the same size. The index itself is defined (Black, 1987) as the difference between the proportion of students answering as expected (i.e., those in the upper group answering correctly and those in the lower group answering wrongly) and the proportion answering contrary to expectation (i.e., those in the upper group answering wrongly and those in the lower group answering correctly):

$$E = \frac{U + (n_2 - L)}{n_1 + n_2} - \frac{L + (n_1 - U)}{n_1 + n_2} \qquad (11.11)$$

where U is the number in upper group answering the item correctly, L the number in the lower group answering the item correctly; n_1 is the total number in the upper group, n_2 the total number in lower group; $n_2 - L$ is the number in the lower group answering the item wrongly, and $n_1 - U$ the number in the upper group answering the item wrongly. By placing all over a common denominator and simplifying, this can be reduced to

$$E = \frac{2U - 2L - n_1 + n_2}{n_1 + n_2} \qquad (11.12)$$

Also, this index actually subsumes the traditional norm-referenced one, D, in that the equation (11.12) for E reduces to equation (11.8) for D above for the special case of a symmetrical (normal) distribution, that is, where the situation $n_1 = n_2$ prevails.

The index, E, is interpreted in the same way as that for norm-referenced tests, ranging from $+1.0$ (a perfectly discriminating question) through 0.0 (a non-discriminating question) to -1.0 (discriminating in reverse). For example, let us consider a trial of an achievement test in mathematics taken by 30 students in a class. The item analysis depends upon the purpose and type of test; therefore, let us consider the consequences of analysing it as if it were norm-referenced and then as if it were criterion-referenced, having produced the same set of scores. The item analysis for an individual item is based upon what is decided to be the dividing score between the upper and lower groups. For a norm-referenced test, this is the test median, 7.5 (half the examinees above this score and half below), which would be close to the mean (here 7.0) for a normal distribution.

For the criterion-referenced test, the dividing point will be the designated pass score chosen by the researchers of 6, with the upper group having 24 and the lower 6. This was decided as the minimum score that would indicate adequate learning and could be considered part of the construct validity of the instrument. The distribution of scores is shown in Figure 11.7, being negatively skewed (the long tail is on the low side).

Table 11.2 provides the item analysis statistics for interpreting the first item on the test in both ways. In part (a), the test was assumed to be norm-referenced and has a difficulty of 0.87, and using formula (11.8) to find the traditional norm-referenced discrimination index, D,

$$D = \frac{14 - 12}{15} = 0.13$$

which indicates a poorly discriminating item.

Considering the item as part of a criterion-referenced test in part (b), where a pass mark of 6 was set, the difficulty remains the same, but using formula (11.12) to find the criterion-referenced discrimination index, E,

$$E = \frac{2(23) - 2(3) - 24 + 6}{24 + 6} = 0.73$$

indicating a relatively highly discriminating item.

Looking at the data on this test and in particular this sample item, it appears that both indices produce results for the data. But the purpose of the test and the

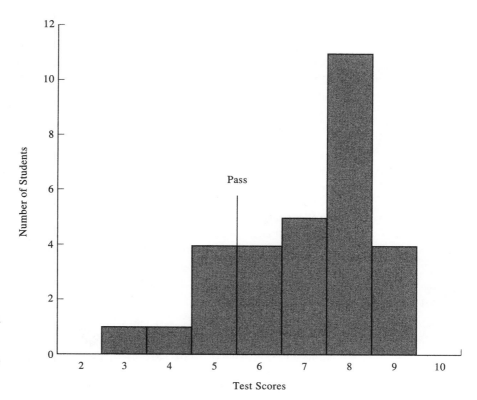

FIGURE 11.7
Distribution of scores for a trial of an achievement test for 30 students, with pass mark 6 or above (5.5 or above using real intervals)

TABLE 11.2
Item analysis of the first item (choice B is correct) in the same test (distribution shown in Figure 11.7) taken by 30 students, analysed as if it were part of (a) a norm-referenced test, (b) a criterion-referenced test (pass mark = 6)

		Numbers making each choice						
	N	A	B*	C	D	E	Omit	
(a) Norm-referenced test								
U	15	0	14	1	0	0	0	Difficulty = 0.87
L	15	0	12	3	0	0	0	Discrim. index, D = 0.13
(b) Criterion-referenced test								
U	24	0	23	1	0	0	0	Difficulty = 0.87
L	6	0	3	3	0	0	0	Discrim. index, E = 0.73

way the marks are interpreted will ultimately determine which index is most appropriate for deciding the relative quality of this item. Thus, if the test were to be used as a dependent variable to compare achievement after different treatments, then it might be most appropriate to aim for a normal distribution so that inferential statistical tests could be used to resolve the hypotheses. Consequently, this test would be considered to be a norm-referenced test, and the items would be evaluated using D accordingly. On the other hand, if this test were to be used as a way of grouping students into two groups as part of an independent variable, then what constitutes 'adequately learned' would be reflected in the chosen pass mark. Thus the test would need to be considered criterion-referenced and the items would need to be evaluated on the basis of how well they discriminated between those who passed and those who did not.

It should be noted that this would become a moot point mathematically if the distribution in Figure 11.7 were perfectly bell-shaped and the pass mark corresponded to the mean, so that D and E had the same value. Also, if the expectation were that the distribution in Figure 11.7 should be normal, then for some statistical tests it would violate that assumption and the data would have to be adjusted, as will be seen in later chapters.

There is always the possibility that an item producing a low value for difficulty or for the discrimination index may indicate wholesale guessing, which in turn may be an indication of a poorly taught concept or idea! Therefore, item analysis may be considered as a valuable source of information about teaching and learning as well as the quality of the test. As with much of teaching and learning, the actual cause(s) of the observed effect will not always be clear and obvious, requiring some detective work on the part of the test developer.

Activity 11.7 provides an opportunity to set up a spreadsheet for evaluating a criterion-referenced test employing these more appropriate coefficients.

Criterion-referenced versus norm-referenced instruments

What are the consequences of choosing items for the final test with a high discrimination index? If the index D is used as a basis, and only items with a value of, say, 0.60 or above are used, then this will help to ensure that the final score distribution is normal. If the index E is used to choose items, then the resulting distribution will more than likely be negatively skewed and a better

Activity 11.7

Now consider the results of the test shown in Figure 11.7. The item analysis using the discrimination index, E, and Livingston's reliability, k^2, are shown in Figure 11.8. To generate this quickly, proceed as follows:

1 Make a copy of Figure 11.4 and add the two rows at the bottom, 25 and 26, with the new data.
2 Change the entries for the test responses to match the new ones for a criterion-referenced test in Figure 11.8. You should get the results shown. If not, check the 'check' values in **B22**, **K22** and **K24** to see if they are the same. If not, look at your raw data again or see if the equations were inadvertently changed.
3 Which items need to be considered for improvement? Why?
4 From the choices that were wrong, can you see any patterns that might give you a clue?
5 It could be argued that the cut-off score is between 5 and 6, so change the cut-off score to 5.5. What happens to k^2?

Answer: 3.   Questions 3, 4, 5 and 6 need improving since $E < 0.40$.
4.   Since choice 3B was made by many in the upper group, it may be that the answer is too close to the correct answer A: check the wording. The same may be true of 6. The other two could have any one of several problems, but may be related to content, for example asking for obscure facts.
5. $k^2 = 0.57$.

discriminator between those who pass and those who fail. Thus, organizations that want a normal distribution of scores on an achievement, aptitude or even IQ test will conduct trials on representative samples of learners and put only items with a discrimination index, D, of, for example, 0.60 or more in their item bank. When a final test is finally made up, they draw from this bank of items which have undergone trial, enhancing the probability that the scores for a representative sample will be normally distributed.

This is the source of a certain amount of controversy, since by using this technique it is possible to construct a test that will produce a normal distribution of scores, regardless of the distribution of the underlying trait. This does not prove that the trait is necessarily normally distributed – such a proof would have to be conducted independently, a difficult task at best. Thus, the case for intelligence being normally distributed is not supported by the fact that IQ tests are normally distributed. IQ tests are *designed* to be normally distributed; whether intelligence is normally distributed is another matter. As Kline (1991) states: 'It is assumed that intelligence has a normal distribution as is the case with most polygenic variables'. In other words, since physiological variables (height, weight, distance between eyeballs, forefinger length) all tend to be normally distributed, so should intelligence. The controversy around the validity of this assumption, and consequently the validity of IQ tests as measures of intelligence, will continue for some time to come until an independent method of measuring intelligence is found on which all can agree.

=(2*B2-2*B3-C$25+C$26)/(C$25+C$26)
and Copy down the column)

	A	B	C	D	E	F	G	H	I	J	K	L	M
1	Quest	Correct	A	B	C	D	E	Omit	Total	Disc E	Diff p	q=(1-p)	p * q
2	1-B	23	0	23	1	0	0	0	24	0.73	0.87	0.13	0.12
3		3	0	3	3	0	0	0	6				
4	2-C	22	0	1	22	1	0	0	24	0.87	0.73	0.27	0.20
5		0	0	0	0	4	2	0	6				
6	3-A	14	14	8	1	0	0	1	24	0.00	0.63	0.37	0.23
7		5	5	1	0	0	0	0	6				
8	4-D	14	1	4	3	14	1	1	24	–0.07	0.67	0.33	0.22
9		6	0	0	0	6	0	0	6				
10	5-B	15	2	15	3	2	0	2	24	0.00	0.70	0.30	0.21
11		6	0	6	0	0	0	0	6				
12	6-E	13	1	1	8	1	13	0	24	–0.13	0.63	0.37	0.23
13		6	0	0	0	0	6	0	6				
14	7-A	21	21	0	1	1	1	0	24	0.80	0.70	0.30	0.21
15		0	0	2	2	0	0	2	6				
16	8-C	20	1	1	20	0	1	1	24	0.73	0.67	0.33	0.22
17		0	2	1	0	1	1	1	6				
18	9-D	20	2	2	0	20	0	0	24	0.73	0.67	0.33	0.22
19		0	1	2	0	0	1	2	6				
20	10-E	21	1	0	1	0	21	1	24	0.73	0.73	0.27	0.20
21		1	2	1	1	0	1	1	6				
22	Total=	210								$n\Sigma p$ =	210.00	$\Sigma(p*q)$ =	2.06
23	Items	N =	10			Mean =	7.00				(check)		
24	Subjects	n =	30			S_x^2 =	2.40			n*mean	210	KR20=	0.16
25	Upper	n_1 =	24		Cut-off	C =	6					k^2=	0.41
26	Lower	n_2 =	6										

=(M24*G24+(G23-G25)^2)/(G24+(G23-G25)^2)

FIGURE 11.8
Item analysis for results in Figure 11.7: 30 subjects answering ten multiple-choice items with raw data in columns **C** to **H** (shaded area) and entries for column **J** providing the criterion-referenced discrimination index, E, and reliability coefficient, k^2

The general point to be made is that the distribution of scores that an instrument generates is *not* proof of the distribution of the trait, something that must be considered when designing an instrument that is a valid indicator of the trait. At the same time, a developer would need to have good reason to choose a cut-off score for a test before deciding to use a criterion-referenced approach.

Analogous to criterion-referenced achievement tests are instruments that employ discrimination at a point on a continuum. As Nunnally and Bernstein (1994) note, the Minnesota Multiphasic Personality Inventory is probably the best known as its intent is to discriminate at a point to detect a pathology. This is a highly specialized area beyond the scope of this text and is mentioned only to suggest the diversity of application of a principle.

Standard error of the measurement

There will be situations where it is desirable to describe the amount of error in individual scores, based upon the reliability of the test. If we solve equation (11.3) for the error variance term by first subtracting 1 from both sides of the equation,

$$r_{xx} - 1 = -\frac{S_e^2}{S_x^2}$$

and then multiply through by -1, we obtain

$$\frac{S_e^2}{S_x^2} = 1 - r_{xx}$$

Multiplying both sides by S_x^2, and taking its square root, we obtain a term known as the *standard error of the measurement*, S_e, which is expressed mathematically as

$$S_e = S_x\sqrt{1 - r_{xx}} \tag{11.13}$$

where S_x is the standard deviation of the set of observed scores and r_{xx} is the reliability coefficient.

While reliability tells us something about the instrument in general, the standard error of measurement can tell us something about the scores of individual subjects: basically how close the true score is to the observed (instrument) score. To illustrate this, consider the example of IQ tests and two individual scores. IQ tests tend to be designed to have a mean of 100 and a standard deviation of 15. How does one interpret individual scores?

Let us take two people whose IQ scores are presented to you, John with 120 and Mary with 125. Is there any *real* difference? On the one hand, John is 1.33 standard deviations above the mean and has done better than approximately 90.8% taking the test, while Mary's score is 1.67 standard deviations above the mean and she has done better than 95.2%. Yet how precise these scores are depends upon the reliability of the test. Table 11.3 provides selected interpretations depending upon the reliability coefficient, r_{xx}. If it is high then the standard error of the measurement, S_e, is low and vice versa. From the last two columns of Table 11.3, it can be seen that the true score (remember that the test provides an observed score which includes errors) will fall within a range around the observed score that gets smaller the more reliable the test. Yet even with a highly reliable test ($r_{xx} = 0.95$) the two true score ranges still overlap, rendering very uncertain the validity of any inferences about differences in IQ between these two people in the way the scores indicate. From such an example, one can see how the reliability of a measuring instrument can influence the interpretation of individual scores.

Finally, it is possible to estimate the proportion of test variance attributable to the true score and to errors, using the standard error of the measurement, since the true score variance is the sum of the observed score variance and the error variance, as given in equation (11.2):

$$S_x^2 = S_t^2 + S_e^2$$

TABLE 11.3
The effect of selected values of reliability coefficient, r_{xx}, on the standard error of the measurement, S_e, and specific score interpretation, for an IQ test with standard deviation, $S_x = 15$

Name (score)	r_{xx}	S_e	True score range with 68% certainty	True score range with 95% certainty
John (120)			113.3–126.7	106.9–133.1
	0.80	6.7		
Mary (125)			118.3–131.7	111.9–138.1
John (120)			114.2–125.8	108.6–130.4
	0.85	5.8		
Mary (125)			119.2–130.8	113.6–136.4
John (120)			115.3–124.7	110.7–129.3
	0.90	4.7		
Mary (125)			120.3–129.7	115.7–134.3
John (120)			116.6–123.4	113.4–126.6
	0.95	3.4		
Mary (125)			121.6–128.4	118.4–131.6

This is illustrated graphically in Figure 11.9 for the two extremes of Table 11.3, for IQ tests with reliabilities of 0.80 and 0.95.

In summary, the above discussion simply tells us that the higher the reliability of an instrument, the more confident one can be that the results reflect an individual's true score. Also, it tells us that most instrument scores are not perfect indicators on any scale. This is something that is intuitively felt by examination boards when reviewing cases that are on the borderline between two letter grades, based on a set of numerical scores. The issue of reliability is one that has consequences for *any* grading system based upon any kind of assessment that might be used for classifying subjects, either norm-referenced or criterion-referenced. Thus when making decisions or grouping subjects on the basis of numerical scores, it is well worth asking what are the reliabilities of the instruments that are used.

VALIDITY INDICATORS

Items on an instrument are only a *sample* of the possible tasks a subject could carry out; we infer from the performance on the sample how well he or she would do on others or in other situations. A test's validity is an indication of how accurate these inferences are, which obviously depends on how skilled we are in writing and selecting questions for the test.

Using the rubrics that were introduced in Chapter 8, let us consider some basic descriptions of the different types of validity and, where possible, how they could be quantified to enhance evaluating validity of an instrument.

Construct validity

This relates to research on various abstract concepts whose constructs have been detailed (such as intelligence, motivation, perception, attitudes) and how

If $r_{xx} = 0.80$,

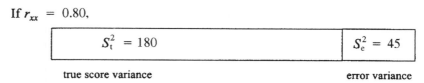

true score variance   error variance

FIGURE 11.9
Sources of total
observed score
variance, $S_x^2 = 225$,
depending upon test
reliability

If $r_{xx} = 0.95$,

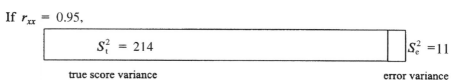

true score variance   error variance

representative the questions in an instrument are of the characteristics making up the construct. For abstract constructs, the test may well be the operational definition of the construct – for example, intelligence (or IQ anyway) is what an intelligence test measures! The three processes for constructing instruments to measure constructs provide different ways of evaluating validity.

The *logical* approach of construct elaboration from a theory or model was described in Chapter 9, with techniques for ensuring the validity of such instruments. The evaluation of such instruments would consist primarily of an analysis of the logical consistency between the definition of the concept, construct elaboration and the resulting instrument. A second analysis would be related to the wording of questions and statements to minimize the possibility of faking, distorted answers due to a tendency towards social desirability, bias, and misinterpretation.

The *factor-analytic* approach basically assumes that of the set of questions piloted, those that are the most valid indicators will be those with the greatest commonality and thus will appear in clusters and consequently would be included in the final instrument. The factor analysis is the source of justification for instrument validity.

The *empirical* approach would require administering the instrument to subjects who have been independently identified as having the characteristic of interest, as well as those who did not. If those who possessed the trait consistently scored higher (or lower) on the instrument than those without, then this would suggest a high validity as an instrument for classifying subjects.

Criterion validity

To check the level of this type of validity requires comparing the new instrument to an existing one, usually by calculating the correlation of scores of subjects on both instruments. Depending on correlations with other instruments as a means for justifying the validity of a new instrument may be of limited value, since this is passing the responsibility for ensuring validity to another researcher or instrument developer. This does not mean that some support cannot be found from such a check, but that it should not be the only justification for validity. The two types of criterion validity reflect the time-scale over which the comparison is made.

Concurrent validity (present performance) for achievement tests is an indicator of accuracy. For example, does a class test indicate student learner performance as accurately as a public or standardized examination? Calculating the correlation between the results on an achievement test and an established examination for a set of subjects would provide an indication of how well the results of the achievement test would correspond to a more established instrument.

Predictive validity (future performance) indicates how well performance on an instrument predicts later performance in another situation. This is of obvious interest to those who design aptitude tests or selection examinations, as the main function of such instruments is to predict the suitability of a person, for example, for a job or training programme. Using existing examinations designed for other purposes can be risky. For example, as noted earlier, a number of studies have shown that, even using public examinations taken at age 18 in England, highly accurate prediction of future university results is unlikely. Several researchers have found low correlations (as low as 0.08 and up to 0.40) between A-level results and university final degree classifications (Chopin, 1972; Murphy, 1981; Bourner and Hamed, 1987), indicating A-levels are poor predictors of the level of higher education success.

Content validity

On an achievement test, this is how well the set of questions represents what content or subject matter the test is supposed to be testing. There are no measures for this type of validity, but the design of a table of specifications, as described in Chapter 10, is probably the best way of ensuring high content validity for achievement and aptitude tests. It also provides a mechanism for evaluating content validity in that one could compare the individual item analysis (such as Figures 11.4 and 11.8) with the corresponding table of specifications (such as Table 10.5). A low difficulty index, for example, may indicate an item that is not testing the concept or skill accurately. Unfortunately, it could also indicate poor teaching, but at least it raises the awareness of the developer to a possible source of lack of validity. For essay questions, there is a need for agreement on the content of the marking scheme and consistency with the table of specifications. Much of the evaluation of content validity will by necessity be a matter of evaluation of consistency and discussion among subject experts of what constitutes reasonable knowledge and skills for a subject and how adequately the questions sample this. A systematic consideration of trial group results compared to original specifications should be more fruitful than an academic argument of content in general.

In addition, you may find *curricular* validity mentioned, which stresses the relationship between what is taught and what is tested. In England and Wales, it is tacitly assumed that syllabuses for public examinations ensure common content coverage in classrooms, and that the National Curriculum will ensure that skills and knowledge to be tested at 7, 11, 14 and 16 will be included in teaching. Classroom teachers, though, do not always test what is taught. The problem often lies in interpreting the syllabus, a National Curriculum description, or the textbook on which a course is based. There is a danger that the syllabus writers think they are implying one cognitive level for a topic while the teacher is inferring another.

TABLE 11.4
Matching needs with coefficients: the *most common* applications of reliability coefficients for different types of questions for achievement tests and attitude/perspective measures

Type of consistency	Stability (test–retest)	Equivalence (parallel forms)	Internal			Across judges (inter-judge)	Over time (intra-judge)
Coefficient	Pearson	Pearson	Split-half: Spearman–Brown	Cronbach's alpha	Kuder–Richardson	Cronbach's alpha and Pearson	Pearson
Figure(s)	11.1	11.1	11.5	11.2	11.4, 11.8	11.6	11.1
Achievement							
Objective (MC, TF, matching)	✓	✓	✓		✓		
Short answer			✓	✓		✓	✓
Essay (long answer)			✓	✓		✓	✓
Observation schedule			✓	✓		✓	✓
Attitudes/perspectives							
Questionnaire (Likert, rating)	✓	✓	✓	✓			
Observation schedule			✓	✓		✓	✓
Structured interviews			✓	✓		✓	✓

Ultimately, it is up to researchers to ensure that the validity of their tests is maintained. Which type of validity will depend on the nature of the research question, and this will govern the focus of the justification for the instrument.

SUMMARY

This chapter has introduced a number of techniques to assist test, examination and questionnaire designers in evaluating and improving their instruments, as summarized in Table 11.4. The advantage of using various indices, such as difficulty, discrimination and reliability, is that they provide objective indicators. These tend to be *flags* that should attract attention rather than values that specify some absolute quality. The interpretation of an index is still up to the designer or evaluator and will depend upon the situation. For example, one would expect a high value for a reliability index on a nation-wide examination, but would accept a lower one for a classroom test. The strength of any inferences made based upon achievement tests or questionnaires by researchers will be affected by the relative reliability of their instruments. Evaluating tests with the intention of maintaining as high a reliability and validity as possible is not an easy task and requires considerable detective work. The tools here provide assistance in carrying out a complex analysis and evaluation, the importance of which cannot be overstressed considering the fact that this is the foundation of any quantitative research. Carry out Activity 11.8 now.

Activity 11.8

1   Describe how you have estimated the reliability of your measuring instrument(s) and why you have chosen the coefficient(s) you have used.
2   Which type of validity are you primarily concerned with maintaining in your instrument(s)? What have you done or do you plan to do to justify their validity?

Part III
Turning Data into Information using Statistics

DESCRIPTIVE STATISTICS USING A SPREADSHEET

12

One of the greatest challenges facing researchers is communicating their results to others. It is one thing to have a study published in a learned journal, where the readership is restricted to those who understand much of what is being described and can interpolate and extrapolate from parsimonious writing. The rest of the world needs more explicit information, and descriptive statistics – in particular, graphs and charts – have the potential to enhance the understanding of the outcomes of quantitative research, if presented with care. Raw data in the form of lists of numbers or even tables mean little to the reader. While learned journals tend to discourage the use of charts and graphs since they appear to occupy large amounts of space, theses, dissertations and reports to contracting organizations will often benefit from graphical presentation. Many of those reading a project report may not be as knowledgeable of the field in which the research is being conducted or as sophisticated in the use of statistical tools as the researchers, but still need to understand the findings as policy decisions may be based on understanding the study's results.

This chapter will address the practical problems associated with presentation of quantitative results graphically using a basic computer-based spreadsheet, one that is widely available and relatively easy to use. In the process, the advantages and limitations of software-generated graphs and tables will be considered, with an emphasis on what appropriate practice is and how to override software defaults that produce potentially deceptive graphs. The chapter will also provide several statistics that describe group characteristics, with some guidance as to when is most appropriate to use them. As a consequence, there will be a number of activities using software to generate various types of graphs, measures of central tendency and indicators of variability for given data. The spreadsheet utility package Excel (version 5.0 or later) will be needed to complete these exercises.

TYPES OF DATA

It is generally helpful to classify all data as being on a nominal, ordinal, interval or ratio scale (see Chapter 2). Recall that variables that are considered to be *nominal* include such categories as sex of respondents, the town or county in which they live, or which football team they support. Even numerals can be nominal if they have naming value only, such as the numbers on the shirts of football players. One example that follows is concerned with the political affiliation of subjects, thus the frequency table will list the parties and how many people associate themselves with each.

Data that are on an *ordinal* scale indicate some ranking, such as, social class, grade/class in school, or position in a management hierarchy. While one category may be higher or 'better' than another, the differences between each adjoining pair are not necessarily the same. This is equivalent to a race where one only notes who came in first, second and third, etc., with no reference to time for running the race. All that is known is the order of finishing.

Data on an *interval* scale are numerical and intervals between numbers mean the same thing, but zero has no meaning. Thus the difference between a score of 90 and 95 should mean the same as the difference between 105 and 110 on an IQ test, though there would be no meaning attached to a score of zero, other than the fact that the person did not take the test.

Data on a *ratio* scale are again numerical data where the intervals on the scale are equal but now zero does have a meaning. Take, for example, the scores on an examination where answering all the questions correctly would result in a score of 100, and not being able to answer any questions would result in zero. Answering 20 points worth of questions would suggest that twice as much had been learned by the examinee as someone answering only 10 points worth. These values would indicate how much each person had achieved.

We will use these categories as one of the criteria for deciding what is the most appropriate type of graph or chart to use, but it is necessary to consider each case with respect to meaningfulness of the data. While the differences in these scales seem to depend exclusively on the nature of the data collected, it is not necessarily that simple. Sometimes it will depend on the interpretation of the results as to which scale is most appropriate.

For example, when asking subjects about salaries, we could request and obtain exact values from a sample group, providing ratio data, and plot a histogram to display a distribution. Alternatively, we could ask respondents to indicate in which of several ranges their salary falls, providing ordinal data. While this may degrade the data (provide less exact numbers than we could potentially acquire), for purposes of interpretation it may be better. To employ salaries as indicators of economic well-being may not be best since some differences in gross incomes are not meaningful. For example, consider the difference between £10 000 and £11 000 per year. Take away graduated income tax, social security, pension deductions, and essentials such as food, clothing, transport to work, etc., and there may not be much left for a family of four from either amount. It might be more desirable to consider *income per person* and use ranges that are indicative of levels of economic security: below survival, bare survival, able to buy a house, able to buy a house and car, etc. Such decisions must be made by the researcher as numbers are just tools and must be employed to convey meaning.

PLOTTING GRAPHS AND CHARTS

Numbers by themselves tell us little about groups, so there have been endeavours to find ways of improving meaning through graphical representation. The first difficulty is that not all types of charts and graphs are appropriate for all types of data. In summary, Table 12.1 outlines what are considered appropriate types for each of the four varieties of graphs and charts commonly used. Others, such as pictographs where objects of various sizes are used (e.g., car sales where different-sized cars represent different numbers of cars sold), tend to be visually deceiving, not to mention very difficult to generate (see Huff, 1954) and are not recommended for serious research presentations. Other issues related to quality and pitfalls are covered in various texts which are commonly available (for example, Black, 1993; Chase, 1985). The focus here is on how can one produce informative tables, graphs and charts without deceiving the reader.

Histograms have their bars touching, indicating equal intervals, whereas in bar charts the bars are separated by some space, suggesting that the categories are not separated by equal intervals. Thus the difference between these is consistent with the differences in the definitions of ordinal and interval/ratio data. In some software that is used for producing graphs, it may take a special effort to make the bars touch to form a histogram, or to separate them with a space to present a bar chart. Pie charts, on the other hand, are only of value when presenting nominal data, since the sections represent percentages of a whole, the full circle encompassing 100%. Frequency polygons (line graphs) are an alternative to histograms for interval/ratio data, providing a clearer picture in some cases. Unfortunately, computer software tends to offer no guidance as to which is most appropriate, so that the uninformed user may well not use these tools to their best advantage.

As each type of chart or graph is presented, there will be opportunities to explore a number of alternative types, shadings and shapes, allowing for a certain amount of aesthetic taste to govern the acceptability of the representations. Before generating graphs and charts, it will be necessary to group the data.

TABLE 12.1
Appropriate usage of charts and graphs for frequency data

	Bar chart	Pie chart	Histogram	Frequency polygon
Nominal	✓	✓		
Ordinal	✓			
Interval			✓	✓
Ratio			✓	✓

Frequency tables

The first step in organizing raw data is to group scores or values and present them as a *frequency table*, as shown in Table 12.2. Each grouping has its associated frequencies of occurrence. With large data sets, this can be an arduous task by hand, but once the data are entered into a worksheet, there are functions that will generate such tables with minimal effort. Basically, there will be the two types of tables shown in Table 12.2, those that are frequencies for nominal or ordinal data (Table 12.2a), and those for interval/ratio data (Table 12.2b).

Displaying nominal and ordinal data

Typically, nominal data are a record of persons and categories to which they belong, such as marital status (married, single, or with partner), sex (male, female), religious affiliation, county of residence, etc. There is no assumed order or ranking. On the other hand, ordinal data assume some intended order of the categories, as for educational qualifications, positions in an organization, or place in a competition. There are some types of data where it may be somewhat contentious as to whether the data are ordinal or interval/ratio – for example, the grades on an essay (A, B, C, etc.). Raw data typically appear as a list of persons' names and columns of characteristics, memberships, classes, scores, etc. Two different types will be used in the examples below. The first will use nominal data: a list of named persons who were patrons of the Green Toad pub on the evening of a survey and the political party for which they say they voted in the most recent election. In the following Activity 12.1, you will be taken through the steps of entering the data into a spreadsheet, and generating a frequency table, a bar chart and a pie chart.

Glancing at the next couple of pages, you may feel that this is a considerable effort to generate graphs and tables. In reality, the bulk of any work such as this is inputting the raw data, a task necessary no matter what software you use. Also, once you have a worksheet set up for nominal or ordinal data (Activity

TABLE 12.2
Frequency tables for responses from a sample: (a) nominal data; (b) interval data

(a)

Residence (county)	Frequency
Surrey	10
West Sussex	18
Somerset	16
Hampshire	9
Devon	20
Somerset	16

(b)

Age	Frequency
20–24	2
25–29	3
30–34	6
35–39	9
40–44	2
45–49	7
50–54	12
55–59	13
60–64	5
65–70	4

	A	B	C	D	E	
1	**Name**	**Choices**				
2	John	L		**Party**	**Frequency**	
3	Henry	C		Labour	8	◄— =COUNTIF(B$2:B$31,"L")
4	Jane	RL		Conserv	6	◄— =COUNTIF(B$2:B$31,"C")
5	Fred	LD		Lib Dem	12	◄— =COUNTIF(B$2:B$31,"LD")
6	Mary	LD		Rav Loony	4	◄— =COUNTIF(B$2:B$31,"RL")
7	Albert	RL		Total	30	◄— =SUM(E3:E6)
8	Sam	L				
9	Ellen	C				
10	Ted	LD				
11	Anne	L				
12	Hilary	L				
13	Barbara	LD				
14	Betty	LD				
15	Terry	LD				
16	Robert	RL				
17	Tom	RL				
18	James	C				
19	Nancy	LD				
20	Peter	L				
21	David	L				
22	Melany	LD				
23	Sonya	LD				
24	Jacob	LD				
25	Sean	L				
26	Shirley	C				
27	Janet	LD				
28	Annette	C				
29	Patsy	L				
30	Ian	C				
31	Sarah	LD				
32	Total:	30				
33						

=COUNTA(B2:B31)

Stage 1: Setting up the data and frequency table

(a) Enter the raw data in columns **A** and **B**, labelling each column.

(b) Set up a frequency table in columns **D** and **E**, entering titles as shown.

(c) There is a convenient function that will count all of the occurrences of any designated set of characters in a set of data:

=COUNTIF(data range,criteria)

where

data range = location of raw data,
here: **B$2:B$31**
criteria   = the text to count – in the first   entry, it is "L" for Labour

Therefore, the first cell entry on the frequency table will be:

=COUNTIF(B$2:B$31,"L")

(d) It can then be **Copy**ed to the other three cells and the criteria changed for the other parties, as shown above.

(e) Once this is set up, if you add new data, all you have to do is to change the data range in each of your functions, and the frequency table will be automatically updated. For the data provided, your frequencies should be the same as those shown on Figure 12.2.

Stage 2: Preparing the frequency table for nominal data

(a) It is useful to build in mechanisms to check to see if you have typed everything correctly. The simplest is to just count up the data entries and the total on the frequency table. This can be done easily with two functions. The total number of data entries can be found using the **=COUNTA** function shown in **B32** and the total in the frequency column can be found using **=SUM** as shown in cell **E7** above. Both of these simply require the range for the data or numbers as shown.

(b) Check your results, obviously the two 'Totals' should be the same.

(c) To display these data graphically proceed to the box describing stage 3.

FIGURE 12.1
Excel worksheet showing nominal data and the first steps for generating a frequency table and graphs/charts

12.1) and one for interval or ratio data (Activity 12.2), you have a skeleton that can be used with other sets of data. All that is needed is to enter new data, change the ranges in the functions, and save the result under a new file name (see Appendix A for guidance on workbook file and worksheet names). Thus all this initial effort can be exploited again and again.

Activity 12.1

This activity will provide you with a set of data to enter into a spreadsheet; you will then generate a frequency table, bar chart and pie chart. You now need to go to a computer, and run Excel version 5 or later. To keep your tables and graphs orderly, start by double-clicking on the tab at the bottom of the page labelled **Sheet 1**. This will give you the opportunity to change the name of this sheet to suit your own scheme; you might call it **Fig 12.1**. Then follow the directions provided for the four stages in Figure 12.1 and the box describing the Excel ChartWizard. Figures 12.2 and 12.3 show you what you should get as a result of having the package plot a bar chart and pie chart from your data.

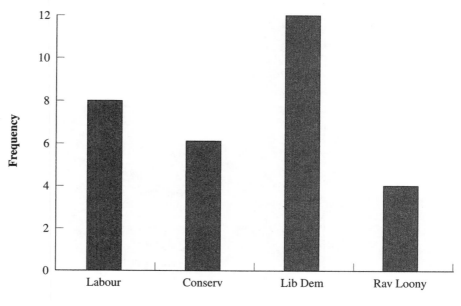

FIGURE 12.2
Bar chart for data in Figure 12.1, generated in Excel (see box 'Stage 3: ChartWizard')

Stage 3: Producing a bar chart using the ChartWizard in Excel

This box will describe how to generate the graph shown in Figure 12.2, using the ChartWizard in Excel. These are the basic steps: you can obviously refine the result by changing colours, patterns, fonts, etc., but that is left to you. Here we will focus on generating the appropriate types of graphs (recall Table 12.1) for the data, changing the default settings where necessary. Excel, like many packages, has preset default settings that are not always correct or necessarily aesthetically pleasing, but these are relatively easy to change once you get to grips with the mouse and the menus it brings up.

In the descriptions that follow, Excel commands appear in the bold sans serif font, such as **Copy**; these can be carried out by placing the mouse pointer on them and clicking the left button.

Call up the ChartWizard by clicking on the icon **⬛**. This will allow you to block out an area on your worksheet where you want your chart to appear by clicking on the point where you want the upper left-hand corner and dragging diagonally, holding the button down until the area is big enough (this can be adjusted later). Upon releasing the button, the first of five menu boxes will appear, and you should proceed as follows:

Step 1 of 5 As you hold the left mouse button down, block the two data columns from **D3** to **E6**. This tells the ChartWizard where the data is that will be used. Then click on the [Next >] button.

Step 2 of 5 Click on the image labelled **Column**. You can try three-dimensional versions later if you want. Click on the [Next >] button.

Step 3 of 5 Click on the image labelled **2**, separated columns, as this is for nominal data. Click on the [Next >] button.

Step 4 of 5 Select the following options:

Use First [1] ⬆⬇ Column(s)
     for Category (X) Axis Labels.

Use First [1] ⬆⬇ Row(s)
     for Legend Text.

Step 5 of 5 Indicate ⊙ **No** for the Legend and insert the Title, x-axis and y-axis labels shown in Figure 12.2, and then click on the [Finish] button.

To edit the final chart on the worksheet, double-click on the component, for example the vertical (y-)axis. A **Format Axis** box will appear giving you various options. For example, to get your chart to look exactly like the one in Figure 12.2, you will have to click on **Scale** tab and change the maximum to 13, one more than the default; leave the minimum at 0. Place the mouse cursor on the top edge of the box around the graph and double-click to get the **Format Plot Area** box. There you should change the Border to ⊙ **None** and in the Area to ⊙ **None**. You can also change fonts, change colours to patterns for the bars, etc. and ultimately copy your chart into a report, but we will stop here with the bar chart.

Stage 4: Producing a pie chart using the ChartWizard in Excel

Somewhere below your bar chart on the worksheet, make a new range of cells active for the pie chart, then click on the ChartWizard icon again. Now proceed as follows:

Step 1 of 5   As you hold the mouse button down, block the two data columns from **D3** to **E6**. This tells the Chart-Wizard what data is to be used. Then click on the | Next > | button.

Step 2 of 5   Click on the image labelled **Pie**. You can try three-dimensional versions later if you want. Click on the | Next > | button.

Step 3 of 5   Click on the image labelled **7**, to have labels and percentages for each section. Click on the | Next > | button.

Step 4 of 5   Select the following options:

Use First | 1 | ▲▼ Column(s)
for Category (X) Axis Labels.

Use First | 1 | ▲▼ Row(s)
for Legend Text.

Step 5 of 5   Indicate ⊙ **No** for the **Legend** and insert the **Chart Title** shown in Figure 12.3, and then click on | Finish | button.

If you want to explode one section, as done for the Raving Loony Party, simply double-click on that section to highlight it, then hold the button down and move it out a bit. You can change various other aspects by double-clicking on them and bringing up the appropriate menu (number of decimal places on percentage, shadings for each section instead of colour, etc.).

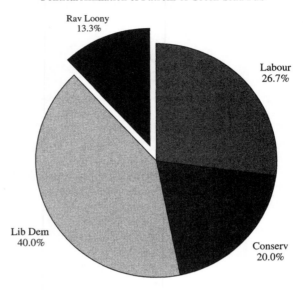

Political Affiliation of Patrons of Green Toad Pub

FIGURE 12.3
Pie chart for data in
Figure 12.3,
generated in Excel
(see box 'Stage 4:
ChartWizard')

Interval and ratio data

Raw interval and ratio data sets usually appear as numbers (scores on a test, annual income, age, weight, height, etc.) for a list of individuals. Initially, these numbers have to be translated into a frequency table in order to glean any information from them. The first task is to establish intervals in which to group the data. As a rule of thumb (Chase, 1985), about 15 intervals are appropriate, though a maximum of 20 and a minimum of 10 are acceptable. Outside this range, the shapes of distributions will tend to be distorted.

Also, it is much more meaningful to have intervals in increments that are easy to follow: steps of 2, 3, 4, 5 or 10 are better than fractional numbers such as 2 ¼. One does not have to start with the lowest score, and choosing carefully where to start may make a graph just that much easier to read. For example, if the range of scores on a test were from 23 to 67, a difference of 44, one could have fifteen intervals of three each (45 point spread). Where do you start? It is possible to work on a sequence of 23–25, 26–28, 29–31, etc., but by habit from our days of learning multiplication tables, it might make easier reading by starting with 21–23, 24–26, 27–29, 30–32, etc. Do not make the task unnecessarily difficult for yourself!

The next issue to be addressed is the one of where the interval boundaries *really* are. If the scores are whole numbers, it may not seem to be an important point, but for fractional or decimal numbers, it will be necessary to make a decision. Take the example above: where is the dividing point between 23 and 24? If there were scores of 23.3 and 23.6, in which interval(s) would they fall? Convention follows the simple rule that if the number is below a half it goes in the lower group and if it is a half or more it goes in the upper group. Therefore, any score below 23.5 is counted in the 21–23 interval (the *apparent interval*), and any score of 23.5 or above is counted in the 24–26 interval. Thus, the *real intervals* are 20.50000 to 23.49999 . . ., 23.50000 to 26.49999 . . ., etc. If you take the difference of the two pairs of real limits, you will get 3 each time. (see Figure 12.4).

There are three conventions for labelling the *x*-axis on a graph of continuous data:

(a)   the midpoints of the intervals, here 22, 25, 28, 31, etc;
(b)   the apparent intervals, here 21–23, 24–26, 27–29, etc;
(c)   the real limits, here 20.5, 23.5, 26.5, 29.5, etc.

Again, the choice is mostly a matter of aesthetics and ease of reading. If one displays data as a histogram, then any of the three is acceptable, though when a frequency polygon is used, the convention is to use (a) the midpoints of the intervals. If the graphs are generated by computer software, you may or may not have a choice, depending on the package. The other problem is space along the *x*-axis to include one or another of these. A bit of trial and error is in order, asking yourself which is easiest to read.

You may also find that you are limited by the graphics facilities in the software package you are using. For example, Excel tends to used midpoints, though with other packages it may be possible to introduce intervals or use real limits. Remember, though, it is not so much the detail, but the overall appearance of the shape of the distribution that will be of greatest interest to the readers. To try this out yourself using Excel, carry out Activity 12.2 now.

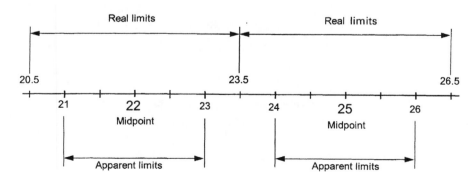

FIGURE 12.4
An example of real limits, apparent limits and midpoints

Activity 12.2

1 Figure 12.5 has a set of raw data and instructions on how to get the spreadsheet to make a frequency table for you. The box that follows will guide you in creating the histogram and frequency polygon in Figures 12.6 and 12.7.

2 Change defaults for your charts to see the results. For example, try a shorter chart, or widen the x-axis. Does this distort results or make them clearer?

Stage 2: Producing a histogram using the ChartWizard in Excel

Call up the ChartWizard by clicking on the icon 📊. This will allow you to drag out an area where you want your chart to appear on the page by clicking at where you want the upper left-hand corner and dragging diagonally, holding the button down until the area is big enough. Upon releasing the button, the following menu boxes will appear in sequence:

Step 1 of 5   Click on the tab for the worksheet with your data and as you hold the mouse button down, block the two data columns from **E3** to **F16**. Excel uses the midpoint for the interval on the x-axis and this tells the ChartWizard where the data are to be used. Then click on the | Next > | button.

Step 2 of 5   Click on the image labelled **Column**. You can try 3-D versions later if you want. Click on the | Next > | button.

Step 3 of 5   Click on the image labelled **8**, combined columns, as this is for interval data. Click on the | Next > | button.

Step 4 of 5   Select the following options:

       Use First | 1 | ⬆⬇ **Column(s)**
       for Category (X) Axis Labels.

       Use First | 1 | ⬆⬇ **Row(s)**
       for Legend Text.

Step 5 of 5   Indicate ⊙ **No** for the Legend and insert the Title, x-axis and y-axis labels shown in Figure 12.6 and then click on the | Finish | button.

	A	B	C	D	E	F
1	Name	Score		Real	Interval	
2	John	21		upper limits	midpoints	Frequency
3	Henry	72		20.50	18	0
4	Jane	37		25.50	23	1
5	Fred	45		30.50	28	1
6	Mary	44		35.50	33	2
7	Albert	67		40.50	38	3
8	Sam	56		45.50	43	4
9	Ellen	54		50.50	48	4
10	Ted	48		55.50	53	5
11	Anne	52		60.50	58	4
12	Hilary	61		65.50	63	2
13	Barbara	56		70.50	68	2
14	Betty	30		75.50	73	1
15	Terry	51		80.50	78	1
16	Robert	39		85.50	83	0
17	Tom	33				30
18	James	50				
19	Nancy	46				
20	Peter	64				
21	David	68				
22	Melany	76				
23	Sonya	55				
24	Jacob	42				
25	Sean	58				
26	Shirley	51				
27	Janet	47				
28	Annette	38				
29	Patsy	60				
30	Ian	44				
31	Sarah	34				
32	Total	30				
33						
34						

=D3–2.5 & **Copy** down the column

=SUM(F3:F15)

=COUNTA(B2:B31)

Stage 1: Making a frequency table for interval data

(a)   Record the raw data in columns **A** and **B** on the worksheet, entering titles for each.

(b)   Set up a set of upper real limits in column **D** and interval midpoints in column **E**, starting with **E3** and **Copy**ing, such that the lowest and highest intervals have 0 frequencies, remembering that you want 10–20 intervals with values > 0. Label the Frequency column **F** in cell **F2**.

(c)   With the mouse, block the cells **F3:F16** (start in **F3**, hold the left button down and highlight the cells). Then click on the Function Wizard icon, [*fx*].

(d)   In the **Step 1 of 2** box, from the list of Statistical Functions, choose **FREQUENCY**, then click on the [**Next >**] button.

(e)   In the **Step 2 of 2** box, use the mouse to indicate the
data_array   B2:B31   (the raw data)
bin_array   D3:D16   (the list of upper real limits)
then click on the [**Finish**] button.

(f)   Don't panic, this is an array function, which means that one more step is required. Place the mouse at the beginning of the text at the top before the **=FREQUENCY** and while holding the < Ctrl > and < Shift > (or < ⇑ >) keys down together, press < Rtn > (or < ↵ >). The set of cells will fill with the frequencies.

(g)   To check the process, find totals as shown in **B32** and **F17**.

FIGURE 12.5
Setting up an Excel worksheet to present a frequency table for interval data

Stage 3: Producing a frequency polygon using the Chart-Wizard

Only the following two steps are different to those for the histogram to implement Figure 12.7:

Step 2 of 5 Click on the image labelled **Line**. You can try other versions later if you want. Click on the ┃ Next > ┃ button.

Step 3 of 5 Click on the image labelled **1**, lines with data points marked, as this is for interval data for which you want to see the midpoints on the graph. Click on the ┃ Next > ┃ button. Carry out the last two steps as before.

Embellishments

In both of the above cases, your charts may not look exactly like those in the Figures 12.6 and 12.7. If you wish to change the defaults on the graph, double-click with the mouse inside the chart and it will become 'active'. Click once on the *y*-axis to activate it then double-click to get the **Format Axis** menu. Under **Scale**, I have made the **Maximum** 6 and the **Major Unit** 1. Click on the ┃ OK ┃ button. Repeat the process for the *x*-axis, where I have changed the **Alignment** to horizontal. Double-click on the top edge of the chart area to get **Format Plot Area** menu, where I have ⊙ **None** for Border and **None** for **Area color**. To prepare to print the histogram, I clicked on the bars to get the **Format Data Series** menu, where I have chosen a light grey colour and a fine dot **Pattern**. You can preview such changes by clicking on the **Axis** tab.

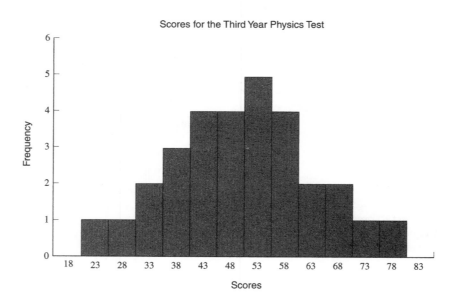

FIGURE 12.6
A histogram for the data in Figure 12.5

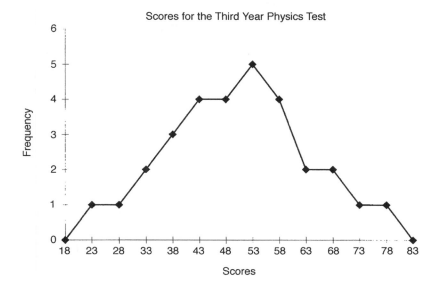

FIGURE 12.7
A frequency polygon
for the data in Figure
12.5

Comparing groups: nominal data

The above exercises have required you to enter a single set of data, generate frequency tables and plot graphs. Often one is collecting data on a number of characteristics related to subjects and it is useful to compare these visually. To display multiple sets of data on a chart, there will be a need to have multiple columns. For example, in Activity 12.1 we displayed election voting patterns for the sample, treating it as one group in a pub. If we want to divide the subjects into two groups on the basis of gender and compare their voting patterns, then we need two sets of bars on the chart. These can be set side by side, as in Figure 12.10, which allows direct comparison, or they can be stacked as in Figure 12.11, such that the total height of each bar is equivalent to those in Figure 12.2. Activity 12.3 guides you through the process of generating the frequency tables and charts.

Activity 12.3

Start up your spreadsheet program again and load the workbook for this chapter.
(a) You will start with the data you entered and saved in Activity 12.1 on voting preferences in the Green Toad pub. Make a copy of the worksheet to use for this activity and change the name on the tab at the bottom to Fig 12.8.
(b) Follow the directions provided in the window in Figures 12.8 and 12.9. You should generate bar charts like the ones in Figures 12.10 and 12.11, comparing the propensities of the two groups.

	A	B	C	D	E	F
1	**Name**	**Choice**	**Gender**		**Frequency**	**Frequency**
2	John	L	m	**Party**	**Male**	**Female**
3	Henry	C	m	Labour		
4	Jane	RL	f	Conserv		
5	Fred	LD	m	Lib Dem		
6	Mary	LD	f	Rav Loony		
7	Albert	RL	m	Total	0	0
8	Sam	L	m			
9	Ellen	C	f			
10	Ted	LD	m			
11	Anne	L	f			
12	Hilary	L	m			
13	Barbara	LD	f			
14	Betty	LD	f			
15	Terry	LD	f			
16	Robert	RL	m			
17	Tom	RL	m			
18	James	C	m			
19	Nancy	LD	f			
20	Peter	L	m			
21	David	L	m			
22	Melany	LD	f			
23	Sonya	LD	f			
24	Jacob	LD	m			
25	Sean	L	m			
26	Shirley	C	f			
27	Janet	LD	f			
28	Annette	C	f			
29	Patsy	L	f			
30	Ian	C	m			
31	Sarah	LD	f			
32	Total	30				
33						
34						

Stage 1: Identifying subgroups

(a) In this exercise, you will divide the group into two based upon the gender of the respondents. First use column **C** to indicate subject gender, typing in the data for each subject. Head the column accordingly, as shown above.

(b) Change the frequency table headings in **E1** to **F2** as shown.

(c) **Copy** the **=SUM** in **E7** to **F7** so that the totals in the frequency distributions can be checked.

(d) Before the frequency table can be created, it is necessary to rearrange the raw data and group subjects according to gender. First, with the mouse, block the data from **A1** to **C31**, including column titles. On the main menu, select **Data** and then **Sort**. At the bottom of the **Sort** menu box, change the **My List Has** setting to ⊙ **Header Row**. Then in the **Sort By** box, select **Gender**. In this case, it does not matter whether it is **Ascending** or **Descending** since the aim is to separate males and females. I have left it **Ascending**, thus the females will be in the first group. Click on the [OK] button and the entire list should rearrange itself so that it looks like Figure 12.9.

FIGURE 12.8
Nominal data with two subgroups to be divided

Comparing groups: interval/ratio data

Similar to the previous subsection, there will be occasions when it will be desirable to compare two groups for traits measured as continuous data. This may occur as the result of random selection or random assignment, or for two traits observed in a single group in a correlational study. Comparing two groups or traits graphically in an effective manner is not easy, since the aim is to show how the two overlap or interact. Using histograms, one will inevitably

	A	B	C	D	E	F
1	**Name**	**Choice**	**Gender**		**Frequency**	**Frequency**
2	Jane	RL	f	**Party**	**Male**	**Female**
3	Mary	LD	f	Labour	6	2
4	Ellen	C	f	Conserv	3	3
5	Anne	L	f	Lib Dem	3	9
6	Barbara	LD	f	Rav Loony	3	1
7	Betty	LD	f	Total	15	15
8	Terry	LD	f			
9	Nancy	LD	f			
10	Melany	LD	f			
11	Sonya	LD	f			
12	Shirley	C	f			
13	Janet	LD	f			
14	Annette	C	f			
15	Patsy	L	f			
16	Sarah	LD	f			
17	John	L	m			
18	Henry	C	m			
19	Fred	LD	m			
20	Albert	RL	m			
21	Sam	L	m			
22	Ted	LD	m			
23	Hilary	L	m			
24	Robert	RL	m			
25	Tom	RL	m			
26	James	C	m			
27	Peter	L	m			
28	David	L	m			
29	Jacob	LD	m			
30	Sean	L	m			
31	Ian	C	m			
32	Total	30				
33						
34						

=COUNTIF(B$17:B$31,"L")

=COUNTIF(B$2:B$16,"L")

Stage 2: Generating frequency tables and plotting charts

(a) Now there are two easily identifiable groups. To create the two frequency charts, simply use the **=COUNTIF** function for each group, as shown above. Note that each one covers only its part of the list.

(b) Activating a cell on the worksheet, call up the ChartWizard. Block out the area where you want your chart.

Step 1 of 5   As you hold down the mouse button, block the three data columns **D2** to **F6**. Click on Next >

Step 2 of 5   Click on the image **3-D Column** and Next >

Step 3 of 5   Click on the image labelled **1** and Next >

Step 4 of 5   As before:

Use First **1** Column(s) for Category (X) Axis Labels.

Use First **1** Row(s) for Legend Text.

Step 5 of 5   Insert the Title, *x*-axis, and *y*-axis labels as shown in Figure 12.10, and click on Finish button.

(c) Activate the chart and double-click on one of the bars to get the **Format Data Series**, choose the **Values and Names** tab and in the **Name** box, enter Male or Female, whichever is appropriate. Repeat the process for the other bars. Using the appropriate menus change the chart to suit yourself.

(d) An alternative way to display the data is to stack the bars so that the total height of a bar is the total for that category, as in Figure 12.11. The only difference is in the choice in **Step 3 of 5** where chart type **2** is chosen. Activate the chart, then to adjust the width of the bars, choose **Format** from the main menu, then **Chart Type** . . . In the menu box, click **Options** then select the **Options** tab and adjust the **Chart Depth**.

FIGURE 12.9
Table for generating charts in Figures 12.10 and 12.11

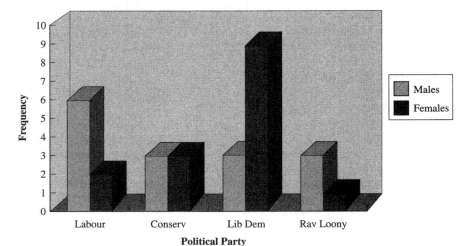

FIGURE 12.10
Bar chart with
adjacent bars for the
two subgroups

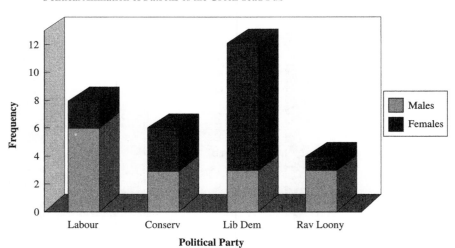

FIGURE 12.11
Bar chart with
stacked bars for the
two subgroups

cover up the other so that only part is visible (you can try this in the Activity 12.4), thus frequency polygons are often used as shown in Figure 12.14.

Occasionally it is possible and desirable to show one set of data as positive values and the other as negative, using histograms as in Figure 12.15. In this example, there were two groups of learners, one which attended an experimental session and one which did not. Their grades on a subsequent test are compared. In Activity 12.4, you will build on data entered for Activity 12.2 to enter the scores for the second characteristic of the students, whether or not they attended the special experimental session.

Both of these will provide a visual comparison of the two groups but neither will be able to provide details on the nature of any relationship between them. For example, had the groups been randomly assigned (attend and not attend), it would take a statistical test to determine whether both groups really belong to a common population and the observed differences are just chance variation, or whether the differences are great enough to be attributable to some variable. On the other hand, had the students initially been a single group and then decided themselves whether to attend or not, then one could ask whether there was any association between choosing to attend and scores on the test. These questions can only be answered by using specific statistical tests, the subject of later chapters. Now we are interested in being able to display the data visually, so carry out Activity 12.4 at this time.

Activity 12.4

For this activity, you will use the data you entered in Activity 12.2. First make another copy of the worksheet in Figure 12.5 and change the tab name to **Fig12.12**.

1   Add a second column of data on whether or not each student attended a special experimental teaching session, column **C**. After creating the appropriate frequency tables, you will plot frequency polygons for both groups on one graph. Follow the directions in the windows in Figures 12.12 and 12.13 and you should end up with a graph like the one shown in Figure 12.14. Also, with a small addition to the frequency table, you will be able to plot the pair of histograms in Figure 12.15.

2   Which do you think best illustrates the situation and why?

If we wish to display demographic data, the same approach can be applied, only rotating the chart in Figure 12.15 by 90°, as shown in the example in Figure 12.16. This is most easily done by using the **Bar** choice and type **8**, then again reformatting the graph, using from the main menu **Format**, **1 Column Group**, **Options**, and changing the **Overlap** to **100**. Depending on how the original data were entered, it may be necessary to select **Categories** in **Reverse order** on the **Scale** tab when formatting the vertical axis.

Data such as these are often available from national censuses for a number of population characteristics, though they are not very meaningful unless displayed graphically. In this case, it is possible to illustrate the differences in school enrolment between boys and girls over the years of schooling. Children take a school leaving examination at the end of P7 for entry selection into secondary school, O-level examinations at the end of S4, and A-level examinations at the end of S6. Such data have helped the government recognize the need to encourage more girls to stay in school.

Now try Activity 12.5 to see how you can put together some of the above skills in a new problem.

	A	B	C	D	E	F	G	H
1	Name	Score	Attend?	Real	Interval	Frequency	Frequency	Frequency
2	John	21	n	upper limits	midpoints	not attended	attended	neg. "not"
3	Henry	72	y	20.50	18			
4	Jane	37	n	25.50	23			
5	Fred	45	y	30.50	28			
6	Mary	44	n	35.50	33			
7	Albert	67	y	40.50	38			
8	Sam	56	y	45.50	43			
9	Ellen	54	y	50.50	48			
10	Ted	48	n	55.50	53			
11	Anne	52	y	60.50	58			
12	Hilary	61	y	65.50	63			
13	Barbara	56	n	70.50	68			
14	Betty	30	n	75.50	73			
15	Terry	51	y	80.50	78			
16	Robert	39	n	85.50	83			
17	Tom	33	n		Total:	0	0	0
18	James	50	n					
19	Nancy	46	y					
20	Peter	64	y					
21	David	68	y					
22	Melany	76	y					
23	Sonya	55	y					
24	Jacob	42	n					
25	Sean	58	y					
26	Shirley	51	n					
27	Janet	47	n					
28	Annette	38	n					
29	Patsy	60	y					
30	Ian	44	n					
31	Sarah	34	n					
32	Total		30					
33								
34								

=COUNTA(C2:C31)

Stage 1: Setting up the data

(a) Make a copy of Figure 12.5 from Activity 12.2 to use here.

(b) Enter the data for each student as to attendance at the special sessions or not, in the shaded cells.

(c) Delete the frequencies in column **F** and set up new titles.

(d) Copy the **=SUM** function in **F7** to **G7** and **H7** so that the totals in the frequency distributions can be checked.

(e) Before the frequency table can be created, it is necessary to rearrange the raw data and group subjects according to gender.

(i) With the mouse, block the data **A1:C31**, including column titles. On the main menu, select **Data** and **Sort**.

(ii) At the bottom of the **Sort** menu box, change the **My List Has** setting to ⊙ **Header Row**. Then in the **Sort By** box, select **Attended**. In this case, it does not matter whether it is **Ascending** or **Descending** since the aim is to separate those who have attended from those who have not. I have left it **Ascending**, thus the non-attendees will be in the first group.

(iii) Click on the [**OK**] button and the entire list should rearrange itself so that it looks like the worksheet in Figure 12.13.

FIGURE 12.12
Data for exercise on comparing groups

	A	B	C	D	E	F	G	H
1	**Name**	**Score**	**Attend?**	**Real**	**Interval**	**Frequency**	**Frequency**	**Frequency**
2	John	21	n	upper limits	midpoints	not attended	attended	neg. "not"
3	Jane	37	n	20.50	18	0	0	0
4	Mary	44	n	25.50	23	1	0	−1
5	Ted	48	n	30.50	28	1	0	−1
6	Barbara	56	n	35.50	33	2	0	−2
7	Betty	30	n	40.50	38	3	0	−3
8	Robert	39	n	45.50	43	3	1	−3
9	Tom	33	n	50.50	48	3	1	−3
10	James	50	n	55.50	53	1	4	−1
11	Jacob	42	n	60.50	58	1	3	−1
12	Shirley	51	n	65.50	63	0	2	0
13	Janet	47	n	70.50	68	0	2	0
14	Annette	38	n	75.50	73	0	1	0
15	Ian	44	n	80.50	78	0	1	0
16	Sarah	34	n	85.50	83	0	0	0
17	Henry	72	y		Total:	15	15	−15
18	Fred	45	y					
19	Albert	67	y					
20	Sam	56	y					
21	Ellen	54	y					
22	Anne	52	y					
23	Hilary	61	y					
24	Terry	51	y					
25	Nancy	46	y					
26	Peter	64	y					
27	David	68	y					
28	Melany	76	y					
29	Sonya	55	y					
30	Sean	58	y					
31	Patsy	60	y					
32	Total		30					
33								
34								

Stage 2: Making frequency tables

(a) With the mouse, block the 'not attended' cells **F3:F16** (start in **F3**, hold the button down and move to **F16**), then activate and select the Function Wizard icon.

(b) In the **Step 1 of 2** box, from the list of Statistical Functions, choose **FREQUENCY**, then click on the ⟨ Next > ⟩ button.

(c) In the **Step 2 of 2** box, use the mouse to indicate the

data_array   B2:B16   (the non-attendees)
bin_array   D3:D16   (the list of upper real limits)

then click on the ⟨ Finish ⟩ button.

(d) Remember, this is an array function, which means that one more step is required. Place the mouse at the beginning of the text at the top before the **=FREQUENCY** and while holding the <Ctrl> and <Shift> keys down together, press <Rtn>. The set of cells will fill with the frequencies. Repeat this process for the 'yes' group.

(e) To plot overlapping frequency polygons, click on ChartWizard icon and set up a new area for a graph. Go through the steps, selecting the block of cells **E2:G16**, choosing chart **Line** type **1**.

(f) An alternative chart is shown in Figure 12.15, which can be achieved by adding the negative values for the 'no' group in Column **H**. Using the ChartWizard:

Step 1 of 5   range: **E3:E16, G3:H16**,
Step 2 of 5   choose **Column**,
Step 3 of 5   choose number **8**,

and complete the process. Activate the graph and from the main menu, select **Format**, **1 Column Group**, **Options** and increase the **Overlap** to **100**.

FIGURE 12.13
Generating frequency tables for comparing groups graphically

Attendance at Experimental Session: Third Year Physics

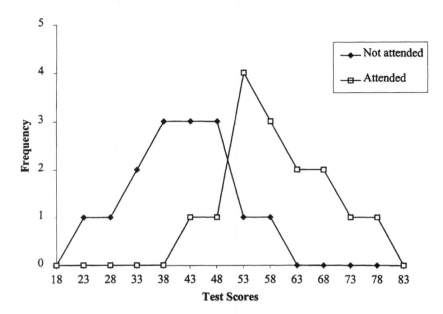

FIGURE 12.14
Frequency polygons
for the data in Figure
12.13

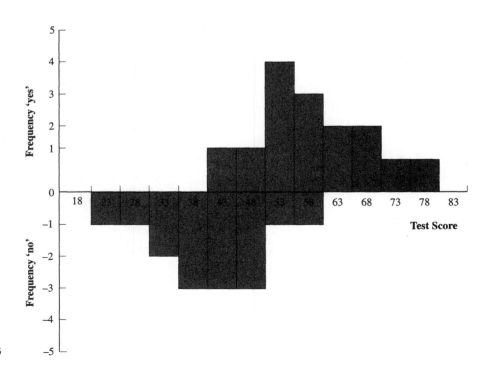

FIGURE 12.15
Histograms for the
data in Figure 12.13

Activity 12.5

1(a) Listed below is a set of data for a group of 30 subjects which includes each person's social class and age in years. Set up a worksheet, entering the raw data in appropriate columns; change the worksheet name tab to **Act12.5**.

	Class	Age		Class	Age
Jones	A	41.3	Browne	E	33.3
Smith	C	33.2	Green	A	65.2
Singh	A	56.7	Rocard	C	52.3
Dubcek	D	33.4	Andretti	B	49.7
Ducette	B	44.3	Plum	C	44.4
Long	E	32.6	Peach	B	50.3
Grey	D	65.4	Jenkins	A	48.4
Alvarez	B	57.1	Grunwald	C	38.2
Orange	E	37.2	Hinkel	B	47.9
McKay	C	50.7	Leong	B	60.9
Wang	C	43.2	Lopez	A	62.3
Baker	E	35.4	Ball	D	51.4
Carlton	B	66.7	Felchet	E	44.3
Hansen	C	52.1	Morton	D	58.9
Norris	E	34.2	Price	A	54.6

(b) Create a frequency table and generate appropriate chart(s) showing the distribution of persons in social classes.

(c) Create a frequency table and generate appropriate chart(s) showing the distribution of ages.

2 Alternatively, carry out a similar activity for data of your own, resulting in at least one set of nominal/ordinal data and charts, and at least one set of interval/ratio data and charts.

3 Display some available demographic data in a similar manner to that shown in Figure 12.16.

Two variables for a single group

There are occasions when it is desirable to display two variables for a single group. For example, if one were to display two variables, primary class and age, for a one-room school that has four levels of children, they could be presented in any of the ways shown in Figure 12.19. The problem is clarity, which is partially due to type of chart and partially due to perspective. Figure 12.19(a) employs a filled frequency polygon, and while it allows the comparison of age distributions for each class, some of the data are obscured.

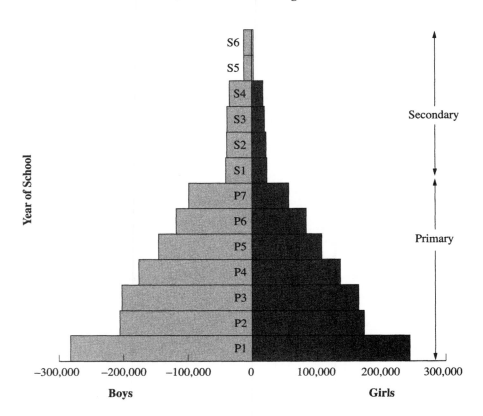

School Enrolment in Uganda

FIGURE 12.16
An example of
demographic data
illustrated
graphically

Figure 12.19(b) shows the data as bars, making it a little clearer what the age
distributions are, but still has the problem of obscured data. Figure 12.19(c) is
similar to the Figure 12.19(a) but does not use solids, thus obscuring less of
the data. Now carry out Activity 12.6.

Activity 12.6

1 Follow the directions in Figures 12.17 and 12.18 to produce the charts
   shown in Figures 12.19. Which do you think best presents the data?
2 Use your data and worksheets for Activity 12.4 to display chart
   equivalent to one of those shown in Figure 12.19.

Summary for graphical presentations

Charts and graphs do provide visual summaries of raw data that would probably be mostly meaningless to us otherwise. Although we have presented a

	A	B	C	D	E	F	G	H
1	**Name**	**Age**	**Class**					
2	John	5	2					
3	Henry	8	1					
4	Jane	6	2					
5	Fred	8	2					
6	Mary	5	1					
7	Albert	7	1					
8	Sam	6	3					
9	Ellen	8	3					
10	Ted	6	1					
11	Anne	10	4					
12	Hilary	7	1					
13	Barbara	7	3					
14	Betty	9	4					
15	Terry	6	1					
16	Robert	8	3					
17	Tom	8	2					
18	James	6	3					
19	Nancy	7	2					
20	Peter	9	3					
21	David	7	2					
22	Melany	9	4					
23	Sonya	8	3					
24	Jacob	7	2					
25	Sean	9	4					
26	Shirley	6	1					
27	Janet	9	3					
28	Annette	10	3					
29	Patsy	7	3					
30	Ian	8	4					
31	Sarah	7	2					
32								
33								
34								

Stage 1: Setting up a two-variable frequency table

(a) Start a new worksheet and save time by copying in the set of names from Figure 12.13.

(b) Type in the age and grade (class) to which each child belongs.

(c) Block the whole set of data, including headings: **A1:C31**. From the main menu, select **Data** and then **Sort**. Set **My List Has** to ⊙ **Header Row**, and select **Class**. If you use **Ascending**, the data will group starting with P1 as shown in Figure 12.18, where you will find the rest of the instructions.

FIGURE 12.17
Data for a one-room school house with a class of 30 children

variety of types and some guidance on appropriate usage, our treatment has not been exhaustive nor does it eliminate the need for some careful judgement based on the data to hand and the aim of the presentation. As you should have noticed, there are a number of alternatives in Excel not used in the above activities. Some would be viable alternatives, but others totally inappropriate. A few more will be introduced later, but many of those untried are variations on themes covered here and the appropriateness of their usage can be judged on the guidelines presented, combined with some good taste.

	A	B	C	D	E	F	G	H
1	Name	Age	Class	Age/Class	P1	P2	P3	P4
2	Henry	8	1	**4**	0	0	0	0
3	Mary	5	1	**5**	1	1	0	0
4	Albert	7	1	**6**	3	1	1	0
5	Ted	6	1	**7**	2	4	2	0
6	Hilary	7	1	**8**	1	2	3	1
7	Terry	6	1	**9**	0	0	2	4
8	Shirley	6	1	**10**	0	0	1	1
9	John	5	2	**11**	0	0	0	0
10	Jane	6	2					30
11	Fred	8	2					
12	Tom	8	2					
13	Nancy	7	2					
14	David	7	2					
15	Jacob	7	2					
16	Sarah	7	2					
17	Sam	6	3					
18	Ellen	8	3					
19	Barbara	7	3					
20	Robert	8	3					
21	Peter	9	3					
22	Sonya	8	3					
23	Janet	9	3					
24	Annette	10	3					
25	Patsy	7	3					
26	James	9	4					
27	Anne	10	4					
28	Betty	9	4					
29	Melany	9	4					
30	Sean	9	4					
31	Ian	8	4					
32								
33								
34								

Stage 2: Generating a frequency table and charts

(a) Set up the headings for classes and the set of ages.

(b) Block the column for P1: **E2:E9**, and click on the Function Wizard, selecting **FREQUENCY**. Use **B2:B8** as the **data_array** (ages of all those in primary class 1), **D2:D9** as the **bin_array**.

(c) Repeat this process for P2, P3 and P4, using the appropriate sets of data for each **data_array**.

(d) Insert a **=SUM(E2:H9)** in **H10** to check your frequency table.

(e) Select the ChartWizard and block off an area for the first of the three charts.

(f) Go to the data above and block the whole set including titles, for the **Range: D1:H9**. Start with **3-D Area** number **5** and set the next menu:

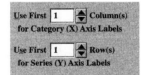

Complete the labels for the axes.

(g) Use **Format**, **Chart Type**, **Options** to change the width of bars, etc., to suit your taste.

(h) To orientate the chart so that it is most effective, activate the chart box by double-clicking anywhere in the chart area. Then click on a top corner of the chart. If you now place the mouse pointer on one of the corners and hold the button down, a + will appear, and as you move the mouse a wire-frame version of the chart will move. At first, it may seem that it has a mind of its own, but with some practice, you will be able to change the orientation to what you think is most appropriate. (*Hint*: if it gets out of control, try using a different corner.)

(i) Repeat the process, but choose the other two types of 3-D chart and try to orientate them the same.

FIGURE 12.18
Generating a
frequency table for
two variables for the
one-room school

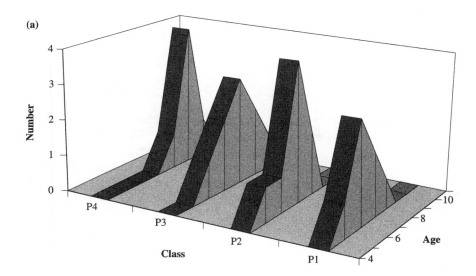

FIGURE 12.19(a)
Solid polygons, one
of three ways of
displaying 3-D
charts for data in
Figure 12.19.

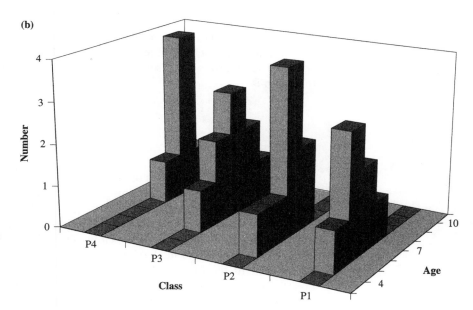

FIGURE 12.19(b)
Solid bars, second of
three ways of
displaying 3-D
charts for data in
Figure 12.19.

GROUP CHARACTERISTICS FOR DISTRIBUTIONS

It is not so much that individuals are not important, but in the world of statistics, one is looking for quantifiable traits and characteristics that are common within groups as well as for differences between groups. Therefore, the need to identify a way of quantifying group characteristics has lead to *measures of central tendency*, numbers that describe the group as a whole and what it tends to do. Each of these is most appropriate for different types of data and distributions:

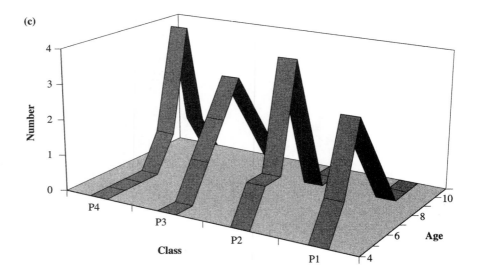

(c)

FIGURE 12.19(c)
Surfaces, third of
three ways of
displaying 3-D
charts for data in
Figure 12.19.

- The *mean* is calculated by adding the scores or values for each subject and dividing by the total number of subjects. In Excel, use **=AVERAGE (range)** to find this for a set of data in a range of cells. The equation for the mean is

$$\bar{x} = \frac{\sum_{i=1}^{n} x_i}{n} \qquad (12.1)$$

where x_i is the individual score or value for person i, and n is the total number of subjects. When this is the population mean, a parameter, the Greek symbol mu, μ, is used instead of $\bar{x}$.

- The *median* is simply the number that divides the group into two, with half falling above this value and half below. Thus if there are 11 subjects, the score for the 6th is the median. For an even number of subjects, take the mean value of the two scores in the middle. Thus if there are 10 subjects, take the mean of the 5th and 6th scores. It is appropriate for interval/ratio data that is not normally distributed, or ranked data. In Excel use the function **=MEDIAN(range)**.

- The *mode* refers to the interval or category with the largest frequency, thus it is appropriate for ordinal or nominal data, and bimodal distributions. Choose the interval or category with the most subjects, always remembering there may be more than one such interval or category.

Given the way the mean and median are defined, note that they will be the same (and equal to the mode) for normal distributions, but not for those that are skewed, as shown in Figure 12.20.

The *variability* or *dispersion* within a sample or population indicates how much spread there is, and in some cases, the implied shape of the distribution.

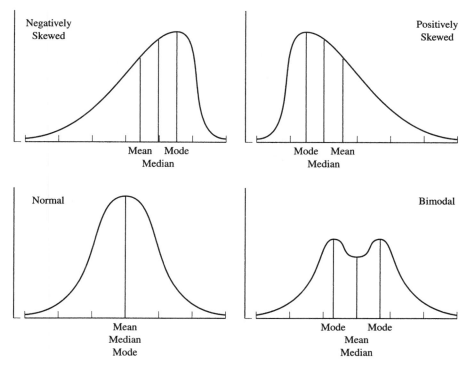

FIGURE 12.20
Mean, median and mode for a variety of distributions

Again, each of these is most appropriate for different types of data and distributions:

- The *standard deviation* is used when the distribution is normal and indicates its width (see Figure 12.21), it tends to be used in conjunction with the mean. Since there are different ways of calculating this, it is discussed in detail below.
- *Quartiles* are an extension of the median, providing the points at which the distribution can be divided into quarters. This is appropriate for non-normal distributions. In Excel use **=QUARTILE(range, 1)** and **=QUARTILE(range, 3)**.
- The *range* is the simplest measure, indicating just the maximum and minimum, appropriate for ordinal data, or non-normal distributions of interval/ratio data. From a set of raw data, these limits can be found in Excel by using **=MAX(range)** and **=MIN(range)**.

Parametric tests (such as the *t*-test and analysis of variance) make use of the means and standard deviations of sample groups, but nonparametric tests (such as the chi-square test) are not distribution-dependent and therefore usually do not use measures of central tendency or variability in their calculations.

The *median* was defined as the number that divides a group in half, regardless of the shape of the distribution, and *quartiles* are the divisions at the first and third quarters. Unfortunately, these measures are not nearly as valuable for inferential statistics as are the mean and standard deviations, but they are much more appropriate as descriptive statistics for non-normal distributions than the latter. The median will also be of use when trying to determine just how skewed a distribution can be before it violates the assumptions of parametric tests.

Activity 12.7

Use the appropriate functions to find the mean, median and mode of the scores data in Figure 12.13 for each of the two groups.

Answer

	Not attended	Attended
Mean	40.9	59.0
Median	42.0	58.0
Mode (intervals)	38–48	53

Standard deviation and variance

If age were a dependent variable, then everyone in the group would be within a defined age range. When age is an independent variable, then the actual distribution of ages within a group (teachers, pensioners, students, clients, or subjects selected on a specific trait) around the mean will have a bearing on the results. If the distribution were normal, then the standard deviation would be the appropriate indicator of variability within the group. Recall that because of the shape of the normal curve, the area under the curve (representing the number of subjects) changes in a nonlinear manner moving away from the mean. Thus the area under the first standard deviation above or below the mean is 34.13%, between the first and second standard deviations is 13.59%, with the remaining 2.28% in the tail beyond the second standard deviation, making up the 50% on each side, as shown in Figure 12.21 for two different standard deviations. As can be seen, these areas are independent of the shape of the curve. The area is equivalent to the total number of subjects in the sample, thus for the idealized histogram in Figure 12.22, it is possible to add the numbers in each set of bars for each standard deviation, divide by the total (200), and arrive at a percentage approximately equal to the percentages in Figure 12.21.

The calculation of the standard deviation is not very straightforward, though many calculators and most spreadsheets will do it for you for a set of data. There are three ways of defining standard deviation (Hays, 1994), resulting in two different calculations based upon raw data, for

- a population, σ,
- a sample of a population, S,
- the unbiased estimate for the population based on sample data, s.

The difference, where there is one, appears in the denominator of the equations. To find the *population standard deviation*, σ, requires data for the entire population:

$$\sigma = \sqrt{\frac{\sum_{i=1}^{n}(x_i - \mu)^2}{n}} \qquad (12.2)$$

where x_i is the score of the individual member, i, of the population, μ is the population mean and n is the size of the population. Using Excel, this is found directly by the function **=STDEVP(range)**.

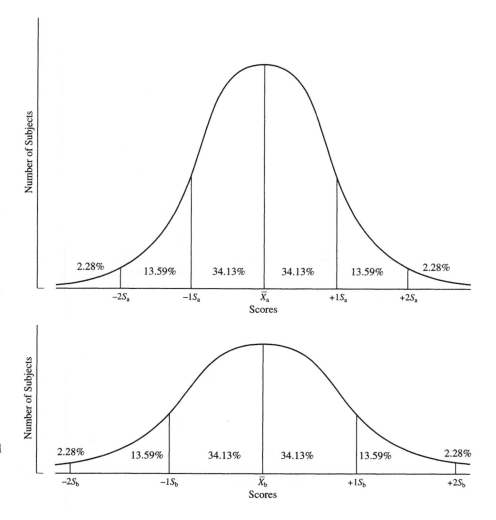

FIGURE 12.21
Areas under normal distributions with two different standard deviations

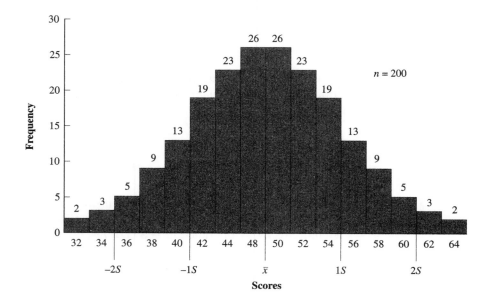

FIGURE 12.22
Idealized normal
histogram. Add the
areas in each
standard deviation
($\cong 6$) and divide by
the sample total of
200

The *standard deviation for a sample* from a population, S, where no inference is being made about the population standard deviation, is calculated in much the same way:

$$S = \sqrt{\frac{\sum_{i=1}^{n}(x_i - \bar{x})^2}{n}} \qquad (12.3)$$

where x_i is the score for the individual member, i, of the sample, $\bar{x}$ is the sample mean and n is the size of the sample. Though this is not discussed in many textbooks, there are situations where this is used. It is found in Excel by using the same function as used for population standard deviation, **=STDEVP(range)**.

If there is a need to have an *unbiased estimate of the population standard deviation*, s, and all that is available is sample data, then

$$s = \sqrt{\frac{\sum_{i=1}^{n}(x_i - \bar{x})^2}{n - 1}} \qquad (12.4)$$

where x_i, $\bar{x}$ and n are as in the definition of S. The unbiased estimate is found in Excel by using the function **=STDEV(range)**.

The reason for the difference between equations (12.4) and (12.3) is that the former compensates for small samples. The $n - 1$ instead of n in the denominator calculation is meant to add a correction factor to err on the large side for small samples. As n gets smaller, the standard deviation gets larger and this is exacerbated for very small samples by the $n - 1$. The distinction between S and s will be maintained throughout the text and the differences in use noted where appropriate.

The standard deviation, though visually meaningful and in the same units of measure as the original scores, is actually a consequence of taking the square root of the *variance*, the average of the squared deviations from the mean. Also, there are situations when it is necessary to combine the variabilities, and this is done by adding variances (*not* standard deviations). The mathematical reasons are similar to those for adding the squares of the sides of a triangle so as to get the square of the hypotenuse. The *population variance*, σ^2, is mathematically defined as:

$$\sigma^2 = \frac{\sum_{i=1}^{n}(x_i - \mu)^2}{n} \tag{12.5}$$

This is obtained in Excel by using the function **=VARP(range)**, as is the biased *sample variance*, S^2, which is defined as:

$$S^2 = \frac{\sum_{i=1}^{n}(x_i - \bar{x})^2}{n} \tag{12.6}$$

Again, while the distinction may seem trivial, it was this form of the variance, you may have noticed, that was used in the calculations for reliability in Chapter 11. The *unbiased estimate of the population variance*, s^2, based on sample data, is defined as:

$$s^2 = \frac{\sum_{i=1}^{n}(x_i - \bar{x})^2}{n - 1} \tag{12.7}$$

This is found in Excel by using the function **=VAR(range)**. A consequence of the different denominator is that for small samples, this estimate will be larger than the sample variance of equation (12.6). To illustrate the differences in values for small samples, carry out Activity 12.8.

Activity 12.8

(a) For the group of 15 subjects in the 'not attended' category in Figure 12.13, find s, S, s^2, and S^2, using the appropriate Excel functions (set the number of decimal places to one, i.e., 12.3). By how much do the pairs differ?

(b) Now repeat the process but only use the data for the first five subjects. What happens to the differences between s and S? Between s^2 and S^2?

Answers: (a) $s = 9.15$, $S = 8.84$, $s^2 = 83.8$, $S^2 = 78.2$. (b) $s = 13.22$, $S = 11.82$, $s^2 = 174.7$, $S^2 = 139.8$. The differences are greater and they are all larger than those for the larger sample. Sample size does influence these values.

SUMMARY

This chapter has introduced a variety of ways of displaying data graphically and describing group characteristics numerically. The focus has been on how to present data in such a way as to inform the reader. There are a number of common practices that intentionally or unintentionally lead to deception, but the reader is referred to other sources for examples (e.g. Black, 1993; Huff, 1954). The graphical techniques will be used in subsequent chapters to explore the consequences of using means and standard deviations to describe data, as well as to introduce new concepts related to inferential statistics.

PROBABILITY AND STATISTICAL SIGNIFICANCE 13

We live in a probabilistic environment: many events *might* happen and some are more likely than others. For certain events for which causes are better understood than others, it may even be possible to establish accurate probabilities of those events occurring. The chances of winning when placing money on specific numbers in the game of roulette are well known as this is an extremely simple system. It is one where all extraneous variables are controlled and only random events dictate the outcomes. On the other hand, while the probability that a person who smokes cigarettes will suffer from a heart condition or lung cancer is higher than for someone who does not, the outcome cannot be known exactly because of the many variables that contribute to these conditions. While there may be some randomness involved, variables such as physical well-being, age, life-style and genetics will contribute to the outcome. Consequently, associated with this probability is the fact that there is also a finite possibility one will *never* suffer from either of these afflictions. We have all heard stories of a friend of Uncle Charlie's who smoked three packs of Old Moose Hide cigarettes a day and lived to be 99 years old, dying an accidental death while hang-gliding. As the nature of such diseases is better understood and the links with genetic propensities that are inherited are determined, it may be possible in the future to run tests on one's DNA and tell even more accurately the probability of contracting certain illnesses as a consequence of specific actions or exposure to known carcinogens. But considering the number of potential variables involved, it is unlikely to go beyond a 'probably'. Epidemiologists, using statistics, tell us the likelihood of suffering dire consequences from smoking and microbiologists identify the actual chemical, physiological and/or genetic mechanisms.

The insurance premiums on your car, life, house, dog, etc., are all calculated based upon predictions of probabilities determined by past experiences with similar conditions, persons, events, etc., plus a bit for profit. Unconsciously, many of life's decisions are based upon probabilities, such as that spending three to eight years as a university student will *probably* improve ones income prospects, *possibly* qualify one for a more personally rewarding job, and *might* make one more appealing to a potential partner. There are no guarantees, and life is not fair – but then we all know that and must make decisions on the data that are available. The plight of the social scientist is not dissimilar, since the data are often not as complete or comprehensive as we would like. The difference arises in the more systematic way research data are collected, processed and interpreted, compared to the haphazard way we process data from everyday experiences. We also have various statistical tests and tools, but this introduces an additional burden of understanding just what these tests can tell us and what their limitations are.

As has been maintained from the beginning, one of the goals of any research-based discipline is to try to determine causal relations. As you hopefully have gleaned by now, statistics and statistical tests alone cannot prove causality, they can only provide support in situations of competing variables. The structure of the design (sampling, control of variables, measurement, etc.) will be as important as the outcome of any statistical test, if not more so. In the case of the links between smoking and heart disease or lung cancer, statistically based research simply told the biologists *where* to look for causes of these afflictions. It was up to the biologists and physiologists to provide the evidence for the actual mechanism.

Correlational studies did not *prove* a causal relationship any more than finding the butler standing over his dead master with a smoking revolver in his hand *proved* he committed the crime. Such an ex post facto design does not provide the comparable conditions of an experimental design where extraneous variables are carefully controlled. The equivalent experimental design would include having witnesses and a home video of the butler performing the dastardly deed. Granted, it is possible to forge such evidence, and there have been a few cases in research where the evidence has been contrived, but then in the situation of research the results should be testable by replicating the study.

Experimental designs employing greater control over potential extraneous variables provide more support in comparable situations for causality than initial searches using correlations. Ex post facto designs use some of the same statistical tests as employed in experimental designs and answer questions about differences between groups, but are less likely to provide unequivocal evidence for causality from the life-experience variables. We will consider a wide range of tools to see how and why they can support hypotheses for a variety of situations and what their limitations are.

This chapter will focus on underlying concepts in mathematical probability that justify the process of random sampling and are the basis for tests of significant differences. All of these are based upon the assumption that our data when plotted as a graph (frequency polygon) have roughly the same shape as a normal distribution (other types of data will be considered later). Parametric statistical tests are based upon a mathematical model that follows an equation of an ideal distribution, and, as with other exercises in the world of numbers, the ideal is rarely, if ever, reached. Mathematicians are able to devise such ideals because they are relatively simple and straightforward, and the resulting mathematics does a pretty good job of predicting the outcomes of truly random events, as we will see. The difficulty comes in trying to apply these models to our own data, and trying to answer the hard question whether we are close enough to the underlying assumptions to make valid use of these mathematical tools or not. This is not a trivial question in such an area as social science research where we are using these models and accompanying mathematical tests just as decision support tools. How far one can deviate from an ideal before the use of a tool becomes invalid is a question that will be considered on a number of occasions in the rest of this book.

The aim of this chapter is to provide a sufficiently sound conceptual background for understanding how probability provides the basis of statistical inference. It is not a detailed presentation of probability, and there are books that go into much greater depth for those who are interested in the topic of probability and its relationship with statistical inference (for example, Hays, 1994; Howell, 1997; Kerlinger, 1986; Moore, 1991).

WHAT IS PROBABILITY?

Statisticians have two approaches to the definition of probability, depending to a large extent on the particular situation being modelled. The one traditionally used is Laplace's classical *a priori* approach, meaning before the event, or independent of experience (see Kerlinger, 1986). Loosely speaking, this treats the probability of something occurring as the number of ways it can occur divided by the number of ways all possible events (expected and unexpected) in the universe of interest can occur; in other words, the approach is in terms of long-term relative frequencies. Such situations are the realm of the mathematician (Blalock, 1979), particularly those predictions of probabilities that cannot be obtained empirically and are not data-dependent. These 'natural' events are ideals – such as tossing coins, throwing dice, perfectly shuffled decks of cards, etc. – and, if carried out honestly, have no contributing external variables. They are based upon truly random events. This definition of probability can be expressed mathematically as

$$\text{probability} \equiv \frac{\text{expected}}{\text{possible}} = \frac{\text{expected}}{\text{expected} + \text{unexpected}}$$

Numerically, this probability ranges from 0.00 (the expected has no chance of happening: the unexpected is certain to happen) to 1.00 (the expected is certain to happen: the unexpected has no chance of happening).

Alternatively, one must consider the *a posteriori* or frequency definition, which is based upon the supposition of having already collected some data. To fit the above equation, the probability calculated is now based on assuming that the expected did happen (note the past tense), resulting in observing the frequency of occurrence. Quite often, *a posteriori* probabilities are used to make *a priori* predictions, and usually life is a combination of these: for example, how does the insurance company arrive at life expectancy; what is the probability one will live to be (say) 95? The predictions are based upon past experiences, which assume that not much has changed in terms of impinging variables.

In addition, there are two fundamental ways of thinking about probabilities that relate to numerical data:

(a) the probability that a person will belong to one group or another – basically nominal (for example, being pregnant or not) or ordinal (such as social class) – the person fits in one of the definable categories; or

(b) the probability distribution of a set of scores or values associated with a trait that one will have (for example, the probability distribution for time for gestation) – such data would consist of interval/ratio numbers.

In the first case, if one looks at a group of women with a common characteristic or combination of traits – such as age, educational background, etc. – there will be a finite probability of some of them being pregnant, based upon existing data. To describe their situation further, we draw upon the second definition. For those who are pregnant, a normal distribution of probabilities of the full gestation period, with a mean around nine months and a standard deviation of about two weeks then about 68% would have their babies between 8½ and 9½ months after conception. These two ways of considering probabilities are important to keep separate in mind, and will be pertinent later when deciding which statistical test is to be used to resolve a hypothesis.

This leads to category systems commonly used to classify data. For the discussion that follows, three types of data will be used:

(a) *Categorical, dichotomous data.* Where the number of occurrences of specific independent separate qualitative categories of events are recorded, such as the number of girls in a class or home, the number of people driving by in Fords.

(b) *Discrete data.* These result from frequencies of events for whole-number (integer) variables, for example a survey of homes to determine the number of occupants would result in frequencies of houses with 0, 1, 2, 3, . . . children. There would not be homes with 2.5 children. The categories under which data are collected are numerical and sequential, and the jumps are equal. Thus, in spite of parental perceptions, the difference between having one and two children is the same as the difference between having two and three children, at least in terms of possession and the person from the census bureau.

(c) *Continuous data.* Such data are numerical, but now any number or part of a number is possible. For example, the length of human pregnancies can be determined quite accurately (assuming you are willing to pry into people's personal lives a bit), and varies around a mean of nine months. The times are not discrete, since births are not restricted to one time of day. Heights, weights, income and age are considered to be continuous data. As seen earlier, to make any sense of this type, we tend to group the results into intervals, and, for all intents and purposes, reduce it to discrete data. Thus one could argue that the distinction between discrete and continuous data is an academic one, but it is useful for understanding some of the rationale provided for using probabilities as the basis for decision-making.

As will be seen in the rest of this section, this scheme overlaps with the earlier way of classifying variables as being represented by nominal, ordinal, interval or ratio data.

Nominal categorical data

Classifying a variable as *nominal* results from a decision about the type of data: if it is possible to decide whether a given datum fits in one category or another, such as gender, political affiliation, or even the numerals on the back of football players' jerseys. As a result, this type of data is sometimes referred to as dichotomous (two categories), classificatory, or categorical data (Chase, 1985; Kerlinger, 1986; Siegel and Castellan, 1988).

The consideration of probabilities of belonging to distinct categories is favoured by mathematicians as a basis for considering probability because of its simplicity. One can test models and theories with events that have well-established expected probabilities, such as tossing coins. Assuming that the coin used is perfectly balanced, there are only two possibilities when it is tossed: it will fall head up or tail up. For a given toss, there is a 50% chance it will come up heads and, assuming a fair toss, there is no better prediction of the outcome. This can be checked by actually tossing a coin repeatedly, seeing how many times it turns up heads and how many times it turns up tails. Moore (1991) related several stories of persons doing this large numbers of times – for example, around 1900, the statistician Karl Pearson tossed a coin 24 000 times to find 12 012 heads, 50.05% of the time.

Not surprisingly, considerable interest has been shown in probability by persons interested in various forms of gambling, and it has been suggested that this is one of the origins of the formal mathematics of probability theory (Howell, 1997; Moore, 1991). Consistent with history, we will also consider probabilities related to dice and cards.

Progressing from a two-sided coin to a single die and remembering that a cube has six sides, the probability that any side will be up is one in six, or 0.1667, or 16.67%. Again there is (for a fair and carefully balanced die) an equal probability of each side appearing up when thrown, noting that the single die would function equally well with six different letters of the alphabet. This does raise an interesting thought: does the die have a memory? In other words, having thrown a die and produced a 2, will it remember and choose another number next time just to be fair? No, each time the die is thrown, there is an equal probability that it will produce any one of the six numbers. So, you might ask, what is the probability before throwing at all, that in two successive throws, there will be two 2's? One in 36. Why? Well, how many combinations of pairs of throws could one have and how many ways can you get two 2's? For convenience, these are listed in Table 13.1. Remembering that die have no memory, any one of the 36 combinations in Table 13.1 is equally possible, thus the probability of any one of these combinations is equal, one in 36, or 0.02778, or 2.778%. What would be the probability of three 2's in a row?

TABLE 13.1					
All possible	1, 1	2, 1	3, 1	4, 1	5, 1	6, 1
outcomes of	1, 2	2, 2	3, 2	4, 2	5, 2	6, 2
successive throws of	1, 3	2, 3	3, 3	4, 3	5, 3	6, 3
a die	1, 4	2, 4	3, 4	4, 4	5, 4	6, 4
	1, 5	2, 5	3, 5	4, 5	5, 5	6, 5
	1, 6	2, 6	3, 6	4, 6	5, 6	6, 6

Well, rather than list all the possibilities, let us accept that, as with two tosses in the above example where it was one in $6 \times 6 = 36$, it is the product of the individual probabilities: one in $6 \times 6 \times 6 = 216$ possibilities, or 1/216 or 0.00463 or about 0.46%. In other words, not very likely! The trouble is that gamblers seem to think that once a number has appeared it is more (or less) likely to appear again. Placing additional bets after winning because they are on a 'run', or increasing a bet because they have lost several times in a row and it is about time to win, seems to imply an underlying pattern. The reality is that the outcome is truly a random event, *each time*.

Nominal or categorical probabilities depend on the potential of the situation. In the examples above, the probabilities of events occurring have been equal, but this could be changed. For example, consider the die with the following numerals on the six sides: 1, 2, 2, 3, 3, 3. What are the probabilities of a 1, a 2 and a 3 appearing? The answer is, of course, one in six, one in three, and one in two. This can be checked by adding all the probabilities together, which should result in 1: $1/6 + 1/3 + 1/2$.

The use of nominal data in the social sciences is more commonly associated with categories characteristic of subjects, but since most data are *a posteriori* in nature, one aim is to show their similarity with a model that is better understood, where outcomes are predictable. Thus it is possible to take a random sample of persons and show that the probability of getting half male and half female is not unlike the outcome from flipping a coin. With our understanding of human reproduction, therefore, it is worrying when a sample with specific characteristics (such as geographic location) produces, for example, many more boys than girls. Do Activity 13.1 now.

Activity 13.1

Carry out a brief survey in your class: find out how many males and females there are not only in the class, but also among the class members' siblings. How does this compare with the expectation that there should be half and half? To what would you attribute any difference?

Ordinal data

As defined earlier, *ordinal* data result from the categories of classification being based on rank ordering, which includes such variables as social class, essay grades (A, B, C, etc.), and finishing in a race (first, second, third). Siegel and Castellan (1988) note that some statistical tests assume that the actual ranking results from discrete categories that have an underlying continuous variable, but that '[f]requently the crudeness of our measuring devices obscures the underlying continuity that may exist'. It may also be the result of tradition and a bit of history: horse racing has been around longer than the clock. Besides, can you imagine the difficulty of trying to work out the odds not on the basis of 'win, place or show' (first, second or third), but on the running time? This would be much too complicated.

Ordinal data provide a rank order but no way of knowing just how much better or faster A is than B, and whether A is the same amount faster than B as B is faster than C. Whether this arises from degradation of data (we know the running time but cannot be bothered), or the nature of the measuring instrument (social class), ordinal data will be skipped over in the present discussion of probabilities, and subsumed under the next category.

Interval and ratio data: discrete values

Instead of one die thrown twice, let us consider two dice thrown simultaneously. Since these are independent of each other, the probabilities for pairs are the same as above, listed in Table 13.1. Also, instead of considering just the numerals on each as nominal categorical data (replaceable by letters of the alphabet), these will now assume values and they will be added, providing discrete data. Thus the outcome of throwing the dice will result in values between 2 and 12. We have all heard of the dice game 'craps' from the movies, and some of us may actually engage in such a recreational activity (shame!). But how many know what the chances of winning or loosing are? The castigation, therefore, is *not* for gambling (it is your money), but for playing without understanding the risk! The rules are simple: if the player 'rolls' a total point score of 7 or 11 on the first try, he wins. If he produces a 2, 3, or 12, he instantly loses. Any other number must be repeated in a subsequent roll *before* a combination that produces a 7 appears. If 7 appears first, he loses. In Activity 13.2, you will now work out some of the probabilities of winning and losing.

Activity 13.2

1 Using Table 13.1, what are the probabilities that the thrower will:
   (a) win on the first throw? (*Hint*: circle all those that add up to 7 or 11.)
   (b) lose on the first throw?
   (c) neither win nor lose on the first throw?
2 Assume an 8 (5 + 3) was thrown on the first roll. What are the probabilities the thrower will, on the very next roll:
   (a) get another 8 and win?
   (b) get a 7 and loose?
   (c) neither win nor lose, but get to throw again?
3 Assuming that you neither win nor lose on the first throw,
   (a) are some numbers (combinations) 'better' to have as a target than others? Why?
   (b) Would you rather throw the dice or bet against the thrower? Why?
   (c) Finally, having considered all of these chances of winning and losing, what do you think would be the likelihood that you will risk your beer money in a crap game?
Answers (rounded to two decimal places). 1(a) 0.22. (b) 0.11. (c) 0.67. 2(a) 0.14. (b) 0.17. (c) 0.69. 3(a) 6 or 8. (b) See discussion that follows.

One way to check the answers in Activity 13.2 is to add all the probabilities up for a given roll: the sum of all possible categories must add up to 1.00 since the dice must show something! Figure 13.1 shows a spreadsheet table providing the probabilities of numbers appearing when single die, a pair of dice and three dice are being thrown; the results are graphed in Figure 13.2. The probability of any side appearing on the throw of a single die is equal, 1/6, thus the bar chart in Figure 13.2(a) shows six bars of equal height. While these have been displayed in numerical order, remember that the data for a single die are really nominal (categorical), since the sides of the die could have the letters A, B, C, D, E and F. Even Table 13.1 is displaying raw data that are basically nominal since they would have the same meaning if each number pair were replaced by the corresponding sequential pairs of letters of the alphabet starting with A. If a probability distribution were plotted using these nominal data, it would result (assuming fair dice) in 36 equal-height bars each representing a 1 in 36 chance.

Now tradition has it that there are numerals on each die. It is only when the numerals take on a value that the data become quantitative with discrete values and begin to show something besides a flat distribution, such as that in Figure 13.2(b). Incidentally, you can check your answers for Activity 13.2 by referring to the spreadsheet distributions for two dice in Figure 13.1. Remember that for any one event (throw of the dice), all the probabilities must add up to one.

Does this mean that throwing dice could generate a normal distribution? Yes, it might, but since one should not assume every distribution is normal, a little effort is needed to produce the third set of data in Figure 13.1 for three dice, the results of $6 \times 6 \times 6 = 216$ possible combinations. The data are more

	A	B	C	D	E	F	G	H	I
1	Die Num	Expected	Probability	Dice Pair	Expected	Probability	3 Dice	Expected	Probability
2	1	1	0.1667	2	1	0.0278	3	1	0.0046
3	2	1	0.1667	3	2	0.0556	4	3	0.0139
4	3	1	0.1667	4	3	0.0833	5	6	0.0278
5	4	1	0.1667	5	4	0.1111	6	10	0.0463
6	5	1	0.1667	6	5	0.1389	7	15	0.0694
7	6	1	0.1667	7	6	0.1667	8	21	0.0972
8	Totals:	6	1.0000	8	5	0.1389	9	25	0.1157
9				9	4	0.1111	10	27	0.1250
10				10	3	0.0833	11	27	0.1250
11				11	2	0.0556	12	25	0.1157
12				12	1	0.0278	13	21	0.0972
13				Totals:	36	1.0000	14	15	0.0694
14							15	10	0.0463
15							16	6	0.0278
16							17	3	0.0139
17							18	1	0.0046
18							Totals:	216	1.0000

FIGURE 13.1
Probability distributions for sets of dice shown on a worksheet

(a)

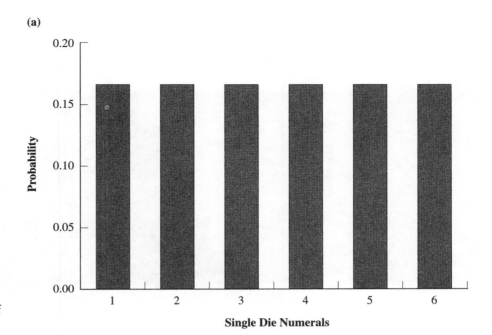

Single Die Numerals

FIGURE 13.2(a)
Graphical displays
of probability
distributions for
various numbers of
dice

(b)

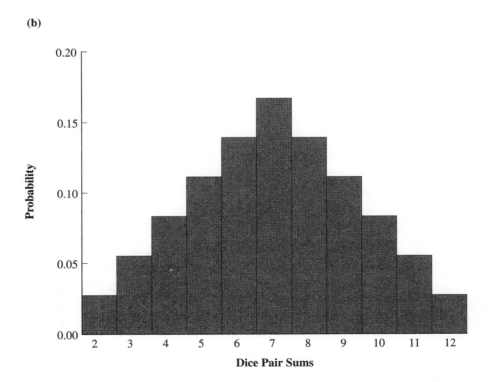

Dice Pair Sums

FIGURE 13.2(b)
Graphical displays
of probability
distributions for
various numbers of
dice

(c)

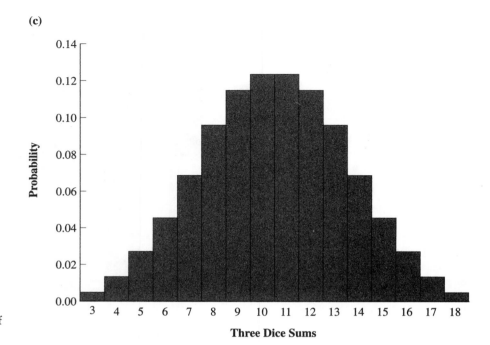

FIGURE 13.2(c)
Graphical displays
of probability
distributions for
various numbers of
dice

(d)

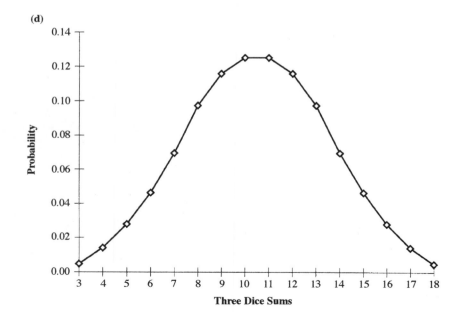

FIGURE 13.2(d)
Graphical displays
of probability
distributions for
various numbers of
dice

convincingly normal when displayed as a frequency polygon than drawn as a bar chart, as seen in Figures 13.2(c) and 13.2(d). Why do they appear normal when the one for two dice does not? Two dice generate 9 intervals while three dice generate 16. The more dice, the more data and the more intervals, and consequently the more normal the distribution will become. You could try it by generating the distribution for four dice, but there will be $6 \times 6 \times 6 \times 6 = 1296$ combinations to sort into 21 intervals!

To answer Question 3(b) in Activity 13.2, remember that in casinos, the house owns the dice and you throw, so there must be some advantage to them. The most likely outcome of the first throw is another throw (0.67), then you winning (0.22), and then the house winning (0.11). After that, it is all to the house's advantage, since the probability of your throwing a 7 is 0.17 and any other combination (4, 5, 6, 8, 9, or 10) is lower.

There are other events that would present distinct and equal probabilities, such as the chance of drawing a card of a given suit – for example, a heart – from a standard deck of 52 playing cards: one-quarter of the cards are of each suit. Thus the bar chart showing probabilities for drawing suits of cards would be four equal-height bars, one for each suit, representing 25% probability. Likewise, the bar chart for the probability of drawing any numbered card (A, 2, 3, . . . , Q, K) would be 13 bars of equal height, one for each number, representing a probability of 1 in 13 or 7.69%. Thus, the probability of drawing a 7 (any suit) from a *full* pack of cards is 1 in 13. The probability of drawing the 5♣ is 1 in 52. Drawing a random sample is a bit like this: one strives for the situation where there is equal probability of selecting any individual in the population.

Harder questions can now be asked. For example, why is drawing to an inside straight so risky in poker? Let us say that you are playing against one other player and are dealt

Thus you need to discard the 9♣ draw a 5♥ to make a straight flush (a sequence of numbers in one suit) to win, and your opponent has five unknown cards. Assuming that the 5♥ is in the remaining 42 cards in the deck (and not in your opponent's hand), you have a 1 in 42 chance of drawing this and only this card. If your opponent holds 5 non-sequential cards, say

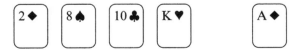

and only discards the A♦ and draws one new card from the 42 in the deck, then, like you, all he needs is a second card to go with any of the other four to make a pair, which could beat you if you fail to get your 5♥. What are the odds of his getting such a card? Any one of three suits of any one of four cards will do – in other words, any one of 12 cards out of the 42 remaining. Consequently, he has

12 times better chance of meeting his goal. In fact you have the same odds of getting a card to make a pair as he does, thus in the end, it could be a matter of who gets the highest pair if you did not get the 5♥. When we look at all the possibilities, it gets much more complicated. Consequently either one plays for fun, or, if you are to be a 'successful' gambler, you must set out all the probabilities and worry a lot. In other words, a professional gambler must be like the insurance company and know what the risks are in each case in order to make the best decisions.

Comparing social science data to discrete *a priori* probabilities is not too difficult, but much of the information collected will possibly take the form of continuous data. It is necessary to see if the same rules and principles apply.

Interval and ratio data: continuous values

Not all probabilities are just a matter of belonging to a group or not; there are situations where it is possible to identify quantifiable gradations of characteristics for which any fractional value is possible. Consider a randomly selected group of 12-year-olds. They could be separated into two dichotomous categorical groups: tall and short. Or they could be divided into three groups: tall, medium and short. We would then have to define what is meant by 'tall', 'medium' and 'short'; but regardless, this results in ordinal data. Consider an example, the raw data for a sample of 35 such 12-year-olds provided in the spreadsheet shown in Figure 13.3. For reference, the population distribution is shown in Figure 13.4(f).

First, let us define three groups: tall, greater than or equal to 1.51 metres; medium, between 1.36 and 1.50 m; and short, less than or equal to 1.35 m. The results of this are summarized in the frequency table on the upper right of Figure 13.3 and shown as the bar chart in Figure 13.4(a) (the procedure for generating this frequency table is the same as that described in Figures 12.1–12.3).

Now what happens if the number of groups increase and the gradations become smaller? Let us use 10 groups and number them 1 to 10; each will include persons in a range of 5 cm, starting with the bottom height of 1.21 m. This results in the frequency table shown second from the top right in Figure 13.3 and the bar chart, and frequency polygon in Figures 13.4(b) and 13.4(c).

This process can be carried one step further to generate a frequency table with 15 intervals, as shown on the lower right of Figure 13.3, the bar chart, in Figure 13.4(d) and the frequency polygon in Figure 13.4(e). Comparing the two frequency polygons to one showing the population in Figure 13.4(f), the graph for the 15 intervals, provides more convincing evidence of a normal distribution than the one for 10 intervals. This is comparable to the situation using discrete data for a pair of dice and three dice shown in Figure 13.1: the more intervals one has the better the evidence for deciding what the shape of the graph is. It also shows the link between discrete data and continuous data, reinforcing the view that what we really are doing when we establish intervals for our sample data is forcing continuous data to become discrete data.

There exists another conflict here. If one were to be very rigorous, all sets of data would be considered ordinal, because the individuals are lost in the intervals (whether 3 or 10 or 15). What is seen here is the fuzzy boundary between

	A	B	C	D	E	F	G	H
1	Name	Height	Group 1	Group 2	Group 3		Group 1	Frequency
2	John	1.21	S	1	1		Short	7
3	Henry	1.32	S	3	4		Medium	21
4	Jane	1.56	T	8	12		Tall	7
5	Fred	1.38	M	4	6		Total	35
6	Mary	1.50	M	6	10			
7	Albert	1.55	T	7	12		Group 2	Frequency
8	Sam	1.38	M	4	6		0	0
9	Ellen	1.26	S	2	2		1	1
10	Ted	1.44	M	5	8		2	3
11	Anne	1.34	S	3	5		3	3
12	Hilary	1.41	M	5	7		4	5
13	Barbara	1.53	T	7	11		5	7
14	Betty	1.30	S	2	4		6	8
15	Terry	1.27	S	2	3		7	3
16	Robert	1.59	T	8	13		8	2
17	Tom	1.51	T	7	11		9	2
18	James	1.40	M	4	7		10	1
19	Nancy	1.42	M	5	8		11	0
20	Peter	1.46	M	6	9		Total	35
21	David	1.65	T	10	15			
22	Melanie	1.46	M	6	9		Group 3	Frequency.
23	Sonya	1.38	M	4	6		0	0
24	Jacob	1.45	M	5	9		1	1
25	Sean	1.50	M	6	10		2	1
26	Shirley	1.48	M	6	10		3	1
27	Janet	1.61	T	9	14		4	2
28	Annette	1.47	M	6	9		5	2
29	Patsy	1.35	S	3	5		6	3
30	Ian	1.43	M	5	8		7	4
31	Sarah	1.41	M	5	7		8	5
32	Kevin	1.40	M	4	7		9	5
33	Carla	1.43	M	5	8		10	4
34	Barbara	1.49	M	6	10		11	2
35	Albert	1.46	M	6	9		12	2
36	Tracey	1.42	M	9	8		13	1
37	Total	35					14	1
38							15	1
39							16	0
40							Total	35

FIGURE 13.3
Three approaches to grouping one set of data

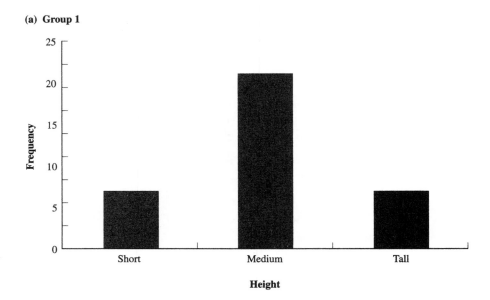

(a) Group 1

FIGURE 13.4(a)
Bar charts and
histograms for data
in Figure 13.3, and
the population (f)

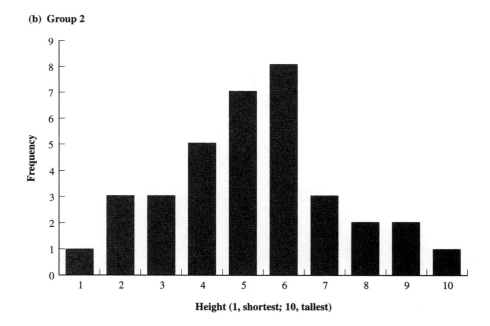

(b) Group 2

FIGURE 13.4(b)
Bar charts and
histograms for data
in Figure 13.3, and
the population (f)

ordinal (discrete with big intervals) data and interval/ratio (discrete with more but smaller intervals) data. As the intervals get smaller, we approach the situation where the individual scores reach the limits of accuracy of measurement. Each is in its own interval and no longer must be combined with near-neighbours (continuous data). When displayed as frequencies for the *y*-axis value, they become points on a graph that fit the ideal equation of the normal distribution that will be provided later. The more subjects there are, and conse-

(c) Group 2

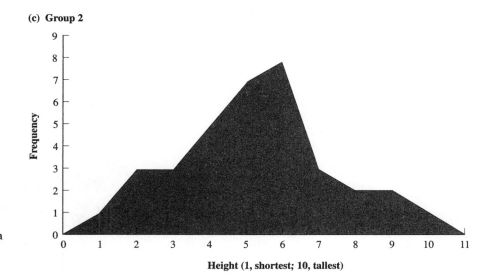

FIGURE 13.4(c)
Bar charts and
histograms for data
in Figure 13.3, and
the population (f)

(d) Group 3

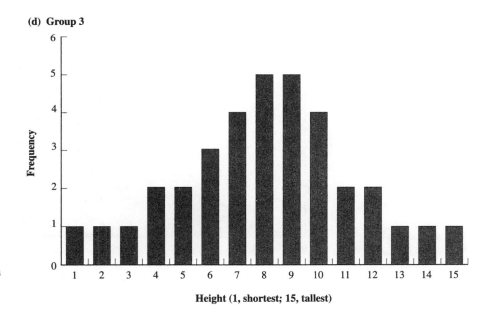

FIGURE 13.4(d)
Bar charts and
histograms for data
in Figure 13.3, and
the population (f)

quently the more intervals there can be, the closer the data come to fitting the curve, which raises the question: at what point do ordinal data become interval discrete data? This is not a trivial question, and the world of applied mathematics is filled with arguments about the appropriateness of approximations and mathematical models that 'almost' match reality. For practical purposes, we will fall back on the rule of thumb presented in Chapter 12, reinforced by the above example, that one needs between 10 and 20 (probably ideally 15) intervals to display sample interval/ratio data without distorting the shape.

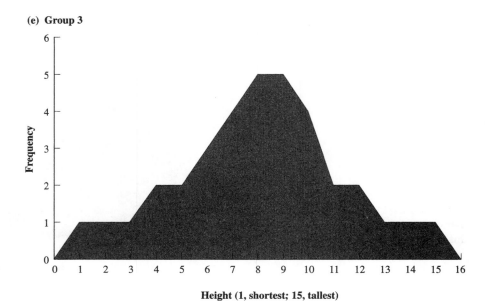

(e) Group 3

FIGURE 13.4(e)
Bar charts and histograms for data in Figure 13.3, and the population (f)

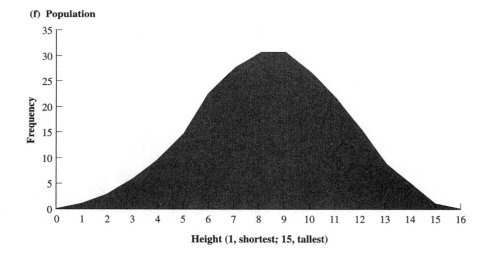

(f) Population

FIGURE 13.4(f)
Bar charts and histograms for data in Figure 13.3, and the population (f)

This requires a minimum sample size of 30 if the shape is going to be decipherable. On the other hand, Siegel and Castellan (1988) maintain that if one is to use the chi-square one-sample test, introduced in Chapter 5, for nominal or ordinal data, one needs at least five in each category for the expected frequencies and between one and four in no more than 20% of the categories. This would obviously place a restriction on the minimum sample size and/or how many categories are identified when using the test. From such criteria, we start to see the beginnings of the intersection of requirements for sampling, data type, and choice of statistical test. We will return to these issues when considering specific tests later.

It must not be assumed that by increasing the number of discrete increments of any ordinal data the result will automatically approach a normal distribution. What the shape of the resulting distribution of any set of data is will ultimately depend on what is being measured and whether or not in reality that *trait* as measured is normally distributed. This may be determined by examining the distribution of sample data to see how closely they conform to a Gaussian shape (the ideal mathematical model), which will be demonstrated in the next section. Rarely does one have the population data to confirm a shape; therefore the larger the number of samples that provide normally distributed data, the stronger the argument that the trait is normally distributed. Even then, this does not necessarily *prove* that the trait is normally distributed, only that the measuring instrument itself will generate a normal distribution of data. This reminds us of the old argument about intelligence: is it really normally distributed across the whole human population, or are only the *IQ test results* normally distributed? In other words, go back to the original question: what does an IQ test actually measure?

All the charts in Figure 13.4, except (f), are based on the one set of raw data in Figure 13.3 and illustrate probabilities of occurrences. If another random sample of 35 twelve-year-olds were taken, we might reasonably expect a similar spread of heights, depending on the number of height categories we use. Note that there is no way of predicting the height of individuals and that the only prediction that can be made is one related to the *relative probability* of an expected height (recall Figure 1.2). Thus, using the data provided, we would *expect* that the next member of a new sample to walk through the door would have about a 20% chance of being short, a 60% chance of being medium, and a 20% chance of being tall. At the other extreme, one could consider the population distribution and virtually determine the probability for any height by using Figure 13.4(f), with the total area underneath equal to 1.00 (that is, the next person will be there somewhere and have a particular height). This requires a deeper consideration of the normal distribution, which we will pursue in the next section; there are other distribution shapes, but these are not so well known and do not seem to apply to as wide a variety of human traits.

Before becoming too concerned about insurance and probabilities, it is worth emphasizing the difference between reality and our models of reality. We use statistics to *model* reality, since the processes employed provide convenient ways of predicting the probabilities of some future events; they do not *cause* events. Carry out Activity 13.3 before proceeding.

Activity 13.3

When measured, a wide variety of human physiological characteristics seem to produce normal distributions. In class, collect the following data and plot them on a histogram: the distance between the pupils of each person's eyes. What decisions must be made as part of the process? How large a group are you and do you think the results justify considering this trait to be normally distributed? Why or why not?

THE NORMAL DISTRIBUTION OF PROBABILITIES AND Z-SCORES

We will now progress to the situation where discrete or continuous data have been collected and we are confident that we are dealing with a normally distributed trait. Even though our sample data may not provide a perfectly normal curve, they are close enough to assure us we can proceed, and we have some independent evidence that the trait is intrinsically normally distributed. The next question is: what can the data reveal?

It is possible to glean a certain amount of information when provided with the mean and standard deviation for a distribution. Such information will assume a normal distribution for the population and therefore will use its intrinsic shape as the basis for discussing probabilities of occurrence of events. For example, IQ tests are actually designed to have a mean of 100 and a standard deviation of 15. Referring to Figure 12.21, one would expect that about 68% of all persons taking an IQ test will have an IQ of between 85 and 115. One way of indicating an individual's performance is to state his or her position on the horizontal axis in terms of the percentage of examinees performing below this position, the *percentile group*. In other words, if John did better than 67% of the other people taking an exam, then John was in the 67th percentile group. If you have an IQ score of 115, one standard deviation above the mean, then your score is better than 84% of all persons taking that examination (50% below the mean plus 34% up to the first standard deviation). This also means that visually, 84% of the area under the curve is to the left, as shown in Figure 13.5.

It is possible to identify where in a distribution an individual score lies when the mean and standard deviation are known. It is relatively easy to convert a raw score into a number of standard deviations, called a *z-score*, which can be found in a table to see exactly in what percentile group that score falls:

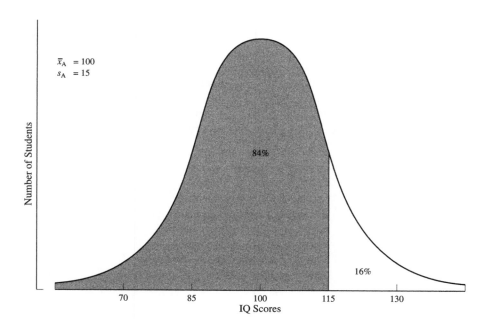

FIGURE 13.5
The 84th percentile group for IQ scores

$$z\text{-score} \equiv \frac{\text{raw score} - \text{mean}}{\text{standard deviation}}$$

Expressed in mathematical symbols,

$$z_i = \frac{x_i - \bar{x}}{S} \tag{13.1}$$

where x_i is the individual score for person i, $\bar{x}$ is the mean of the distribution of scores and S is the standard deviation of the distribution from equation (12.4). For example, an IQ score of 92 would be:

$$z = \frac{92 - 100}{15} = \frac{-8}{15} = -0.53$$

or 0.53 standard deviations *below* the mean. Looking this up in Table B.1 in the Appendix B, reveals that the score corresponds to a percentage score of 20.19% below the mean. Subtracting this from the 50% total below the mean results in this score being in the 29.81 percentile. In other words, this person scored higher than 29.81% of the persons taking this test and 70.19% did better than this person. This simply tells how an individual with this score performed with respect to all the others. What decisions are made based upon such results is the domain of the researchers or other persons using these data. Now try Activity 13.4, where you are asked to find equivalent z-scores for raw scores.

Activity 13.4

Find the percentile group for IQ scores of 110, 98 and 120, using Table B.1 in Appendix B.
Answers (rounded values): $z = 0.67$ thus 75%; $z = -0.13$ thus 45%; $z = 1.33$ thus 91%.

The IQ score distribution is based upon population data, whereas in many situations one would be finding z-scores based upon an estimate of the population mean and standard deviation provided by sample data. The assumption is that the distribution will not be greatly different if the sample is truly representative. As noted earlier, in most situations, population data will simply not be available anyway.

STATISTICAL INFERENCE

Now that we have established a background in probability and have seen what a normal distribution can reveal, what can a statistical test tell a researcher? It *cannot* prove that a change in one variable caused a change in another, but it can tell whether the difference in mean scores observed between those experiencing one treatment and the usual population that did not could have occurred as a random event. If the test says that it is unlikely that the difference occurred by chance alone, it is still up to the researcher to prove that the one variable was the only possible cause. Statistical tests are like the 'idiot lights' on the dashboard of your car: they only tell you that *something* has happened, but not exactly why. For example, if the oil light comes on, we assume something is not right. It could mean the engine is low on oil, the engine bearings have worn out, the oil pump has perished, the signal-sending device on the engine is broken, or a wire has shorted out to the light. The motorist obviously checks the oil level first, but if that is adequate, then it is time to call the mechanic, who will try to find the reason for the light being on. In the social sciences, the researcher should plan a study such that when the light comes on (the statistics indicate that something probably happened), then there is only one predicted, defensible link or potential cause. As seen in Chapters 1–7, designing a study to resolve such issues is not trivial.

The term *inferential statistics* refers to the process of using data collected from samples to make inferences about a larger population or populations. The research process introduces complications since:

- most research involves samples (which are *probably* representative);
- the traits usually result in distributions of scores, thus the group characteristics or tendencies are best described as measures of central tendency, such as means;
- the natural variability (with hopefully little error due to low reliability of the instrument) is best indicated by standard deviations.

Using this information, there is a desire to compare groups to determine relationships that will ultimately extend back to the original population(s). Thus any comparisons will require the nature of the distribution to be considered as well as the central tendency of the group. All of this depends heavily upon probability, and it is never possible to speak about relationships with absolute certainty, a fact that causes a distinct amount of mental anguish for most people who feel that events should have some degree of certainty.

There is a need to state the expected outcomes of inferential statistical research in terms of the *null hypothesis*: that there will *not* be any statistically significant difference. In other words, it is expected that any differences or changes or relationships found will be attributable to chance alone. Even if the null hypothesis is rejected, it only means that the difference or occurrence witnessed *probably* did not occur by chance alone. This probability level traditionally has been set at a critical level of 5%, which basically means that if a statistical test says that the probability of this event occurring by chance alone is less than 5%, then it probably did *not* occur as a random event. At this level, there is something probably influencing the event(s), or at least the event(s) has/have occurred as the result of some external influence other than natural random fluctuation. Exactly what this influence is, is not made clear by the statistical test. As noted before, it is still up to the researcher to justify that what he or she did or the variables identified, were the only possible source of influence.

This section will bring together earlier concepts from probability and combine them with research questions and hypotheses, and apply them to the cases where the variables are normally distributed. Before the actual choice of statistical tests can be considered, it is necessary to take a brief mathematical look at what underlies statistical inference and significance. This will be done graphically as much as possible, since most decisions are made on the basis of where the means of sets of data are in a normal distribution. It will provide a basis for later chapters that will continue the review of inferential statistics by considering a variety of specific tests which can be used as part of experimental, quasi-experimental and ex post facto designs to decide the acceptability of stated hypotheses.

Linking probability to statistical inference

Just as individual scores for a trait vary around a mean to form a normal distribution, the means of samples themselves will vary if a number of representative samples are taken from a population. Thus, if the frequencies of these means are plotted on a graph it is not surprising that we find yet another normal distribution. This *distribution of sampling means* will be quite useful in making inferences about the population. This was introduced earlier in Chapter 5 with reference to sampling error. Figure 13.6 shows all three types distributions for IQ scores: (a) an exemplar population distribution with parameters provided; (b) a single-sample distribution with its statistics; and (c) a distribution of sampling means.

The IQ score is used here simply because it is one distribution for which the population parameters are known, since the tests are designed to produce a mean of 100 and a standard deviation of 15. As will be seen later, this is the exception, since we rarely know what the population mean is. The situation where the population mean is known is used here primarily because it is the simplest and easiest to use to illustrate the principles behind statistical significance. Once this foundation is laid, all the others are basically variations on this ideal.

Remember that when the term *population* is used, it refers to a group sharing a limited set of common characteristics. In social sciences, these are often not

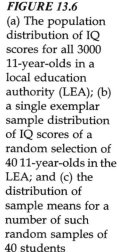

FIGURE 13.6
(a) The population distribution of IQ scores for all 3000 11-year-olds in a local education authority (LEA); (b) a single exemplar sample distribution of IQ scores of a random selection of 40 11-year-olds in the LEA; and (c) the distribution of sample means for a number of such random samples of 40 students

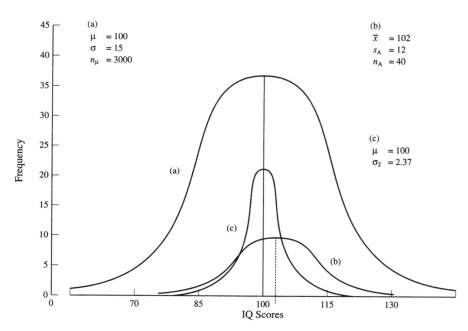

obvious to the casual observer and require some form of detailed observation, measurement or questioning of the subjects. So initially, the issue is whether or not a sample as a group is similar enough to the population for the trait or characteristic in question to be considered representative. A statistical test should be able to resolve what is enough.

The first thing to notice in Figure 13.6 is that the standard deviation (and width of the bell-shaped curve) for the distribution of sample means is relatively small compared to the standard deviations for the population and any single sample. Thus it is very unlikely that a truly representative sample will have a mean very different from that of the population. This fact is used in the most basic of inferential statistical tests, deciding whether a sample is to be considered part of a defined population, or part of some other population. To distinguish this standard deviation from that of a sample of the population, the standard deviation of the distribution of sampling means is used, which is known as the *standard error of the mean* (SEM). This will be designated by $\sigma_{\bar{x}}$ if it is calculated from the population parameter and is found by

$$\sigma_{\bar{x}} = \frac{\sigma}{\sqrt{n}} \qquad (13.2)$$

where σ is the population standard deviation (equation (12.2)), and n is the sample size. Obviously, the standard error of the mean depends on the sample size: for a very large sample size the standard error of the mean, and consequently the width of the curve for the sampling distribution, will be very small.

It is illustrative to consider an example: in order to carry out a study, a researcher selects a sample of 40 students from the LEA population of 11-year-olds described in Figure 13.6. They are given an IQ test: the group mean is found to be 106. Is this group typical? Let us first state this question as a null hypothesis:

H_0: There is no significant difference between the IQ of the sample group and that of the population.

In everyday English, we would say that we expect that the sample *is* representative of the population for this trait. Here the sample mean will be used to resolve the issue. To make the decision, it is necessary to zoom in on distribution (c) in Figure 13.6, the sample means, shown enlarged in Figure 13.7. The question now becomes one that is stated in terms of probabilities:

What is the probability that a sample with a mean of 106 would be randomly chosen from the population?

Recall that the area under the distribution for a range of scores represents the percentage of people having scores within that range (see Figure 12.21). In this situation, we are considering a distribution of sample means. Using Table B.1 in Appendix B, the number of standard deviations of sampling means (SEMs) can be used to determine what percentage of sample means one would expect below this group's. Here, a sample mean of 106 is 2.40 standard deviations (SEMs) above the population mean, as marked on Figure 13.7. From Table B.1, this

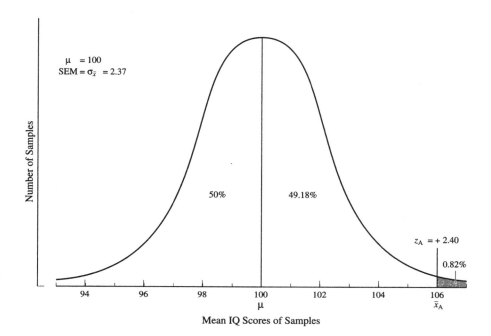

FIGURE 13.7
Distribution of
sampling means
(each sample size =
40), showing the
position of a single
sample mean, $\bar{x}_A$

tells us that 49.18% of the sample means would be expected to be between this
score and the population mean. Add to this the 50% below the population mean
and we find that 99.18% of the sample means should be below this, as shown in
Figure 13.7. To put it another way, the probability of this event or any one
beyond it occurring as a random event is $100\% - 99.18\% = 0.82\%$, or 0.82 of
a chance in 100 or 8.2 chances in 1000. Thus this sample mean does seem to
be a highly unlikely outcome for a random sample, but what is *unlikely
enough* for researchers?

Testing the null hypothesis

For normally distributed traits, those that produce sample means out in either
of the tails of a distribution of sampling means are highly unlikely. Social
science researchers commonly accept that events which occur less frequently
than 5% of the time are unlikely to have occurred by chance alone and consequently are considered statistically significant. To apply this to a normal distribution would mean that the 5% must be divided between the top and the
bottom tails of the distribution, with 2.5% for each (there are occasions when
all 5% would occur in one tail, but that is the exception, to be discussed
later). Consulting Table B.1 in Appendix B, the top 2.5% is from 47.5%
onward, or (interpolating) 1.96 standard deviations (SEMs) or more from the
mean. The two ranges of sample means that would be considered *statistically
significant*, and result in the rejection of the null hypothesis since they probably
did not occur as part of the natural chance variation in the means, are shown
shaded in Figure 13.8.

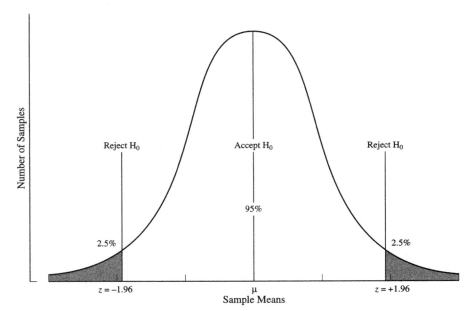

FIGURE 13.8
Normal distribution
of sample means
with 5% significance
levels, where μ is the
population mean

Thus for the situation above involving the mean IQ of the sample of 11-year-olds, the null hypothesis and the statement of expected outcomes need an addition:

. . . and, is the probability that the difference between the sample mean and the population mean would occur naturally more or less than 5% (the chosen level of significance that will be used as the test criteria)?

The cut-off point of 1.96 standard deviations (SEMs) would correspond to $1.96 \times 2.5 = 4.9$ points above or below the mean. Thus a sample mean IQ of less than 95.1 or greater than 104.9 would be considered significant and the sample not representative of the population. Therefore, in the example, the group with a mean IQ of 106 would be considered statistically significant and the group not typical, and it is unlikely that they are a representative sample of the whole population, for IQ.

Some researchers present results that are supported by an even lower level of probability, usually designated by the Greek letter α, to support their argument, such as 1% ($\alpha = 0.01$), 0.5% ($\alpha = 0.005$), or even 0.1% ($\alpha = 0.001$). Two problems arise with such a practice. First, for the test to be legitimate, one school of thought says the level of significance should be set *before* the test (or even the study) is conducted. Remember that the hypothesis is a statement of expectation, one that should include what will be expected in terms of statistical outcome. It is not fair to write the rules after the game has begun. Second, there is a feeling that a lower significance level than 5% ($p < 0.05$), such as 1% ($p < 0.01$), provides greater support for the results. In other words, if the probability of the relationship existing is only 1 in 100, that must be a stronger statement than if it were only 1 in 20. This supposition will be challenged in Chapter 14 when the concept of the power of a statistical test is introduced.

The one-sample comparison: z-test

The preceding arguments provide us with the most basic inferential statistical test related to testing for evidence of causality. In the situation where we know what the population parameters are, we can ask whether what has happened to a representative sample group has caused it to become different from the population. The above situation is just a matter of finding the z-score for the sample mean on the distribution of sampling means. This is expressed as

$$z = \frac{\bar{x} - \mu}{\sigma_{\bar{x}}} \tag{13.3}$$

where $\bar{x}$ is the mean of the sample, μ is the population mean and $\sigma_{\bar{x}}$ the standard error of the mean from equation (13.2).

For example, the research and design team of a computer manufacturer produced a keyboard that had a new pattern of keys, different from the usual QWERTY layout. The team maintained that, with a bit of practice, a typist could exceed the accepted mean speed of 60 words per minute (standard deviation of 5), and that this would be a good selling point for the product. In order to test the claim, a random sample of 40 typists in the company were asked to adopt the new keyboard and master it. After four weeks, they were tested and found to have a mean typing speed of 64 words per minute with no effect on their level of accuracy. The null hypothesis was that there would be no significant difference between the sample group and the population of typists. To be 'rigorous', the significance level was set at 0.01 (or 1%); thus from Table 1 (assuming 0.005 in each tail) the critical value was set to be, $z_{\text{crit}} = 2.58$. First, the standard error of the mean for the distribution of sampling means was calculated using equation (13.2):

$$\sigma_{\bar{x}} = \frac{5}{\sqrt{40}} = 0.79$$

This in turn was used in equation (13.4) for the z-test:

$$z = \frac{64 - 60}{0.79} = 5.06$$

This exceeded z_{crit}, so the company put the keyboard into production. With respect to this example, consider the questions in Activity 13.5.

The z-test can reveal differences between a sample and the population, but, as seen above, the underlying design is very weak and not always going to provide sufficient evidence to support a hypothesis. This is not the fault of the z-test, but one must consider carefully its appropriateness if statistical validity is to be maintained. As was seen in Chapter 5, it is of considerable value in testing whether a sample belongs to a population when trying to justify its representativeness with respect to a measurable trait. There one would hope for a non-significant result.

Activity 13.5

1 Which of the designs in Tables 3.3 and 3.4 does this study exemplify?
2 What sources of invalidity (see Figure 6.2 for a summary) can you identify?
3 What does this result tell us and what does it not tell us about the typing speeds of secretaries using the two different keyboard?
4 Devise a new null hypothesis and suggest an improved design to test the question of which keyboard potentially enhances typing speed.

Suggested answers: 1. It might be argued that this is a variation on design B3 (post-test/observation only), where the population is the control group. On the other hand, it could be argued that this is design A1 (one group post-test/ observation only), since the population is not a valid control (the typists are not new learners) in this case.
2. Sources: 1, 8 (since they all came from the company) and 10.
3. The trial group type faster than the population, but not why.
4. Design B2 (two equivalent groups of non-typists), but the nature of the training could be a factor; or B3 (two equivalent groups of typists), with control group set an equivalent task, such as improving speed.

One-sample comparison when σ is not known: t-test

There will be situations where the population standard deviation, σ, is not known and the only estimate will be that based upon the sample. This will lack the accuracy of a standard deviation found directly from population data. If an estimate of the standard error of the mean is subsequently calculated using these sample statistics, then it will be designated as and calculated from

$$s_{\bar{x}} = \frac{s_A}{\sqrt{n_A}} \tag{13.4}$$

where s_A is the estimate of the population standard deviation based upon the single sample group A, using equation (12.4), and n_A is the size of the sample group A.

In such situations, the test for significance must depend upon a slightly different sampling distribution from the normal one, the t-distribution, since the standard error of the mean is an estimate. The t-distribution, which will be discussed in detail in Chapter 15, is actually a family of distributions whose critical values vary with the size of the sample. The shapes of these distributions are very similar to the normal distribution, but tend to be shorter with tails that extend farther before approaching the axis. Consequently, when n_A is small (up to 30), the critical values can be considerably larger than those found by using the normal distribution. The formula for determining a t value for the difference between population and sample means is

$$t = \frac{\bar{x} - \mu}{s_{\bar{x}}} \qquad\qquad (13.5)$$

With samples over 30, the differences are small and the normal distribution critical values are used, since the standard deviations, s_A and $s_{\bar{x}}$, become more accurate estimates of the population ones, σ and $\sigma_{\bar{x}}$. For example, questioning a dozen patrons of the local pub on a randomly selected evening resulted in a mean consumption of 20 pints of beer in the previous week, with a standard deviation of 5.6. The landlord had been keeping a record of the number of patrons for that week and from his records knew how much beer he had sold. This suggested an average consumption of 15 pints per person for that week. Were the patrons sampled likely to be a representative sample? First, to find the population estimate of the standard deviation, we convert the standard deviation for the sample (compare equations (12.3) and (12.4)):

$$s = 5.6\sqrt{\frac{12}{11}} = 5.85$$

From this we can find the standard error of the mean:

$$s_{\bar{x}} = \frac{5.85}{\sqrt{12}} = 1.69$$

The t-test then produces the following ratio:

$$t = \frac{20 - 15}{1.69} = 2.96$$

Considering Table B.2 in Appendix B, we have $12 - 1 = 11$ degrees of freedom, therefore the critical value at the 5% level would be, $t_{crit} = 2.201$. Therefore, it is unlikely that this group was representative of patrons.

Confidence intervals

An alternative way of testing the null hypothesis is to describe the outcome as an interval in which we would expect to find the population mean based upon the sample mean. In other words, if the sample mean is one that would indicate the sample was representative of the population, then we should find that the population mean falls within the predicted range, referred to as the *confidence interval*. The outcome is expressed as a probability that the population value will appear in the interval, with the sample mean at the centre. In the typing speed example above, the sample mean was 64 words per minute and the population standard deviation resulted in a standard error of the mean of $\sigma_{\bar{x}} = 0.79$. To find the 99% confidence interval, we use the expression

$$\bar{x} \pm 2.58\sigma_{\hat{x}}$$

Inserting these values results in a 0.99 confidence interval

$$64 \pm 2.58 \times 0.79 = 64 \pm 2.04$$

Alternatively, we can express this as an expectation that the population mean as indicated by this sample should be between 61.96 and 66.04. Since the known population mean, $\mu = 60$, is outside the range, this provides an argument for rejecting the null hypothesis. In other words, one would suspect that the sample belongs to a different population with a mean in this range. Before going on to consider the ideal normal distribution in greater detail, try one more example in Activity 13.6.

Activity 13.6

It was suspected that the life expectancy of university academics who had been in psychology departments was greater than that of academics in general. The national pension plan was consulted and it was found that average life expectancy of male academics was 73 years. A random sample of 20 psychology academics revealed that their life expectancy was 75 years, with a standard deviation of 5 years.

1   State the null hypothesis for this situation.
2   What type of design is this: experimental, quasi-experimental or ex post facto? Why?
3   Carry out a test, using the 5% level for significance. Would you reject the null hypothesis?
4   Identify any sources of invalidity. Do they affect the validity of your conclusion?
5   Express this outcome as a 95% confidence interval.
6   The question arose whether the pension plan should raise the contribution rate for psychologists while they are employed since they will cost the plan more in the long run. How would you answer this? Defend your response.

Answers: 1. There is no difference in life expectancy for psychology academics from all other academics.
2. Ex post facto.
3. $S = 5$, therefore $s \cong 5.13$, $s_{\bar{x}} = 1.15$, $t = 1.74$, and since $t_{crit} = 2.093$, n.s. ($p > 0.05$), accept the null hypothesis.
4. Source 9: just being a psychologist is unlikely to have any effect by itself, though some aspect of the profession might.
5. $75 \pm 2.093 \times 1.18 = 75 \pm 2.47$.
6. No evidence to this effect, another sample could even have a mean less than 73.

THE IDEAL NORMAL DISTRIBUTION

There has been frequent reference to the 'ideal' normal distribution, the bell-shaped curve, in the text. To explore what this means, it is necessary to delve into some mathematics, which looks more frightening than it is. The equation for the normal distribution or Gaussian curve is:

$$y(x) = \frac{1}{\sigma\sqrt{2\pi}} e^{-\frac{1}{2}\left[\frac{x-\mu}{\sigma}\right]^2} \tag{13.6}$$

where $y(x)$ is the height of the curve, a function of x, x is the independent variable as plotted on the horizontal axis, μ is the mean of the distribution, σ is the standard deviation of the distribution, e is the constant, 2.71828 . . . and π is the constant, 3.14159 . . . .

Fortunately, Excel has a function that allows the calculation of all the points $y(x)$ for a given value of x if we know σ and μ for the distribution, so it will be easy to generate 'ideal' normal distributions. But such a complex equation requires some digesting if one is going to be able to see how it could produce a bell-shaped curve. Recalling that a minus sign in the exponent means that that part is really in the denominator, allows equation (13.6) to be rewritten as follows:

$$y(x) = \frac{1}{\sigma\sqrt{2\pi}\, e^{\frac{1}{2}\left[\frac{x-\mu}{\sigma}\right]^2}}$$

From this it is a little easier to see that how a bell shape is generated. First note that the only variable in the equation that changes is x; everything else remains constant. Thus, as x gets farther away from the mean, μ, the difference gets larger, making the exponent larger, which makes the denominator larger. Consequently the overall value of $y(x)$ becomes smaller, creeping ever closer to the x-axis, but never quite touching. As x gets closer to the mean, the difference gets smaller, and, when $x = \mu$, then the exponent of e is zero: any number raised to the power zero equal 1.00. Thus, when $x = \mu$,

$$y(x) = \frac{1}{\sigma\sqrt{2\pi}\, e^0} = \frac{1}{\sigma\sqrt{2\pi}}$$

which is the maximum height of the curve. This maximum can be changed so that the curve generated is equivalent to the original data and the two graphs can be superimposed on each other to see how close the raw data are to a true normal distribution. To accomplish this, equation (13.6) requires small modifications substituting statistics for parameters and an adjustment for the maximum, as follows:

$$y'(x) = \frac{\Delta x n}{S\sqrt{2\pi}}\, e^{-\frac{1}{2}\left[\frac{x-\bar{x}}{S}\right]^2} \tag{13.7}$$

where n is the number of subjects in the sample and Δx is the interval width in the frequency distribution.

Why does this work? Recall that the area under a frequency polygon is the number of persons in the sample. Therefore, by multiplying the general bell-shaped curve inside the square brackets by a term that is the area for the ideal maximum interval, the total area under the curve will still add up to be equal to the sample size. Consequently, it is possible, knowing the mean and standard deviation, to set up a table of x values and calculate $y(x)$ values, to plot them against each other on a graph.

To set up a data table calculating each point by hand would be difficult, but on a spreadsheet it is relatively easy. In Activity 13.7, this is what is done, using the Excel function for equation (13.5) to allow you to generate a curve that corresponds to any mean, standard deviation, sample size and interval width in real data that you might collect.

Activity 13.7

1 Set up a worksheet as described in Figure 13.9 and enter data from Figure 12.5 as directed to produce the graphs shown at the bottom of Figure 13.9.

2 Now change the mean, standard deviation and interval width to those for the data below: $\bar{x} = 78.63$, $S = 10.25$. Plot the two graphs: raw data frequency polygon and ideal. These will be discussed in the next activity:

Midpoint	Frequency	Midpoint	Frequency
44	0	72	6
48	1	76	8
52	1	80	10
56	2	84	15
60	2	88	12
64	3	92	6
68	4	96	0

Remember, you may have to extend the axis beyond the range given to obtain a good overlay of graphs.

WHAT IS *NOT* NORMAL?

The set of numbers in Question 2 of Activity 13.7 produced a distinctively lop-sided distribution, one that has a long tail on the left and virtually no tail on the right, which should be recognized as a negatively skewed distribution. If the tail had been on the other side (see Figure 12.20), then it would have been positively skewed. For such non-normal distributions as these, there are more appropriate measures of central tendency and variability, since these are not symmetrical and the mean no longer truly provides us with the dividing line between the upper and lower halves of the group.

It is often *assumed* that most human traits and characteristics are normally distributed, so of what relevance is a discussion on skewed distributions? Take, for example, salaries in organizations: a few very large ones can distort the mean salary paid (but not the median) and provide a false indicator of what is 'typical'. For example, the following 16 salaries (in pounds sterling) could be for a small school, organization, or section of an organization:

12 000	14 500	18 000	22 000
12 500	15 000	19 000	26 000
14 000	16 000	20 000	30 000
14 000	16 000	20 000	35 000

	A	B	C
1	mean =	50	
2	s..d. =	12.84	
3	n =	30	
4	int. width =	5	
5			
6		Fig. 12.5	Ideal
7	x	Freq	y(x)
8	13.0		0.07
9	18.0	0	0.21
10	23.0	1	0.51
11	28.0	1	1.07
12	33.0	2	1.94
13	38.0	3	3.01
14	43.0	4	4.02
15	48.0	4	4.60
16	53.0	5	4.54
17	58.0	4	3.84
18	63.0	2	2.79
19	68.0	2	1.74
20	73.0	1	0.94
21	78.0	1	0.43
22	83.0	0	0.17
23	88.0		0.06
24	Total =	30.0	29.95

The aim is to generate an ideal normal curve for a set of data, given only values for the mean, standard deviation, the number of subjects and the interval width. It will then be possible to overlay this with the curve generated by the original raw data to see how they compare. The data from Figure 12.5 will be used to illustrate the procedure.

(a) Set up the first four rows of the table as shown. Then starting with row **8**, enter the interval midpoints under x, beginning at least one if not two below the last one having a frequency greater than 0 in the original data. For Figure 12.5, the lowest occupied interval midpoint was 23, so this table begins at 13 and goes down to two below the last occupied interval, here to 88.

(b) In cell **C8**, enter the following, which is equation (13.3) using cell designations for the constants (those with **B$**) and the x variables in **A**:
= (int.width)* (n)* NORMDIST(x, mean, s.d., 0)
=B$4*B$3*NORMDIST(A8.B$1.B$2,0)

(c) Use **Copy** to put this in cells below. Note that each time, the term **A8** changes by 1 to **A9**, **A10**, etc. The others have **$** so do not change when copied.

(d) Now type in the raw data from Figure 12.5.

(e) Next use the ChartWizard to plot line graphs of the data on one graph as an **XY (Scatter)**. If you choose [x] Smoothed line for the ideal graph it will look better, and if you choose a dashed line it is more easily distinguished as shown below. How close are they?

(f) Use =**SUM** in cells **B24** and **C24** to total the frequencies. Why are they so different?

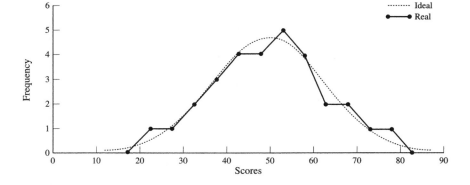

FIGURE 13.9
Comparing raw data and the assumed ideal normal distribution

The mean is easily found to be £19 000, and just counting up the line, the median is between £16 000 and £18 000, or simply £17 000. No matter the situation, such distributions usually do not have tails on the left, but tend to have them on the right. To spoil the fun, the accountant is only worried about the total cost of wages, but a researcher might be wanting to compare organizational salaries. Which measure of central tendency should be used? The choice is primarily one of what is to be done with the results, and may depend on what questions are to be answered. It should be noted, though, that the longer the tail on a skewed distribution, the greater the difference will be between the mean and the median. From a measurement point of view, most salary distributions do tend to be positively skewed, but there can be occasions when they appear normal. For example, a survey across socio-economic groups might result in a distorted, more normally appearing distribution because of 'volunteers', with low-income subjects preferring not to participate. This is a good example of why there is an emphasis on ensuring that the underlying population distribution of the trait or characteristic is truly normal and that the sample data distribution is not just a result of how the data were collected. Let us consider another example in Activity 13.8.

Activity 13.8

1   Figure 13.10 shows what you should have as a result of Activity 13.7, Question 2. It also takes you through the process of using frequency data to determine mean, standard deviation, median and quartiles of a distribution. This is a useful tool for situations where you wish to check someone else's graphs or frequency tables. Figure 13.11 shows the graph, with mean and median indicated.
2   Does the difference between the mean and median seem to be a good indicator of the skewness seen in the graph?

In the data in Activity 13.8, a few extreme scores pulled the mean to the left. This has even been exaggerated by the score range which had a ceiling of 100 and therefore there was no possibility of scores to balance them. There may be other data-gathering situations that are skewed in this way because of lower or upper limits to the scale. This is one reason why, when planning a measuring instrument, if you want a normal distribution, you must ensure that the score range can extend equally on both sides of the mean. One way of achieving this is to choose items that have a high discrimination index, D, on achievement tests (see Chapter 11); this automatically prevents skewed distributions because of bunching of scores at one extreme or another.

Quantifying skewness

The difference between the values for the mean and median in Figure 13.10 (78.63 and 81.20, respectively) does not seem to warn one of the visual difference in Figure 13.11 between the two curves: the real skewed and the ideal normal. How skewed is too skewed? At what point does the degree of skewness become so large as to invalidate the use of certain parametric statistical tests? This is not an easily answered question, and most tests that will be used in later chapters are more concerned with the homogeneity of the variances of the sample groups being compared. Academic journals do not tend to allow graphs of data such as the ones presented above (though they are instructive

	A	B	C
1	mean =	78.63	
2	s..d. =	10.25	
3	$n =$	70	
4	int. width =	4	
5		Activity 13.5	
6	x_i	$freq_i$	$y(x)$
7	40.0		0.01
8	44.0	0.0	0.04
9	48.0	1.0	0.13
10	52.0	1.0	0.37
11	56.0	2.0	0.95
12	60.0	2.0	2.09
13	64.0	3.0	3.94
14	68.0	4.0	6.36
15	72.0	6.0	8.84
16	76.0	8.0	10.55
17	80.0	10.0	10.80
18	84.0	15.0	9.50
19	88.0	12.0	7.18
20	92.0	6.0	4.65
21	96.0	0.0	2.59
22	100.0	0.0	1.24
23	104.0		0.51
24	108.0		0.18
25	Total =	70.0	69.93
26			
27	$\Sigma freq*x =$	5504	
28	$\Sigma freq*x^2 =$	440128	
29	mean =	78.63	
30	std.dev. =	10.25	
31	median =	81.20	

=78+(B3/2–SUM(B8:B16))*B4/B17

=SQRT((B28–B27^2/B3)/B3)

=B27/B3

Given a frequency table, find descriptive statistics

While considering the shape of a distribution, this activity will also provide a way of finding descriptive statistics from a frequency table when the raw data are not available.

(a) Assume that cells **B1** and **B2** are empty: how could these values be determined? There are computational formulae (for derivations, see, for example, Chase, 1985) that facilitate their calculation in a worksheet. The *mean* is found by adding all the products of the frequencies and the interval midpoints:

$$\bar{x} = \frac{\sum_{j=1}^{m} freq_j * x_j}{n} \quad \text{for } m \text{ intervals} \quad (13.8)$$

The *standard deviation* is found using the formula:

$$S = \sqrt{\frac{\sum_{j=1}^{m} freq_j * x_j^2 - \frac{1}{n}\left(\sum_{j=1}^{m} freq_j * x_j\right)^2}{n}}$$

$$(13.9)$$

(b) These are based on two summations for which there are Excel equivalents:

$$\sum_{j=1}^{m} freq_j * x_j \text{ in this example is}$$

=SUMPRODUCT(B8:B21,A8:A21)

$$\sum_{j=1}^{m} freq_j * x_j^2 \text{ here is (note how } x^2 \text{ is achieved)}$$

=SUMPRODUCT(B8:B21,A8:A21,A8:A21)

(c) The calculations are now quite easy, using the contents of the cells as indicated for cells **B29** and **B30**.

(d) The median is found from frequency data by

$$median = l + \frac{(n/2 - f_b)\Delta x}{f_w} \quad (13.10)$$

where l is the lower real limit of the interval containing the median, 78.0; f_b is the sum of the frequencies below the interval containing the median, **SUM(B8:B16)**; and f_w is the frequency of the interval containing the median **B17**. Thus a slightly messy equation appears in cell **B31**.

(e) These are shown on the graph in Figure 13.11.

FIGURE 13.10
Finding descriptive statistics from frequency data

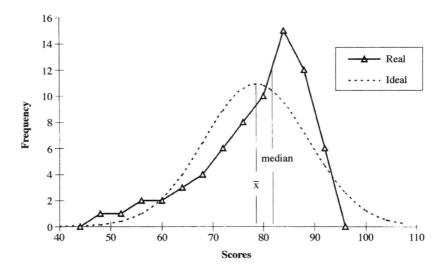

FIGURE 13.11
Graphs for data in
Figure 13.10: the
mean implies the
ideal curve

and commonly found in reports, dissertations and theses). Therefore it is left to
the reader and researcher to consider this issue. A better indication of skewness
than just comparing the mean and median is available using a formula, for
example (Blalock, 1979):

$$\text{Skewness} = \frac{3(\bar{x} - M)}{S} \tag{13.11}$$

where $\bar{x}$ is the mean, M is the median and $S =$ the standard deviation. For
example, for the distribution in Figure 13.11,

$$\text{Skewness} = \frac{3(78.63 - 81.20)}{10.25} = -0.75$$

At a glance, it is obvious that a normal distribution will have skewness of 0.0,
and that the larger the difference with respect to the standard deviation, the
larger the index. A negatively skewed distribution will have negative values
and a long tail to the left, while a positively skewed distribution will have positive values and a long tail to the right. This index leaves us none the wiser about
what is acceptable skewness. The best that can be said is that a measuring instrument which produces a skewed distribution of scores for a trait that is known to
be normally distributed for a representative sample may be faulty. On the other
hand, if the distribution of the trait is not fully understood, then this may be an
indication of non-normality.

Another coefficient is also used, particularly in computer packages, including
Excel. Its origins are complex (see, for example, Glass and Hopkins, 1996) and
its range is not the same as that for equation (13.11), nor is it any easier to interpret. In Excel, the **=SKEW** function uses the original data and not the distribution statistics:

$$\text{skew} = \frac{n}{(n-1)(n-2)} \sum \left(\frac{x_i - \bar{x}}{s} \right)^3 \tag{13.12}$$

We will return to this characteristic of distributions later when considering the choice of statistical tests since many tests assume a normal distribution of scores, not only in the samples being tested but also in the population trait.

Homogeneity of variance

There will be occasions later when there will be tests involving more than one group and both will have traits that are normally distributed. Unfortunately, even this is sometimes not enough to satisfy the requirements for justifying the use of some statistical tests. There are tests that assume that while the means of the two (or more) groups under consideration will differ, the variances (and standard deviations) are the same. In this situation, there are tests to determine the limits of acceptability of non-equality and they vary somewhat, so these will be covered with the appropriate tests.

SUMMARY

In order to lay the foundations for decision-making using statistical tests, some basic concepts in probability were provided. This was followed by an introduction to statistical inference, presenting the one-sample z-test as the most basic parametric test. As part of considering the underlying assumptions of such tests that assume a normal distribution, its characteristics were explored. As part of this process, a method for generating a graph of the ideal normal distribution (using Excel) for a given mean, standard deviation and sample size was presented.

Though the role of statistical inference in resolving hypotheses has been defined, there are still some unanswered questions. Before considering a greater variety of tests that apply to more complex designs, we will consider one aspect of statistical tests that provides a basis for deciding on such issues as the choice of level for statistical inference and size of samples needed: the power of a statistical test.

POWER, ERRORS AND CHOOSING α 14

It was suggested in the previous chapter that it is not necessarily beneficial to the argument for causality to report a probability for statistical significance smaller than 5% (or $p < 0.05$). Intuitively, it may seem that a level of significance of $p < 0.01$ is a stronger argument than $p < 0.05$, and that $p < 0.001$ is even better. Unfortunately, intuition is not necessarily the best way of making such a choice in this case, and the process requires some consideration of the alternatives to rejecting the null hypothesis. Keep reminding yourself that statistical tests do not make decisions for you, they simply provide support for a decision. Ultimately, the level chosen will have to be based upon the consequences of making 'right' or 'wrong' decisions based on the data, which will depend on the nature of the research. If you are looking for variables, you may set one level, but if, on the basis of the outcomes, decisions will be made that affect people's lives, then a different level might be more appropriate.

To make the most appropriate choice for a study requires examining in greater depth the nature of decision-making based upon statistical tests. To achieve this in as clear and straightforward manner as possible, you will set up a simulation that will allow you to change values and see the consequences. Again, many of the outcomes will be probabilities, but these will be expressed as graphs, providing a visual representation of a mathematical situation.

It is also worth reminding ourselves that there will always be a difference between statistical significance and academic or practical significance. Finding a difference that is not attributable to chance may be interesting, but the nature of the variables and the size of the difference may be more important with respect to the value of the outcome.

STATISTICAL INFERENCE: A DEEPER LOOK

In the previous chapter, it was noted that researchers commonly use different probability limits when carrying out statistical tests. Specified by the Greek letter alpha, α, each has a corresponding limit on a normal distribution of sampling means (like Figure 13.8). The number of standard deviations from the mean, expressed in z-scores as seen in Table 14.1, corresponds to the probability chosen as being indicative of 'not likely to have happened by chance alone'. Thus, as the level of significance becomes more stringent, the z-score cut-off point moves farther out into the tails of the distribution.

As a first step to deciding which of the levels to choose for a study, let us see how the decision on statistical significance is made by generating a graph of the possible sampling means for the population. Using Excel, this is not difficult and allows us to investigate the consequences of changing such variables as the sample mean or the size of the sample. To achieve this an example will be used and a series of worksheets and graphs will be devised in stages.

For this and subsequent activities, we will use the following problem as an example. All 300 final-year students in a school have taken a test on mathematical reasoning and for all of these final-year students in that school a population mean of $\mu_0 = 50$ is found, with a standard deviation of $\sigma = 12$. Now a teacher has a group of 30 students who she feels are, as she puts it, 'not normal, but exceptional'. When their scores on the test are extracted, their mean is calculated: $\bar{x}_A = 54$, and fortuitously, their standard deviation is the same as the population: $S_A = 12$. It was agreed to test this supposition and consequently, the null hypothesis was stated as:

H_0: This sample group A is not significantly different from the population for the trait, mathematical reasoning.

To investigate the basis for a statistical decision in detail, we will set up a simulation on a spreadsheet that will allow us to change variables and to investigate this and other possible classes. Carry out Activity 14.1 now.

Activity 14.1

1   Follow the directions in Figure 14.1 to generate an ideal graph based on the population mean and standard deviation, and an ideal graph based on the sample mean and standard deviation. This should produce the two graphs together like the ones in Figure 14.2. Do this now before proceeding.
2   To see how the simulation works so far, go to cell **C3** and change the value for the mean for sample A to 57, then look at the graphs. What has changed?

TABLE 14.1
Probability levels, α, and corresponding z-scores for a normal distribution of sampling means (two-tailed)

α	$z(\alpha)$
0.10	± 1.64
0.05	± 1.96
0.02	± 2.33
0.01	± 2.58
0.001	± 3.29

	A	B	C	D
1		Data		
2		Population	Sample A	
3	mean =	50	54	
4	s.d. =	12	12	
5	n =	300	30	
6	int. width =	5	5	
7				
8		y(x)	y(x)	
9	x	Ideal pop.	Ideal samp.	
10	8.0	0.11	0.00	
11	13.0	0.43	0.01	
12	18.0	1.42	0.06	
13	23.0	3.97	0.18	
14	28.0	9.29	0.48	
15	33.0	18.28	1.08	
16	38.0	30.25	2.05	
17	43.0	42.07	3.28	
18	48.0	49.18	4.40	
19	53.0	48.33	4.97	
20	58.0	39.93	4.72	
21	63.0	27.73	3.76	
22	68.0	16.19	2.52	
23	73.0	7.95	1.42	
24	78.0	3.28	0.67	
25	83.0	1.14	0.27	
26	88.0	0.33	0.09	
27	93.0	0.08	0.03	
28	50.0	0		Population
29	50.0	50		mean
30	54.0		0	Sample
31	54.0		5	mean
32	Total =	299.95	30.0	

Stage 1: Setting up the simulation

(a) Type in the data and headings for rows **1** to **8** as shown, and the interval midpoints in column **A**. The range has been chosen on the rule of thumb that you need a range of roughly +3.5 standard deviations to display a normal curve: ±3.5 × 12 = ±42, so 50 − 42 = 8, 50 + 42 = 92. Note

=C$6*C$5*NORMDIST(A10,C$3,C$4,0)

=B$6*B$5*NORMDIST(A10,B$3,B$4,0)

92 − 8 = 84 conveniently divided by 5 gives 18 intervals, 9 either side of the mean. Also add the references to the means at the end as these will put lines for the means on the graphs.

(b) In the same way as was done in Figure 13.9, insert the Excel **NORMDIST** function with additions in cells **B10** and **C10** (you can use the Function Wizard, but go back and add the needed **$**) then **Copy** them down the column.

(c) The numbers in cells **A28:C31** will provide automatic markers on the graph for the means, even if the means change.

(d) Use the **=SUM** function in Row 32 to check the entries for Rows 10 to 27.

=C3

=B3

=SUM(C10:C27)

=SUM(B10:B27)

FIGURE 14.1
The first stage in setting up the example for the spreadsheet simulation

As might be suspected, though Figure 14.2 does present a visual representation of the two distributions, it does not provide us with sufficient information to decide whether the sample is representative. In fact, the sample does not look much different from the population, except smaller. As was seen in the previous chapter, it is necessary to consider the position of the mean on the *distribution of*

Stage 2: Drawing the graph

1   Use the ChartWizard (see Appendix A for assistance) to plot the two distributions together on the same graph,

    Step 1   Use the **Range A9:C31**, including column headings.
    Step 2   Choose **XY (Scatter)** this time.
    Step 3   Choose format **2**.
    Step 4   Set the following:

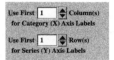

    Step 5   Label the axes as shown in Figure 14.2.

2   Keep the legend and it will use the column headings automatically. By double-clicking on each curve, you can adjust the types of lines and remove data point markers, if you wish.

You should now have a table like the one in Figure 14.1 and the graphs shown below.

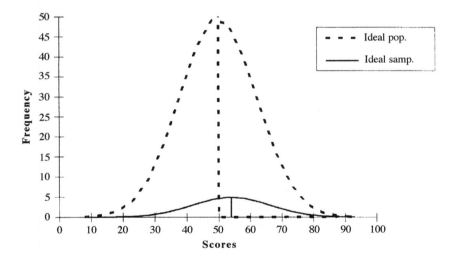

FIGURE 14.2
Simulation curve for the worksheet in Figure 14.1

sampling means to see if this sample is significantly different from the set of possible sample classes of 30 students. Thus it is necessary to generate one of these for our data.

This will involve generating a graph equivalent to Figure 13.5, only here the mean will be the population mean, $\mu_0 = 50$, and the distribution of sampling means will have a standard deviation equal to the standard error of the mean (SEM), using equation (13.2):

$$\sigma_{\bar{x}} = \frac{\sigma}{\sqrt{n}} \qquad (14.1)$$

Here, the population standard deviation is $\sigma = 12$, and the samples will have $n = 30$. With this graph, it will be possible to determine whether the group is statistically significantly different from the population. To do this, carry out Activity 14.2.

Activity 14.2 Stage 3: Setting up the simulation

Follow the directions for setting up the simulation below. You will generate a worksheet like that in Figure 14.3, which in turn will be used to generate an ideal distribution of sampling means. You should obtain a graph like that in Figure 14.4, then decide whether or not the group is statistically significantly different from the population. To generate a *distribution of sampling means*, new values and a frequency table must be added, as shown on the worksheet in Figure 14.3. To do this:

1 Set up the area **E1:I7** as shown, including using equation (14.1) for the SEM, as shown.
2 On the new graph, we will want the cut-off points for α shown, so enter the formulae for the intervals in **E10:E13** and the corresponding values in column **H**. Also add the reference to the value for the sample mean in **E14:E15** and the values in column **I**. By using references to the shaded boxes, when these are changed the graph will change.
3 To obtain a reasonable graph, it is again advisable to use about ± 3.5 standard deviations for the range, here about ± 7.7 (**F7**), so 50 ± 8 is from 42 to 58.
4 Generate an ideal normal distribution using the **NORMDIST** function, as shown, **Copy**ing down the column.

Save this as there is one column to add to complete the full simulation.
The worksheet is now ready for generating the graph. Go to Figure 14.4 for instructions to do this. We will change the numbers in the four shaded cells later to see the effect on the graphs. After you have a graph generated, then proceed as follows:

5 In order further to illustrate the simulation's functionality, go to cell **C3** again and change the mean for sample A, say to 57 as suggested in Activity 14.1, Question 2, then check to see what has happened to the graph. Try changing the $z(\alpha)$ to that for $\alpha = 0.001$. What happens to the graph?

As can be seen, the mean for group A, $\bar{x}_A = 54$, is within the range of means that one would expect 95% of the time, thus the null hypothesis was not rejected and the group was deemed to be part of the population. Having set this up, let us

Annotations (cell formulas):
- I4: `=−NORMSINV(13/12)`
- F3: `=B3`
- G3: `=C3`
- F4: `=B4/SQRT(C5)` — Which is equation (14..1)
- F7: `=3.5*F4`
- E10: `=F3-I4*F4`
- E12: `=F3+I4*F4`
- E14: `=C3`
- F16: `=F$6*F$5*NORMDIST(E16,F$3,F$4,0)` and **Copy** down the column

	A	B	C	D	E	F	G	H	I
1		Data			Sampling	Means			
2		Population	Sample A			Population	Sample A	Tails =	2
3	mean =	50	54		mean =	50	54	α =	0.05
4	s.d. =	12	12		SEM =	2.19		z(α) =	1.96
5	n =	300	30		samples =	100			
6	int. width =	5	5		int. width	1			
7					3.5*SEM =	7.7			
8		y(x)	y(x)		Sample				
9	x	Ideal pop.	Ideal samp.		Means	Expected	Sample A	Alpha	
10	8.0	0.11	0.00		45.7			6	mean −
11	13.0	0.43	0.01		45.7			0	z(α)*SEM
12	18.0	1.42	0.06		54.3			0	mean +
13	23.0	3.97	0.18		54.3			6	z(α)*SEM
14	28.0	9.29	0.48		54		0		Sample
15	33.0	18.28	1.08		54			10	mean
16	38.0	30.25	2.05		42	0.02			
17	43.0	42.07	3.28		43	0.11			
18	48.0	49.18	4.40		44	0.43			
19	53.0	48.33	4.97		45	1.35			
20	58.0	39.93	4.72		46	3.44			
21	63.0	27.73	3.76		47	7.13			
22	68.0	16.19	2.52		48	12.00			
23	73.0	7.95	1.42		49	16.41			
24	78.0	3.28	0.67		50	18.21			
25	83.0	1.14	0.27		51	16.41			
26	88.0	0.33	0.09		52	12.00			
27	93.0	0.08	0.03		53	7.13			
28	50.0	0			54	3.44			
29	50.0	50			55	1.35			
30	54.0		0		56	0.43			
31	54.0		5		57	0.11			
32	Total =	299.95	30.0		58	0.02			

FIGURE 14.3
The third stage in setting up the distribution of sampling means for the simulation

now explore some other possibilities, to see whether it is just the mean that influences the decision or other factors contribute. Consider the following response to the results. Not to be outdone, another teacher comes along and says that his group really is *superior* and therefore they deserve a new computer for his class to maximize on these skills (a good line, true or not). It is found that his class, group B, had a mean, $\bar{x}_B = 56$, and standard deviation, $S_B = 12$. Is his group 'superior', or at least statistically significantly different from the population? Why or why not? To find the answer, carry out Activity 14.3.

Activity 14.3

1   To test whether group B is statistically different, all you need to do is change the means in cell **C3**, which will cause the entire distribution and graph to change automatically. Your new graph should look like Figure 14.5.

2   Now use the simulation to consider the effect of changing some of the other variables. First, go back to having the sample mean as 54.
    (a)   What would the outcome be if the sample were $n = 60$ (say, two classes)?
    (b)   What would the outcome be if the sample $n = 30$, but the s.d. $= 10$?
    (c)   What if the second teacher's class was small, 12 students, and their mean score was 56 (s.d. $= 12$)? Would his argument be as strong?
    (d)   Consider the second teacher's class of 25, mean of 56, s.d. of 12, but the criterion for significance was $\alpha = 0.01$? How does this affect his case? Note the new cut-off z-score.

Answers: (a)   SEM = 1.55 (smaller); sample A mean is now beyond the new 5% cut-off.
(b)   SEM = 1.83; sample A mean is also beyond this 5% cut-off.
(c)   SEM = 3.46; sample B mean is now within 95% range.
(d)   SEM = 2.40; new sample B mean is within 99% range, thus for this criterion the sample could be representative of the population and not 'special'.

The easier way . . .

Obviously, it is not necessary to plot a graph every time one has to make such a decision, as was demonstrated in Chapter 13. To test whether a sample belongs to a population simply requires that the z-score for the given sample mean is calculated (based on the sampling distribution of the means) and compared to that for the chosen α in Table 14.1. Equation (13.4) was

$$z = \frac{\bar{x} - \mu}{\sigma_{\bar{x}}} \tag{14.2}$$

where $\sigma_{\bar{x}}$, the SEM, is found from equation (14.1). Using the example above, where the sample mean for group B was 56,

$$\sigma_{\bar{x}} = \frac{12}{\sqrt{30}} = 2.19 \quad \text{and} \quad z = \frac{56 - 50}{2.19} = 2.74$$

which exceeds the critical z-score for $\alpha = 0.05$ of 1.96. Since the probability of it belonging to the population is less than 5%, the null hypothesis that the sample belongs to the population could be rejected ($p < 0.05$).

Stage 4: Drawing the graphs

The following will generate the new line graphs:

1   Use the ChartWizard to plot the two distributions together on the same graph:

Step 1   Use the whole block **E9:H37**, including column headings, for **Range** (we will   use rows **33:37** later).

Step 2   Choose **XY (Scatter)** again.

Step 3   Choose type **2** format.

Step 4   Set the following:

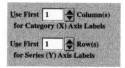

Step 5   Label the axes as shown below.

2   Keep the legend and it will use the column headings automatically. By double-clicking on each curve, you can adjust the lines and remove data point markers, if you wish.

Your graph should look like that below. The vertical α lines will automatically appear, even when $z(\alpha)$ changes on the worksheet.

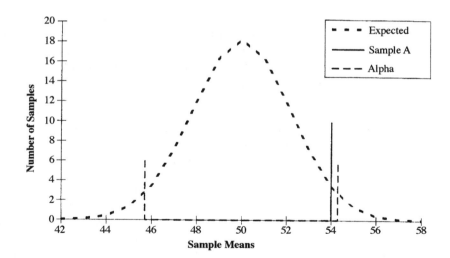

FIGURE 14.4
Graph of distribution of sampling means for the population parameters, with the mean of Sample A, $\bar{x}_A = 54$, shown with respect to the upper $\alpha = 5\%$ cut-off

Let us now consider the important issue of levels of significance. Do we report this as ($p < 0.02$), since the z-score also exceeds this limit (see Table 14.1)? As noted earlier, to play the game fairly, you set the rules out ahead of time – in other words, before starting the study – you decide what α to use as the cut-off for accepting or rejecting the null hypothesis. Let us now see why the decision as to what level to choose is not a simple one.

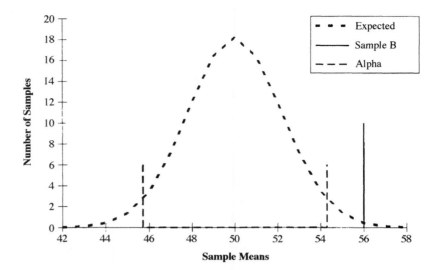

FIGURE 14.5
Result of Activity
14.3 (a) for Sample B,
$\bar{x}_B = 56$ and $\alpha = 0.05$

RESEARCH ERRORS

Since all inferential statistics results in probabilities and not certainties, it is reasonable to expect that it is possible to make a wrong decision based upon the outcome of a test. For example, when we choose $\alpha = 0.05$ as the critical value, there is still a 5% probability that any difference *did* happen by chance. In fact, there are two possible 'mistakes' or errors that could be made, depending on what is actually the truth. The problem is that we rarely know what the truth is, since that is what we are trying to determine. Therefore, we are back to describing what is *probably* true. Table 14.2 presents the problem of two possible alternative realities in tabular form, showing the consequences of making decisions based upon statistical tests.

Consider the logic of these alternatives. The first reality is that the null hypothesis, H_0, is really true (first column) – in other words, there was no difference between the sample mean, $\bar{x}$, and the population mean, μ_0, (the sample does belong to the population). Thus, either our test will lead us correctly to accept the null hypothesis, making no error, or wrongly to reject the null hypothesis, thus making a Type I error. On the other hand, the other reality could exist, where the H_0 is false. In this case, the sample actually belongs to a different population, with a mean μ_1. Consequently, based upon the statistical

TABLE 14.2
Possible
consequences of
decisions based on
two possible
alternative realities

		Possible realities	
		H_0 true	H_0 false
Decisions	H_0 accepted	Correct decision	Type II error
	H_0 rejected	Type I error	Correct decision

test, we could correctly reject the null hypothesis, or we could incorrectly accept it, thus committing a Type II error. And, as with all things statistical, it is possible to suggest the probabilities of making each of these four decisions. Since we do not know what reality is, we talk about the *risk of making a Type I or Type II error*. These will be considered in pairs, based on decisions made for the two different possible realities.

Possible reality: H_0 is true

First consider the left-hand possible reality of Table 14.2, where the null hypothesis H_0 is really true: the sample is representative of the population in question. This would be most likely if the sample were randomly selected from the population, but not impossible if a convenience or purposive sample were used. Consider the example in earlier activities, which described the school population that took a mathematical reasoning test that produced a population mean of 50. Let us consider a third sample, C, whose mean, $\bar{x}_C = 54.3$, which results in an interesting z-score:

$$z_C = \frac{54.3 - 50}{2.19} = 1.96$$

In other words, the sample mean sits right on the α border and a decision has to be made as to whether or not the null hypothesis is to be accepted or rejected. The graph of this from the simulation looks like that in Figure 14.6 with the mean of group C right on top of the critical z. The consequences of the decision are shown in Table 14.2: if H_0 is accepted, then this would be a correct decision, but if rejected, a Type I error would be made. Now the researcher does not know which reality prevails, and therefore must consider what probabilities (risks) are associated with each of the decisions. There is a $1 - \alpha = 0.95$, or 95% probability that accepting the H_0 would result in correctly identifying the group as being part of the population, *if it really were part of the population*. This corresponds to the area under the graph between the two $z(\alpha)$ lines. Alternatively, if the decision were made to reject H_0, since $\alpha = 0.05$ there would be a 5% probability that a Type I error would be made. This means there would be a 5% risk

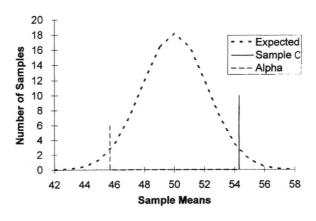

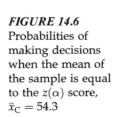

FIGURE 14.6
Probabilities of making decisions when the mean of the sample is equal to the $z(\alpha)$ score, $\bar{x}_C = 54.3$

that the group would be incorrectly identified as not belonging to the sample when it really did. But we only have half the picture, so the other possible reality must also be considered in this case.

Possible reality: H_0 is false

The researcher must also consider the opposite possible reality: H_0 is really false, the sample does not belong to the population. This would correspond to the two situations in right hand column in Table 14.2. The first alternative for our unique situation where the mean is on the $z(\alpha)$ line on the distribution of sampling means would be to make the decision not to reject the null hypothesis, H_0. The probability of incorrectly classifying the group as belonging to the original population when it did not, a Type II error, is designated by the Greek letter beta (β), which will be found shortly. The alternative situation is correctly accepting the null hypothesis H_0 that the sample does not belong to the original population, but a different one. The probability of being correct in this situation is $1 - \beta$, commonly referred to as the *power*. In other words, the higher the probability of correctly rejecting H_0, the more powerful the test is considered to be. Traditionally, the calculation of β and *power* has been considered too difficult, but recently there have been devised some means of estimating these, which actually provide an elegant way of exploring these concepts (Cohen, 1988; Hays, 1994; Howell, 1997; Welkowitz *et al.*, 1991). We will employ the functionality of Excel to simplify the process even further.

To find β requires one to interpret this alternative reality in such a way that the sample actually belongs to a different population altogether. Thus the sample mean, $\bar{x}$, really belongs to a *different* distribution of sampling means, for a population whose mean we can only estimate by assuming that it is equal to the sample mean, $\mu_1 = \bar{x}$. To determine a value for β necessitates finding the overlap of these two sampling distributions. Thus we need to replace the single line for the mean for the sample in Figure 14.6 with a second sampling distribution (referred to as the *non-central* distribution) of means for the second population with mean μ_1. In order better to understand how various factors affect β, and consequently the power of a statistical test, Activity 14.4 will extend the spreadsheet simulation to generate *both* sampling distributions on one graph, the one for the known population, the central distribution, and one for the population implied by the sample, the non-central distribution.

In Figure 14.8, the choice of a mean is such that it equals the α critical value for the example. Thus it becomes apparent that β is equal to the area under the left half of the sampling distribution of means based on an estimate from Sample C, and that the power $1 - \beta$ is equal to the area under the right half. Thus both $\beta = 0.50$ and power $= 0.50$. Now let us carefully interpret the contents of the four cells of our table on the right of Figure 14.8, For the mean for sample C:

- If H_0 is *accepted*, there is a 95% probability that the group would be correctly classified as a group that belongs to the original population, if it really did belong to it. Also, there is a 50% probability that the group would be wrongly classified as belonging to this population if it really belonged to a different population, a Type II error.

Activity 14.4

Continue with the example used in Activity 14.3 of the school population taking a mathematical reasoning test, using sample C, $\bar{x}_C = 54.3$. To establish the non-central distribution for the hypothesized second population, even as an estimation, it will be necessary to assume that the population mean, μ_1, is approximately equal to the sample mean, $\bar{x}_C$. Thus $\mu_1 \approx 54.3$.

1   Referring to Figure 14.7 as a guide for extending the simulation, all that is needed is to add the second distribution of sampling means based upon the mean for sample C. In cell **G20**, enter the equation based upon the Excel function **NORMDIST**, then **Copy** it down to row **37**, ensuring the **$** are where they should be so those values do not change. Only the first term, **E20**, the x-axis value, should change as this is copied down the column.

2   To produce a graph equivalent to that in Figure 14.8 should require nothing extra since the original chart included the entire range of cells **E9:H37**. In this new extension, all the changes have been made within that range. Note that the shaded area under the sampling distribution for population C is equal to β, the probability of making a Type II error for the decision based on these data. You will not get the shading in Figure 14.8 in Excel; that was added in a graphics package to clarify the three areas of the graphs that are equivalent to α, β and power.

- If H_0 is *rejected*, there is a 5% probability that the group would be incorrectly classified as not belonging to the original population if it really did, a Type I error. On the other hand, if the group really belonged to the alternative population, there would be a 50% probability that it would be classified as such correctly, equal to the power of the test.

This all seems a bit bizarre because neither the rows nor all four cells sum to 1.00, which one might suspect ought to happen. This is because the four cells do not describe the probabilities of making absolutely correct/incorrect decisions, but decisions with respect to the unknown possible realities. To be able to make absolute statements about the decisions would require our knowing the overall probability in reality of sample C belonging to the original population or to an alternative population. In other words, we would need to know the probability of the two possible realities.

For example, if there were an equal prevalence of the two populations, then we could multiply all the probabilities in Figure 14.8 by 50%, resulting in Table 14.3. Thus in absolute terms, there would be a 47.5% chance of correctly classifying the sample as belonging to the original population, a 25% chance of wrongly classifying it as belonging to the original population, a 2.5% probability of wrongly classifying it as belonging to the alternative population, and a 25% chance of correctly classifying it as belonging to the alternative population.

Add all four probabilities together and the result is 1.00. All probabilities for decisions are included and no probability for a decision is omitted, which is intuitively more acceptable. Unfortunately, we simply do not know what the prevalence of the two populations is, so we must be satisfied with the less specific probabilities of Figure 14.8, which seem less intuitively acceptable, but are appropriate descriptions of the risks associated with the decisions.

	A	B	C	D	E	F	G	H	I
1		**Data**			**Sampling**	**Means**			
2		Population	Sample C			Population	Sample C	Tails =	2
3	mean =	50	54.3		mean =	50	543	alpha =	0.05
4	s.d. =	12	12		SEM =	2.19	2.19	z(alpha) =	1.96
5	n =	300	30		samples =	100	100		
6	int. width =	5	5		int. width =	1	1		
7					3.5*SEM =	7.7			
8		y(x)	y(x)		Sample				
9	x	Population	Sample C		Means	Expected	Sample C	Alpha	
10	8.0	0.11	0.00		45.7			6	mean −
11	13.0	0.43	0.01		45.7			0	z(α)*SEM
12	18.0	1.42	0.05		54.3			0	mean +
13	23.0	3.97	0.17		54.3			18	z(α)*SEM
14	28.0	9.29	0.45		54.3		0		Sample
15	33.0	18.28	1.03		54.3		10		mean
16	38.0	30.25	1.98		42	0.02			
17	43.0	42.07	3.20		43	0.11			
18	48.0	49.18	4.34		44	0.43		=G\$6*G\$5*NORMDIST(E20,G\$3,G\$4,0)	
19	53.0	48.33	4.96		45	1.35			
20	58.0	39.93	4.76		46	3.44	0.01		
21	63.0	27.73	3.83		47	7.13	0.07		
22	68.0	16.19	2.60		48	12.00	0.29		
23	73.0	7.95	1.48		49	16.41	0.98		
24	78.0	3.28	0.71		50	18.21	2.65		
25	83.0	1.14	0.29		51	16.41	5.86		
26	88.0	0.33	0.10		52	12.00	10.49		
27	93.0	0.08	0.03		53	7.13	15.27		
28					54	3.44	18.04		
29					55	1.35	17.30		
30					56	0.43	13.48		
31					57	0.11	8.52		
32					58	0.02	4.37		
33					59		1.82		
34					60		0.62		
35					61		0.17		
36					62		0.04		
37					63		0.01		

FIGURE 14.7
Spreadsheet demonstration of relationships among α, β and power

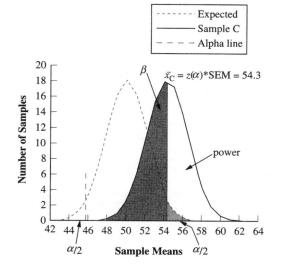

FIGURE 14.8
Graphical
representation of
relationships among
α, β and power

Possible realities		
	H₀ true	H₀ false
H₀ accepted	**Correct decision** $p = 1 - \alpha$ $p = 0.95$	**Type II error** $p = \beta$ $p = 0.50$
H₀ rejected	**Type I error** $p = \alpha$ $p = 0.05$	**Correct decision** $p = 1 - \beta$ $p = 0.50$ (power)

TABLE 14.3
Contrived table of
probabilities based
on the assumption
that a sample has
equal probability of
belonging to the two
populations

		Possible realities	
		50% H₀ true	50% H₀ false
Decisions	H₀ accepted	Correct decision $p = 0.475$	Type II error $p = 0.25$
	H₀ rejected	Type I error $p = 0.025$	Correct decision $p = 0.25$ (power)

Calculating β

As we have seen in the special example in Figure 14.8, the α critical line for the central sampling distribution of means based on the original population cuts the non-central distribution of sampling means for the alternative population in half. Rarely is this the case, therefore we need a more general way to determine a value for β, the area under the curve. To accomplish this, it is necessary first to calculate the z-score, $z(\beta)$, from the actual score on the x-axis resulting from the z-score for α, $z(\alpha)$. Starting with $z(\alpha)$ from Table 14.1, the actual score, $x(\alpha)$, on the x-axis can be expressed as

$$x(\alpha) = \mu_0 + z(\alpha)\sigma_{\bar{x}_0} \qquad (14.3)$$

where μ_0 is the mean for the original known population and $\sigma_{\bar{x}_0}$ is the standard error of the mean for the original population. With $x(\alpha)$, the process is simply reversed for the non-central distribution, starting with the analogous equation,

$$x(\alpha) = \mu_1 + z(\beta)\sigma_{\bar{x}_1} \qquad (14.4)$$

where μ_1 is the mean of the alternative population, which equals the sample mean, $\bar{x}$, and $\sigma_{\bar{x}_1}$ is the standard error of the mean for the alternative population. Solving for the z-score for β,

$$z(\beta) = \frac{x(\alpha) - \mu_1}{\sigma_{\bar{x}_1}}$$

Substituting in equation (14.3) for $x(\alpha)$,

$$z(\beta) = \frac{\mu_0 - \mu_1 + z(\alpha)\sigma_{\bar{x}_0}}{\sigma_{\bar{x}_1}}$$

If we accept that the two standard errors of the mean are equal and that the best estimate of the mean for the non-central distribution is the sample mean, $\mu_1 \cong \bar{x}$, then the equation simplifies to one that contains values readily determined:

$$z(\beta) = \frac{\mu_0 - \bar{x}}{\sigma_{\bar{x}}} + z(\alpha) \qquad (14.5)$$

For the example above,

$$z(\beta) = \frac{50.0 - 54.3}{2.19} + 1.96 \approx 0.00$$

Not surprisingly, when we look up this value, 0.00, on the z-score table, we find that 0.50 of the area is above and 0.50 of the area is below this point, thus $\beta = 0.50$, and the power $= 1 - \beta = 0.50$. Equations (14.3) and (14.5) will be used to find β in the next examples.

Typical results

It is useful to consider other situations – in particular, where the sample mean does not equal the α cut-off score and is either above or below. Two examples will be used. For sample D, we have $\bar{x}_D = 54.0$, a score obviously below the cut-off, resulting in a decision to accept H_0 and take this group as representative of the original population, as shown in Figure 14.10, where

$$z(\beta) = \frac{50.0 - 54.0}{2.19} + 1.96 = 0.13$$

From Table B.1 in Appendix B, the area for β would be $0.50 + 0.05 = 0.55$. Thus the probability of making a Type II error is 55%, the probability of wrongly classifying groups that have this mean and were really part of the alternative population as belonging to the original population. On the other hand, the probability of making the correct decision with respect to groups really from the original population with this mean remains at 95%.

Sample E, where $\bar{x}_E = 56.0$, a score obviously above the cut-off, results in a decision to reject H_0, and to assume that this group comes from an alternative population, as shown in Figure 14.10, where

$$z(\beta) = \frac{50.0 - 56.0}{2.19} + 1.96 = -0.78$$

Since the minus indicates a point below the mean, from Table B.1 in Appendix B, the area for β would be $0.50 - 0.28 = 0.22$. Thus the probability of making a Type I error and wrongly classifying a group with this score as belonging to the alternative population when they belong to the original population is still 5%. The probability of correctly classifying samples with this mean as belonging to the alternative population when they really do is now $1 - \beta = 0.78$, or 78%, which is the *power*.

The graphs in Figure 14.10 can be generated by your worksheet in Figure 14.7 by simply changing the sample mean. For sample D, where $\bar{x}_D = 54.0$, the obvious decision is to accept H_0, so only the top row of the decision box is of relevance to that decision. Similarly, for sample E, where $\bar{x}_E = 56.0$, the obvious decision is to reject H_0, thus only the bottom row provides any information on that decision. But both of these are post hoc, and only of interest in terms of seeing the consequences of decisions that had to be made *before* data were collected and someone carried out the statistical tests. Now in Activity 14.5 we add all these calculations to your worksheet so that it is not necessary to carry out the z-test, find β in a table, and calculate power by hand.

Activity 14.5

1 Bring up the spreadsheet in Figure 14.7 and refer to Figure 14.9 when adding the β and power calculations. In the last column I, add the equations shown.
2 Now you can change the values in the shaded cells and the whole sheet will change. This allows you to try other combinations of statistics and parameters, as well as changing the α value.

Effect of choice of α on power

As has been noted before, to follow the rules so that statistical validity is maintained, it is necessary to decide before carrying out the statistical test just what level of α is going to be used. One of the criteria may be that the test has high statistical power – in other words, a high probability of correctly rejecting the null hypothesis. As you might have suspected from the graphs, there is a link between choice of α and β, but the relationship is not simple. To illustrate it, let us consider just one more group, sample F, which has a mean score of 57.5. In Activity 14.6, you will find the β that corresponds to two different values for α, $p = 0.05$ and $p = 0.001$. Conventional wisdom or intuition might suggest that there would be an advantage to the second, which may be true in some situations but not all.

Activity 14.6

1 Using your worksheet, consider sample F, which has a sample mean of 57.5. Would you accept or reject H_0? Note what the value of the power is for this sample, and print out a graph.
2 Then on the worksheet, change the critical level from $p = 0.05$ ($z(\alpha) = 1.96$) to $p = 0.001$ ($z(\alpha) = 3.29$). Would you still reject H_0? What is the power value associated with this level of significance?

After you have carried this out, compare your results with those in Figure 14.11.

3 Which α would be most appropriate? Recall the original question at the beginning of this chapter, related to whether or not the samples were typical of the whole population. Can you think of other cases where the reverse situation could exist?

Answers: 1.   Reject H_0 with power very high at 93%.
2.   Reject H_0 but the power is now marginal at 55%.
3.   For this case, I would choose the first option, wishing for power. There may be other situations where the risk of making a Type I error should be reduced due to the nature of the decision made, thus the power would be potentially lower for the same outcome.

Thus a consequence of a seemingly more impressive value for α is a much lower value for power, one where there is only a 55% probability of detecting a significant difference when it existed! Unfortunately the situation is still not just a matter of opting for the highest power, any more than it is always better to have a smaller α. We will consider two other factors that influence power before combining everything that might influence our choice of α.

Effects of sample size and standard deviation on power

It is also possible to use this approach to estimate the sample size necessary to achieve a desired level of power as part of planning a study. Recall equation (14.5):

$$z(\beta) = \frac{\mu_0 - \bar{x}}{\sigma_{\bar{x}}} + z(\alpha)$$

It is necessary to estimate an expected value for the sample mean, $\bar{x}$, to provide an estimate of μ_1, and assume that $\sigma_{\bar{x}_0} = \sigma_{\bar{x}_1} = \sigma_{\bar{x}}$. Estimates of values for a sample mean can be obtained from other research or trials. Since the standard error of the mean, $\sigma_{\bar{x}}$, in the denominator is the only term to contain the sample size, n, we solve for it first:

$$\sigma_{\bar{x}} = \frac{\bar{x} - \mu_0}{z(\beta) - z(\alpha)}$$

From equation (14.1) for the standard error of the mean,

$$\frac{\sigma}{\sqrt{n}} = \frac{\bar{x} - \mu_0}{z(\beta) - z(\alpha)}$$

Inverting both sides, we obtain

$$\frac{\sqrt{n}}{\sigma} = \frac{z(\beta) - z(\alpha)}{\bar{x} - \mu_0}$$

	A	B	C	D	E	F	G	H	I
1		**Data**			**Sampling**	**Means**			
2		**Population**	**Sample D**			**Population**	**Sample D**	tails =	2
3	mean =	50	54		mean =	50	54	alpha =	0.05
4	s.d. =	12	12		SEM =	2.19	2.19	z(alpha) =	1.96
5	n =	300	30		samples =	100	100	z(mean) =	1.83
6	int. width =	5	5		int. width=	1	1	z(beta) =	0.13
7					3.5*SEM =	7.7		beta =	0.55
8		**y(x)**	**y(x)**		Sample			power =	0.45
9	**x**	**Population**	**Sample**		**Means**	**Expected**	**Sample D**	**Alpha**	
10	8.0	0.11	0.00		45.7			6	mean –
11	13.0	0.43	0.01		45.7			0	z(α)*SEM
12	18.0	1.42	0.06		54.3			0	mean +
13	23.0	3.97	0.18		54.3			18	z(α)*SEM
14	28.0	9.29	0.48		54		0		
15	33.0	18.28	1.08		54		10		
16	38.0	30.25	2.05		42	0.02			
17	43.0	42.07	3.28		43	0.11			=ABS(B3–C3)/F4
18	48.0	49.18	4.40		44	0.43			=I4–I5
19	53.0	48.33	4.97		45	1.35			NORMSDIST(I6)
20	58.0	39.93	4.72		46	3.44	0.02		=1–I7
21	63.0	27.73	3.76		47	7.13	0.11		
22	68.0	16.19	2.52		48	12.00	0.43		
23	73.0	7.95	1.42		49	16.41	1.35		
24	78.0	3.28	0.67		50	18.21	3.44		
25	83.0	1.14	0.27		51	16.41	7.13		
26	88.0	0.33	0.09		52	12.00	12.00		
27	93.0	0.08	0.03		53	7.13	16.41		
28					54	3.44	18.21		
29					55	1.35	16.41		
30					56	0.43	12.00		
31					57	0.11	7.13		
32					58	0.02	3.44		
33					59		1.35		
34					60		0.43		
35					61		0.11		
36					62		0.02		
37					63		0.00		

FIGURE 14.9
Completed
worksheet for
carrying out z-test
and calculating β
and *power* of the test

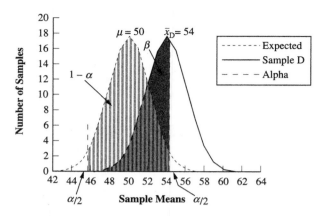

$\bar{x}_D = 54.0$	H_0 true	H_0 false
H_0 accepted	**Correct decision** $p = 1 - \alpha$ $p = 0.95$	**Type II error** $p = \beta$ $p = 0.55$
	$p = \alpha = 0.05$	$p = 1 - \beta = 0.45$

$\bar{x}_E = 56.0$	H_0 true	H_0 false
	$p = 1 - \alpha = 0.95$	$p = \beta = 0.22$
H_0 rejected	**Type I error** $p = \alpha$ $p = 0.05$	**Correct decision** $p = 1 - \beta$ $p = 0.78$ (power)

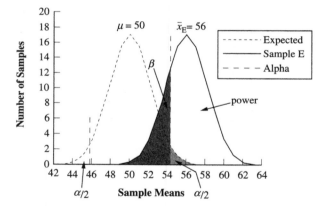

FIGURE 14.10
Comparing the error
probabilities for two
outcomes

and solving for n,

$$\sqrt{n} = \frac{\sigma[z(\beta) - z(\alpha)]}{\bar{x} - \mu_0}$$

Finally, squaring both sides of the equation,

$$n = \left[\frac{\sigma[z(\beta) - z(\alpha)]}{\bar{x} - \mu_0} \right]^2 \tag{14.6}$$

For our example of the mathematical test used earlier, let us assume the following situation. When planning the study, it is decided to aim for a power (prob-

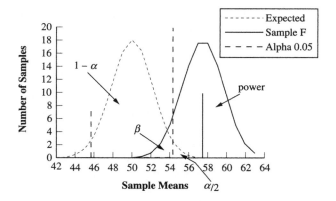

$\bar{x}_F = 57.5$	H_0 true	H_0 false
	$p = 1 - \alpha = 0.95$	$p = \beta \cong 0.08$
H_0 rejected	**Type I error** $p = \alpha$ $p = 0.05$	**Correct decision** $p = 1 - \beta$ $p \cong 0.92$ (power)

$\bar{x}_F = 57.5$	H_0 true	H_0 false
	$p = 1 - \alpha = 0.999$	$p = \beta \cong 0.45$
H_0 rejected	**Type I error** $p = \alpha$ $p = 0.001$	**Correct decision** $p = 1 - \beta$ $p \cong 0.55$ (power)

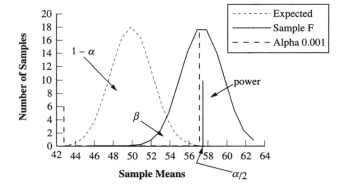

FIGURE 14.11
Comparing the Type I Error and *power* probabilities for different α

ability of correctly rejecting H_0) of 0.90. Using the original population mean of 50, it is assumed that the sample mean score will be about the same as before, 56 (and thus the mean for the alternative population). All other values will remain the same. If the power is 0.90, then $\beta = 0.10$. Consulting Table B.1 in Appendix B, this results in a z-score (area beyond z) of about -1.28. Thus we have:

$$\sigma = 12$$
$$z(\beta) = z(0.10) = -1.28 \quad \text{(negative since } below \text{ its mean, } \bar{x})$$
$$z(\alpha) = z(0.05) = +1.96 \quad \text{(positive since } above \text{ its mean, } \mu_0)$$
$$\bar{x} = 56.0$$
$$\mu_0 = 50.0$$

Then, the estimate of the optimum sample size to achieve this would be

$$n = \left[\frac{12(-1.28 - 1.96)}{56.0 - 50.0}\right]^2$$

$$= 42 \quad \text{(nearest whole number)}$$

This result would seem reasonable, since the original situation had a sample of 30 resulting in a power estimate of 0.78, for the same sample mean. This result can also be obtained by trial and error using the worksheet in Figure 14.7, therefore the process can be used as part of planning. After entering estimates for the means and standard deviation, simply enter a variety of values for n until you reach the desired power. Try this by carrying out Activity 14.7.

Activity 14.7

Using the worksheet in Figure 14.9, predict the sample size required for the following situation. From observing children in school, Sharon Surenough suspected that spelling ability would be influenced by the use of word-processors. She wanted a group of 11-year-olds just starting that year to learn to use the word-processor for six weeks before all the rest started to use them. At the end of the time, she would compare their scores on a common spelling test to those of the rest of the 11-year-olds. Scores on this type of test in the past had a mean of 65 with a standard deviation of 10. She felt that a mean score difference for the trial group of at least 5 points would be educationally significant (either better or worse). How large a sample would be needed to achieve a power of 0.80 for a two-tailed test? (Since $\bar{x} < \mu$, graph will be strange: ignore it.)
Answer: n = 31.

Equation (14.6) conveniently allows us to see another relationship between sample size and standard deviation: the smaller the standard deviation, the smaller the sample one needs to maintain the same test power. Upon what does the standard deviation of a set of scores depend? These are *observed* scores, which from Chapter 11 we recall were defined as a combination of true scores plus error. This was reflected in the description of associated variances expressed in equation (11.2)

$$S_x^2 = S_t^2 + S_e^2$$

The true score variance, S_t^2, is due to natural variation in the trait. Thus, the smaller the error variance, S_e^2, the smaller the observed score variance, S_x^2, and the smaller the standard deviation, S_x, will be. Recall that the way to reduce the error variance is to increase the reliability of the instrument. This is shown by substituting the above equation into the denominator of equation (11.1), the definition of reliability,

$$r_{xx} = \frac{S_t^2}{S_x^2}$$

which when rearranged provides

$$S_e^2 = S_t^2 \left(\frac{1}{r_{xx}} - 1 \right)$$

Thus, the closer the reliability of the instrument is to 1.00, the smaller the error variance, and the smaller the sample needed to achieve the same power. This provides a solid link between measurement and sampling, showing their interdependence. Now carry out Activity 14.8.

Activity 14.8

Using your worksheet simulation, try varying each of the following to see the consequences for the graphs and ultimately power:
(a)   the level of α,
(b)   sample size, n,
(c)   standard deviation,
(d)   size of difference between the means. (Keep $\bar{x} > \mu$)
You may find it useful to print out graphs and compare them, so include a title for each.

Enhancing statistical power

It becomes obvious that it is possible to control *some* of the factors that influence what the power of a test will be, but not all. The four explored using the worksheet in Activity 14.8 are really just the tip of the iceberg, since these can be governed by decisions made by the researcher. Cohen (1988) has suggested that ideally, for realistic resources, one should aim for a Type II error that is four times that of a Type I, thus for $\alpha = 0.05$, β would be 0.20 and power 0.80. Even then, 20% of truly significant differences could be missed! In any event, to achieve this would require careful planning and execution.

As an aid to making a link with the discussions in earlier chapters, recall the relationship between the total variance in observed scores, S_x^2 (thus the standard deviation of a set of measures), and the true score variance, S_t^2, and error variance, S_e^2, as expressed in equation (11.2) and provided above. The influences on power are directly related to four processes that are part of the planning stage of a study: sampling procedures, measurement procedures, statistical test decisions, and treatments. Each of these contribute as follows:

1   *Sampling* procedures that are employed. These have two types of influence:
   • *sample size*. This is one of the variables that determines the size of the standard error of the mean.
   • *sample quality*. The more homogeneous and representative a sample is for the designated traits, the more likely those in the sample will respond as would the whole population that they represent. Loss of the representativeness can contribute to the error variance and increase the observed score variance and thus the standard deviation. Thus it is expected that

quasi-experimental studies will probably have lower power than true experimental designs.

2 *Measurement* procedures. These provide an influence from two different directions:

   • *reliability* of the instrument. By definition, this is an indicator of the amount of error variance, S_e^2, in the total variability of a group, shown above.

   • *instrument design*. This will determine whether the data are interval, ratio, ordinal or nominal, which in turn will influence the type of statistical test.

3 *Statistical test* decisions. There are two of these:

   • *choice of test*. This could be applied to a given design, noting that parametric tests tend to be more powerful than nonparametric tests. From this we can see the link with the type of data generated by instruments.

   • *choice of α*. As demonstrated earlier, this influences β and in turn, power.

4 *Treatment*. In experimental and quasi-experimental designs, the treatment needs to be such that it maximizes the difference between the means of the potential populations, particularly if power is to be above 0.80 (recall the case described in Figure 14.10). This is sometimes referred to as *treatment effects*, and indicated by the effect size, *ES*, (Lipsey, 1990), given by

$$ES = \frac{\mu_0 - \mu_1}{\sigma} \tag{14.7}$$

In designs having control group, ensuring their isolation from the treatment is essential. For ex post facto designs, this will be directly influenced by the choice and definition of life events that constitute the independent variables, and sampling of these groups. Thus the results of these studies are vulnerable to lower power due to these added challenges.

Budgets and availability may limit sample size, but error variance can be reduced by ensuring sample quality, piloting instruments and enhancing reliability. The choice of α, though, may depend on other factors, as we will see in the next section. Small effects resulting in minimal differences in means may seem trivial, but often lead to more refined variables. And the use of nonparametric tests may reduce the power, but, more often, it is instrument design and sampling that are the sources of most of the loss. The interrelationships among this rather cumbersome collection of variables influencing power are shown in Figure 14.12, which suggests how one would maximize it, if this were the only goal.

ONE- OR TWO-TAILED TEST?

Up to this point, we have used only two-tailed tests in the examples, suggesting that the sample mean might be greater or less than the population mean. The anticipated direction of the difference between the sample and the population has not been certain enough to state the hypothesis directionally. This raises an issue that generates considerable discussion in research circles and must be resolved for each study. The choice, like that of what α to use, ought to be made before the statistical analysis is carried out. Some authors recommend that any study that has any inkling of directionality should use a one-tailed

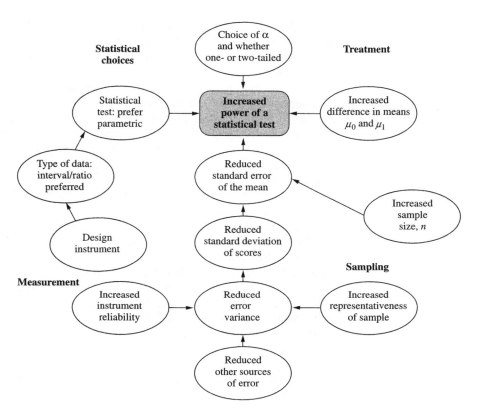

FIGURE 14.12
Enhancing the *power*
of a statistical test

test, since the power increases greatly. For example, a one-tailed test at 5% is equivalent to a two-tailed test at 10%. Like most decisions, it is hardly that simple and one must consider the following consequences of choosing a one-tailed test:

- The test will not detect significant differences in the other direction, thus unanticipated significance in that direction could be missed.
- The statement of the hypothesis and H_0 will be different than for non-directional tests: you are hypothesizing $\mu_1 > \mu_0$, rather than $\mu_1 \neq \mu_0$.
- The nature of the statistical test changes, providing a much less conservative test.
- It inflates the probability of making a Type I error, the consequences of which for theory testing could lead one up a blind alley due to potentially unreplicable results.
- It provides greater power and reduces probability of making a Type II error, since the critical α moves closer to the mean of the first distribution, thus decreasing the β area and increasing the power area under the second distribution.

Generally a one-tailed test should not be used when testing a theory since the reverse directional relationship would be as important to identify as the expected. This is particularly true for weak theories or ones that lack an empirical underpinning that would strongly suggest a direction. On the other hand, a one-tailed test would be valuable if the direction could only be one way and the difference in the other direction would be meaningless. For example, if a group of subjects receive training, it would be unlikely they would get worse, but it might not be significantly effective and might not result in skill acquisition greater than that possessed by the untrained population. This rationale would not necessarily apply to seemingly parallel situations, such as counselling. An ineffective counselling technique could result in a decline in the state of clients with respect to a population receiving no treatment.

On the other hand, a one-tailed test may be appropriate for a comparative study where direction is part of the hypothesis based upon prior evidence. For example, there will be situations where informal observations of those treated indicate that they always improve more quickly than the population which is left to its own devices.

In the end, there is always the temptation to apply a one-tailed test when no significance is found for the two-tailed test because the difference is too small for the latter. Remember, tests are only valid if the H_0 is stated *before* results are analysed, and there is sufficient justification for the choice of test and level of significance. Stating the hypothesis, choosing α, and making it directional after the data have been collected and analysed is like placing your bets *after* the roulette wheel has stopped. It is called cheating.

If it is any consolation, Fisher (1966) always maintained that an experimenter never accepts H_0, he merely fails to reject it on the basis of his data, leaving the possibility for it to be rejected in another study. In other words, you may have just committed a Type I error and there is nothing (except resources) to prevent you trying again.

Choosing an appropriate α

The discussion up to this point in the chapter has focused on enhancing the potential power of a study, to ensure the highest probability that if there are two populations then the test will correctly detect this. The examples have all been related to determining whether a group is part of a population, but this can be extended to comparing two or more groups, particularly where there is a control group. Those whose writings have focused on ensuring that the power of statistical tests is high (such as Cohen, 1988; Lipsey, 1990) have assumed that this is the main goal of design, identifying an effect through correctly rejecting a null hypothesis. Undoubtedly this is an important goal of researchers, but other factors must be considered as well.

As a researcher planning a study, imagine yourself having to decide what level of statistical significance, α, you are going to employ in your tests. How do you decide? In addition to the power of the test, it is necessary to consider the consequences, good and bad, of any action that may be taken as a result of such a decision. In particular, it is necessary to consider the potential repercussions associated with making a Type I or Type II error. While much of academic research may aim at identifying variables for the sake of enhancing theories, there will be practical situations where the research results will be used as the basis for decisions about people's lives.

As Rowntree (1981) notes, resolving this issue is analogous to the following dilemma that arises in courts of law: if weak evidence is accepted, there is a danger many innocent people will go to jail. This is like changing the significance level from $\alpha = 0.05$ to $\alpha = 0.10$, increasing the risk of a Type I error. Here the court could be rejecting the null hypothesis that there is no significant difference between those on trial and innocent people, when in reality it is true. The advantage would be that a greater proportion of villains would be convicted (increased power).

Alternatively, by making the demands on the quality of evidence more stringent so that fewer innocent people are convicted, the probability of more guilty persons not being convicted would increase, increasing the risk of making a Type II error. This is parallel to changing the significance level to $\alpha = 0.01$, thus more frequently accepting the null hypothesis that there is no difference between these people and the innocent, when it should be rejected. This dilemma is often summarized in courtroom dramas by the statement 'guilty beyond a reasonable doubt'. What is ultimately accepted as evidence is based upon the balance between making Type I and Type II errors, and, as most people have noticed, this is dependent to some extent upon what a given society will tolerate.

In quantitative research, for a given sample mean that is indicative of some population mean, μ_1, making α smaller would increase β by moving the α and sample mean lines on the graph of sampling means closer together. Thus while decreasing the probability of making a Type I error, this would increase the probability of making a Type II error and decrease the potential power of the test. Thus, one only wants to make α more stringent if there are severe consequences for making a Type I error (finding a difference when it does not really exist).

In such cases, it is necessary to return to the research question and ask what are the consequences of any decisions made based upon this study. For example, if a potential drug were being tested for curative effects, the H_0 would be no greater frequency of cures than for those taking no drug. If, in addition, it had harmful side-effects then the focus of the study would be on the frequency of these side-effects. For example, most drugs for parasites such as worms or malaria are poisons, since parasites are animals and the secret is to poison the parasite and not the host. Here it would be desirable to reduce the chance of making a Type I error, to reduce the chance of approving a drug that in reality might harm more people than would be acceptable. Again, the issue is what is acceptable. If the criteria were that no one would suffer, then most drugs would disappear from the pharmacist's shelf. Unfortunately, there can be a wide variety of reactions and allergies to drugs, some of which are extremely rare.

Let us alter the example: what if there were a study to see if a family of drugs with side-effects were potentially beneficial, knowing that if it were proven so, then a less harmful derivative could be developed? In this situation, any hint of success would be of potential benefit and the consequences of making a Type II error (not finding a difference that existed) and not following a potentially productive lead would be worse than mistakenly investing some additional effort in a dead end. Thus even increasing the level for significance to $\alpha = 0.10$ might be justified.

Where does social science research fit in this pattern? Maybe it is fortunate that the conclusions of a single piece of social science research are rarely used as the basis of a radical decision affecting vast numbers of people! How do other professions that use statistics as a decision-making tool – for example, chemists testing new medicines – protect themselves? They replicate the study *several times* using different samples of persons. Getting the same results time after time reduces the overall probability of making a decision error. One could argue that research which is trying to verify potential variables should not set excessive constraints on the outcomes, and that it is better to have a relatively high risk of a Type I error (find a significance that does not really exist) and raise the potential power of a test, thus lowering the risk of making a Type II error (not finding a difference that existed). Research that would form the basis of major policy decisions, on the other hand, might require just the opposite strategy. Each situation will have to be considered on its own merits, but there is little benefit to reporting a higher significance level for the sake of looking more impressive, if it potentially reduces the power of the test.

The factors influencing the decision about what α to use are summarized in Figure 14.13. Thus, going back to Figure 14.12, the oval at the top might result in a choice that would not necessarily enhance the power of the study, though all of the other contributors would.

SUMMARY

Over the past two chapters, an attempt has been made to weave a long thread from basic concepts in probability, through the foundations of statistical inference, right up to considering the probabilities of making errors. It must be emphasized that statistical testing constitutes another decision support tool, it does *not* make the decisions for you. Researchers must resolve issues for each study, such as what level of significance to set, and they have to consider all the contributing factors and outcomes relevant to such a decision. For example, the sample size and choice of significance level will affect the probability of drawing the wrong conclusions. Usually, researchers do not know which type

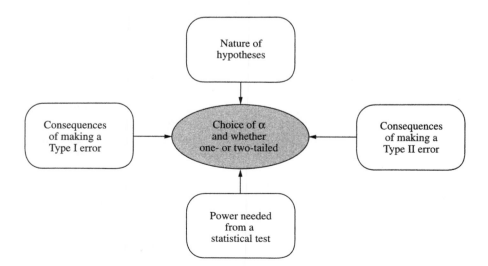

FIGURE 14.13
Factors influencing
the choice and
nature of
significance level, α

of error is actually made, but they should be concerned about which type to *risk* making. This means that a decision will be made as to which type of error a researcher can best tolerate in a study and this in turn will determine the choice of significance level and influence the sample size. To play the game of statistical inference honestly, the decision about the significance level should really be made *before* the statistical test is carried out, when the null hypothesis is stated. Though widely practised, reporting just the most significant level found as the statistical tests are performed is not proper, since this implies that the criterion for acceptance/rejection of the null hypothesis was not set ahead of time. It also often indicates a lack of understanding of decision errors and power.

These issues will be raised again for the statistical tests that are considered in subsequent chapters; each time, the necessity to consider all the contributing factors will be raised. Now carry out Activity 14.9.

Activity 14.9

1   Since prolonged exposure to electric motor noise (for example, electric drills, saws, etc.) can reduce sensitivity to higher-frequency sounds, Edward Earful wanted to know whether or not the noise from the fans in desktop computers would do the same. These do not tend to be anywhere near as loud as, say, a drill, but computer users are exposed to the noise for long periods of time.

    (a)   If he were to measure the maximum frequency detectable for a random sample of computer users of a given age group (this deteriorates somewhat with age anyway) and compared the results with known population values, what would be an appropriate level for α?

    (b)   Should the test be one-tailed or two-tailed? Why?

    (c)   What sampling problems will he have to face?

2   Over the years, data have been collected at Aardvark Aviation showing a mean time per page for producing external letters. Albert Ant, manager in charge of computer software purchases, has been to lunch with a sales representative who claims that his software, Speedwrite, will reduce the time 'significantly.' Albert is concerned because of the cost not only of the software but also of retraining staff. He decides to conduct a study using 15 new secretaries who will learn Speedwrite. Their average time for 10 letters each will be compared to that of the company for existing software.

    (a)   What would be an appropriate level for α?

    (b)   Should the test be one-tailed or two-tailed? Why?

Model Answers

1(a)   An argument for having $\alpha = 0.05$ would be that there is a need to detect even small damage to ears, thus a need to reduce Type II error and increase power, even if there is an increased risk of a Type I error. Since it is likely that if damage is detected, there would be further studies, then the *consequence of making a Type I error would be the unnecessary cost of more research, whereas the consequence of making a Type II error would be to fail to detect a common source of damage to ears. (b) Since there is some evidence that exposure to sound can reduce hearing sensitivity at higher frequencies, the test could be one-tailed. (c) Sampling difficulties arise not only because of age of participants, but also the number of hours exposed per day and the type of computer, since they do tend to have different fans. 2(a) Since making a Type I error (finding a difference when it did not exist) could cost the company unnecessarily, he could argue that a more conservative test, say $\alpha = 0.001$, is required. (b) Considering he has no more than the sales representative's word (and a free lunch) for any difference, a two-tailed test would allow for the possibility that rates would be worse than with the present software. Even if there were a significant difference in favour of Speedwrite, he would still need to consider whether the speed difference was of sufficient magnitude to merit the expenditure, and carry out a cost–benefit analysis.*

PART IV
EX POST FACTO, EXPERIMENTAL AND QUASI-EXPERIMENTAL DESIGNS: PARAMETRIC TESTS

Comparing Two Groups: *t*-test

15

One of the most basic situations in research is the one where we want to compare two groups for some trait to see if they are sufficiently dissimilar that we can say they do not belong to the same population. Something different has happened to each, whether it was a life experience or a planned treatment, and we want to know if, for the trait of interest, they can still be considered alike. If not, then, reflecting on earlier chapters, have we controlled all the extraneous variables so that the one isolated cause is the only one possible? All that a statistical test can answer is the first question, whether the two groups probably belong to the same population.

The rationale for establishing a statistical test to resolve this question is analogous to that introduced in Chapter 13 for deciding whether a sample is part of a population. Here we will ask whether or not the difference between the means for the two groups is sufficiently large that we can say they are from two separate populations. How this will be decided will depend on which of the underlying conditions of the statistical tests the situation most closely meets:

- the samples are independent (if not, the test is modified);
- the variances are nearly equal (if not, again there is another modification);
- the samples are large (over 30, if not then a new distribution other than the normal one must be used);
- the samples are equal (if not, a different way of combining variances will be used).

Each time an adjustment is made for deviating from the basic assumptions, it becomes more difficult to find statistical difference. Thus for the same difference in the two means, the potential power of the test will decline slightly if one has to compensate by modifying the test. Ultimately we will consider four versions of the *t*-test in this chapter, and others under nonparametric tests for comparing two groups in Chapters 19 and 20. In this chapter, you will be able to set up a simulation to explore the relationship among these assumptions and compare outcomes for different situations. You will also have at the end a worksheet into which you can enter raw data and generate the results for any one of the four tests, including an assessment of the power of each.

FROM ONE GROUP TO TWO

Having established a way of determining the likelihood of a sample belonging to a known population rather than a separate unknown one, it would seem that this could be extended to comparing two samples. There are definite similarities and the issue is much the same: if we have two samples, do they belong to one population or do they belong to two separate ones for the trait in question? For example, two random samples of employees are selected, one provided with a programme of motivation counselling to improve self-image and therefore productivity, and a second control group. Both groups respond to a written instrument to measure self-image both before and after the treatment period. At the end of the study, do both groups belong to the same population for the characteristic of interest, self-image, based on gain scores on the instrument? Assuming all extraneous variables were controlled, did the counselling have any effect and make them different?

When testing the question of whether a sample belongs to a known population, the sample mean is compared to a distribution of possible sample means to see if it is within an acceptable range, often the 95% range of $\pm 1.96\sigma_{\bar{x}}$, the standard error of the mean (SEM). This assumes we know what the standard deviation of the population is for the trait and therefore can test this for the mean of sample A by using equation (13.4):

$$z(\bar{x}_A) = \frac{\bar{x}_A - \mu}{\sigma_{\bar{x}}} \tag{15.1}$$

This is checked against the chosen $z(\alpha)$, which for $\alpha = 0.05$ is 1.96 (two-tailed test); if it exceeds it, this is evidence that the sample is probably not typical of the population. Yet to extend this to two samples is not possible since both means would be sample means and either is an estimate of the population mean. In the example above, it is unlikely that the tests on motivation are going to be administered to the entire population of employees, and in much research the population could be very large indeed. Recalling the adaptation of the one-sample test when the population standard deviation is not available, described by equation (13.5),

$$t = \frac{\bar{x}_A - \mu}{s_{\bar{x}}} \tag{15.2}$$

where

$$s_{\bar{x}} = \frac{s_A}{\sqrt{n_A}} \tag{15.3}$$

is the estimate of the SEM, and using the second sample mean as an estimate of the population mean will provide misleading results, as we will soon see.

Consequently, a replacement gauge for the SEM is needed for comparing the difference between two sample means. This will be a different standard deviation for the denominator that reflects the following:

- The standard deviations of both samples are only estimates of the hypothesized single-population standard deviation, and could be different from each other.
- Both the means are estimates of one common or two separate population means.
- The focus here is on the potential magnitude of the difference between means.

The new approach involves the *standard error of the difference*, s_{diff}, the standard deviation of a *distribution of differences in sample means*. In other words, if all the possible independent sample pairs were taken from a single population and the *differences* in their means were found, they would also form a normal distribution. This time there would be a grand mean of 0, since overall there should be no difference in the means. Consequently, we can calculate for a *t*-score that tells us just how far apart the means are with respect to this distribution:

$$t(\bar{x}_A - \bar{x}_B) = \frac{\bar{x}_A - \bar{x}_B}{s_{diff}} \tag{15.4}$$

The test will now compare this ratio to the appropriate *t*-distribution to check the likelihood of the two samples belonging to a single population that would tolerate such a difference. Now if we were to know the population standard deviations associated with the two samples, then the two SEMs for the sampling distributions could be combined as follows (Blalock, 1979; Hays, 1994):

$$\sigma_{diff} = \sqrt{\sigma_{\bar{x}_A}^2 + \sigma_{\bar{x}_B}^2} \tag{15.5}$$

This can be written using the definitions for each of the SEMs from equation (13.2):

$$\sigma_{diff} = \sqrt{\frac{\sigma_A^2}{n_A} + \frac{\sigma_B^2}{n_B}}$$

Considering that, in the case of two samples, the sample standard deviations are only estimates of the populations' standard deviations, then the SEMs will only be estimates. Thus, the standard error of the difference is just the combination of these two estimates, whereby the unbiased estimates of the standard deviations of the samples are used (see equation (12.5)). This is the simplest form of s_{diff} and assumes that the variances for samples A and B are much the same. Since there is no compensation for any difference, it is referred to as using *unpooled variances*. Therefore, it will be expressed as

$$s_{diff\ unpooled} = \sqrt{\frac{s_A^2}{n_A} + \frac{s_B^2}{n_B}} \tag{15.6}$$

This is the equation that will be used in many calculations. Such comparisons are usually between estimates of population parameters and often are based on small samples, thus usually the *t*-distribution is used for comparison. As a consequence, the basic equation (15.2) is written as

$$t_{unpooled} = \frac{\bar{x}_A - \bar{x}_B}{s_{diff\ unpooled}} \tag{15.7}$$

TABLE 15.1
Summary data for
Kelvin Climate's
study on children's
height

	Norway	Italy
$\bar{x}$	160	170
s	34	32
n	50	50
$s_{\bar{x}}$	4.81	4.53
s_{diff}	6.60	

Having laid out the rules, you might still have a nagging doubt as to why we cannot use the SEM. Let us use an example to see how the two approaches do produce different results.

Kelvin Climate wanted to see if children living in the far north grew more slowly than those living in sunnier regions. His null hypothesis was there would be no significant difference in height between two samples of 14-year-olds selected from northern Norway and southern Italy. Fortunately, his cousin taught in Tromsø and his sister-in-law was a secondary teacher in Naples. Fifty children aged 14 years were randomly selected from each of the two schools and their heights measured and recorded in centimetres. A summary of the results is provided in Table 15.1.

From the two values for the SEM, $s_{\bar{x}}$, two distributions can be plotted, as shown in Figure 15.1. Using the values from the sample from Norway to represent the population, cut-off lines are added for $\alpha = 0.05$. It becomes apparent that, applying this approach, it would be possible to conclude that there was a significant difference between the two groups, since the mean of the Italian sample is beyond the critical point.

On the other hand, if the standard error of the difference, s_{diff}, is used to generate a distribution of sampling mean differences for the pair, we have the graph

FIGURE 15.1
Two distributions of
sampling means
based upon separate
samples, for Kelvin
Climate's study

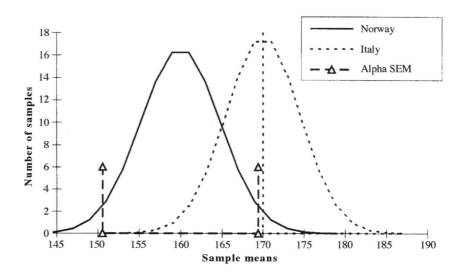

FIGURE 15.2
Sampling
distribution based
upon differences
between sampling
means, with the
difference for the
sample means in
Kelvin Climate's
study

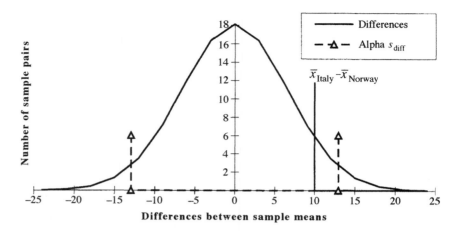

in Figure 15.2. When the difference in the means of the samples is included, we see that it falls inside the cut-off lines for $\alpha = 0.05$. Therefore, it would be reasonable to conclude that there is no difference between the groups, other than that which could be attributed to chance. Thus the two groups probably come from a common population for this trait.

Overlooking the fact that this is not a well-designed study due to its poor sampling and lack of control of extraneous variables, it is possible to see the conflict in conclusions. The *t*-test based upon the difference in the means and combined estimates of the population standard deviation, assumes both samples provide estimates, rather than using a model that tells us to treat one of them as a good estimate of the population. This results in a more conservative test, one that has lower power, but is less likely to result in a Type 1 error. Now let us see what differences there are between the normal distribution and the family of *t*-distributions.

Student's *t*-distribution

While representative samples greater than 30 in size for normally distributed traits seem to provide data that result in normal distributions, samples smaller than 30 tend to incur greater sampling errors. In an endeavour to compensate for this, W.S. Gosset, who was employed by the Guinness Brewery in Dublin and publishing under the pen name 'Student', in 1908 devised an equation that would compensate for small samples. It produces a curve equivalent to the normal distribution provided by equation (13.2) when samples are large (Hays, 1994), but when they are small the distribution becomes shorter and flatter with extended tails. This means that the 2.5% of the area in each tail is farther from the mean than for the normal distribution. Thus, it is harder to find significance, requiring a greater difference between the means than equivalent situations with large samples. The distribution still assumes that the underlying population is normally distributed. A simplified version of the *t*-distribution is given by

$$y(\Delta\bar{x}; \nu) = \frac{G(\nu)}{\left[1 + \frac{1}{\nu}\left(\dfrac{\Delta\bar{x}}{s_{\text{diff}}}\right)^2\right]^{\frac{\nu+1}{2}}} \tag{15.8}$$

Here $\Delta\bar{x}$ is the difference in the means for the x-axis, $\bar{x}_B - \bar{x}_A$; ν stands for the degrees of freedom (df), explained below, but here given simply by $n_A + n_B - 2$; $G(\nu)$ is a function that depends on the degrees of freedom, which will produce a constant for a given situation (but there is a slightly different curve for each situation with different degrees of freedom); and s_{diff} is the standard error of the difference, constant for a given situation. The mathematically minded will see that as $\Delta\bar{x}$ increases in the denominator, the value of $y(\Delta\bar{x}; \nu)$ becomes smaller. When $\Delta\bar{x}$ is zero, then $y(\Delta\bar{x}; \nu)$ attains its maximum, which is equal to $G(\nu)$. Also, since $\Delta\bar{x}$ is in brackets and squared, the curve will be symmetrical since it will not matter whether $\Delta\bar{x}$ is positive or negative. Since $y(\Delta\bar{x}; \nu)$ depends on two variables, $\Delta\bar{x}$ and ν, for each ν there will a different curve for all the possible values of $\Delta\bar{x}$.

We will use an approximation of this equation, available through Excel functions, to show its relationship with the normal distribution, but first let us consider one important detail.

Degrees of freedom

The degrees of freedom for a set of data are best described as the number of observations free to vary at one time without affecting the result. For example, how many observations in a sample could vary from sample to sample if we are to have the same value for the mean? Consider the following sample of five observations:

$$6 \quad 8 \quad 4 \quad 9 \quad 6$$

which has mean

$$\bar{x} = \frac{6 + 8 + 4 + 9 + 6}{5} = \frac{33}{5} = 6.6$$

How many of these observations can be changed and how many must be left to adapt if the resulting mean is going to remain 6.6? As many as any four can be altered, and changing the first four here for convenience, for example to the following,

$$7 \quad 9 \quad 5 \quad 10$$

has the consequence that the last number, 6, must become

$$33 - (7 + 9 + 5 + 10) = 33 - 31 = 2$$

so that the mean is still

$$\bar{x} = \frac{7 + 9 + 5 + 10 + 2}{5} = \frac{33}{5} = 6.6$$

Since four out of five is the maximum, we say we have four degrees of freedom. Thinking about it, logic dictates that for any number of observations, we can change all but one and still have the same mean (or standard deviation, for that matter). Thus the number of degrees of freedom are stated as $df = n - 1$.

For our present situation of two samples, the t-test depends upon the combined degrees of freedom,

$$df = (n_A - 1) + (n_B - 1)$$
$$= n_A + n_B - 2 \tag{15.9}$$

For other tests the number of degrees of freedom will vary depending on what is being compared. For example, if we were to ask whether a very small sample belonged to a population, as in Chapter 13, then it would be necessary to use the t-distribution instead of the normal distribution. The population parameters are fixed and we are considering only one sample, thus when consulting the table of critical values for t (Appendix B, Table B.2), we would use

$$df = n_A - 1 \tag{15.10}$$

The number of degrees of freedom is a value that will appear in most statistical tests since it allows the test to take into account that in such situations we are using sample statistics to estimate population parameters. Now let us compare the z- and t-distributions graphically in Activity 15.1.

Activity 15.1

1   Start a new worksheet and begin by entering labels in the first two rows and column **A** rows **1** to **12**, and all those in row **13** (Figure 15.3). Also enter the numbers in the shaded cells. These will be the only ones changed when exploring the relationship between the distributions.

2   Now insert the formulae shown for s_{diff}, degrees of freedom, $t(\alpha)$ and $z(\alpha)$ cut-offs, $3.5 * s_{diff}$ and interval width. Using **B8*2/B7** for the α values allows you to change from one-tailed to two-tailed tests just by changing the entry in **B7**. You are now ready to generate the data for the two graphs.

3   Rows **14** to **23** generate vertical lines for the two sets of αs and the line for the difference in the means on the graphs. The values in columns **D**, **E** and **F** simply make the lines tall enough.

4   In column **A**, the centre of the graph is fixed by having the difference in the means, 0, in cell **A36**. Then above and below, enter what is indicated and **Copy** up and down. Row values without **$** will change automatically.

5   In column **B**, enter the normal distribution function, taking care to include **$** where indicated. **Copy** this down the column to **B48**.

6   To generate an approximate t-distribution is a bit more complicated, since the function used, **TDIST**, is a cumulative distribution. (For those interested, to find the area for each interval it is necessary to find the area up to the upper real limit and subtract the area below the lower real limit.) In **C35**, enter and **Copy** the long formula up the column. Enter the formula in **C36** to get the peak at the centre. Finally, in **C37**, enter the formula indicated and **Copy** down the column.

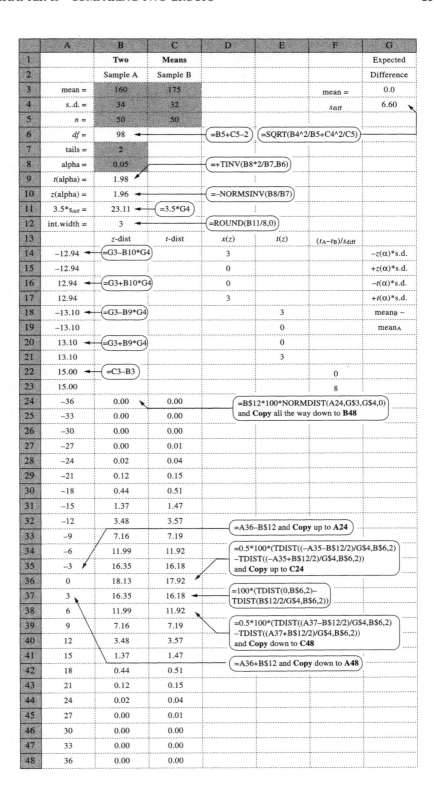

	A	B	C	D	E	F	G
1		**Two**	**Means**				Expected
2		Sample A	Sample B				Difference
3	mean =	160	175			mean =	0.0
4	s..d. =	34	32			s_{diff}	6.60
5	n =	50	50				
6	df =	98		=B5+C5–2	=SQRT(B4^2/B5+C4^2/C5)		
7	tails =	2					
8	alpha =	0.05		=+TINV(B8*2/B7,B6)			
9	t(alpha) =	1.98					
10	z(alpha) =	1.96		=–NORMSINV(B8/B7)			
11	3.5*s_{diff} =	23.11	=3.5*G4				
12	int.width =	3		=ROUND(B11/8,0)			
13		z-dist	t-dist	x(z)	t(z)	$(t_A - t_B)/s_{diff}$	
14	–12.94	=G3–B10*G4		3			$-z(\alpha)$*s.d.
15	–12.94			0			$+z(\alpha)$*s.d.
16	12.94	=G3+B10*G4		0			$-t(\alpha)$*s.d.
17	12.94			3			$+t(\alpha)$*s.d.
18	–13.10	=G3–B9*G4			3		$mean_B$ –
19	–13.10				0		$mean_A$
20	13.10	=G3+B9*G4			0		
21	13.10				3		
22	15.00	=C3–B3				0	
23	15.00					8	
24	–36	0.00	0.00	=B$12*100*NORMDIST(A24,G$3,G$4,0) and **Copy** all the way down to **B48**			
25	–33	0.00	0.00				
26	–30	0.00	0.00				
27	–27	0.00	0.01				
28	–24	0.02	0.04				
29	–21	0.12	0.15				
30	–18	0.44	0.51				
31	–15	1.37	1.47				
32	–12	3.48	3.57	=A36–B$12 and **Copy** up to **A24**			
33	–9	7.16	7.19	=0.5*100*(TDIST((–A35–B$12/2)/G$4,B$6,2) –TDIST((–A35+B$12/2)/G$4,B$6,2)) and **Copy** up to **C24**			
34	–6	11.99	11.92				
35	–3	16.35	16.18				
36	0	18.13	17.92	=100*(TDIST(0,B$6,2)– TDIST(B$12/2/G$4,B$6,2))			
37	3	16.35	16.18				
38	6	11.99	11.92	=0.5*100*(TDIST((A37–B$12/2)/G$4,B$6,2) –TDIST((A37+B$12/2)/G$4,B$6,2)) and **Copy** down to **C48**			
39	9	7.16	7.19				
40	12	3.48	3.57				
41	15	1.37	1.47	=A36+B$12 and **Copy** down to **A48**			
42	18	0.44	0.51				
43	21	0.12	0.15				
44	24	0.02	0.04				
45	27	0.00	0.01				
46	30	0.00	0.00				
47	33	0.00	0.00				
48	36	0.00	0.00				

FIGURE 15.3
Setting up a
simulation for
graphically
demonstrating
t-tests

7 Use the ChartWizard to generate the graph (remember, you can refer to Section A.3 in Appendix A for assistance). After marking out a space for the graph, the five ChartWizard steps will have the following entries:

Step 1 Set the **Range** to be **A13:F48**.
Step 2 Select **XY (Scatter)**.
Step 3 Select **format 2**.
Step 4 Set

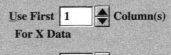

Use First 1 Column(s)
For X Data

Use First 1 Row(s)
for Legend Text.

Step 5 Enter titles.

You should get the graph shown in Figure 15.4(a). Print it out if possible.

8 Change the values for n to 30 (thus $df = 58$) and then to 5 (thus $df = 8$) to generate the graphs in Figures 15.4(b) and 15.4(c). How do the z- and t-distributions begin to differ?

9 Try other numbers and see what happens, printing each out if possible, so that you can compare them.

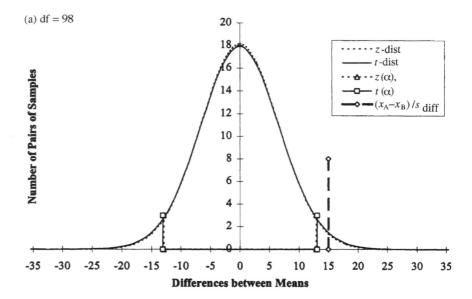

FIGURE 15.4(a)
Three comparisons of z- and t-distributions for different df

(b) df = 58

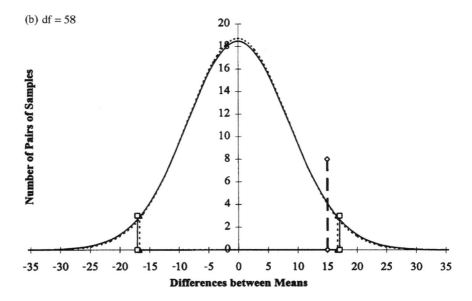

FIGURE 15.4(b)
Three comparisons
of *z*- and
t-distributions for
different *df*

(c) df = 8

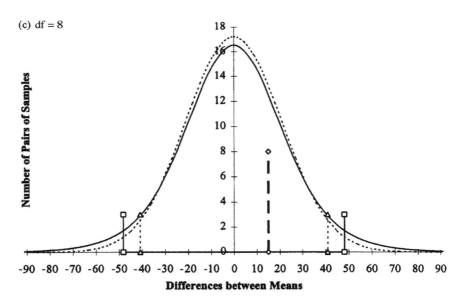

FIGURE 15.4(c)
Three comparisons
of *z*- and
t-distributions for
different *df*

The three pairs of graphs in Figure 15.4 allow you to see how the $t(\alpha)$ and $z(\alpha)$ critical points diverge as the samples become smaller in spite of the observation that there is little difference in the shapes. This shows why the test becomes more conservative as the sample size declines: Figure 15.4(a) suggests a significant difference for $n_A = n_B = 50$, while Figures 15.4(b) and 15.4(c) suggest a non-significant difference when the samples are smaller. These hide an even more interesting fact about the two distributions.

A better way of illustrating how the *z*- and *t*-distributions change with changes in *df* would be to plot the above three distributions on one graph, as

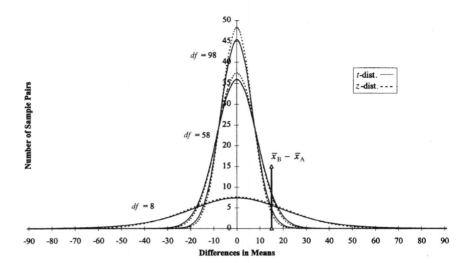

FIGURE 15.5
Comparison of the three *t*-distributions, dependent on *df*

shown in Figure 15.5. Note that while the maxima on the vertical axes have changed to allow this comparison, the areas under the graphs are all equal. While the three separate graphs hide a major change since they have different interval sizes and different ranges for the horizontal axis, this representation does not. From Figure 15.5, the three graphs show that the normal distributions change in much the same way as the *t*-distribution, getting shorter and fatter as the samples (and *df*) become smaller. What is to be noticed is that as the samples become smaller, the *t*- and *z*-distributions become increasingly different, particularly in the tails, influencing where the cut-off is for the last 2.5% in each. From both sets of graphs, it becomes more apparent why it is harder to find significance when samples are smaller: both distributions become shorter and fatter; and the *t*-distribution becomes even fatter and shorter than the *z*-distribution. Thus while the *t*-distribution compensates for greater sampling error due to small samples, both are sensitive to small samples.

Interpreting *t*-tests

The *t*-distribution necessitates a new set of tables giving the cut-off points for various degrees of freedom, as shown in Table B.2 in Appendix B, which was generated using the Excel functions indicated. Alternatively, after calculating a value for the *t*-ratio, one simply uses the Excel function to determine the probability level for that value. If it is less than the level set up *before* the test, then one can reject H_0, whereas if it is greater than this value, then one must accept H_0. For example, in the example above, using equation (15.7),

$$t_{\text{unpooled}} = \frac{\bar{x}_A - \bar{x}_B}{s_{\text{diff unpooled}}}$$

$$t_{\text{unpooled}} = \frac{175 - 160}{6.60} = 2.27$$

which is greater than the minimum value for $p = 0.05$, $t_{df=98} = 1.99$, thus this is significant ($p < 0.05$). If this were used in the Excel function to determine the probability of obtaining such a t-ratio, we would find

$$p = \textbf{TDIST}(\textbf{value}, \textit{df}, \textbf{tails}) = \textbf{TDIST}(\textbf{2.27, 98, 2}) = 0.025$$

which is less than 0.05. Remember that for $p = 0.05$, $z = 1.96$, always. If the second case is calculated for samples of 30 for each, then

$$t_{\text{unpooled}} = \frac{175 - 160}{8.52} = 1.76$$

which is less than the minimum value for $p = 0.05$, $t_{df=58} = 2.00$, thus this is not significant. Using the Excel function, the probability of obtaining a t-ratio of this size is

$$p = \textbf{TDIST}(\textbf{value}, \textit{df}, \textbf{tails}) = \textbf{TDIST}(\textbf{1.76, 58, 2}) = 0.084$$

which is greater than 0.05. Finally, for the last of the three examples, where the samples were only 5 each,

$$t_{\text{unpooled}} = \frac{175 - 160}{20.88} = 0.72$$

which is much less than the minimum value for $p = 0.05$, $t_{df=8} = 2.31$, thus this is not significant. Using the Excel function,

$$p = \textbf{TDIST}(\textbf{value}, \textit{df}, \textbf{tails}) = \textbf{TDIST}(\textbf{0.72, 8, 2}) = 0.492$$

which is much greater than 0.05. Now carry out Activity 15.2 to explore some of the traits of and influences on the outcomes of t-test.

Activity 15.2

Using the simulation of Figure 15.3, try the changes described below one at a time, keeping the other variables constant and reflecting on how this relates to research:

1   Change the sample sizes, n_A and n_B to see how sample size influences the potential of identifying a significant difference. Which contributes more, the effect on s_{diff} or the influence of using the t-distribution? Is it uniform for all sample sizes?
2   Change the difference between the means by increasing and decreasing the one for sample B. This will demonstrate the influence of *size of effect*.
3   Change the standard deviations, keeping them close to each other for now, as we will explore the consequences of big differences later.

CALCULATING BASIC t-TEST RESULTS

Now that the characteristics of t-distributions have been established, let us consider how we can calculate results of tests quickly and efficiently. What must be realized is that not every situation is as perfect at the ones described above. In other words, we may not meet all the assumptions above of equal sample sizes, equal variances and independent samples.

Therefore, there are four slightly different ways of carrying out the *t*-test, one for situations that meet all the assumptions, and three that compensate for situations that do *not* meet the assumptions. To facilitate the calculation of these, a data-processing worksheet will be developed in stages, that will allow you to enter either means, standard deviations and sample sizes directly, or raw data. The first will allow you to perform calculations quickly to compare the effects of violating the three assumptions, as well as quickly check calculations in published research. The second, a simple addition to the basic sheet, will allow you to enter raw data and generate the results. There will still be decisions to be made as to which of the three is most appropriate for the design, but this will also show you the consequences of design choices. To start the process, carry out Activity 15.3.

Activity 15.3

In this activity, you will set up a worksheet that can be used to process data for the *t*-tests, one that is somewhat better than standard software packages since it will also provide estimates of the power of the tests for planning. This will be done in three stages, the first shown in Figure 15.6. In this worksheet, the shaded boxes will eventually be the only ones in which you will have to make changes. It will also generate graphs of the distribution of differences in sampling means, as in Figure 15.7.

1　Go to your copy of the worksheet for Figure 15.3. With the mouse, block out the cells **A1:G9**, then **Copy** them either through **Edit** on the main menu or the **Copy** icon. Go to a new worksheet and with the cursor in cell **A1**, **Paste** this set of cells.

2　Add the new title at the top. As noted, there will be several versions of the *t*-test, therefore space will be left on the sheet for additions in later activities. In cell **D3** place the calculation for the difference in the means. In **C6** put the calculation for the degrees of freedom, and shade the area for **B6**, since we will have the possibility of more than one source for *df* later. Add 'unpooled' to the s_{diff} label in cell **F4**.

3　In columns **D** and **E**, enter the first *Results* as shown. The *t*-statistic, $t_{unpooled}$, is calculated using equation (15.7) and the critical value employs the Excel function = TINV(**probability, df**). The probability in this function is determined by **2*B8/B7** to obtain a critical value for either a one-tailed or two-tailed test, since **B7** can be 1 or 2.

4　The outlined box area **B15:C18** will eventually contain the final results of the chosen test, with you selecting the appropriate one of the four that will eventually be included. Therefore the cells **D15:D18** contain the cell references but typed in as text, that is, each preceded by a single quotation mark. To enter the set as the one chosen, the three cells are **Copy**ed to **C16:C18** and the quotation

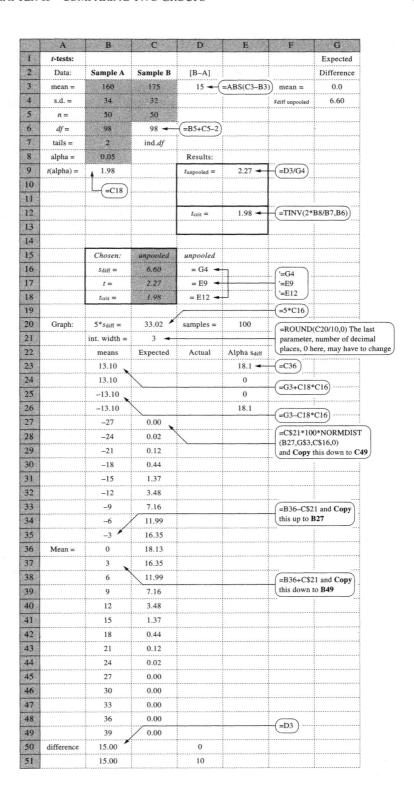

FIGURE 15.6
First stage in
developing a data
processing
worksheet for *t*-tests

marks deleted in each cell. The numbers then appear. At this point, we have included only one test, *unpooled*, therefore the cell designations are those shown in adjoining column **D**. We also need to use the value for t_{crit} for the graphs so it also appears in cell **B9**.

5 To provide the data necessary to generate the graph for the distribution of differences in the means ('Expected'), rows **22** downwards in column **C** contain the necessary numbers and functions, as shown. Added to this are the α critical lines and a line for the 'Actual' difference in the sample means. In cells **C27** and below, we will use the normal distribution function, recognizing that it really should be a *t*-distribution. This is because the *t*-distribution is (as we saw earlier) messy to generate in Excel, and the little difference in the graphs is not significant here since the purpose is to give a rough illustration of the results. The initial set of data is from the example above, which shows a significant *t*-test result, $p < 0.05$, since *t* is greater than t_{crit}. Now let us see how to generate the graph.

6 This shows the relationship of the actual difference between the sample means to the assumed population difference of zero. After marking out an area for the graph, proceed using the ChartWizard as follows:

Step 1 Set the <u>R</u>ange to be **B22:E51**.
Step 2 Select X<u>Y</u> (<u>S</u>catter).
Step 3 Choose **format 2**.
Step 4 Set

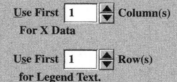

Step 5 Add the titles.

Your graph will probably be in colour. You can remove data point markers if you want and change the *x*-axis scale to integers.

7 Try entering data for the other situations shown earlier and consider the resulting graphs. You may find it useful to print these out, labelling each carefully using the Chart Title facility.

SMALL SAMPLES: THE POOLED VARIANCE APPROACH

When the samples are very small, then there is a need to compensate even more for the error introduced, by adjusting for the estimate of the standard error of the difference, s_{diff}. This is achieved by pooling data from both samples to generate new estimates of the population value for the standard error of the mean.

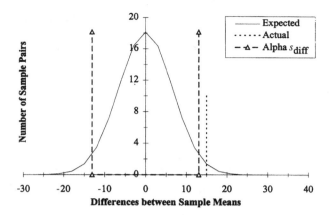

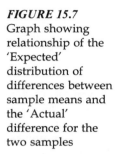

FIGURE 15.7
Graph showing relationship of the 'Expected' distribution of differences between sample means and the 'Actual' difference for the two samples

We start with equation (15.3), which we re-write to suit our needs:

$$\sigma_{\text{diff}} = \sqrt{\sigma_{\bar{x}_A}^2 + \sigma_{\bar{x}_B}^2}$$

$$= \sqrt{\frac{\sigma_A^2}{n_A} + \frac{\sigma_B^2}{n_B}}$$

The estimate assumes that the variances are equal since both samples belong to a common population: $\sigma_A^2 = \sigma_B^2 = \sigma^2$. Thus the equation becomes

$$\sigma_{\text{diff}} = \sqrt{\sigma^2\left(\frac{1}{n_A} + \frac{1}{n_B}\right)} \tag{15.11}$$

Pooling the sample data tends to reduce the sampling error, and results in an expression for estimating σ^2 (see Hays, 1994, for the derivation),

$$\text{est } \sigma^2 = s_{\text{pooled}}^2 = \frac{(n_A - 1)s_A^2 + (n_B - 1)s_B^2}{n_A + n_B - 2} \tag{15.12}$$

Substituting this into equation (15.9) provides the new estimate for the standard error of the difference for small samples:

$$s_{\text{diff pooled}} = \sqrt{\frac{(n_A - 1)s_A^2 + (n_B - 1)s_B^2}{n_A + n_B - 2}\left(\frac{1}{n_A} + \frac{1}{n_B}\right)} \tag{15.13}$$

It does not take very much effort to show that if $n_A = n_B$, then this equation is exactly equal to equation (15.6). Thus the real advantage of using this equation appears *when the samples are small and unequal.*

As daunting as this equation may seem, we will find that Excel, as well as standard statistical packages, will provide the results of this for you. Let us demonstrate the consequences of using this by working an example, before seeing how the hard work is done for us.

In a desperate attempt to test the null hypothesis that there would be no difference in the gain scores on an instrument that measures motivation between a

TABLE 15.2
Summary of results
of Professor
Encouragem's study
employing
counselling sessions
for increasing
motivation (x was a
gain score)

	Experimental group A	Control group B
$\bar{x}$	14.25	12
s	2.5	1.8
n	10	7

control group and a group that received a series of counselling sessions, Professor Encouragem secured two small groups. These were randomly selected from the undergraduate psychology class, and while he started with ten in each group, he lost three from the control group, all having withdrawn from university due to financial problems. Since the reason for withdrawal seemed unrelated to the study, he decided to carry out the study anyway. The results were as shown in Table 15.2. First, calculating the standard error of the difference using equation (15.6), we get

$$s_{\text{diff unpooled}} = \sqrt{\frac{(1.8)^2}{7} + \frac{(2.5)^2}{10}} = 1.043$$

Finding t is straightforward:

$$t_{\text{unpooled}} = \frac{14.25 - 12}{1.043} = 2.157$$

Comparing this with the critical value in Appendix B, Table B.2, for $\alpha = 0.05$ and $df = 17$ of 2.131 for a two-tailed test, then $p < 0.05$ and the result could be considered significant, rejecting H_0. This would encourage Professor Encouragem to accept his treatment as having a recognizable effect, assuming that all extraneous variables were adequately controlled. On the other hand, if we use equation (15.11) to find s_{diff},

$$s_{\text{diff pooled}} = \sqrt{\frac{(7-1)(1.8)^2 + (10-1)(2.5)^2}{7+10-2}\left(\frac{1}{7} + \frac{1}{10}\right)}$$

$$= \sqrt{\frac{19.44 + 56.25}{15}(0.243)} = 1.107$$

and obtain the t-ratio using equation (15.5) as before, we have

$$t_{\text{pooled}} = \frac{14.25 - 12}{1.107} = 2.033$$

This does *not* exceed the critical value, thus the results are not significant and the difference could be attributed to chance alone. So we see that using the pooled variance approach can influence the outcome of a test.

On the other hand, if Professor Encouragem had obtained previous evidence that the experimental group would surely be greater than the control, he would have declared a one-tailed test with a critical value of 1.573, and the results would have been significant. We will consider two more commonly encountered situations when testing pairs of means, and the adjustment that is applied.

Unequal sample variances and small samples

The above approach was able to compensate for small samples, but assumed that the variances were roughly the same and reasonable indicators of the population variance. What happens if the variances differ by a large amount, and how much is 'large'? As with previous criteria, some compensation has to be made for this violation of the assumptions underlying the test. As before, this will make the test more *conservative*, in other words, make it more difficult to find a significant difference by reducing the value for the t-ratio. From a practical viewpoint, this is easier than increasing the critical value and generating tables for all the possible variations and combinations. First let us consider a test for 'how much is too much?'.

Testing for homogeneity of variance

The hypothesis that is being tested, that the two samples belong to the same population, uses a statistical test that assumes that even if there are two populations, they have equal variances, $\sigma_A^2 = \sigma_B^2$. We talk about *homogeneity of variance* just to avoid saying the sample variances must be exactly equal. Consequently, it is necessary to establish some criteria for what will be accepted as homogeneous *enough*. As the statisticians say, the t-test is *robust*, as it will tolerate some difference in the variances, and even some non-normality (for example, skewness) in the distributions, without increasing the probability of making a Type I error (Winer *et al*, 1991). The homogeneity of variance test that is used is based upon the F-distribution, one that we will consider in detail in the next chapter. This simply requires finding the ratio of the two sample variances, with values inserted as indicated:

$$F = \frac{s_{\text{largest}}^2}{s_{\text{smallest}}^2} \qquad (15.14)$$

This is checked against the appropriate F_{crit} value table, where $df = n - 1$ for each group, as if it were a one-tailed test. Since critical value tables for F-distributions, such as Table B.3 in Appendix B, are two-tailed, then one must take care to use the correct value of α. For example, to check the homogeneity of the variances in the example in Table 15.2, with $\alpha = 0.10$,

$$F = \frac{2.5^2}{1.8^2} = 1.93$$

From Table B.3, Appendix B, we find that $F_{0.05}(9, 6) = 4.10$. Since our value for F-ratio does not exceed this value, the variances can be taken to be sufficiently homogeneous to use the t-test unaltered.

Adjusting for different sample sizes and heterogeneity of variances

If the F-ratio were to exceed the critical value, thus violating the assumption of the t-test, and the sample sizes are different, then a correction must be made (Hays, 1994). There are a number of adjustments available, which usually result in either finding an adjusted value for the t-ratio, or the determination of a new value for the degrees of freedom, df, either of which would allow existing tables to be used. A commonly used approach (Winer et al, 1991; Sirkin, 1995; Howell, 1997; Blalock, 1979; Hays, 1994) involves an awesome-looking equation that generates a new value for the df, identified as df^*, which can be put into a worksheet with a little effort, as we will see:

$$df^* = \left[\frac{\left(\frac{s_A^2}{n_A} + \frac{s_B^2}{n_B} \right)^2}{\frac{\left(\frac{s_A^2}{n_A} \right)^2}{n_A + 1} + \frac{\left(\frac{s_B^2}{n_B} \right)^2}{n_B + 1}} \right] - 2 \qquad (15.15)$$

The answer is truncated to the integer value and must be considered an estimate, but is used to identify a new df value for t_{crit}^*, as long as it is less than the maximum, $df = n_A + n_B - 2$. The standard error of the difference in this situation is calculated using the unpooled variance approach (Equation (15.6)). If the sample size is large this will probably provide little difference in the value of df. What effect this does have can be seen by changing sample sizes in the spreadsheet that includes this calculation (see Activity 15.4 below).

INTERRELATED SAMPLES

There will be situations where it is not possible, or even desirable, to have independent samples and yet there is a need to test whether the two samples belong to the same population. Because of the nature of the samples, there will be some sort of relationship between them, therefore while they may differ on the independent variable, they are not entirely independent samples, a violation of one of the assumptions of the t-test. Most studies will be one of three types.

The first will involve a single group over time (sometimes referred to as *repeated measures*), where measures before and after treatment are compared. This could be considered to be a test for a time series design with only two measures. Using such an approach may be necessary when samples are difficult to acquire, when first developing a treatment and trying to refine it, or when not providing treatment could present ethical problems (the control group would definitely suffer). For example, a study of the potential effects of counselling young people who are substance abusers, where we are interested in whether the level of abuse declines, would involve using one group, measuring before and after the session. As a first step, this would provide some information about the treatment (see pre-experimental design A2 in Chapter 3), but it would not be as good as two groups, one being a control (design B2 or even C2 in Chapter 4). On the other hand, it is not very defensible to use such an approach simply because it is more convenient to have just one group. The numerous sources of confounding described in Chapter 3 can make the validity of the results questionable, though this approach is tempting since, as will be seen later, the statistical power is increased. It might be most justifiable for a pilot, using the results as a basis for a better structured study with a control group (see design B2).

Studies of the second type involve two groups *intentionally matched* (referred to as *matched pairs*), where the members of the two groups are assigned to the experimental and control groups based upon some trait that will influence the dependent variable. For example, Grommet Electronics wants to determine the best training programme for its staff by using a sample of employees. Being concerned about the influence of educational background and rank within the company on the apparent effectiveness of the programmes, the random sample of staff were divided into two matched groups so that staff from all levels of the company were equally represented. Thus there were matched pairs of upper management, middle management, shop-floor supervisors, and assembly-line workers, one of the pair in each group. This is a B2 design with a twist, thus a different statistical test is required.

The final study type again involves *matched pairs*, but now with two groups *closely related*, thus having traits in common that influence the measured outcomes of the study. This is common in ex post facto designs where comparisons across family members are to be made and may constitute a desirable situation, but one that also requires special statistical treatment. The study appears to have the structure of design B2 (or possibly C2), but one underlying assumption of the *t*-test is not met: the samples are not independent of each other. For example, to resolve the hypothesis that there is a gender difference in prejudice, it was decided to compare men's and women's attitudes towards ethnic minorities. Realizing that couples will influence each other, it was decided to select couples purposefully and recognize this relationship. While this has the advantage that both individuals are exposed to many of the same influences in society, it acknowledges that they are not totally independent in their views. Thus a random sample of couples was selected to test the hypothesis.

Due to the interrelatedness of samples, an adjustment must be made to the way the *t*-test is applied to resolve the null hypothesis. The logic goes something like this: the *t*-test assumes two independent samples, so we treat our data as one of the samples and use the *difference* between the two measures, finding the mean of the differences, $\bar{D}$, and assume the other measure would generate no difference, and therefore have a mean of zero. Thus the equation would be

$$t = \frac{\bar{D} - 0}{s_{\text{diff}}}$$

The standard error of the difference, though, would have to be found from the standard deviation of the one set of data, the differences, s_D, thus, analogous to equation (15.3), it becomes

$$s_{D_{\text{diff}}} = \frac{s_D}{\sqrt{n}} \tag{15.16}$$

but with *df* equal to the number of pairs less one, thus halving the degrees of freedom, since this is the number of *independent* measures. Thus the *t*-statistic would be

$$t_{\text{related}} = \frac{\bar{D}}{s_D / \sqrt{n}} \tag{15.17}$$

TABLE 15.3
Summary of results
of a study to
determine existence
of difference in
prejudice between
men and women

	Men	Women	Difference
$\bar{x}$	5.44	6.33	0.89
s	2.65	2.50	1.05
n	9	9	9
df	16		8

To see what effect this has on the outcome of a test, consider the ex post facto study of the possible effect of gender on racial prejudiced described above. The results of the study are provided in Table 15.3. If the results were taken to be from two independent samples, then equation (15.7) would result in

$$t_{\text{unpooled}} = \frac{6.33 - 5.44}{\sqrt{\dfrac{2.65^2}{9} + \dfrac{2.50^2}{9}}} = \frac{0.89}{1.21} = 0.74$$

whereas if they were considered to be matched pairs, then equation (15.17) would result in

$$t_{\text{related}} = \frac{0.89}{1.05/\sqrt{9}} = \frac{0.89}{0.35} = 2.54$$

From Table B2 in Appendix B, for $p = 0.05$, we have $t_{\text{crit}}(df = 16) = 2.12$ for unrelated samples, and $t_{\text{crit}}(df = 8) = 2.31$ for interrelated samples; it is evident that, in some cases, there will be a distinct advantage (statistically) in recognizing matched pairs. The disadvantage is that the inference is now limited to gender differences for couples and *not* gender differences in general. You will be able to work out further examples on the extended version of the worksheet in Activity 15.4 that follows.

Activity 15.4

Bring up the worksheet that you started in Activity 15.3. You will now add the calculations for the other three varieties of *t*-test. First type in the data into the shaded cells from the example in Table 15.3, as shown in Figure 15.8.

1 In column **D**, add the shaded cell and *df* for related samples. (If this is not to be used, leave a number in cell **D4** as a place holder.)
2 In cell **G5** add the Excel version of equation (15.13) for the standard error of the difference for pooled variances. In cell **G6** add the Excel version of equation (15.17) for the standard error of the difference for related data. Both of these refer to data in the shaded boxes on the left.
3 In cell **E10** add the Excel version of the *t*-test using the pooled standard error of the difference in **G5**. In cell **E11** add the Excel version of the *t*-test using the standard error of the difference for related variables, **G6**.

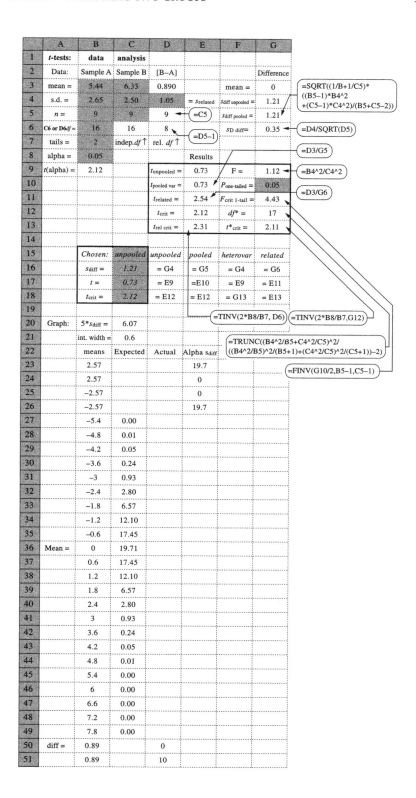

FIGURE 15.8
Second stage in developing a data processing worksheet for *t*-tests

4   To test for homogeneity of variance, set up the F-test in cell **G9** and prepare the next cell for the probability level that will be used. Then in cell **G11**, enter the function will return the critical value = **FINV(probability, df_{num}, df_{den})**. The probability value in cell **G10** is divided by 2 since the F-statistic is two-tailed and this test is one-tailed.

5   Next in **G12** is the rather long equation (15.15) for degrees of freedom for heterogeneous samples, that is truncated (rounded down) to the nearest whole number. This value must be *less than* that in **C6** for the critical value in the next cell, **G12**, to be used.

6   In cell **E13** add the Excel function for the critical value for related means, $t_{rel\ crit}$, which varies only in which df is used, **D6** instead of **C6**, since there is a choice.

7   Add all the alternative cell designations in **E15** to **G18**. Type these in as a *string* (a set of characters interpreted as a label and not a formula), for example, $'= G5$. After **Copy**ing a set as a block to **C15:C18**, in each cell the $'$ can be deleted to change the cell contents from a string to a proper cell reference, which will then be interpreted and display the appropriate number.

8   The results for the example should be for *unpooled* variances. Make sure that the df in cell **B6** corresponds to **C6** and that the chosen results **C15:C18** are *unpooled* (see 7 above). These should be the results for the first alternative in the example above and are shown in Figure 15.9. Now change the df in **B6** and **Copy** the *related* cell addresses into **C15:18** to find the second set of outcomes for related samples. How do they differ?

Before going any further, let us consider the calculation of the estimate of *power* for such tests.

Answer: 8. See Figure 15.10.

POWER AND CHOOSING α

Finding the power of a t-test is analogous to the process used in Chapter 14 where it was found for the one-sample test of belonging to a population. For the t-test, we are concerned with two samples and the differences in their means. Therefore the power calculations will be based upon the two possible distributions of differences in sampling means.

Recall that the quantification of power is based upon the overlap of two distributions. Illustrations such as Figure 15.7 show the relationship between the distribution of differences in sampling means, with an expected grand mean of 0, and the difference in the means for the two samples. The central distribution is based upon the assumption that the difference in population means for the samples is zero, that is, they belong to a single population. A second, *noncentral* distribution can be generated, based upon the assumption that the

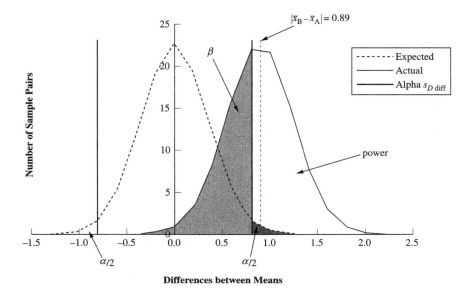

FIGURE 15.9
Relationship
between α, β, and
power, illustrated
graphically, based
on Figure 15.8
worksheet, where
$s_{D_{\text{diff}}} = 0.35$, since
samples are related

difference is indicative of a second population and H_0 is false. Thus the non-zero difference in sample means forms the mean of the non-central distribution. Using the difference in means from the worksheet in Figure 15.7 as the mean for the non-central distribution and the corresponding standard error of the difference (in this case the samples are related), the two distributions would appear as in Figure 15.9. The α cut-off of the central distribution extends into the non-central distribution to divide the area into β and power, as shown by the vertical line. It is obvious that the power area is greater than half the area under the non-central distribution. The difference in the sample means that is the basis for the non-central distribution is shown by the dashed vertical line. Thus the power is greater than 50%. You will generate this pair of curves in Activity 15.5, but first let us consider how to calculate β and power based upon these curves directly.

To quantify β and power, it is necessary first to find the position of α on the horizontal axis using an expression analogous to equation (14.3), with reference to the first distribution:

$$x(\alpha) = \Delta\mu_0 + t_{\text{crit}}s_{\text{diff}} \tag{15.18}$$

where $\Delta\mu_0$ is the expected difference in sampling means if H_0 is true, i.e., zero; t_{crit} is the critical value for the situation from Appendix B, Table B2, s_{diff} is the standard error of the difference for the test to be used. Expressing this in terms of the second distribution, like equation (14.4), we have

$$x(\alpha) = \Delta\mu_1 + z(\beta)s_{\text{diff}}$$

where $\Delta\mu_1$ is an estimate of the expected difference in sampling means if H_0 is false, not zero, given by

$$\Delta\mu_1 = |\bar{x}_B - \bar{x}_A|$$

that is, the absolute value (always positive) of the difference in sampling means.

Solving for the z-score for β gives

$$z(\beta) = \frac{x(\alpha) - \Delta\mu_1}{s_{\text{diff}}}$$

Substituting in equation (15.18) for $x(\alpha)$ and the estimate for $\Delta\mu_1$,

$$z(\beta) = \frac{\Delta\mu_0 + t_{\text{crit}}\, s_{\text{diff}} - |\bar{x}_B - \bar{x}_A|}{s_{\text{diff}}}$$

which reduces to the following, since $\Delta\mu_0 = 0$:

$$z(\beta) = t_{\text{crit}} - \frac{|\bar{x}_B - \bar{x}_A|}{s_{\text{diff}}}$$

This becomes simply

$$z(\beta) = t_{\text{crit}} - t\text{-ratio} \tag{15.19}$$

Which t-ratio and which df for t_{crit} are used will depend upon the design and situation. To find β, the area under the curve is found from the table of z-scores, Table B1 in Appendix B, and power is found from the definition, $1 - \beta$. For example, using the values from Figure 15.9 originally provided in the worksheet in Figure 15.8, the samples are related, therefore, from the worksheet, you should find

$$z(\beta) = t_{\text{rel crit}} - t\text{-ratio}$$

$$= t_{\text{rel crit}} - \frac{|\bar{x}_B - \bar{x}_A|}{s_{D_{\text{diff}}}}$$

$$z(\beta) = 2.31 - \frac{0.89}{0.35} = -0.23$$

Consulting Table B1 in Appendix B, we find that for this value the area between the mean and $z(\beta)$ results in $\beta = 0.5 - 0.0910 = 0.4090$, thus the power is about 0.59. This indicates that there was about a 41% probability of committing a Type II error and a 59% probability that any true significant difference would have been correctly identified. This is consistent with the areas under the curves in Figure 15.9.

What would have been the consequence of treating the data as unrelated and using pooled variances? We saw in the original worksheet example that the difference was not statistically significant. To calculate the power of correctly rejecting H_0 on the basis of such contradictory evidence,

$$z(\beta) = t_{\text{crit}} - t\text{-ratio}$$

$$= t_{\text{crit}} - \frac{|\bar{x}_B - \bar{x}_A|}{s_{\text{diff unpooled}}}$$

$$z(\beta) = 2.12 - \frac{0.89}{1.21} = 1.38$$

Table values tell us that $\beta = 0.5 + 0.4162 = 0.9162$, thus the power is about 0.08. In other words there would be a very large probability of making a Type II error.

Now up to this point you will have noticed that we have been using the normal distribution for z-scores, when we really ought to have been using t-distributions. Since the equivalent tables were not available for carrying out the examples, these have been used as estimates. As you will see in activity 15.5, where t-distributions are used, the results are much the same, though they will increasingly diverge, the smaller the samples. The calculations will now be added to the worksheet, as the capacity to display the graphs, by carrying out Activity 15.5 now.

Activity 15.5

First we will call up the worksheet in Figure 15.8 and add the β and power calculations, then formulae to generate the non-central distribution graph as shown in Figure 15.10.

1   In row **10**, insert the Excel version of equation (15.19) for $t(\beta)$.
2   A value for β is found by referring to the t-distribution using the Excel function in one of two forms:= **TDIST**$(-t(\beta),$ **df, tails**$)$ for negative values of $t(\beta)$ when the power is greater than 0.50; and = **1 − TDIST**$(t(\beta),$ **df, tails**$)$ for positive values of $t(\beta)$ when the power is less than 0.50. Two versions are necessary because of the nature of the function, which provides an error message **#NUM!** when $t(\beta)$ is negative. Thus, when the difference in sample means is greater than α, then the first will appear, and vice versa. Also, since it is a cumulative distribution, this is the only way to obtain values on either side of a mean. In any case, only one of the pairs of cells will have numbers in them, the other will have **#NUM!** In this case, the number of tails does not refer to our statistical test; here we are looking for the area under the second curve beyond the α line from the first (see Figure 15.9). Thus we are using only one half the distribution and this is equivalent to a one-tailed situation, so in the above two formulae, tails = 1.
3   To generate a graph of the non-central distribution whose mean equals the difference in means for the two samples, insert the function shown in **D27** and **Copy** as indicated. Again, since it is simpler to use the normal distribution function, we use it instead of the t-distribution for purposes of illustration. Though slightly inaccurate in terms of areas, none of us will be able to detect it. The above calculations are accurate and the visual representation is there to illustrate what they mean.
4   Simply by adding the formulae in column **D**, the chart should generate the pair of graphs like the ones in Figure 15.11(a), though without all the labels. Make sure that the df in cell **B6** is for related samples since the data illustrate the second situation in the example above, showing the t-test for interrelated samples in Table 15.2. You may have to adjust the scale on the x-axis. Print out your results and save them.

	A	B	C	D	E	F	G
1	*t*-tests:	**data**	**analysis**				
2	Data:	**Sample A**	**Sample B**	[B–A]			Difference
3	mean =	5.44	6.33	0.890		mean =	0
4	s.d. =	2.65	2.50	1.05	= $s_{related}$	$s_{diff\ unpooled}$	1.21
5	*n* =	9	9	9		$s_{diff\ pooled}$ =	1.21
6	**C6/D6***df* =	8	16	8		$s_{D\ diff}$=	0.35
7	tails =	2	indep.*df*	rel. *df*			
8	alpha =	0.05			Results	F =	
9	*t*(alpha) =	2.31		$t_{unpooled}$ =	0.73	$P_{one\text{-}tailed}$ =	1.12
10	*t*(beta) =	–0.24		$t_{pooled\ var}$ =	0.73	$F_{crit\ 1\text{-}tail}$ =	0.05
11				$t_{related}$ =	2.54	df^* =	4.43
12	*beta* =	0.41	#NUM!	t_{crit} =	2.12	t^*_{crit} =	17
13	*power* =	0.59	#NUM!	$t_{rel\ crit}$ =	2.31		2.11
14							
15		*Chosen:*	*related*	*unpooled*	*pooled*	*hetero var*	*related*
16		s_{diff} =	0.35	= G4	= G5	= G4	= G6
17		*t* =	2.54	= E9	=E10	= E9	= E11
18		t_{crit} =	2.31	= E12	= E12	= G13	= E13
19							
20	Graph:	5*s_{diff} =	1.75				
21		int. width =	0.2				
22		means	Expected	Actual	Alpha s_{diff}		
23		0.81			22.8		
24		0.81			0		
25		–0.81			0		
26		–0.81			22.8		
27		–1.8	0.00	0.00			
28		–1.6	0.00	0.00			
29		–1.4	0.01	0.00			
30		–1.2	0.06	0.00			
31		–1	0.38	0.00			
32		–0.8	1.67	0.00			
33		–0.6	5.24	0.00			
34		–0.4	11.86	0.03			
35		–0.2	19.36	0.18			
36		0	22.80	0.90			
37		0.2	19.36	3.27			
38		0.4	11.86	8.56			
39		0.6	5.24	16.17			
40		0.8	1.67	22.06			
41		1	0.38	21.70			
42		1.2	0.06	15.40			
43		1.4	0.01	7.89			
44		1.6	0.00	2.91			
45		1.8	0.00	0.78			
46		2	0.00	0.15			
47		2.2	0.00	0.02			
48		2.4	0.00	0.00			
49		2.6	0.00	0.00			
50		0.89		0			
51		0.89		10			

Annotations (callout boxes):
- =C18–C17 → *t*(alpha) (B9)
- =TDIST(–B10,B6,1) → *t*(beta) (B10)
- =1–B12 → *beta*/power (B13)
- =1–TDIST(B10,B6,1) → (row 14)
- =1–C12 → (D12/D13 area)
- =C$21*100*NORMDIST(B27,D$3,C$16,0) and **Copy** down to **D49** → (D27)

FIGURE 15.10
Worksheet for carrying out *t*-tests, with power calculations

5 Now go back and **Copy D15:D18** for unrelated data, *Unpooled,* into **C15:C18** and remove the ' marks, remembering also to change *df* in cell **B6**. This provides the results if one were not to consider the data related, as originally done in Figure 15.8. You may have to adjust the scale on the *x*-axis. How does your graph of the two distributions compare to the interrelated situation? Yours should look like that in Figure 15.11(b), with the power being the area to the right of the vertical line. What are the graphical and power consequences of treating the data these two ways?

A number of additional problems (with answers) will be available to try at the end of the chapter after all the decision issues have been covered.

Influence of instrument reliability on *t*-test results

To demonstrate how instrument reliability can affect the outcome of a statistical test, let us consider an example. Alice Inwonderland wanted to know if there were a difference across social classes in attitudes towards the consumption of marijuana. She devised a questionnaire to quantify respondents' overall feelings towards its use, which she hypothesized would be different for two random samples (an ex post facto design C3 - see Chapter 7) of university students from social classes A and C. During trials of the instrument, she found its reliability to be $r_{xx} = 0.50$. To improve the instrument would take considerable effort, so she was wondering whether it would be worth the effort before collecting all the data and carrying out a *t*-test to determine if there were a significant difference between the groups.

To help her make the decision, let us go back to the definition of reliability from equation (11.1):

$$r_{xx} \equiv \frac{S_t^2}{S_x^2} \qquad (15.20)$$

where S_t^2 is the true score variance and S_x^2 is the observed score variance (equal to the standard deviation of the set of scores squared). Since the reliability coefficient is an estimate, we can only get an estimate of the true score variance. We will use S and s interchangeably here since the sample size is large and we are using approximations,

$$\text{est } S_t^2 = r_{xx} S_x^2 \qquad (15.21)$$

Now let us imagine two scenarios, one where Alice does not improve the instrument and a second where she does. Without improvement, the results were as shown in Table 15.4, below, where no significant difference between the groups was found, $t_{crit} = 1.98$. From this we can get estimates of true score variances:

$$\text{est } S_{tC}^2 = 0.50 \times 30^2 = 450$$

$$\text{est } S_{tA}^2 = 0.50 \times 28^2 = 392$$

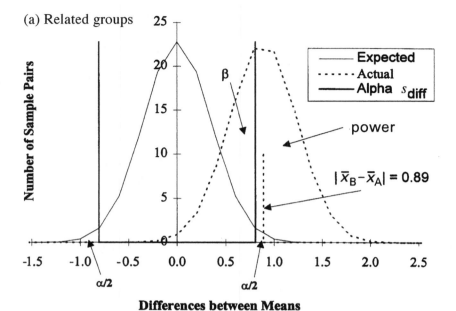

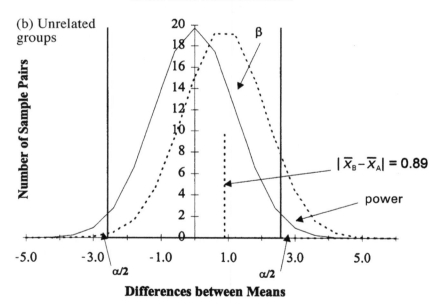

FIGURE 15.11
Graphs of sample
distributions and
difference
distributions
(illustrating β and
power) for the
example in Figure
15.10

TABLE 15.4
Summary of results
of Alice
Inwonderland's
study of attitudes
toward use of
marijuana
($r_{xx} = 0.50$)

	Soc. class C	Soc. class A
$\bar{x}$	80	90
s	30	28
n	50	50
t	1.72*	

*Not significant

Next we can speculate what would have happened had she improved her instrument and acquired a reliability of, say, $r_{xx} = 0.75$. Rearranging equation (15.22) to solve for observed scores variance and taking the square root, it is possible to get a projected value for the standard deviations of observed score sets with the improved questionnaire:

$$S_x = \sqrt{\frac{\text{est } S_t^2}{r_{xx}}} \qquad (15.22)$$

Substituting in the values for est S_t^2 and the new value for r_{xx}, we get

$$S_C' = \sqrt{\frac{450}{0.75}} = 24.5$$

$$S_A' = \sqrt{\frac{392}{0.75}} = 22.9$$

With the same means and sample sizes, the t-ratio becomes, $t = 2.11, p > 0.05$, a significant difference. Thus by reducing the error (and subsequently the error variance) in the instrument, Alice would be able to identify a significant difference in the groups for the same difference in scores and sample size. Now carry out Activity 15.6.

Activity 15.6

1 Use the data-analysis worksheet in Figure 15.10 to set up the above example, finding t for both situations. What is the difference in s_{diff} for the two situations? What is the difference in the power? How would you revise Alice's hypothesis, considering her sample?

2 We will add one more facility to the worksheet, a place to enter raw data instead of means, standard deviations, etc., and graphs of the raw data.

   (a) Bring up the worksheet and move to empty column **I** (leave **H** blank just for neatness). Figure 15.12 shows the layout, with columns **I** and **J** shaded for raw data entry. In column **K**, starting in row **3**, is the difference between **I** and **J**, for situations where the t-test for related or correlated data will be used. This will have to be copied down as far as needed.

   (b) In column **P**, rows **3** to **5**, add the equations indicated and **Copy** them to columns **O** and **N** (they will change appropriately). Add the equations for setting the interval width and ideal area for the graphs.

   (c) In column **L**, set out the intervals, starting with the mean in cell **L25** and one on either side, then just **Copy** up and down as needed.

   (d) In columns **M** and **N**, install the **FREQUENCY** function (see Section A.2 in Appendix A for help), using the same intervals from column **L**, but different raw data.

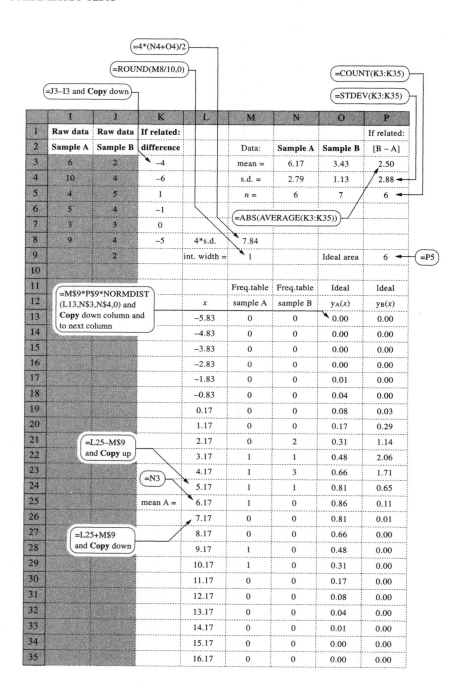

FIGURE 15.12
Extension of data processing worksheet for raw data entry

(e)   Starting in row **13** in columns **O** and **P**, insert the **NORMDIST** function as shown and **Copy** it down the page to provide the ideal distributions.

(f)   Mark out an area on the worksheet. Then follow the five Chart-Wizard steps (see Section A.3):

Step 1   Select the data **Range**, including headings, **L12:P35**.
Step 2   Select **Combination**.
Step 3   Choose **format 1**.
Step 4   Set

Use First ⎹ 1 ⎹ ⬍ Column(s)
For X Data

Use First ⎹ 1 ⎹ ⬍ Row(s)
for Legend Text.

Step 5   Add titles, *x*- and *y*-axis labels.

You should have a graph like that in Figure 15.13 (with coloured lines and possibly different shading and axis scales), that shows not only the raw data, but also the normal distributions assumed by using the mean and standard deviation.

3   If you want, you can change the source of means, standard deviations, and *n* in cells **B3:D5** from direct entry to the appropriate cell designations in **N3:P5**.

4   The given set of raw data was collected to test the hypothesis that there would be a difference in number of units of alcohol consumed per day by residents of hostels A and B, depending on the nature of the counselling programmes in each. Check the test for homogeneity of variance, and select the appropriate options to resolve the hypothesis. (Figure 15.14 contains the answer.)

Sample size: How big is big enough?

Predicting the optimal sample size for a study is not a trivial problem. If the sample is too large then resources are wasted; if it is too small there is a risk of not finding a significant difference when it does exist (the power would be too low). Previous and related research can help the researcher in making decisions about sample size. The most obvious situation is where you are replicating an earlier study that you think should have found a significant difference, but did not since it used small samples. The question is relatively simple: how large would samples need to be to find a significant difference with the same difference in the means? The solution can be found by using the worksheet, trying larger sample sizes while keeping other sample statistics the same. While it is

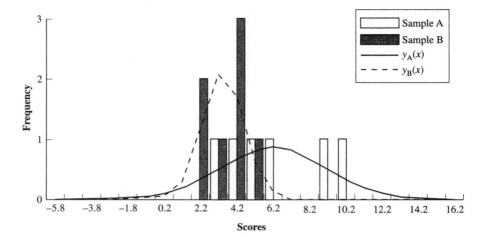

FIGURE 15.13
Plots of raw data and implied normal distributions for two samples, with data from Figure 15.12

possible to determine when the power would just exceed 0.50, it is often held that one should strive for a power of around 0.80. Larger samples would probably result in smaller standard deviations in the sample data, but, to err on the conservative side, one could just leave them the same.

Is this not cheating, I hear you say? No, one possible reason, though not the only, for not finding significant difference is the power of the test was too low due to small n. Obviously, the other is that there is no significant difference. By increasing n, you are potentially raising the power of the test, the probability of finding a significant difference if it were to exist. This approach to estimating the optimal sample size works when you have some indication of the size of the difference in the means and the standard deviations of the scores. While other studies can give you some indications of the size of these, alternative sources are possible. Previous applications or even trials of an instrument can provide an indication of standard deviations. It is harder to estimate the size of the difference in the means unless similar instruments have been used with samples from the target groups. Also, one should consider the *other* significance when determining the possible difference in means: psychological, educational, sociological, etc. For example, what sort of difference in mean gain scores on a mathematics test between two groups using different learning approaches would be considered *educationally* significant? What magnitude of improvement in self-confidence scores over a control group would be considered *psychologically* significant? Do not lose sight of the fact that determining statistical significance is only a tool for determining whether support for a hypothesis exists. It is still up to you to establish a respectable hypothesis. Thus an estimate of the size of the difference in the means may be more appropriately found back in the original question and from considering the ramifications of the outcomes. Small but statistically significant differences can result in a 'So what?' response from colleagues in your field.

ONE- OR TWO-TAILED TEST?

This was discussed in Chapter 14, so it only remains to remind you of the need to have a reasonably strong case for expecting a difference between two samples to be in only one direction. As noted, when testing a theory or the extension of a theory into a new domain, a one-tailed test would prevent the identification of a significant difference in the opposite direction. On the other hand, referring to the previous discussion, there will be situations where previous or related studies indicated that differences are likely only in one direction, in which case it would be justified. The recommendation of some texts that if you have any suspicion of the direction of difference, then use of the one-tailed test is *not* advised. The aim, remember, is to resolve a *sound* hypothesis, not just find statistical significance!

DESIGN B2: PRE- AND POST-TEST/OBSERVATIONS, USING GAIN SCORES

In the past, researchers using this design have carried out two *t*-tests, one comparing pre- and post-test results for the experimental group and one for the control group, maintaining that if significance existed for the former and not the latter, then the treatment was effective (Campbell and Stanley, 1963). This does not even compare the experimental group with the control before testing, thus it is not an appropriate test. Other researchers have statistically compared gain scores, the difference between pre- and post-test results. While this may be appropriate in some situations, in Chapter 18 an alternative to this test will be introduced which can be more powerful: the analysis of covariance. We will see then how to determine which of the two would be most appropriate for the conditions that prevail.

USING EXCEL DATA ANALYSIS TO CARRY OUT *t*-TESTS

If you have installed the appropriate Data Analysis tools, Excel will carry out *t*-tests and the *F*-test for homogeneity of variance on raw data, but they do not plot graphs or provide power calculations. The facility is menu-driven and provides a set of outcomes such as those shown in Figure 15.14, which was generated from the raw data in Figure 15.12. Note that Excel refers to 'homoscedasticity' (which really refers to homogeneity of variance in regression analysis) when it should be homogeneity of variance for the two distributions in question. Also, the test is really for twice the α given, since it is a one-tailed test.

SUMMARY: WHICH TEST TO USE?

Though there are only four possible tests for pairs of samples that have continuous data, the criteria for choosing may seem a bit complicated. The decision

	Sample A	*Sample* B
Mean	6.1666667	3.4285714
Variance	7.7666667	1.2857143
Observations	6	7
Hypothesized Mean Difference	0	
df	6	
*t*Stat	2.2521329	
$P(T< = t)$, one-tail	0.0326248	
*t*Crit one-tail	1.9431809	
$P(T< = t)$, two-tail	0.0652497	
*t*Crit two-tail	2.4469136	

FIGURE 15.14
Output for the Data
Analysis tool in
Excel, using raw data
from Figure 15.12 as
an example

requires one to consider three factors together: independence of samples; homogeneity of variance; and sample size. The decision-making process is quite logical and therefore can be easily summarized in the decision chart in Figure 15.15. Each of the diamond-shaped boxes requires you to respond according to the nature of your data and follow a path to one of the boxes. Though this seems simple and logical, there are numerous other issues to consider when choosing the test, based upon the original design and potential sources of invalidity, as you will see when answering the questions in Activity 15.7.

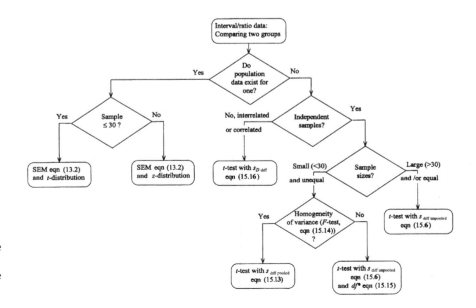

FIGURE 15.15
Decision chart for
selecting appropriate
statistical test for
studies that compare
two means

Activity 15. 7

Now let us try some new examples on the 't-test data analysis' worksheet. In addition to solving a statistical problem, you will be asked to identify the design type from Tables 3.3 and 3.4, consider which of the 15 sources of internal and external invalidity summarized in Figure 6.2 may be at work, and decide which test is the most appropriate.

1 Ben Smallbudget conducted a study to resolve the hypothesis that one word-processing package tended to encourage users to make fewer grammatical errors than another. His null hypothesis was that there would be no significant difference in number of errors per 10 000 words between the groups of randomly selected users from each group in his organization. The analysis of a major document from a random selection of members of the two groups of devotees (he started with seven in each) resulted in the following:

A	21	17	16	18	10	
B	10	13	12	13	13	11

(a) Which design from Tables 3.3 and 3.4 has been employed?
(b) Work through each t-test for pooled and unpooled variances, and check for non-homogeneity of variance: is each significant?
(c) How does the power change as one is compelled to use the most appropriate test due to low sample size and lack of homogeneity of variance?
(d) Which validity would be threatened by an inappropriate choice?
(e) The documents for the three 'lost' subjects appear late: in group A, 16 and 15; and in Group B, 17 mistakes per 10 000 words. What are his results now?
(f) Which source of invalidity almost damaged Ben's study?

2 Freddy Finagle wanted to find out if teaching approach made any difference on attitudes towards use of statistics. He acquired a new text and exercises which he tried with a small group of six students, having them complete a questionnaire before and after the course. His first null hypothesis, H_{01}, was that there would be no significant difference in the scores before and after for the sample group. As he contemplated the problem, he decided it might be better to have a control group (but he could only get five subjects) and use gain scores as his measure, resulting in a new null hypothesis, H_{02}, the results are summarized below. Carry out the appropriate statistical tests for both approaches.

Exp. before:	55	52	56	51	53	52
Exp. after:	61	58	56	54	61	64
Control before:	56	53	55	52	53	
Control after:	57	55	57	56	56	

(a) Write out a null hypothesis for each of the strategies.
(b) These are examples of which designs in Tables 3.3 and 3.4?
(c) Which approach generates statistical significance? Determine the power of each.
(d) What conclusion can be drawn in each case?
(e) Which is most valid and why?

3 Previous experience had convinced Frances Nightingale that continuity of nursing staff in a ward would enhance patient recovery time, but she needed more substantial evidence. Rather than have nurses just fill any available shift vacancy on eight-hour shifts, it was planned that each nurse would work a 12-hour shift assigned to a limited range of patients. Thus, in ward A, each patient would have only two nurses over a three-day period, while ward B (with equivalent patients) would continue the procedure of assigning nurses to eight-hour shifts and no specific patients. The hypothesis was that recovery time would be reduced, and the null hypothesis therefore stated that the new scheme would not produce significantly *lower* recovery times. As a consequence, a one-tailed test would be used when comparing recovery times in the two wards over a period of time. After one week, she had accumulated the following recovery times:

Ward A:	2	4	3	1	2	3	4	2	1
Ward B:	2	4	5	4	3	4	2	4	

(a) Which design has Frances adopted?
(b) Is she justified in using a one-tailed test? Why?
(c) Did she find a significant difference? Would she have done so using a two-tailed test?
(d) What sources of invalidity exist?

4 Harry Hardsell wanted to see if it was possible to determine whether the self-confidence of his sales team would vary because of the way new insurance policy information was presented. While both sets of materials provided by the company presented all the relevant information, one employed more examples than the other. In addition to testing team members knowledge at the end of a course, he wanted to determine their level of confidence in selling the new policy. He had developed a confidence measure for another study that produced a mean of around 50 and a standard deviation of about 15. The original version had a reliability of 0.60. For the difference to be significant in terms of its impact on sales performance, he expects at least 10 points between those using each package.

(a) Which design does this study employ?
(b) What would the sample sizes have to be to find a significant difference with a power of approximately 0.90?
(c) Determine the effect of improving the instrument and increasing the reliability to 0.80: how large would the samples have to be now?

(d)   Which sources of invalidity are potentially at work?

5   Two groups of students are randomly selected, based upon IQ scores, for a study to determine the differential effect of a treatment purported to improve IQ. The two groups are: low IQ (85–95) and high IQ (105–115).

(a)   Identify the design.

(b)   If the low-IQ group were to show an increase greater than the high-IQ group, is this evidence of differential benefit, or would there be a possible source of invalidity? If so, how could it be controlled?

Answers

1. (a)   D3, ex post facto: the independent variable is word-processor used; the dependent variable is the number of errors per 10 000 words.

   (b)   Both $t_{\text{unpooled}} = -2.34$ and $t_{\text{pooled}} = -2.55$ are significant ($t_{\text{crit}} = 2.26$), but there is heterogeneity of variance, and $t^*_{\text{crit}} = 2.78$, which is greater than t_{pooled}, thus not significant (n.s.).

   (c)   Power(unpooled) = 0.53, power(pooled) = 0.61, power(hetero) = 0.34.

   (d)   Statistical validity: due to the nature of the results Ben must choose a more conservative test, which in this case returns a non-significant result.

   (e) $t_{\text{unpooled}} = -2.26$, $t_{\text{crit}} = 2.18$, $df = 12$, $p < 0.05$, power = 0.53.

   (f)   Source 6. Sample stability.

2. (a) H_{01}: there will be no significant difference in the performance of the group under treatment before and after.

   H_{02}: there will be no significant difference in gains in the performance between two groups, one receiving the treatment, the other not.

   (b) H_{01}: test–retest with a single group (design A2), and

   H_{02}: test–retest with two groups, one as control, using gain scores (design B2).

   (c) H_{01}: $t_{\text{related}} = 3.47$, $t_{\text{rel crit}} = 2.57$, $p < 0.05$.

   H_{02}: heterogeneity of variance, $t_{\text{unpooled}} = -1.95$, $t^*_{\text{crit}} = 2.45$ ($df^* = 6$), n.s.

   (d) H_{01}: the group improved, though the reason for this is not unambiguous.

   H_{02}: the group did not improve more than usual due to the new strategy (i.e., both improved, but there were possible common reasons for the improvements other than the treatment since the gain scores did not differ significantly).

   (e)   To ensure statistical validity, H_{01} used t_{related} and H_{02} used t_{pooled} with t^*_{crit}, but the design with the fewest sources of invalidity (greater control over possible extraneous variables) for the situation would be H_{02}, thus the one most likely to answer the question.

3. (a) Design B3 (post-test only with a control group), but quasi-experimental since groups were not random samples.

   (b) Yes, if you are willing to accept her informal observations as a basis for the decision.

   (c) $t_{pooled} = 1.97$, t_{crit}(one-tailed) $= 1.75$ ($p < 0.05$), t_{crit}(two-tailed) $= 2.13$ (n.s.), power(one-tailed) $= 0.58$, power(two-tailed) $= 0.44$.

   (d) Source 4: are the samples representative of patients? A longer period of time and greater number of patients would strengthen her case. Also Source 10: the nurses may have greeted the new shift regime with enthusiasm in the week, improving their disposition and bedside manner. The difficulty is if the latter were true, it may not result in a sustainable effect.

4. (a) Design B3.

   (b) $n_A = n_B \cong 48$.

   (c) $n_A = n_B \cong 36$, twelve fewer in each group.

   (d) This illustrates how source 12 instrument reliability can directly influence the overall validity of the conclusions of a study and even the size of the sample required (related to Source 4 – size is related to sampling error).

5. (a) Design D3, ex post facto, *not* C2; the question is whether the response to treatment, the gain scores (dependent variable, **O**), depend on IQ group (independent variable, *X*)?

   (b) Source 5 could explain the results since the upper group could have regressed down towards the mean, minimizing apparent gains, and the lower group regressed up towards the mean, inflating gains. A more complex structure, such as design B5 (Solomon Four) would be needed to control for regression towards mean in this case.

ONE-WAY ANALYSIS OF VARIANCE

16

So far we have encountered two types of statistical test: the first determining the likelihood of one sample belonging to a population; and the second considering the probability of two samples belonging to a common population. To extend our testing capability to situations where there are three or more samples demands a new test. This one will require a slightly different approach in order to determine the likelihood that all the samples share a common trait. The approach will compare the sample means for the measured characteristic indirectly using estimates of population variances instead, which is why it is referred to as analysis of variance (ANOVA).

In this chapter, we will consider studies that wish to compare three or more groups, traits, or treatments that are variations of a variable, such as educational background (ex post facto) or types of counselling received (experimental). In the next chapter, two-dimensional studies will be considered, where the interaction of traits or treatments would be of interest. For example, if investigating the influence of gender and educational background on income at age 40, one would want to know if combinations of gender and each of three types of education made a difference (a 2×3 design). A design considering three different counselling techniques for those addicted to heroin may wish to compare the consequences of the approaches for subjects in clinics, in hostels, and day clients (a 3×3 design). In Chapter 18, we will also see how these tests apply to time series and Solomon four designs.

A number of issues related to the use of ANOVA will be addressed, including

- the use of unequal sample sizes;
- homogeneity of variance and transformations of data that overcome lack of it;
- post hoc analysis, techniques for comparing pairs of sample means if an overall significance is found using ANOVA;
- the power of the test.

A number of simulations are presented that will allow you to explore the models behind each of these tools.

APPLICABLE DESIGNS

The use of three or more levels or categories of a variable corresponds to an extension to two of the sets of designs considered in Chapter 3. First are the designs B2 and C2 (pre- and post-test/observation, experimental and quasi-experimental), employing gain scores $(O_2 - O_1)$, extended to allow for three or more treatments or groups with varying levels of traits:

$$(\mathbf{RS}) \rightarrow \begin{cases} \mathbf{RA_a} \rightarrow \mathbf{O_{a1}} \rightarrow \mathbf{X_a} \rightarrow \mathbf{O_{a2}} \\ \mathbf{RA_b} \rightarrow \mathbf{O_{b1}} \rightarrow \mathbf{X_b} \rightarrow \mathbf{O_{b2}} \\ \mathbf{RA_c} \rightarrow \mathbf{O_{c1}} \rightarrow \mathbf{X_c} \rightarrow \mathbf{O_{c2}} \\ \quad\quad\quad\quad \vdots \\ \mathbf{RA_o} \rightarrow \mathbf{O_{o1}} \rightarrow \mathbf{X_o} \rightarrow \mathbf{O_{o2}} \end{cases}$$

Alternatively, there will be occasions when the designs B3 and D3 (post-test only with control group) will include three or more groups with a single measure for each (using **R** to represent either random assignment after the random selection for an experimental design, or random selection from each population in the case of an ex post facto design):

$$(\mathbf{RS}) \rightarrow \begin{cases} \mathbf{R_a} \rightarrow \mathbf{X_a} \rightarrow \mathbf{O_a} \\ \mathbf{R_b} \rightarrow \mathbf{X_b} \rightarrow \mathbf{O_b} \\ \mathbf{R_c} \rightarrow \mathbf{X_c} \rightarrow \mathbf{O_c} \\ \quad\quad \vdots \\ \mathbf{R_0} \rightarrow \mathbf{X_0} \rightarrow \mathbf{O_0} \end{cases}$$

The aim of any statistical test would be first to resolve whether all the groups belong to a single common population. If they do not, then the next question would concern, which *pairs* of groups are sufficiently close together to belong to one population and which are far enough apart to be considered in different populations. This is exemplified by Professor Boffin's study in Chapter 4 (see Table 4.4), on question-asking tendencies of teachers. The issue being addressed is simply whether the differences in means can be attributed to chance alone, or to some variable. As we have seen before, not all the means from random samples from a population will be exactly the same, due to natural variations – but there are limits. The first test will simply determine whether the overall differences are sufficiently great to exclude them from belonging to a single population. As can be seen from Figure 16.1, in the case of Professor Boffin's study, if the normal distributions implied by the means and standard deviations for the three groups are displayed, the answer is not obvious.

Later, in Chapter 18, we will consider an alternative to the analysis of variance as a potentially more powerful test for design B2, analysis of covariance, and identify difficulties in analysing data from the quasi-experimental version C2.

ONE-WAY ANALYSIS OF VARIANCE

The question of membership of a sample in a given population (Chapter 13) was resolved by comparing the mean of the sample to the expected *distribution of sampling means* for that population. The question of membership of two sam-

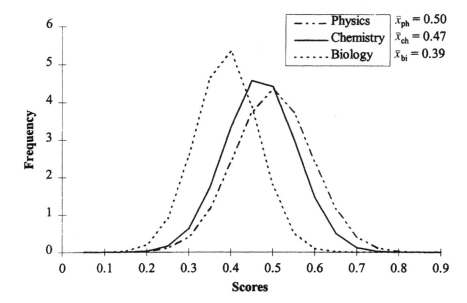

FIGURE 16.1
Ideal distributions for the means and standard deviations from the three samples in Professor Boffin's study (see Table 4.4)

ples in a common population (Chapter 15) was resolved by locating the difference between the two sample means on an expected *distribution of differences in sample means* for a population that had the combined characteristics of the two samples. Now we have gone one step further, the question is about the probable membership of three or more samples in a single population. Using the differences in means (repeated t-tests on pairs) is not practical simply because it would require the use of each mean more than once, raising the probability of committing a Type I error. What is needed is a single test that includes all the means together.

There is more than one way mathematically to arrive at a definition of the F-test, the basis for ANOVA (for example, Sirkin, 1995; Howell, 1997; Winer *et al.*, 1991; Ferguson, 1976). The descriptions that follow will be the least complex mathematically and the simplest conceptually to enhance continuity with the definitions of earlier tests. The approach that has been taken is one that involves providing two separate estimates of the variance for the single population, σ^2, to which all the samples would be assumed to belong if the null hypothesis were accepted. To begin, it is worth recalling that sample variances are calculated involving the mean, from equation (12.7),

$$s^2 = \frac{\sum_{i=1}^{n}(x_i - \bar{x})^2}{n - 1} \tag{16.1}$$

and that variances (but *not* standard deviations) can be combined by addition.

The first estimate stems from recalling the characteristic of distributions of sampling means. When samples are taken from a population, they will not all have the same mean but will display a normal distribution of means, with a standard deviation referred to as the standard error of the mean (SEM). This is estimated from the population standard deviation and the size of the samples as

$$\text{SEM} = \frac{\text{population standard deviation}}{\sqrt{\text{sample size}}}$$

which in equation (13.2) was written in mathematical symbols as

$$\sigma_{\bar{x}} = \frac{\sigma}{\sqrt{n}}$$

Expressing this in terms of variances gives

$$\sigma_{\bar{x}}^2 = \frac{\sigma^2}{n}$$

Solving for the population variance, we get

$$\sigma^2 = n\sigma_{\bar{x}}^2$$

For this we need an estimate of the standard error of the mean using sample data. For a set of samples in a study, we will assume that the variance of the means will be the estimate of the variance of all possible samples, thus

$$\text{est } \sigma_{\bar{x}}^2 = \text{variance of sample means} = s_{\bar{x}}^2$$

$$= \frac{\sum_{j=1}^{k}(\bar{x}_j - \bar{X})^2}{k - 1}$$

where $\bar{x}_j$ is the mean of the jth sample, k is the number of samples and $\bar{X}$ is the grand mean, or mean of all the data. Thus an estimate of the population variance, referred to as the variance based upon variance between means, can be found from

$$\text{est } \sigma^2 = s_{\text{between}}^2$$

$$s_{\text{between}}^2 = ns_{\bar{x}}^2 \tag{16.2}$$

$$s_{\text{between}}^2 = n\frac{\sum_{j=1}^{k}(\bar{x}_j - \bar{X})^2}{k - 1} \tag{16.3}$$

for equal n. In Excel, this is nothing more than n***VAR(means)**.

A second estimate of the population variance can be found from simply taking the average of all the variances of the samples. Considering a set of data for a study, it is relatively simple to find the variance for each sample using equation (16.1). Then all that is necessary is to add them together and divide by the number of groups, to give the estimate of the population variance using variances within the groups, s_{within}^2:

$$s_{\text{within}}^2 = \frac{\sum_{j=1}^{k} s_j^2}{k} \tag{16.4}$$

again for equal n. In Excel, this is found simply by **AVERAGE(variances)**.

As estimates of the population mean, these two should be approximately equal if all the samples were to belong to that population. As a consequence, it would seem reasonable for their ratio to be approximately 1, which is how the F-ratio is defined and what is expected for samples from a single population:

$$F \equiv \frac{s^2_{\text{between}}}{s^2_{\text{within}}} \qquad (16.5)$$

We would expect, $F \cong 1.0$ if all samples belong to one population. We would also expect there to be an acceptable range of ratios around 1.0 that would allow us to conclude that the samples belong to a single population. Therefore, this value for a set of samples is compared with the F-distribution, which requires two different degrees of freedom, one for the numerator and one for the denominator,

$$df_{\text{between}} = k - 1$$

$$df_{\text{within}} = k(n - 1)$$

based upon the number of samples. This F-test was devised by Fisher and published in 1923 and it preceded Gosset's t-test, which only later became the accepted way of comparing two means. Before looking in detail at this F-distribution of values, let us first consider an example by carrying out Activity 16.1.

Activity 16.1

Professor Bloggs carried out a study to see if there was a difference in the number of hours spent per week in the library by students who were studying various subjects. He randomly selected eight students each from biology (sample A), psychology (B), English (C), chemistry (D), and history (E). Each was asked to keep a record of hours per week for ten weeks and report the average.

1 The data and their analysis are shown in Figure 16.2. Enter this into a worksheet. Were the groups different?
2 What would the results have been if he had chosen α to be 0.005 instead?
3 Restore α, to its original value of 0.05, then remove group E by deleting cells **F1:F14**. What does this do to the results? (When finished, simply select **Edit** and **Undo Clear** to restore the original data and calculations.)
4 Delete the data in rows **2** and **3**, cells **B2:F3**, the first two subjects in each group, thus reducing sample size. What consequence does this have for the results? Undo the delete and try another set. Are the consequences the same?

If you want to use this worksheet for more than nine subjects per group, simply **Insert Rows** while in row **9** or **10** and the formulae will change to include these.

Answers
1. Yes.
2. $F_{\text{crit}} = 4.62$, not significant (n.s.).
3. $F = 4.27$, $F_{\text{crit}} = 3.01$, still $p < 0.05$.
4. $F = 2.11$, $F_{\text{crit}} = 2.47$, n.s.; no, some are still significant.

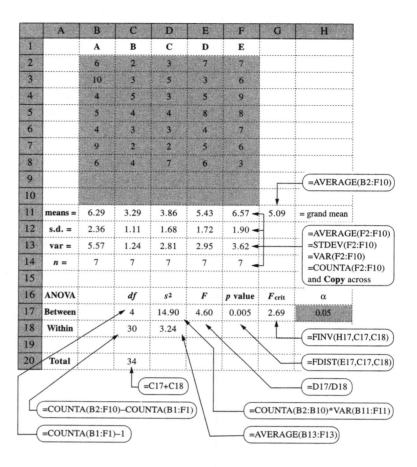

FIGURE 16.2
Analysis of variance
calculation (equal
cell size) on a
worksheet

Again, to answer how close to 1.0 one would expect this ratio of estimates of
the population variance to be in order to consider samples to be part of a single
population requires a family of distributions of possible F-ratios. Just for interest, the equation is

$$y(F, df_{\text{between}}, df_{\text{within}}) = \frac{cF^{\frac{df_{\text{between}}}{2} - 1}}{(df_{\text{within}} + df_{\text{between}}F)^{\frac{df_{\text{between}} + df_{\text{within}}}{2}}}$$

where $df_{\text{between}} = k - 1$ and $df_{\text{within}} = k(n - 1)$, which has the following characteristics:

- It has a mean of 1.0.
- It is positively skewed with the amount of skewness dependent on the number
  of groups, k, and the nature of the tail dependent on the total size of each of
  the samples, n.

This is best illustrated by some examples of distributions, as shown in Figure
16.3, where an approximation for the above equation is implemented by
using the Excel cumulative F-distribution function, **FDIST**(**F**, **df_{within}**,
df_{between}). Comparing the three sets of graphs, it becomes apparent that the

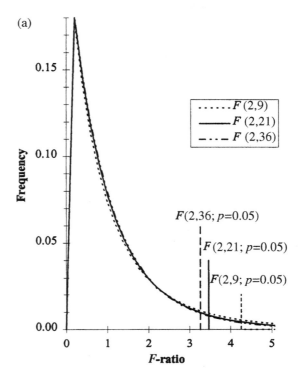

FIGURE 16.3(a)
F-distributions for two groups/ treatments, $k = 3$, $df_{between} = 2$, for three cases where sample sizes per cell, n, are 4 ($df_{within} = 9$), 8 ($df_{within} = 21$), and 13 ($df_{within} = 36$)

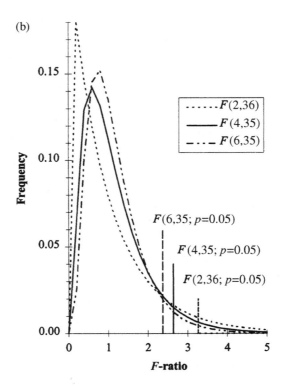

FIGURE 16.3(b)
F-distributions for three cases where the number of groups, k, are 3 ($df_{between} = 2$), 5 ($df_{between} = 4$), and 7 ($df_{between} = 6$), and the total sample is about 40 (13, 8, and 6 in each group respectively) such that df_{within} is about the same for each (35 or 36)

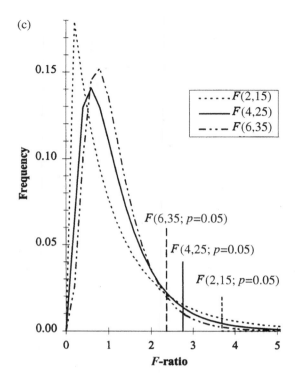

FIGURE 16.3(c)
F-distributions for
three cases where the
number of groups, k,
are 3, 5 and 7 with 6
subjects in each
group,
$df_{within} = k(n - 1)$,
with $F_{crit}(0.05)$
shown for each case

skewness is influenced mainly by the number of samples, while how far out F_{crit} is depends on the total sample size.

In Figure 16.3(a), the three curves for the three-group situation with $df_{between} = 2$, the curves are virtually indistinguishable visually. The difference is in how the tail approaches the x-axis and consequently how far out the last 5% under the curve is. The larger the sample and the larger df_{within}, the closer in F_{crit} is and the easier it is to find a significant difference across groups. Considering previous statistical tests, this is not very surprising.

In Figure 16.3(b), the total sample size is kept constant close to 40, but divided among 3, 5 and 7 groups, having sample sizes of 13, 8 and 6 respectively, leaving df_{within} approximately the same (35 or 36). Thus the sample size of each group gets smaller as the number of groups increases. Here both the shapes of the curves and F_{crit} vary with the number of groups. Though F_{crit} is smallest for a larger number of groups, this does not mean that one should strive for many groups, as there is a tendency for the variance across the means to decrease as the number of groups increases, just as we found that the variance tends to decrease as sample size increases. This situation illustrates the case where a fixed sample could be divided into a number of treatment groups.

In Figure 16.3(c), the situation is such that even though the number of groups increases, the group sizes remain at 6. This means that F_{crit} is smallest for the largest overall sample, again not a surprising outcome. You can generate other F-distributions for other df and different α using the procedure described in Activity 16.2.

Activity 16.2

Figure 16.4 provides a worksheet and corresponding graph for generating any three F-distributions with F_{crit} for a designated α.

1　Enter this into a new worksheet. Type in each of the formulae in column **D** and then **Copy** them to the other columns. Then **Copy** all of row **13** down the page to row **37**. Add the formulae and numbers in the remaining cells to produce the F_{crit} lines and the total area under each curve. Ideally they should be 1.00, but these approximations should be close.

2　Using ChartWizard, generate an **XY Scatter**, format **2** graph. You should get one close to Figure 16.3(b).

3　Vary the degrees of freedom by changing the number of groups and sample size in the shaded cells to see how they change the shape of a distribution, as well as where F_{crit} appears. If the degrees of freedom are very small, F_{crit} becomes large and it may be necessary to change the interval width in cell **B9** to 0.4 to get a reasonable set of graphs.

4　Set all three k groups to 3 and all three sample sizes to 8. Then change α in the first column to 0.001 and in the second to 0.01, leaving the third at 0.05. This allows you to see what happens to F_{crit}.

Assumptions behind the F-test

The one-way ANOVA assumes a single independent variable with three or more categories/treatments to investigate the possibility of differential impact on the dependent variable (integer/ratio measure). There are three basic assumptions which underlie the F-test, similar to those for the t-test:

- The dependent variable generates interval/ratio data and the data for each treatment group or sample are normally distributed (this test is reasonably robust to some deviation from normality).
- There is homogeneity of variance across groups (if not, there are ways of compensating for this deficiency which are covered below).
- There is independence of observations (it is possible to have interrelated observations – for example, for repeated measures designs, which are described in Chapter 18).

Assuming these are met, the test focuses on differences in means. It is assumed that the sample means are indicators of potential population means, thus H_0 is really saying that these are all the same:

$$\mu_A = \mu_B = \mu_C = \mu_D = \ldots = \mu_0$$

Before considering how we can contend with non-homogeneity of variance, the general equations for the F-test need to be developed, in order to allow unequal sample size.

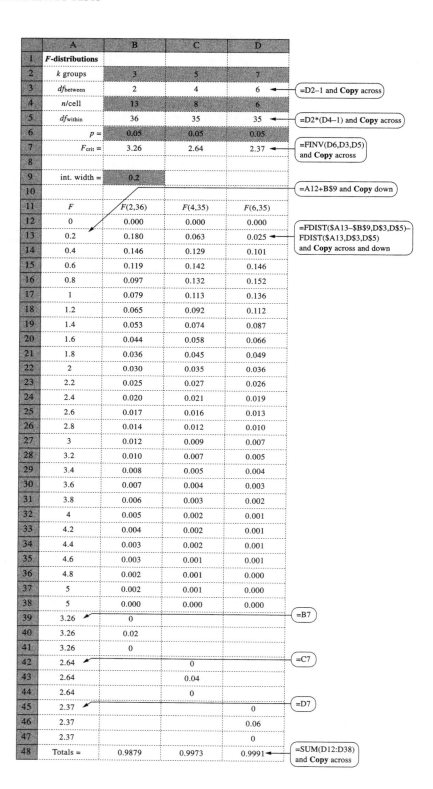

	A	B	C	D
1	*F*-distributions			
2	*k* groups	3	5	7
3	$df_{between}$	2	4	6	← =D2−1 and **Copy** across
4	*n*/cell	13	8	6
5	df_{within}	36	35	35	← =D2*(D4−1) and **Copy** across
6	*p* =	0.05	0.05	0.05
7	F_{crit} =	3.26	2.64	2.37	← =FINV(D6,D3,D5) and **Copy** across
8				
9	int. width =	0.2		
10					=A12+B$9 and **Copy** down
11	*F*	F(2,36)	F(4,35)	F(6,35)
12	0	0.000	0.000	0.000
13	0.2	0.180	0.063	0.025	← =FDIST($A13−$B$9,D$3,D$5)−FDIST($A13,D$3,D$5) and **Copy** across and down
14	0.4	0.146	0.129	0.101
15	0.6	0.119	0.142	0.146
16	0.8	0.097	0.132	0.152
17	1	0.079	0.113	0.136
18	1.2	0.065	0.092	0.112
19	1.4	0.053	0.074	0.087
20	1.6	0.044	0.058	0.066
21	1.8	0.036	0.045	0.049
22	2	0.030	0.035	0.036
23	2.2	0.025	0.027	0.026
24	2.4	0.020	0.021	0.019
25	2.6	0.017	0.016	0.013
26	2.8	0.014	0.012	0.010
27	3	0.012	0.009	0.007
28	3.2	0.010	0.007	0.005
29	3.4	0.008	0.005	0.004
30	3.6	0.007	0.004	0.003
31	3.8	0.006	0.003	0.002
32	4	0.005	0.002	0.001
33	4.2	0.004	0.002	0.001
34	4.4	0.003	0.002	0.001
35	4.6	0.003	0.001	0.001
36	4.8	0.002	0.001	0.000
37	5	0.002	0.001	0.000
38	5	0.000	0.000	0.000
39	3.26	0			=B7
40	3.26	0.02		
41	3.26	0		
42	2.64		0		=C7
43	2.64		0.04	
44	2.64		0	
45	2.37			0	=D7
46	2.37			0.06
47	2.37			0
48	Totals =	0.9879	0.9973	0.9991	=SUM(D12:D38) and **Copy** across

FIGURE 16.4
Worksheet for generating any set of three *F*-distributions for comparison (this data should generate Figure 16.3(b))

The general *F*-ratio, including unequal sample size

Equations (16.3) and (16.4) for s^2_{between} and s^2_{within} are the most basic and assume that all the samples are the same size, n. To generalize to any situation, we will start with equation (16.3), for constant n:

$$s^2_{\text{between}} = n \frac{\sum_{j=1}^{k}(\bar{x}_j - \bar{X})^2}{k-1}$$

When using summation notation, we often simplify equations by applying mathematical rules. One of these rules says that if we want to add a set of k numbers, g_i, together, when each number is multiplied by a constant, n, then the following shorthand applies:

$$ng_1 + ng_2 + ng_3 + \ldots + ng_k = \sum_{j=1}^{k} ng_j$$

In turn, this can be simplified by extracting the constant, n, to give

$$n(g_1 + g_2 + g_3 + \ldots + g_k) = n\sum_{j=1}^{k} g_j$$

Now equation (16.3) above is equivalent to this last term, so what we want to do is go back one step, because in our case, all the values for n are not the same. What we want is the equivalent to the more general expression

$$n_1 g_1 + n_2 g_2 + n_3 g_3 + \ldots + n_k g_k = \sum_{j=1}^{k} n_j g_j$$

where $n_1 \neq n_2 \neq n_3 \neq \ldots \neq n_k$. Thus, equation (16.3) becomes, for unequal n,

$$s^2_{\text{between}} = \frac{\sum_{j=1}^{k} n_j (\bar{x}_j - \bar{X})^2}{k-1} \tag{16.6}$$

The numerator is referred to as the *sum of squares between*, SS_{between}. When divided by df_{between}, this gives s^2_{between}, often shown as *mean square between*, MS_{between}, in texts and computer printouts.

To find the general expression for s^2_{within}, we start with equation (16.4), multiplying both the numerator and denominator by n:

$$s^2_{\text{within}} = \frac{n\sum_{j=1}^{k} s_j^2}{nk}$$

and, as above, moving n inside the summation, we do not change the value of the expression:

$$s^2_{\text{within}} = \frac{\sum_{j=1}^{k} n s_j^2}{nk} \tag{16.7}$$

$$s_{\text{within}}^2 = \frac{\sum_{j=1}^{k} \left(\dfrac{\sum_{i=1}^{n}(x_{ij} - \bar{x}_j)^2}{n-1} \right)}{k} = \frac{\sum_{j=1}^{k}\sum_{i=1}^{n}(x_{ij} - \bar{x}_j)^2}{k(n-1)}$$

$$= \sum_{j=1}^{k}\sum_{i=1}^{n} \frac{(x_{ij} - \bar{x}_j)^2}{N - k} \tag{16.8}$$

where $kn = N$. This is the equation that frequently appears in statistical tests, showing the source of the *sum of squares within*, SS_{within}, in the numerator, with $df_{\text{within}} = N - k$, in the denominator. Strictly speaking, this is only true for constant n, all samples being the same size. Going back to equation (16.7), it is true that for the situation of all k samples having n subjects, the expression nk is equal to the total number of subjects involved in the study. But to change the situation from n being a constant, to n_j, which can vary with each sample, the equation simply changes to become

$$s_{\text{within}}^2 = \frac{\sum_{j=1}^{k} n_j s_j^2}{\sum_{j=1}^{k} n_j} \tag{16.9}$$

for unequal n. If this is expanded in a similar way as above, entering the definition for the individual sample standard deviations to arrive at an expression as close to (16.8) as possible, we get

$$s_{\text{within}}^2 = \frac{\sum_{j=1}^{k} \left(\dfrac{n_j}{n_j - 1} \right) \sum_{i=1}^{n}(x_{ij} - \bar{x}_j)^2}{\sum_{j=1}^{k} n_j}$$

This is *not* equal to equation (16.8), even though (16.8) is often used to calculate s_{within}^2 in software such as Excel and SPSS, even for unequal sample sizes. The difference is usually minuscule and the reason for using this seems to be a hangover from the pre-computer days when such calculations were carried out with desk calculators. Equation (16.8) was simply much easier to use to generate an answer and provides an obvious display of df_{within} related to the sums of squares within. With the use of computers, equations (16.6) for s_{between}^2 and (16.9) for s_{within}^2 take no effort to calculate. The difference in results will be demonstrated in Activity 16.3 below.

The advantage of considering equations (16.6) and (16.9) is in the understanding of the meaning of the F-ratio. It is still

$$F = \frac{\text{estimate of population variance based on variance between sample means}}{\text{estimate of population variance based on average of sample variances}}$$

The degrees of freedom are partitioned as indicated and sum to one less than the total sample, $\sum n_j - 1$, for the reason presented in Chapter 15. How many observations can we change and how many must be left to adapt if the overall results are to remain the same? The same question is then applied to the numerator and denominator. Since the numerator is considering sample means, how many can vary without changing the numerator? One less than the total number of samples for the numerator $df_{between} = k - 1$. The individual sample variances depend on the individual samples, so the number of degrees of freedom depends on the sum of the sample sizes less one in each case, since this is how each of the standard deviations is calculated:

$$df_{within} = \sum(n_j - 1) = N - k$$

Now carry out Activity 16.3 to set up your worksheet for general one-way ANOVA.

Activity 16.3

When Professor Bloggs' assistant scrutinized the collected results of the study, she noticed that several of the returned forms contained data that looked inaccurate. When asked, the students admitted they had not honestly recorded their times, so these entries had to be removed, leaving unequal sample sizes.

1   Make a copy of the worksheet in Figure 16.2. Remove selected data in rows **7** and **8** as shown in Figure 16.5.
2   Rows **11** to **14** are the same; change only the labels in column A.
3   **Insert** two rows for **15** and **16**. Add the formulae indicated and **Copy** them to the other cells.
4   In the ANOVA section rows **19** and **20**, add the simple calculations for sums of squares so that you can compare these results with other software output. Also change the calculations for s^2 (MS), which are just equations (16.6) and (16.9), respectively.
5   Excel can generate its own ANOVA table. To check yourself, open the **Tools** menu and select **Data Analysis**. Choose **Anova: Single Factor** and click on **OK**. The following window will appear to be completed as shown, placing the results below work area.

Anova: Single Factor

Input
Input Range: $B$1:$F$10
Grouped By: ● Columns
                    ○ Rows
☒ Labels in First Row
Alpha: 0.05

Output options
● Output Range: $A$25
○ New Worksheet Ply:
○ New Workbook

OK
Cancel
Help

Partitioning the variances

What are the sources of these variances? We described the sources of variance for measuring instruments in Chapter 11 in equation (11.2) as follows (with obvious changes to notation):

$$s^2_{\text{observed}} = s^2_{\text{true}} + s^2_{\text{error}}$$

In the case of the estimate of the population mean in the numerator of the *F*-ratio, based upon the average of the sample variances, *within groups*, this is equivalent to equation (16.9) for the measurements or observations. This is because we are assuming only two sources of variance and the true score variance is attributable simply to individual differences within groups, so it is described here as

$$s^2_{\text{within}} = s^2_{\text{ind diff}} + s^2_{\text{error}} \tag{16.10}$$

In the case of the estimate in the numerator using the variance of the group means, *between groups*, the true score variance can be described in two different ways:

$$\text{if } \mathbf{H_0} \text{ is true:}\quad s^2_{\text{true}} = s^2_{\text{ind diff}}$$
$$\text{if } \mathbf{H_0} \text{ is false:}\quad s^2_{\text{true}} = s^2_{\text{treatment}} + s^2_{\text{ind diff}}$$

Thus there are two possible explanations for the estimate of the population variance based upon the variance of group means, *between groups*:

$$s^2_{\text{between } H_0 \text{ true}} = s^2_{\text{ind diff}} + s^2_{\text{error}} \qquad \text{for } H_0 \text{ true} \tag{16.11}$$

If the H_0 were to be false, the assumption is that this is attributable to the difference in treatments, thus this would add an additional source of variance:

$$s^2_{\text{between } H_0 \text{ false}} = s^2_{\text{treatment}} + s^2_{\text{ind diff}} + s^2_{\text{error}} \qquad \text{for } H_0 \text{ false} \tag{16.12}$$

Not surprisingly, equations (16.10) and (16.11) are the same and therefore we would expect the two estimates of $s^2_{\text{ind diff}} + s^2_{\text{error}}$ to be much the same,

$$F = \frac{s^2_{\text{between}}}{s^2_{\text{within}}} = \frac{s^2_{\text{ind diff}} + s^2_{\text{error}}}{s^2_{\text{ind diff}} + s^2_{\text{error}}} \cong 1 \qquad \text{for } H_0 \text{ true}$$

and

$$F = \frac{s^2_{\text{between}}}{s^2_{\text{within}}} = \frac{s^2_{\text{treatments}} + s^2_{\text{ind diff}} + s^2_{\text{error}}}{s^2_{\text{ind diff}} + s^2_{\text{error}}} > 1 \qquad \text{for } H_0 \text{ false}$$

This partitioning of variances allows us to identify sources of variances so as to reflect on how we might influence the probability of making the right decision based upon an *F*-test. Three factors influence this:

	A	B	C	D	E	F	G	H
1	ANOVA data:	A	B	C	D	E		
2		6	2	3	7	7		
3		10	3	5	3	6		
4		4	5	3	5	9		
5		5	4	4	8	8		
6		4	3	3	4	7		
7		9	2	2		6		
8		6		7		3		
9								
10								grand mean
11	means: M_j =	6.29	3.17	3.86	5.40	6.57	5.09	= GM
12	s.d.: s_j =	2.36	1.17	1.68	2.07	1.90		
13	var: s^2_j =	5.57	1.37	2.81	4.30	3.62		
14	n_j =	7	6	7	5	7		
15	$n_j (M_j - GM)^3$ =	9.95	22.28	10.70	0.47	15.28	◀ =F14*(F11–$G11)^2	
16	ns^2_j =	39.00	8.20	19.67	21.50	25.33	◀ =F14*F13 and **Copy** across	
17								
18	ANOVA	SS	df	s^2 (MS)	F	p value	F_{crit}	α
19	Between	58.69	4	14.67	4.13	0.010	2.73	0.05
20	Within	95.93	27	3.55				
21								
22	Total	154.62	31					

=C19*D19

=C20*D20

=SUM(B15:F15)/C19

=SUM(B16:F16)/SUM(B14:F14)

FIGURE 16.5
Worksheet for general one-way ANOVA ($n_{ij} \neq$ constant)

Anova: Single Factor						
SUMMARY						
Groups	Count	Sum	Average	Variance		
A	7	44	6.2857143	5.5714286		
B	6	19	3.1666667	1.3666667		
C	7	27	3.8571429	2.8095238		
D	5	27	5.4	4.3		
E	7	46	6.5714286	3.6190476		
ANOVA						
Source of Variation	SS	df	MS	F	P-value	Fcrit
Between groups	58.685417	4	14.671354	4.1248861	0.0097873	2.7277665
Within groups	96.033333	27	3.5567901			
Total	154.71875	31				

FIGURE 16.6
Sample output from the **Tools** menu, **Data Analysis,** and **Anova: Single Factor** option in Excel, for the data in Figure 16.5, for comparison

- $s^2_{\text{ind diff}}$ will be influenced by the quality (representativeness) of the samples.
- For $s^2_{\text{treatment}}$ to be maximized requires as great a difference in the means for the different treatments or levels of treatment (for an experimental study) or experiences (ex post facto study) of the sample groups.
- s^2_{error} depends, as before, upon the measuring process, including the reliability of the instrument itself and how the data were collected.

Thus we can again expect the power of a test (the probability of correctly identifying a significant difference when it exists) to depend heavily upon the design *and* the execution of that design. Recalling Figure 6.2, it is now possible to see how the sources of invalidity and confounding influence the validity of conclusions through the statistical test. Table 16.1 lists the relevant sources and their impact on the three component variances when H_0 is rejected, plus the consequences for making a Type II error (β) and the probability of correctly rejecting the null hypothesis (power). Now carry out Activity 16.4.

Activity 16.4

Henry Horsefeathers was preparing to conduct a study to see if there was any difference in self-confidence across social classes. As a result of the trial of his measuring instrument, the Horsefeathers Self-confidence Scale, he established that it would probably have a reliability of 0.50 as it was. He then sent the instrument to a random sample of subjects from each social class, based upon groupings according to property tax lists.

1 (a) What is his null hypothesis?
   (b) What type of study is this?
   (c) How valid is his independent variable?
   (d) What sort of relationship is he likely to establish if he were to find a significant difference across the classes?

2 What would be the potential consequences of each of the following actions for $s^2_{\text{ind diff}}$, $s^2_{\text{treatment}}$ and/or s^2_{error}, and consequently F?

   (a) He rewrites the instrument and its reliability is improved to 0.70.
   (b) He has 60% of his sample respond.
   (c) His classification of social class is not clear enough and not as mutually exclusive as it should be, thus some subjects are put in the wrong group.

Answers
1 (a) There will be no difference across social class for self-confidence. (b) Ex post facto. (c) The size of house may not be the best indicator, and he is likely to end up with volunteers. (d) Not causal, but whether there is a difference that can be associated with class.
2 (a) Lower s^2_{error} and increased F. (b) Increased $s^2_{\text{ind diff}}$ and lower F. (c) reduced overall 'effect' and consequently $s^2_{\text{treatment}}$ decreased, reducing F.

	Sources of invalidity and confounding	Influence on variances, β and power
$s^2_{\text{ind diff}}$		
4	Selection: sample and assignment	A poor sample can increase individual difference variance in the F-ratio, overshadowing treatment variance, thus increasing β and reducing power.
5	Selection: regression	If samples were based on a trait whose measurement was susceptible to regression towards the mean, this could reduce individual difference variance unnaturally, exaggerating the treatment variance influence, decreasing β and invalidly increasing power.
6	Selection: sample stability	Loss of sample members lowers representativeness, thus could increase individual difference variance and the possibility of overshadowing treatment variance, thus increasing β and decreasing power.
$s^2_{\text{treatment}}$		
8	Interaction of independent variable with sample	If it differentially increased treatment effects with some groups, it would have the apparent effect of increasing treatment variance, increasing F-ratio, and invalidly increasing power.
10	Unnatural/invalid experiment/treatment	Poor procedure can reduce differences across means, thus reducing treatment variance, reducing F-ratio, and consequently reducing power.
s^2_{error}		
2	Time: other events	If all groups did better, then this would hide the treatment effects and increase error variance, increasing β and reducing power.
3	Time: maturation	If all groups did better, then this would hide the treatment effects and increase error variance, increasing β and reducing power.
7	Interaction of time with sample	If the source of differences in sample means were differentially attributable to time, there could be increased error variance, increasing β and reducing power.
11	Invalid measurement of variables	If an instrument did not measure the consequences of the treatment, then differences across means would not be attributable solely to treatment: increased error variance, increased β and reduced power.
12	Instrument reliability	Low reliability results in increased error variance, with an increase in β and reduction in power.
13	Learning from instrument	The source of any differences in means can be uncertain, thus increased error variance, increased β and reduced power.
14	Instrument reacts with independent variable	The source of difference in means may not be due only to treatment, increasing error variance, increasing β and reducing power.

TABLE 16.1
Influence of sources of invalidity and confounding

Homogeneity of variance

Recall the three assumptions for the F-test:

- The trait measured should be normally distributed for the underlying population(s).
- These distributions of scores should be much the same (homogeneity of variance) and this should be reflected in the samples.
- The measures should be independent.

While the test is a robust one, tolerating some violation of the first two, there are limits. It is possible to generate a histogram of sample distributions and check them visually to see if they approach a normal distribution, but this is not very practical for small samples (less than 20). An obvious skew may be apparent, yet little can be determined from a relatively flat distribution of, say, six scores, so the first assumption is not easy to check. The consequence for the F-test is in the estimate of the population variance in the denominator s^2_{within}, since this is determined by the average of the sample variances. Heterogeneity of variance would make one suspicious of the accuracy of this estimate.

The deviation from homogeneity of variance is testable using data from the samples, and there are acceptable differences and unacceptable ones. In experimental designs, one is most likely to find heterogeneity of variance for small, unequal samples with measures that have non-normal distributions.

There are several tests for homogeneity of variance ranging in conservativeness, thus allowing differing degrees of heterogeneity to be tolerated. There has also been considerable discussion over which is most desirable and appropriate, with some writers suggesting that one does not worry too much about it since analysis of variance is a robust test. While the arguments rage on, two tests suggested by Winer *et al.* (1991) will be described here. It is left to the reader to decide, along with other factors, whether it is necessary to worry about increasing the probability of making a Type I error by ignoring heterogeneity of variance. I would test for it if I thought there were a risk, but then nervousness runs in the family. In any event, let us see how these are carried out.

The first is a simple test to apply for situations where the sample sizes are the same, in other words, for n constant. Hartley's test for homogeneity of variance involves finding the ratio of the largest of the sample variances to the smallest:

$$F_{max} = \frac{s^2_{largest}}{s^2_{smallest}} \qquad (16.13)$$

The degrees of freedom are simply $df_{num} = k$ and $df_{den} = n - 1$, using the critical values tabulated by Hartley in Table B.4 in Appendix B. For *small* differences in sample size, this test can be used with the largest n_j being used for df_{den}.

Bartlett's test for homogeneity of variance takes into account unequal sample sizes, but no sample should be less than 3 and most should be over 5 (Winer *et al.*, 1991), since the test is based upon χ^2. While the equation is rather daunting in appearance, once entered into the worksheet, checking data is simple.

$$\chi^2 = \frac{df_{within} \ln s^2_{within} - \sum_{j=1}^{k}(n_j - 1) \ln s^2_j}{1 - \frac{1}{3(k-1)}\left(\sum_{j=1}^{k}\frac{1}{n_j - 1} - \frac{1}{df_{within}}\right)} \tag{16.14}$$

This is checked against the χ^2 critical value in Table B.9, Appendix B, with $df = k - 1$. To implement these tests on a worksheet, carry out Activity 16.5.

Activity 16.5

1 Make a copy of the worksheet in Figure 16.5, developed in Activity 16.3.
2 As shown in Figure 16.7, first delete the contents of cells **E1:F16**, since we will use only three samples for the illustration. Then replace the data in the shaded area with those for the three samples. To this we will add what is necessary to carry out Bartlett's tests for homogeneity of variance.
3 **Insert** two more rows for **17** and **18**. Add the formulae indicated for column **C** and **Copy** them to the other cells in those rows.
4 In rows **26** to **29**, add the formulae for Bartlett's test. In this case, the test suggests that there is heterogeneity of variance since 8.78 > 5.99.

Correcting for heterogeneity of variance: Transformations

The next question is obvious: what do we do if one of the above tests shows that the sample variances indicate heterogeneity in the underlying population variances? The consequences of ignoring them may be an increased risk of making a Type I error, finding a significant difference when it does not exist. Thus any action should be aimed at redressing this possibility. This is accomplished most directly by changing the nature of the original data. For example, we could multiply each subject's score, x_{ij}, by some constant, but all this would do is to move them all along an axis, not change the relationship among the sample variances. Therefore, transformations have been developed that tend to 'bunch up' the scores, reducing the differences in the distributions and making the variances more alike. This also has the effect of making it slightly harder to find a significant F-ratio, simply because it also reduces the differences between the means, thus reducing the numerator, s^2_{within}.

Four common transformations are considered here (Winer *et al.*, 1991; Montgomery, 1991; Howell, 1997), arranged roughly in ascending order of their impact on the data (the further down the list, the greater the change to the shape of the distribution):

- *Arcsine*. Create a new set of data by using the mathematical operation that is the reverse of the *sine*, pulling data together:

$$x'_{ij} = 2 \arcsin \sqrt{x_{ij}} \tag{16.15}$$

	A	B	C	D	E	F	G	H
1	ANOVA data:	A	B	C				
2		3	6	7				
3		5	3	6				
4		3	5	13				
5		4	7	10				
6		2	4	7				
7		3		4				
8		4		2				
9								
10							grand mean	
11	means: $M_j =$	3.43	5.00	7.00			5.16	= GM
12	s.d.: $s_j =$	0.98	1.58	3.65				
13	var: $s^2_j =$	0.95	2.50	13.33				
14	$n_j =$	7	5	7				
15	$n_j (M_j - GM)^2 =$	20.93	0.12	23.75				
16	$n_j s^2_j =$	6.67	12.50	93.33				
17	$(n_j-1) \ln (s^2_j) =$	−0.29	3.67	15.54				
18	$1/(n_j-1) =$	0.17	0.25	0.17				
19								
20	ANOVA	SS	df	MS	F	p value	F_{crit}	α
21	Between	44.81	2	22.41	3.78	0.045	3.63	0.05
22	Within	94.74	16	5.92				
23								
24	Total	139.55	18					
25								
26	Bartlett's test			df(Bartlett's) =	$df_{between}$			
27	num =	9.54		chi.sq. =	8.78			
28	denom =	1.09		chi-sq.prob. =	0.012			
29				chi-sq.crit. =	5.99			

Annotations:
- Row 17: =(D14−1)*LN(D13)
- Row 18: =1/(D14−1) and **Copy** across
- =C22*LN(D22)−SUM(B17:F17)
- =B27/B28
- =CHIDIST(E27,C21)
- =1+(SUM(B18:F18)−1/C22)/(3*C21)
- =CHINV(H21,C21)

FIGURE 16.7
Worksheet including Bartlett's tests for homogeneity of variance

This is effective when the measure is a proportion (decimal values less than 1.0) – for example, the fraction of the responses answered in a certain way, the proportion of actions in a specific category, the percentage of time spent on an activity. This has the smallest effect on the data and may not result in homogeneity of variance across the transformed sample.

- *Square root*. Create a new set of data by taking the square root of every score or trait value:

$$x'_{ij} = \sqrt{x_{ij}} \qquad (16.16)$$

This is most appropriate when there is a pattern of the sample variances increasing as the sample means increase. In other words, if the means go up by half, do the variances increase by the same proportion $(s^2_j \propto \bar{x}_j)$? For example, if one mean were 3.0 with a variance of 2.0, and the next mean were 4.5, is the second variance also half as large again, that is, 3.0?

- *Logarithmic.* Create a new set of data by taking the log of each score:
$$x'_{ij} = \log x_{ij} \qquad (16.17)$$

This transformation is most effective for positively skewed distributions (long tail to the right), not uncommon when time is the measure, as in reaction time. It is also appropriate for samples whose standard deviations (instead of the variances) increase in the same proportion as the means $(s_j \propto \bar{x}_j)$. For example, if the means increase from 2.0 to 4.0, you would expect the standard deviations to double as well.

- *Reciprocal.* Create a new set of data by taking the reciprocal of each score:
$$x'_{ij} = \frac{1}{x_{ij}} \qquad (16.18)$$

This is appropriate for samples whose standard deviation increases in the same proportion as the square of the means increases $(s_j \propto \bar{x}_j^2)$. In other words, if the square of the mean were to increase from 4.0 to 12.0, you would expect the standard deviation to triple.

There are variations on these (see the references above), and since many cases of heterogeneity of variance occur with non-normality, transformations tend to cure both ills. After carrying out the transformation, the analysis of variance is then repeated with the transformed data. If the results appear still to be heterogeneous, then a second test of homogeneity of variance should be carried out. If there is still a lack of sufficient homogeneity, a different transformation could be tried. Not always is the need for transformations a consequence of poor design or execution of a study (though these are possibilities). It may be due to the nature of the impact of the independent variable on the dependent variable. This may be particularly true for ex post facto studies where the groups may have experienced rather different extremes of life experiences (the treatment, the independent variable) and consequently the variances may differ considerably as well as the means for the dependent variable. Such differences would be considered due to differing natural variabilities for the trait in the groups.

Figure 16.8 shows graphically the consequences of transforming the three sets of heterogeneous distributions implied by data in Figure 16.7. Now carry out Activity 16.6 to implement transformations in a worksheet.

Activity 16.6

1 Block the analysis section **A1:H29** in the worksheet in Figure 16.7 and **Copy** it to the lower part of the same sheet starting in cell **A31** (see Figure 16.9).
2 Transform this new copied data set using the square root transformation (equation (16.15)), by entering the formula in cell **B32** and **Copy**ing it to all the other data cells:
   (a) Is there homogeneity of variance now?
   (b) Does the new ANOVA produce a significant result?
   (c) Do any other transformations produce homogeneity of variance and significant results?

Answers
2. *(a) Yes, $5.42 < 5.99$. (b) Yes, $3.67 > 3.63$, $p < 0.05$. (c) If either log or reciprocal used, homogeneity of variance, but F n.s.*

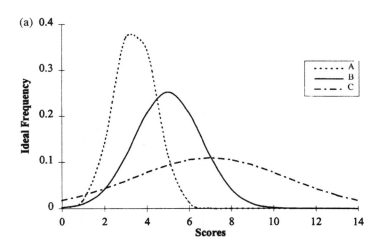

FIGURE 16.8
Illustration of
consequences of
applying
transformations.
(a) raw data from
means and standard
deviations in Figure
16.7

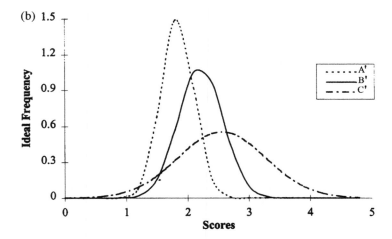

FIGURE 16.8
Illustration of
consequences of
applying
transformations.
(b) square root
transformation (see
Figure 16.9)

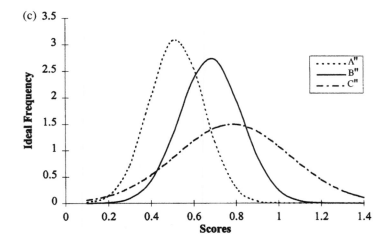

FIGURE 16.8
Illustration of
consequences of
applying
transformations.
(c) logarithmic
transformation

=SQRT(B2) and **Copy** to all cells with data

	ANOVA data:	A	B	C			grand mean	
31	ANOVA data:	A	B	C				
32	Square root	1.73	2.45	2.65				
33	transformed	2.24	1.73	2.45				
34		1.73	2.24	3.61				
35		2.00	2.65	3.16				
36		1.41	2.00	2.65				
37		1.73		2.00				
38		2.00		1.41				
39								
40							grand mean	
41	means: $M_j =$	1.84	2.21	2.56			2.20	= GM
42	s.d.: $s_j =$	0.27	0.36	0.72				
43	var: $s^2_j =$	0.07	0.13	0.52				
44	n_j	7	5	7				
45	$n_j (M_j - GM)^2 =$	0.94	0.00	0.90				
46	$n_j s^2_j =$	0.49	0.65	3.63				
47	$(n_j-1) \ln (s^2_j) =$	−15.90	−8.16	−3.94				
48	$1/(n_j-1) =$	0.17	0.25	0.17				
49								
50	**ANOVA**	**SS**	**df**	**MS**	**F**	**p value**	**F_{crit}**	**α**
51	Between	1.84	2	0.92	3.67	0.049	3.63	0.05
52	Within	4.02	16	0.25				
53								
54	Total	5.86	18					
55								
56	**Bartlett's test**			df(Bartlett's) =	$df_{between}$			
57	num =	5.89		chi.sq. =	5.42			
58	denom =	1.09		chi-sq.prob. =	0.066			
59				chi-sq.crit. =	5.99			

FIGURE 16.9
Worksheet with transformed data with second ANOVA and Bartlett's test

For all the transformations shown in Figure 16.8, the resulting variances were not significantly different, as indicated by a subsequent Bartlett's test. In other words, the transformed data passed the test for homogeneity of variance. Interestingly, though, while the original data and the square root transformation both produced significant F-tests, analysis of variance of the logarithmic and reciprocal transformations gave a non-significant result. There has been some criticism of tests for homogeneity of variance based upon research suggesting that they can be excessively conservative. On the other hand, if heterogeneity of variance were identified and, even after a transformation was applied, the data still showed heterogeneity of variance, it could be argued that the data should be treated as ranked (instead of interval or ratio) and a nonparametric test employed.

MULTIPLE COMPARISONS

As a result of the ANOVA test, you decide that there is a difference across the three or more samples for the trait under investigation, but this does *not* indicate that they are all significantly different from each other. For example, in the worksheet in Figure 16.2, there are five groups which the *F*-test suggests are not all from the same population. Considering the five means,

	A	B	C	D	E
Means	6.14	3.43	3.86	5.29	6.43

we might suspect that there is no significant difference between A and E, nor between B and C. We also might suspect that there is a difference between E and D and reject H_0, and even conclude incorrectly that the two belong to different populations. Underlying such a collection of decisions is the risk of making a Type I error, which can be expressed in terms of the probability of making one error out of the whole set of decisions. The consequences are sometimes referred to as the *family wise* probability of making at least one Type I error in a set of tests (Hays, 1994; Howell, 1997). This can be expressed mathematically, where α_{FW} represents the overall probability,

$$\alpha_{FW} = 1 - (1 - \alpha)^c \qquad (16.19)$$

and α is the probability level for any single comparison for c comparisons. Thus for the example above, the overall probability of committing a Type I error by using a repeated *t*-test for all ten possible comparisons, using $\alpha = 0.05$ each time, would be

$$\alpha_{FW} = 1 - (1 - 0.05)^{10}$$
$$= 1 - 0.95^{10}$$
$$= 1 - 0.60$$
$$= 0.40$$

Put simply, there would be a 40% probability of incorrectly rejecting the null hypothesis that there was a difference in at least one of the comparisons, if it were really true. We would also be correct in expecting a big rise in the power of this test as compared with the original *F*-test. This reasoning has prompted mathematicians to devise more conservative tests – in other words, ones that would not have such a high probability of making a Type I error. Before considering these, let us think about what we might expect as outcomes.

A priori versus post hoc tests

There is the possibility that you may expect certain relationships prior to carrying out a study investigating differences across three or more groups. This is analogous to the situation where you would choose a one-tailed *t*-test if there were strong reasons to believe the difference in a single pair of groups could only be in one direction (recall Chapter 14). In the situation where specific differences are anticipated, it would be reasonable to hypothesize relationships among the means of the sample groups. For example, in an ex post facto study, the amount of living expenses among university students is hypothesized to be different across specific pairs of social classes. In fact, the researcher expects that students from social class A families will have significantly more money to spend than those from all others. On the other hand, there will not necessarily be a significant difference between class B, C and D students. At the other extreme, it is expected that students from social class E families will be on scholarships or loans and have only the bare minimum, thus they too will be different from each of the other groups. Making the decision to limit the number of tests *before* the data are collected, a priori, automatically reduces the probability of a Type I error. Since this results in less conservative, more powerful tests, it would be cheating to make the decision after seeing the data.

In most cases, we do not know which pairs will be significant, therefore tests are carried out on all the pairs after the data have been collected, so they are referred to as post hoc. This results in tests that compensate for the fact that *all* pairwise comparisons will be made. There are a number of such tests, ranging in conservativeness, which again places the researcher in the position of asking what the consequences are of making Type I and Type II errors in order to decide which to employ.

A priori tests

An acceptable alternative to multiple *t*-tests when relationships are predicted ahead of data collection is *Dunn's test* (also called the *Bonferroni t*). This is based upon the *t*-test equation for pairwise comparisons,

$$t' = \frac{\bar{x}_B - \bar{x}_A}{\sqrt{\dfrac{2MS_{\text{within}}}{n}}} \qquad \text{equal } n_j \qquad (16.20)$$

where the mean square within, MS_{within}, comes from the ANOVA results table. For unequal sample sizes, this becomes

$$t' = \frac{\bar{x}_B - \bar{x}_A}{\sqrt{\left(\dfrac{1}{n_B} + \dfrac{1}{n_A}\right) MS_{\text{within}}}} \qquad \text{unequal } n_{ij} \qquad (16.21)$$

The critical value is found on a special table of modified t'_{crit} that depends not only on degrees of freedom but also on how many pairs are being considered. It is more powerful than some post hoc tests, but only if less than all the possible comparisons are made. Interestingly, SPSS (version 6.1) provides *only* for all possible comparisons, which counteracts any power advantage from being able to predict comparisons and results in a very conservative test.

The table of critical values is based upon using the *t*-distribution, but uses an altered level of significance so that α_{FW} does not rise with the number of comparisons. This is based upon the premise that the error rate per comparison, α_{PC}, is dependent on the number of comparisons, *c* each using a level α:

$$\alpha_{\text{PC}} = c\alpha$$

If the overall error is to be maintained, then

$$\alpha_{\text{FW}} \leq \alpha_{\text{PC}}$$

Thus the critical value can be found by simply using a table of critical values for t, but at the following maximum level of significance, α:

$$\alpha = \frac{\alpha_{FW}}{c}$$

If, for example, the aim was to have α_{FW} the same as for the analysis of variance, $p < 0.05$, for a study with four comparisons, then the α for each comparison would be

$$\alpha = \frac{0.05}{4} = 0.0125$$

This presents a difficulty, since standard tables of t_{crit} usually do not provide for values of α other than 0.10, 0.05, 0.025, 0.01, 0.005 or 0.001, therefore special tables are often provided. This is not a problem when using Excel since the function **TINV(prob, df)** can cope with any probability; this is how Table B.5 in Appendix B was generated.

Post hoc tests

Choosing to make all pairwise comparison after data have been collected and the F-test has been carried out still leaves the researcher with decisions. Many post hoc tests are based upon the studentized range statistic, q_r, but with different tables of critical values depending on the rationale for the test. The statistic is calculated similarly to the t'-statistic,

$$q_r = \frac{\bar{x}_B - \bar{x}_A}{\sqrt{\dfrac{MS_{within}}{n}}} \qquad \text{equal } n_j \qquad (16.22)$$

For unequal sample sizes, the Tukey–Kramer approach (Howell, 1997) modifies the equation as follows:

$$q_r = \frac{\bar{x}_B - \bar{x}_A}{\sqrt{\left(\dfrac{1}{n_A} + \dfrac{1}{n_B}\right) \dfrac{MS_{within}}{2}}} \qquad \text{unequal } n_j \qquad (16.23)$$

The different tests have q_{crit} depend on various combinations of factors to make them by varying degrees more conservative than implementing multiple t-tests. The differences are based upon various alterations to the critical scores as a consequence of:

- changes in the degrees of freedom, df_{within}, though only a few depend on this alone;
- the number of comparisons, c;
- the rank order of the means, taking into account how many steps there are across the samples being compared, r.

These different combinations and adjustments result in a series of tests that vary in terms of overall conservativeness, thus decreasing α_{FW} and consequently decreasing the power. Table 16.2 lists some of these tests, with the post hoc tests in order of increasing conservativeness. The rationale for each is elaborated briefly before looking at how the tests are applied.

TABLE 16.2
Some multiple
comparison
techniques, in order
of conservativeness
for the six possible
post hoc tests

Test	Comparison	Description	A priori/ post hoc
Multiple t-tests	pairwise	Standard t-test (not recommended)	Either
Duncan	pairwise	q-statistic, where q_{crit} is dependent on df and an α that increases with number of steps apart, r	Post hoc
Newman–Keuls	pairwise	q-statistic, where q_{crit} is dependent on df and r, the number of steps in the range, α=constant	Post hoc
Tukey B	pairwise	q-statistic, where q_{crit} is the average of those for Tukey A and Newman–Keuls	Post hoc
Tukey A	pairwise	q-statistic, where q_{crit} is constant no matter how many steps apart	Post hoc
Scheffé	any combination	F-statistic, where F'_{crit} is constant and based upon F_{crit} (eqn (16.24))	Post hoc
Bonferroni t (Dunn's)	any combination*	Modified t-test, where t'_{crit} is dependent on df and number of comparisons to be made	A priori
Dunnett's	against a control	Modified t-test, between each group with a control (or a single group), where t'_{crit} is dependent on df_{error} and number of means, constant α_{FW}	Post hoc

(left margin, top to bottom: **least** / **conservative** / **most**)

*See Howell (1997) for details of contrasts among combinations of groups.

NEWMAN–KEULS TEST   The critical value for this test is based directly on the critical values for the studentized range statistic (Table B.6 in Appendix B) and its associated sampling distribution. Since this depends on the stated α, df_{within}, and the number of samples spanned, then as the number of means in the range increases, so does q_{crit}. We will see an easier way below than to calculate q_r for each pair and compare it to a table.

DUNCAN'S MULTIPLE RANGE TEST   This test was designed to keep a *protection level* α_{prot} constant for a set of data, thus α for individual pairs of means is dependent on the number of groups, r, spanned by the test. This is expressed mathematically as

$$\alpha = 1 - (1 - \alpha_{prot})^{r-1}$$

Consequently, if $\alpha_{prot} = 0.05$, then for two adjacent groups, $\alpha = 0.05$, but for two groups with one in between, $\alpha = 1 - (1 - 0.05)^2 = 0.0975$, and so on. Therefore the more groups spanned, the greater the α corresponding to the number of groups is when consulting the table of critical values for the studentized range statistic. The critical value still increases as the number of means spanned increases, but not nearly as fast as for the Newman–Keuls test. As suggested by Table 16.2, Duncan's test is more powerful than the Newman–Keuls test. Since it is not possible to obtain critical values directly from the table of critical values for the studentized range statistic because of the different values for α, a special table has been created (Table B.6, Appendix B). The consequence for such an approach is that α_{FW} will be quite high, resulting in a greater risk of making a Type I error, but a higher power when means are more than two steps apart.

TUKEY'S TESTS   There are two versions of this test. Tukey A simply uses the maximum value of q_{crit} for the Newman–Keuls test for *all* pairwise comparisons, regardless of how many means are spanned. As a compromise, Tukey B uses the average of Tukey A and Newman–Keuls. Consequently, both of these tests are more conservative than the Newman–Keuls test.

SCHEFFÉ COMPARISONS   Scheffé's test sets α_{FW} to be a maximum for all comparisons and depends on the total number of samples. Its critical value is therefore constant for all pairwise comparisons, no matter how many means are spanned. It is the odd one, in that it is based on a modified F-distribution, assuming equal n:

$$F' = \frac{\left(\bar{x}_{\text{larger}} - \bar{x}_{\text{smaller}}\right)^2}{\dfrac{2MS_{\text{within}}}{n}} \tag{16.24}$$

As well as pairwise comparisons, there is a modified version of this that allows comparisons between groups of samples – say, the two highest and two lowest in a set of four samples. In this case the equation becomes (assuming unequal n)

$$F' = \frac{\left(\dfrac{n_1\bar{x}_1 + n_2\bar{x}_2}{n_1 + n_2} - \dfrac{n_3\bar{x}_3 + n_4\bar{x}_4}{n_3 + n_4}\right)^2}{\dfrac{MS_{\text{within}}}{n_1 + n_2} + \dfrac{MS_{\text{within}}}{n_3 + n_4}} \tag{16.25}$$

with the critical value being determined indirectly from the table of critical values for F:

$$F'_{\text{crit}} = \sqrt{2df_{\text{between}}\ F_{\text{crit}}(df_{\text{between}}, df_{\text{within}})} \tag{16.26}$$

Scheffé's test is more conservative than Tukey A, though it does allow comparisons of groups of means.

DUNNETT'S TEST FOR STUDIES WITH A CONTROL GROUP   This is unique in that it allows only comparisons with a single group, typically the control group, therefore it is not equivalent to the other post hoc tests. Dunnett's test uses the t-statistic of equations (16.20) and (16.21) and a constant critical value. The critical value is found by using a value for α for a set of means such that α_{FW} is held constant, for example that used in the ANOVA. This has resulted in another table of critical values, Table B.8 in Appendix B. It is possible to see the logic behind this test by starting with equation (16.19):

$$\alpha_{FW} = 1 - (1 - \alpha)^c$$

We can solve for α having decided on α_{FW}:

$$(1 - \alpha)^c = 1 - \alpha_{FW}$$

$$1 - \alpha = \sqrt[c]{1 - \alpha_{FW}}$$

$$\alpha = 1 - \sqrt[c]{1 - \alpha_{FW}}$$

For example, for a set of seven samples for which $\alpha_{FW} = 0.05$, there will be six possible comparisons with the control group, therefore

$$\alpha = 1 - \sqrt[6]{1 - 0.05} = 1 - \sqrt[6]{0.95} = 1 - 0.9915 \cong 0.01$$

Thus, to estimate the critical value directly from a table of critical values for t, in this case we would look in the $p = 0.01$ column to find approximate values for $\alpha = 0.05$. As noted earlier, this will not work for probabilities for which there are not tables and this is only an approximation. You could confirm the above by comparing the values in the two tables to see if they are close: is one-tailed $t_{\text{crit}}(0.01, df) \cong t'_{\text{Dunnett}}(6, 0.05, df)$ true? If you look, they are closest for large df.

WHICH TEST TO USE?   Let us consider an example to help understand how one would decide on a test. First of all, finding a minimum difference between means for significance is easier than calculating the critical values for all possible comparisons. By taking equations (16.20) and (16.22) and rearranging them, it is possible to generate for each test a set of values for the minimum difference in pairs of means to be considered significant. For those based upon the modified t-statistic,

$$t' = \frac{\bar{x}_B - \bar{x}_A}{\sqrt{\dfrac{2MS_{\text{within}}}{n}}}$$

$$\bar{x}_{\text{larger}} - \bar{x}_{\text{smaller}} = t'\sqrt{\frac{2MS_{\text{within}}}{n}}$$

$$\Delta\bar{x}_{\text{min}} = t'_{\text{crit}}\sqrt{\frac{2MS_{\text{within}}}{n}} \tag{16.27}$$

Then, depending on the test, the level of significance, and df, a value for t'_{crit} is used to find the minimum difference in means for a significant difference.

Similarly, for those based upon the studentized range statistic, q_r it is possible to determine a minimum significant difference in means from equation (16.22):

$$q_r = \frac{\bar{x}_{\text{larger}} - \bar{x}_{\text{smaller}}}{\sqrt{\dfrac{MS_{\text{within}}}{n}}}$$

$$\bar{x}_{\text{larger}} - \bar{x}_{\text{smaller}} = q_r\sqrt{\frac{MS_{\text{within}}}{n}}$$

$$\Delta\bar{x}_{\text{min}} = q_{r\,\text{crit}}\sqrt{\frac{2MS_{\text{within}}}{n}} \tag{16.28}$$

Again, depending on the test, the level of significance, df, and in some cases, number of comparisons, c, or range of means, r, a value for $q_{r\,\text{crit}}$ is used to find the minimum difference in means for a significant difference.

Scheffé's test can be presented in this same format by rearranging equation (16.24):

$$F' = \frac{\left(\bar{x}_{\text{larger}} - \bar{x}_{\text{smaller}}\right)^2}{\dfrac{2MS_{\text{within}}}{n}}$$

to give

$$\bar{x}_{\text{larger}} - \bar{x}_{\text{smaller}} = \sqrt{\frac{2F'MS_{\text{within}}}{n}}$$

To obtain a minimum significant difference, we substitute in equation (16.26) for $F' = F'_{\text{crit}}$, giving us

$$\Delta\bar{x}_{\text{min}} = \sqrt{\frac{2MS_{\text{within}}\, df_{\text{between}}\, F_{\text{crit}}\left(df_{\text{between}}, df_{\text{within}}\right)}{n}} \qquad (16.29)$$

For purposes of comparison across post hoc tests on the spreadsheet, the equivalence

$$q = \sqrt{2}\,t = \sqrt{2F}$$

and the equivalent q for each test will be calculated. This will be used to find the minimum significant difference in means for each pair,

$$\Delta\bar{x}_{\text{min}} = q_{\text{crit}}\sqrt{\frac{MS_{\text{within}}}{n}}$$

by using the appropriate q_{crit} or its equivalent in each case,

$$q_{\text{crit}} = \sqrt{2}\,t'_{\text{crit}} = \sqrt{2F'_{\text{crit}}} \qquad (16.30)$$

Table 16.3 (after Winer *et al.*, 1991) provides critical values for each test based upon the situation described in our example above from Figure 16.2 for five samples. This results in $c = 10$ possible comparisons, thus for the Bonferroni test to be of any advantage, it is necessary to choose less than this, so for this example, $c = 5$. For other tests, the value of $r = 2, 3, 4, 5$, depending on how many means are in the range. Table 16.3(a) sets out the means in descending order and puts their differences in a table. The linking lines indicate those that have a common span of means (equal r). Table 16.3(b) is the result of using equations (16.27), (16.28) and (16.29) to find all the $\Delta\bar{x}_{\text{min}}$, allowing a direct match to Table 16.3(a). Table 16.3(c) provides the actual critical values for each test. Table 16.3(d) indicates which of the pairwise comparisons for each test were significant. One interesting artefact is in the Dunnett's test column: since this only compares other samples with the control, even though the differences E–C and A–C were less than the minima, they are not included since neither of these included the control group, B.

The ordering of the post hoc tests by conservativeness in Table 16.2 is clearly exemplified here: as we move 'down' the list, fewer comparisons are classified as significantly different. This still leaves the question which to use? The answer, unfortunately, is the same as before: one must consider the consequences of making Type I and Type II errors and decide accordingly. If the aim is to identify possible variables for developing a theory, then a less conservative test may be quite appropriate. On the other hand, if major decisions are to be made as

TABLE 16.3
A comparison of post hoc tests for the data in Figure 16.2, $MS_{within} = 3.24$, $df_{within} = 30$

(a) Difference between pairs of means

Differences	E 6.57	A 6.29	D 5.43	C 3.86	B 3.29	r
E		0.29	1.14	2.71	3.29	5
A			0.86	2.43	3.00	4
D				1.57	2.14	3
C					0.57	2

Means= ; $\alpha = 0.05$; $n = 7$; $c = 10$

(b) Minimum differences for significance for each $= q_{crit}\sqrt{\dfrac{MS_{within}}{n}} = q_{crit} \times 0.68$

r	Multiple t-tests	Bonferroni $t(\alpha = \alpha_{FW}/c)$	Duncan	Newman–Keuls	Tukey B	Tukey A	Scheffé	Dunnett's B = control
5	1.96	2.56	2.18	2.79	2.79	2.79	3.15	2.16
4	1.96	2.56	2.12	2.62	2.70	2.79	3.15	2.16
3	1.96	2.56	2.07	2.37	2.58	2.79	3.15	2.16
2	1.96	2.56	1.97	1.97	2.38	2.79	3.15	2.16

(c) Critical values for each test, q_{crit}

r	Multiple t-tests $=\sqrt{2}t_{crit}$ Table B.2	Bonferroni $=\sqrt{2}t'_{crit}$ (c=4) Table B.5	Duncan Table B.7	Newman–Keuls Table B.6	Tukey B =(Tukey A +NK)/2	Tukey A $= NK_{max}$	Scheffé $=\sqrt{2F'_{crit}}$ eqn (16.26) and Table B.3	Dunnett's $=\sqrt{2}t_{D_{crit}}$ (p=4) Table B.8
5	2.89	3.76	3.20	4.10	4.10	4.10	4.64	3.18
4			3.12	3.85	3.98			
3			3.04	3.49	3.80			
2			2.89	2.89	3.50			

(d) Significant pairs as identified by each test

r	Multiple t-tests	Bonferroni	Duncan	Newman–Keuls	Tukey B	Tukey A	Scheffé	Dunnett's
5	E–B	E–B	E–B	E–B	E–B	E–B	E–B	E–B
4	E–C, A–B	E–C, A–B	E–C, A–B	E–C, A–B	E–C, A–B	A–B	A–B	A–B
3	A–C, D–B		A–C, D–B	A–C				
2								

part of a real-world study, then the consequences become more important and one must reflect carefully before deciding.

Reporting results of multiple comparisons meaningfully is a challenge. The more pairs there are, the more difficult it is to make sense of the results. It is suggested that a sort of Venn diagram be used to display the results. For example, to show those that are not significantly different for Newman–Keuls in Table 16.3, the letters are listed in order of declining means and boxed according to those who belong to the same populations,

$$\boxed{\text{E} \quad \text{A} \quad \boxed{\text{D}}\ \text{C} \quad \text{B}}$$

Therefore, if two groups (E + A, and C + B) are in different boxes, they are significantly different. Here D is in both boxes, therefore it is not significantly different from either group.

We can now add this facility to our worksheet for the ANOVA. In Activity 16.7, this will be done for the more general situation of unequal n_j, but this will simply mean using the appropriate equations encountered earlier for each case.

Activity 16.7

1 Using the data in Table 16.3, create a box diagram for the outcomes for

   (a) Duncan's test,
   (b) Tukey's B test (same outcome as Bonferroni t).

2 Having found a significant difference across the five groups of students (Activity 16.1 and modified in Activity 16.3), Professor Bloggs wanted to find out which groups differed from each other.

   (a) Start with his refined data by making a copy of the worksheet for basic ANOVA (n_{ij} not equal), Figure 16.5.
   (b) Add multiple comparisons to the worksheet as shown in Figure 16.10, using equations for n_{ij} not equal:
       (i) In **H24**, the formula for the *harmonic mean* is used as a best estimate of sample size, as long as the n_j do not vary too much from each other:

$$\tilde{n} = \frac{k}{\dfrac{1}{n_1} + \dfrac{1}{n_2} + \dfrac{1}{n_3} + \ldots + \dfrac{1}{n_k}}$$

       (ii) In **A24:F29**, a table of differences in sample means is set up. If the group labels and means are placed in the shaded areas in descending order, then formulae for differences can be placed in the other cells. Two have been provided; you can supply the rest. The little link lines can be added using the **Drawing** facility in Excel:

(iii) In **H26** the general formula for $\Delta \bar{x}_{min}$, equation (16.28), is inserted. This depends on the value in the next column which will be a q_{crit} value from the test statistic copied into that column. The formula in **H26** should be **Copy**ed to the other three cells below.

(iv) In the last section, the formulae (where possible) are the q_{crit} values for each test from equation (16.30), dependent on $\tilde{n}$, α and appropriate degrees of freedom. Those in the shaded cells must be taken from the appropriate tables in Appendix B.

(c) To carry out each test, **Copy** the appropriate sets of cells for other tests into cells **I25:I29**. How many significant pairwise comparisons are found for each? Try each before looking at the answers below.

(d) Which test would be most appropriate for Professor Bloggs' question?

Answers

1. (a)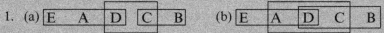

2. (c) Multiple *t*: 5, Bonferroni *t*: 2, Duncan: 4, Newman–Keuls: 2, Tukey B: 2, Tukey A: 2, Scheffé: 0, Dunnett's: 3. (d) Probably Duncan since it is least conservative and no important decisions will be made on the basis of this study.

POWER

To find β, the probability of making a Type II error, and thus the power, the probability of correctly rejecting H_0, we will again overlay the sampling distribution with an alternative non-central distribution based upon the sample data. As we saw earlier, the *F*-distributions of possible sample ratios of the two estimates of the population variance have a mean of about 1.0 and are highly skewed (see Figure 16.3). What does it mean graphically, then, if we reject the null hypothesis? We can then imagine that there is actually a second population, one that has its own sampling distribution, analogous to that of the *z*- and *t*-tests. This non-central distribution would have an expected $F \gg 1$ and can be shown in relation to the central distribution similar to previous illustrations: overlapping distributions with the critical α line for the central distribution delineating the division between β and power on the non-central distribution. This allows us to describe power graphically, as before, in Figure 16.11.

Using this as a basis, a mathematical expression that would allow us to consider the interactions among sample size (*n*), level of significance (α), the relative magnitude of the differences across means, and the power of the test, would be of value in planning research. Being able to see the consequences of changing each would provide sufficient information on which to make decisions. We will start with the *non-centrality parameter*, λ, which, as Winer *et al.* (1991),

	A	B	C	D	E	F	G	H	I
1	ANOVA	A	B	C	D	E			
2	data	6	2	3	7	7			
3		10	3	5	3	6			
4		4	5	3	5	9			
5		5	4	4	8	8			
6		4	3	3	4	7			
7		9	2	2		6			
8		6		7		3			
9									
10								grand M	
11	means: M_j =	6.29	3.17	3.86	5.40	6.57	5.09	= GM	
12	s.d.: s_j =	2.36	1.17	1.68	2.07	1.90			
13	var: s^2_j =	5.57	1.37	2.81	4.30	3.62			
14	n_j =	7	6	7	5	7			
15	$n_j (M_j - GM)^2$ =	9.95	22.28	10.70	0.47	15.28			
16	ns^2_j =	39.00	8.20	19.67	21.50	25.33			
17									
18	ANOVA	SS	df	s^2 (MS)	F	p value	F_{crit}	α	
19	Between	58.69	4	14.67	4.13	0.00974	2.73	0.05	
20	Within	95.93	27	3.55					
21									
22	Total	154.62	31						
23	post hoc								
24	means =	6.57	6.29	5.40	3.86	3.17	$\tilde{n}$ =	6.2874	Test
25	differences	E	A	D	C	B	r	ΔM_{min}	Tukey (b)
26	E		0.29	1.17	2.71	3.40 — 5		3.10	4.13
27	A			0.89	2.43	3.12 — 4		3.01	4.00
28	D				1.54	2.23 — 3		2.87	3.82
29	C					0.69 — 2		2.64	3.52
30	q_{crit} values								
31	r	Multi-t	Bonferroni	Duncan	NK	Tukey B	Tukey A	Scheffé	Dunnett's
32	5	2.90	3.78	3.21	4.13	4.13	4.13	4.67	3.20
33	4	2.90	3.78	3.15	3.87	4.00	4.13	4.67	3.20
34	3	2.90	3.78	3.05	3.50	3.82	4.13	4.67	3.20
35	2	2.90	3.78	2.90	2.90	3.52	4.13	4.67	3.20
36		= sqrt(2)t	= sqrt(2)t'	q_r	q_r	q_r	q_r	= sqrt(2F')	=sqrt$t$(2)$_D$
37			4			= (TA + NK)/2	= NK_{max}	eq (16.26)	
38	Appendix B:	Table B.2	Table B.5	Table B.7	Table B.6			& Table B.3	Table B.8

Callout annotations:

- (H21): =126*SQRT($D$20/$H$24) and **Copy** down column
- (row 23): =5/(1/B14+1/C14+1/D14+1/E14+1/F14)
- (C26): =B24–C24
- (C28): =B24–D24
- =SQRT(2)*TINV($H$19,$C$20) and **Copy** down
- =SQRT(2)*TINV($H$19/$C$37,$C$20) and **Copy** down
- =SQRT(2*$C$19*FINV($H$19,$C$19,$C$20)) and **Copy** down
- =$E$32 and **Copy**
- =($G$32+$E$32)/2
  =($G$32+$E$33)/2
  =($G$32+$E$34)/2
  =($G$32+$E$35)/2

FIGURE 16.10 Worksheet with one-way ANOVA and post hoc analysis: shaded cells require entries, the rest are the results of equations

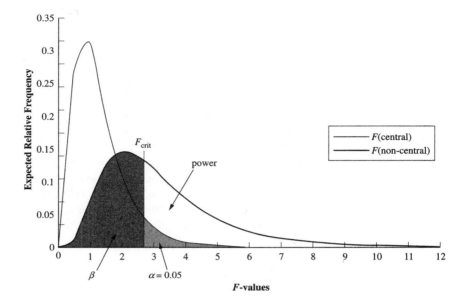

FIGURE 16.11
An example of a central *F*-distribution and the corresponding *non-central* *F*-distribution for a study showing how they illustrate β and power when F_{crit} is added

Howell (1997) and Glass and Hopkins (1996) note, is defined as

$$\lambda = \frac{n \sum_{j=1}^{k} \tau_j^2}{\sigma_{within}^2} \tag{16.31}$$

where $\sum \tau^2$ is the *treatment effect* such that

$$\tau_j = \mu_j - \mu$$

in which μ_j is the mean of treatment population j and μ is the grand mean of all populations. If the treatment did not introduce a significant change, then we would expect $\sum \tau^2$ to approach zero, as would λ. The difficulty is that this is an expression involving population parameters, which are unlikely to be known. As Winer *et al.* (1991) note, an appropriate estimate for this in terms of sample (pilot) data is

$$\sum \tau_j^2 \cong \frac{k-1}{n}(MS_{between} - MS_{within})$$

and, combined with a second estimate,

$$\sigma_{within}^2 \cong MS_{within}$$

it is possible to derive a simple expression for the non-centrality parameter:

$$\lambda \cong \frac{n \left[\dfrac{k-1}{n}(MS_{between} - MS_{within}) \right]}{MS_{within}}$$

$$\cong (k-1)\left(\frac{MS_{between}}{MS_{within}} - 1 \right)$$

$$\cong (k-1)(F-1) \tag{16.32}$$

There are other definitions of the basic non-centrality parameter, one of which is based upon using equation (16.31) with sample data, not necessarily an appropriate choice, which results in $\lambda \cong (k-1)F$. This produces inflated values of power and is not recommended. Also, it can be shown that equation (16.32) provides values of power that are generally lower than what would be expected. For example, for the unique situation where it so happens that $F = F_{\text{crit}}$, the value of power is considerably less than the 50% that would be expected (Black, 1997b). This is not consistent with what was found either for the z-test or the t-test. Therefore, a slight modification in this basic assumption is used that provides estimates of power equal to 50%, as expected for situations where $F = F_{\text{crit}}$. This takes into account the fact that the shape of the F-distributions is influenced greatly by the number of treatment groups, k, as seen in Figure 16.3. The introduction of a correction factor, cf, results in values of power for $F = F_{\text{crit}}$ to be 50% for any number of treatment groups when group sizes are five or more ($n \geq 5$),

$$\lambda = (k-1)\left(\frac{F}{cf} - 1\right) \tag{16.33}$$

where

$$cf = \frac{k}{k + 0.4} \tag{16.34}$$

This allows us to describe the relationship between the two sampling distributions as two separate F-distributions:

$$F(\text{central}) = F(df_{\text{between}}, df_{\text{within}}) \qquad \text{for } H_0 \text{ true}$$

$$F(\text{non-central}) = F(df_{\text{between}}, df_{\text{within}}, \lambda) \qquad \text{for } H_0 \text{ false}$$

As we have seen, the first distribution is relatively easy to generate, but the second is not. Therefore we will resort to an interesting approximation that allows us to calculate power directly. This will provide two procedures, the first to estimate the power of a study based upon the outcomes, and second to use a desired value of power to estimate required sample sizes.

Estimating the power of the outcome of a study

This estimate is easily found from the ANOVA results. To calculate the power directly, rather than referring to a set of tables such as those provided by Cohen (1988) or Howell (1997), requires another estimating procedure. This is based on expressing the non-central distribution as a specific central distribution (Winer *et al.*, 1991),

$$F(\text{non-central}) = F(df_{\text{between}}, df_{\text{within}}, \lambda) \cong F'(df'_{\text{between}}, df_{\text{within}})$$

where

$$df'_{\text{between}} = \frac{(df_{\text{between}} + \lambda)^2}{df_{\text{between}} + 2\lambda} \tag{16.35}$$

The area that will represent power is that beyond the modified critical point, F_{crit}/k', where

$$k' = \frac{df_{between} + \lambda}{df_{between}} \tag{16.36}$$

Now we have all the parameters for determining power. If we substitute F_{crit} into the Excel cumulative distribution for F, along with the degrees of freedom, we get

$$\textbf{FDIST}(\textbf{\textit{F}}_{\textbf{crit}}, \textbf{\textit{df}}_{\textbf{between}}, \textbf{\textit{df}}_{\textbf{within}}) = \alpha$$

the area under the shaded tail of the F-distribution for H_0 true in Figure 16.11. We can also get an approximate value for power using the values from the equations above

$$\textbf{FDIST}(\textbf{\textit{F}}_{\textbf{crit}}/\textbf{\textit{k}}', \textbf{ROUND}(\textbf{\textit{df}}'_{\textbf{between}}, \textbf{0}), \textbf{\textit{df}}_{\textbf{within}}) \cong \text{power} \tag{16.37}$$

For example, using the values in Figure 16.10, $F = 4.13$, and the value for the correction factor for five groups is

$$cf = \frac{5}{5 + 0.4} = 0.926$$

Therefore, equation (16.38) gives a value for the non-centrality parameter,

$$\lambda = (5 - 1)\left(\frac{4.13}{0.926} - 1\right) = 13.84$$

From equations (16.39) and (16.40), we find

$$df'_{between} = \frac{(4 + 13.84)^2}{4 + 2 \times 13.84} = 10.05$$

$$k' = \frac{4 + 13.84}{4} = 4.46$$

Combining with $F_{crit} = 2.73$, the result is

$$\textbf{power} \cong \textbf{FDIST}(\textbf{2.73/4.46}, \textbf{ROUND}(\textbf{10.05}, \textbf{0}), \textbf{27}) \cong \textbf{0.790}$$

Had the correction factor not been used, then $\lambda = 12.52$ and power $= 0.736$, lower than above. If we had used the alternative estimating procedure that used the sample data as population data, then the non-centrality parameter would have resulted in $\lambda = (k - 1)F = 16.52$, and power $= 0.864$. This is a rather higher value and we will see how this approach produces less meaningful results later.

There are several other coefficients that will be provided in the power section of the final ANOVA worksheet in Figure 16.12. These are coefficients used by other authors in determining power, thus if you wish to check this approximation against other sources, Winer *et al.* (1991) and Howell (1997), use ϕ in their authoritative tables, and Cohen (1988) uses **f** in his extensive tables, where

$$\phi = \sqrt{\frac{\lambda}{k}} \quad \text{and} \quad \textbf{f} = \frac{\phi}{\sqrt{n}}.$$

You will find that the values found by the approximation method above are very close to those from the tables for values of ϕ. For example for the case above,

$$\phi = \sqrt{\frac{13.84}{5}} = 1.664$$

the value of power would be about 0.78, interpolating between table values in Howell (1997) or Winer *et al.* (1991). This compares with the value of 0.862 found using SPSS, since its calculations are apparently based upon the alternative assumption that the sample data are an estimate of the population data.

Now carry out Activity 16.8 to complete the worksheet for a one-way ANOVA with multiple comparisons and calculation of power.

Instructions for use of ANOVA worksheet in Figure 16.12

(a) Enter data in top shaded cells. If there is insufficient space ($n_i > 9$), then block a set of cells in a row from column **B** to **H** and **Insert Cells**; or groups (if $k > 5$), then block a set of cells in one column from row **2** to **16** and **Insert Cells**, to include space for calculations to be **Copy**ed over in rows **11** to **16**. Repeat either of these as many times as needed. As long as this is done in the shaded area, the equations below will adjust automatically.

(b) Set α level in cell H19. You must consider the consequences of making Type I and Type II errors, as well as desired power when deciding what to use.

(c) Choose a post hoc test. Again, you must consider the consequences of making Type I and Type II errors, as well as desired power when deciding which one to use. Copy the appropriate set of cells from below into **I25:I29**. Also, if using Duncan's test, Newman–Keuls, either of the Tukey tests (which depend upon Newman–Keuls studentized range statistic), or Dunnett's test, their critical values for the *df* must be entered before the results will be accurate. If using the Bonferroni *t*, decide which and how many comparisons you plan to make in cell **C37** (you will have to justify these in your report).

(d) Power. This is generated automatically for the overall ANOVA.

Activity 16.8

1 Bring up Figure 16.10, which will be added to so that it includes power calculations as shown in Figure 16.12. Add the formulae shown for the power section and the sheet will be complete. Refer to the 'Instructions for use of ANOVA worksheet' above when you want to use it later.

	A	B	C	D	E	F	G	H	I
1	ANOVA	A	B	C	D	E			
2	data	6	2	3	7	7			
3		10	3	5	3	6			
4		4	5	4	5	9			
5		5	4	4	4	8			
6		4	3	3	4	7			
7		9	2	2		6			
8		6		7		3			
9									
10								grand M	
11	means: M_j =	6.29	3.17	3.86	5.40	6.57	5.09	= GM	
12	s.d.: s_j =	2.36	1.17	1.68	2.07	1.90			
13	var: s^2_j =	5.57	1.37	2.81	4.30	3.62			
14	n_j =	7	6	7	5	7			
15	$n_j\,(M_j - GM)^2$ =	9.95	22.28	10.70	0.47	15.28			
16	ns^2_j =	39.00	8.20	19.67	21.50	25.33			
17									
18	ANOVA	SS	df	s^2 (MS)	F	p value	F_{crit}	α	
19	Between	58.69	4	14.67	4.13	0.0097	2.73	0.05	
20	Within	95.93	27	3.55					
21									
22	Total	154.62	31						
23	post hoc								
24	means =	6.57	6.29	5.40	3.86	3.17	$\tilde{n}$ =	6.2874	Test
25	differences	E	A	D	C	B	r	$\Delta M_{\min}$	Duncan
26	E		0.29	1.17	2.71	3.40 —	5	2.41	3.21
27	A			0.89	2.43	3.12 —	4	2.37	3.15
28	D				1.54	2.23 —	3	2.29	3.05
29	C					0.69 —	2	2.18	2.90
30	q_{crit} values								
31	r	Multi-t	Bonferroni	Duncan	NK	Tukey B	Tukey A	Scheffé	Dunnett's
32	5	2.90	3.78	3.21	4.13	4.13	4.13	4.67	3.20
33	4	2.90	3.78	3.15	3.87	4.00	4.13	4.67	3.20
34	3	2.90	3.78	3.05	3.50	3.82	4.13	4.67	3.20
35	2	2.90	3.78	2.90	2.90	3.52	4.13	4.67	3.20
36		= sqrt(2)t	= sqrt(2)t'	q_r	q_r	q_r	q_r	= sqrt(2F)	=sqrt(2)t_D
37			4			= (TA + NK)/2	= NK$_{\max}$	eqn (16.26)	
38	Appendix B:	Table B.2	Table B.5	Table B.7	Table B.6			& Table B.3	Table B.8
39	Power cf =	0.926		k' =	4.46				
40	λ =	13.84		power =	0.79				
41	φ =	1.66		β =	0.21				
42	df_{between} =	10.05	f =	φ/sqrt(ñ) =	0.663				

Formula annotations (right side):
=(C19+B40)/C19
=FDIST(G19/E39,ROUND(B42,0),C20)
=1-E40
=B41/SQRT(H24)

Formula annotations (bottom):
=(C19+1)/(C19+1.4)
=C19*(E19/B39–1)

=SQRT(B40/(C19+1))
=(C19+B40)^2/(C19+2*B40)

FIGURE 16.12
Final integrated worksheet for one-way ANOVA

> 2   Change the significance level, $\alpha = 0.01$. What happens to the power? If the scheme where sample data are used in equation (16.31) were used for defining λ, you would find a value for power of 0.529. If the correction factor is omitted, then the power is 0.468. Which seems more reasonable, considering the value of F?
>
> **Answer**
>
> 2.   Power $= 0.529$, not unexpected since F is just over F_{crit}.

What are desirable values for n and r_{xx}?

In previous chapters, it was demonstrated that power was influenced by sample size. The power of the ANOVA test is also susceptible to the size of the samples, partly because a drop in n causes a drop in df_{within} and partly because this also contributes to a rise in sample variances. The other way to increase sample variances would be to increase s^2_{error}, which, as we have seen before, is easily done by having a measuring instrument with low reliability. Again, we see mathematically how poor sampling (or loss of subjects) and weak measuring instruments directly influence the probability of correctly rejecting H_0. It should be a little more obvious why in Figure 2.15 **Statistical Validity** is linked to the 'Design instruments' (instrument reliability) and 'carry out plan' (potential loss of subjects) stages. No amount of statistical fiddling can make up for our sins, and in fact it is the statistical tests that suffer and ultimately the likelihood of our correctly identifying statistically significant differences.

Now that the statistical tools have been developed, let us return to two of the most common questions that are asked when planning research:

- How big should the sample be?
- How reliable should the measuring instrument be?

The answers to both of these will determine the demand on resources, both time and money. Though neither question can be answered with absolute certainty, rough estimates can be made on the basis of the trial of the instrument, a few assumptions, and some prior knowledge of the measured trait and target groups. It has been suggested that it would be desirable to have power $= 0.80$, in other words an 80% probability that we will correctly reject H_0. In summary, the power of an F-test depends on

- the size of any treatment effect (reflected by the range of means of samples);
- the chosen α;
- the variance of the samples, which in turn depends on the reliability of the instrument and the sample size.

To answer the two questions above is not easy, so a model will be set up that takes into account the interrelationships among these five variables. When it is on a worksheet, you can then vary each one to see what it will take to obtain the desired outcome.

Unfortunately, this is not the most desirable situation to be in, since it is obvious that any number of different combinations of four of the variables will produce a potential power of 0.80. To minimize the problem, first establish some reasonable value for the variance of the samples from the trial of the instrument in order to determine reliability (Chapter 11) using a small representative sample. Second, your knowledge of the traits being investigated will help you estimate the range of the means and how much impact any treatment might have. Third, the value of α will be determined by the nature of the research question and consequences of any decisions. This leaves only the sample size to vary in the model on the worksheet until the desired level of power is achieved. The model will also allow you to indicate an improved level of reliability for the instrument to see the consequences on power.

Using the same approximation as in Figure 16.12, the impact of an estimated value for the F-ratio manifests itself in its impact on the estimated value of the non-centrality parameter λ, from equation (16.33),

$$\lambda = (k-1)\left(\frac{F}{cf} - 1\right)$$

where the correction factor, cf, depends on the number of groups as shown in equation (16.34). Since value of the F-ratio is in turn influenced by the magnitudes of the difference in the means (effect size) and their variances, an estimate of this can be influenced by estimates of expected outcomes. As seen earlier, the magnitudes of variances are in turn influenced by the reliability of the measure. Thus, the estimate of an F-ratio depends on the range of expected means and the variance of the trial data, plus a means of correcting for an improved reliability coefficient. This last relationship is based upon the definition of reliability in equation (11.1), which can be written as

$$S^2_{\text{true}} = r_{xx} S^2_{\text{observed}}$$

A second version of this that reflects a test with improved reliability, r'_{xx}, would be

$$S^2_{\text{true}} = r'_{xx} S'^2_{\text{observed}}$$

Since S^2_{true} would be the same for both, dividing one equation by the other results in

$$1.0 = \frac{r_{xx} S^2_{\text{observed}}}{r'_{xx} S'^2_{\text{observed}}}$$

Solving for S'^2_{observed}, provides an estimate of the variance if the reliability were to change from r_{xx} to r'_{xx}:

$$S'^2_{\text{observed}} = \frac{r_{xx}}{r'_{xx}} S^2_{\text{observed}}$$

Assuming that the trial s^2 is S^2_{observed} above, then this could be expressed as

$$s^2_{\text{predicted}} = \frac{r_{xx}}{r'_{xx}} s^2_{\text{trial}} \qquad (16.38)$$

Some liberty has been taken by using s^2 (an unbiased estimate of population variance) from the trial as an estimate of S^2_{observed} (variance of sample data from measurement calculations) on the worksheet, but this it the best source for making predictions. These equations are included in the Figure 16.13, which can be set up by carrying out Activity 16.9.

Activity 16.9

1   Start a new worksheet and set up the labels shown in Figure 16.13. Normally the data in the shaded cells will come from trials of the instrument and prior knowledge of the trait. Consider Mary Smith's situation: she is planning an experimental study to investigate whether or not students from major cities, towns, suburbia, small rural villages and farms have different views on the environment. She has devised a questionnaire to determine a relative level of commitment to action on environmental issues. Her trial of the instrument with six representative subjects has resulted in a mean of 6.0 and standard deviation of 1.4. The reliability of this first version of the instrument was found to be 0.50. She expects the range of means for the five groups to be from about 5 to 7, so these data have been entered on the worksheet. As can be seen, with five groups and six in each group, with this range of means there is little chance of finding a significant difference with a predicted power of 0.28.

2   First change n until you get a value of power of at least 0.80. How many subjects will she need?

3   Mary wondered if improving the reliability would make a difference. To see what would happen if the instrument reliability were increased, change 'desired r'_{xx}' to 0.70. What can n be reduced to so that power remains at least 0.80?

Keep this worksheet for future use when planning a study.

Answers

2. $n = 13$ thus 65 subjects total.
3. $n = 9$, a total of 45 subjects.

SUMMARY

This chapter has provided an overview of analysis of variance as a test of significance across three or more groups. The violations of the original assumptions of equal sample size and homogeneity of variance have been recognized as common enough to deserve adjustments that compensate for them. As a consequence, the calculations were modified for unequal sample sizes, and a test for heterogeneity of variance has been provided. Several data transformations have been given to allow an analysis of variance when heterogeneity of variance exists. Also, a number of tests for comparisons across pairs of groups were presented. Finally, the power of the analysis of variance test was considered. In each situation, a worksheet has been provided to allow the exploration of the test, as well as ultimately providing templates for new sets of data. Where possible, links have been drawn to earlier chapters on the design of studies, highlighting the consequences for statistical test of decisions made during the planning stages. In the following chapter, the application of analysis of variance to more complex designs will be considered.

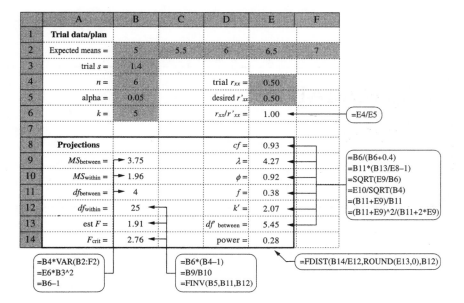

FIGURE 16.13
Worksheet to
estimate sample size
and required
instrument
reliability

FACTORIAL DESIGNS

In Chapter 15, four alternative *t*-tests for resolving null hypotheses were introduced. These determined whether differences between pairs of samples (variables) existed. In Chapter 16, this was extended to three or more groups, or three or more levels of one variable, with the introduction to the analysis of variance as a test. Even so, life is rarely so simple that our questions can be satisfactorily answered with just these tests. Often the most exciting questions not only involve several independent variables, but also express an aim to determine if they combine or interact to influence outcomes as indicated by the dependent variable. Thus there is a need for a new set of statistical tests to answer the question not only whether there is a difference in impact across individual variables, but also whether two or more variables can interact to produce different outcomes. Such a test, therefore, must be able to resolve not just one, but several null hypotheses.

These extensions of the analysis of variance will provide the opportunity to extend original designs, for example B3/D3 (post-test only with a control group) to include two or more potentially interacting variables. They will also provide the means to test combinations of life experience variables (ex post facto) with treatment variables (experimental), extending the potential to investigate more real-life hypotheses. As before, issues of homogeneity of variance, unequal cell size, pairwise comparisons, and power will be covered for the tests.

WHAT IS A FACTORIAL DESIGN?

Over the previous two chapters, we have progressed from comparing two groups to situations where we would want to compare three or more groups to test if their life experiences or treatments leave them significantly different for some trait. These experiences or treatments have been drawn from one category, such as type of counselling programme, educational background, type of production-line process, or variations on teaching approach. Many of life's exciting questions involve more than one variable or *factor* and whether the interactions between these different factors make an impact on outcomes. An example will be used to illustrate such a factorial design, one that includes two variables, one experimental and one life events.

Let us take the question of teaching science in schools. It has been widely recognized that in many countries there seems to be a shortage of science, engineering and technology graduates. Nevin Nucleus decided to try to develop learning materials that would change this, but also wanted to be able to determine whether an impact on attitudes could be made. When he sketched a variable map, as shown in Figure 17.1, he noted a potential extraneous variable, the type of class (single-sex or mixed). This was of interest since not only did the literature indicate a shortage of graduates, but also there were fewer girls following careers in science, engineering and technology than boys. Also, some studies indicated that girls are put off by being in classes with boys. On the one hand, if the study were to control all other possible extraneous variables it could be done by sampling. The study would focus just on teaching approaches and would control class gender as a potential variable simply by sampling so that each group had some of each type of class. The study would have a structure like that of design B3, with two innovative programmes and a traditional one as control:

$$RS \rightarrow \begin{cases} RA_a & \rightarrow & X_a & \rightarrow & O_a \\ RA_b & \rightarrow & X_b & \rightarrow & O_b \\ RA_o & \rightarrow & X_o & \rightarrow & O_o \end{cases}$$

The outcomes, group attitudes, would be analysed using a one-way analysis of variance.

This unfortunately ignores the important issues of gender as reflected in the type of class, single-sex or mixed, in which students encounter science. It would be much more interesting to add class type as a variable in its own right to see if the learning materials worked better with one type of class than with another. To conduct a study that included this variable would require combinations of single-sex classes, mixed classes and types of programmes. Nevin

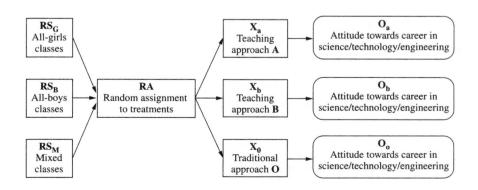

FIGURE 17.1
Variable map for a study on possible effects of teaching programmes on career choice

decided he would need to have an expanded version of Figure 17.1, a total of at least nine groups, where B indicates boys only, G indicates girls only, M indicates mixed classes, and a, b and o are the approaches:

$$RS_B \rightarrow \begin{cases} RA_{Ba} & \rightarrow & X_{Ba} & \rightarrow & O_{Ba} \\ RA_{Bb} & \rightarrow & X_{Bb} & \rightarrow & O_{Bb} \\ RA_{Bo} & \rightarrow & X_{Bo} & \rightarrow & O_{Bo} \end{cases}$$

$$RS_G \rightarrow \begin{cases} RA_{Ga} & \rightarrow & X_{Ga} & \rightarrow & O_{Ga} \\ RA_{Gb} & \rightarrow & X_{Gb} & \rightarrow & O_{Gb} \\ RA_{Go} & \rightarrow & X_{Go} & \rightarrow & O_{Go} \end{cases}$$

$$RS_M \rightarrow \begin{cases} RA_{Ma} & \rightarrow & X_{Ma} & \rightarrow & O_{Ma} \\ RA_{Mb} & \rightarrow & X_{Mb} & \rightarrow & O_{Mb} \\ RA_{Mo} & \rightarrow & X_{Mo} & \rightarrow & O_{Mo} \end{cases}$$

Yes, this is messy, which is why such studies are usually described diagrammatically as in Table 17.1. This highlights the two individual variables as well as the possible interactions between them, which in this case may be of the greatest interest.

Such a design would allow Nevin Nucleus to test differences across types of class regardless of programme, differences across programmes regardless of type of class, and interactions between these two *main effect* variables. This is called a 3×3 *factorial design* and would require a *two-way analysis of variance* to resolve the hypotheses. This could be followed by multiple comparisons similar to those carried out with one-way ANOVA, to determine significant pairwise differences. As you might guess from looking at Table 17.1, this will generate considerable data, and even with, say, 10 subjects per cell, would require 90 students. If intact classes were to be used and these tend to have between 20 and 30 students, such a study could grow to have 180–270 subjects just using existing purposively selected representative classes (quasi-experimental). For this study, the main interests would be in determining not only whether the programmes had any differential impact on learning, but also in particular whether single-sex classes had an advantage. It was therefore decided that there was a need

TABLE 17.1
Variables and interactions for a study on possible effects of teaching programmes on student career choices

	Programme a	Programme b	Control o	Main effect: class type
Boys only	$\bar{x}_{Ba}$ s_{Ba} n_{Ba}	$\bar{x}_{Bb}$ s_{Bb} n_{Bb}	$\bar{x}_{Bo}$ s_{Bo} n_{Bo}	$\bar{x}_B$
Girls only	$\bar{x}_{Ga}$ s_{Ga} n_{Ga}	$\bar{x}_{Gb}$ s_{Gb} n_{Gb}	$\bar{x}_{Go}$ s_{Go} n_{Go}	$\bar{x}_G$
Mixed	$\bar{x}_{Ma}$ s_{Ma} n_{Ma}	$\bar{x}_{Mb}$ s_{Mb} n_{Mb}	$\bar{x}_{Mo}$ s_{Mo} n_{Mo}	$\bar{x}_M$
Main effect: programme	$\bar{x}_a$	$\bar{x}_b$	$\bar{x}_o$	$\bar{X}$

for coherent classes rather than a collection of randomly selected subjects (students), since the latter could introduce an extraneous variable due to unfamiliarity of learners with each other. Also, using a collection of randomly selected students could reduce the generalizability of the results to the real world of classroom teaching. It was assumed that 20–30 randomly selected students would constitute an unnatural situation in which to learn. Even providing complementary materials to be used outside class would not necessarily constitute a situation that was easily transferable back to real life. Thus here, *not* having a random selection of students was considered desirable. Consequently, cluster sampling was used to obtain three representative classes of each type, which in turn were randomly assigned to a treatment. The implications of using non-equivalent groups in a quasi-experimental design will be considered later.

Benefits of factorial designs over one-way ANOVA

Before considering the problems of interpreting the possible outcomes and the rationale for the statistical tests, let us consider the benefits of a factorial design. It is obvious that any changes in attitudes resulting from the study on science teaching in schools could be tested using a one-way ANOVA with nine parallel treatments, one for each cell. The post hoc pairwise comparisons would allow testing of all possible combinations. But such an approach would *not* allow testing of the main effects: whether there is an overall difference across learning materials; and whether there is an overall difference across types of class, mixed or single-sex. Thus a factorial design is potentially more comprehensive in its coverage of individual variables and possible interactions. Such a design can be extended to three or more variables, though the complexity of both interpretation and statistics increases, accompanied by a demand for more subjects. Resource limitations and access to subjects are often the greatest restriction on the level of complexity of studies, since the number-crunching for the statistics can be done by computers. Having said this, there is another seemingly contradictory advantage in factorial designs over several one-way studies. Consider the alternative to testing the main variables only in the study using two one-way designs: Nevin Nucleus would need three groups of students for each of the three treatments and three more groups of all-boys, all-girls and mixed classes to achieve the same power. Remember that the probability of rejecting H_0 when it is false (power) is dependent on the number of subjects. A two-way factorial design with 30 students per cell (a class) would result in $3 \times 90 = 270$ students for each of the two main effects, since there would be 90 for each level. The equivalent would be two one-way designs that would need 90 students for each treatment and 90 students for each of three classes. This pair of tests would require a total of $2 \times 3 \times 90 = 540$ subjects and would not include interactions.

In summary, a two-way factorial design allows the testing for both significant differences across both main factors (variables) and possible interactions, more economically than several one-way designs, with the same power. Such a design also makes it possible to generalize to realistic settings, enhancing external validity.

INTERPRETING THE RESULTS: INTERACTIONS

The novel aspect of factorial over one-way designs is the addition of the possibility to investigate interactions. This presents some challenges for interpretation. First, we will consider a graphical technique that is widely used to show possible relationships, then later provide statistical tests that will confirm or refute the statistical significance of suspected differences across variables or between cells. The aim is to make sense of the relationships among the combinations of treatments. Though a table of means in the format of Table 17.1 may provide clues, plotting the results on a graph such as the one in Figure 17.2 makes it easier to understand relationships. The situation illustrated there is one where there were absolutely no differences across the three programmes since the lines are parallel to the horizontal axis (they all have the same mean gain scores). There is also no difference between groups, since they are very close to each other, and there are no interactions since they are parallel to each other.

Rarely does one get such unexciting results, and even if there were no significant differences across programmes, there would probably be some differences resulting in lines not quite parallel to the horizontal, lines not quite parallel to each other, and lines that were close but not so obviously close to each other as to suggest no significant difference. Thus there is the need for statistical tests to tell us when the deviations are 'enough'. For now, we will use the line graphs as a way of discussing different types of outcome. It should be recognized that this is just a way of visually analysing data and the graphs are potentially misleading. The lines connect single points between means of categories and *not* continuous data, thus they do not imply a smooth transition between categories. This is just a graphical technique for highlighting relationships, so do not read any more into them than that. On the other hand, it does provide a visual way of displaying results in a report or article.

For a two-factor design, there are six possible combinations of results:

1   There are no significant differences across either of the factors, nor are there any significant interactions.

	Programme			Main: class
	a	b	o	
Boys Only	22	22	22	22.0
Girls Only	21	21	21	21.0
Mixed	20	20	20	20.0
Main: programme	21.0	21.0	21.0	21.0

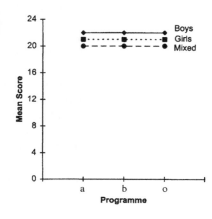

FIGURE 17.2
Summary of means and graphical representation

2   There is a significant difference across one factor but not the second, and there are no significant interactions.
3   There are significant differences across each of the factors but no significant interactions.
4   There is a significant difference across one factor but not the second, and there are possible significant interactions.
5   There is a significant difference across each of the factors and there are possible significant interactions.
6   There is no significant difference across either of the factors, but there are possible significant interactions.

Each of these outcomes will be displayed graphically, starting with the simplest situation of a more realistic version of no significant outcomes at all, as shown in Figure 17.3. Here one of the potential main effects, type of programme, is plotted along the horizontal axis and a line for each of the three types of class is again generated. The lack of significance is indicated by the three lines being very close together: there are only small differences across the types of class. The lines are almost horizontal, thus there is no difference across the programmes. The little kink for programme b is not significant. With no crossing lines and no singularly deviant cells, they are parallel, there are no interactions.

The second situation consists of a significant difference across one of the main effects but not the other, and there are no significant interactions, as illustrated by Figure 17.4. For the example, here there was a significant difference across gender composition of classes, whereas there was no significant difference across the different programmes. Obviously, the situation could be reversed. The interesting aspect of using the graphs comes in the choice of variable to plot on the horizontal axis. If the same scheme were used as in Figure 17.3, with programmes on the axis, the graph would look like Figure 17.4(a), with the resulting line for the Girls-Only classes distinctly apart, but all of them nearly horizontal across the different programmes. Alternatively, if type of class were on the axis with different lines for programmes, the graph would look like Figure 17.4(b), where there is a distinct set of peaks or a shift away from the horizontal for the Girls-Only class, yet the lines are parallel across the three programmes. The difference between Figures 17.3 and 17.4(a) is

FIGURE 17.3
Summary of means and graphical representation for situation 1 – no significant main effects and no significant interactions

	Programme			Main: class
	a	b	o	
Boys Only	22	21	23	22.0
Girls Only	21	20	22	21.0
Mixed	20	19	21	20.0
Main: programme	21.0	20.0	22.0	21.0

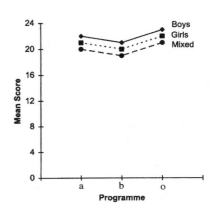

obvious, though some would suggest the uniqueness of the Girls-Only classes is more apparent in Figure 17.4(b). Visual inspection of the table does indicate that the marginal mean for Girls-Only classes is considerably higher than the others. Had all three types of class been different from each other, the mixed class being even lower, then the three lines in Figure 17.4(a) would have all been separated by two large gaps and in Figure 17.4(b) the three parallel lines would have produced a gradual sloping set of parallel lines.

Activity 17.1

Sketch another version of Figure 17.3(b) with the order of the types of classes changed to boys only, mixed, girls only. Is the interaction any more apparent? Does it matter what the order is?

The third situation to consider has significant differences across both main effects, but no significant interaction. This indicates differences, but not specific differences that depend on an interaction between variables. This is illustrated in Figure 17.5, again with two ways of displaying the outcomes. Note the cell means and marginal means for Girls-Only classes and Programme a, since these have been chosen as the significantly different groups. In Figure 17.5(a) the graphical consequences are that the lines are no longer horizontal, with all the Programme a means higher than the others, and the Girls-Only classes

	Programme			Main:
	a	b	o	class
Boys Only	22	21	23	22.0
Girls Only	28	27	29	28.0
Mixed	20	19	21	20.0
Main: programme	23.3	22.3	24.3	23.3

FIGURE 17.4
Summary of means and graphical representation for situation 2 – one significant main effect (class gender) and no significant interactions – with alternative ways of displaying the results

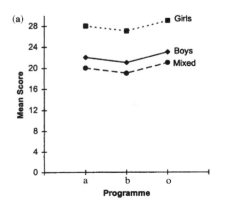

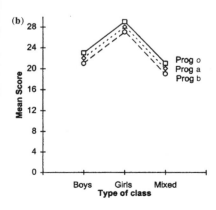

line is well above the other two. In Figure 17.5(b) the lines are not parallel *and* there is a definite rise in all the Girls-Only class means.

Activity 17.2

Try sketching the two graphs using different orders for the horizontal axes. Is there a better arrangement? Does it make any difference to the interpretation?

While it has been maintained that the distinct advantage of factorial designs is the identification of interactions between variables, little has so far been said about the interpretation of these. In many cases this is not trivial, considering all the possible outcomes of such a design. Recall that with a two-factor design, three of the six possible combinations of outcomes listed earlier can result in significant interactions. These interactions can be the product of various combinations of cells, which for large two-dimensional studies can make interpretation difficult. The examples will continue to use the 3×3 study, with some exercises at the end to allow you to interpret some outcomes of 2×2 and 2×3 designs.

Interactions add another complication to the interpretation of graphical representations. A significant main effect plus a significant interaction may result in a different interpretation about the main variable than the previous

	Programme			Main:
	a	b	o	class
Boys Only	26	21	23	23.3
Girls Only	29	27	28	28.0
Mixed	25	19	20	21.3
Main: programme	27.0	22.3	23.6	24.2

FIGURE 17.5
Summary of means and graphical representation for situation 3 – two significant main effects but no significant interactions – with alternative ways of displaying the results

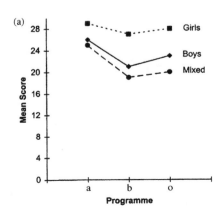

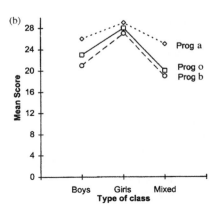

situation where there was a significant main effect and no significant interaction. In the former, the significant main effect may be due to a single cell that also flags up the significant interaction, rather than an overall difference across treatments. Thus it would not necessarily be valid to say there was a general difference across the main effect, as we will see in the example below. This does not mean that if there is a significant interaction the significant main effect would be ignored, but that it is a possibility.

Graphically, interactions will often appear as one or more distinct lines diverging from the rest. These are illustrated through some examples of representative situations, which are presented below, though they are not exhaustive of possible visual outcomes. Also, the existence of suspected interactions will need to be confirmed by appropriate statistical tests, described later.

A word of caution is in order. Finding and confirming a significant interaction is a mechanical process, while making sense of these can sometimes be difficult or impossible. In other words, some interactions may not have a logical or academically significant interpretation for a study. It is up to the researcher to interpret these in light of the original hypotheses and the variables involved.

While there may be such a thing as meaningless interactions, let us consider how the last three possible outcomes of a two-factor study that include significant interactions could possibly manifest themselves graphically. First to be considered is the situation where there is a significant difference across one of the main effects but not the other, and there is a significant interaction. This is illustrated in Figure 17.6, where there is a significant difference across the programmes and a significant interaction. Looking at the graph and the table of

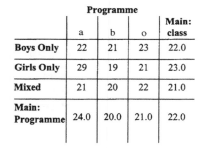

	Programme			Main: class
	a	b	o	
Boys Only	22	21	23	22.0
Girls Only	29	19	21	23.0
Mixed	21	20	22	21.0
Main: Programme	24.0	20.0	21.0	22.0

FIGURE 17.6
Summary of means and graphical representation for situation 4 – one significant main effect (across programmes) and a significant interaction (at least two cells of the nine will be significantly different) – with alternative ways of displaying the results

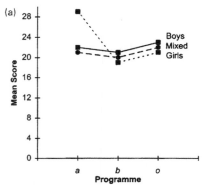

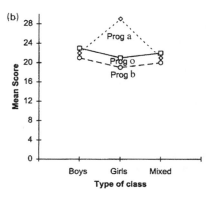

means, it is apparent that both of these are the result of the Girls-Only class responding to Programme a much better than any other group. Interpreting this, one would not necessarily be able to say Programme a was universally better, but that the Girls-Only classes responded significantly better. The outcome appears obvious in Figure 17.6(a) by the isolated point for the combination of Programme a and Girls-Only. In Figure 17.6(b) it is again made apparent by the single data point out by itself.

Activity 17.3

1   Sketch Figure 17.6(a) with the order of programmes changed to b, a, o. Is the interaction still reasonably apparent?
2   Sketch Figure 17.6(b) with the order of class type changed to Girls Only, Boys Only, Mixed. Is the interaction still reasonably apparent?

In the fifth situation, where both main effects are found to be statistically significant and there is a significant interaction, the results become more difficult to interpret. First, this indicates a significant difference across the levels of each of the main effect variables, plus some sort of interaction between them. To illustrate this, the simplistic example of three teaching programmes in three different types of class will be taken one step further. In Figure 17.7, this situation is shown as Programme a producing significantly different attitude changes from b and the Control o. Also, the members of the single-sex classes have shown a greater change in attitude than those in the mixed class. The interaction between these two variables would suggest the significantly larger improvements in attitude were in Boys-Only classes in Programme a, and Girls-Only classes in Programmes a and b. Thus the most reasonable conclusion would be that there are potentially positive attitude changes towards careers in science engineering and technology in single-sex classes if taught using Programme a, and the attitudes of girls in a single-sex class would also tend to improve if taught in Programme b.

Coming to these conclusions from the graphs in Figure 17.7 is another matter. While it is fairly obvious that Programme a provides a greater increase than b or the Control o for single-sex classes, the benefit of Programme b for Girls-Only classes is less obvious in Figure 17.7(a) than in Figure 17.7(b).

Activity 17.4

See if you can improve the visual impact of Figure 17.7(b) by changing the order of the types of class on the horizontal axis.

The sixth and final possible outcome is the somewhat anomalous one of no significant differences across either of the main effects, but a significant inter-

	Programme			Main: class
	a	b	o	
Boys Only	28	21	23	24.0
Girls Only	29	25	21	25.0
Mixed	19	20	22	20.3
Main: Programme	25.3	22.0	22.0	23.1

FIGURE 17.7
Summary of means
and graphical
representation for
situation 5 – both
main effects are
significant and there
is a significant
interaction – with
alternative ways of
displaying the
results

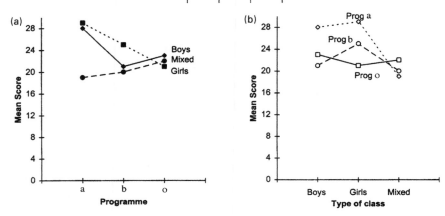

action. This is illustrated here with the situation where only one cell stands out from the rest: Girls-Only classes taught using Programme a. This is different from the one above with one significant main effect and a significant interaction in that the other groups under Programme a produced sufficiently lower changes in attitudes that there was no significant difference across that main effect. The interesting aspect of this result is that it is fairly obvious from either of the graphs in Figure 17.8.

One other situation of interest remains, often referred to as *disordinal interaction*, where the results for one cell are the opposite to those for another. This results in crossed lines, as shown in Figure 17.9. Here, the significant benefits in attitude change in Girls-Only classes under Programme a contrast with the much lower results for Boys-Only and Mixed classes for that programme. For Programme b, however, the opposite has occurred, with the Boys-Only and Mixed classes improving much more than the Girls-Only classes. Here there was no difference across Programme o. Such results have the potential of providing a strong basis for drawing conclusions, if the variables are meaningful and the interactions suggest strong contrasts.

Activity 17.5 provides an opportunity to interpret some additional data and graphs, before moving on to the statistical tests. These cover a variety of combinations of experimental and ex post facto components, which you should identify. Also, keep in mind that these are contrived studies, not real ones, and you are not asked to agree with the results, just to interpret them as they are presented. Some are intentionally counterintuitive, but then what would

	Programme			Main: class
	a	b	o	
Boys Only	21	24	23	22.7
Girls Only	29	20	19	22.7
Mixed	19	22	21	20.7
Main: Programme	23.0	22.0	21.0	22.0

FIGURE 17.8
Summary of means and graphical representation for situation 6 – no significant difference across either main effect but there is a significant interaction – with alternative ways of displaying the results

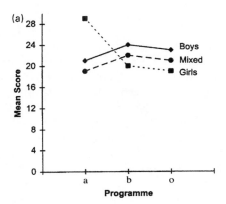

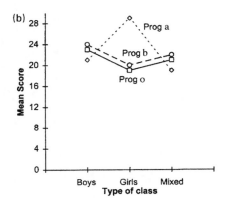

	Programmes			Main: class
	a	b	o	
Boys Only	21	29	22	24.0
Girls Only	29	20	19	22.7
Mixed	19	28	21	22.7
Main: Programme	23.0	25.7	20.7	23.1

FIGURE 17.9
Summary of means and graphical representation for the situation with a disordinal interaction – here there is a significant difference across only one of the main effects (Programmes) and there is a significant interaction – with alternative ways of displaying the results

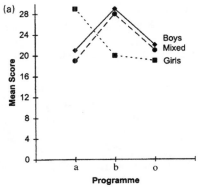

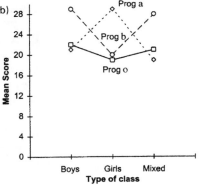

research be if we were not surprised occasionally? You should also consider the validity of the measures in relation to the research questions and possible conclusions that could be drawn.

Activity 17.5

1   David Doctor wanted to compare two therapy approaches on institutionalized patients, but also wanted to know if the use of medication would influence their effectiveness. The dependent variable was percentage of waking time spent in activity or socializing, as opposed to sitting alone, daydreaming or withdrawn. He arranged to have a team of observers spend a week collecting data on patients, not knowing which regime they were undergoing. The results are shown in Figure 17.10. Which of the six types of result does this appear to represent? How would you interpret the results if the differences were significant?

2   Patricia Personnel was concerned about the possible effects of strong coffee on the work of staff, particularly when deadlines were placed upon them. She felt that strong coffee made them 'fidgety' and unable to work. She installed three coffee machines and randomly assigned 30 word-processing staff to each one from which to take their coffee for a period of two weeks, ostensibly to rate the coffee on taste. She then divided the group into two, giving one a strict deadline for a DTP task over a two-day period towards the end of the two weeks, and the other group she set the same task but just with a request that it be done by the end of the two days. She used the percentage of completion as the dependent variable. Her results are summarized in Figure 17.11. Which of the six outcomes does this appear to represent? How would you interpret the results if the differences were significant? Is there an ethical problem here, not telling staff the purpose of the study? Would telling them have a possible impact on the outcomes?

3   Anne Adviser in the Careers Counselling Service was frequently asked if choice of degree subject at university made a big difference in starting salary after graduation. She also wanted to know if gender made any difference. In collaboration with the placement bureau in Lifeskills University, she randomly selected 20 recent male and 20 recent female graduates in each of arts, science/engineering and humanities. She contacted them to find out what the salary was for their first job after graduation. The results and alternative plots of marginal means are shown in Figure 17.12. Which of the two graphs is the most meaningful? What conclusions can you draw? Is it possible to describe any causal relationships?

4   Using the following written description and data for a study, draw graphs and suggest conclusions.

     Miracle Microprocessors was anticipating a cut in profits due to increased legislation that would require the company to improve by-product disposal and reduce environmental pollution. This would inevitably result in no salary or wage increase for the coming year. It was felt that it would be worthwhile explaining this to staff to enhance morale and prevent loss of productivity, but that this would be a costly exercise.

To justify the expenditure, trial groups across the income spectrum were provided with explanatory materials, while control groups were not. Both were asked to complete a questionnaire on environmental awareness: the higher the score, the 'greener' the respondent. Plot the means and suggest conclusions, analysing their validity.

Income	Explanation	None
High	60	40
Medium	50	55
Low	35	60

Part answers: 1 Type 4. 2 Type 2. 3 Type 5. 4 Type 6 (disordinal).

RATIONALE BEHIND ANOVA

Although we have now seen a variety of different combinations of outcomes that could occur from a factorial design, we still need statistical tests to confirm or refute the apparent differences in cells seen graphically. In other words, do these really exist, or are they within the realm of chance occurrences? What follows is not a rigorous description, but one that is conceptually easier to grasp than some of the more mathematical derivations while still providing the appropriate equations.

	A_1	A_2	Dose means
Placebo	0.90	0.30	0.60
Half dose	0.60	0.75	0.68
Full dose	0.25	0.40	0.33
Therapy means	0.58	0.48	0.53

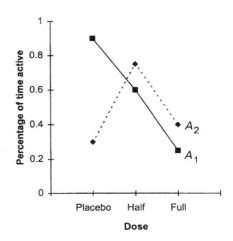

FIGURE 17.10
The results of David Doctor's comparison of two therapy approaches

	Strict	Re-quest	Caffeine means
Decaf.	0.72	0.65	0.69
Low caf.	0.90	0.80	0.85
High caf.	0.58	0.50	0.54
Deadline means	0.73	0.65	0.69

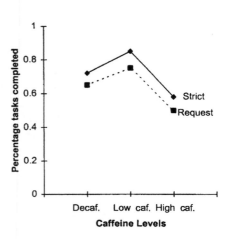

FIGURE 17.11
The results of Patricia Personnel's study of the effects of coffee on staff performance

	Arts	Hum.	Sci/Eng.	Gender means
Male	12	15	18	15.0
Female	14	13	13	13.3
Subject means	13.0	14.0	15.5	14.2

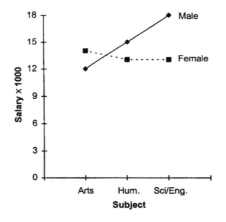
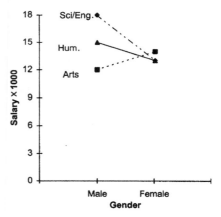

FIGURE 17.12
The results of Anne Adviser's study of the relationship between degree subject and starting salary

There are now *four* possible sources of estimates of the population variance, three of which could include components that would allow the rejection of the null hypothesis, that the groups are not different from each other. If we take the idealized study of two 'treatments' with different levels for each, such as exemplified above, we will have estimates that include variability:

- within the groups, taking into account only individual differences and measurement error;

- due to treatment A, plus individual differences and error;
- due to treatment B, plus individual differences and error;
- due to any interaction between A and B, plus individual differences and error.

This is graphically illustrated in Figure 17.13. To contend with the mathematical rationale for two dimensional studies, a notation must be established based upon the data. As before, we will need values for cell means, cell variances and cell sizes, but now there is also a need for the means for each treatment, the row and column means. This notation is outlined in Table 17.2, which shows the summary of results that will be required.

As with the one-way ANOVA, there is an estimate based upon all the variances of all the cells, the *within-group* variance. This is assumed to reflect only two variance components: that from individual differences and error variance. As a consequence, the calculation of this estimate is the same as for the one-way

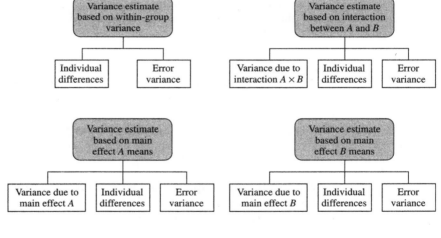

FIGURE 17.13
Four sources of estimates of population variance for a two-dimensional factorial design

TABLE 17.2
Summary statistics displayed using subscript notation

B_l / A_j	B_1	B_2	$\cdots$	B_m	Main effect A
A_1	$\bar{x}_{11}$ s_{11}^2 n_{11}	$\bar{x}_{12}$ s_{12}^2 n_{12}	$\cdots$	$\bar{x}_{1m}$ s_{1m}^2 n_{1m}	$\bar{x}_{A1}$
A_2	$\bar{x}_{21}$ s_{21}^2 n_{21}	$\bar{x}_{22}$ s_{22}^2 n_{22}	$\cdots$	$\bar{x}_{2m}$ s_{2m} n_{2m}	$\bar{x}_{A2}$
$\vdots$	$\vdots$	$\vdots$		$\vdots$	$\vdots$
A_k	$\bar{x}_{k1}$ s_{k1}^2 n_{k1}	$\bar{x}_{k2}$ s_{k2}^2 s_{k2}	$\cdots$	$\bar{x}_{km}$ s_{km}^2 n_{km}	$\bar{x}_{Ak}$
Main effect B	$\bar{x}_{B1}$	$\bar{x}_{B2}$	$\cdots$	$\bar{x}_{Bm}$	$\bar{X}$

ANOVA, which assumes that the average of all the sample variances constitutes a reasonable estimate of the population variance. Thus, similar to equation (16.4), we have

$$s_{\text{within}}^2 = \frac{\sum_{j=1}^{k} \sum_{l=1}^{m} s_{jl}^2}{km} \qquad \text{for equal } n \qquad (17.1)$$

where s_{jl}^2 is the variance of data in cell jl, with $j = 1, 2, \ldots, k$ and $l = 1, 2, \ldots, m$, indicating rows and columns. This simply tells you to add up all the variances, s_{jl}^2, and divide by the total number of cells, km, which in Excel will simply be **AVERAGE(cell variances)**.

To obtain estimates of the population variance based upon the two possible main effects variables, it is assumed as before that there is a possible significant contribution to these variance estimates due to the variables themselves. As indicated in Figure 17.13, these 'treatment' or 'main effect' contributions would be in addition to that of individual differences and error variance. Similar to the one-way ANOVA between-groups estimate, it is assumed that a reasonable estimate of the population variance would have its roots in an estimate of the standard error of the mean, the standard deviation of the sample means, but expressed as a variance, s_x^2,

$$\text{est } \sigma^2 = n s_{\bar{x}}^2$$

Thus, finding an estimate of the population variance for a main effect would use the marginal means, providing an equation analogous to (16.3) for effect A,

$$s_{\text{A}}^2 = \frac{nm \sum_{j=1}^{k} (\bar{x}_{\text{A}j} - \bar{X})^2}{k - 1} \qquad \text{for equal } n \qquad (17.2)$$

which in Excel is simply $n \times m \times$**VAR(marginal means A)**. Note the summation is multiplied by m columns, as well as n subjects per cell, since the marginal means include all the cells in that row. Similarly, for the other main effect B,

$$s_{\text{B}}^2 = \frac{nk \sum_{l=1}^{m} (\bar{x}_{\text{B}l} - \bar{X})^2}{m - 1} \qquad \text{for equal } n \qquad (17.3)$$

which in Excel is simply $n \times k \times$**VAR(marginal means B)**.

The difficult part is finding an estimate of population variance based purely upon the interactions. What is needed here is a variance that takes into account the interaction without individual contributions from each of the main effects. Mathematically this is achieved by finding the sum of each of the differences between the cell means and the grand mean, but then removing the variance contributions of each of the individual main effects by subtracting the difference of each marginal mean and the grand mean. Think of it as the pure interaction variance being the total interaction variance contribution, $\bar{x}_{jl} - \bar{X}$, less the individual contributions of the main effects, shown in square brackets in the following,

$$s^2_{A \times B} = \frac{n \sum_{j=1}^{k} \sum_{j=1}^{m} (\bar{x}_{jl} - \bar{X} - [\bar{x}_{Aj} - \bar{X}] - [\bar{x}_{Bl} - \bar{X}])^2}{(k-1)(m-1)}$$

which is simplified by removing the square brackets inside the parentheses and combining terms to produce

$$s^2_{A \times B} = \frac{n \sum_{j=1}^{k} \sum_{l=1}^{m} (\bar{x}_{jl} - \bar{x}_{Aj} - \bar{x}_{Bl} + \bar{X})^2}{(k-1)(m-1)} \qquad \text{for equal } n \qquad (17.4)$$

This does not have a simple formula in Excel, but it is not difficult to calculate on a worksheet, as we will see.

Now that we have equations for the four estimates of the population variance, it is possible to test the null hypothesis for each of the three cases. The degrees of freedom for the denominator in each case will be

$$df_{\text{within}} = km(n-1) \qquad (17.5)$$

Thus for the 3×3 study above with 20 in each cell, $df_{\text{within}} = 171$. The F-ratio for each part, with corresponding degrees of freedom for the numerators, is as follows:

$$F_A = \frac{s^2_A}{s^2_{\text{within}}} \qquad (17.6)$$

$$F_B = \frac{s^2_B}{s^2_{\text{within}}} \qquad (17.7)$$

$$F_{A \times B} = \frac{s^2_{A \times B}}{s^2_{\text{within}}} \qquad (17.8)$$

where $df_A = k - 1$, $df_B = m - 1$ and $df_{A \times B} = df_A df_B$. In every case the question is asked whether the F-ratio is within the range expected on a sampling distribution with the appropriate degrees of freedom for the specified α. If the ratio were found to be beyond the specified critical value, then it would be assumed that the differences were attributable to something other than chance. Assuming all other variables were controlled, for a significant F_A, it would mean that there was a real difference across the levels of A, and similarly for F_B. If $F_{A \times B}$ were found to be significant, then this would indicate that there was one or more possible significant interactions. Thus, the results would indicate there was an outcome that was the consequence of combined influence of both variables, such as shown in Figures 17.6–17.9.

The same assumptions about the measurement of the dependent variable apply as for one-way ANOVA:

- Underlying population distributions are normal for the traits.
- There is homogeneity of variance across groups.
- All measures are independent of each other.
- Component variances are additive.

Up to this point, we have assumed equal cell sizes, but this is rarely appropriate. The best laid plans of researchers never quite work out, consequently some subjects always disappear, even when we start with equal cell sizes in our samples. As long as this has nothing to do with the purpose of the study, then it must simply be accepted. While there is the possible situation where the proportion of the sample is relevant to the study, this will not be included here. This leaves us with the equally weighted means solution and the least-squares solution. Most computer packages, such as SPSS, employ the latter, but it requires a mathematically sophisticated approach. Results very close to those acquired by this approach can be achieved with the equally weighted means approach. This simply uses the *harmonic means*, $\tilde{n}$, of appropriate sample sizes as the value for n in the above equations. This is found by (note the tilde $\tilde{ }$ over n, $\tilde{n}$)

$$\tilde{n}(k) = \frac{k}{\frac{1}{n_1} + \frac{1}{n_2} + \frac{1}{n_3} + \ldots + \frac{1}{n_k}} \qquad (k \text{ marginal means}) \qquad (17.9a)$$

$$\tilde{n}(m) = \frac{km}{\frac{1}{n_1} + \frac{1}{n_2} + \frac{1}{n_3} + \ldots + \frac{1}{n_m}} \qquad (m \text{ marginal means}) \qquad (17.9b)$$

$$\tilde{n}(\text{cells}) = \frac{km}{\frac{1}{n_{11}} + \frac{1}{n_{12}} + \frac{1}{n_{13}} + \ldots + \frac{1}{n_{km}}} \qquad (\text{interactions}) \qquad (17.9c)$$

To see an example of the difference, the results in the worksheet that will be set up in Activity 17.6, shown in Figure 17.14 can be compared to the ANOVA analysis on the same data carried out in SPSS-PC, shown in Figure 17.15. Now let us see how to set up a worksheet for carrying out a two-way ANOVA.

TWO-WAY ANOVA: SAMPLE PROBLEMS ON A WORKSHEET

If all of the equations presented above were implemented as Excel formulae, the ANOVA table would contain those shown in Table 17.3. These are implemented in a worksheet in an example in Activity 17.6 for a 3 × 3 design. This will be used subsequently to extend to the situation where cell sizes are not necessarily equal, to show pairwise comparisons and for the calculation of power. While some of these are included in Excel data analysis tools and SPSS-PC version 6.1, not all are there together in any one place. Therefore, the final sheet will not only provide an illustration of ANOVA calculations, but also leave you with a useful tool for future calculations based on your own data.

Activity 17.6

Valerie Verbatim wished to know if the expansion of vocabulary in learning a new language could be enhanced by different approaches. Language students seemed to have difficulty in keeping extensive vocabulary in their memory, particularly since they are not continually using the language. Therefore, she arranged a three-day special course, dividing the participants into nine groups, isolated from each other. Her experiment was based on two variables. The first, A, was the level of immersion in the new language: A_1 total, A_2 partial, A_3 none. The second variable, B, was the type of practice language tapes used each day: B_1 vocabulary drill, B_2 conversations, B_3 recorded news reports. All groups were tested at the end on a set of 15 new nouns introduced over the time and the number of words correctly translated was used as the dependent variable.

(a) Start a new worksheet and enter the raw data shown in rows 1 to 16 in Figure 17.14. In cells **G4:G6**, include the formulae for the harmonic mean, equations (17.9).

(b) Add formulae to calculate means, variances, cell sizes and $A \times B$ diffs[2] (what is summed up in the numerator of equation (17.4) for calculating $MS_{A \times B}$) tables as shown. Add the formulae for ANOVA, which correspond to Table 17.3.

(c) Produce graphs (sketches by hand) for interactions using the means table.

(d) Excel's **Data Analysis** function cannot cope with unequal cell sizes when carrying out factorial ANOVA: it assumes all empty cells have zero in them and averages these in as well. To check the spreadsheet model, initially add some dummy numbers (such as a 5) in the four empty cells and carry out ANOVA for comparison, from the menu using: **Tools, Data Analysis, Anova: Two-Factor with Replication**. Include the entire data table and select a space to display the results to the right by specifying the upper left:

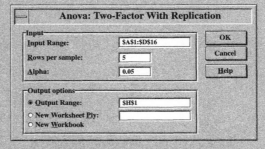

(e) When the two ANOVA tables match, go back and remove the dummy data and continue with the analysis. What would you conclude from the results of the problem above?

MULTIPLE COMPARISONS

As noted earlier, it is possible to illustrate the results of a factorial study graphically, but it is still necessary to check that apparent differences are significant. Pairwise comparisons can be carried out using the same tests as introduced in Chapter 16, the decision as to which being based upon the willingness to risk Type I and Type II errors. While it is possible to carry out all comparisons on marginal means to test the source of significance across main effects, and all possible combinations of interactions, the choice should depend on the variables and the interpretations that would result. Also, as seen before,

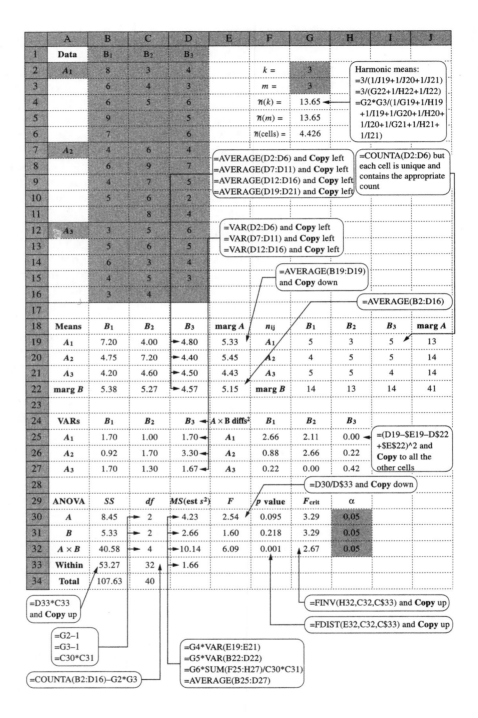

FIGURE 17.14
Worksheet for calculating two-way ANOVA, including unequal cell sizes

FIGURE 17.15
SPSS-PC (version
6.1) analysis of
variance output for
data in Figure 17.14
(having been
modified for input):
from the main menu
select **Statistics,
ANO̲VA Models,
General Factorial**

* * * * * * Analysis of Variance – design 1 * * * * * *

Tests of Significance for VARI using UNIQUE sums of squares

Source of Variation	SS	DF	MS	F	Sig of F
WITHIN CELLS	55.35	32	1.73		
A	8.46	2	4.23	2.45	.103
B	5.34	2	2.67	1.54	.229
A BY B	38.10	4	9.53	5.51	.002
(Model)	57.77	8	7.22	4.18	.002
(Total)	113.12	40	2.83		

R-Squared = .511
Adjusted R-Squared = .388

- -

Effect Size Measures and Observed Power at the .0500 Level

Source of Variation	Partial ETA Sqd	Noncen- trality	Power
A	.133	4.891	.456
B	.088	3.088	.303
A BY B	.408	22.028	.954

- -

TABLE 17.3
Calculations for two-
way ANOVA, with
unequal cell sizes

	df	MS (est s^2): Excel functions	F
A	$k-1$	$s_A^2 = s_{\text{across A}}^2 + s_{\text{ind diff}}^2 + s_{\text{error}}^2$ $MS_A = \tilde{n}(k)*\textbf{VAR(marginal means A)}$	$\dfrac{MS_A}{MS_{\text{within}}}$
B	$m-1$	$s_B^2 = s_{\text{across B}}^2 + s_{\text{ind diff}}^2 + s_{\text{error}}^2$ $MS_B = \tilde{n}(m)*\textbf{VAR(marginal means B)}$	$\dfrac{MS_B}{MS_{\text{within}}}$
$A \times B$	$(k-1)(m-1)$	$s_{A\times B}^2 = s_{\text{int-AB}}^2 + s_{\text{ind diff}}^2 + s_{\text{error}}^2$ $MS_{A\times B} = \tilde{n}(\textbf{cells})*\textbf{SUM(differences)^2/}$ $((k-1)*(m-1))$	$\dfrac{MS_{A\times B}}{MS_{\text{within}}}$
Within	$\sum n_{jl} - km$	$s_{\text{within}}^2 = s_{\text{ind diff}}^2 + s_{\text{error}}^2$ $MS_{\text{within}} = \textbf{AVERAGE(cell variances)}$	
Total	$\sum n_{jl} - 1$		

by designating a limited number of pairwise comparisons ahead of time, it is possible to increase the power of the outcome by an appropriate choice of test. Carrying out all possible pairwise comparisons, as presented by some software packages, may increase the probability of making a Type II error.

Carrying out pairwise comparisons across individual cells is equivalent to treating them as constituents of a large one-way ANOVA. If you do find significant differences in cells, the combinations are confounded: you will not be able to determine which of the two variables is the source, though it may be the combinations themselves that are of interest. Unfortunately, these designs can generate a large number of combinations, as can be seen from Table 17.4. On a modest 3 × 3 design (three levels for each of two factors), there would potentially be six comparisons for main effects and 36 pairwise comparisons across cells. So while two-way ANOVA provides a tool for investigating potential interactions, it also generates some work in the form of mathematical and interpretative effort.

The choice of tests is much the same as described in Chapter 16, though the implementation must be carried out with some care since there are differences in the calculations for the marginal means and the cell means. If there are only two levels for either or both of the two variables, then there is no need for additional tests because the ANOVA indicates whether there is a difference across the pair. If there are three or more levels for either or both, then pairwise comparisons across levels of the main effects are possible.

The following new considerations must be borne in mind for each of the tests provided before carrying out the activity to implement them in the worksheet:

- The *Bonferroni t-test* (Dunn's) is very conservative and only of value if the number of comparisons is limited and planned prior to data collection. For example, if a limited number of planned comparisons were of interest in a 3×3 design out of the possible 36 pairs of cells, then this would be an appropriate test. Considering that for some studies, some pairs of cells may not have any meaning, planning ahead and considering how the outcome would be interpreted could result in using this test. On the other hand, it is not appropriate for all possible pairwise comparisons as its power is too low for large numbers of these.
- The *Newman–Keuls test* can be used for either marginal means or pairwise comparisons of cells. Since the critical value is dependent on the number of means across which a comparison is made, the more cells spanned, the larger the critical value is. Therefore, the more cells, the more difficult it is to find a significant difference.
- *Duncan's multiple range test* is less conservative than the Newman–Keuls, and as the number of means spanned increases, it becomes more difficult to find a significant difference.
- *Tukey's tests* differ, with test A having a constant critical value no matter how many means are spanned. Test B is a compromise between Tukey A and Newman–Keuls. It is dependent on the number of means spanned and more conservative than the Newman–Keuls test.
- *Scheffé comparisons* have a fixed critical value regardless of the number of means spanned and are very conservative. Their advantage is that they can be used to compare blocks of means to each other.

TABLE 17.4
Numbers of possible comparisons for two-dimensional factorial designs

Design $(A \times B)$	Number of cells	Possible marginal comparisons for factors	Possible pairwise comparisons for cells
2×2	4	1 and 1	6
2×3	6	1 and 3	15
3×3	9	3 and 3	36
4×4	16	6 and 6	120
$k \times m$	km	$\dfrac{k(k-1)}{2}$ and $\dfrac{m(m-1)}{2}$	$\dfrac{km(km-1)}{2}$

- *Dunnett's test* is limited to designs with a control group. It is of value for testing main effects where one level is a control group not receiving a treatment. It is *only* of value in testing across rows or down columns when one level of a variable is the control. For example, consider $A_1 \times B_2$ as the control group in the example in Figure 17.16.

There is a valid question about post hoc analysis that the researcher needs to ask: should *all* pairwise comparisons be considered? The answer really depends on the variables and the research question. If the interactions and comparisons help to resolve the question (the rejection of a null hypothesis makes sense), then of course testing across cell means is in order. On the other hand, if they do not, you will not impress anyone by just carrying out more statistical tests and reporting more significant differences. Consider the example in Activity 17.7, which provides the worksheet extension to include all possible multiple comparisons, using the example from Activity 17.6. Not only will you be shown how to carry out the mechanics of determining whether the differences are significant, you will also be asked to decide whether they mean anything.

Activity 17.7

1 Consider the results of applying the Newman–Keuls test shown in Figure 17.16 and list all the *significant* pairwise comparisons. Are they all interpretable? Do all the 36 pairwise comparisons of the cell means potentially tell Valerie Verbatim anything more about desirable strategies than the simple analysis of the marginal means?

2 If you want to be able to carry out multiple comparisons on your worksheet, add the section shown in Figure 17.16 to provide a way of carrying out pairwise comparisons, allowing a choice of methods.

The contents of shaded cells are determined by the user, the rest are automatically generated once the formulae are inserted. When **Copy**ing values for a test to column **M**, use the menu and **Paste Special**, **Values**, otherwise the formulae will change the values when copied.

Answer: 1. In this case, yes because each is a sensible combination of treatments. While neither of the treatments alone seems to provide an advantage, combinations $A_1 \times B_1$ and $A_2 \times B_2$ do appear to do so.

$A_1 \times B_1$	$A_2 \times B_2$	$A_1 \times B_3$	$A_2 \times B_1$	$A_3 \times B_2$	$A_3 \times B_3$	$A_2 \times B_3$	$A_3 \times B_1$	$A_1 \times B_2$

HOMOGENEITY OF VARIANCE

As with the one-way analysis of variance, it is assumed that all the sample variances are homogeneous. Bartlett's test for homogeneity of variance to estimate the likelihood that all the variances can again be used are sufficiently alike, with a few small changes to equation (16.14):

$$\chi^2 = \frac{df_{\text{within}} \ln s^2_{\text{within}} - \sum_{j=1}^{k}\sum_{l=1}^{m}(n_{jl}-1)\ln s^2_{jl}}{1 - \frac{1}{3(km-1)}\left(\sum_{j=l}^{k}\sum_{l=1}^{m}\frac{1}{(n_{jl}-1)} - \frac{1}{df_{\text{within}}}\right)} \tag{17.10}$$

This is checked against the χ^2 critical value in Table B.9, Appendix B, with $km - 1$ degrees of freedom. Again, refer to the discussion in Chapter 16 on the use of this test.

Activity 17.8

If you want to introduce this calculation into the worksheet, place it on the right of the ANOVA table, as indicated in Figure 17.17. Transformations would have to be carried out as before (see Figure 16.8), if it were deemed necessary.

=G4 harmonic mean A

=G38*SQRT($D$33/$F$36) and **Copy** down the column

=G5 harmonic mean B

=N38*SQRT($D$33/$M$36) and **Copy** down the column

	A	B	C	D	E	F	G	H	I	J	K	L	M	N
36	**Marginal**	5.45	5.33	4.43	$\tilde{n}$ =	13.650	Test	**Marginal**	5.38	5.27	4.57	$\tilde{n}$ =	13.650	Test
37	**means** ***A***	A_2	A_1	A_3	r	$M_{\min}$	NK	**means** ***B***	B_1	B_2	B_3	r	$M_{\min}$	NK
38	A_2		0.12	1.02	9	1.22	3.49	B_1		0.12	0.82	9	1.22	3.49
39	A_1			0.90	8	1.01	2.89	B_2			0.70	8	1.01	2.89
40														
41	**Cell**	7.20	7.20	4.80	4.75	4.60	4.50	4.40	4.20	4.00	$\tilde{n}$ =	4.426	Test	
42	**means**	$A_1 \times B_1$	$A_2 \times B_2$	$A_1 \times B_3$	$A_2 \times B_1$	$A_3 \times B_2$	$A_3 \times B_3$	$A_2 \times B_3$	$A_3 \times B_1$	$A_1 \times B_2$	r	$M_{\min}$	**NK**	
43	$A_1 \times B_1$		0.00	2.40	2.45	2.60	2.70	2.80	3.00	3.20	9	2.89	4.72	
44	$A_2 \times B_2$			2.40	2.45	2.60	2.70	2.80	3.00	3.20	8	2.82	4.60	
45	$A_1 \times B_3$				0.05	0.20	0.30	0.40	0.60	0.80	7	2.74	4.46	
46	$A_2 \times B_1$					0.15	0.25	0.35	0.55	0.75	6	2.64	4.30	
47	$A_3 \times B_2$						0.10	0.20	0.40	0.60	5	2.51	4.10	
48	$A_3 \times B_3$							0.10	0.30	0.50	4	2.36	3.84	
49	$A_2 \times B_3$								0.20	0.40	3	2.14	3.49	
50	$A_3 \times B_1$									0.20	2	1.77	2.89	
51														
52		r	Bonferroni	Duncan	NK	Tukey B	Tukey A	Scheffé	Dunnett's					
53		9	3.74	3.35	4.72	4.72	4.72	4.62	3.58					
54		8	3.74	3.32	4.60	4.66	4.72	4.62	3.58					
55		7	3.74	3.29	4.46	4.59	4.72	4.62	3.58					
56		6	3.74	3.25	4.30	4.51	4.72	4.62	3.58					
57		5	3.74	3.20	4.10	4.41	4.72	4.62	3.58					
58		4	3.74	3.13	3.84	4.28	4.72	4.62	3.58					
59		3	3.74	3.03	3.49	4.11	4.72	4.62	3.58					
60		2	3.74	2.89	2.89	3.81	4.72	4.62	3.58					
61			q=sqrt(2)t'_{crit}	$q_{r\ \text{crit}}$	$q_{r\ \text{crit}}$	$q_{r\ \text{crit}}$	$q_{r\ \text{crit}}$	q=sqrt(2F')	q=sqrt(2)t_d					
62			4	(table)	(table)	(TA+NK)/2	(NKmax)	eqn(16.26)	(table)					
63			no comp.											

=G6 overall harmonic mean

Using cell means in row 41, insert formulae to find cell differences here

=SQRT(2)*TINV ($H$32/$C$62,$C33)

=(G53+E53)/2

=$E$53

=M50*SQRT($D$33/$L$41) and **Copy** up the column

=SQRT(2*$C$32*FINV ($H$30,$C$32,$C$33)) and **Copy** down the column

FIGURE 17.16 Section of worksheet to be attached to Figure 17.14, for carrying out pairwise comparisons

	K	L	M	N	
18	$I/(n_{ij}-1)$	B_1	B_2	B_3	
19	A_1	0.25	0.50	0.25	=1/(I9–1) and **Copy** to other cells
20	A_2	0.33	0.25	0.25	
21	A_3	0.25	0.25	0.33	
22					
23					
24	$(n-1)\ln s^2$	B_1	B_2	B_3	
25	A_1	2.12	0.00	2.12	=(I19–1)*LN(D25) and **Copy** to other
26	A_2	–0.26	2.12	4.78	
27	A_3	2.12	1.05	1.53	
28					=C33*LN(D33)–SUM(L25:N27)
29	**Bartlett's**		df(Bart) =	$km-1$	=1–(SUM(L19:N21)–1/C33)/(3*(G2*G3–1))
30	num =	0.72	chi sq. =	0.81	=L30/L31
31	den =	0.89	chi-sq. prob. =	0.999	=CHIDIST(N30,G2*G3–1)
32			chi-sq. crit. =	15.51	=CHIINV(0.05,G2*G3–1)

FIGURE 17.17
Bartlett's test for
homogeneity of
variance in the
worksheet

POWER

Estimates of the power of each F-test can be made using the same approach as in Chapter 16, resulting in the Excel formula analagous to (16.37) for each *source* (treatment or interaction)

$$\text{power (source)} \cong \text{FDIST}(F_{\text{crit}}/k', \text{ROUND}(df'_{\text{source}}, 0), df_{\text{within}}) \quad (17.11)$$

where F_{crit} is the critical value for that source, using the appropriate degrees of freedom, from the ANOVA table, and

$$k' = \frac{df_{\text{source}} + \lambda}{df_{\text{source}}} \quad (17.12)$$

$$df'_{\text{source}} = \frac{(df_{\text{source}} + \lambda)^2}{df_{\text{source}} + 2\lambda} \quad (17.13)$$

$$\lambda \cong df_{\text{source}}\left(\frac{F_{\text{source}}}{cf} - 1\right) \quad (17.14)$$

in which

$$cf = \frac{df_{\text{source}} + 1}{df_{\text{source}} + 1 + 0.4}$$

is the correction factor, expressed as degrees of freedom. The df_{source} represents the degrees of freedom for that source from the ANOVA table, and F_{source} is the F-ratio for that source from the ANOVA table.

When carried out for a main effect as a source, this provides an estimate of the power of the test across that main effect's means. When it is used for interactions, then an estimate of the power of the overall $A \times B$ interaction test is provided. In all cases, β, the probability of making a Type II error, can also be found. Obviously, if the appropriate values for each case are inserted into the worksheet in Figure 17.16, an estimate of the balance across sample sizes, effects and standard deviations necessary for a high probability of finding significance when it exists, can be found.

As categorically stated earlier, factorial designs are more powerful than one-way designs. This becomes apparent when considering the nature of the calculation of the F-ratio. When a factorial design has two or more variables (dimensions), then there is the potential for more of the 'natural' variance (individual differences) to be accounted for by these variables. Thus one would expect the F-ratio to be larger since this component in each of the mean squares (MS_{within}, MS_A, MS_B and $MS_{A \times B}$) should be smaller, a consequence similar to reducing the error variance by increasing the reliability of the instrument, as seen earlier (Activity 16.9). Using the directions in Activity 17.9, you can add power calculations, as shown in Figure 17.15, to your factorial ANOVA worksheet, as well as analyse the results of a new study. In addition to using the formulae above, calculations for ϕ and $\mathbf{f}$ are again included to allow comparisons of results with various power tables, since this is an estimate. These are the same as those defined in Chapter 16, though the use of ϕ with the tables seems to produce conflicting results with the interaction term.

Activity 17.9

1   Enter the formulae shown to calculate power on the worksheet, to right of ANOVA, as shown in Figure 17.18.
2   Now consider a new problem: in the age of innovative taxation, the local tax authority of Blodge County wanted to find a way of raising money for schools. It was felt that the voters would resist less if the proceeds were known to go directly to education and not to become just general revenue, but it was also deemed necessary to test this. It was decided that the variables to be included were children (parents, grandparents, none) and type of home (public housing/council house, rented flat or apartment, owned home). Leaflets describing the tax and its implications were distributed to a random sample of 6 for each cell which was followed by a questionnaire addressing the consequences of the tax: the higher the score, the greater support for the tax. The results are presented as shown in Figure 17.19.
    (a)   Enter these into the worksheet for Figure 17.14 with the enhancements of Figures 17.16–17.18, and analyse the results.
    (b)   What other independent variables could have been used?

Answers:
2(a) See Figures 17.20 and 17.21
The Newman–Keuls test across marginal means indicates that public housing people showed significantly greater support for the tax than people with rented and owned houses. Also the parents and grandparents showed significantly greater support for the tax than those who had no children.

| P×Pa | R×GP   P×N   O×Pa   P×GP   R×Pa | O×GP | O×N | R×N |

In summary, the above boxes tell us that cell means for the 'support for the tax' scores resulted in the following significant differences across groups: Public × Parents was greater than Owned × None and Rented × None; while Rented × Grandparents, Public × None, Owned × Parents, Public × Grandparents, Rented × Parents, Owned × Grandparents were all greater than Rented × None. The rest were not significantly different from each other (those within a single box). While the marginal means are not surprising, alone they could be misleading (equivalent to two one-way ANOVAs). Considering cell differences, most dissent would seem to come from childless people who rent.
(b) Possibilities include income, social class, education, number of children.

HIGHER-ORDER FACTORIAL DESIGNS

Obviously, it is possible to have factorial designs that include three or more dimensions (recall, for example, Figure 7.11), though these can increase the difficulty of interpreting results with interactions. Significant differences across the main effects still indicate that, for the variable in question, there is a difference across the levels or categories. Not only does the demand for more subjects increase, but so also does the difficulty in sampling for each cell, row and/or column, particularly for designs that include life events (such as gender, marital status, social class, education, number of children).

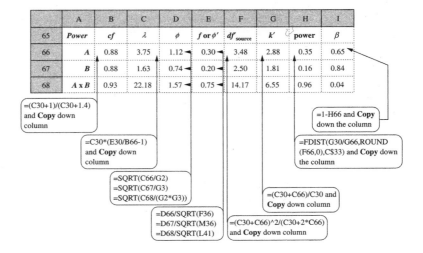

FIGURE 17.18
Power calculations for the factorial ANOVA worksheet

1	**Data**	B Parents	C GrandParents	D None
2	Public	60	62	54
3		65	54	63
4		58	56	56
5		55	54	61
6		62		53
7	Rented	56	60	45
8		54	55	53
9		57	59	50
10		60	63	46
11		55		48
12	Owned	55	55	50
13		57	51	48
14		65	58	52
15		49	56	56
16		60	50	

FIGURE 17.19
Testing support for Blodge County's new local education tax

	A	B	C	D	E	F	G	H
29	**ANOVA**	*SS*	*df*	*MS* (s^2)	*F*	*p* value	F_{crit}	α
30	**Housing**	115.02	2	57.51	3.89	0.030	3.28	0.05
31	**Children**	223.34	2	111.67	7.56	0.002	3.28	0.05
32	*A × B*	174.58	4	43.64	2.95	0.034	2.66	0.05
33	**Within**	487.73	33	14.78				
34	**Total**	1000.66	41					

FIGURE 17.20
ANOVA solution for Activity 17.9, Question 2, using Figure 17.14 worksheet: voters' views on a possible new tax

Interactions can be analysed with the aid of simple two-dimensional graphs of means, as before, but by generating sets for one variable. For example, a three-dimensional design A × B × C, where there are 3 × 3 × 3 levels, would have 27 cells. To display all the interactions, one could display three graphs, A × B, for each of the three levels of C. Obviously one could alternatively display three A × C graphs, one for each B, or three B × C graphs, one for each A, depending on what would be most meaningful.

FIGURE 17.21
Power calculations
for Activity 17.9,
Question 1

		A	B	C	D	E	F	G	H	I
	65	*Power*	*cf*	λ	ϕ	*f* or ϕ'	*df* ${}_{source}$	*k'*	power	β
	66	*A*	0.88	6.82	1.51	0.40	4.97	4.41	0.60	0.40
	67	*B*	0.88	15.13	2.25	0.60	9.09	8.56	0.93	0.07
	68	*A* × *B*	0.93	8.76	0.99	0.46	7.56	3.19	0.58	0.42

For the ANOVA calculations and additional guidance on interpretation of designs employing three or more variables for factorial analysis of variance, see such texts as Edwards (1972), Glass and Hopkins (1996), Hays (1994), Keppel (1973) and Winer *et al.* (1991).

SUMMARY

This chapter has extended the use of analysis of variance for detecting differences in means to two-dimensional designs. This not only allows two variables to be considered simultaneously, but also potential interactions between them. The development of a worksheet has provided a tool that provides the usual ANOVA calculations, and also a variety of pairwise comparison tools, a check for homogeneity of variance and calculations of power. The analyses of variance for one-way and factorial designs are very useful statistical tests, but they do not cover all the eventualities. Therefore, in the next chapter, we will encounter some modifications that will allow us to provide statistical tests for situations that are often typical of real-life situations in the field rather than in the laboratory.

RANDOMIZED BLOCK DESIGNS AND ANALYSIS OF COVARIANCE   18

The statistical tests of the previous chapter cover the obvious, tightly controlled experimental situations of design B3/D3 (Post-test/observation only), but much potentially interesting social science research needs more flexibility. We often want to use life-event variables, such as social class, IQ and education, in our studies since these are what is of greatest interest, the interaction of controlled external events with the varied characteristics of subjects. In such situations, it is either suspected or there is some tentative evidence that life-event variables make a considerable contribution to attitudes, choices and responses to treatments. The statistical need is for tests that will allow the detection of differences due to the variable(s) of interest (treatment), separating this effect from that of subject characteristics. At the same time, they should not allow the extraneous variables either to counteract the effect of these, or to fool us into thinking that the treatment was the cause when the extraneous variable was the real reason for the difference. For interval/ratio measures, several tests have been developed that are modifications of the analysis of variance, many of them quite complex. In this chapter, some of the more basic but powerful tests will be covered, along with any necessary alterations in the designs.

These tests will potentially enhance the control of extraneous variables that could be introduced through the design itself. This includes situations when a single group is to be observed more than once and designs where it is necessary to vary sampling approaches to ensure groups are homogeneous by matching subjects or repeated measures (randomized blocked designs). We will also introduce analysis of covariance for situations where it is not possible to measure a potential extraneous variable ahead of the study and group subjects accordingly, and for design B2 (pre- and post-test/observation). Finally, some statistical tests for the special cases of designs C2 (non-equivalent control group), C6 (time series) and B5 (Solomon four) will be introduced.

RANDOMIZED BLOCK AND ANALYSIS OF COVARIANCE DESIGNS

Simple one-way and factorial ANOVA designs are quite desirable as long as there are sufficient resources and the researcher has control over all extraneous variables. They have the potential to answer the questions asked, if samples are available and the sampling procedure and sample size protect against extraneous variables, thus enhancing internal validity. But these conditions cannot always be fulfilled. Three additional variations of designs B3/D3 (post-test/observation only) will be considered here since there will be situations where control of extraneous variables by random sampling and random assignment is potentially not sufficient. In such situations where outcomes are influenced by uncontrolled extraneous variables, internal validity would be threatened, resulting in conclusions that are not justifiable and probably not replicable. The new tests are intended to prevent confounding of variables and will derive from two variations on the ANOVA test, one of which will be covered in detail.

The aim of any design based upon B2 and B3 is to control potential extraneous variables so that any differences across groups in the dependent variable can be unequivocally attributed *only* to the independent variable(s) (treatment). One-way and factorial designs can achieve this if random selection is followed by random assignment to cells. Research being the way it is, things sometimes do not work out perfectly and adjustments have to be made. This is particularly true when the background of subjects contributes extraneous life-event variables. Some of these will have ramifications for the choice of statistical test. We will consider four representative classes of designs that deviate from the ideals of previous designs, and necessitate choosing a different test or a modification of these. This will include design D3 the ex post facto approach where at least one of the independent variables is not a treatment, but a life experience. Quasi-experimental design C2 presents some unique problems to be considered separately later.

Simple blocked design

First let us consider ex post facto designs where a life event is one of the variables. In such designs, there would be random selection from each category for the life-event variable, since in this situation it is not possible randomly to assign subjects as life has assigned them already, so to speak. The result is a factorial design where subjects are randomly selected for one life-event variable (D3), and the other variable is a treatment to which they are randomly assigned (B3). For example, recall the earlier experiment where randomly selected classes of girls only, boys only and mixed were then randomly assigned to different types of teaching. This is referred to as *blocking* on a variable, here the type of class (single-sex or mixed), and there are many subjects per cell. In such a study, there is interest in variation across subjects, as well as across the treatment. Also, there is a need to determine whether the groups of subjects interact with the treatment. Therefore, the combination design (D3+B3) employs a simple two-way factorial ANOVA, the same as if there were two experimental treatment variables.

Matched sample design

There will be other situations where we may wish to block on a variable, in other words, specifically select subjects from a group, but for different reasons. Not always will random sampling ensure that we have obtained homogeneous groups for potential extraneous variables. For example, would a small random sample of eight students in each of three groups provide subjects with equivalent and representative ranges of IQ for a study on different learning approaches? There may be a need to block on IQ just to ensure homogeneity of groups. Thus here it would be desirable to select from several IQ ranges and randomly assign subjects to different learning approaches. This is necessary to reduce the impact of what Hays (1994) quaintly calls *nuisance* variables, extraneous variables potentially not controlled by sampling. In this example, it would be because a small random sample of students would not ensure that the researcher had an appropriate range of IQ scores in each treatment group, which could ultimately influence outcomes.

In such cases, we are *not* concerned with detecting inherent variability across life experiences, just across the levels of treatment. On the other hand, if there is not an association between the blocking variable and the dependent variable (it is not an extraneous variable), this effort would be a waste of resources and the results may suffer a loss of power. The researcher must have identified and measured the blocking variable *before* treatment so as to be able to select and assign subjects. The blocking variable can be categorical or continuous, though the latter must be divided into discrete ranges.

In general, this approach avoids the possible introduction of an extraneous variable when you want to make sure that the variable is included and accounted for in proportions related to the population, or when a random sample is not going to ensure that you would have an even spread and would have all the variables represented as they should. In other words, it is possible or even likely that a random sample would result in a predominance of one or more levels of the extraneous variable and the exclusion of others. Each of these *blocks* of subjects is representative of one of the levels of the extraneous variable that may contribute to the outcome. Such a study is referred to as employing a *matched sample* design. This is shown below, where $RS_1 + RS_2 + RS_3$ make up the representative sample of the whole single group, but each has been randomly sampled from defined subgroups:

Thus each group receiving treatment would be like the others, at least for the potential extraneous variable. In the case above, the researcher could randomly sample (**RS**) from three IQ ranges, randomly assigning (**RA**) equal numbers to each treatment group. The three ranges could be equal probabilities from the population. To determine the ranges, it is necessary to find the IQ scores that divide the distribution into three equal parts. Recalling that the mean is 100 and the standard deviation is 15, we consult Table B.1 in Appendix B. Half of 33.33% is 16.67%, so from the table we see that this corresponds to about 0.43 standard deviations, here 6.45 IQ points. Thus our three ranges would be: below 93.55, from 93.55 to 106.45, and above 106.55.

This is analogous to a one-way ANOVA, but, because of blocking, we will have to modify this statistical test. Before considering it, let us look at another situation that will employ the same statistical test.

Repeated treatments and measures

There will be situations where it is not possible or may not be desirable to have more than one group, thus more than one measure would be made on a single group, typically to determine whether changing the treatment makes a difference. Situations arise when, there may be a limited number of subjects with the appropriate characteristics, a complex skills, or restricted traits. The following are some examples:

- Police officers needing to identify the best communication protocol for radio-telephones could try three different schemes and complete a questionnaire on each.
- To determine which of several counselling or medical treatments would be most effective for short-term relief of symptoms in mentally ill persons, each person would encounter the treatments over an extended period of time.
- As part of a consumer survey, persons are asked to complete questionnaires about trial usage of different brands of a single common product, such as automobiles, cameras, or computers.

While this could be resolved by using a one-way or factorial design, in some cases it is not necessary, desirable or even possible to use different groups for each of the treatments. Therefore, a single group may receive several unrelated treatments and multiple observations will be made, such as the three illustrated here (Hays, 1994):

$$\textbf{RS} \longrightarrow \textbf{X}_a \longrightarrow \textbf{O}_a \longrightarrow \textbf{X}_b \longrightarrow \textbf{O}_b \longrightarrow \textbf{X}_c \longrightarrow \textbf{O}_c$$

The order in which the individuals in the group receive each treatment may be completely random so as to avoid the possibility of order effects. In any case, variation across individuals will likely occur due to natural traits, even for a random sample. Thus this is equivalent in structure to the matched sample, but instead of a number of groups we have a spread of individuals. For the situation where order is controlled by randomly assigning subjects, the design could be described as follows:

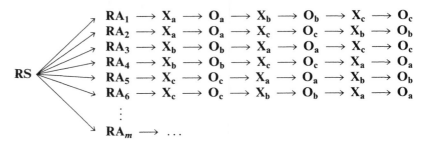

for a random sample of size m. Again it is recognized that there will be a difference across subjects that may influence the outcome (dependent variable) just as there was with blocks, and this will have an impact on the nature of the statistical test. It does not matter here that there is a difference across the individuals, since overall the group is representative of the population. (If the order in which they encounter the treatments becomes a factor, then a different approach is needed. See Keppel (1973) for a discussion on this possibility).

Another design that falls into this structure is C6 (Howell, 1997; Wright, 1997), where all subjects are observed or measured on a number of occasions. The treatment may occur at one or more times during the study, depending on the nature of the hypothesis. The researcher is looking for either a one-off change or a gradual improvement with increased number of treatments. Again, this depends upon a random selection and there may well be an underlying trait that influences the strength of the outcome, but this is assumed and not of prime interest. The aim of the statistical test is to determine whether a difference has occurred over time. This design will be discussed in greater detail later in the chapter.

Neither of these two designs precludes using more than one sample. For example, a second group could be used as a control group in addition to the experimental group, except that the subjects would receive no treatment or a placebo, or a different treatment.

Such designs are referred to as *repeated measures* designs since each group is measured more than once. They are also sometimes referred to as *within-subjects designs*. With such designs, it is possible to take advantage of the fact that instead of several groups, only one group is used, resulting in situations where measurements will be highly correlated across time or treatments; consequently, there will be a reduction in the denominator term in the F-test, and fewer subjects will be needed.

Matched sample and repeated measures designs will be grouped together because the modified ANOVA test is the same as for both of them; they will be referred to collectively as *randomized block* designs. There are several characteristics of these approaches that result in some unique statistical outcomes, providing enhanced power over simple one-way and factorial designs. In matched sample designs, homogeneous sets of persons replace the individuals, instead of measures taken on the same persons for each treatment as in the repeated measures.

But what if. . .?

What if it is not possible to identify the extraneous variable or, even if so, not possible to measure it before so as to group subjects according to the variable, but that variable would potentially overshadow the possible effect of an independent variable of interest? The alternative is to carry out an analysis of covariance (ANCOVA). The constraints are that the potential extraneous variable (covariate) must be continuous, not categorical, and it should have a linear relationship with the independent variable. Thus, data on subjects for the covariate could be collected *after* treatment, possibly at the same time as the measure on the dependent variable is made. The researcher must ensure that treatment does not contaminate the covariate and that it is truly independent.

In general, this procedure can reduce the denominator in the *F*-test for main effect variables or treatment(s) when there is a covariate, even when random sampling and random assignment are employed, primarily because these rarely produce perfectly equivalent groups anyway. There are limitations to the value of ANCOVA, and the power of this test will be greatly reduced when the relationship is non-linear, though adjustments could be made. On the other hand, the randomized block design has no such restrictions (Huitema, 1980). Also, for factorial designs, the advantage of employing ANCOVA is dependent on the magnitude of the correlation between the covariate and the independent variable, being greatest when the correlation is high. Thus we have two new statistical tests to consider, randomized block ANOVA and analysis of covariance. The criteria for the choice of which to employ are summarized in Figure 18.1.

The modified analysis of variance for randomized blocks follows similar logic to that for simple ANOVA, so this will be explained in much the same way as for simple one-way and factorial designs. Analysis of covariance is mathematically much more complex and beyond this text. It will be conceptually described

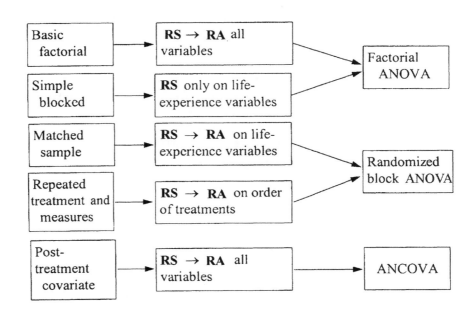

FIGURE 18.1
Alternative statistical analyses for factorial-type designs

and an example presented with output from SPSS, but if you are interested in the mathematics behind this test, then you are directed to such texts as Howell (1997), Hays (1994) and Huitema (1980).

RANDOMIZED BLOCK ANOVA

The statistical test for significant difference across the measures can be thought of as an extension of the *t*-test for two interrelated groups. A one-factor ANOVA test for these situations will be demonstrated here, taking into account three or more measurements on a single group or block. For two-way designs (for example, employing a control group or one with contrasting traits of interest), see other texts, such as Howell (1997), Winer *et al.* (1991) or Ferguson (1976).

The test is somewhat different from the two-way ANOVA, since there is essentially only one group, even if made up of selected blocks experiencing all of the treatments, or individuals being treated and measured over time. Thus the variance across the sample is just individual differences, since there is in reality only one sample. Therefore, not all of the four possible estimates of the population variance considered for the factorial design have any value in testing hypotheses.

Let us consider first what the aim of this test is in relation to the two designs described above: to determine whether there is a difference across the observations/measures, either when these are after different treatments, *or* simply over time on either side of a treatment. Consequently, let us consider how an estimate of the population variance which potentially contains this can be found. The four sources are analogous to those described for the two-dimensional ANOVA in Figure 17.13, but slightly different in their coverage:

- *Within-groups variance*, s^2_{within}, can only include the average variances across the treatments/time plus error variance of the measures, but not across subjects:

$$s^2_{\text{within}} = s^2_{\text{across-T}} + s^2_{\text{error}}$$

This is because there are not cell variances where each cell contains a different sample, but one sample. Thus this only takes into account some of the variance.

- *Variance between subjects*, $s^2_{\text{btwn-S}}$, does not provide an estimate of the population variance that tells us anything about a potential variable, as it can only include the variance of individual differences and error variance of the measures:

$$s^2_{\text{btwn-S}} = s^2_{\text{ind diff}} + s^2_{\text{error}}$$

We know there will be some differences across subjects, but it does not help us in this case.

- *Variance between treatments/time*, $s^2_{\text{btwn-T}}$, should give an estimate that includes variance due to the treatments/time (main effect) and the interactions between treatments/time and the subjects, plus error variance of the measures:

$$s^2_{\text{btwn-T}} = s^2_{\text{across-T}} + s^2_{\text{int-TS}} + s^2_{\text{error}}$$

The individual differences variances are part of the interactions variance.

- *Variance due to interaction of treatments/time and subjects,* $s^2_{\text{T}\times\text{S}}$, which should include just the interaction effects alone, plus error variances:

$$s^2_{\text{T}\times\text{S}} = s^2_{\text{int-TS}} + s^2_{\text{error}}$$

This is of use since it includes interaction and error terms but not across treatment.

These are summarized in Figure 18.2, which highlights the problem: what is needed is a ratio that allows the one potential variable, treatments/time, to provide the only difference. This means that we need a denominator for the between groups due to treatments/time variance. The within-groups variance is able to take into account the variance across groups but does not include an interaction term, therefore it is unsuitable as the denominator for the ratio as its analogue was for factorial analysis. Interestingly, it appears that since there is only one sample, the between-subjects variance includes individual differences, but no interactions, so it is not a suitable denominator. This leaves the groups (treatments/time) × subjects variance, which should provide an appropriate denominator since it includes only the interaction variance.

Thus to test the null hypothesis that there is no difference across groups (treatments/time), we need an estimate of the population that would potentially include all the effects of this for the numerator and one for the denominator that has all the other contributions. Therefore, the only F-ratio for repeated measures designs will be

$$F = \frac{s^2_{\text{across-T}} + s^2_{\text{int-TS}} + s^2_{\text{error}}}{s^2_{\text{int-TS}} + s^2_{\text{error}}}$$

$$= \frac{MS_{\text{btwn-T}}}{MS_{\text{T}\times\text{S}}} \qquad (18.1)$$

FIGURE 18.2
Partitioning of variance for randomized block designs: matched samples and repeated measures, where groups can be time, measures or treatments

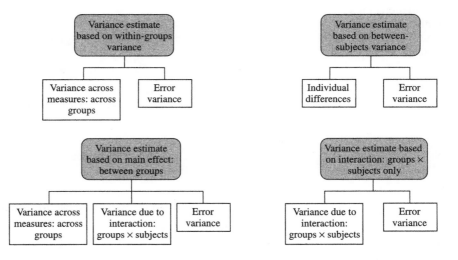

Having argued that this is the appropriate ratio, now it is necessary to find actual values. Remember that we can only determine variances that are *observed score variances*, and these contain components that cannot be separated. Thus it is necessary to justify that the variances determined from the data do represent the variances described above. While only two are of interest, it is possible to determine the others, based upon the definitions in Figure 18.2:

- The *within-groups variance* is found from the average of variances of measures over groups or time; in Excel this will be

AVERAGE(variances over groups/treatments/measures/time)

- The *between-subjects variance* is found from the variance of means across subjects, in Excel this will be

$$k \times \textbf{VAR(marginal means subjects)}$$

where k is the value in the cell containing the number of treatments or measures over time.

- The *between-treatments/time variance* is given by the variance of means across time; in Excel this will be

$$m \times \textbf{VAR(marginal means groups/treatments/measures/time)}$$

where m is the value in the cell containing the number of subjects.

- The *treatments/time × subjects variance* is found from the modified variance that includes marginal means and grand mean, $\bar{x}_{Sj}$, $\bar{x}_{Tl}$, and $\bar{X}$, as before, but using individual subject scores, x_{jl}, instead of cell means:

$$s_{T \times S}^2 = \frac{\sum_{j=1}^{k} \sum_{l=1}^{m} (x_{jl} - \bar{x}_{Sj} - \bar{x}_{Tl} + \bar{X})^2}{(k-1)(m-1)} \tag{18.2}$$

This is all summarized in Table 18.1, which outlines the components of the ANOVA table, though it includes unused variance estimates. As you

TABLE 18.1
Calculations for randomized block ANOVA (single factor)

	df	MS(est s^2): Excel functions	F
Between treatments/ time	$k-1$	$s_{\text{btwn-T}}^2 = s_{\text{across-T}}^2 + s_{\text{int-TS}}^2 + s_{\text{error}}^2$ $MS_{\text{btwn-T}} =$ $m * \textbf{VAR(marginal means treatments/time)}$	$\dfrac{MS_{\text{btwn-T}}}{MS_{\text{T} \times \text{S}}}$
Between subjects	$m-1$	$s_{\text{btwn-S}}^2 = s_{\text{ind diff}}^2 + s_{\text{error}}^2$ $MS_{\text{btwn-S}} = k * \textbf{VAR(marginal means subjects)}$	
Groups × subjects	$(k-1)(m-1)$	$s_{\text{T} \times \text{S}}^2 = s_{\text{int-TS}}^2 + s_{\text{error}}^2$ $MS_{\text{T} \times \text{S}} =$ $\textbf{SUM(differences)}\hat{} \textbf{2}/((k-1) * (m-1))$	
Within groups	$km - k$	$s_{\text{within}}^2 = s_{\text{across-T}}^2 + s_{\text{error}}^2$ $MS_{\text{within}} =$ $\textbf{AVERAGE(variances for treatments/time)}$	
Total	$km - 1$		

might have guessed, this test is the analysis of variance analogue of the correlated means *t*-test encountered in Chapter 15, and similarly, when appropriately used, is more powerful than a simple one-way ANOVA, as will be seen in Activity 18.1 below, which should be carried out now.

Activity 18.1

1   Set up a worksheet as in Figure 18.3, for randomized block (matched samples/repeated measures) ANOVA, based upon Excel formulae in Table 18.1. Consider the following example as a trial source of data: Elvira English wanted to compare the effectiveness of four sets of complementary materials for teaching grammar (prepositional phrases) to 14-year-olds. To ensure that the groups were equivalent, she used a matched sample design of randomly selected children from each of five ranges of IQ in proportions roughly equivalent to the normal distribution. Thus, there would be in each group (in parentheses): top, 118.5 and above (1); upper, 118.5–106.5 (2); mid, 106.5–93.5 (3); lower, 93.5–81.5 (2); and bottom: 81.5 and below (1). The results are shown and will be used again later.

   (a)   Insert formulae for row and column means and variances as shown.
   (b)   Set up a differences table for interactions calculation as indicated.
   (c)   Set up the ANOVA table as shown.
   (d)   Set up pairwise comparisons: only main effects as in a one-way design.
   (e)   Add power calculations as shown.

2   Check the basic ANOVA with Excel. From the main menu select: **Tools, Data Analysis, Anova: Two-Factor Without Replication**, where the **input Range: A1:E10** includes column and row labels. Click on the box for ☒ **Labels**. Place the output to the side on the worksheet.

3   Repeat the analysis as a plain one-way ANOVA using the worksheet in Figure 16.12, assuming a random sample and random assignment to each group, or, in Excel, select **Tools** from the main menu, and **Data Analysis, One Factor Anova**. You should get the same total sum of squares (SS). Would a significant difference be identified using a one-way ANOVA? Why or why not? How do these results compare?

Applying randomized block ANOVA to repeated measures designs

In repeated measures designs, there is one violation of the three basic assumptions associated with any analysis of variance test introduced in Chapter 16: we no longer have independence of observations. If we have observed Bloggs once,

	A	B	C	D	E	F	G	H	I
1	Group	A	B	C	D	Mean	Var		
2	Top	70	72	67	72	70.3	5.58		
3	Upper	65	70	72	74	70.3	14.92		
4	Upper	60	56	76	70	65.5	83.67		
5	Mid	45	50	55	58	52.0	32.67		
6	Mid	50	48	58	59	53.8	30.92		
7	Mid	46	51	54	56	51.8	18.92		
8	Lower	42	38	45	47	43.0	15.33		
9	Lower	38	44	48	48	44.5	22.33		
10	Bottom	30	36	32	38	34.0	13.33		
11									
12	Mean	49.6	51.7	56.3	58.0	53.9	$k =$	4	
13	Var	171.53	159.50	193.25	152.75		$m =$	9	
14							$m/(m-1) =$	1.125	
15	Diffs^2	A	B	C	D				
16	Top	16.7	15.8	32.4	5.6				
17	Upper	0.8	3.9	0.5	0.1				
18	Upper	1.4	53.0	64.9	0.2				
19	Mid	7.1	0.0	0.3	3.6				
20	Mid	0.3	12.4	3.3	1.3				
21	Mid	2.0	2.2	0.0	0.0				
22	Lower	11.1	7.7	0.2	0.0				
23	Lower	4.7	3.0	1.1	0.4				
24	Bottom	0.1	17.8	19.8	0.0				
25									
26									
27		SS	df	MS	F	p value	F_{crit}	α	
28	Btwn Grps	419.33	3	139.78	11.42	0.0001	3.009	0.05	
29	Btwn Subj	5122.56	8	640.32					
30	Interaction	293.67	24	12.24					
31	Within	5416.22	32	169.26					
32	Total	5835.56	35						

Annotations (columns H/I and callouts):
=AVERAGE(B2:E2)
=VAR(B2:E2) and **Copy** both down the columns
=COUNTA(B3:E3)
=COUNTA(B2:B11)
=H13/(H13–1)
=AVERAGE(B2:E11)
=AVERAGE(E2:E11)
=VAR(E2:E11) and **Copy** both across the rows
=(E2–$F2–E$12+$F$12)^2 and **Copy** to all other cells
=D28*C28 and **Copy**↓
=H12–1
=H13–1
=(H12–1)*(H13–1)
=H12*(H13–1)
=D28/D30
=FDIST(E28,C28,C30)
=FINV(H28,C28,C30)
=H13*VAR(B12:E12)
=H12*VAR(F2:F11)
=SUM(B16:E25)/C30
=AVERAGE(B13:E13)
=C28+C31
=I36*SQRT($D$30/$H$34) and **Copy** down the column
=H13

	A	B	C	D	E	F	G	H	I
33									
34	post hoc	58.00	56.33	51.67	49.56		$\bar{n} =$	9.00	Test
35	differences	D	C	B	A		r	M_{min}	NK
36	D		1.67	6.33	8.44		4	4.55	3.90
37	C			4.67	6.78		3	4.12	3.53
38	A				2.11		2	3.40	2.92

Insert formulae for differences
=($G$42+$E$42)/2
=SQRT(2)*TINV($H$28/$C$47,C30)
=SQRT(2*$C$28*FINV($H$28,$C$28,C30))

	r	Bonferroni	Duncan	NK	Tukey B	Tukey A	Scheffé	Dunnett's
42	5	3.82	3.23	4.17	4.17	4.17	4.25	3.04
43	4	3.82	3.16	3.90	4.04	4.17	4.25	3.04
44	3	3.82	3.08	3.53	3.85	4.17	4.25	3.04
45	2	3.82	2.93	2.92	3.55	4.17	4.25	3.04
	=(C28+1)/(C28+1.4)	q=sqrt(2)t'	q_r crit	q_r crit	q_r crit	q_r crit	q=sqrt(2F')	q=sqrt(2)t_d
	=C28*(E28/B49–1)	4	(table)	(table)	(TA+NK)/2	(NKmax)	eqn(16.26)	(table)
	=SQRT(B50/(C28+1))	no.comp						
	=(C28+B50)^2/(C28+2*B50)							

=$E$42

	A	B	...	E	F	...
49	Power: $cf =$	0.91		$k' =$	12.57	
50	$\lambda =$	34.70		**power =**	1.00	
51	$\phi =$	2.95		$\beta =$	0.00	
52	$df_{treat} =$	19.63		$f=\phi/\text{sqrt}(\bar{n})$	0.982	

=(C28+B50)/C28
=FDIST(G28/E49,ROUND(B52,0),C30)
=1–E50
=B51/SQRT(H34)

FIGURE 18.3
Worksheet for randomized block ANOVA

having performed under the first treatment, then his performance under the second treatment is hardly independent. As we saw earlier in this chapter, this is the basis for determining the sources of variances and the basis for the modified F-test above. This does not leave us, though, with one less assumption, but by necessity we replace it with a new one. The three assumptions are:

- interval/ratio data normally distributed;
- homogeneity of variance across treatments;
- compound symmetry of the covariance matrix.

This last assumption requires some further explanation. Covariances are the analogue of variances for pairs of sets of data, instead of a single set of data. The covariance of two sample groups A and B, is defined as

$$\text{cov}_{AB} = \frac{\sum_{i=1}^{n}(x_{Ai} - \bar{x}_A)(x_{Bi} - \bar{x}_B)}{n - 1} \tag{18.3}$$

If you compare this equation with that for the variance, you will see that instead of one term in the numerator, squared for a single distribution, you have two terms, one for each distribution. A major difference between variances and covariance is while variances are always positive since the numerator is squared, it is possible to have negative covariances. This will occur when positive differences with one group pair with negative differences in the other, indicating a negative relationship between them. This will be considered in Chapter 21 on correlations, but it is worth mentioning here that the Pearson product moment correlation can be defined as

$$r_{AB} = \frac{\text{cov}_{AB}}{s_A s_B}$$

and therefore an alternative equation for covariance that reflects this relationship is

$$\text{cov}_{AB} = s_A s_B r_{AB}$$

To test the three assumptions above, it is simply a matter of generating a matrix of values that includes all possible variances along the diagonal and covariances off the diagonal. Figure 18.4 illustrates this schematically for four treatments/measures. In Activity 18.2 that follows, you will add the matrix to the repeated measures version of Figure 18.3.

For our purposes, it is sufficient to use a visual check of the matrix to see if the covariances are roughly equal. It is *not* a requirement that they be exactly the same as the variances, just equivalent to each other. The reason why this has not been mentioned with respect to analysis of variance is that, while the requirement is still there, when the observations are independent the covariances will approach zero. With repeated measures designs, they will not be zero and should be roughly equal for all pairs. According to Keppel (1973), one potential source of heterogeneity of covariance comes from interaction between subjects and successive treatments due to carry-over effects in time series designs. While it may be possible to reduce these through the design and execution of the study, when it is not, there are alternative tests or modifications that can be applied, though these are beyond this text (see, for example,

FIGURE 18.4
Variance–covariance
matrix and cells for
inserting into the
worksheet of Figure
18.3. (*Hint*: type in
the contents of **H16**,
Copy this into **I16**
and **J16**, then change
the first range
column letters back
to **B**. Now you can fill
the rest of the matrix
by **Copy**ing these to
diagonal cells and the
ranges will change
automatically and
appropriately.)

	F	G	H	I	J
15	Var/Covar	A	B	C	D
16	A	=B13	=$H$14*COVAR (B$2:B$10,C$2:C$10)	=$H$14*COVAR (B$2:B$10,D$2:D$10)	=$H$14*COVAR (B$2:B$10,E$2:E$10)
17	B		=C13	=$H$14*COVAR (C$2:C$10,D$2:D$10)	=$H$14*COVAR (C$2:C$10,E$2:E$10)
18	C			=D13	=$H$14*COVAR (D$2:D$10,E$2:E$10)
19	D				=E13

Howell, 1997; and Keppel, 1973). The consequences of not correcting for heterogeneity will likely be a reduction in power ($F_{critical}$ lower than it should be), though this may not be apparent in the numerical results. The difficulty is that corrected $F_{critical}$ values tend to be excessively conservative, thus when the situation arises, one possibility is to not adjust, but to report the heterogeneity, since the true value for α may only be, say, 0.08 instead of 0.05 (Keppel, 1973). Now carry out Activity 18.2.

Activity 18.2

1   Make a copy of the randomized block worksheet in Figure 18.3 and apply it to the following *repeated measures* design. Larry Lumen was concerned about the arrangement of library lighting and its potential effect on concentration. He arranged for three library carrels to be set aside for an experiment and invited eight randomly selected students to use them free of charge for six weeks, indicating he wished to try different designs and monitor their effects. He used sensors in the chairs and logged continuous sitting time that included up to five minutes' absence as the measure of concentration time. He then changed the lighting every two weeks, rotating it across the three styles. The average concentration time per session for each student for each lighting style (A, B, C) is given in Table 18.2. Was there a difference, and if so, was it also architecturally significant (that is, would it justify changing all the lights)? Was his measure of concentration the best or can you think of another that might be better?
2   Add the cells shown in Figure 18.4 to the worksheet and consider whether there is homogeneity of variance and covariance.

Answers

1

	SS	df	MS	F	p-value	F-crit	α
Btwn grps (treat/time)	157.0	2	78.5	5.56	0.0167	3.739	0.05
Btwn subj.	586.0	7	83.7				
Interaction	197.7	14	14.1				
Within	783.6	21	37.3				
Total	940.6	23					

Using Newman–Keuls, only A and C are significantly different.

2 This would suggest homogeneity of variance and covariance.

Var/Covar	A	B	C
A	31.0	22.1	20.3
B		29.7	27.2
C			51.3

ANALYSIS OF COVARIANCE

From the beginning, there has been an emphasis in the designs considered on controlling extraneous variables. In other words, we want to make sure that variables other than the ones of interest are not influencing the measured outcomes and hiding the effects of the variables of interest, thus jeopardizing internal validity. Random selection and random assignment can achieve this in most cases, but, as we have seen above, there are situations where this may not be achieved unless a randomized block design is employed. An alternative statistical way of controlling the effects of extraneous variables not controlled by the design, or due to practical limitations, is through analysis of covariance. Like randomized block designs, this requires the identification of the variable that we are fairly sure influences or is correlated with the outcome, but may not be controlled by random assignment. Unlike the randomized block design, this does not have to be done before the collection of the data for the dependent variable. Situations will arise where it is not possible to acquire the data on the

TABLE 18.2
The results of Larry Lumen's lighting experiment

	A	B	C
S_1	30	35	40
S_2	32	33	35
S_3	40	38	41
S_4	45	50	55
S_5	36	43	34
S_6	44	43	45
S_7	35	38	45
S_8	33	43	50

extraneous variable ahead of time, or it may not be possible to block subjects according to the variables to control them.

The limitation to this approach is the requirement that the extraneous variable of interest, referred to in this situation as the *covariate,* must be continuous (quantifiable) and not categorical (a classification). Consider the example above used for the randomized block design, but imagine that Elvira English was not able to block the students before the experiment. We would assume that the higher the IQ, the higher the score, regardless of the treatment – in other words, scores would be correlated with IQs. Even if the results came out much the same in terms of distributing the students evenly across the treatments according to IQ, there is still a need to differentiate between the impact of the treatment and the influence of IQ. To verify this, the left half of Figure 18.5 presents the raw data with the actual IQ scores as well as the category system used in the randomized block design. On the right are the results of the analysis of covariance for these data, using IQ scores as the covariate.

Activity 18.3

Figure 18.5 presents the data from Figure 18.3 with actual IQ scores, arranged for input into SPSS and the corresponding SPSS ANCOVA results. How do the results differ? Can you suggest reasons why? Would the ANCOVA interpretation be different from the parallel situation of matched samples that used the randomized block design?

Comparing the three analyses – simple ANOVA, randomized block ANOVA, and ANCOVA – for the same data provides some insight into the consequences of selecting an appropriate design and statistical test. If IQ had not been taken into account as a covariate by either blocking or ANCOVA, then there would have been no indication that the treatment made any difference with ANOVA ($F = 0.83$, $p \cong 0.49$). With the ANCOVA test, the differential effect of the materials has been detected, but with slightly reduced power. The difference is most obvious with the randomized block design, since the individual blocks (ranges) are assumed to be homogeneous from treatment to treatment. The ANCOVA test will be more sensitive to differences in sampling. In this case, the difference in results between the randomized block ANOVA and ANCOVA is probably as much to do with the small numbers and the blocking into just five groups that allows the F-ratio in the randomized block to be larger than for the ANCOVA. Are the mean IQ scores and standard deviations roughly equivalent for the three groups? The two tests would probably be more consistent in outcomes with larger samples, but this does highlight the possibility of varying results due to choices of design and test.

On the other hand, had the four groups in the example not had roughly the same mean IQ, then ANCOVA would have been indispensable in compensating for this. In such situations, one might find the reverse to our example, that simple ANOVA detects a significant difference, where the ANCOVA says

	Group	iq	score	treat
1	Top	130	70	1
2	Upper	116	65	1
3	Upper	108	60	1
4	Mid	105	45	1
5	Mid	100	50	1
6	Mid	95	46	1
7	Lower	90	42	1
8	Lower	85	38	1
9	Bottom	75	30	1
10	Top	125	72	2
11	Upper	115	70	2
12	Upper	107	56	2
13	Mid	104	50	2
14	Mid	101	48	2
15	Mid	93	51	2
16	Lower	85	38	2
17	Lower	82	44	2
18	Bottom	79	36	2
19	Top	128	67	3
20	Upper	117	72	3
21	Upper	112	76	3
22	Mid	105	55	3
23	Mid	100	58	3
24	Mid	95	54	3
25	Lower	88	45	3
26	Lower	90	48	3
27	Bottom	80	32	3
28	Top	120	72	4
29	Upper	118	74	4
30	Upper	108	70	4
31	Mid	105	58	4
32	Mid	99	59	4
33	Mid	94	56	4
34	Lower	88	47	4
35	Lower	85	48	4
36	Bottom	79	38	4

*** ANALYSIS OF VARIANCE ***

SCORE
by TREAT
with IQ   UNIQUE sums of squares
         All effects entered simultaneously

Source of Variation	Sum of Squares	DF	Mean Square	F	Sig of F
Covariates	4741.739	1	4741.739	217.935	.000
IQ	4741.739	1	4741.739	217.935	.000
Main Effects	405.912	3	135.304	6.219	.002
TREAT	405.912	3	135.304	6.219	(.002)
Explained	5161.072	4	1290.268	59.302	.000
Residual	674.484	31	21.758		
Total	5835.556	35	166.730		

Covariate	Raw Regression Coefficient
IQ	.784

36 cases were processed.

0 cases (.0 pct) were missing.

FIGURE 18.5
SPSS-PC (version 6.1) data sheet and analysis of covariance, ANCOVA, output for data in Figure 18.2 (having been modified for input). From the main menu: **Statistics**, **ANOVA Models**, **Simple Factorial**, using **iq** as the covariate, were chosen

there is none primarily because the apparent difference is due to IQ (or some other covariate). For example, in spite of randomly selecting and assigning subjects to experimental and control groups, it is possible to have an imbalance in a potential covariate. Take the situation of Marvin Muchmore, who wished to test to see if there were any difference in the effectiveness of two sets of independent learning materials for a specific topic. He randomly divided his class into two groups and measured their learning through a post-test and obtained the results in Figure 18.6. He tested the difference in achievement using a *t*-test, as shown, but then thought he ought to take into account the students' IQ and checked again using analysis of covariance. Comparing the two sets of results, it becomes obvious that he did not have equivalent groups and the analysis of covariance was sensitive to this, showing no significant difference between them due to the treatment.

This is why not only carrying out random assignment but checking that one has equivalent groups is such an important aspect of the design and execution of a study. It also points up the need for statistical validity (selecting the appropriate test) in order to ensure validity of the conclusions.

In addition to the assumptions for analysis of variance, there are two new assumptions associated with employing analysis of covariance, both of which

	iq	treatmen	score
1	120.00	1	65.00
2	105.00	1	50.00
3	100.00	1	48.00
4	131.00	1	70.00
5	95.00	1	45.00
6	105.00	1	48.00
7	100.00	2	45.00
8	100.00	2	50.00
9	82.00	2	33.00
10	85.00	2	30.00
11	110.00	2	53.00
12	82.00	2	35.00

t-tests for Independent Samples of TREATMEN

Variable	Number of Cases	Mean	SD
SCORE			
TREATMEN 1	6	54.3333	10.443
TREATMEN 2	6	41.0000	9.612

Mean Difference = 13.3333

Levene's Test for Equality of Variances:
F = .046 P = .834   95%

t-test for Equality of Means

Variances	*t*-value	df	2-Tail Sig	SE of Diff
Equal	2.30	10	.044	5.795

*** ANALYSIS OF VARIANCE ***

SCORE
by TREATMEN
    with IQ   UNIQUE sums of squares
          All effects entered simultaneously

Source of Variation	Sum of Squares	DF	Mean Square	F	Sig of F
Covariates	940.911	1	940.911	127.491	.000
IQ	940.911	1	940.911	127.491	.000
Main Effects	1.856	1	1.856	.252	.628
TREATMEN	1.856	1	1.856	.252	.628
Explained	1474.245	2	737.122	99.878	.000
Residual	66.422	9	7.380		
Total	1540.667	11	140.061		

Covariate   Raw Regression Coefficient
IQ   .765

FIGURE 18.6
SPSS-PC data and two versions of analysis for Marvin Muchmore: *t*-test of scores and ANCOVA including IQ as covariate (note circled results)

will be explained and will help in understanding how analysis of covariance can find significant difference that exists when a plain ANOVA cannot:

- The relationship between the dependent variable and the covariate is linear – in other words, as the covariate increases so does the dependent variable. This indicates that we assumed that as IQ increases, so would scores on a test and if a graph were plotted between IQ and scores, the best-fit line would be straight and not curved.
- The regression coefficients across treatments are equal – in other words, if a set of graphs were plotted, one for each treatment, the best-fit straight lines formed would all have the same slope and consequently the lines would be parallel.

In order better to understand the implications of this, let us use the original data to illustrate *linear relationship* and *equal regression coefficients*. This will also provide a way to test these assumptions. If the data from SPSS are displayed in Excel and the four sets of dependent variables (scores) are moved to separate columns as shown in Figure 18.7, then it is possible to plot the scatter diagrams of IQ versus scores for each variable shown in Figure 18.8(b). Using an approach suggested by Huitema (1980), we will 'look' at the scatter diagram as the two tests do. The ANOVA test does not recognize the influence of IQ and, as far as it is concerned, IQ does not exist, therefore it 'sees' only four distributions that overlap greatly compared to their means, as shown in Figure 18.8(a), and assumes they are one distribution. Unknown to the ANOVA, each sample mean's observed score variance is made up of the score true variance, the IQ variance and error variance:

$$s^2_{\text{ANOVA obs}} = s^2_{\text{IQ}} + s^2_{\text{score}} + s^2_{\text{error}}$$

thus the square roots of the variances, the standard deviations, are also very large.

On the other hand, the ANCOVA test sees the data differently, as if it were 'looking' along the regression lines, as shown in Figure 18.8(c), and it has eliminated the variance contribution due to IQ to the observed score:

$$s^2_{\text{ANCOVA obs}} = s^2_{\text{score}} + s^2_{\text{error}}$$

Consequently the square roots, the standard deviations, are much smaller. With the narrower distributions, it is not surprising, then, that the ANCOVA test detects a significant difference across the four means when the ANOVA test does not.

The ANCOVA also adjusts for any horizontal displacement of the means due to larger variations from group to group in covariate means and adjusts the score means accordingly. As can be seen from Figure 18.7 data and 18.8(b) graphs, these do not differ much from the raw score means here, since all the IQ means are about 100. The adjusted mean values for each score are shown in Figure 18.7 in column H and these are reflected in Figure 18.8(c) graphs, where the mean for A has been shifted up slightly and that for D down slightly, spreading the means just that much more. The calculations and more details on the ANCOVA can be found in Huitema (1980), which provides the mathematics behind this test for those who are interested. Now carry out Activity 18.4.

REVISITING SOME OF THE DESIGNS

There are a few unresolved issues that need to be addressed before going on to nonparametric tests, including some possible controversies that have been glossed over above. Factorial ANOVA is quite appropriate for design B3 but more complex approaches may be better for some of the other experimental, quasi-experimental and ex post facto designs introduced earlier in this book. Since the development and refinement of statistical tests are continuous processes, judgements about appropriateness of these for types of designs may change with time and may vary with the text that you consult. Thus do not be surprised to find that some texts and possibly even your teacher may disagree about some of the finer points on applications of tests. We present here some contemporary views on what are seen as the most appropriate tests and problems of interpretation.

Interpreting studies that use gain scores

While gain scores present us with some advantages, they also introduce pitfalls other than the ones already described. As with many situations, the source of the problem of interpretation may reside in the choice of measuring instrument for the situation. For example, if the choice of task or instrument for measuring has a ceiling, in other words a maximum possible score or maximum possible achievement, then the results could be as shown in Figure 18.9(b). If it is not even possible for the control group to improve, how do we know that it was the treatment that caused the improvement and not something else? Remember that the role of the control group is to be exposed or susceptible to any extraneous variables that the treatment groups would be, in order to differentiate

	A	B	C	D	E	F	G	H
1	Group	IQ	A	B	C	D		
2	Top	130	70					
3	Upper	116	65					
4	Upper	108	60				s.d. A =	13.10
5	Mid	105	45				mean A =	49.56
6	Mid	100	50				r =	0.76
7	Mid	95	46				adj. s.d. A =	3.62
8	Lower	90	42				adj. mean A =	49.34
9	Lower	85	38				s.d. IQ =	16.65
10	Bottom	75	30				mean IQ =	100.44
11	Top	125		72				
12	Upper	115		70				
13	Upper	107		56			s.d. B =	12.63
14	Mid	104		50			mean B =	51.67
15	Mid	101		48			r =	0.76
16	Mid	93		51			adj. s.d. B =	4.34
17	Lower	85		38			adj. mean B =	52.58
18	Lower	82		44			s.d. IQ =	15.60
19	Bottom	79		36			mean IQ =	99.00
20	Top	128			67			
21	Upper	117			72			
22	Upper	112			76		s.d. C =	13.90
23	Mid	105			55		mean C =	56.33
24	Mid	100			58		r =	0.80
25	Mid	95			54		adj. s.d. C =	6.46
26	Lower	88			45		adj. mean C =	55.16
27	Lower	90			48		s.d. IQ =	15.35
28	Bottom	80			32		mean IQ =	101.67
29	Top	120				72		
30	Upper	118				74		
31	Upper	108				70	s.d. D =	12.36
32	Mid	105				58	mean D =	58.00
33	Mid	99				59	r =	0.83
34	Mid	94				56	s.d. D =	3.13
35	Lower	88				47	mean D =	58.48
36	Lower	85				48	s.d. IQ =	14.40
37	Bottom	79				38	mean IQ =	99.56

FIGURE 18.7
Data for scatter plots to display regression lines to determine linearity and equality of regression coefficients for covariate relationships in analysis of covariance in Figure 18.2

(a) The view from the side   (b) Regression lines for each variable and covariate

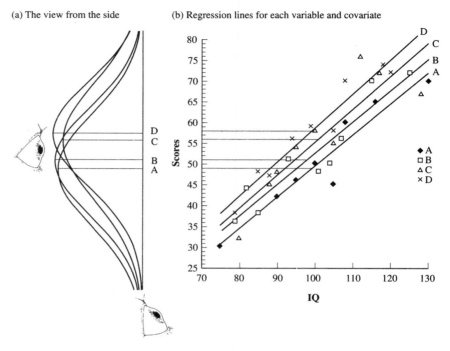

(c) The view up the regression lines

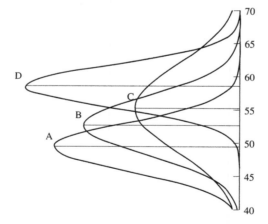

FIGURE 18.8
Different 'views' of
the data in (b):
(a) how ANOVA
sees the data, as if
there were no IQ
influence, and
(c) how ANCOVA
sees the data with
compensation for IQ

between effects due to treatments and extraneous variables. The opposite, a floor, could also exist where there is a desire to reduce a trait. The graph in Figure 18.9(a) shows a parallel situation where there is no obvious ceiling to the performance and, if the design were carried out properly, the influence of extraneous variables would have been apparent in the control group. While these look like the simple graphs used earlier to facilitate interpretation of factorial designs, do note that here it is the gain scores that would be the statistically analysed values.

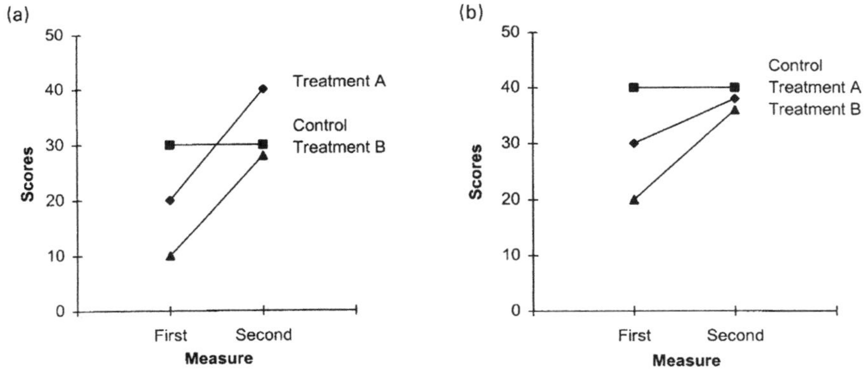

FIGURE 18.9
Some interpretable and uninterpretable results for studies using gain scores: (a) interpretable; (b) uninterpretable, due to ceiling effect

Experimental design B2 (pre- and post-test/observation) gain scores or ANCOVA?

Instead of using gain scores in a one-way or factorial design, it is possible to use the pre-test score as the covariate and the final scores as the dependent variable, employing analysis of covariance as the statistical test. Huitema (1980) maintains that there will be increased power from using ANCOVA when:

- the slope of the overall regression line is *not* equal or close to 1.0;
- the individual regression lines are (nearly) parallel.

This will be illustrated with two contrived examples, one where the overall regression coefficient (slope) for pre-versus post-test scores is approximately equal to 1.00 (thus the correlation between the pre-test and gain scores approaches zero), and the other when it is much greater than 1.00 (about 1.25). Imagine that, in the previous example, a pre-test was administered instead of an IQ test. Figure 18.10 contains the raw data, which uses the same post-test scores as for the ANCOVA example above, but the pre-test scores have been devised to provide an overall regression slope of about 1.00 (note the circled value: 0.988). The SPSS analysis for this, the first case, shows the difference.

By comparing the relevant F probabilities (in ovals), $0.0309 < 0.033$, we can infer that the ANOVA test is slightly more powerful than the ANCOVA since its probability is the lesser of the two. Considering the trial A data in Table 18.3, it is apparent that the slopes of all the regression lines are approximately equal

TABLE 18.3
Summary of descriptive statistics for the two trial situations

	Trial A				Trial B			
	1	2	3	4	1	2	3	4
Mean pre	43.11	44.89	48.33	48.22	43.11	44.89	48.33	48.22
Mean post	49.56	51.67	56.33	58.00	49.56	51.67	56.33	58.00
Adj. mean post	52.60	52.92	54.13	55.91	53.40	53.25	53.55	55.35
Adj. s.d. post	4.21	2.19	4.51	3.71	0.82	1.79	1.76	1.66
Mean gain	6.44	6.78	8.00	9.78	6.44	6.78	8.00	9.78
S.d. gain	2.07	2.39	2.45	2.91	2.88	3.07	3.24	3.11
b (slope)	1.01	0.93	1.10	0.93	1.27	1.25	1.25	1.27

	pretesta	posttesa	treata	gaina
1	65	70	1	5
2	59	65	1	6
3	52	60	1	8
4	40	45	1	5
5	40	50	1	10
6	38	46	1	8
7	35	42	1	7
8	32	38	1	6
9	27	30	1	3
10	65	72	2	7
11	64	70	2	6
12	52	56	2	4
13	43	50	2	7
14	44	48	2	4
15	44	51	2	7
16	30	38	2	8
17	32	44	2	12
18	30	36	2	6
19	54	67	3	13
20	63	72	3	9
21	66	76	3	10
22	50	55	3	5
23	52	58	3	6
24	46	54	3	8
25	38	45	3	7
26	40	48	3	8
27	26	32	3	6
28	60	72	4	12
29	64	74	4	10
30	60	70	4	10
31	51	58	4	7
32	54	59	4	5
33	48	56	4	8
34	36	47	4	11
35	33	48	4	15
37	28	38	4	10

*** ONE WAY ***

Variable GAINA
by Variable TREATA

Analysis of Variance

Source	DF	Sum of Squares	Mean Squares	F Ratio	F Prob.
Between Groups	3	61.4167	20.4722	3.3538	.0309
Within Groups	32	195.3333	6.1042		
Total	35	256.7500			

*** ANALYSIS OF VARIANCE ***

POSTTESA
by TREATA
with PRETESTA

UNIQUE sums of squares
All effects entered simultaneously

Source of Variation	Sum of Squares	DF	Mean Square	F	Sig of F
Covariates	5221.708	1	5221.708	832.191	.000
PRETESTA	5221.708	1	5221.708	832.191	.000
Main Effects	62.138	3	20.713	3.301	.033
TREATA	62.138	3	20.713	3.301	.033
		4			
Explained	5641.041	31	1410.260	224.755	.000
Residual	194.514	35	6.275		
Total	5835.556		166.730		

Covariate	Raw Regression Coefficient
PRETESTA	.988

FIGURE 18.10
Results comparing ANOVA on gain scores with ANCOVA on post-test scores with pre-test as covariate: trial A

and therefore the lines are roughly parallel, satisfying the basic requirement for ANCOVA. Also note the differences in s.d. between Trials A and B.

Now look at Figure 18.11, where the same post-test scores and the same mean gain scores are used, but the pre-test scores have been devised to generate regression line slopes of about 1.26. When the SPSS analyses are compared, not only has the ANCOVA test detected a difference when the ANOVA using gain scores has not, but we can infer that it has much greater power by comparing the relevant F probabilities (circled), noting that $0.027 << 0.1121$. Looking at the summary data for this in Table 18.3, (trial B), the lines should again be parallel, but the slope is about 1.26, as indicated by the circled value in Figure 18.11. If the gain scores are the same, what has changed so that the ANOVA does not recognize a difference across the treatments?

This is where comparing the raw data in Figures 18.11 and 18.12 gives a clue. In trial A, the increases followed no relationship between gain score and pretest, whereas in trial B the subjects with lower pre-test scores tended to have smaller gains than those with higher pre-test scores. In other words, those

	pretestb	posttesb	treatb	gainb
1	59	70	1	11
2	55	65	1	10
3	51	60	1	9
4	41	45	1	4
5	44	50	1	6
6	40	46	1	6
7	37	42	1	5
8	34	38	1	4
9	27	30	1	3
10	59	72	2	13
11	59	70	2	11
12	50	56	2	6
13	45	50	2	5
14	42	48	2	6
15	46	51	2	5
16	32	38	2	6
17	39	44	2	5
18	32	36	2	4
19	55	67	3	12
20	60	72	3	12
21	65	76	3	11
22	47	55	3	8
23	51	58	3	7
24	45	54	3	9
25	40	45	3	5
26	44	48	3	4
27	28	32	3	4
28	58	72	4	14
29	59	74	4	15
30	59	70	4	11
31	50	58	4	8
32	50	59	4	9
33	47	56	4	9
34	38	47	4	9
35	40	48	4	8
37	33	38	4	5

*** ONE WAY ***

Variable GAINB
by Variable TREATB

Analysis of Variance

Source	DF	Sum of Squares	Mean Squares	F Ratio	F Prob.
Between Groups	3	61.4167	20.4722	2.1597	.1121
Within Groups	32	303.3333	9.4792		
Total	35	364.7500			

*** ANALYSIS OF VARIANCE ***

POSTTESB   UNIQUE sums of squares
by TREATB   All effects entered simultaneously
with PRETESTB

Source of Variation	Sum of Squares	DF	Mean Square	F	Sig of F
Covariates	5337.801	1	5337.801	2110.041	.000
PRETESTB	5337.801	1	5337.801	2110.041	.000
Main Effects	26.610	3	8.870	3.506	.027
TREATB	26.610	3	8.870	3.506	.027
Explained	5757.134	4	1439.284	568.951	.000
Residual	78.421	31	2.530		
Total	5835.556	35	166.730		

Covariate   Raw Regression Coefficient
PRETESTB   1.258

FIGURE 18.11
Results comparing ANOVA on gain scores with ANCOVA on post-test scores with pre-test as covariate: trial B

who started out high did even better than those who started out low. Thus the interpretation of the results would need to reflect such relationships. The problem is it would be easy to interpret the ANCOVA results for both of these the same: 'there was a significant difference across the treatments, with learners doing better for some treatments than others, where the pre-test was the covariate'. More accurately, this would need to be qualified in trial B to say: 'but learners who had lower pre-test scores did not tend to gain as much as those with higher pre-test scores for all treatments'.

Thus, not only is the ANCOVA test more likely to find a significant difference in some cases (greater power), but it does so for a sound reason: when there is a definite relationship (correlation) between pre-test scores and gain scores. Interestingly, this can be shown another way, by plotting a scatter diagram for pre-test versus gain scores for the two trials, as shown in Figure 18.12. Note the slope for trial A is almost zero, and the distribution of diamonds shows no relationship, where the distribution of squares (trial B) shows a trend upwards and the slope is about 0.27. Yes, if you add 1.00 to each of these you get the regression slope between pre-test and post-test, so you see why it is said that ANCOVA is more powerful when the slope is much different from 1.00. It takes into account these hidden relationships. The same would be true of situations where there was a negative relationship between the pre-test scores and gain scores: the lower the pre-test the greater the gain. These would result in overall regression slopes of much less than 1.00.

Thus to test whether or not ANCOVA or ANOVA is the most appropriate test for experimental design B2, all that is necessary is to find the slopes of the regression lines between pre- and post-test scores. (If this is not an obvious process to you now, it is covered in Chapter 21.) If they are roughly equal, thus the regression lines are parallel, *and* much different from 1.00, then there is a

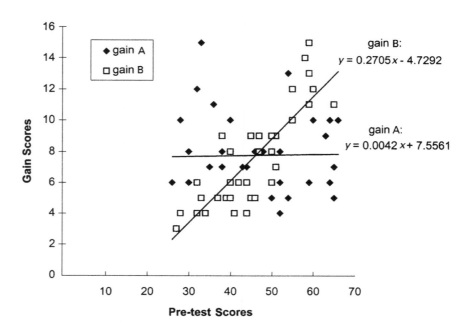

FIGURE 18.12
Scatter diagrams for gain scores versus pre-test for the example

definite advantage to using analysis of covariance, but one must take care when interpreting the results.

Until recently, one argument for using ANOVA with gain scores rather than ANCOVA was the difficulty in carrying out the calculations. Assuming that one can struggle through using occasionally unfriendly software, there are sufficient packages available to do the ANCOVA computations to eliminate this reason. The issues are now reduced to ones parallel to those which govern the use of other statistical tests:

- Which test is most appropriate?
- Have the assumptions been met?
- Are the results interpretable?
- Which is the more powerful?

This requires the researcher to understand the nature of his or her design, the variables and the measuring instruments, and to anticipate the nature of alternative conclusions, depending on the possible outcomes of the statistical tests.

Quasi-experimental design C2 (non-equivalent groups with pre- and post-tests)

Recall that this design involves using intact groups assigned to treatments, such as classrooms, work groups, therapy groups and even social groups. While this can result in enhancing external validity since the sample situation is closer to reality than randomly selecting individuals and unnaturally grouping them, threats to other forms of validity arise. This design presents some unique problems for control of potentially extraneous variables which can reduce internal validity. Such studies may also violate the assumption of independence of observation. For example, student responses in a class may not be the product of just their thinking, and interactions in a therapy session may be due to the constituents of the group as much as the approach employed. This would threaten the validity of using any test based upon analysis of variance.

The lack of random selection may reduce external validity and the ability to generalize to people though it may enhance generalization to situations, but lack of random assignment even with matched sample groups would jeopardize internal validity due to lack of control of life-event variables. In such cases, even ANCOVA would not preserve the validity of the conclusions (see Huitema, 1980). If the groups are randomly assigned to treatments *and* the group means for the covariate are very close, then ANCOVA becomes more justifiable.

As was seen above, the ANCOVA process produces *adjusted means* for the independent variable for treatment groups. These are based upon the covariate means that correspond to the means for the independent variable, and *project* what the means for treatment groups would be if all groups had the same grand covariate mean. In the example above, the adjusted means were little different from the original group means for scores simply because all of the covariate means were very close to the grand mean. But note the use of the word *project*, as these values are no more than predications based upon correlational relationships. There is no assumption of causality, thus it is not assumed that IQ *causes* higher scores, though we would expect higher scores for those with higher IQ. Why this is true could be due to one of at least three reasons:

- IQ does cause higher scores.
- The experience of learning and getting higher scores increases IQ.
- A third factor, say aptitude (defined as time needed to learn) or the quality of the schools from which each group comes contributes to both.

The jury is still out, the arguments still continue about the relative roles of nature and nurture in determining IQ and what aspects or components of learning IQ influences. The correlational relationship exists, but any causal links are still being argued. Thus for non-equivalent groups, it is not sufficient to say that because the adjusted means are equivalent, the results from the ANCOVA test can be used to support causality, but that at best the results support a correlational relationship. Even worse, the groups could be so far apart that there would be no justification for extrapolating to a point where the covariate means were equal to the grand mean. For example, comparing treatments on two existing groups where one is a special education class whose mean IQ is 70 and the other an 'advanced' class whose mean IQ is 115, ignores so many other variables by simply extrapolating to the situation of a common mean of, say, 92. These situations would not exist in reality. Lack of control over extraneous variables in situations of non-equivalent groups should temper the interpretation of any results. If you intend to pursue such an approach, you are encouraged to consider such sources as Huitema (1980), who provides more detailed discussion of typical situations and the problems that may arise.

Viewing it another way, the problem is one of burden of proof that lies with the researcher. Either provide some justification for accepting that the groups are equivalent, or it must be assumed that they are not. If pre-test scores are roughly equivalent for the trait, then this offers some support for equivalence, but, as will be noted below, even this is not foolproof. If they are grossly different, then using gain scores may still result in uninterpretable results for non-equivalent groups.

For example, Figure 18.13 provides some examples of interpretable and uninterpretable results. What we are looking for here is the nature of the underlying changes, which may be the source of uninterpretability. In Figure 18.13(a), it is assumed that the gain score for treatment A is significantly different from those for treatment B and the control. This is interpretable because their pre-test scores are almost the same, thus it could be maintained that the three groups started off equivalent for the trait.

In Figure 18.13(b), treatment A gain is again significantly different from the control, but the groups do not start off the same. Also, each of the second scores is double the first, thus the differences were probably due to something other than the treatments (for example, time or maturation). Had there been little or no increase in the control group over the same period of time, then the significant differences might have been interpretable. One cannot trust statistical significance alone in situations such as this.

Additional in-depth discussion of the alternative tests for and problems associated with this design can be found in Reichardt (1979) and Huitema (1980: Chapters 14 and 15). These are worthwhile references to consult if this design is to be used, as they discuss the advantages and disadvantages of various tests depending on different conditions.

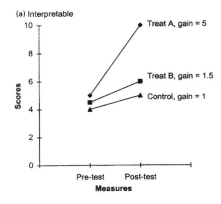

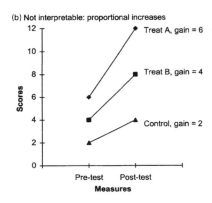

FIGURE 18.13
Some interpretable and uninterpretable results for quasi-experimental studies:
(a) interpretable;
(b) uninterpretable, due to proportional increases

Ex post facto designs and life-event variables: D3 (post-test/observation only)

Interpreting the outcomes of designs that include at least one life-event variable can present some interesting challenges. When formulating hypotheses and testing for significance across such life-event variables, it is often not reasonable to speak of these in terms of causality. It is difficult to justify saying that gender *causes* a difference in performance of a task, or that education level *causes* people to consume certain products at different levels. For example, even if gender differences resulted in different responses to learning approaches in computing, this would not indicate that being a girl *causes* one to learn less well under an approach than if one were a boy. While there may be a gender-associated cause, such as culturally biased attitudes that encourage boys more than girls to participate in computing, or there are learning materials that are more appealing to boys than girls, being a girl does not cause the difference. If there were an identifiable cause, it would more than likely be something like cultural influences, societal expectations, peer pressure, etc. What could be said is there is a high association between the variables, tendencies that allow predictions. This sounds more like the outcome of a correlational study, and some authors would maintain that ex post facto studies, or ones employing life-event variables, should be considered correlational (see, for example, Grimm, 1993). Alternatively, it could be said the designs provide much stronger evidence for relationships than correlations, but that, since the variables are macro-variables and there is a longer chain of events involved, one must simply take care in wording the hypotheses and conclusions. Direct causality can be an elusive relationship to establish, and it is even more complicated when life-event variables are involved. It may well be that only differences can be confirmed without establishing causal links.

Time series designs

As described in Chapter 7, time series designs consist of a series of observations or measures on a single group, with a treatment in the sequence. The research question tends to ask whether the treatment makes a difference over time. Designs of this type demand a number of measures on one or more groups to resolve the issue. The simplest time series designs, such as C6 described in Chapter 7, employ only one group and are described as follows:

$$(RS) \rightarrow O_1 \rightarrow O_2 \rightarrow O_3 \rightarrow X \rightarrow O_4 \rightarrow O_5 \rightarrow O_6$$

Obviously, a second control group with no treatment, for comparison, would be advantageous, but we will focus on the basic single-group design. The choice of statistical test will depend on the number of observations and the nature of the outcome.

A number of analytic approaches depend on regression lines and their analysis, which will be considered later. McCain and McCleary (1979) provide an extensive discussion of procedures that are appropriate when a large number of observations are made (more than 50), but suggest that, for a small number of observations, repeated measures analysis of variance is appropriate. Howell (1997) elaborates on the design, maintaining the need for ensuring the homogeneity of variance and covariance for such studies to preserve internal validity. Though this is not the only statistical test that may be appropriate for such a design, it is assumed that for most small- to moderate-scale research this test will be one of the most likely to be used and will be described here.

Let us first consider a range of possible outcomes and how they might be interpreted. If the outcomes were as clear as those illustrated in pattern (a) or (b) in Figure 7.8, then life would be simple: just use a t-test where the change is. While a repeated measures ANOVA with post hoc comparisons might detect differences in all four of the situations (a)–(d) illustrated in Figure 7.8, each presents its own problem of interpretation of the sets of six measures:

(a)   If the first three were significantly different from the last three, then one could conclude that there was a sustained difference, at least for the time period shown.

(b)   If the first four were significantly different from the last two, then the delay in the effect being felt would be confirmed.

(c)   If the fourth one were the only one significantly different from the other five, then the non-sustainable nature of the effect would be confirmed.

(d)   Even if some of these were different – say, the first two and the last two observations – the nature of the progressive increase suggests there was no impact from the treatment.

The reality is that there is usually considerably more 'noise' in the data than is seen in these simple graphs, and data appear more akin to the situation in Figure 7.9. When the noise – the seemingly random ups and downs – is considerable, it may be more appropriately analysed using regression-based techniques. The problem with many of these situations is the same for any design without a control group; it is a challenge to ensure that this did not happen because of some other event that coincided with the treatment of interest. Also, this design is highly prone to measurement effects, and consequently would benefit from non-intrusive observation techniques. In other words, a measure consisting of a series of questionnaires over time could constitute a serious extraneous variable, though in others it might be just a matter of becoming used to completing the instrument.

Try Activity 18.5 which presents a simple time series design that can be resolved by using the repeated measures ANOVA in the randomized block worksheet, checking the variance–covariance matrix.

Activity 18.5

Professor Inno Vate wanted to explore the impact of use of colour in overhead transparencies on student attitudes. He approached one of his classes and asked them to complete a short questionnaire on his lectures as part of a self-improvement programme. For the first three weeks, he used overhead transparencies designed with a professional software package but in monochrome (black and white with grey shading). For the last three weeks, he produced them using a colour laser printer. The results from the questionnaires are provided in Table 18.4.

Expand a copy of the worksheet in Figure 18.3 to six observations.

1   Sketch a graph of means over time to illustrate the results.
2   Carry out a repeated measures ANOVA, checking the variance–covariance matrix. Choose an appropriate post hoc analysis for pairwise comparisons. Show the results as treatments in overlapping boxes as before (Venn diagrams).
3   Interpret the results: did using colour influence the class's attitudes?
4   Identify the limitations of this study, including sources of invalidity. How could it be improved?

Answers
2   See Figure 18.14.
3

| O6   O5 | O4 | O3   O2   O1 |

Yes, but there was an apparent time delay of a lesson.
4   What else might have influenced the results? For example, improved lectures or more relaxed lecturer, change of subject matter, etc. A parallel 'control' group which did not have colour transparencies might provide the evidence needed to resolve the hypothesis.

TABLE 18.4
The results of Inno Vate's experiment

	O1	O2	O3	O4	O5	O6
a	10	9	11	10	11	12
b	8	7	9	10	11	11
c	11	10	12	13	14	13
d	10	9	7	9	11	12
e	8	14	12	14	14	15
f	11	13	12	11	12	13
g	11	8	9	12	9	10
h	9	11	11	11	14	13
i	12	10	13	12	15	14
j	13	12	10	12	14	14

	SS	df	MS	F	p value	F_{crit}	α
Btwn Grps (treat/time)	59.00	5	11.80	6.99	0.0001	2.42	0.05
Btwn Subj	97.60	9	10.84				
Interaction	76.00	45	1.69				
Within	173.60	54	3.21				
Total	232.60	59					

post hoc	12.70	12.50	11.40	10.60	10.30	10.30	$\tilde{n} = 10.0$		Test
differences	**O6**	**O5**	**O4**	**O3**	**O2**	**O1**	r	M_{min}	NK
O6		0.20	1.30	2.10	2.40	2.40	6	1.83	4.22
O5			1.10	1.90	2.20	2.20	5	1.75	4.03
O4				0.80	1.10	1.10	4	1.64	3.78
O3					0.30	0.30	3	1.49	3.43
O2						0.00	2	1.24	2.86

FIGURE 18.14
Repeated measures for ANOVA for Question 2 of Activity 18.5

Solomon four design

This design was put forward as the 'ideal' basic experimental design because it allowed for the control of testing effects that was lacking in design B2. Diagramatically, the basic design was as follows:

$$RS \longrightarrow \begin{cases} RA_a \longrightarrow O_{a1} \longrightarrow X_a \longrightarrow O_{a2} \\ RA_0 \longrightarrow O_{01} \longrightarrow X_0 \longrightarrow O_{02} \\ \\ RA'_a \longrightarrow \quad\quad\quad\quad X_a \longrightarrow O'_{a2} \\ RA'_0 \longrightarrow \quad\quad\quad\quad X_0 \longrightarrow O'_{02} \end{cases}$$

Though a single test is unlikely to answer all the questions, Campbell and Stanley (1963) and Kerlinger (1986) support Solomon's (1949) original suggestion that the appropriate test would be a 2×2 factorial ANOVA using all four O_2 measures (see Figure 7.7). Campbell and Stanley suggest that if there were no difference between the pre-tested and not pre-tested groups, then the full results of first two groups should be used in an ANCOVA test with the pre-tests as covariate. Though the added cost in resources seems to have restricted the implementation of this design, it does present an interesting possibility. Activity 18.6 provides an example to consider for those who wish to investigate this design further.

Activity 18.6

Mary Smith worked for a government agency that assisted new immigrants in finding employment. Some complaints had been made that staff were not sympathetic to the adjustment problems of clients. Mary had acquired some informal evidence that a film which aimed at increasing understanding of the backgrounds of new immigrants improved viewers' attitudes and responsiveness. She wished to confirm this before distributing the video throughout the organization, but she was concerned that any pre-test measure might antagonize subjects, making them less receptive to the 'treatment'. She decided to carry out a study employing a Solomon four design. She randomly assigned 24 employees to four groups; two groups saw a travel film on the South Sea islands (control) and two saw the video in question. The results of the post-viewing attitude measure are provided below.

Post-test	So. Sea	video
pre-test	25	36
	30	32
	34	34
	29	24
	21	30
no pre-test	26	34
	33	30
	36	37
	25	30
	27	28

Use the factorial ANOVA worksheet in Figure 17.14, or **Data Analysis, Anova: Two-Factor with Replication** in Excel (with the input range including labels), to determine whether the pre-test did influence the outcomes.

Answers

There appears (see Figure 18.15) to be no pre-test influence. Though there is no significant difference between the treatment and control group post-tests, an ANCOVA test should be carried out to determine whether there is a significant difference between the pre-test and post-test scores: did the attitudes *improve*? If you have access to SPSS, the data are provided in Figure 18.16 and you should find $F = 5.976$ ($p < 0.05$).

ANOVA	SS	df	MS (s^2)	F	p value	F_{crit}	α
Test	6.05	1	6.05	0.29	0.595	4.49	0.05
Treatment	42.05	1	42.05	2.04	0.172	4.49	0.05
A × B	1.25	1	1.25	0.06	0.809	4.49	0.05
Within	329.60	16	20.60				
Total		19					

FIGURE 18.15
Factorial ANOVA
for Activity 18.6

pre-test	post-test	treatment
24	25	1
30	30	1
35	34	1
28	29	1
20	21	1
26	36	2
28	32	2
33	34	2
22	24	2
24	30	2

FIGURE 18.16
Data format for SPSS
ANCOVA

SUMMARY

In Chapters 13–18 a wide range of statistical tests for interval/ratio data have been presented, with reference to the designs described in Part I of the book. These have covered experimental, quasi-experimental and ex post facto designs, and combinations of these. Obviously, it is possible to devise even more complex schemes that require extensions of the statistical tests presented here. The foundation skills and understanding acquired should make it possible to understand and use more advanced tests presented in specialist texts. Also, like most academic areas, statistics is evolving and changing. The understanding of the parametric tests presented here should provide you with the basis for keeping up with advancements and new applications that appear in the future.

Furthermore, the aim of engaging you in decision-making about the most appropriate test for a given study should provide a basis for planning statistical tests for your own research. The criteria are sometimes numerous, but taking them into account should help to ensure a high level of statistical validity and, in turn, enhance the overall validity of any conclusions.

Related to this has been the inherent difficulty in interpreting results. While the problems presented in activities have been contrived in order best to illustrate statistical principles, there has also been the aim to expose you to a variety of issues. There have been situations where the statistics seem to do their job of resolving the hypotheses but the choice of variables could have been better. Poor sampling and loss of subjects can be compensated by some statistical manipulation, but not always. Controlling extraneous variables requires a combination of careful planning and execution, sometimes necessitating a decision on the most appropriate statistical test. Poor choices can result in finding ghosts or missing valuable opportunities.

By now, it is hoped that you have acquired a healthy respect for the potential of statistical tests as well as an understanding of their limitations. Like any intellectual tool, they can be used to great benefit for further understanding and decision support, or for deception, either intentional or accidental. They cannot make decisions for you. In the planning of research, the application of statistics requires as much attention as any of the other tools introduced here.

Up to now, all the tests have been *parametric* tests, involving dependent variables that result in interval or ratio data. There will be numerous situations where such data do not exist and ordinal or nominal data will be the most meaningful measure of dependent variables. While determining how strongly people feel about different political parties may be of great interest in some situations, just how many voted for each one will be of prime interest to other research. Analysis of frequencies for nominal or ordinal categories requires a different type of statistical test, the subject of the next two chapters.

PART V
NONPARAMETRIC TESTS:
NOMINAL AND
ORDINAL VARIABLES

NONPARAMETRIC TESTS: ONE AND TWO SAMPLES

19

There will be times when the data collected for variables will not meet the assumptions on which parametric tests are based. The distributions may be extremely non-normal and/or lack homogeneity of variance. Alternatively, the data may not be continuous (being ordinal or categorical instead) and, in any case, will not be appropriately described by means and standard deviations. At the most basic level, consider the following two examples that illustrate the problem of determining whether a sample can be considered part of a population:

- We wish to know if a minority group tended to have incomes *consistent* with those of the overall population. If the random sample from the group were asked to report their income exactly and comparable population data existed, then the question could be answered using a *z*-test that used means and standard deviations. On the other hand, had the question asked respondents to indicate in which of 10 unequal income ranges theirs fell, then the data would be ordinal and a different test would be needed.

- To investigate whether a group was as politically conservative as the population, an instrument measuring 'conservativeness' could be devised that would provide a sufficiently large range of scores to be considered interval data. Therefore the issue could be resolved using the *z*-test. Alternatively, a possibly less precise indicator would be voting patterns and the group's voting record for conservative candidates or political parties as compared to the population. Here the voting frequencies for candidates or parties would be nominal, again requiring a test other than the *z*-test.

As we will see, there are parallels that use frequencies for ordinal and nominal categories for all the experimental, quasi-experimental and ex post facto designs considered earlier. While the nonparametric tests that correspond to the parametric ones introduced in the previous chapters tend to have lower power, there are often very good reasons for using nominal or interval data. In the first example above, it may well be that because of buying power and tax structures, carefully chosen income ranges are actually more meaningful indicators of economic well-being than raw income to test consistency between the group and the population. As to the second example, one might argue that actions speak louder than words and if you really want to know how a person feels about politics, look at how he or she votes. Both sides of this argument have pitfalls, but it does place the resolution of the issue in the province of the research question and measuring instrument rather than simply arguing over which is the most powerful statistical test. The literature is not without ardent proponents of parametric and nonparametric tests, sometimes to the extreme of advocating the exclusion of the 'opposition'. Taking the view that statistical tests are tools, selecting the best one for the job seems a more rational approach, one that requires weighing up all the implications and interrelations between the various aspects of the research design. Choosing to collect ordinal data may lower the statistical power, but this may be the best operational definition of the concept, increasing both construct and statistical validity. Taking into account all the influences on the overall validity of the outcomes of a study is much more difficult than having a simple answer to the question of what statistical test to employ based upon power alone.

This chapter will introduce a number of tests that allow us to use nominal and ordinal data and to resolve hypotheses involving representativeness of a sample, and comparing two independent groups, design B3/D3 (post-test with control group). The next chapter will consider analogues to two matched groups and the analysis of variance. The tests covered here are, for one-sample cases (comparing a group with the population),

- the chi-square χ^2 goodness-of-fit test, for nominal dependent variables and
- the Kolmogorov–Smirnov test for ranked dependent variables;

for cases of two independent samples (comparing two groups to each other for levels of the independent variable),

- the Kolmogorov–Smirnov test for ordinal dependent variables;
- the Wilcoxon–Mann–Whitney test for independent samples from ordinal dependent variables and
- the χ^2-test for independent samples from nominal dependent variables.

Table 19.1 summarizes the roles of these tests, showing their parametric counterparts, and also the tests to be covered in the next chapter, again with their parametric counterparts. This chapter will start in the lower left-hand corner and work around the four cells clockwise, in order best to compare and contrast the techniques.

ONE-SAMPLE TESTS

Chi-square test

Since many nonparametric tests are based upon this one, we will start with the *chi-square* (χ^2) *test*. Historically this has its origins in a very old test, but since

TABLE 19.1
Nonparametric tests to be covered in this chapter and the next, with parametric counterparts covered earlier [chapter numbers in brackets]

Measure (optimal)	One sample	Two groups Independent	Two groups Related/ matched	Three or more groups Independent	Three or more groups Related/matched
Interval/ ratio	z-test [13] t-test ($n < 30$)	t-tests [15]	t_{rel}-test [15]	one-way ANOVA [16] factorial ANOVA [17]	randomized block ANOVA [18] ANCOVA [18]
Ordinal	Kolmogorov–Smirnov test [19]	Kolmogorov–Smirnov test Wilcoxon–Mann–Whitney test [19]	Wilcoxon signed ranks test [20]	Kruskal–Wallis one-way analysis of variance [20]	Friedman two-way analysis of variance by ranks [20]
Nominal	χ^2-test, goodness of fit [19]	χ^2-test, $k \times 2$ tables [19]	McNemar change test [20]	χ^2-test for $m \times k$ tables [20]	Cochran Q-test [20]

parametric tests were introduced first in this text, it is more meaningful to use them as the starting point. Recall from Chapter 13 that the z-test for determining the likelihood of a sample belonging to a population based upon the sample and population means score is expressed as equation (13.3):

$$z = \frac{\bar{x} - \mu}{\sigma_{\bar{x}}} \tag{19.1}$$

where $\sigma_{\bar{x}}$ is the standard deviation of the distribution of sampling means for all possible samples of a given size. The value of the z-score tells us how many standard deviations away from the population mean score the mean of the sample in question is, which in turn can be translated into the probability that sample would have been selected at random from the population. This assumes that the values for x are normally distributed.

For the present discussion, as we will see, this has more value to us if expressed as a square:

$$z^2 = \frac{(\bar{x} - \mu)^2}{\sigma_{\bar{x}}^2} \tag{19.2}$$

where the denominator now contains a variance instead of a standard deviation (the squared standard error of the mean). Imagine that a population is randomly sampled a large number of times, the values for $\bar{x}$ being recorded and each of the z^2 values calculated, and the frequency plotted on a graph. This would result in something like Figure 19.1. Not surprising, the most likely $\bar{x}$ will be close to μ, resulting in z^2 being maximum as it approaches 0 (in other words, no difference). This is seen from the curve rising sharply as z^2 approaches zero.

Now if the sample were from a distribution that did not represent continuous data, but frequencies of occurrences, then we would have to change equation (19.2). These are situations where instead of measuring a trait on a scale producing a score for each subject, a subject simply either belongs to a group or does

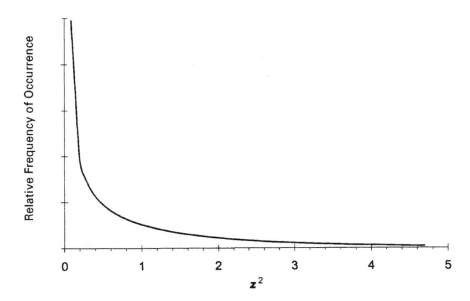

FIGURE 19.1
Consequences of
repeated sampling
from a population

not, as in the case of tossing a fair and balanced coin or being male or female, where there are only two equally possible outcomes. Let us consider an example to show how this works. If we were repeatedly to take random samples of 12 subjects from the population of all people, we would be able to generate a frequency table of how many times there would be 1, 2, 3, 4, 5, 6, 7, 8, 9, 10, 11 and 12 females in a group. If this were plotted on a graph, a distribution such as the one shown in Figure 19.2 would be produced. Not surprisingly, 6 females in a sample of 12 is the most common occurrence, but others are possible and probable. It turns out that the mean and standard deviation of such distributions (referred to as *binomial* since there are only two possible categories to belong to) are found by

$$\text{mean} = Np$$
$$\text{variance} = Npq$$
$$\text{standard deviation} = \sqrt{Npq}$$

where N is the sample size, p is the probability of occurrence of the event whose distribution we are interested in, and q is the complement of p, that is, $1 - p$. Thus, for the example in Figure 19.2, p is the probability of the person being female, and q the probability of that person not being female. Obviously since we are dealing with equally possible outcomes, we have in this case $q = p = 0.50$. So, we would expect

$$\text{mean} = 12 \times 0.50 = 6$$
$$\text{variance} = 12 \times 0.50 \times 0.50 = 3.0$$
$$\text{standard deviation} = 1.73$$

In other words, we would expect on average six females in a group. Looking at Figure 19.2, this is not an unreasonable result.

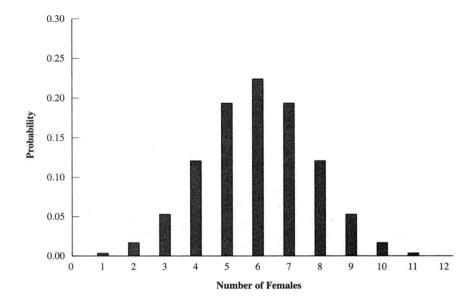

FIGURE 19.2
Probability
distribution of
females for samples
of 12 from the whole
population of people
in the world

Now let us consider what would happen if we were to sample a *special* population, such as the nursing profession where there tends to be more females than males (let us assume 80% female). Now the distribution would be different. The expected mean number of females for samples of 12 nurses would be

$$\text{mean} = 12 \times 0.80 = 9.6$$
$$\text{variance} = 12 \times 0.80 \times 0.20 = 1.92$$
$$\text{standard deviation} = 1.386$$

As an example of how this can be used, let us ask whether a hospital ward with 12 nurses, only six of whom are female, would be considered representative of the nursing population. If we plot a normal curve with mean 9.6 and standard deviation 1.386, on top of the sampling distribution, we obtain the graph shown in Figure 19.3. If our ward sample value of 6 is taken as the 'mean' of the sample and is located on the graph, it would be possible to determine the probability of this sample being part of the population. Looking at the graph it is difficult to tell, but referring to the z-table (Table B.1 in Appendix B), using the equivalent z-score,

$$z = \frac{6 - 9.6}{1.386} = -2.60$$

the area beyond which is 0.0047. In other words, it is highly unlikely, and using our standard of $p = 0.05$, which is $p = 0.025$ in each tail, it would be concluded that this group is not typical of the nursing profession with respect to gender proportions. Obviously, this is an approximation, one that gets better as the sample size increases and the number of columns under the curve increases.

This is basically the same procedure as used in Chapter 13 to determine whether a sample is probably representative of a larger population based

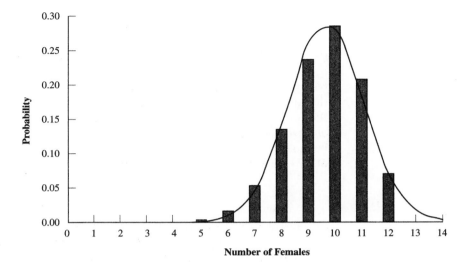

FIGURE 19.3
Sampling distribution for nurses (assuming 80% of nurses are female) for samples of 12, with the ideal normal distribution superimposed

upon a characteristic that generates interval data. Alternatively, we could calculate z^2 using equation (19.2), which would be

$$z^2 = \frac{(6 - 9.6)^2}{1.92} = 6.75$$

and consult the distribution of relative frequency of occurrence versus z^2 in Figure 19.1. Here we see that this sample would show up well out into the tail on the right, making it highly unlikely. This distribution is referred to as the *chi-square* (or χ^2) distribution. Since tables for all values are not readily available, we can determine what the probability is most easily by consulting the appropriate Excel function for this distribution. The degrees of freedom are 1, since there are two alternatives, male and female. If we know how many females there are, then the number of males is known, and as before, *df* is equal to the number of possible categories less one, that is, one. Thus, we have in Excel,

CHIDIST(value, *df*) = CHIDIST(6.75, 1) = 0.0094

This is exactly twice the probability for the z-test carried out above, since the z-distribution is a two-tailed distribution. Using the χ^2-distribution offers greater flexibility and ease of calculation, therefore we will use it for nominal data.

To make this possible requires a new equation that will be easier to use to calculate a result. First, let us alter our z^2 equation (19.2) to take into account that we will be using frequency data. Assume, as we did before, that the frequency observed for the category, designated as O, is used as the mean for the sample. Inserting this and our binomial values for population means and standard deviations, equation (19.2) becomes

$$\chi^2 = z^2 = \frac{(O - Np)^2}{Npq}$$

which, by some devious algebra, can be shown to equal

$$\chi^2 = \frac{(O - Np)^2}{Np} + \frac{(N - O - Nq)^2}{Nq} \qquad (19.3)$$

(If you really want to show they are equal, start with equation (19.3) and expand it, then place everything over the common denominator Npq. While working backwards, remember that $p + q = 1$, so substitute $q = 1 - p$). If we recognize that a group must belong to one category or the other, then we can write O, the number *observed* belonging to one category, as O_1; $N - O$, the number *observed* belonging to the other category, as O_2; Np, the number *expected* to belong to one category, as E_1; and Nq the number *expected* to belong to the other category, as E_2. Thus, rewriting in terms of our newly named variables,

$$\chi^2 = \frac{(O_1 - E_1)^2}{E_1} + \frac{(O_2 - E_2)^2}{E_2} \qquad (19.4)$$

To illustrate this let us return to the example about nurses in a hospital ward where there are $O_1 = 6$ female nurses observed in the hospital, $O_2 = 6$ male nurses observed in the hospital, $E_1 = 9.6$ female nurses expected if 80% of nurses are female, and $E_2 = 2.4$ male nurses expected if 20% of nurses are male, Therefore, from equation (19.4), not surprisingly, we get the same value found for z^2 above:

$$\chi^2 = \frac{(6 - 9.6)^2}{9.6} + \frac{(6 - 2.4)^2}{2.4} = 1.35 + 5.40 = 6.75$$

Now the real advantage of using this form is that we can increase the number of groups and equation (19.4) simply acquires more terms, one for each category. This means that the general equation for χ^2, also known as the Pearson chi-square statistic, after its inventor, Karl Pearson, is

$$\chi^2 = \sum_{i=1}^{m} \frac{(O_i - E_i)^2}{E_i} \qquad (19.5)$$

where O_i represents the observed frequencies, from the sample; E_i the expected frequencies, determined from population values; and i stands for the categories, ranging from 1 to m. This statistic is referred to a table of critical values such as Table B.9 in Appendix B, and has $m - 1$ degrees of freedom.

To illustrate this, let us consider another example. Samuel Sucker kept loosing at 'craps' and accused Charlie Casino of playing with loaded dice. To test one of the dice, Samuel threw it 100 times and obtained the results shown in Table 19.2. Remembering that the numbers on a single die are nominal (categories) and have no intrinsic quantitative value, it would be expected that each side on a 'fair' die would have an equal probability of coming up, in other words, one in six, or 16.67% (rounded) of the time. To answer the question of fairness of the die, we need to look at the χ^2-distribution more closely.

Chi-square distribution

Figure 19.1 shows the χ^2-distribution for $df = 1$ for two groups (male and female in our example), and it was noted that to evaluate the ratio from equation (19.5) the corresponding distribution would be dependent on the df. As has

TABLE 19.2
Data for exemplar
χ^2-test

Face numeral on die	Observed, O_i: Samuel's 'test'	Expected, E_i: a fair die*	$\dfrac{(O_i - E_i)^2}{E_i}$
1	22	16.67	1.704
2	13	16.67	0.808
3	11	16.67	1.929
4	19	16.67	0.326
5	21	16.67	1.125
6	14	16.67	0.428
Totals:	100	100	6.319

* Rounded to 2 decimal places

been the practice, the actual equation for the χ^2-distribution is presented, with no obligation except to consider it with some awe:

$$y(\chi^2; df) = \frac{(\chi^2)^{(df/2)-1} e^{-(\chi^2)/2}}{2^{df/2} \Gamma(df/2)} \qquad (19.6)$$

Here χ^2 is given by equation (19.5), when samples are very large, df is the number of degrees of freedom (number of categories less one) and $\Gamma(df/2)$ is a 'gamma' function which depends only on degrees of freedom. For our purposes, we do not have to know what a gamma function is, just that this one varies only with the degrees of freedom. Thus the whole distribution depends only on the χ^2-ratio and the degrees of freedom. This again results in a family of curves where there is a plot of $y(\chi^2)$ for each df, four of which are shown in Figure 19.4. As can be seen, these change rather radically for each different df, resulting in the critical value for each moving farther out the distribution as df increases. For the four shown,

$$\chi^2(1, 0.05) = 3.84$$
$$\chi^2(2, 0.05) = 5.99$$
$$\chi^2(4, 0.05) = 9.49$$
$$\chi^2(8, 0.05) = 15.51$$

as can be found from Table B.9. Thus we can see that for our example at the end of the previous section, Samuel Sucker's suspicions about Charlie Casino's die are not well founded, since this χ^2-ratio, 6.319, is less than $\chi^2(5, 0.05) = 11.07$. If we recall Activity 13.2 and the probabilities of even winning, it becomes obvious that while Samuel asked the right question – 'Why am I losing?' – he could have had a better hypothesis.

Carry out Activity 19.1 to set up a worksheet for doing χ^2 calculations.

Characteristics of the χ^2-test for one sample

The one-sample χ^2-test described so far is sometimes referred to as the *goodness-of-fit test*, since the question being answered is how well the sample data fit the expectations established by the population. As we have seen, this is analogous to the *z*-test for integer and ratio data. Though the test is without the limitations of its parametric counterpart, obviously there are some limitations and assumptions. These are as follows:

- The data are categorical (frequencies observed for categories). Ordinal data could be used, though there are more appropriate tests available.
- The observations are independent (basically only one tally per subject).
- Sufficient categories exist to contend with *all* responses from subjects (this may require a category of *no response*).
- The sample is sufficiently large.

These last two requirements overlap but are emphasized in a specific limitation for this test. If there are just two categories ($df = 1$), the expected frequency for each category should be at least 5; for situations where there are three or more categories for the variable ($df > 1$), then not less than 20% of the expected frequencies should be less than 5 (Siegel and Castellan, 1988). Considering the worksheet in Figure 19.5, it is apparent that an expected frequency less than 5 is most likely to occur if

- the overall sample is small, and/or
- the expected probability for a category is small.

Activity 19.1

1   To simplify the process, let us set up a worksheet for carrying out the χ^2-test, as shown in Figure 19.5. The data used are those from Table 19.2. Column **C** allows us to insert whatever set of probabilities might exist for population values.
2   As another example to try, insert the data from Table 5.2 in the shaded area and check your answer against Table 5.3.
3   Peter Politics wanted to know whether the patrons of his local pub voted consistently with the constituency, so on one Saturday night he did a survey to find out how many voted for each party in the last election. From the results published in the newspaper, he found the percentage each party received in the last election.

Parties	Local patrons	Last election
Labour	24	32%
Conservative	18	30%
Liberal Democrat	33	32%
Raving Loony	12	6%
Totals:	87	100%

Were the pub patrons typical?
Copy Figure 19.5 to a new worksheet, **Delete** rows **6** and **7**, then enter the new data.
Answer: 3. $\chi^2 = 12.81$, $p < 0.05$, *not likely.*

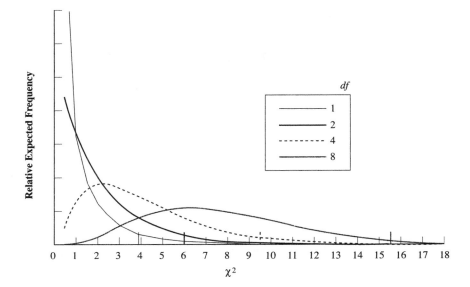

FIGURE 19.4
The χ^2-distributions for four different degrees of freedom with the $p = 0.05$ critical points indicated

	A	B	C	D	E	F
1	**Category**	***O***	**Exp. prob.**	***E***	$(O\text{-}E)^2/E$	
2	1	22	0.1667	16.67	1.707	
3	2	13	0.1667	16.67	0.807	
4	3	11	0.1667	16.67	1.927	
5	4	19	0.1667	16.67	0.327	
6	5	21	0.1667	16.67	1.127	
7	6	14	0.1667	16.67	0.427	
8	Totals:	100	1.0000	100	6.320	$= \chi^2$-ratio
9	*df* =	5			0.28	$= p$
10	$\alpha =$	0.05			11.07	$= \chi^2(\alpha)$

=1/6 and **Copy** down column

=B$8*C2 and **Copy** down column

=(B2-D2)^2/D2 and **Copy** down column

=SUM(E2:E7) and **Copy** across rows

=COUNTA(A2:A7)-1

=CHIDIST(E8,B9)

=CHIINV(B10,B9)

FIGURE 19.5
Worksheet for basic χ^2-test (note that differences in values compared with table 19.2 are due to the spreadsheet not rounding numbers when calculating)

Thus it should be possible to anticipate the situation and plan for a sufficiently large sample. If this is not done, it may be possible to combine categories, but such action may distort the meaning of the categories or the new combined categories may jeopardize the validity of the operational definition of the variable, reducing construct validity. This is an act of last resort and should be avoided if possible.

The reason for this restriction lies in the fact that the χ^2-distributions of equation (19.6) are reasonable representations of the possible distribution of χ^2-ratios from equation (19.5) *when the total sample is large* (they would be exact if the sample were infinitely large). Thus for most situations, testing the results of a χ^2-ratio against the expectations of one of the χ^2-distributions is an approximation. This is quite acceptable as long as the expected frequencies are sufficiently large, as noted above. This is one of those areas where not all agree and some statisticians would argue for even larger minima than 5 (see, for example, Hays, 1994). Before going on to other tests, let us consider the issue of power.

Power

While there is considerable reference to the tendency for nonparametric tests to have lower power than their parametric counterparts, few texts offer any way to compare. Cohen (1988) has produced sets of tables from which it is possible to determine the power of selected parametric and non-parametric tests, which will be assumed to be accurate. Unfortunately, using these tends to be tedious as they require separate calculations before it is possible to consider values in the tables, and some of the underlying assumptions are contentious. As has been the case in previous chapters, a technique for approximating the power of tests on a post hoc basis will be developed.

Starting with the concept of power as the probability of correctly rejecting the null hypothesis, it is possible to develop a method for producing a value analogous to that in Chapter 14. First we assume that the distribution of χ^2-ratios for the situation where H_0 is true corresponds to the χ^2-distribution for the degrees of freedom of the test. Such distributions have a number of characteristics that will be used to develop alternative distributions that correspond to the situation where H_0 is false. Each distribution is characterized by

$$\text{mean} = df$$
$$\text{variance} = 2df$$
$$\text{mode} = df - 2 \ (\text{for } df \geq 2)$$
$$\text{median} \cong df - 0.65 \ (\text{for } df \geq 2)$$

Recall that in the derivation of the calculation of a value for the power of F-tests in Chapter 16, the most likely value of F-ratio if H_0 were true was approximately the value of the median. Similarly, for χ^2-tests, for the situation when H_0 is true, the *most likely value* would be

$$\bar{\chi}^2_{H_0\text{true}} = df - 1 \tag{19.7}$$

In other words, since the χ^2-distribution is positively skewed, the most likely value will be somewhat below the mean. Consider an example where there were five categories for a variable ($df = 4$) and it was found that $\chi^2 = 14.0$. In this case,

$$\bar{\chi}^2_{H_0\text{true}} = 3$$

This is more apparent when considering the probability distribution shown for $df = 4$ in Figure 19.4, where the peak is closer to 3 than 4. On the other hand, if H_0 were false, then one must assume that another distribution would better represent the possible values for the ratio, whose most likely value would be

$$\bar{\chi}^2_{H_0\text{false}} = \chi^2$$

Analogous to equation (19.7), the degrees of freedom for the non-central distribution, df', can be found from

$$\bar{\chi}^2_{H_0 \text{false}} = df' - 1$$

$$df' = \chi^2 + 1$$

Thus a visual representation of the non-central distribution would be a graph of the $\chi^2_{(df=15)}$-distribution. Both of these are shown in Figure 19.6, with the critical value for H_0, $\chi^2_{df=4}(0.05) = 9.49$, indicated on the graph. This allows us to visualize the relationships among α, β and power. Unfortunately, this has little meaning since it suggests that the true situation is one where there should be 16 categories instead of 5, but it does give us a way to picture the mathematical relationship.

As before, the idea of a non-central distribution has associated with it a non-centrality parameter, λ, which has been defined as equal to the χ^2-ratio (Patnaik, 1949; Cohen, 1988). Interestingly, even though the mathematical derivation is rigorous, this ultimately provides some rather bizarre estimates of power, as we shall see later. An alternative definition for the non-centrality parameter, designated here as λ', is offered which corrects for this and will be established from a relationship between the two *most likely values* of the χ^2-ratio (Black, 1997a),

$$\bar{\chi}^2_{H_0 \text{false}} = \bar{\chi}^2_{H_0 \text{true}} + \lambda' \qquad (19.8)$$

Substituting in equation (19.7), this can be expressed as

$$\chi^2_{H_0 \text{false}} = df - 1 + \lambda'$$

If the value of the χ^2-ratio for the study is substituted for $\bar{\chi}^2_{H_0 \text{false}}$, then

$$\chi^2 = df - 1 + \lambda'$$

Solving for λ', we have the following for a post hoc analysis of *power*:

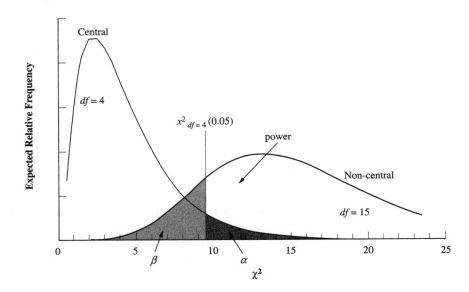

FIGURE 19.6
The χ^2-distribution for $df = 4$, and the imagined non-central distribution for a χ^2-ratio of 14.0, with critical value:

$$\chi^2_{df=4}(0.05) = 9.49,$$

showing α, β and power as areas under the graphs

$$\lambda' = \chi^2 - df + 1 \qquad (19.9)$$

Thus for the example above,

$$\lambda' = 14.0 - 4 + 1 = 11.0$$

As with the F-test, to provide an estimate of the power, a new value for the df (Patnaik, 1949; Winer $et\ al.$, 1991) can be found to insert in the existing χ^2-function in Excel to determine an estimate for $power$ directly:

$$df' = \frac{(df + \lambda')^2}{df + 2\lambda'} \qquad (19.10)$$

Also, a correction factor is needed for the χ^2_{crit} value:

$$c = \frac{df + 2\lambda'}{df + \lambda'} \qquad (19.11)$$

To include the power calculation in the worksheet requires a bit more effort than for the earlier parametric tests. Since the **CHIDIST(ratio, df)** function takes all values of df and truncates them to a whole number (in other words, cuts off the decimal values without rounding), the jumps are rather radical. This is reflected in the table of values in Table B.9, and the problem becomes more obvious as you run your finger down any column: the value changes are fairly large from one df to the next. Since the new degrees of freedom, df', will inevitably not be a whole number much of the time, it is necessary to interpolate between the jumps from one whole value for df' to the next. To do this a three-step process is required: it is necessary to find two values of power, the high value from rounding up df' and the low value from rounding down df', then interpolate between them based upon the decimal portion of df', as shown below:

$$p_{hi} = \textbf{CHIDIST}(\chi^2(\textbf{df}, \alpha)/\textbf{c}, \textbf{ROUNDUP}(\textbf{df}', 0))$$
$$p_{lo} = \textbf{CHIDIST}(\chi^2(\textbf{df}, \alpha)/\textbf{c}, \textbf{ROUNDDOWN}(\textbf{df}', 0))$$
$$\text{power} = p_{lo} + (df' - \textbf{TRUNC}(\textbf{df}')) * (\textbf{p}_{hi} - \textbf{p}_{lo})$$

For the example above, substituting in the following values,

$$\chi^2 = 14.0\ (p < 0.05)\ \text{since}\ \chi^2(4, 0.05) = 9.49$$
$$df' = \frac{(4 + 11.0)^2}{4 + 2(11.0)} = \frac{225}{26} = 8.654$$
$$c = \frac{4 + 2(11.0)}{4 + 11.0} = \frac{26}{15} = 1.733$$

we obtain,

$$p_{hi} = \textbf{CHIDIST}(\textbf{9.49/1.733}, \textbf{ROUNDUP}(\textbf{8.654}, \textbf{0})) = \textbf{0.791}$$
$$p_{lo} = \textbf{CHIDIST}(\textbf{9.49/1.733}, \textbf{ROUNDDOWN}(\textbf{8.654}, \textbf{0})) = \textbf{0.706}$$
$$\text{power} = \textbf{0.706} + (\textbf{8.654} - \textbf{TRUNC}(\textbf{8.654})) * (\textbf{0.791} - \textbf{0.706}) = \textbf{0.76}$$

As a test of the validity of these equations, we would expect, as before, that the value of power would be 50% when $\chi^2 = \chi^2(df, \alpha)$, the critical value.

You will be able to demonstrate in Activity 19.2 that this is true for the above process (the calculations of both Patnaik (1949) and Cohen (1988) indicate that power $\gg 50\%$ for all distributions except $df = 1$, since they use $\lambda = \chi^2$). Obviously, it is easier to do such calculations on a worksheet, so carry out Activity 19.2 now and consider another example. Here it is necessary to use ordinal instead of nominal data in order to generate an example that allows us to compare the power of parametric and nonparametric tests. There are more powerful tests for ordinal data, as we will see, but this example allows a direct comparison.

Activity 19.2

1 Peaceful Valley School has had problems with its finances and the accountant wants to know if the school is 'typical'. Salary data were collected on all 20 staff. Set up the worksheet in Figure 19.7 which has the salaries as both ordinal and interval data: raw incomes and income ranges that correspond to the three grades of teacher. The z-test compares the mean of all basic salaries with the national average (all teachers are on a common basic pay scale) and standard deviation. The χ^2-test compares the three salary ranges using the same national distribution of salaries as the source for the three expected frequencies. The z-test (using t_{crit} since $n < 30$) detects a significant difference, but the χ^2-test does not. What are the different questions being answered by the two tests?

2 Instead of using the top salary of each range as the upper limits in cells **D7:D9**, change them so that the range extends to just under the next salary increment: 13 300, 21 139 and 34 300. What are the effects on the results?

3 Now change the top salary of each range to the midpoint between the two salaries either side of the category border, that is, in cells **D7:D9**, change them so that the ranges are: 12 311, 19 842, and 33 422. What are the effects on the results?

(*Hint*: When starting with raw data, first compile them into frequency tables as shown in Figures 12.1 and 12.2 for single samples, then Copy values as a block to Figure 19.7, adjusted beforehand for number of categories.)

Answers: 1. The parametric test is asking: 'Is there a difference in mean salary for this school from that of the population mean, and is it typical?' The nonparametric test is asking: 'Is there a difference in the types of teachers in this school as compared with the national trend?' The answers are roughly: yes there is a mean salary difference; but no, the distribution of type of teaching staff is typical.
2. Now the χ^2-test detects a difference, $\chi^2 = 11.867$, power = 0.86, but notice the expected value for group C is less than 5. 3. Now the result is more modest, $\chi^2 = 6.061$, just above $\chi^2(2, 0.05)$, so power = 0.50.

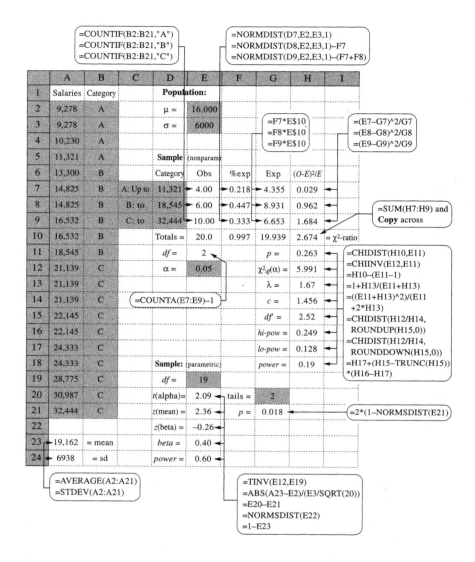

FIGURE 19.7
Worksheet for comparing the power of parametric and nonparametric one-sample tests

The results of Activity 19.2 point up a problem with using the χ^2-test with ordinal data: if we change the limits for the categories, the significance changes. When using ordinal data it is difficult to know where to place the boundaries, thus the 'measure' could be said to have questionable validity. Remember that the χ^2-test assumes mutually exclusive categories for both the observed and the expected, which can be difficult to establish for ordinal categories. Let us consider an alternative test that does not appear to suffer from this dilemma.

Kolmogorov–Smirnov one-sample test for ranked data

Several alternatives for one-sample tests involving ordinal data are available (Siegel and Castellan, 1988; Gibbons and Chakraborti, 1992) with advantages that vary slightly with the situation. The reader is referred to these texts for tests in addition to the one described here. The Kolmogorov–Smirnov one-sample test has been chosen for three reasons: it is purported to be more powerful than the χ^2-test for the same data, particularly when the sample is small; it tends to be used frequently; and it appears in SPSS. The test is appropriate for ranked data though it is truly a test for the match of the distribution of sample data to that of the population and consequently the distributions can include those other than the normal distribution for populations. It also assumes an underlying continuous distribution even though the data may be in unequal steps (see Gibbons and Chakraborti, 1992), which leads to alternative calculations, as will be seen below.

The test itself compares the *cumulative* distribution of the data with that for the expected population distribution. It assumes an underlying continuous distribution and has a definite advantage over the χ^2-test when the sample size is small, due to the limitation of the minimum expected value. The maximum magnitude of the divergence between the two distributions is the test factor and is determined simply by the largest absolute difference between cumulative *relative* frequencies, the fractions of the whole. This is checked against a table of maximum differences expected to be found for various α.

The difficulty in appropriately applying this test lies in the nature of the intervals for the ranks. There are basically two types of problems illustrated in the literature, each resulting in different applications of the Kolmogorov–Smirnov test.

- The intervals are well defined, mutually exclusive and population data exist for them by interval, thus the population data are stepped as well as those for the sample (see Siegel and Castellan, 1988). This makes it equivalent to the two-sample test where both samples are stepped.
- The intervals for the ranks are not well defined and the underlying distribution is *assumed*, therefore it is mathematically determined by a continuous function – for example, a normal or even a flat distribution (see Gibbons and Chakraborti, 1992; Kraft and van Eeden, 1968). Here the sample data are stepped and the population 'data' are continuous.

Both of these are presented as *the* way of applying the test by some texts. Some examples will be used to clarify this issue for what first appears to be a rather simple test. We will start with the second situation, where the underlying population distribution is continuous.

Continuous population data from a mathematical distribution

Using the data from the earlier example on school salaries presented in Figure 19.7, it is possible to devise a table of cumulative relative frequencies for these sample data, and also provide a cumulative relative distribution for the population based upon a normal distribution, as shown in Figure 19.8. Plotting these

FIGURE 19.8
Observed (CF_o) and
expected (CF_e)
cumulative relative
frequency
distributions,
corresponding to the
sample and the
population, when
the population
distribution is
assumed and
generated from a
mathematical
function

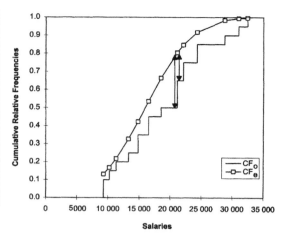

Salary	f_o	CF_o	CF_e
9,278	2	0.10	0.13
10,230	1	0.15	0.17
11,321	1	0.20	0.22
13,300	1	0.25	0.33
14,825	2	0.35	0.42
16,532	2	0.45	0.54
18,545	1	0.50	0.66
21,139	3	0.65	0.80
22,145	2	0.75	0.85
24,333	2	0.85	0.92
28,775	1	0.90	0.98
30,987	1	0.95	0.99
32,444	1	1.00	1.00
Total=	20		

data, it becomes apparent that there are two possible points of comparison for
each data point: the interval above and the interval below. This is shown by the
two arrows for one point on the continuous population distribution which
could be considered to be matched with either of the steps below for the
sample data. Therefore, the Kolmogorov–Smirnov test checks both steps by calculating both differences for all points. Then the *maximum difference* from the
complete set is compared to that for the appropriate corresponding α value.
Now carry out Activity 19.3 to set up a worksheet to do this.

Activity 19.3

1   Set up the example in the worksheet as shown in Figure 19.9, which
     has all the calculations for the Kolmogorov–Smirnov test first for
     each salary range. What question is being answered?
          The *critical maximum difference*, D_{max}, can be closely estimated
     from Table 19.3.

2(a) In the lower part of the worksheet, the test uses the same three
     groups as used for the χ^2-test in Activity 19.2. How do these results
     compare?

 (b) Try it for the other two interval sets, as was done for the χ^2-test.
     How do they compare?

*Answers: 1. Is the distribution of grades of teachers consistent with the
national distribution?*
*2(a) The results show a significant difference, $p < 0.01$. (b) Each is very
large: $D_{max} = 0.497, 0.604, 0.539$. It seems that the Kolmogorov–Smirnov
test is less sensitive to the ranges for the intervals and more sensitive to
the overall ranks.*

TABLE 19.3
Critical maximum
difference, D_{max}, for
use in the
Kolmogorov–
Smirnov test

Sample size	α		
	0.10	0.05	0.01
$25 > n > 10$	$\dfrac{1.22}{\sqrt{n+1}}$	$\dfrac{1.36}{\sqrt{n+1}}$	$\dfrac{1.63}{\sqrt{n+1}}$
$n \geq 25$	$\dfrac{1.22}{\sqrt{n}}$	$\dfrac{1.36}{\sqrt{n}}$	$\dfrac{1.63}{\sqrt{n}}$

FIGURE 19.9
Worksheet for
Kolmogorov–
Smirnov one-sample
test for ranked data
where the
population
distribution is a
mathematical
function

	A	B	C	D	E	F	G	H
1	**Population**		μ =	16,000	=NORMDIST(B6,D$1,D$2,1)		=E6–F7 and	
2			σ =	6000	**Copy** down the column		**Copy** down	
3			=E6+C7/C$19		=C6/C19	=E6–F6 and		=0–F6
4	**Sample**		and **Copy** down			**Copy** down		
5		Salary	f_0	f_{pop}	CF_o	CF_e	CF_{oi}–CF_{ei}	$CF_{o(i-1)}$–CF_{ei}
6		9,278	2		0.100	0.131	–0.031	–0.131
7		10,230	1		0.150	0.168	–0.018	–0.068
8		11,321	1		0.200	0.218	–0.018	–0.068
9		13,300	1		0.250	0.326	–0.076	–0.126
10		14,825	2		0.350	0.422	–0.072	–0.172
11		16,532	2		0.450	0.535	–0.085	–0.185
12		18,545	1		0.500	0.664	–0.164	–0.214
13		21,139	3		0.650	0.804	–0.154	–0.304
14		22,145	2		0.750	0.847	–0.097	–0.197
15		24,333	2		0.850	0.918	–0.068	–0.168
16		28,775	1		0.900	0.983	–0.083	–0.133
17		30,987	1		0.950	0.994	–0.044	–0.094
18		32,444	1		1.000	0.997	0.003	–0.047
19		Total =	20				$p<$	.05
20					D_{max} (0.05) =	0.297	=1.36/SQRT(C19+1)	
21					D_{max} (0.10) =	0.266	=1.22/SQRT(C19+1)	
22					D_{max} (0.01) =	0.356	=1.63/SQRT(C19+1) {equation (19.12)}	
23						=NORMDIST(B26,D$1,D$2,1)		
24	**Sample**					and **Copy** down		
25		Salary	f_0	f_{pop}	CF_o	CF_e	CF_{oi}–CF_{ei}	$CF_{o(i-1)}$–CF_{ei}
26	Up to	11,321	4		0.200	0.218	–0.018	–0.218
27	to	18,545	6		0.500	0.664	–0.164	–0.464
28	to	32,444	10		1.000	0.997	0.003	–0.497
29		Totals =	20				$p<$	.01

=C26/C29
=E26+C27/C29
=E27+C28/C29

=E26–F26
and **Copy**
down

=0–F26
=E26–F27
=E27–F28

As can be seen, the choice of intervals for the Kolmogorov–Smirnov test, in this case, is less sensitive to the ranges chosen for ordinal data, unlike the χ^2-test, but more sensitive to the *number* of ranks. Again, the two tests in Figure 19.9 are actually answering two different questions: the top one about the distribution of salary levels with respect to the population, the second about the distribution of the three grades of teachers with respect to the population. It is not simply a matter of collapsing or not collapsing categories, but what the research question is asking.

Interestingly, in the example the results for the Kolmogorov–Smirnov test appear to be much more powerful than those for the *t*-test, but again the questions being answered are different in each case. The test also assumes that the distribution of ranks is normal and the underlying continuous distribution has a mean between 15143 and 16532, which may not be strictly true.

The point to focus on is that four tests have been presented for a given set of data, providing different levels of power, but also answering essentially three different questions! Thus, as a researcher, you must be somewhat wary of the enthusiasm some statisticians have for the use of one test over another. The important deciding issue is still: what is the research question and what is the null hypothesis?

As a final point, it should be mentioned that SPSS only allows comparisons for three distributions: normal, uniform (flat) and Poisson. With the worksheet template above, you can insert *any* mathematically generated distribution. Now we will consider the situation where the population distribution is based upon 'real' data and not limited to predetermined mathematical ones.

Stepped population data from a full survey

In this situation, we wish to compare sample data with actual population data, where the frequencies for each of the ordinal categories for both are known. To illustrate this, let us use the sample data set as before, but compare it to a national register of teachers. The data (with the population contrived to have a mean of 16000 and standard deviation of 6000) and corresponding stepped graphs are shown in Figure 19.10, where it becomes obvious that only data within intervals are to be compared. For example, the double-ended arrow shows the difference between one pair of intervals. Therefore, the Kolmogorov–Smirnov one-sample test will only use the differences in column G of Figure 19.9, and the largest difference will be compared with the minimum for the chosen α. Such a distribution-free comparison will have advantages in many situations where data do not fit a predetermined distribution. To carry out the equivalent test in SPSS, it is necessary to use the two-sample function, where one of the sets of data is that of the population. Carry out Activity 19.4 and set up the test on a worksheet.

TESTS FOR TWO INDEPENDENT SAMPLES

Not always will designs of studies involving the comparison of two groups produce interval/ratio data and lend the resolution of the hypotheses to a *t*-test.

Activity 19.4

Add the column for population frequencies from Figure 19.10, then **Copy** column **E** (in other words, **E6:E18**) to column **F** to generate the cumulative relative frequencies from the population data instead of an equation. Check only the differences in column **G**. Is the school significantly different? Also, plot a graph of the population frequencies against the salaries. What is its shape?

Answer: The largest difference should be −0.278 which is less than the 5% minimum, thus no significant difference. The population distribution is highly negatively skewed.

Recall the basic designs – experimental (B3) and ex post facto (D3) – where we would wish to employ two groups, either experimental and control groups or two groups receiving different treatments. The difference will depend on the nature of the independent variable, whether it is manipulated (B3) or a life-experience (D3), one over which the researcher has no control, except through sampling. The null hypothesis is basically that the nature of the frequency distributions across the categories or levels of the dependent variable is the same for both of the groups. In other words, does the differentiating characteristic of the two groups (independent variable) influence the nature of the distribution of the levels/categories of the dependent variable? As mentioned earlier, for life-experience variables it may be more valid to describe the relationship as associational rather than causal. Therefore the question may be: is there a difference between the groups for the variable? This could be described as an association between the characteristics of the groups and the nature of the distribution of frequencies for the levels/categories of the other variable.

FIGURE 19.10
Observed and expected cumulative relative frequency distributions, corresponding to the sample and the population when both sets of data are stepped (that is, population data are from a real survey)

Salary	f_o	f_{pop}	CF_o	CF_e
9,278	2	260	0.10	0.10
10,230	1	287	0.15	0.21
11,321	1	320	0.20	0.33
13,300	1	350	0.25	0.46
14,825	2	365	0.35	0.59
16,532	2	287	0.45	0.70
18,545	1	208	0.50	0.78
21,139	3	145	0.65	0.83
22,145	2	125	0.75	0.88
24,333	2	100	0.85	0.92
28,775	1	85	0.90	0.95
30,987	1	74	0.95	0.98
32,444	1	64	1.00	1.00
Total=	20	2670		

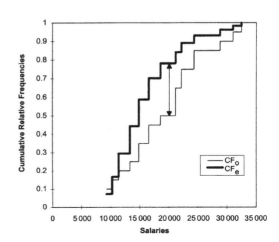

Kolmogorov–Smirnov test for two independent samples

This is a test to see if the two samples have been drawn from same population, again with assumption of underlying continuous distribution (see Gibbons and Chakraborti, 1992). The process is the same as above in Figure 19.9 and explained in Activity 19.4, except in this case one is comparing CF_A to CF_B. This also requires a set of maxima that can be calculated when $n > 25$ and $m > 25$; then

$$D(0.05) = 1.36\sqrt{\frac{m+n}{mn}} \qquad (19.12)$$

For small samples, special tables are needed (see, for example, Siegel and Castellan, 1988). Alternatively, the probabilities are calculated automatically when using SPSS. Siegel and Castellan (1988) maintain that this test is 'slightly more efficient' than the Wilcoxon–Mann–Whitney test, which we will consider before carrying out an activity. When the samples are large, the reverse tends to be true.

Wilcoxon–Mann–Whitney (WMW) test for two independent samples

This is a frequently used test which is considered to be one of the most powerful nonparametric tests available and is appropriate for data that are at least ordinal. Three statisticians, Mann, Whitney and Wilcoxon, developed what is essentially the same test, the *Mann–Whitney U-test* and the *Wilcoxon rank-sum test* (Gibbons and Chakraborti, 1992), and indeed references in the literature tend to refer to them as one test. The actual calculations may vary from one reference to another, but the same end is achieved. The WMW test is also of use as an alternative to the *t*-test when its assumptions of normality and homogeneity of variance cannot be met (Siegel and Castellan, 1988). We will consider situations where the sample sizes are of sufficient size to use existing tables for the normal distribution to test the hypotheses. When the sample sizes are small, it is necessary to have special tables, or depend on a computer-based statistical package to tell you what the probability is.

We will treat the situation as if the data are ordinal and make no assumptions about their underlying distribution homogeneity of variance. Obviously, this implies that we could also use the test for interval/ratio data that were not normally distributed or the pairs so heterogeneous with respect to variance that normal corrections would be ineffective. Conceptually, the issue being addressed is whether the two samples come from the same population, thus the question asked is: are the two underlying population distributions the same? As usual, it is unlikely that they are identical and the statistical test is asking whether they are close enough to be considered the same or so different as to be considered two different distributions. Figure 19.11 illustrates the questions, showing that they cannot be resolved simply by visual inspection.

Though some authors would say that the WMW test does not even assume a random sample, it is difficult to argue that the sample can be a valid source of an

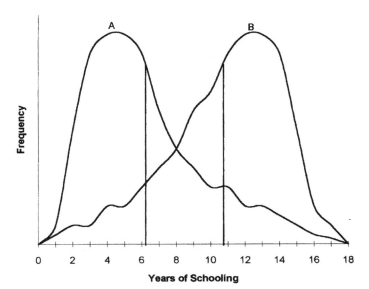

FIGURE 19.11
Two overlapping
sample distributions
with means shown
as vertical lines: are
they indicative of
one single or two
separate population
distributions?

inference about the structure of some population distribution if it is not
random. While the source of the sample might not threaten statistical validity,
it surely would have an adverse impact on external validity.

The test is based upon the rank order of the data and is asking whether the
sum of the ranks of one sample is sufficiently different from the overall mean
of the ranks of both of the groups to indicate that it is not part of a common
population. The sampling distribution again says that any sample from a population will have a sum of ranks close to the population mean but not necessarily
identical. The distribution of the sum of ranks for 'large' samples is assumed to
be normal with a population mean defined as

$$\mu = \frac{1}{2}n_1(n_1 + n_2 + 1) \tag{19.13}$$

and a standard error of the mean found by

$$\text{SEM} = \sqrt{\frac{n_1 n_2(n_1 + n_2 + 1)}{12}} \tag{19.14}$$

Some texts suggest that 'large' can mean 10 or more in each group; others will
maintain a minimum of 25. In any case, the following approximation is more
accurate the larger the sample. It is not difficult to see that the test is based
upon the z-test,

$$z = \frac{\bar{x} - \mu}{\text{SEM}}$$

which, when using the sum of the ranks, W_1, for one of the groups as the sample
mean, becomes

$$z(\text{WMW}) = \frac{W_1 - \frac{1}{2}n_1(n_1 + n_2 + 1)}{\sqrt{\dfrac{n_1 n_2(n_1 + n_2 + 1)}{12}}} \qquad (19.15)$$

where W_1 is the sum of the ranks for one of the two groups, n_1 is the sample size of one group and n_2 is the sample size of the other group. Thus, to carry out the test on sample data, the first task is to arrange all the raw data in rank order and use the order as the data. This will require that when 'ties' in scores occur, the subjects having identical scores be assigned equivalent ranks. Let us consider an example to illustrate the process.

Betty Binder, Chief County Librarian, wanted to find a way of encouraging children to read more and had discovered two possible approaches. To decide which to implement, she randomly selected four local libraries and randomly assigned them to two groups. In libraries in group A she enhanced the children's reading area and shelving as suggested in one plan, and in group B libraries this area was enhanced according to the other plan. After a year, she collected data on how many books each member of two randomly selected groups of 20 subscribers borrowed over the period. The data are shown in Figure 19.12. Unfortunately, several young people from each group had moved from the area, but she did note that the distributions both appeared highly skewed. Also, even if they read all the books taken out, the data would have to be considered ordinal to reflect the amount of reading, since the books were not necessarily the same size.

To carry out the WMW test to resolve the null hypothesis that there was no difference between the impact of the two library enhancements, it is necessary to assign ranks to the data. Since the first four were different (30, 31, 32, 33), assigning ranks was simple, as shown in the tabular part of Figure 19.13, but both groups had the same next value. Thus they each became 5.5 (*not* 5 and 6), and the next one was 7. This is one way of settling 'ties' in the data, though some authors suggest that an alternative is randomly to assign each with a common value to a rank – that is, randomly to break ties. Further

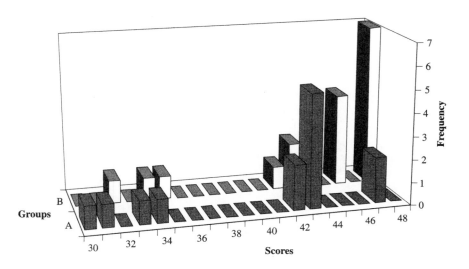

FIGURE 19.12
Bar charts of raw data showing non-normal distributions

down the line, there were three numbers the same, which were each assigned the rank of 9 (*not* 8, 9 and 10). This is followed by a set of seven numbers the same, each becoming 14.0, since

$$\frac{11 + 12 + 13 + 14 + 15 + 16 + 17}{7} = 14.0$$

As can be seen from the worksheet, this type of expression is relatively easy to enter when necessary. If the numbers really do come from interval/ratio data, few if any will be ties, but if the data are truly ordinal (for example, responses on questionnaire are ticks indicating value in a range), then the data will be ordinal and many ties will be possible. The rest of the equations are straightforward, even the one for equation (19.15) for W.

It appears from the results, that there is a difference in the consequences of applying the two approaches and the samples are no longer part of the same population. Thus, Betty Binder decided to implement approach **B** in the county's public libraries.

FIGURE 19.13
Worksheet for Betty Binder's study: for $\alpha = 0.05$ the Wilcoxon–Mann–Whitney test is significant, but for t-ratio $= -1.93$, where $t_{crit} = 2.05$ for $\alpha = 0.05$, it would be non-significant

	A	B	C	D	E
1		Data A	Rank A	Data B	Rank B
2		30	1	32	3
3		31	2	34	5.5
4		33	4	35	7
5		34	5.5	42	9
6		42	9	43	14.0
7		42	9	43	14.0
8		43	14.0	46	19.5
9		43	14.0	46	19.5
10		43	14.0	46	19.5
11		43	14.0	46	19.5
12		43	14.0	48	27
13		47	22.5	48	27
14		47	22.5	48	27
15				48	27
16				48	27
17				48	27
18				48	27
19	$W=$		145.5		319.5	SUM(E2:E18)
20	$n =$		13		17	=COUNTA(E2:E18)
21	Mean =	40.1		44.1	
22	sd =	5.89		5.36	
23	$\alpha =$	.05			
24	$z\,(\alpha) =$	1.96		Total $W =$	465	=C19+E19
25	$z\,(WMW) =$	–2.34		Check =	465.0	=(C20+E20)*(C20+E20+1)/2

=–NORMSINV(B23/2)

=(C19–0.5*C20*(C20+E20+1)/SQRT(C20*E20*(C20+E20+1)/12))

Note that the same data analysed using SPSS-PC provide the same value for W_1, but then generate $z(\mathrm{WMW}) = -2.3778$, $p = 0.0174$. Such discrepancies will arise, since statistical packages will employ different techniques for correcting for sample size and even ties that include both groups (see for example, Gibbons and Chakraborti, 1992), but do not always inform the user which ones. Carry out Activity 19.5 to install this test on a worksheet and try a new example.

Activity 19.5

1   Set up the worksheet as shown in Figure 19.13. Since the process of assigning ranks to tied scores could be prone to error, a check on our entries is needed. One way of doing this is to compare the sum of the two W values with the total of all ranks: $48 + 47 + 46 + \ldots + 2 + 1$. This would be tedious, except there is a replacement formula that does it for us and copes with unequal sample sizes:

$$\text{Total of ranks} = \frac{(n_1 + n_2)(n_1 + n_2 + 1)}{2}$$

which appears in cell **E16**. Also, it does not matter which group is n_1 and which is n_2, but the sum W_1 must be for group 1. The only difference will be in the sign of $z(\mathrm{WMW})$; the value should be the same.

2   It would be instructive to consider limitations of Betty Binder's study and to even suggest possible improvements. Should she really make the changes based upon the evidence to hand?

3   Melvin Monetary wanted to know if there was any relationship between parental income and success in school. He randomly selected 40 children in his secondary school, 20 from the top third and 20 from the bottom third, based on their academic grades (marks on last year's examinations). He then asked them to take a questionnaire home for their parents to complete. One of the questions was about their income, which asked them to indicate in which range their total income was. The results were shown as frequency data in columns **B** and **D** in Figure 19.14, which require a slightly different approach to ranking if the table is to be kept simple. Instead of turning this back into a long list of raw data, in the rank columns when there are ties, simply multiply the frequency by the tie rank. For example, for the interval in row **4**, there was 1 for the high achiever group and 5 for the low achiever group, a total of 6 covering ranks 3, 4, 5, 6, 7 and 8. Thus any one entry would be

$$\frac{3 + 4 + 5 + 6 + 7 + 8}{6} = 5.5$$

and all five together in the low-achiever group would come to 27.5.

(a)   Do the two groups have different parental income?

(b)   How would you describe the consequences of this study: causal or associative?

(c)   Are there other explanations for this outcome? are there other extraneous variables?

Answers: 2. What was the population doing at the same time? Was either of these an improvement over existing practice? Was Betty able to control for other extraneous variables, such as those arising from sources of invalidity/confounding (e.g., time: other events)? 3(a) No, z(WMW) > 1.96, p < 0.05. (b) Associative, the reason being as follows. (c) There are any number of other extraneous variables that have not been controlled plus this is likely to be an artefact, with other possible variables being the cause of both higher achievement and parental income.

Power

The easiest way to compare the power of this test with that of the parametric equivalent is to carry out a *t*-test on the raw data, even though the skewness violates one of the assumptions of the test. Since the standard deviations of the raw data for Betty Binder's study are close, it can be assumed that the variances are homogeneous. For this set of data, the *t*-test does not show a significant difference, suggesting that the WMW test is the more powerful. While often it is said that parametric tests in general tend to be more powerful than their nonparametric counterparts, this assumes that the data meet all the assumptions of the parametric test. In this example, it is obviously not true, since both distributions are skewed. Had they been close to normal, then it is likely the *t*-test would have been the more powerful.

FIGURE 19.14
Worksheet for Wilcoxon–Mann–Whitney test for data from a frequency table for Melvin Monetary's study

Chi-square test for two independent samples

We will now return to situations where the variable consists of a collection of nominal categories instead of ranks or interval values. Again, the aim will be to compare two independent groups: either a treatment and a control group, or just two different groups. Let us consider two examples to illustrate this, the first a truly experimental design. Research in human–computer interaction (HCI) suggests that colours used in computer screen designs elicit different emotions. For example, red implies danger or something to be avoided and so should be used for warnings but not positive messages as this would generate a mental conflict. Martin Monitor wanted to determine whether teaching about the principles of colour usage as part of his teaching of HCI (independent variable) had any real impact on student use of colour in screen design (dependent variable). He asked a colleague who taught business studies, where he knew they used the Windows environment, to duplicate the request he would make to his class six weeks after he had taught about colour:

In Windows 3.1, if you choose **Control Panel, Color**, you will find that there are over 20 different colour designs available for menus. Set up and use each of the six listed below for one week and at the end of the six weeks, choose the one you think is best:

Windows Default (pale blue and grey)
Ocean (dark blue and grey)
Designer (dark green and grey)
Patchwork (maroon, blues and yellow)
Fluorescent (cyan and green)
Hot Dog Stand (red and yellow)

If you have access to a computer with Windows 3.1 environment, you can view the six choices yourself. (In Windows 95, this is buried in **Settings, Control Panel, Display, Appearance**, where equivalent combinations can be customized.) His null hypothesis was that there would be no difference in preference between the two groups. What he hoped was that the HCI group would tend to choose from the first three, these being closest to 'good practice'. His results for this quasi-experimental design will be presented and discussed later.

As a second study, let us consider the results of an ex post facto study conducted by a medical practice. The team was trying to decide if the psychologist they were going to bring into the practice was to be a man or a woman. It was felt (rightly or wrongly) that if female patients tended to have more psychological problems than males, then the person should be a woman, and vice versa. This was translated into: men and women (a life-event independent variable) do not differ in the types of complaints that compel them to go to the doctor's office (general practitioner's surgery). The records for all the doctors in the practice were reviewed by a research assistant for three randomly selected weeks over the past year. Each patient was classified as having one of three complaints as recorded by the four doctors (two men and two women): disease (viral or bacterial), physiological (e.g., injury, tumours, arthritis) or psychological. The results are summarized in Table 19.4 below and the hypothesis will be resolved in Activity 19.6.

TABLE 19.4
Data from the survey
of patient complaints

Complaint	Male	Female
Disease	149	169
Physiological	108	91
Psychological	84	105

In general, to determine whether there was a difference between two groups, we use much the same equation (19.5) as before, but it is necessary to work out *expected* values by combining the frequencies. This is analogous to the *t*-test where the standard error of the difference was based upon the combined standard deviations of the two samples. Here it is assumed that if the two groups are part of the same population, then the two distributions will not differ significantly from one that is made up of the characteristics of the two. The equation is

$$\chi^2 = \sum_{i=1}^{m} \sum_{j=1}^{2} \frac{(O_{ij} - E_{ij})^2}{E_{ij}} \tag{19.16}$$

where the O_{ij} are the observed frequencies, from both of the samples; the E_{ij} are the expected frequencies, determined by combining the expected frequencies for the two groups (see below); i represents the categories, ranging from 1 to m, where m is at least 2; and j represents the treatment groups, here ranging from 1 to 2. The statistic has $m - 1$ degrees of freedom, and can be checked against Table B.9 in Appendix B. It may be easier to understand it in a slightly expanded form,

$$\chi^2 = \sum_{i=1}^{m} \frac{(O_{i1} - E_{i1})^2}{E_{i1}} + \sum_{i=1}^{m} \frac{(O_{i2} - E_{i2})^2}{E_{i2}}$$

one element for each treatment group. This still means that there will be $2 \times m$ calculations to do before adding them altogether, thus there is an advantage to setting up the procedure on a worksheet. Before doing this, the determination of the expected frequencies, E_{ij}, requires some explanation.

Referring to Figure 19.15, the rows are staggered for each category so that there is a single column containing the χ^2-ratios. Each expected frequency is determined by first finding the total number of respondents in each category for the two groups, the 'Combined' column. This is used to determine the expected percentage for each category. The expected frequencies are then determined by multiplying the category expected percentage by the *total for that group*. Therefore, when the samples are of different sizes, the expected frequencies will differ accordingly.

The assumptions that underlie the test are the same as for the one-sample case:

- Independence of observations – all subjects must belong to one and only one of the categories.
- The data are categorical (frequencies observed for categories). Ordinal data could be used, though there are more appropriate tests available.

FIGURE 19.15 Worksheet for χ^2-test for two independent samples and their choices of Windows colour schemes

Callouts:
- =E3*B\$15 and **Copy** down
- =D3/D\$15 and **Copy**
- =B2+C3 and **Copy**
- =E3*C\$15 and **Copy** down
- =(B2–F2)^2/F2
  =(C3–G3)^2/G3 and **Copy** down as a pair of cells
- =SUM(B2:B13) and **Copy** across
- =COUNTA(B2:B13)–1
- =CHIDIST(H15,E16)
- =CHIINV(E17,E16)

	A	B	C	D	E	F	G	H	I
1		HCI	Bus Stud	Combined	Exp prob	Exp HCI	Exp BS	$(O{-}E)^2/E$	
2	Windows	12				8.00		2.000	
3	Default		4	16	0.167		8.00	2.000	
4	Ocean	10				8.00		0.500	
5			6	16	0.167		8.00	0.500	
6	Designer	10				8.00		0.500	
7			6	16	0.167		8.00	0.500	
8	Patchwork	6				8.00		0.500	
9			10	16	0.167		8.00	0.500	
10	Fluorescent	4				7.00		1.286	
11			10	14	0.146		7.00	1.286	
12	Hot Dog	6				9.00		1.000	
13	Stand		12	18	0.188		9.00	1.000	
14									
15	Totals:	48	48	96	1.000	48	48	11.571	= χ^2–ratio
16				$df =$	5		p =	0.04	
17				$\alpha =$	0.05	$\chi^2(5,0.05) =$	11.070		

- Sufficient categories exist to contend with *all* responses (this may require a category of *no response*).
- The sample is sufficiently large such that no more than 20% of expected frequencies are less than 5, and in no case less than 1.

The test is a non-directional test, since it is based upon absolute differences in observed and expected frequencies. This is apparent since the differences are squared in the calculation. Now let us consider the first example and set it up on the worksheet, as described in Activity 19.6.

Activity 19.6

1 We will use Martin Monitor's study of colour usage in Windows in setting up the general worksheet for the χ^2-test for two samples (Figure 19.15).
  (a) What does the outcome tell Martin?
  (b) What would he have concluded if there had been no significant difference?

(c) What other possible studies come to mind as a consequence of
     this research?
(d) How might the sample influence the conclusions?
2   Try another example. This time input the data from the ex post facto
    study carried out in the doctors' practice, described above with the
    data in Table 19.4. (*Hint:* In a copy of the worksheet in Figure
    19.15, block cells **A8:H13**, **Delete** them and **Shift cells up**,
    before entering the new data.)
    (a) What was the outcome?
    (b) There is potentially a measurement problem here: what is it?
    (c) What role does sampling play in this study?
    (d) If there were a significant difference, what would it tell the doc-
         tors?

(*Hint:* When starting with raw data, first compile them into frequency
tables using the procedure shown in Figures 12.9 and 12.10 for two samples. Then Copy the values to a new worksheet like Figure 19.15.)

*Answers: 1(a) There does appear to be a difference, though because of the
nature of the samples, he ought to be a little suspicious of the results, asking
whether there are any other possible causes. (b) Whatever has happened to
these students, it was not enough to make them different. (c) The fact that
the untrained class has a view could be considered contrary to 'good practice'
and seemingly based on 'common sense' might suggest a study to see if some
possible sources of influence on their choices are greater than others — for
example, to shock or be outrageous, to mimic other software seen, or to
use colour combinations found in contemporary art or posters. Even if this
showed a difference, would it suggest generational taste difference or that
the original theory was not correct? (d) Were there any traits of the two
classes that could account for this, rather than the teaching?
2(a) $\chi^2 = 4.232$, $\chi^2(2, 0.05) = 5.991$, thus not significant (n.s.). (b) How
consistent were the doctors' diagnoses, especially for psychological complaints: interjudge reliability. (c) Were the patients typical? Should the
sample have been taken in complete weeks or scattered randomly? (d)
This study does not answer the question of causality, but it would describe
a significant association. Further research would be required to resolve the
true source.*

Power

As we will see in Activity 19.7, adding the power calculation to the worksheet is
a simple matter of copying formulae. The difficulty lies in the comparison of the
power of the χ^2-test with that of the t-test. As we saw earlier, the choice of interval bands is crucial when comparing tests, since the χ^2-test is very sensitive to
this. Therefore, as before, a test for ordinal data rather than nominal data
would be more appropriate. Though the power of the χ^2-test is not so obviously
dependent on sample size in the same way as the t-test was from its equation, do
remember that the sampling distribution approximates a χ^2-distribution. Therefore, the larger the sample the closer the approximation will be. The limit of no

less than 5 per expected frequency for more than 20% of the cells is a consequence of this 'rule'. Therefore, for a small sample where the rule is violated, there would be an increased chance of committing a Type I error as well as an inflated power. Also, external validity could be jeopardized since the smaller the original sample the less likely it is going to be representative and the less likely the two randomly assigned groups will be equivalent.

The second factor to influence power is the reliability of the classification scheme. As was suggested in Activity 19.8, if the doctors were not consistent in classifying patients' complaints (for example, male doctors diagnosing complaints of pain by women patients as psychological when female doctors might consider physiological causes), then the reliability would be low. This in turn could influence the differences between observed and expected frequencies, which in turn could increase the probability of a Type I or Type II error, depending on the error in classification. Recall Chapter 11 and the section on scorer or rater reliability.

Having mentioned the minimum expected frequency several times, as with other tests there are corrections that have been proposed. One of these, *Yates's correction*, has frequently been advocated, particularly for 2×2 tables (two samples with a dependent variable with two categories). Its use, though, is a matter of debate (see Haviland, 1990; Howell, 1997; Minium *et al.*, 1993). The correction is simple, subtracting 0.5 from the absolute value of the difference of each observed–expected pair. This essentially consists of changing equation (19.16) to

$$\chi^2 = \sum_{i=1}^{m} \sum_{j=1}^{2} \frac{(|O_{ij} - E_{ij}| - 0.5)^2}{E_{ij}} \qquad \text{(corrected for small } E_{ij}) \qquad (19.17)$$

Obviously, this reduces any χ^2-ratio, making the resulting test more conservative. The consensus seems to be that it unnecessarily makes the test more conservative (reducing the power) than it already is, but it is still an option in most computer programs. With the above discussion in mind, carry out Activity 19.7 now.

Activity 19.7

(a) Add power calculations to the worksheet in Figure 19.15, as shown in Figure 19.16.

(b) Reduce each data frequency in columns **B** and **C** of the worksheet in Figure 19.15 by half so the total in each group is 24. What happens to the power?

(c) Now take each of the cell values in (b) and triple them so the group totals are 72 and 72. What is the power now?

(d) What are the outcomes for the second example in Activity 19.6?

Answer: (b) $\chi^2 = 5.786$, *power* $= 0.14$; *also note that all expected frequencies are less than 5.* (c) $\chi^2 = 17.357$, *power* $= 0.82$. (d) *Not surprisingly, since the results were n.s., power is less than 50%: 0.33.*

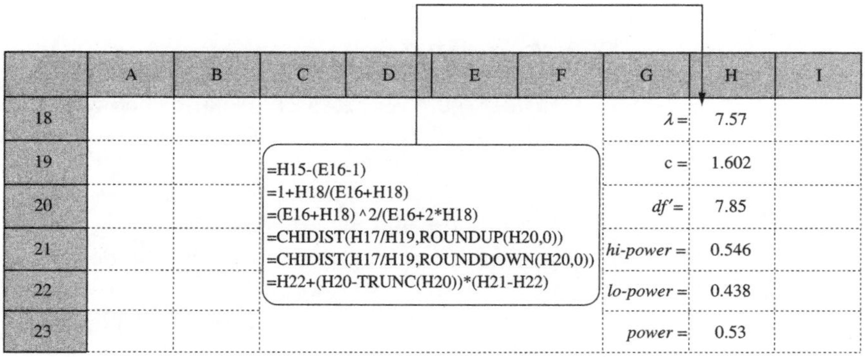

	A	B	C	D	E	F	G	H	I
18							$\lambda =$	7.57	
19			=H15-(E16-1)				$c =$	1.602	
20			=1+H18/(E16+H18)				$df' =$	7.85	
21			=(E16+H18)^2/(E16+2*H18)				$hi\text{-}power =$	0.546	
22			=CHIDIST(H17/H19,ROUNDUP(H20,0))				$lo\text{-}power =$	0.438	
23			=CHIDIST(H17/H19,ROUNDDOWN(H20,0)) =H22+(H20-TRUNC(H20))*(H21-H22)				$power =$	0.53	

FIGURE 19.16
Power calculations
to be added to
worksheet in Figure
19.15

SUMMARY

This chapter has introduced the five nonparametric tests in the lower left-hand section of Table 19.1. We now have at our disposal a set of tests that allow us to determine the likelihood of a sample belonging to a population, and of two independent samples belonging to a common population, where the dependent variables are represented by nominal characteristics or ordinal levels, instead of interval/ratio data summarized by means and standard deviations. These, therefore, are the counterparts to the parametric z- and t-tests.

While many texts emphasize the tendency for nonparametric tests to be less powerful than corresponding parametric ones, it has been emphasized here that often the choice is not that simple. It is necessary to consider two important issues when you think you are confronted with a choice:

- What is the research question, and consequently what is the most valid operational definition of the variables?
- Have all the assumptions (normality, homogeneity of variance) for the parametric tests been met?

The answers to these two questions may override a simple decision based upon potential power of a test alone.

A final note on worksheets: when using raw data, first compile them into frequency tables as shown in Figures 12.1 and 12.2 for single samples, and Figures 12.9 and 12.10 for two samples. To practise deciding which test would be most appropriate for a situation, carry out Activity 19.8 before going on to the next chapter.

Activity 19.8

Consider the seven research scenarios below with the tests in the first two columns of Table 19.1 in mind, and, for each, answer the following questions:

(a) State the null hypothesis.
(b) Identify proposed independent and dependent variables.
(c) Select the most appropriate test for the situation described, providing a defence of each choice (it is possible to answer 'none of the tests').
(d) Identify potential pitfalls and limitations of each design.

1 Happy Valley Hospital wanted to know whether its pattern of childbirth was typical. The hospital collected data over the previous year on how many births were 'natural' (e.g., Lamaze), under anaesthetic, and Caesarean, comparing this to national trends.

2 The hospital also wanted to know whether there was a difference in the labour time before childbirth for 'natural' and anaesthetic childbirths.

3 A survey was conducted among a random selection of 30 students and 30 teachers to see if there was a difference in their perception of the role of secondary school education. They were asked to choose among general education, vocational training and life skills. The results were as shown in the following table:

	Teachers	Students
General education	18	9
Vocational training	10	20
Life skills	17	12
Totals	45	41

4 George Geographer wanted to compare the achievement of two groups of 60 equivalent students learning map reading for the first time, one using paper-based individualized learning materials, and the others a computer-based learning package. The results were both highly negatively skewed for the criterion-referenced test.

5 Terry Teacher was concerned that children in his class (11–12-year-olds) were watching too much television. He found a study that said the national average was 15.3 hours per week (3.4). He asked his students to keep a record of how many hours they watched television each day for three weeks.

6 Calvin Clean wanted to know if there was any difference in responses between men and women to rubbish on the walkway. In a shopping mall, he placed a special bin, monitored by a concealed video camera. The bin contained a number of empty drink cans, and when no one was around would eject one from a door at the bottom. The video would record the reaction of passers-by. If the

can was picked up and placed in the bin, after a pause it would eject another into the path. The responses of 63 men and 75 women were recorded and coded as 'ignored', 'put in bin', 'took away'.

7   The *Daily Bumble* advertised itself as 'The newspaper for everyone'. To check this, it published a questionnaire to be returned by readers. Using the responses to questions on income, education, etc., it classified readers as belonging to one of five social classes. These results were compared with national demographic data.

Suggested answers: 1(a) There is no difference in the birthing pattern at the hospital from national trends. (b) Birthing pattern different for the hospital. (c) χ^2-goodness of fit, one sample. (d) While it might identify an anomaly, it would not say why.

2(a) There is no difference in labour times for natural and anaesthetic births. (b) The choice of anaesthetic or natural childbirth influences labour time. (c) t-test. (d) Measurement problem: when does labour start, twinges, waters break, can they remember?

3(a) There is no difference in perception of purpose between teachers and students. (b) Perception is dependent on position in system. (c) Trick question: note that the totals in the table exceed the sample numbers: some subjects responded more than once, thus responses are not independent, no test is appropriate. (d) See (c), questionnaire did not give clear instructions, data can be presented only descriptively.

4(a) There was no difference in how much each group achieved. (b) Achievement depends on media. (c) Reasonably large number but non-normal distributions, Wilcoxon–Mann–Whitney.

5(a) There is no difference in amount of television watching between his class and the rest of the children in the country. (b) Television time is different for the class. (c) z-test. (d) This does not answer his question about 'too much', all children in the country could be watching too much.

6(a) There is no difference in the response to litter by men and women. (b) Response to litter depends on gender. (c) χ^2-test for two samples. (d) Convenience sample, representativeness questionable. Would they respond the same way to dirty paper? Cans can have monetary value in some places.

7(a) There is no difference in social class of readership from national distribution. (b) Readership is different for this paper. (c) Ordinal data, one-sample Kolmogorov–Smirnov test. (d) Volunteers. What other traits might be investigated other than social class?

NONPARAMETRIC TESTS: MULTIPLE AND RELATED SAMPLES

20

This chapter will introduce a number of tests that allow us to consider hypotheses that have possible dependent variables which are described by frequencies for nominal or ordinal categories. One set of tests will be employed to resolve hypotheses comparing multiple samples analogous to the analysis of variance, for designs B3/D3 (post-test/observation only with control group). Other tests will be for two or more matched or related groups (including one group measured more than once), for designs B2/C2 (pre- and post-test/observation with control group). The tests covered here are, for cases of three or more independent samples (comparing three or more groups for levels of the independent variable, treatments),

- the χ^2-test for $m \times k$ tables, independent samples for nominal dependent variables and
- Kruskal–Wallis one-way analysis of variance, for independent samples for ordinal dependent variables;

for one sample with two measures over time, or one measure on each of two matched/related samples,

- the McNemar change test for a categorical (nominal) dependent variable and
- the Wilcoxon signed-rank test for a dependent variable on an ordinal scale;

for one-sample cases (three or more measures) or three or more matched/related samples,

- the Cochran Q-test for a nominal (binary) dependent variable and
- Friedman two-way analysis of variance for a ranked dependent variable.

The situations where these apply are summarized in the six cells in the lower right-hand corner of Table 19.1 in the previous chapter. In each case below, examples will be provided to illustrate the appropriate use of the tests.

THREE OR MORE INDEPENDENT SAMPLE CASES

There will be situations where comparing three or more groups for a potential independent variable (treatments) is necessary when the nominal or ordinal dependent variable generates frequency data. This means there is a need for a nonparametric counterpart to ANOVA for designs B3/D3. This could be used for such studies as comparing the impact of three or more different campaign approaches on voting patterns, counselling techniques on student choices of courses, and degree choice on subsequent job choice. Some results can be interpreted as causal relationships, others as association, depending on the nature of the variables and whether the study is experimental or ex post facto. The tests determine whether there is a difference across treatments or life events, but it is still up to the researcher to interpret the meaning. If the samples are based upon random selection and random assignment, with appropriate control of extraneous variables, then either way the strength of the conclusions will be enhanced.

There are a number of limitations that arise as a consequence of using nonparametric tests rather than parametric ones for multiple samples. One of these is the difficulty of carrying out the analogues to the post hoc analysis: even if a difference is found across three or more treatment groups, it is not always simple to determine which pairs are significantly different from each other. Also, as noted earlier, in many situations, nonparametric tests are less powerful than their parametric counterparts, reducing the probability of finding a significant difference if it exists. In most cases, this is not a large difference and what is more important is the validity of the operational definition of the dependent variable. In simple terms, given the choice, is it more meaningful to define the variable in such a way as to provide ordinal data (for example, social class or income in a range) or interval/ratio data (absolute income)? This can only be answered by the researcher.

Two tests, one each for nominal and ordinal variables, will be considered. Others exist and the criteria for deciding are often subtle and not unimportant. However, due to the growing variety, the choice has been restricted to the most common. Understanding the nature of these will allow you to consider the others if the need arises.

Chi-square test for $m \times k$ tables

A consequence of the versatility of the χ^2-test is that it can be extended to situations where there are more than two levels (groups) for the independent variable, as long as the dependent variable is nominal or possibly ordinal (though there are other tests for the latter). The extension of this test to k treatment groups for a potential dependent variable with m categories is best described using an example. Bungles Bakery had a new product it wished to franchise and sell on a national market, the Breakfast Blob, a sort of diet chocolate doughnut with jelly inside (something that, to the amazement of Mr Bungles, his 12- and 14-year-old children loved). The company felt its success would depend on advertising and was willing to consider an approach other than the one used in the past employing child actors to sell its products. The

Samuel Sellem Agency suggested two new approaches based upon cartoons and animated clay puppets. To determine which would be most effective to use on a larger scale, the bakery worked with the agency to supply Blobs in three of its distribution areas in separate cities. Each city had a different advertising campaign. The shops kept a record of purchases of Blobs as compared to other breakfast purchases (sweet rolls, doughnuts, etc.) or no breakfast purchases, for a week after the weekend campaigns on the three local television stations. The results are shown in the left-hand shaded area of Figure 20.1.

The test is simply an extension of that used for two independent groups, which compares the observed frequencies to the expected, the latter based upon the overall combined distribution of frequencies. The null hypothesis being tested is that all the samples could have come from one population, based upon whether the differences in proportions would be greater than that expected by chance. The equation is

$$\chi^2 = \sum_{i=1}^{m}\sum_{j=1}^{k}\frac{(O_{ij}-E_{ij})^2}{E_{ij}} \tag{20.1}$$

where the O_{ij} are the observed frequencies from each category, from 1 to m, of all groups, from 1 to k; the E_{ij} are the expected frequencies, determined by combining the expected frequencies for all the groups (see below); i represents variable categories, ranging from 1 to m, where m is at least 2; and j stands for the treatment groups, here ranging from 1 to k, where k is at least 3. This statistic is referred to in Table B.9 in Appendix B, and has $(m-1)(k-1)$ degrees of free-

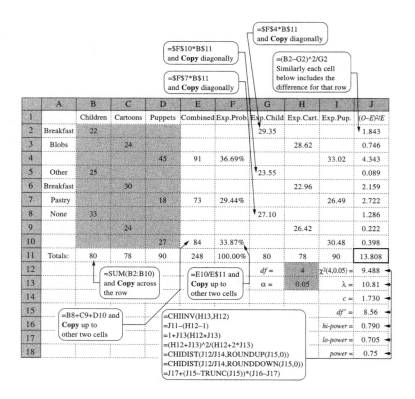

FIGURE 20.1
Worksheet for three
advertising
campaigns for
Breakfast Blobs

dom. The expected frequencies are again found by first combining all the observed frequencies to determine the expected probabilities for each category as shown in Figure 20.1. This is illustrated as an example to be set up on a worksheet in Activity 20.1, which should be carried out now.

Activity 20.1

1 Set up the Bungles Bakery example as shown on the worksheet in Figure 20.1. Note that the χ^2 table has some built-in checks: the sums for the observed and expected frequencies should be equal. Once this is set up, changes can be made by changing values in the shaded cells as follows:

   (a) Mr Bungles wanted to be 'really sure', so changed the significance level, $\alpha = 0.01$. Are the results still significant? Does this tell him any more than the other test?

   (b) Identify any pitfalls in this study.

   (c) What other information might Bungles Bakery want to gather before investing in large scale production and a national sales campaign?

   (d) Investigate what would have happened had Bungles collected data for only half a week by cutting each observed score in half (rounding up any resulting fractions). Would there still be a significant difference? What would the power be?

2 The Dean of Science at Freedonia University wondered whether there was a difference across the four departments in the nature of the jobs new undergraduates found upon graduation. In particular, did they tend to get jobs in the area of their degrees? Fifty graduates randomly selected from each of the departments for one year were sent questionnaires on the nature of their employment. If the jobs were related to their degree subject, they were classified as 'consistent', and if not then 'inconsistent'. Examples of inconsistent jobs included physicists becoming accountants, biologists selling life insurance, mathematicians becoming pop music stars. The results were as follows:

	Biology	Chemistry	Physics	Maths
Consistent	32	22	33	38
Inconsistent	4	9	11	2

   (a) What is the research question?

   (b) What conclusions were reached? (*Hint*: make a copy of Figure 20.1 on a new worksheet, activate rows **8:10** and press the ⟨Delete⟩ key to clear the contents. **Insert Column** for Expected at **H** and a corresponding column for the data at **C**, and **Insert Rows** at **6** and **3**, in that order. Add the new raw data and change the two formulae under Combined to include these, **F5** and **F9**. Copy the sums formula to **I13** and **C13**. **Copy** diagonally the formulae for the new Expected column to **I3** and **I7**. Add the formulae under the $(O - E)^2/E$ column. Check that the sums under the two sets of four columns match and that the Combined Total matches the original total for the above data.)

(c)   Identify limitations and any pitfalls in this study.

Suggested answers: 1(a) The results are still significant, but they do not tell him any more and may possibly tell him less, since now the power would be 0.52, a lower probability of being correct. What is more important is whether there will be a significant difference in sales. (b) Are the three areas representative of the rest of the country? (c) Questions need to be answered such as whether enough children really like them and whether parents will buy them in sufficient volume. Will the product stand on its own or will it need continual advertising? (d) No, $\chi^2 = 7.34$, power = 0.34.

2(a) Is there any difference in terms of job choice across graduates in different subjects? (b) Yes, there seems to be, $\chi^2 = 10.036$, $p < 0.05$. (c) While it started with a random sample, it ended with volunteers. Why did non-respondents not respond? The study does not tell us why there is a difference, just that there is one.

Post hoc analysis for chi-square tests

As Siegel and Castellan (1988) note, a significant χ^2 for the situation of k independent groups for m levels of the dependent variable only tells us that there is a significant difference in the frequencies from that which would be expected. One would assume that procedures would be available analogous to those for the one-way analysis of variance to carry out pairwise comparisons across treatment groups. Unfortunately, there is less consensus as to what should be done, though a few ways of resolving the source of overall significance and how to interpret the results will be considered.

PAIRS OF CHI-SQUARE TESTS ON NEW GROUPS   Daly *et al.* (1995) suggest that a new χ^2-test could be carried out on two new groups created by regrouping the others according to a new common trait. For the example above, the advertisement approaches for Bungles could be regrouped into the two groups that used television cartoons and the one group that used real people. This does look a bit like data snooping, changing the actual research question and hypotheses after the data has been collected, not unlike moving your bets on the roulette table after the ball has settled into a slot on the wheel.

PARTITIONING   This is a procedure whereby the contingency table is subdivided into a series of 2×2 tables equal to the number of degrees of freedom (Siegel and

Castellan, 1988). Thus for the above example, there would be six 2×2 tables. Since there can be a large number of possible combinations, the actual subtables would need to be identified *before* processing the data in order to answer meaningful questions. The new χ^2 calculation is rather complex and since this process does not necessarily resolve the issue of pairwise comparisons of the independent groups, it is left to the reader to pursue it further in the reference provided.

RESIDUALS   This allows the identification of specific 'cells' in the contingency table as the sources of the overall significance (Siegel and Castellan, 1988), by considering the individual differences between observed and expected frequencies. Again, this does not resolve the issue of pairwise comparisons of groups. This procedure is of greater relevance when applying χ^2-tests to single samples and endeavouring to identify associations.

COMPENSATED PAIRS OF CHI-SQUARE TESTS, WHERE ONE IS THE CONTROL GROUP
This approach is the closest to pairwise comparisons analogous to those for the one-way ANOVA, but applies only to the special case of k independent groups with a binary (two-level) category for the dependent variable. A procedure that allows the use of multiple pairwise χ^2-tests using a compensated value of α is described in Everitt (1977). This essentially entails carrying out all the possible 2×2 χ^2-tests, but using the following critical value for each:

$$\alpha' = \frac{\alpha}{2(k-1)} \tag{20.2}$$

which allows for an overall level of significance of α. If, for the example above, there had been only two levels, buy Blobs or buy something else, then the two χ^2-tests for the pairwise comparisons would each be evaluated against ($\alpha=0.05$),

$$\alpha' = \frac{0.05}{2(3-1)} = 0.0125$$

and, using the Excel function,

$$\chi^2(1, 0.0125) = \textbf{CHIINV}(\textbf{.0125}, \textbf{1}) = \textbf{6.24}$$

This is considerably higher than $\chi^2(1, 0.05) = 3.84$, increasing the conservativeness of the test to compensate for multiple comparison, analogous to pairwise tests seen earlier. To try this, carry out Activity 20.2 now.

Activity 20.2

1   Set up a chi-square worksheet using just the data for the first two entries for Bungles: 2×3 contingency table.

   (a)   Is there a difference across the three advertising approaches? (*Hint*: on a copy of the worksheet in Figure 20.1, simply **Delete** rows **8:10** (for None) and change *df*.)

(b)   Is either of the two new approaches better than the usual? Set up a worksheet area with three 2×2 tables. (*Hint*: Create one and then **Copy** it twice, changing the data numbers and headings). Compare it to Figure 20.2.

(c)   Is the question being answered by this exercise different from that answered in Activity 20.1, Question 1? If so, what is the difference?

2   What groups are significantly different in the study of science and mathematics graduates in the example in Activity 20.1? Set up a series of 2×2 tables and calculate a new α for pairwise comparisons.

Answers: 1(a) Yes, $\chi^2 = 10.10$, $\chi^2(2, 0.05) = 5.99$. (b) Puppets seem to have a higher response than either of the other two; see Figure 20.2. (c) Yes, this one is asking if the districts subjected to the different advertising have different patterns of buying breakfast pastry, while the original question included not buying any breakfast pastry at all. Thus the original question would potentially include all customers, not just those buying breakfast pastry, and would reflect differences in overall consumption of breakfast pastry. The structure of this second study ignores considerable data and would better reflect the possible effect if the second two categories had been combined regrouping other pastries and no pastry into a single category not buying Blobs.
2 Only mathematics and chemistry graduates are significantly different, with mathematics having a smaller proportion of graduates deviating from a subject-based career. The question remains as to whether the samples reflect the different sizes of the graduate populations.

Kruskal–Wallis one-way analysis of variance (ranks)

The Wilcoxon–Mann–Whitney test covers the two-sample situation, and this test is for three or more independent samples/treatments. It is based upon medians and answers the question whether several groups belong to a single population, their differences within expectation or not. The null hypothesis is that the medians are not different from that for the population, the statistical test checking to see if they are close enough, allowing for natural variation in samples. The variable is assumed to be at least ordinal and there is a single underlying continuous distribution (Siegel and Castellan, 1988).

As with other tests based on rank, this one requires that all the raw data from all the samples be placed in order and assigned a rank, starting with 1 for the smallest, going to N, the number of independent observations for all k samples. The sum of all the ranks for each sample is found and the mean rank for each group calculated. The assumption is that if the samples are really from the same population with a common mean, then these average ranks should be much the same, allowing for random variation. This is best seen in the following expression of the Kruskal–Wallis statistic, which reminds one of the calculation of variance:

	A	B	C	D	E	F	G	H
17		Children	Cartoons	Combined	Exp.Prob.	Exp.Child	Exp.Cart.	$(O–E)^2/E$
18	Breakfast	22				21.41		0.016
19	Blobs		24	46	45.54%		24.59	0.014
20	Other	25				25.59		0.014
21	Pastry		30	55	54.46%		29.41	0.012
22	Totals	47	54	101	100.00%	47.00	54.00	0.057
23	:				$df =$	1	$\chi^2(1,0.0125) =$	6.238
24					$\alpha =$	0.05		
25								
26		Children	Puppets	Combined	Exp.Prob.	Exp.Child	Exp.Pup.	$(O–E)^2/E$
27	Breakfast	22				28.63		1.534
28	Blobs		45	67	60.91%		38.37	1.145
29	Other	25				18.37		2.391
30	Pastry		18	43	39.09%		24.63	1.783
31	Totals:	47	63	110	100.00%	47.00	63.00	6.853
32					$df =$	1	$\chi^2(1,0.0125) =$	6.238
33					$\alpha =$	0.05		
34								
35		Cartoons	Puppets	Combined	Exp.Prob.	Exp.Cart.	Exp.Pup.	$(O–E)^2/E$
36	Breakfast	24				31.85		1.933
37	Blobs		45	69	58.97%		37.15	1.657
38	Other	30				22.15		2.779
39	Pastry		18	48	41.03%		25.85	2.382
40	Totals:	54	63	117	100.00%	54.00	63.00	8.751
41					$df =$	1	$\chi^2(1,0.0125) =$	6.238
42					$\alpha =$	0.05		

=SUM(B36:B39) and **Copy** across the row

=B38+C39 and **Copy** up to other cells

=D39/D40

=E39*B40 and similarly for other Exp cells

=CHIINV(F42/(2*(3–1)),F41) and **Copy** to other cells

=(C39–G39)^2/G39 and similarly for other cells in column

FIGURE 20.2
Worksheet for pairwise comparisons for Figure 20.1

$$KW = \frac{12\sum_{j=1}^{k} n_j(\bar{R}_j - \bar{R})^2}{N(N-1)}$$

The statistic is also calculated by a form of the equation that makes it easy to use on a spreadsheet (Howell, 1997):

$$KW = \left[\frac{12}{N(N+1)} \sum_{j=1}^{k} \frac{R_j^2}{n_j} \right] - 3(N+1) \tag{20.3}$$

where R_j is the sum of ranks in group j (with $j = 1, \ldots, k$), n_j is the number in group j and N is the total number of subjects in all groups. When the number of groups is greater than 3 and the number in each group is greater than 4 (or even when it is 3 but the sample is large), then the sampling distribution is close to the χ^2-distribution. Also, there is a correction that can be applied if there are a large number of ties (over 25% of the samples), which increases the size of the KW-statistic (see Siegel and Castellan, 1988). We will assume a sufficiently large sample with less than 25% ties here and leave these special cases for those who have a need to pursue them. If all values of R_i are equal to each other, then $KW = 0$.

An example of design D3 (quasi-experimental) for which this test would be appropriate is a study conducted by Dr B. Kalm, a psychiatrist with the counselling service at Freedonia University. He had identified a number of new undergraduate students who said they suffered from 'examination panic' and they felt they were not performing as well as they could on timed examinations. Though he had read that a new tranquillizer was supposed to help, he also had a colleague who was keen to try a new therapy approach. He was concerned that the tranquillizer would actually have an adverse effect on performance, so decided to include a control group in his test of these two approaches. He randomly divided the students into three equal groups that would carry out a timed test as part of one of three treatment programmes: one to undergo therapy sessions before the test day; the second to receive the tranquillizer just before the test; and the third to receive a placebo (a sugar tablet) just before the test.

When the results were collected, as shown in Figure 20.3, it was found that the distributions of scores were highly irregular, neither normal nor showing homogeneity of variance, therefore a one-way ANOVA was not appropriate. Thus the Kruskal–Wallis test was chosen since the data were at least ordinal and the underlying distribution was continuous. As with other tests that have been encountered, the calculation is not as awesome as it looks once it is set up on a worksheet. Carry out Activity 20.3 to perform the analysis of the data as shown in Figure 20.3.

Activity 20.3

1 (a) Set up the worksheet as shown in Figure 20.3. There is a function in Excel for automatically assigning a rank to data,

=RANK(⟨score⟩,⟨list of scores⟩, 0 or 1 ⟨descending or ascending⟩)

but it is not entirely consistent with accepted convention. This can be adjusted after the function is used, as shown in Figure 20.3. In Excel, when there is a tie, say between two scores, they are both assigned the next rank and not the average. Thus, if there are two scores for rank 4, then both are assigned 4 instead of 4.5. The next rank is 6, leaving out 5. This requires an adjustment to conform with what nonparametric tests use. In each case of ties, it is a matter of adding one of the values on the left to Excel's value, depending on the number and continuing in a like manner if there are more than four:

Numbers tied	Add to each Excel rank
2	0.5
3	1.0
4	1.5

To check your values, simply add all the sums (cell **G12**) and compare this value to $N(N+1)$ in cell **G13**. If they do not agree, there is an error.

(b) For this example, what conclusions could be drawn? Are these justified or could a better design have been used? If so, what?

(c) Investigate the consequences of a smaller sample by removing row **10**.

2 The Committee for Improvement of Teaching at Freedonia University wanted to improve teaching quality in the university. Having conducted an induction programme for new staff, the committee wanted to compare student ratings for these staff against others in the University: totally untrained staff and those who by virtue of earlier experiences (for example, trained school teachers who subsequently came to Freedonia as staff) had some training. The results, for eight members of staff randomly selected from each group, were as follows:

Induction	33	35	34	34	30	24	47	42
Trained	65	44	54	45	44	43	64	56
None	56	24	32	28	23	22	45	34

Make a copy of the worksheet in Figure 20.3 and enter the new data. Delete any corrections for ties from the previous data. Finding ties is easier if the data are in order, so, after blocking each column, use **Data Sort** from the main menu. When the **Sort Warning** comes up, click **Continue with current selection** and **Sort** by **Score, Descending**. Then add corrections for ties as needed.

(a) Was there a difference across the groups?

(b) What might threaten the validity of any conclusions?

Answers: 1(b) There is a difference across the three, but it is not obvious where. Dr Kalm has used an entire population, so it is questionable to whom he could extend his results, unless he can somehow justify that this year's group is typical of new undergraduates with problems. Ideally, he would randomly select groups from a number of universities for such a study. (c) This may seem surprising, $W = 12.76$, but remember this test is sensitive to the relative distributions of ranks. This does not mean that the power is insensitive to sample size, but that it is very sensitive to ranks. 2(a) Yes, $W = 10.00$. (b) Since the 'none' lecturers may be older, like cheese they may have simply improved with maturity. Also, are student ratings the most reliable and valid way of judging teaching quality? What other forms of measurement of quality might be used?

> =RANK(E3,($A$3:$A$11,$C$3:$C$11,$E$3:$E$11),1)
> and **Copy** to all *Rank* column cells,
> then adjust individual cells for ties

	A	B	C	D	E	F	G
1	**Tranquil**		**Therapy**		**Placebo**		
2	Score	*Rank*	Score	*Rank*	Score	*Rank*	
3	70	21	80	24	48	11	
4	64	19	79	23	46	10	
5	63	18	74	22	45	9	
6	57	16.5	67	20	40	5	
7	55	15	57	16.5	38	4	
8	51	12	54	14	34	3	
9	44	8	52	13	27	2	
10	42	6.5	42	6.5	21	1	
11							ΣR_i
12	$R_i =$	116		139		45	300
13	$n_i =$	8		8		8	300
14	$R_i^2/n_i =$	1682		2415.125		253.125	
15	$R_i/n_i =$	14.5		17.375		5.625	
16	$N =$	24					=SUM(B12:F12)
17	$W =$	12.01	$\alpha =$	0.05			=B16*(B16+1)/2
18	$\chi^2(2,0.05) =$	5.99					

> =B13+D13+F13
> =(12/(B16*(B16+1)))*
> (B14+D14+F14)–3*(B16+1)
> =CHIINV(D17,2)

> =SUM(F3:F10)
> =F12^2/F13
> =F12/F13
> and **Copy** these left

FIGURE 20.3
Worksheet for an example employing Kruskal–Wallis one-way analysis of variance

Post hoc analysis for Kruskal–Wallis

To carry out pairwise comparisons, it is simply a matter of testing the differences between pairs of averages of ranks against a standard that has been adjusted to take into account that these are not independent. When the samples are large, then their differences are approximately normally distributed (Siegel and Castellan, 1988) and the critical value is found by

$$\Delta(R_i/n_i)_{\text{crit}} = z(\alpha/k(k-1))\sqrt{\frac{N(N+1)}{12}\left(\frac{1}{n_A}+\frac{1}{n_B}\right)} \quad (20.4)$$

Assuming that all the sample sizes are the same, this calculation has to be carried out only once. There is an adjustment that can be made if the comparisons are to be done only between each treatment and a control, but not between treatments (analogous to Dunnett's post hoc test for ANOVA), but in our example comparisons were desired between the two treatments (Siegel and Castellan, 1988). Applying this to the example is more easily done in Excel than by hand, since the value of $z(\alpha/k(k-1))$ can be time-consuming to interpolate from a z-table. To add this to the worksheet, carry out Activity 20.4.

Activity 20.4

1 The three rows in Figure 20.4 are all that is needed to carry out pair-wise comparisons. The data are shown for the example in Figure 20.3. How would you interpret the results in this situation?

2 Add this analysis to the worksheet set up for Question 2 in Activity 20.3, comparing student ratings of academic staff. How would you interpret these results?

Answers: 1 Both the therapy and tranquillizer groups performed significantly better than the control group, but even though the scores of the therapy group were higher than that for the tranquillizer group, this difference could be attributed to chance.

2 [None Inducted] [Trained] There was no significant difference between the induction and none groups (1.75), though there was between the trained and none groups (10.44) and between the trained and induction groups (8.69). This still does not totally negate any possible value for the induction course due to the measuring instruments, though if the experience trained and none groups were of comparable age, time would have less credence as an extraneous variable.

ONE SAMPLE WITH TWO MEASURES OR TWO RELATED/MATCHED SAMPLES

There are analogues to *t*-tests for related samples for data that do not meet the requirements of parametric tests. Two tests will be considered here, one for situations where the dependent variable is nominal and a second for when it is ordinal.

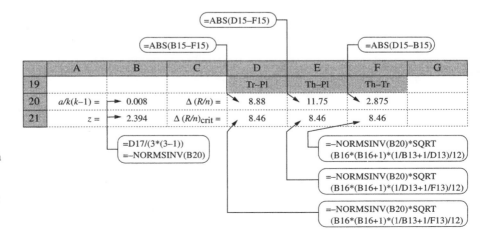

FIGURE 20.4
Worksheet addition for pair-wise comparisons for Kruskal–Wallis test in worksheet in Figure 20.3

McNemar change test

This test is literally looking for a significant change in classification of subjects due to a treatment. To illustrate this, consider the Psychology and Sociology Departments at Freedonia University. They decided to recruit students into a common first-year social sciences programme, letting the students select their degree subject at the end of the year. There was some suspicion that the Sociology Department would benefit more than Psychology from this process in terms of students changing their minds. Sociology suggested that it be left to a trial year and a check be made at the end of the year based upon the number of students changing, presenting Psychology with a test of their 'faith' in statistics. At the beginning of the year, they randomly selected two groups of 24 students claiming a strong commitment to pursuing one degree or the other, from those in the class of 250. At the end of the year, they compared this to which department they selected for the next year. The results are shown in Table 20.1. Was Psychology always going to lose out since it ended up with 16 students and Sociology with 32, or was this just a difference that was within the realm of random fluctuation?

This could be considered an example of design B2/C2 on two groups using a dichotomous variable, where each subject belongs to one of two alternative groups. The 'treatment' here was seemingly the first-year course, though it could be said that it was the collective experience of learning what the two disciplines *and* teaching staff were really like.

The really important students to this test are the ones who changed their minds, the nine in cell C who went from sociology to psychology and the 17 in cell B who went from psychology to sociology. While one would expect some changes, if the first year exercised no differential effect on the students, one would expect as many going one way as the other. In other words, the expected change would have been

$$E = \frac{B + C}{2}$$

Obviously, not every sample would produce exactly this number, so we resort to a statistical test to see what would be an acceptable variation from this. As this is a matter of categories, the χ^2-test is appropriate. If we use B and C as the observed frequencies, these can be substituted into equation (19.5) for χ^2,

$$\chi^2 = \sum_{i=1}^{m} \frac{(O_i - E_i)^2}{E_i}$$

which would become

$$\chi^2 = \frac{\left(B - \dfrac{B+C}{2}\right)^2}{\dfrac{B+C}{2}} + \frac{\left(C - \dfrac{B+C}{2}\right)^2}{\dfrac{B+C}{2}}$$

which reduces to

$$\chi^2 = \frac{(B - C)^2}{B + C} \quad , \quad df = 1 \tag{20.5}$$

TABLE 20.1
Before and after first-year course choices for degrees

		Beginning choice		Totals after
		Psych.	Soc.	
End-of-year choice	Psych.	*A* 7	*C* 9	16
	Soc.	*B* 17	*D* 15	32
	Totals before	24	24	

Thus for the example above,

$$\chi^2_{\text{ratio}} = \frac{(17-9)^2}{17+9} = \frac{64}{26} = 2.46$$

Since $\chi^2(1, 0.05) = 3.84$, the result was considered non-significant, in other words, this was a chance occurrence. It was argued that this scheme would ultimately not influence the balance of student numbers changing their minds over a year. The argument did not end here – see Activity 20.5 for the conclusion.

Activity 20. 5

1 (a) The Psychology Department still felt hard done by and demanded that α should have been 0.10. Would it have proven its case had this been the accepted level of significance?

   (b) If you put these results into a simple 2×2 table using the final totals of 16 and 32 as *observed* and the original 24 and 24 as *expected*, then equation (19.5) for the χ^2-test produces a significant result, $\chi^2 = 5.33$. Does this contradict the above results? Why or why not?

2 Consider the plight of Virgil Verbosity who wished to be a Member of Parliament. His election campaign as an independent attracted little money and therefore what he had needed was to be spent wisely. He decided to make a videotape, but wanted to determine its effectiveness before paying for it to be broadcast. He gathered together a group of 38 volunteers from the local pub and asked them to fill out a ballot. He then had them watch the videotape, followed by a second ballot. The results are summarized in Table 20.2.

   (a) Was there a significant change?
   (b) Should he pay for his videotape to be broadcast on television?

Answers: 1(a) No, $\chi^2(1, 0.10) = 2.71$. (b) No, since it is answering a different question: Is there a significant difference in enrolment from what was expected? The original test asks: Was there a significant difference in the numbers who changed their minds?

2(a) While there was a statistically significant change, $\chi^2 = 3.6$, these were volunteers. (b) Even if they were representative, a change of this proportion is unlikely to get him elected. He should get more than 5% of the votes so would not lose his election deposit, but it still could be a waste of money. It depends on how much money he can afford to spend and still lose.

Wilcoxon signed-rank test for two matched groups

While this test could be used with a single sample, the pre-experimental design A2 (one group pre- and post-test/observations), as could its parametric counterpart, the t-test, the design itself is not encouraged. The other application, which will be emphasized here, is two groups with *matched pairs of subjects*, a variation on design B3. The reason for employing matched pairs instead of two independent samples was discussed in Chapter 15 and is a valid approach when the intent is to eliminate extraneous variables.

Ideally, the researcher would randomly select a group, identify matched pairs, and then randomly assign each pair to one of the two treatments. To obtain matched pairs randomly is not always feasible, and studies can be reduced to purposively selecting representative subjects so that matched pairs can be acquired. There is then the obligation on the researcher to ensure and justify that no extraneous variables have been introduced that could contribute to the outcome.

The Wilcoxon signed-rank test to be used here has few assumptions, but for the results to be meaningful, it is necessary that the pair differences are meaningful and constitute ordinal data. For example, is it true that the difference of five between 15 and 20 means the same as the difference between 30 and 35?

Let us consider an example (based upon design B2) to see how this test is carried out and the ramifications of the underlying assumptions. Two groups were needed to test which of two approaches would be most effective in reducing subjects' dependence on cigarettes. From a large group of volunteer students who professed to wanting to give up smoking at Smogmoor University, subjects were randomly selected until a set of 16 pairs matched on present level of dependence were selected. Each member of a pair was randomly assigned to one of the two treatment groups. It was assumed that, for the range of reduction expected, the

TABLE 20.2 Effect of Vergil Verbosity's videotape on a sample of the electorate

		Before video		Totals after
		Others	Self	
After video	Others	20	2	22
	Self	8	8	16
	Totals before	28	10	

ranking of these would be meaningful. When the results were collected, as shown in columns **A** to **D** in Figure 20.5, it was found that the *differences in decline* in number of cigarettes per day ranged from 1 to 9. When the declines in consumption for each group were displayed in columns **E** and **F**, the narrow range from 10 to 21 per day supported the feeling that it was reasonable to rank-order the differences in declines in dependency. Using the **=FREQUENCY** function in Excel and plotting the distributions as shown in Figure 20.6, it was seen that these were very flat, so a nonparametric test was needed.

To determine whether the decline for group B was really significantly different (in this case, greater) than that for group A, signifying a 'better' treatment, a test is needed that resolves whether the difference in drop in consumption could have occurred by chance or not. In other words, could we have such a difference for two samples from a common population? The Wilcoxon signed-ranks test compares the sizes of the differences in ranks, against a range that would be expected as a result of chance variation. This means that more weight is given to pairs with large differences than to those with

	A	B	C	D	E	F	G	H	I	J	K
1	Pair	Start	Finish A	Finish B	Δ A	Δ B	ΔA−ΔB	|ΔA−ΔB|	Rank of |ΔA−ΔB|	W+	W−
2	1	50	39	30	11	20	−9	9	16		16.0
3	2	48	38	33	10	15	−5	5	9		10.5
4	3	45	26	31	19	14	5	5	9	10.5	
5	4	44	33	28	11	16	−5	5	9		10.5
6	5	44	27	25	17	19	−2	2	2		2.5
7	6	44	34	26	10	18	−8	8	15		15.0
8	7	40	26	20	14	20	−6	6	13		13.0
9	8	40	25	30	15	10	5	5	9	10.5	
10	9	39	25	28	14	11	3	3	4	4.5	
11	10	39	22	18	17	21	−4	4	6		7.0
12	11	37	20	22	17	15	2	2	2	2.5	
13	12	35	21	22	14	13	1	1	1	1.0	
14	13	32	20	16	12	16	−4	4	6		7.0
15	14	32	21	14	11	18	−7	7	14		14.0
16	15	30	15	12	15	18	−3	3	4		4.5
17	16	30	18	14	12	16	−4	4	6		7.0
18	136	= total			219	260			125	29.0	107.0
19										n =	16
20										z (W) =	2.02

=B17−C17 and **Copy** up

=B17−D17 and **Copy** up

=E17−F17 and **Copy** up

ABS(E17-F17) and **Copy** up

=RANK(H17, H$2:H$17,1) and **Copy** up

=(K18−0.25*K19*(K19+1))/SQRT(K19*(K19+1)*(2*K19+1)/24)

FIGURE 20.5
Worksheet for Wilcoxon Signed-Ranks Test for ordinal data

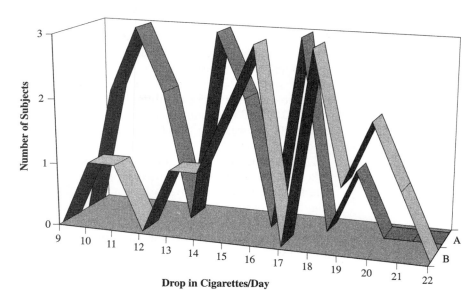

FIGURE 20.6
Distributions of drop
in consumption as a
result of treatments

small differences. Thus the probability of a significant difference would be enhanced not only by the number of differences in a given direction, but also by the size of the differences.

When the number of sample pairs is sufficiently large, the sampling distribution of the sum of differences in ranks compares well to the z-distribution, using the equation

$$z(W) = \frac{\sum W_+ - 0.25n(n+1)}{\sqrt{\dfrac{n(n+1)(2n+1)}{24}}} \tag{20.6}$$

where n is the number of pairs and $\sum W_+$ is the sum of the ranks for differences in one direction.

This equation has similarities, not surprisingly, to equation (19.17) for the Wilcoxon–Mann–Whitney test for two independent samples, and similar origins. Complete the setting up of the worksheet shown in Figure 20.5, answer the questions about the study to hand and try another problem in Activity 20.6 now.

Activity 20.6

1 Set up the worksheet as shown in Figure 20.5, with the raw data for the matched pairs. Find the differences between the gain scores for the two groups and rank them. Recall the problem of ties and Excel's **=RANK** function: when there are ties, the resulting ranks have to be corrected by adding the amounts shown in the table in Activity 20.3.

These are placed in the last two columns, depending on whether the difference in column **G** was (+) or (−).

(*Hints*: Either $\sum W_+$ or $\sum W_-$ can be used in the calculation: the only difference will be in the sign of the value for z. Thus this provides a check for you: try both. Also, the total of $\sum W_+$ and $\sum W_-$ should equal the sum of the ranks, which is why the total under column **A** is provided.)

(a) Considering the nature of the variables, might there be a more appropriate matching variable?

(b) Can you suggest a better way of achieving a representative sample?

2   Melvin Monetary wanted to see if being the first-born male of a male–male sibling pair had an influence on ambition in life, since it is said that parents expect more of the first-born and relax when raising subsequent children. He obtained a record of salaries for 16 pairs of male siblings when each was 45 years old, adjusted for the different years. The results were (salaries are in 1000s of whatever currency you like):

Elder	43.1	39.5	33.4	44.6	42.3	32.1	40.1	43.4
Younger	39.8	22.5	35.6	43.1	45.6	33.1	27.6	44.2
Elder	38.9	33.5	46.8	41.4	46.1	40.5	35.8	39.9
Younger	39.2	35.1	36.1	43.2	30.2	41.2	36.3	24.8

(a) Using the Wilcoxon signed-rank test, is there a significant difference?

(b) What limitations are there to this study and how could it be improved?

(c) Generate a frequency table and graph like Figure 20.6, and check the homogeneity of variance. Would a t-test have been appropriate? What would a t-test for matched pairs have indicated?

Suggested answers: 1(a) Possibly a measure of commitment to stopping or reducing smoking. (b) Neither can I. Considering the population is students who want to stop smoking, it would be hard to get them any other way than if they volunteered. The random sample and assignment should give a representative range of addiction for each of the treatment groups.
2(a) No difference, $z(W) = 0.96$. (b) Is raw salary the best measure of ambition? Even a percentage of maximum salary or rank in organization might be more meaningful since different careers pay differently for similar levels of responsibility and position in a hierarchy. (c) The graphs are skewed and there is heterogeneity of variance: the t-test would not be justified. If used, it says there is a significant difference, $t = 2.15$.

ONE-SAMPLE CASES (THREE OR MORE MEASURES) OR THREE OR MORE MATCHED/RELATED SAMPLES

These tests are analogous to the parametric randomized block ANOVA discussed in Chapter 18, and serve the same function of controlling extraneous variables. Situations covered include the following:

- the *repeated measures* (and treatments) design on one sample, where it is not desirable to have several groups but a single group to be observed/measured after receiving each of the several treatments;
- the *matched sample* design for several treatments, to ensure equivalence of samples that is unlikely to be achieved by simple random sampling and random assignment.

The aim is to control for specific extraneous variables by having the same subjects (or matched subjects with the suspect traits) in each treatment group. Such variables need to be taken into account since they might influence the dependent variable instead of or in addition to the proposed independent variable. The only difference here is the measurement of the dependent variable as frequencies of categories or ordinal data instead of interval data. There is not an exact nonparametric equivalence to analysis of covariance.

Cochran Q-test

This is an extension of the McNemar test for two related samples, described in the previous section. The Cochran Q-test covers situations where the columns are different measures (three or more) on each subject (or matched set of subjects) in a row. The dependent variable is a binary category (has it, does not have it; votes for Smith, does not vote for Smith), thus is recorded as either 0 or 1. This is analogous to the randomized block designs of Chapter 18, but the dependent variable is categorical instead of interval/ratio. To resolve the null hypothesis of whether there is a significant difference across the treatments or measures, the equation for the Q-test is

$$Q = \frac{(k-1)\left[k\sum_{j=1}^{k} G_j^2 - \left(\sum_{j=1}^{k} G_j\right)^2\right]}{k\sum_{i=1}^{N} L_i - \sum_{i=1}^{N} L_i^2} \qquad (20.7)$$

where G_j is the total number in a column, the jth treatment, and L_i is the total number in a row, the ith subject (or matched set). The value of Q for samples is distributed approximately as χ^2, with $df = k - 1$, as long as the product of the sample size and number of 'treatments' is greater than 24 (Siegel and Castellan, 1988).

For example, City High School wanted to conduct extra English classes for students to enhance their reading ability, but was concerned that many who needed such help in the past did not attend. It was recognized that there were a large number of contributing factors that might prevent students attending, such as peer pressure, convenience, subject matter of classes, and who was teaching them. Since they felt it was a motivational problem, the teachers decided to try 'theme' sessions to see if they could identify one that was more effective than the others in attracting those who needed help. Ms Helpum, the teacher in charge, identified 16 students who would benefit and invited them to attend at a time that was determined to be convenient for all. Three themes were identified that were seen as potentially appealing to teenagers: history of pop music; the making of TV soap operas; and alien abduction. Special reading materials were collected at a suitable level and discretely distributed ahead of time. The students were invited to attend all three sessions. Each session was offered one afternoon each week over a three-week period and attendance recorded. The results are shown in columns **A:D** of Figure 20.7. Carry out Activity 20.7 to see how it was determined whether there was a significant difference.

	A	B	C	D	E	F
1	Student	Pop	Soap	Alien	L_i	L_i^2
2	Henry	1	0	0	1	1
3	Jane	0	1	1	2	4
4	Fred	1	0	0	1	1
5	Mary	0	0	1	1	1
6	Albert	1	0	1	2	4
7	Sam	1	1	0	2	4
8	Ellen	1	0	0	1	1
9	Ted	0	0	1	1	1
10	Anne	1	0	1	2	4
11	Hilary	0	0	0	0	0
12	Barbara	0	0	1	1	1
13	Betty	1	0	1	2	4
14	Terry	1	1	0	2	4
15	Robert	0	0	1	1	1
16	Tom	1	0	0	1	1
17	James	1	0	1	2	4
18	Nancy	1	1	0	2	4
19	Peter	1	0	1	2	4
20	$G_j =$	12	4	10	26	44
21	$G_j^2 =$	144	16	100		
22	$k =$	3	$\alpha =$	0.05		
23	$Q =$	6.12				
24	$\chi^2(2,0.05) =$	5.99				

=SUM(B2:D2) and **Copy** down
=E2^2 and **Copy** down
=SUM(F2:F19) and **Copy** across
=D20^2 and **Copy** across
=CHIINV(D22,B22–1)
=(B22–1)*(B22*SUM(B21:D21)–SUM(B20:D20)^2)/(B22*E20–F20)

FIGURE 20.7
A worksheet for carrying out Cochran's Q-test

Activity 20.7

1 Set up the worksheet in Figure 20.7 as shown to determine a value for Cochran's Q.

    (a) Was there a real difference in attendance?
    (b) Was there anything that might jeopardize the results?
    (c) Did this resolve the issue or should something else be done?

2 Professor Albert Educator recalled a piece of research from 20 years ago that suggested young people from farming families tended to choose teaching as a career more often than others, since they could find employment close to home. To see if this was still true, he randomly selected new students from the Cornbelt University database according to home address – urban, suburban and rural – until he had 15 sets matched on entry qualifications, age and gender. He then noted whether they had chosen teacher education as their degree subject. His results are shown below:

Urban	1	0	0	0	1	0	1	0	1	0	0	0	0	0	1
Suburban	0	1	0	1	0	1	0	0	0	0	0	0	1	0	0
Rural	1	1	0	1	1	1	0	1	1	0	1	1	0	1	1

    (a) Was there a difference across the three groups?
    (b) Did this entirely answer his question?
    (c) How might he improve his study?

Answers: 1(a) Yes, $p < 0.05$. (b) There was no random assignment of order in which the sessions were available, thus the first attendance could influence subsequent attendance. (c) A questionnaire to find out whether they liked the sessions and what they did like about them. Attendance alone is not enough, they may have been too polite to leave once there.
2(a) Yes, $Q = 6.62$, $p < 0.05$. (b) Not really, since the population is Cornbelt University students, not all students. (c) Include other universities, add a questionnaire or interviews to find out why.

Friedman analysis of variance for related samples

This test is appropriate for matched samples or repeated measures on a sample when the dependent variable is ordinal. The test will determine whether the several treatments on a single group result in differences according to treatment or condition, *or* whether the matched groups respond differently to the treatments or conditions. In the latter, the members of each set would be randomly assigned to a treatment. In the former, the subjects should encounter the treatments in a random order, in other words they should not all receive treatment A as the first. What is recorded is the ranks of the matched groups or the order chosen as the result of repeated measures. For example, if each individual were to be asked to perform under four conditions, then the quality of the performances would be ranked from 1 to 4 for each. Alternatively, if the members of a matched group were to rank a set of four consumer products, then each would rank them from 1 to 4, or their score would be translated into a rank from 1 to 4.

The Friedman test is an extension of the Kruskal–Wallis one-way analysis of variance for independent samples, with the test of the variation in sums of ranks for each treatment or condition calculated by

$$F_r = \left[\frac{12}{Nk(k+1)} \sum_{j=1}^{k} R_j^2 \right] - 3N(k+1) \qquad (20.8)$$

where R_j is the sum of ranks in a column, the jth treatment or condition (from 1 to k), N is the number of subjects (or matched sets) and k is the number of 'treatments', or conditions measured or observed. This test, like others, can be evaluated using the χ^2-distribution, with $df = k - 1$. It is analogous to the randomized block ANOVA for interval/ratio data, without the constraint of having a normal distribution, but the data must be at least ordinal and are reduced to an order.

For example, Bungles Bakery was unsure about which of three possible recipes for Breakfast Blobs would have the greatest appeal. The company randomly selected four of its outlets and distributed sets of all three types, baked so that their appearance was identical. The shops then asked youngsters between the ages of 8 and 14 to try each one and rank-order them in terms of their appeal. The results are shown in Figure 20.8, where ties have been dealt with as before. Carry out Activity 20.8 to see how to set up the sheet to carry out the test.

Activity 20.8

1   Set up the worksheet shown in Figure 20.8. Note that there are blank columns for raw scores which are not used in this example, but since they may be needed for other cases, we will set up the basic worksheet to include them. Note also column **H**, which is simply a check that all the ranks add up and equal what is expected, shown in cell **H22**.

   (a)   Is there a difference across the three recipes for Blobs?
   (b)   What threats are there to any conclusions because of the design or the way the study was conducted? How would you improve it?
   (c)   Temporarily remove (**Clear, Contents**) the last four rows of 'samplers'. How does this influence the outcome? What relationship appears to exist between sample size and power? (When finished, choose **Edit, Undo Clear**.)

2   Members of 16 matched sets of three MBA students were randomly allocated to one of three mini-courses employing different learning

materials and strategies for teaching the use of spreadsheets for designing budgets. The sets were matched on age, experience and undergraduate grades so that these variables would not enter into the study. It was not seen as reasonable to compel each student to sit through three courses teaching the same thing. Each person ranked the mini-course on a scale of 1 to 20 as to its apparent effectiveness in teaching them. The results were as follows:

Self-instruct	13	16	11	9	16	16	8	13
	12	14	9	15	4	15	6	13
Video-based	7	8	6	9	5	9	9	10
	10	13	8	11	8	12	5	12
Teacher-led	12	17	6	8	15	12	11	15
	13	16	10	12	14	9	10	11

(*Hint*: This time the scores should be translated to ranks of 1 to 3.)
(a) Was there a difference?
(b) Would this be enough evidence for selecting a single style? Why or why not?
(c) Also try the data in the worksheet for Figure 18.3, randomized block ANOVA. Why might this not be a better test?

Answers: 1(a) Yes, 8.53 > 5.99. (b) A random sample of shops, it became a convenience/volunteer sample, though it would be difficult to improve on the sample. (c) $W = 5.61$, not significant (n.s.); it would appear that, as with other tests, power depends on sample size.
2(a) Yes, $W = 9.41$, $p < 0.05$. (b) No, since we do not have evidence on how much they learned, only whether they thought it was effective. (c) One reason for reducing the ratings to ranks instead of using the raw scores is the potential lack of consistency in rating across raters: it is a crude measure.

Pairwise comparisons for Friedman two-way analysis of variance by ranks

The initial test only tells us whether there is a difference across the groups, but it does not tell us which pairs differ significantly. This requires a further test, adjusted to reduce the probability of making a Type II error, as was done for the Kruskal–Wallis test. The critical value for any pair of differences can be found by

$$\Delta R_{crit} = z(\alpha/k(k-1))\sqrt{\frac{Nk(k+1)}{6}} \qquad (20.9)$$

In our example above of Bungles Bakery's Breakfast Blobs, a difference was found across the three types, but it was not clear whether one was a clear first choice. Therefore, in Activity 20.9, this pairwise comparison is added.

=C2+E2+G2 and
Copy down

	A	B	C	D	E	F	G	H
1	Tasters	Score A	*Rank A*	Score B	*Rank B*	Score C	*Rank C*	Row sums
2	1		*1*		*2*		*3*	6
3	2		*1*		*2*		*3*	6
4	3		*2*		*2*		*2*	6
5	4		*3*		*1*		*2*	6
6	5		*2*		*3*		*1*	6
7	6		*1*		*3*		*2*	6
8	7		*1*		*2*		*3*	6
9	8		*2*		*3*		*1*	6
10	9		*2*		*3*		*1*	6
11	10		*1*		*3*		*2*	6
12	11		*1.5*		*1.5*		*3*	6
13	12		*2*		*3*		*1*	6
14	13		*1*		*3*		*2*	6
15	14		*1*		*2.5*		*2.5*	6
16	15		*2*		*3*		*1*	6
17	16		*2*		*3*		*1*	6
18	17		*1*		*2*		*3*	6
19	18		*1*		*3*		*2*	6
20	$R_i =$		27.5		45		35.5	108
21	$R_i^2 =$		756.25		2025.00		1260.25	
22	$N =$	18	$k =$	3			Check=	108
23	$F_r =$	8.53	$\alpha =$	0.05				
24	$\chi^2(2,0.05) =$	5.99						

=CHIINV(23,D22–1)

=COUNTA(A2:A19)

=SUM(G2:G19)
=G20^2 and
Copy across left

=6*B22

=(12/(B22*D22*(D22+1)))*
(C21+E21+G21)–3*B22*(D22+1)

=SUM(C20:G20)

FIGURE 20.8
Worksheet for
Friedman's test for
related samples

Activity 20.9

1   Figure 20.9 shows the addition to make to the worksheet in Figure
20.8. Are there any significant pairwise differences? If so, which and
what conclusion might the bakery make?
2   In the second example in Activity 20.8, was there any single teaching
approach that seemed to be best?

Answers: 1 Yes, between A and B, but not between B and C or between
A and C ⎢ B ⎢ C ⎢ A ⎢ In other words, A is seen as better than B, but not
necessarily better than C. If one has to be chosen, it would probably be A.

> 2 Both the self-instructional and teacher-led were rated higher than video-based approach. This does not necessarily condemn the approach, it may just be that video did not address the learning needs specific to this topic.

Pairwise comparisons with a control group for Friedman

There will be occasions when the desire is to compare the existing practice or situation to an innovation or new approach or treatment. Thus the desired post hoc test would be between each of the new treatments and the control group. This requires a test analogous to Dunnett's test (see Table 16.2), which has the advantage of being less conservative, but restricts the testing to treatments against a control and no comparisons between treatments.

Reconsidering our Bungles Bakery Breakfast Blobs recipes, let us consider A to be the standard production type, with B and C the new variations. The question could be asked: were the new recipes received as well as or better than the standard? The adjustment in critical difference is dependent on the number of comparisons, $k - 1$, resulting in a critical difference of

$$\Delta R_{\text{crit}} = t_{\text{D}}(\alpha, k - 1)\sqrt{\frac{Nk(k + 1)}{6}} \qquad (20.10)$$

where $t_{\text{D}}(\alpha, k - 1)$ is the critical value in Table B.8 in Appendix B for Dunnett's test, using $df_{\text{within}} = \infty$, and α since this is a one-tailed test.

Now carry out Activity 20.10 to implement this on the worksheet.

SUMMARY

Referring back to Table 19.1, we have now covered all the tests indicated. These two chapters have provided a set of nonparametric tests that correspond to the parametric ones presented earlier. This is not an exhaustive coverage, there are others which can be used, though the advantages and disadvantages are left for the interested reader to pursue.

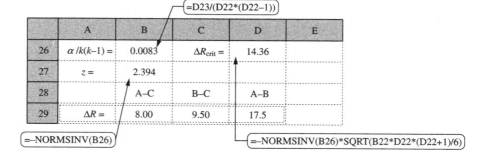

FIGURE 20.9
All pairwise comparisons for Friedman's test, using data from the example in Figure 20.8

It is reasonably obvious when comparing the calculations for comparable tests that the nonparametric ones are much easier to carry out. While some advocates would say this is a good reason to use them even for interval and ratio data that are normally distributed, do remember that these tests tend to be less powerful than their parametric equivalents. With the availability of the worksheets developed here or statistical packages such as SPSS, this is really no longer an issue. With the computational tools now available, you should be able to select the most appropriate test not only for the design, but also for the type of data for the proposed dependent variable. To practise your decision-making skills as to which test would be most appropriate for a given situation, carry out Activity 20.11 before going on to the next chapter.

Activity 20.10

1   Add the worksheet section shown in Figure 20.10 to that in Figures 20.8 and 20.9. It is necessary to look up the value for $t_D(\alpha, k - 1)$ in Appendix B (Table B.8). How would you interpret these results?
2   For the second example of teaching about budgets, consider the teacher-led option as the control, as that is what was done before. Add the section in Figure 20.10 and determine the appropriate value for $t_D(\alpha, k - 1)$. Was either of the trial approaches seen as better by the students?

Answers: 1 There was no difference in the results: recipe B was seen as significantly less popular than A and there was no difference between A and C. The difference between A and B is of no interest here.
2   $\Delta R_{crit} = 7.68$, thus the video was felt to be less effective than class teaching and there was no significant difference between the self-instructional and teacher-led classes. The difference between the video and self-instruction classes is not determined.
   Note: In both cases there seems to be no advantage to this test. In the end, it is a matter of what the research question is and what you want to find out about the relationships. Also, it should be a two-tailed test.

FIGURE 20.10
Friedman's test for comparing treatments with control (using Dunnett's test)

	A	B	C	D
31	With control:	A		
32	$t_D(\alpha, k{-}1) =$	1.92	ΔR_{crit}	8.15

$$=B32*SQRT(B22*D22*(D22{-}1)/6)$$

Activity 20.11

For each of the following scenarios, work through the following questions:

(a)   Describe the hypothesis and null hypothesis.
(b)   Choose a test from Table 19.1 for each of the situations described and write a brief justification of statistical validity before looking at the model answers.
(c)   Carry out the test and interpret the results.
(d)   Identify any problems and suggest any improvements that could be made.

1   McDougal Burgers in Waterloo Station, London, wanted to know if there was any difference in customer patterns during the week so as to be able to allocate staff most efficiently. A sample of a week and three weekends provided an average number of customers per day for each of the periods shown in the table. These corresponded to times that were felt to reflect peaks and low times for commuters, shoppers and revellers.

Period	Weekdays	Saturday
5:30–9:00	40	20
9:00–12:00	15	30
12:00–2:00	20	10
2:00–4:00	10	15
4:00–7:30	39	31
7:30–11:30	25	35

2   A music teacher, Frances Flute, felt her students lacked enthusiasm for classical music. While classes consisted of listening to high-quality recordings on an excellent sound system, this did not seem to impress them. She wanted to find out if attending a full orchestra concert would make a difference so arranged for the class to attend one. She gave the class a short questionnaire on the day before and again the day after the concert, which asked them if they would buy a classical CD. The results were as follows:

		Before concert	
		Yes	No
After	Yes	10	10
concert	No	2	2

3   The attention span of hearing-impaired children tends to be low, so Ivan Innovate investigated different media – computer-assisted learning (CAL), a video with subtitles – to see if they would persevere longer with these than in traditional teacher-dominated classes. He chose a topic for which he could obtain equivalent content coverage

and randomly selected three groups of children from hearing-impaired units in schools. He observed each child's usage of the video and CAL material, timing (in minutes) how long they spent on it. He also unobtrusively observed class sessions with teachers on the same topic, noting when attention lagged for each child. The perseverance times for each child were as below:

Teach	30	33	25	28	31	27	26	28
Video	35	36	44	33	40	38	36	37
CAL	45	40	36	38	34	39	37	38

4   Professor Fireball was a little annoyed at the fact that some students tended to fall asleep during his lectures for his first-year class on 'Rubber Chickens in History', but suspected that it had something to do with the environment. Every week he gave a lecture to a group of about 100 students, each time, in different lecture theatres: A, B and C, on Monday, Wednesday and Friday. He had one of his colleagues count sleepers in each class for four weeks and the totals are shown in the following table.

Theatre	Sleepers
A	20
B	8
C	16

5   Students employ a number of techniques for learning concepts and remembering facts when reading, particularly in courses with large amounts of reading. Professor Freemarket wanted to know if any of three techniques enhanced learning at this level: taking notes; using highlighter pens to mark words/passages in the text; typing notes into a database that would allow keyword searching later. He randomly divided his first-year economics class into three groups of eight and organized training sessions for them, providing the highlighter pen group with pens whose colour would fade after two months, allowing them to resell their books without marks. The computer group members were lent laptops for the trial period. He gave them a reading assignment and warned them of a test after three weeks. This consisted of 50 multiple choice questions testing their understanding of the new concepts. The students' results were in terms of how many concepts were understood and are shown in the following table:

									Mean	s.d.
Notes	41	33	28	27	24	15	12	6	23.25	11.59
Highlighter	35	33	30	29	28	28	25	24	29.00	3.70
Computer	46	45	40	38	34	34	27	21	35.63	8.57

6   Simon Sceptical had doubts about the Piagetian view that children will not be able to appreciate the concept of conservation of volume (that is, be convinced that two different shaped containers will hold the same amount when a liquid is poured from one to the other) until they have physiologically matured. He felt that to achieve volume conservation was simply a matter of teaching. In his primary school, he arranged for two classes of 5–6-year-olds to use two different teaching packages involving exercises on liquids and containers, then he tested a random selection of 10 children from each of these classes and 10 from his own which received no teaching. The test consisted of demonstrating that a short fat cup contained more than a tall thin one, then filling them both with a desirable drink and offering it to them. If they chose the short fat one, they were seen as being able to conserve volume. The results are shown below.

	Package A	Package B	No Learning
Conservers	8	9	4
Non-conservers	12	11	16

7   A hospital wanted to know if the number of days patients occupied post-operative beds was consistent with hospitals in general. They randomly chose a month and recorded the number of patients staying for the numbers of days shown and compared it to national percentages.

Up to	1	2	3	4	5	6	7	8	9	10	> 10
Hosp. freq.	31	45	31	18	14	8	8	5	2	1	8
Pop. %	16.4	20.8	15.6	10.4	9.3	7.5	5.6	3.5	2.9	1.3	6.7

8   Researchers at the Widget-Digit company needed a quick check to determine which of three tools for assembling a tiny component would produce the smallest percentage of failures in a week. A salesperson has lent them sets of two new tools to compare with the existing one. They took 14 assemblers and had them use each of the three tools for a week, randomly assigning the order of encounter. The results are shown below, with tool A being the one presently used.

Tool A	3	5	7	6	5	6	4	4	1
	3	4	5	6	4				
Tool B	2	4	3	5	7	6	5	6	7
	6	5	5	7	5				
Tool C	1	4	3	2	1	4	3	5	6
	4	3	2	3	4				

9   Still being indecisive about the tools, the Widget-Digit test laboratory researchers decided to see how many of the tiny components could be assembled fault-free in a day. The 14 assembly workers were randomly divided into two groups and the results are provided below.

Tool A	26	30	24	31	30	27	28
Tool C	34	33	31	29	30	28	35

10 Charlie Café wanted to determine whether coffee influenced recall ability or not. He randomly assigned matched (on first-year grade average) pairs of volunteer second-year psychology students who were coffee drinkers to one of two groups. Before lunch, he gave each subject a list of 50 words and definitions, all new to their vocabulary. Charlie provided lunch for all and allowed one group real coffee, the other decaffeinated coffee. He then gave them a multiple choice test. The results for the matched pairs were as follows:

Grades	A	A	A–	A–	B+	B+	B	B	B–	B–	C+	C+	C	C	C–	C–
Real	43	39	41	33	31	35	37	26	25	30	21	24	20	17	21	25
Decaffeinated	36	33	34	28	27	30	32	31	23	33	20	22	19	18	26	23

11 Percy Political found from interviews that it seemed that as young people started families, their politics became less conservative. He selected 20 young professional couples without children who agreed to participate in the study, only having to tell the interviewers when they had children and completing a questionnaire then and after each child. The key piece of information was which party the mother voted for in any election before having children, after the first and after the second. This was coded as: Conservative, 1; Liberal Democrats or Labour, 0. After five years, the results were as follows:

None	0	1	1	0	1	1	0	1	1	0	1	1	0	1	1
One	0	0	1	0	1	0	0	1	0	0	0	0	0	0	0
Two	1	0	0	1	0	0	0	0	1	0	1	0	0	0

12 When confronted with national exams with timed multiple-choice questions, Sarah Support always tried to get her students to go through them answering the easy ones first, skipping hard ones and returning to them later. Students did not seem to believe her so she conducted a study where a group of 40 who were about to do an examination were divided into two groups at random so they would fit in two classrooms. As part of the examination instructions on the day, one group was told to find and answer the easy questions first and return to others later. The other group was not told this. The results are shown below:

Informed	46	46	46	46	42	42	40	39	39	39	38	38	38	35	35
Not informed	45	44	44	43	43	42	39	39	38	38	36	36	36	36	36

Suggested Answers:

1(a) H_0: there is no difference in customer patterns between weekdays and Saturday. (b) Although the periods may look like interval data, they are really nominal since time is not continuous but the periods are convenient blocks, thus χ^2-test for two unrelated samples. (c) $\chi^2 = 18.37$, $p < 0.05$ (if the Kolmogorov–Smirnov test were done, n.s.). (d) Was the sample representative of weeks? Also, even though there was a difference, is it large enough to use to determine differential staffing?

2(a) H_0: attendance at a concert will make no difference in attitude. (b) McNemar change test, two related samples, nominal. (c) $\chi^2 = 5.33$, $p < 0.05$. (d) Would this work for all classes, was this one representative? Did it depend on the piece of music?

3(a) H_0: attention span will not vary across teaching media. (b) ANOVA, interval, homogeneity of variance. (c) $F = 24.36$, $p < 0.05$, with both innovations significantly different from teacher-dominated situations, no matter what post hoc test is used. (d) Could improve study by matching children on degree of deafness, age, IQ, etc., then use randomized block design. Also, could replicate the study with other teachers and other topics, result could be topic-dependent or even depend on who teaches.

4(a) H_0: the number of sleepers will not differ across lecture rooms. (b) χ^2-test, goodness of fit, one sample, nominal; expect equal probability of sleeping in each. (c) $\chi^2 = 5.09$, n.s. (d) Other causes may be responsible for sleepers, some of which he may be able to control. Even if he had found a significant difference, with a small sample of classes, it might not be the theatre, but the topic, or even his reaction to having to use the theatres.

5(a) H_0: there will be no difference in test scores across learning techniques. (b) Kruskal–Wallis one-way analysis of variance, ordinal, since non-normal distributions with heterogeneity of variance. (c) $W = 5.67$, n.s., no difference; if ANOVA is used, a difference, though unjustified, is found. (d) Small groups may reduce the power so much as to fail to find significance when it might be there. Also, is the sample representative of all economics classes, or even typical of those he has? In other words, to whom could he extrapolate his results?

6(a) H_0: there will be no difference in conservation patterns across the three groups. (b) χ^2 for three or more samples since dependent variable is nominal. (c) $\chi^2 = 3.08$, n.s., no difference across the groups. (d) Convenience sample, with no apparent justification for them to be representative of all 5–6-year-olds. Also, are the learning packages effective? This could be tested with a group of young adults who were not volume conservers (assuming you could find them), for whom age and maturation was not an issue. Also, Simon assumed they were not conservers beforehand.

7(a) H_0: there will be no difference between the hospital and national patterns. (b) Kolmogorov–Smirnov one-sample test, ordinal, continuous underlying highly skewed distribution. (c) $D_{max} = 0.099$, when $D_{max}(0.05) = 0.102$, thus n.s. (d) Is the month 'typical'? Would a longer period or different time of year reflect a different pattern? For example, is there a time of year when secondary infections are more prevalent?

What of the age, social class, etc., distributions of patients and catchment area: are they consistent with the national distributions? There are a number of possible confounding variables, no matter what the outcome.

8(a) H_0: there will be no difference in failure rate for the three tools. (b) Friedman two-way analysis of variance by ranks for three or more related samples. (c) $Fr = 11.8$, $p < 0.05$, there was a difference, $\Delta R(A–C) = 17.5$, C was significantly better than A, no significant difference between A and B. (d) Another question must be asked: is it cost-effective to replace the tool or cheaper to live with a higher failure rate, assuming quality control can catch all the bad ones? Also, was a week long enough to master the new tools equally well?

9(a) H_0: there will be no difference in the number assembled for the two tools; (b) t-test, interval data, homogeneity of variance. (c) $t = 2.49$, $p < 0.05$, C seems better, but see comments in 8(c) above. (d) Small sample, difficult to identify a larger population to which to extend the results.

10(a) H_0: there will be no difference in recall ability between groups. (b) Wilcoxon signed-rank test for two related samples, at least ordinal, non-normal. (c) $z(W) = 2.02$, $p < 0.05$; if t-test (related) used, $t = 2.10$, n.s. (d) Volunteers, how do we know they are representative of a larger group? Does the cross-section of grades even match those of the class?

11(a) H_0: there will not be a difference in voting across women as number of children increases. (b) Cochran Q-test, three or more related samples, nominal data. (c) $Q = 7.17, p < 0.05$, there appears to be a difference. (d) Does this mean the Conservative Party should discourage childbirth among young professionals? Time (history) is a source of confounding, events other than childbirth could influence voting.

12(a) H_0: there will be no difference across test approaches in performance. (b) Wilcoxon–Mann–Whitney test, two independent samples, at least ordinal, non-normal distributions. Could use Kolmogorov–Smirnov test. (c) $z(WMW) = -0.73$, n.s. (Kolmogorov–Smirnov also n.s.). (d) Though surprising, how do we know that (some of) the others have not been given the same advice before? This would be a difficult variable to control.

PART VI
DESCRIBING
NON-CAUSAL
RELATIONSHIPS

21

Correlation and Association

Correlations are based upon pairs of measure or scores for members of a single sample and provide an indication of the strength of the relationship between two variables that represent characteristics of or performances by that group. Alternatively, a high correlation between scores on two tests taken by a group, measuring the same thing, indicates there is a high level of agreement between the two instruments. Correlations can in some cases also be used in the process of making predictions of values for one variable based upon values of the other. For example, since there is a high correlation between height and weight among adults, it is possible to predict someone's weight given his or her height. On the other hand, if the size and density of the bones were known, the accuracy of the prediction would be greater, since those correlations are even higher.

Yet there are limitations to what can be inferred from such relationships, since both the variables are measured for each subject in a single sample. Even if there is a relationship between the two variables, it still would not be clear whether the first influences the second, the second influences the first, or a third variable influences both. With respect to height and weight, we know that one does not cause the other, but they are both 'caused' by a combination of inherited traits and diet. We have already encountered some uses of correlations in Chapter 11, as a measure of inter-judge reliability and as an indicator of predictive validity. In the first situation, a value was the degree of agreement between judges when assessing a common set of work, or the degree of agreement of scores for the same subjects on two versions of the same test. In the second, the correlation indicates how accurately one is likely to be able to predict future scores based upon an earlier measurement, based upon data from a single sample.

A fundamental question is often asked: when should correlations be employed and when should inferential statistical tests comparing pairs of variables (such as a t-test, Kolmogorov–Smirnov test, or χ^2-test) be used? The answer lies in the nature of the research question and the nature of the sample(s). We can think of three basic situations that consider two variables, which correspond to the designs considered earlier in the text.

If the question is related to the consequences of *manipulating* one of the variables, then a random sample is taken from a population and the researcher randomly assigns subjects to two groups. One would receive a 'treatment' and another would be considered the control (two levels of the independent variable: with and without treatment). Depending on the nature of the measure of the dependent variable, one of the inferential statistical tests would determine whether the two groups still belong to a single population for that trait: an experimental design. The answer would determine whether the variable did 'cause' a change. The researcher may even use several levels as the independent variable (ordinal) rather than categories (nominal). In other words, the focus is on *differences* across treatments, levels or categories of the independent variable.

Alternatively, if 'life experiences' within a limited category (such as levels of education, ranges of income, or achievement groups) were the hypothesized independent variable, then the random samples would be taken from two (or more) distinct groups (populations) who have had different levels or variations of that 'life experience'. Both (or all) are measured for a trait that is considered a potential dependent variable, then again an appropriate inferential test will determine whether the two or more groups probably belong to a single population for that trait: an ex post facto design. The answer would tell whether or not there was any *differences* across the 'life experiences'. This still leaves the researcher with the task of interpreting any statistically significant differences found. Is there an association between the level or type of 'life experience' and the measured outcome? Or is there possibly a justifiable causal link? The statistical test will not tell which is the best description, only that a difference exists. The nature of the variables and the design will have to be used to rationalize which is the most appropriate interpretation.

A third approach would be to take a random sample from a single population and measure a number of variables, looking at pairs of values or observations for each subject. It is then possible to determine the degree of association between the two variables: a correlational, pre-experimental design. This too is an ex post facto design, since the data are collected after the fact, but since the data are from a single group, there is little or no control over possible extraneous variables. The focus is on the possibility of relationships between pairs of variables, showing the degree to which one variable is a function of the other, but not necessarily 'depending on' it in a causal sense.

The distinction lies in the question being asked, the degree of control over the independent variable, sampling, and the strength of the justification for any causal links. In a carefully designed experimental study, a researcher has the greatest potential for providing justification and support for causal links.

Ex post facto designs employing two (or more) randomly selected groups and inferential tests potentially provide some support for causality, but these are greatly dependent on the sampling process and the nature of the variables. Time can confound the results since many things can happen when considering life events, and the variables studied can be so complex as to allow only the description of associational relationships. For example, if we were to find that 16-year-old girls performed better on French examinations than boys of the same age, equal intelligence, the same social class, and taught using the same language teaching methods, it would be foolish to think that genetic sexuality is the only cause. Physiology may result in girls' brains maturing earlier than boys' so that they learn faster at this age. Cultural influences may have an impact on boys' motivation to learn French: they may not perceive it as a 'macho' enough language for them. Self-fulfilling prophecy may have an impact if most of the French teachers are women and enough of the boys did not see them as appropriate 'role models', thus reducing their enthusiasm and ultimate performance. Time, other events and maturation could have a great impact, and the difference could disappear with increased age. This does not detract from the potential value of such a study, but should influence the nature of the conclusions and recommendations for further research. Other ex post facto studies may involve much more restrictive variables and the potential for identifying and justifying causal relationships may be greater.

Correlational studies, on the other hand, should make no pretence about identifying causality. Each subject in the sample is measured for both of a pair of variables, and the group results will provide an indication of whether one variable tends to increase with the other, decrease as the other increases, or neither.

CHOOSING BETWEEN CORRELATIONAL AND EXPERIMENTAL/EX POST FACTO DESIGNS

A single research study may not necessarily fall easily into either an experimental or non-experimental category. Not all traits or characteristics of interest will lend themselves to identification ahead of time to be used as an independent variable in a tightly controlled study. There will be situations where it will be possible, worth the effort, or there will be sufficient previous research to justify conducting a highly structured experimental study. In others, for some variables, there will not.

Correlational studies are a way of 'scanning' the field, to consider the possibility of interrelations among a number of pairs of variables, to see if future research into possible causality is worthwhile. Surveys are often associated with correlational studies, since the instrument (questionnaire, interviews, etc.) tends to collect data on several variables for each subject. Correlations between the various *meaningful* pairs are calculated to see if any relationships exist.

The choice of research strategy also depends on the question being asked, whether one is looking for a way to quantify the strength of a *relationship*, or whether one is looking for a *difference* in the impact of levels or categories of one variable on another. Related to the design to be employed is the question whether one can even control one of the variables.

An even finer and more rigorous distinction is made by Howell (1997) for situations where both independent and dependent variables are measured on continuous (interval or ratio) scales. In *correlational studies*, the researcher has no control over either variable and simply measures both for each subject. In *regression studies* the researcher changes one variable (assumed to be the independent variable, or x) to see the consequences on the other (the dependent variable, or y), to establish a pattern in order to be able to make extrapolations and interpolations using a mathematical relationship. Thus knowing a value for x, a value for y can be predicted. The implication is that correlational studies are pre-experimental and true regression studies are experimental.

In reality, the two mathematical tools are not used strictly according to these criteria. It is quite possible to determine regression equations for correlational studies where both variables are out of the control of the researcher, but still one is used to predict the other. Thus a more common distinction is made between studies that simply wish to express quantitatively a relationship between two variables (correlation) and those which wish to use the data to establish a model that will allow the prediction of one variable based upon the other (regression). If the model aims at describing a causal relationship, then the regression equation would have to be based upon data collected as part of a well-structured experimental design. This chapter will focus on correlations, while predictions through regression equations will be described in Chapter 22.

CORRELATIONAL RESEARCH

Surveys of cross-sections of populations often employ correlations between variables to describe the outcomes. These are based upon a *single* random sample and several measures on each subject. This can include factual data such as age, income, or education, or some classification based upon these such as social class. Other variables may generate data as a result of an instrument that measures such variables as achievement or attitude. In any case, the aim is to see if any relationships exist among selected pairs of variables. For example, in social science surveys, opinions on and attitudes towards specific issues (nuclear power, tax schemes, schools and education, immigration, political parties) are measured and correlations between these and other characteristics (age, social class, education, income, political preference, etc.) are determined. These exemplify variables that are virtually impossible to manipulate and often have multiple causes.

As was noted earlier, correlations can range from -1.00 to $+1.00$, indicating strength of association between the two variables in question. If the value is positive, between 0 and $+1.00$, there is an indication that as one variable increases in value, the other does too. If the value is negative, between 0 and -1.00, then as the value of one variable increases, the other decreases. What is of most interest about a correlation is its *size*, not whether it is positive or negative. Thus a correlation of -0.83 may be more impressive than one of $+0.32$, for reasons we will soon see.

Interpreting what the value of a correlation means is not trivial. First of all, it does *not* describe the magnitude of a relationship, thus one cannot say that if $r = 0.60$, this indicates that x and y are twice as close as when $r = 0.30$. It is also not possible to say that the difference between $r = 0.45$ and $r = 0.65$ is the same as the difference between $r = 0.65$ and $r = 0.85$. Rather it is an index of closeness of data. We have already used the correlation coefficients for predictive validity, where it indicated *how well* one score predicted another.

It was also used as a reliability coefficient to tell how close was the agreement between the results for two versions of a test taken by subjects. As Guilford and Fruchter (1973) note, reliabilities tend to be higher than predictive validities. Yet being able to predict does not 'prove' causation. There may be a causal chain, but there is insufficient evidence to support that from a correlation. The variables under consideration may be artefacts of some relationship, but its exact nature is usually not obvious.

Similarly, Glass and Hopkins (1996) point out that a zero correlation does not necessarily mean there is no causal relationship. They cite studies that show, in cross-sections of students, there is no correlation between hours spent studying for examinations and subsequent performance. Does this mean studying is a waste of time? Not likely, but in a cross-section of students we would expect that so-called bright students would study little to achieve an average score while the less gifted might spend hours to achieve the same. An experimental design that was able to control for inherent ability to learn would certainly show a difference in achievement for time spent. This is another case of a need to ask the 'right' question.

Blalock (1979) points out that the focus of a study may be on *which* variables are potentially related, rather than on making predictions, thus the study would be taking an exploratory approach. Any correlation should be interpreted with reference to the situation and the variables involved. In some situations it may be important to the study if the correlation is large, whereas for others size is not everything nor is it absolute in its meaning. In an exploratory study, any correlation that can be shown not to be a chance event may be of interest. We would be surprised, for example, if there was a large correlation anywhere near 1.00 between the heights of husbands and wives. This would suggest that there was great uniformity and one could predict one spouse's height from the other very accurately, since husbands are always (say) about 7 centimetres taller than wives. On the other hand, we would not be surprised to find a correlation of 0.50, which suggests there is a relationship, but there is also considerable variation and predictions will not be too accurate. This we know from

TABLE 21.1
Some real exemplar correlational relationships

Potential relationship	Typical *r*
IQ scores and elementary school grades/achievement tests (Atkinson *et al.*, 1990)	0.60 to 0.70
Grades in mathematics and mathematics self-concept in a sample of Flemish primary school children (Muijs, 1997)	0.50 to 0.60
Scholastic Aptitude Test (SAT) and freshman (first-year) university results (USA): predictive validity (Atkinson *et al.*, 1990)	0.31 to 0.50
IQ scores and graduate school achievement (Atkinson *et al.*, 1990)	0.30 to 0.40
A-level results and first-year university results: predictive validity (Bourner and Hamed, 1987)	0.00 to 0.28
Liking for electronic voice response systems and age of US respondents (Katz *et al.*, 1997)	−0.29
Authoritarianism and aestheticism among US high school seniors (final-year secondary) (Minium *et al.*, 1993)	−0.42

casual observations and that in most societies there are usually variables other than height involved in choosing a spouse. Table 21.1 provides a selection of exemplar correlations from the literature, many of which are of interest in their own right and not for the purpose of considering predictions.

Scatter diagrams

One way of enhancing the interpretation of correlations is through graphical representation. When we have two characteristics for each subject and these data pairs are plotted on a graph, the results will usually not be a perfect straight line, but a cloud of data points, referred to as a *scatter diagram*. What does a correlation tell about this? Basically, it indicates how tight the cloud is around an imaginary best-fit straight line and, consequently, the relative accuracy of any prediction that might be made using such a set of data. Figure 21.1 shows a set of scatter diagrams for contrived data collected on an imaginary group of children in a school. In each case, data pairs for each child are marked on the graph as a point. As can be seen from the corresponding

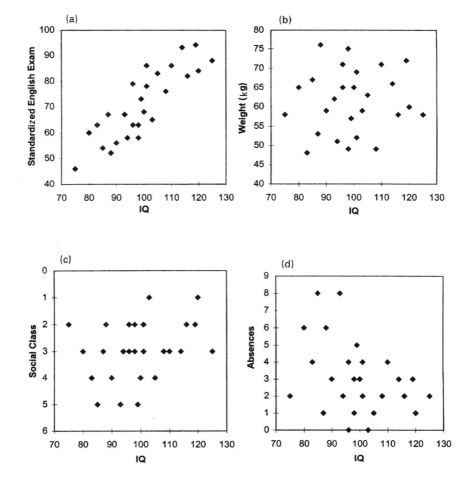

FIGURE 21.1
Four scatter diagrams with (contrived) correlations:
(a) $r_{xy} = 0.85$;
(b) $r_{xy} = 0.08$;
(c) $r_S = 0.30$;
(d) $r_S = -0.35$

values for the correlation coefficients, the *sign* tells us the relative relationship between the two variables: plus (+) indicates that as one increases so does the other, while minus (–) indicates that as one increases the other decreases. The *magnitude* of the correlation indicates how closely grouped the data are around an imaginary straight line. A correlation of 1.00 would represent data points lying in a perfectly straight line, whereas a correlation approaching 0.00 would be a nondescript cloud of points (for example, Figure 21.1 (b)). The closer a correlation is to 1.00 (or −1.00), the more tightly the data points will tend to cluster around the imaginary straight line. Carry out Activity 21.1 now to see how such graphs are plotted using a worksheet.

Activity 21.1

Figure 21.2 shows the raw data for the scatter diagrams in Figure 21.1. Enter these into a new worksheet. Call up the ChartWizard by clicking on the icon 📊. This will allow you to block out an area where you want your chart to appear on the page by clicking on where you want the upper left-hand corner and dragging diagonally, holding the button down until the area is big enough. Upon releasing the button, a sequence of five menu boxes will appear:

Step 1 of 5   With the mouse, sweep the two columns containing the data for the chosen variables, *without* the first row labels. If they are not adjacent, remember to type a comma between sweeps. Then click on the [Next >] button.

Step 2 of 5   Select the **XY (Scatter)** chart. Click on the [Next >] button.

Step 3 of 5   Click on the image labelled **1**. Click on the [Next >] button.

Step 4 of 5   Select the following options:

U̲se First [1] ▲▼ Column(s)
for Category (X) Axis Labels.

U̲se First [0] ▲▼ Row(s)
for Legend Text.

Step 5 of 5   Indicate ⊙**No** for the Legend and insert any **Title**, *x*-axis and *y*-axis labels shown in Figure 21.1, and then click on [Finish] button.

Activate the chart (double-click on it), activate each of the axes in turn and adjust their maximum and minimum values as shown in Figure 21.1.

	A	B	C	D	E	F
1	Name	IQ	Weight	Std Eng	Social class	Absences
2	John	75	58	46	2	2
3	Diana	80	65	60	3	6
4	Tina	83	48	63	4	4
5	Bob	85	67	54	5	8
6	Albert	87	53	67	3	1
7	Sam	88	76	52	2	6
8	Donald	90	59	56	4	3
9	Rose	93	62	67	5	8
10	Jane	94	51	58	3	2
11	Mary	96	65	79	2	0
12	Anne	96	71	63	3	4
13	James	98	49	63	2	1
14	David	98	75	58	3	3
15	Charles	99	57	73	5	5
16	Nancy	100	65	68	4	3
17	Alice	101	69	86	2	2
18	Louise	101	52	78	3	4
19	Henry	103	59	65	1	0
20	Martin	105	63	83	4	1
21	Gail	108	49	76	3	2
22	Betty	110	71	86	3	4
23	Tom	114	66	93	3	3
24	Fred	116	58	82	2	2
25	Martha	119	72	94	2	3
26	Sarah	120	60	84	1	1
27	Russ	125	58	88	3	2

FIGURE 21.2
The raw data from which the scatter diagrams of Figure 21.1 were produced

CHOOSING AN APPROPRIATE CORRELATION OR INDEX OF ASSOCIATION

This chapter will consider five different coefficients and how to calculate them, recognizing that they are not the only ones possible. The choice of test is based on how the variables are measured, as indicated in Table 21.2. There are a number of other nonparametric tests, but the ones provided here give a basic set for use and descriptions of others can be found in more specialized literature.

The table can be considered to encompass just six combinations of data which cover most eventualities. These are listed below, with examples for each:

TABLE 21.2
Decision table for selecting an appropriate coefficient of association/correlation, depending on measures of variable pairs (see also Breakwell *et al.*, 1995: 358)

	Interval/ratio	Ordinal	Nominal $m \geq 2$	Nominal $m = 2$
Interval/ratio	Pearson product moment, r_{xy} (linear relationship) (if non-linear, monotonic: both reduced to ordinal)	(interval/ratio variable reduced to ordinal) $\Downarrow$		Point biserial, r_{pb}
Ordinal		Spearman's *rho*, r_s (linear relationship)	(ordinal variable reduced to nominal) $\Downarrow$	
Nominal $k \geq 2$			Cramér's C (V, ϕ_c)	
Nominal $k = 2$				Phi, ϕ (dichotomies)

- *Interval–interval*: weight versus height. Both interval variables can take any value (within a reasonable range), thus collecting weight and height data on each member of a sample would result in using Pearson product moment correlation to determine the strength of relationship. While one might rightfully expect that, for a random sample of children, this would result in a high positive correlation, this might not be true of a sample of persons suffering from some hormonal or genetic defects.
- *Ordinal–ordinal*: social class and number of children a family has. This requires a coefficient that treats the data as ordinal values (class is ordinal and children come in whole numbers, with not all children being the same for many traits), thus this will require Spearman's *rho*.
- *Nominal–nominal*: gender versus voting for a specific political party or any of the other parties (dichotomies). Categorical relationships that consist of dichotomous variables such as these require the use of the *phi* coefficient. If the question required comparing several parties and included another category for gay persons (multiple categorical levels for each variable), then this would require Cramér's *C*.
- *Interval–ordinal*: speed in completing an assembly task (time to assemble a circuit board: interval) versus number of trials (ordinal) required to reach criterion of quality in production (less than five rejects per 100). Here, the interval data would be turned into ranks as well and Spearman's rho employed.
- *Interval–nominal*: time to run a kilometre versus gender. This special situation can be best described using the point biserial coefficient.
- *Ordinal–nominal*: income range versus original university degree subject. Again, this is a case where the data need to be reduced to a simpler form

and the ordinal data, income range, is considered to be nominal, so that Cramér's *C* can be used.

Other cells in the table would require reduction of data in order to find a coefficient that would describe any possible relationship. In the rest of the chapter, the calculation of each of the five coefficients will be presented.

As before, we will be using the spreadsheet and exploit any built-in functionality. Pearson's product moment correlation is available as a function and the other statistics are reasonably easy to set up on a worksheet. All five can be found in various statistical packages, such as SPSS-PC. The first question is: what is a correlation and what constitutes association? Up to this point, the terms have been used almost interchangeably, but we will now make the following distinction. *Correlation* refers to a direct mathematical link between variables measured on ordinal or interval/ratio scales. Thus it can be said that as one increases, so does the other (or as one increases the other decreases) – for example, the relationship between IQ test scores and those for a standardized English exam.

Association, on the other hand, refers to tendencies for one nominal variable to be linked with another variable – for example, gender and who does the cooking in households: while men do cook, the trend is for women to do most of the cooking. Men and women are nominal variables, as are cooking and not cooking. As we go through each, we will consider any differences in the interpretation of the five coefficients that have been selected, recognizing that there are others described in the literature – for nominal and ordinal data, in particular, see Siegel and Castellan (1988).

PEARSON PRODUCT MOMENT CORRELATION, r_{xy}, FOR INTERVAL/RATIO DATA

This is probably the most commonly used coefficient for sets of data pairs, as social scientists endeavour to investigate possible correlations between carefully designed measures of traits, abilities and characteristics. Some physiological traits, such as age, are naturally interval data and of direct interest as variables with respect to development and changes in life. Others, such as raw income, are often used as operational definitions of other traits, such as success or achievement. In any case, the aim is to see how closely pairs of data from a cross-section (the sample) of a population vary together.

We used the Pearson product moment correlation in Chapter 11 without considering its origins, so the derivation will be presented here. There are several ways to approach this, but let us start with covariance. This was presented earlier as a way to describe the relationship between two variables using a descriptor analogous to variance. In terms of variables x and y measured as a pair for each member of a sample of n subjects, we can write the covariance as

$$\text{cov}_{xy} = \frac{\sum_{i=1}^{n}(x_i - \bar{x})(y_i - \bar{y})}{n - 1} \tag{21.1}$$

This looks similar to the equation for variance (12.7), and has a denominator term of $n - 1$ since we are describing a sample of a population.

Like the variance, the size of the covariance will be related to the magnitude of the means and raw scores. For example, using the **COVAR** function in Excel (which differs slightly in that it uses n in the denominator), it is easy to determine the covariances for the first two pairs of variables in Activity 21.1, shown in the scatter diagrams of Figures 21.1(a) and 21.1(b):

$$\mathrm{cov}_{\mathrm{IQ\ wt}} = 8.36$$

$$\mathrm{cov}_{\mathrm{IQ\ Eng}} = 146.78$$

Thus, since there is a very small relationship between IQ and weight, the covariance is small; and since there is a close relationship between IQ and the standard English test, the covariance is large.

The difficulty with using covariance as a coefficient to describe the relationship between variables is that the size is limited by the nature of the variables measured. It does not allow us to compare the nature of one relationship with another that has been measured on different numerical scales. If instead of using raw differences in the numerator, we use z-scores,

$$z_x = \frac{x_i - \bar{x}}{s_x}$$

then, put simply, everyone is on the same scale, much as when using percentages. This is the origin of the definition of the Pearson product moment correlation, which can be expressed in three different, but equivalent, ways:

$$r_{xy} = \frac{\sum_{i=1}^{n} z_x z_y}{n - 1} \tag{21.2}$$

$$= \frac{\sum_{i=1}^{n} \left[\frac{x_i - \bar{x}}{s_x}\right]\left[\frac{y_i - \bar{y}}{s_y}\right]}{n - 1}$$

$$r_{xy} = \frac{\sum_{i=1}^{n} (x_i - \bar{x})(y_i - \bar{y})}{(n - 1)s_x s_y} \tag{21.3}$$

$$r_{xy} = \frac{\mathrm{cov}_{xy}}{s_x s_y} \tag{21.4}$$

Here x_i and y_i are data pairs for subject i, $\bar{x}$ and $\bar{y}$ are the means for the data for variables x and y, n is the sample size, s_x and s_y are unbiased estimates of population standard deviations for variables x and y based upon sample data, and cov_{xy} is the covariance of variables x and y from equation (21.1) above. Thus, from equation (21.4) we see that if two variables covary together, they will have a high value of r_{xy}, and if they do not covary together, then r_{xy} will approach zero.

Now unfortunately, there is not total agreement on the use of the above equations. Taking a sample of contemporary texts (Howell, 1997; Daly *et al.*, 1995; Coolican, 1994; Sirkin, 1995), each employs one of these or a derivation when calculating Pearson's product moment correlation. On the other hand, others (Minium *et al.*, 1993; Chase, 1985; Excel version 6.0) assume population data, defining covariance with n in the denominator of equation (21.1) and use the following instead,

$$R_{xy} = \frac{\sum_{i=1}^{n}(x_i - \mu_x)(y_i - \mu_y)}{(n)\sigma_x\sigma_y} \qquad (21.5)$$

or the equivalent expression to (21.3) for sample data,

$$r_{xy} = \frac{\sum_{i=1}^{n}(x_i - \bar{x})(y_i - \bar{y})}{(n)S_xS_y} \qquad (21.6)$$

Here μ_x and μ_y are population means for variables x and y, σ_x and σ_y are population standard deviations for variables x and y, and S_x and S_y are sample standard deviations for variables x and y.

Before panic sets in, let us see just how different these might be. First of all, substituting in equation (12.4) for s_x and s_y, equation (21.3) becomes

$$r_{xy} = \frac{\sum_{i=1}^{n}(x_i - \bar{x})(y_i - \bar{y})}{(n-1)\sqrt{\dfrac{\sum_{i=1}^{n}(x_i - \bar{x})^2}{n-1}}\sqrt{\dfrac{\sum_{i=1}^{n}(y_i - \bar{y})^2}{n-1}}}$$

Cancelling out the $n - 1$,

$$r_{xy} = \frac{\sum_{i=1}^{n}(x_i - \bar{x})(y_i - \bar{y})}{\sqrt{\sum_{i=1}^{n}(x_i - \bar{x})^2 \sum_{i=1}^{n}(y_i - \bar{y})^2}} \qquad (21.7)$$

Similarly, starting with equation (21.6) and substituting in equation (12.3) for S_x and S_y, we find

$$r_{xy} = \frac{\sum_{i=1}^{n}(x_i - \bar{x})(y_i - \bar{y})}{(n)\sqrt{\dfrac{\sum_{i=1}^{n}(x_i - \bar{x})^2}{n}}\sqrt{\dfrac{\sum_{i=1}^{n}(y_i - \bar{y})^2}{n}}}$$

Cancelling out the n, this reduces to equation (21.7) as well. Thus, the two approaches provide equivalent values for r_{xy} for a given set of data, assuming appropriate use of standard deviations. One assumes that this is not a problem with computer programs and that they have been consistent with whichever approach they have chosen. Other textbooks avoid the issue altogether by simply providing 'computational' formulae. The panic is over, only one value for r_{xy} is generated.

There is one small caveat proposed by Howell (1997). If the data are *not* for a whole population, then r_{xy} is not an unbiased estimate of the population correlation coefficient, even if s_x and s_y, unbiased estimates of population standard deviations, have been used. He maintains that the *adjusted correlation* coefficient (r_{adj}) is the best estimate, where

$$r_{adj} = \sqrt{1 - \frac{(1 - r_{xy}^2)(n - 1)}{n - 2}} \qquad (21.8)$$

For our example above, this would result in

$$r_{adj} = \sqrt{1 - \frac{(1 - (0.85)^2)(26 - 1)}{26 - 2}} \cong 0.84$$

This is a slightly reduced value. The value is also supplied with some computer-based analysis tools (such as Excel), but the importance of the difference should be confined mainly to small samples.

In summary, the calculation is straightforward and produced by many computer packages, though the values are valid only if the underlying assumptions have been met:

- Each pair of values for each subject is independent of that for other subjects.
- The data consist of interval/ratio numbers.
- The relationship is linear.

Carry out Activity 21.2 now, to find Pearson's product moment correlation for some data sets, using a worksheet.

Activity 21.2

1   Call up the worksheet in Figure 21.2. Place the cursor in cell **C28** and click on the Function Wizard icon $\boxed{f_x}$. Under **Statistical** functions, find either **CORREL** or **PEARSON** (they produce the same results!) and click on the $\boxed{\text{Next >}}$ button. Holding down the left button, highlight each of the columns of data in turn for each **array 1** and **array 2**, then click on the $\boxed{\text{Finish}}$ button. You can then adjust the number of decimal places to 2.
2   Now find r_{xy} for IQ versus the standard English exam on the above data.
3   Academics can be competitive too, and John Backhand did not like losing at handball. He suspected that older colleagues would have lower endurance, so he timed a group in the courts and matched their times with age. The data provided below are the data acquired (keep this, we will see how John tried using it later to select people to play against).

Age	28	30	31	33	35	37	39	40	42	45	46
Time	60	58	51	56	61	62	58	52	53	53	55
Age	50	56	57	58	58	59	61	62	63	64	65
Time	55	50	45	52	33	40	40	30	30	23	20

Find the Pearson product moment correlation and comment on its appropriateness.

4   As computer games are found everywhere, Roberta Response thought this would be a good way of investigating the possible change in reaction time to stimuli with age. She acquired a group of volunteers from Freedonia University's staff, students and children of staff and students, to get a range of ages. She acquired a computer game that awarded points for rapid reaction to 'alien invaders' on the screen. After two practice runs, the score and age of each subject was recorded, as follows:

Age	5	7	8	9	12	14	65	17	18	20	24
Score	23	32	40	45	48	58	37	55	48	62	56

Age	28	30	32	38	42	48	53	55	58	60	63
Score	52	55	62	52	58	51	48	61	39	48	22

Find the Pearson product moment correlation and comment on its appropriateness for this data set.

Answers:

1 and 2 See Figure 21.1.

3 $r_{xy} = -0.83$, but with a curved scatter diagram. Though some sort of relationship exists, as can be seen from the tight cluster, Pearson's is probably not the best coefficient. We will compare this to a different coefficient next.

4 $r_{xy} = -0.03$, not a very good indicator since a relationship does exist, as can be seen from the scatter diagram. We will address this problem again in Chapter 22, so keep the data.

Question 4 in Activity 21.2 points out an interesting characteristic of the Pearson product moment correlation. When $r_{xy} \cong 0$ (or is so small as to have probably occurred by chance) it does indicate that no *linear* relationship exists, but it does *not* say that no other type of relationship exists. Though non-linear relationships are not as common as linear ones (Mitchell and Jolley, 1988; Blalock, 1979) they do occur, particularly when comparing various traits with age. As seen in this case, another type of relationship of interest could exist and a different coefficient will be needed as r_{xy} will yield a gross underestimate of the true degree of clustering of points around a line. For the data for both Questions 3 and 4, we will first try Spearman's rho, the next coefficient to be described, to see if it might be more appropriate.

There are two important issues associated with the interpretation of correlation coefficients:

- *size*, which is of academic interest, telling us the strength of the relationship;
- *statistical significance*, which will tell us whether it could have happened by chance and the probability it did not (power).

Since these two types of significance, academic and statistical, seem to be the source of some confusion, we will consider them in greater detail.

Interpretation of size

While it is not possible to say that a correlation of 0.80 indicates a relationship twice as close as one of 0.40, the Pearson product moment correlation can be interpreted with a more mathematical emphasis. Matters become clearer when the relationship is expressed as r_{xy}^2, the proportion of the variability of one variable which is associated with the other variable. In other words, if $r_{xy} = 0.70$, then 49% of the variance in x, S_x^2, can be associated with the variance in y, S_y^2. While it is emphasized that this does not imply causality, it does provide a more meaningful indication of the magnitude of the link between variables through shared variance.

This still leaves the question of how much is academically significant. This is not an easy question to answer. While r_{xy}^2 may be more meaningful than r_{xy}, it is still up to the researcher to decide whether its magnitude provides a significant contribution to the answer to the research question. While at what might be considered a lower limit of $r_{xy} = 0.10$ there is an indication that only 1% of variance is shared between the two variables, a higher correlation of $r_{xy} = 0.25$ indicates a shared variance of 6%. This might be of considerable interest in a study trying to identify possible links between a pair of proposed variables for two reasons: first, because it says there is a small link; and second, because it tells one to look elsewhere as well!

For example, several studies were described in Chapter 11 where the values for predictive validity of A-level examination results taken at age 18 in England as indicators of university success were of this magnitude. To university staff selecting potential undergraduates, it is worth noting that only 6–7% of the variance in success levels is attributable to A-level results and that other factors should be found and considered if a valid selection procedure is to be established. Also, it might be worth considering the nature of the measuring instrument: are all A-level subject grade cut-offs equivalent and do all universities award grades using the same standards? Both of these issues are frequently discussed in England in newspapers as well as by academics. On the other hand, if a study were to find, among other results, a correlation of this magnitude between a measure of self-esteem and achievement, the results would provide encouragement to the researcher to pursue more experimental studies to establish ways of enhancing students' self-esteem.

Also, the nature of the sample may contribute to the control (or lack of control) of certain extraneous variables and a different sample may increase or decrease a correlation. For example, while the overall correlation between school achievement and university achievement may be around 0.25, looking at students who pursue individual subjects reveals correlations up to 0.38. Again, we must go back to what the research question is asking.

The difficulty with considering the relationship between variables using r_{xy}^2 is the non-linear nature of its relationship with r_{xy}. As can be seen from the values in Table 21.3, the percentage of variability that links two variables drops off quite quickly as r_{xy} declines. Thus the difference between r_{xy} values of 0.80

TABLE 21.3
Comparing r_{xy} with
corresponding r_{xy}^2

r_{xy}	r_{xy}^2	Δr_{xy}^2
0.10	0.01	
0.20	0.04	0.03
0.30	0.09	0.05
0.40	0.16	0.07
0.50	0.25	0.09
0.60	0.36	0.11
0.70	0.49	0.13
0.80	0.64	0.15
0.90	0.81	0.17
1.00	1.00	0.19

and 0.90 is much greater in terms of shared variance than between 0.20 and 0.30, which may be of importance when comparing correlations. Still, using only the numbers as a means for judgement is not enough; one must consider the nature of the question being asked. We will return to the interpretation of correlation coefficients in the next chapter when considering regression.

Testing for significance

It is necessary to determine whether the set of data pairs could have produced a correlation by chance alone. Since any correlation based upon a sample is an estimate of a population value, it is conceivable that a non-zero value could be the result of sampling. Consequently, it is possible to imagine distributions of possible non-zero values of r that could be so close to zero as to be considered zero. Instead of generating such distributions, it is easier to have a statistic that uses an existing sampling distribution. For the Pearson product moment correlation, this is the familiar t-distribution, where the standard error of the difference term is estimated from

$$s_{\text{diff }r} = \sqrt{\frac{1 - r_{xy}^2}{n - 2}}$$

The null hypothesis is simply that the population value of r_{xy} is zero, written as $\rho_{xy} = 0$, and therefore the statistic for the test of significance is calculated from

$$t_r = \frac{r_{xy} - \rho_{xy}}{s_{\text{diff }r}}$$

$$= \frac{r_{xy} - 0.00}{\sqrt{\dfrac{1 - r_{xy}^2}{n - 2}}}$$

$$t_r = \frac{r_{xy}\sqrt{n - 2}}{\sqrt{1 - r_{xy}^2}} \tag{21.9}$$

The value found from equation (21.9) is compared to the t-distribution for $df = n - 2$, for the appropriate α. It is usually a two-tailed test: this assumes that the test is non-directional and that there was no expectation as to the sign of the population value, ρ_{xy} – in other words, whether $\rho_{xy} > 0$ or $\rho_{xy} < 0$. Obviously, if there were some justification, based upon logic or previous research, for expecting one or the other, then a one-tailed test would be appropriate. In either case, just looking at equation (21.9), it is fairly obvious that t_r is going to be sensitive to the sample size, n. Thus the larger the sample, the more likely it is that a small correlation will be significant.

For example, if the results of the correlation found between IQ and the standardized English exam from Figure 21.1 and Activity 21.1 are tested, where $r_{xy} = 0.85$ for the sample of 26 students,

$$ t_r = \frac{0.85\sqrt{26 - 2}}{\sqrt{1 - 0.85^2}} = 7.90, \qquad p < 0.05 $$

Thus, it is highly unlikely that this correlation occurred by chance alone, since $t_{crit} = 2.064$, for $df = 24$ and $\alpha = 0.05$.

If we start with equation (21.9), it is possible to generate an equation that will allow us to determine ahead of time the smallest significant correlation possible for a given sample size. The derivation that follows is in big steps, but the interested reader should be able to fill in the gaps. First, if we multiply both the numerator and denominator by $1/r_{xy}$ and rearrange, we get

$$ t_r = \frac{\sqrt{n - 2}}{\sqrt{\dfrac{1}{r_{xy}^2} - 1}} $$

Squaring both sides and rearranging gives

$$ \frac{1}{r_{xy}^2} - 1 = \frac{n - 2}{t_r^2} $$

Solving for $1/r_{xy}^2$ results in

$$ \frac{1}{r_{xy}^2} = \frac{n - 2 + t_r^2}{t_r^2} $$

Inverting this and taking the square root of both sides gives an expression for r_{xy}, which is a minimum when $t_r = t_{crit}$ for sample size, n:

$$ \min r_{xy} = \frac{t_{crit}}{\sqrt{t_{crit}^2 + n - 2}} \tag{21.10} $$

For the example above where the sample size was 24, then

$$ \min r_{xy} = \frac{2.064}{\sqrt{2.064^2 + 24 - 2}} = 0.40 $$

Thus, the smallest significant correlation for a sample of 24 will be $r_{xy} = 0.40$, but even then the probability of this being truly significant, the power, is only 50%. It soon becomes apparent that small samples can be very limiting in correlational research. This equation can obviously be turned round and solved for sample size. Therefore, if we wanted to replicate a study that had found a non-significant correlation which we suspected was significant, it would be possible to estimate the required minimum sample. Solving for n,

$$\text{est } n = t_{\text{crit}}^2 \left(\frac{1}{r_{xy}^2} - 1 \right) + 2 \qquad (21.11)$$

This can only be an estimate since t_{crit} also depends on n, but for samples over 30 this is about 2.0, using $\alpha = 0.05$. For example, if a study had been conducted using a sample of 20 and found a correlation, $r_{xy} = 0.26$, but it was not statistically significant, how large a sample would be needed for a correlation of this size to establish that it probably did not occur by chance? Rounding up to the nearest whole number,

$$\text{est } n = 2.0^2 \left(\frac{1}{0.26^2} - 1 \right) + 2 \cong 58$$

Power

Now this raises another issue: what is the power of the test? In other words, what is the probability that the test would correctly identify a statistically significant correlation coefficient? To be able to answer this would also provide a way of determining a more appropriate minimum sample size, one that would be based on a power greater than 50%, as found above. Figure 21.3 provides a simple worksheet based calculation of the t-ratio for determining the significance of a correlation and the power of that test based upon derivations provided in Chapter 15. This can be copied and added to any set of data, or used as it is to determine values of power for different situations.

For example, to test for significance and find the *power* of a correlation, the values for the correlation and the sample size are inserted. On the other hand, it is possible to ask 'what if. . .?' questions about sample size by simply trying different combinations of r_{xy} and n until the desired level of power is achieved.

FIGURE 21.3 Worksheet for testing significance of r_{xy} and power of the test

	A	B	C
1	Pearson r =	0.85	
2	alpha =	0.05	
3	n =	26	
4	t-ratio =	7.90	
5	t_{crit} =	2.06	
6	t (beta) =	−5.84	
7	beta =	0.00	#NUM!
8	power =	1.00	#NUM!

=B1*SQRT(B3−2)/SQRT(1−B^2)
=TINV(B2,B3−2)
=B5−B4
=TDIST(−B6,B3−2,1)
=1−B7

=1−TDIST(B6,B3−2,1)
=1−C7

Before going on to consider some other coefficients, carry out Activity 21.3 to use this facility.

Activity 21.3

1   Set up the worksheet in Figure 21.3, which uses the correlation between the standardized English exam and IQ, $r_{xy} = 0.85$, in Figure 21.1 and Activity 21.1 There are two sets of values for β and power, one of which will always be **#NUM!**, due to an idiosyncrasy of Excel. The left one will report power values above 0.50 and the right one values below 0.50.

    (a)   What would be the smallest sample required for this to be minimally significant?
    (b)   What would be the smallest sample required for the power of the test to be at least 0.80?

2   Test whether the correlation between weight and IQ, $r_{xy} = 0.083$, from Figure 21.1 and Activity 21.1, is significant.

3   (a)   What would be the smallest value that r_{xy} could be and still be significant at $\alpha = 0.05$, for our sample of 26?
    (b)   With a power of 0.80?

4   (a)   What would be the smallest sample for a correlation of $r_{xy} = 0.38$ for it to be significant at $\alpha = 0.05$?
    (b)   At $\alpha = 0.01$?
    (c)   To have a power of 80%, for the significance test, $\alpha = 0.05$?

Answers: 1(a) 6. (b) 7.
2 Since $t_r = 0.41$ and $t_{\text{crit}} = 2.06$, for $df = 26$ and $\alpha = 0.05$, $p > 0.05$, no, the population value is probably 0.00, there is no correlation between weight and IQ.
3(a) $r_{xy} = 0.39$. (b) $r_{xy} = 0.51$.
4(a) est $n \cong 28$. (b) est $n \cong 46$; (c) est $n \cong 50$.

Confidence intervals

As noted in Chapter 13, this is an alternative way of viewing and describing the outcome of statistical tests. As a consequence of determining an r_{xy}, it is possible to describe a *confidence interval*, a range of possible values in which we could be (say) 95% certain that the population correlation, ρ_{xy}, would occur. This will also be useful if we wish to compare the correlations of two groups for the same pair of traits to see if they are significantly different. The mathematical difficulty lies in the fact that the sampling distribution is not normal for the full range of possible values of ρ_{xy} from -1.00 to $+1.00$, becoming increasingly skewed as it approaches ±1.00. This is also true for comparing two correlations where it is necessary to find their difference. Glass and Hopkins (1996) provide graphs to illustrate this.

As we saw earlier, non-normality is a violation of the underlying assumptions of most tests and transformations of the data can sometimes overcome this. R.A. Fisher developed an elegant transformation in the 1920s (Howell, 1997; Glass and Hopkins, 1996) that results in r'_{xy} being normally distributed around ρ'_{xy} (also transformed) using the equation

$$r'_{xy} = \tanh^{-1} r_{xy} \tag{21.12}$$

where $\tanh^{-1}$ is the hyperbolic arctangent function (if you are not familiar with this, do not worry about it) with a standard error of

$$s_{r'_{xy}} = \frac{1}{\sqrt{n-3}}$$

This makes it possible to test whether the difference between two correlations, r_1 and r_2, is significant (or is so small as to be attributable to chance) by simply referring to a z-distribution:

$$z = \frac{r'_1 - r'_2}{\sqrt{\dfrac{1}{n_1 - 3} + \dfrac{1}{n_2 - 3}}} \tag{21.13}$$

The usual critical values of z for a sampling distribution now apply – for example for $\alpha = 0.05$, $z_{\text{crit}} = 1.96$. If the same question were asked about the difference between r_{xy} and the population value, ρ_{xy}, then we would assume that n_2 in equation (21.13) would be very, very large. Thus the second term would approach zero, leaving

$$z = \frac{r'_{xy} - \rho'_{xy}}{\sqrt{\dfrac{1}{n-3}}}$$

Now this can be solved for ρ'_{xy}, and, when z becomes the critical value, provides an expression for the confidence interval

$$\rho'_{xy} = r'_{xy} \pm \frac{z_{\text{crit}}}{\sqrt{n-3}} \tag{21.14}$$

Thus, for the example above, where $r_{xy} = 0.85$, when $n = 26$,

$$\rho'_{xy} = 1.256 \pm \frac{1.96}{\sqrt{26-3}} = 1.256 \pm 0.409$$

or, more meaningfully expressed,

$$0.847 \le \rho'_{xy} \le 1.665$$

and converting the two extremes back to ρ_{xy}, using the inverse of equation (21.12),

$$r_{xy} = \tanh r'_{xy} \tag{21.15}$$

we have the confidence interval (rounded) of

$$0.69 \le \rho_{xy} \le 0.93$$

Thus, there is a 95% probability that ρ_{xy} is between 0.69 and 0.93. Since 0.00 is not within the confidence interval, it is also possible to say that the value of r_{xy} is significantly different from 0.00 as well, which is the same conclusion arrived at above. Now this rather tedious process can be encapsulated on a worksheet, as shown in Activity 21.4.

Activity 21.4

1 (a) Set up the worksheet in Figure 21.4 (left-hand side) to determine whether there is a significant difference in the correlations between age and reading ability for boys ($r_{xy} = 0.63$, $n = 45$) and girls ($r_{xy} = 0.73$, $n = 51$), as found for samples in the Happy Valley Primary School.
   (b) How large would the samples have to be for this difference to be significant?
   (c) If the two correlations were significantly different from each other, what would it tell us?

2 (a) Set up the worksheet in Figure 21.4 (right-hand side) to determine the confidence interval for $r_{xy} = 0.85$, $n = 26$.
   (b) What would the confidence interval be with a sample half this size?

3 Determine the confidence interval for ρ_{xy} for the correlation between weight and IQ from Figure 21.1 and Activity 21.1, where $r_{xy} = 0.08$, $n = 26$.

Answers: 1(b) $n \cong 222$ each group. (c) That there was not as much consistency within one group as within the other for the relationship between age and reading ability. It would not tell us that girls read better than boys.
2(b) $0.56 \leq \rho_{xy} \leq 0.95$.
3 $-0.32 \leq \rho_{xy} \leq 0.45$.

FIGURE 21.4
Worksheet for determining significance between two correlations and establishing a confidence interval for a correlation

	A	B	C	D	E	F
1	**Pair of Correlations**				**Confidence Interval**	
2		Boys	Girls		$r_{xy} =$	0.85
3	$r_{xy} =$	0.63	0.73		$r'_{xy} =$	1.256 ← =ATANH(F2)
4	$r'_{xy} =$	0.741 ←	0.929		$n =$	26
5	$n =$	45	51		$\rho'_{xy}(max) =$	1.665
6	$z =$	−0.88652 ←			$\rho'_{xy}(min) =$	0.847
7	$\alpha =$	0.05			$\rho_{xy}(max) =$	0.93
8	$z_{crit} =$	1.960 ←			$\rho_{xy}(min) =$	0.69

=F3+B8/SQRT(F4−3)
=F3−B8/SQRT(F4−3)
=TANH(F5)
=TANH(F6)

=ATANH(C3)

=ATANH(B3)
=(B4−C4)/SQRT(1/(B5−3)+1/(C5−3))
=−NORMSINV(0.5*B7)

Spearman's rho for ordinal data

There will be situations parallel to those using parametric correlations (design E1) where the variable pairs are measured at least as ordinal or directly as ranks. Exemplar variables include incomes or ages recorded as being in a series of ranges, the rankings of judges or observers of overall ability or severity of a disability, and short score ranges for questionnaires that are not considered interval/ratio. The data are either collected as ranks, represented by integers (except for ties) or ranked after collection. Like Pearson's product moment correlation, Spearman's *rho*, denoted r_s can range from -1.00 to $+1.00$. Table 21.4 illustrates the nature of data that will produce the extremes of the coefficient. Spearman's rho is essentially the same as Pearson's product moment correlation and it can be shown that, for this situation, they are mathematically equivalent.

Spearman's rho is appropriate for any *monotonic* increasing or decreasing pairs of variables. In other words, as x increases (or decreases), so does y, but as we are considering all data to be ordinal, the requirement for linearity is not an issue. By definition, though, this does exclude ∩- or ∪-shaped relations, since they are not consistently increasing or decreasing, but first one then the other for different intervals. As we consider how Spearman's rho is calculated, a number of examples will be provided.

Calculating Spearman's rho

There are two equations used to calculate Spearman's rho. One of them is simply equation (21.7) but with ranks substituted for the raw data:

$$r_s = \frac{\sum_{i=1}^{n}(x_i - \bar{x})(y_i - \bar{y})}{\sqrt{\sum_{i=1}^{n}(x_i - \bar{x})^2 \sum_{i=1}^{n}(y_i - \bar{y})^2}} \tag{21.16}$$

where x_i and y_i are pairs of *ranks* for the variables x and y for subject i. Thus the most straightforward way of calculating Spearman's rho is to carry out the Pearson's product moment calculation on the data converted to ranks, with tied ranks adjusted. The following 'simplified' formula appears in many texts,

TABLE 21.4
Three simplified sample sets of data to illustrate Spearman's rho (after Gibbons and Chakraborti, 1992, and Kerlinger, 1986)

$r_S = +1.00$		$r_S = 0.04$		$r_S = -1.00$	
x	y	x	y	x	y
1	1	1	3	1	7
2	2	2	4	2	6
3	3	3	7	3	5
4	4	4	5	4	4
5	5	5	1	5	3
6	6	6	2	6	2
7	7	7	6	7	1

but is only accurate if there are only a few ties (Siegel and Castellan, 1988; Howell, 1997; Daly *et al.*, 1995), as will be illustrated later:

$$r_S = 1 - \frac{6 \sum_{i=1}^{n} D_i^2}{n(n^2 - 1)} \tag{21.17}$$

Here n is the number of subjects in the sample. D_i is the difference in ranks for the two variables for subject i; it is squared so that the sum of all the differences will not equal zero.

The mathematical equivalence of equations (21.6) and (21.17) is demonstrated in all the above references. Equation (21.17) was a useful computational formula in the days of number crunching on the calculator, but of less value now that most calculations will be done using computer software.

Testing the significance

For samples below about 15, special tables are needed to determine the significance of values of Spearman's rho (see, for example, Grimm, 1993; Siegel and Castellan, 1988). Above 15, the values provided by such tables produce virtually the same results as using the process in Figure 21.3 for Pearson's product moment correlation, thus this is a convenient way of checking the significance of rho assuming your sample is not too small. We will use the set of data provided earlier for investigating a possible relationship between social class and absences in the data for Activity 21.1. Carry out Activity 21.5, using the data in Figure 21.5.

	A	B	C	D	
1		x	y	$D^2 = (x-y)^2$	
2		1	3	4	=(B2–C2)^2 and **Copy** down the column
3		2	4	4	
4		3	7	16	
5		4	5	1	
6		5	1	16	
7		6	2	16	
8		7	6	1	=SUM(D2:D8) and **Copy** across
9	Total =	28	28	58	
10	n =	7	r_S =	−0.03571	=1–6*D9/(B10^3–B10)
11			$r_S(P)$ =	−0.03571	=PEARSON(B2:B8,C2:C8)

FIGURE 21.5
Worksheet for ranked data for Spearman's *rho*

Activity 21.5

1 To confirm the equivalence of equations (21.6) and (21.17) for data with no ties, enter the middle set of data in Table 21.4 on a spreadsheet as shown in Figure 21.5. Add a column for differences in ranks squared, D_i^2, as shown in Figure 21.5 and enter the formula for equation (21.17) as shown. Below this, simply enter the **PEARSON** function using the Function Wizard. How do the results compare?

2 Copy the names, social classes and absences data from Figure 21.2, columns **A**, **E** and **F** to a new worksheet, into columns **A**, **B** and **D**, as shown in Figure 21.6(a).

   (a) Enter the **RANK** function in **C2** using the Function Wizard, add **$** to the data reference so it becomes **=RANK(B2, B$2:B$27,1)**, then **Copy** this down the column. This will generate whole numbers and several ties.

   (b) Do the same in **D2**, adding **$** as indicated, and **Copy** down the column.

   (c) Using the mouse, block all the data including titles, then select **Data**, **Sort**, **Rank Soc**, **Ascending**. This will sort all the data in the order shown in Figure 21.6(b).

   (d) Since Excel uses an unconventional ranking process, adjust ties for the *Rank Soc* column in the same way as you did in Question 1(a) of Activity 20.3 in Chapter 20.

   (e) Block all data again, then select **Data**, **Sort**, **Rank Abs**, **Ascending**, ordering the data.

   (f) Adjust ties for the *Rank Abs* column.

   (g) Compare totals of ranks columns with the check value in cell **B30**. If they are not the same, then there is an error in resolving ties.

   (h) Insert the **PEARSON** function using the Function Wizard.

   (i) Add column **F**, sum and add equation (21.17) for comparison in **F29**.

   (j) Is the correlation significant? What is the power of the test?

3 Recall from Table 21.2 that for mixed variables where one is interval/ratio and the other ordinal, Spearman's rho is appropriate. Both sets of data will be turned into ranks before finding the coefficient. The data for Figures 21.1(c) and 21.1(d) are provided in Figure 21.2, columns **B** and **E**, and columns **B** and **F**, respectively. Follow the directions above and use these to calculate Spearman's rho.

Answers: 2 In this case they are virtually the same, 0.58 and 0.60, particularly when correlations are usually reported only to two decimal places. (j) The *t*-ratio is 3.45, $p < 0.05$, power $= 0.91$.

3 See Figure 21.1. If the simplified equation is used, the values would be, for Figure 21.1(c) $r_s = 0.33$, and Figure 21.1(d) $r_s = -0.33$, somewhat different. For $r_s = 0.30$, the t-ratio is 1.55, $p > 0.05$ (not significant), power = 0.34; and for $r_s = -0.35$, the t-ratio is 1.84, $p > 0.05$, (not significant) power = 0.45. Thus neither is significantly different from zero for this small sample.

Other applications for Spearman's rho

There may be other situations when, even though the data are interval/ratio, Spearman's rho may be more appropriate than Pearson's product moment correlation since the assumptions of the latter have not been met. Earlier it was mentioned that the data should be monotonic increasing or decreasing, and there will be interval/ratio variable combinations that produce non-linear scatter diagrams of this sort. Again, the data would be ranked and Spearman's rho calculated using these. Plotting the ranks may also show a linear relationship, but remember this is a relationship between ranks, not the raw data, and therefore must be interpreted as such. Guilford and Fruchter (1973) suggest Spearman's *rho* can be used as an alternative to Pearson's correlation when samples are small (less than 30) and possibly having a small range of scores with many ties as a consequence.

Carry out Activity 21.6 to see how well Spearman's *rho* applies to some non-linear data as examples.

Activity 21.6

1   Use the data from Activity 21.2, Question 3 and find Spearman's rho, since the scatter diagram showed this to be non-linear (monotonic decreasing).
2   Plot the equivalent scatter diagram using the ranked data. How would you describe the results?
3   Use the data from Activity 21.2, Question 4 and find Spearman's rho, since the scatter diagram showed this to be non-linear.

Answers: 1 $r_s = -0.87$, thus slightly higher than Pearson's.
2 The ranked data are more linear, but this describes a relationship based on age ranks, not age itself.
3 $r_s \cong 0$ as well, but this does not fit our intuition, which says such a close clustering ought to have some coefficient to describe it appropriately. As we will see in Chapter 22, there are even better descriptions of non-linear relationships, ones that eventually allow a more accurate prediction of values for such situations as described here. We will use these data again then.

Other tests for ordinal data

Kendall's *tau*, τ, is sometimes suggested as an alternative, but where Spearman's rho is interpreted in the same way as the Pearson product moment correlation, Kendall's rank-order correlation coefficient is not. This coefficient is an indication of the difference between the probability that the two ranked variables are in the same order, and that they are in different orders. Therefore, if paired ranks are exactly in the same order, then $\tau = +1.0$, and if they are in exactly reverse order to each other, then $\tau = -1.0$. While this coefficient still allows us to decide whether the two variables are related, the nature of the coefficient is not directly comparable and tends to have lower values than Spearman's rho. See Siegel and Castellan (1988) for a detailed discussion of this coefficient, and Gibbons and Chakraborti (1992) for comparisons with Spearman's rho.

	A	B	C	D	E
1	**Name**	**Soc class**	*Rank Soc*	**Absences**	*Rank Abs*
2	John	2	*3*	2	*7*
3	Diana	3	*10*	6	*23*
4	Tina	4	*20*	4	*18*
5	Bob	5	*24*	8	*25*
6	Albert	3	*10*	1	*3*
7	Sam	2	*3*	6	*23*
8	Donald	4	*20*	3	*13*
9	Rose	5	*24*	8	*25*
10	Jane	3	*10*	2	*7*
11	Anne	2	*3*	0	*1*
12	Mary	3	*10*	4	*18*
13	James	2	*3*	1	*3*
14	David	3	*10*	3	*13*
15	Charles	5	*24*	5	*22*
16	Nancy	4	*20*	3	*13*
17	Louise	2	*3*	2	*7*
18	Alice	3	*10*	4	*18*
19	Henry	1	*1*	0	*1*
20	Martin	4	*20*	1	*3*
21	Gail	3	*10*	2	*7*
22	Betty	3	*10*	4	*18*
23	Tom	3	*10*	3	*13*
24	Fred	2	*3*	2	*7*
25	Martha	2	*3*	3	*13*
26	Sarah	1	*1*	1	*3*
27	Russ	3	*10*	2	*7*

=RANK(B2,B$2:B$27,1) and **Copy** down column

=RANK(D2,D$2:D$27,1) and **Copy** down column

FIGURE 21.6(a)
First step in setting up worksheet for calculating Spearman's *rho*, starting with raw data and initial ranking

	A	B	C	D	E	F	
1	**Name**	**Soc class**	*Rank Soc*	**Absences**	*Rank Abs*	$D=(x-y)^2$	An example of adjusted ranks: =RANK(B2,B$2:B$27)+0.5
2	Henry	1	1.5	0	1.5	0	
3	Sarah	1	1.5	1	4.5	9	=(C2–E2)^2 and **Copy** down the column
4	Anne	2	6	0	1.5	20.25	
5	James	2	6	1	4.5	2.25	
6	Louise	2	6	2	9.5	12.25	
7	Fred	2	6	2	9.5	12.25	
8	John	2	6	2	9.5	12.25	
9	Martha	2	6	3	15	81	
10	Sam	2	6	6	23.5	306.25	
11	Albert	3	14.5	1	4.5	100	
12	Jane	3	14.5	2	9.5	25	
13	Gail	3	14.5	2	9.5	25	
14	Russ	3	14.5	2	9.5	25	
15	Tom	3	14.5	3	15	0.25	
16	David	3	14.5	3	15	0.25	
17	Betty	3	14.5	4	19.5	25	
18	Alice	3	14.5	4	19.5	25	
19	Mary	3	14.5	4	19.5	25	
20	Diana	3	14.5	6	23.5	81	
21	Martin	4	21.5	1	4.5	289	
22	Donald	4	21.5	3	15	42.25	
23	Nancy	4	21.5	3	15	42.25	
24	Tina	4	21.5	4	19.5	4	
25	Charles	5	25	5	22	9	
26	Rose	5	25	8	25.5	0.25	
27	Bob	5	25	8	25.5	0.25	
28	Total =		351		351	1174	=PEARSON(C2:C27,E2:E27)
29	n =	26			r_s = 0.576	0.599	=1–6*F28/(B29^3–B29)
30	check =	351			(Pearson)	(Simple)	

=26*(26+1)/2

FIGURE 21.6(b) Second step in setting up worksheet for calculating Spearman's *rho*, adjusted ranks after Sorting

CRAMÉR'S C (OR V OR ϕ_c) FOR NOMINAL DATA

Moving across and down Table 21.1, we arrive at situations where the data are nominal (categories with no order) for an attribute. For example, to see if there were any relationship between type of education and career choice among the citizens of Bloggsville, Patsy Pattern randomly selected *one* sample of 50 adult subjects from the population. Each subject was classified into one of several categories for type of secondary school education – public, private or church-based – and into one of several professional career areas – technical (e.g., science, engineering, computing), administrative/managerial or service (teaching, nursing, social services). The question of association between career and type of education was considered to see if there was any relationship.

The inference would be to assume that the pattern extended to all the professionals in Bloggsville, as shown in Table 21.5(a).

On the other hand, had Patsy asked a different question, whether there was a difference across educational background in subjects' choice of careers, she would have chosen *three* random samples, one sample from each of the populations that went to the different types of school. Subjects' career type would contribute to the appropriate cell of the contingency table. Then the χ^2-test would have been appropriate to determine if there was a difference in career choices across school background. The inference about any differences would have been extended to the three populations: professionals who went to the three types of secondary school. The results in this case would have looked like those shown in Table 21.5(b). For purposes of illustration, the same frequencies have been used.

Alternatively, had Patsy asked whether there was a difference in educational background of people who chose each of the career types, then she would have randomly selected *three* groups based upon career choice and then determined the frequency of attendance in different schools. The χ^2-test would have to be used to determine whether there was a difference across choice of careers in educational background. Again the inference would be extended to the three populations, those who had pursued the careers in the three areas. Again, the contingency table is shown in Table 21.5(c), using the same frequencies, just for comparison.

TABLE 21.5
Three ways of collecting data on the same variables, answering three different questions

(a)   One sample, from the whole population of Bloggsville: association, Cramér's $C = 0.34$

	Public	Private	Church
Technical	10	3	3
Administrative	4	9	4
Service	4	4	9

(b)   Three samples, one from each of the educational backgrounds: difference, $\chi^2 = 11.77$ ($p < 0.05$)

	Public	Private	Church
Technical	10	3	3
Administrative	4	9	4
Service	4	4	9

(c)   Three samples, one from each of the career areas: difference, $\chi^2 = 11.77$ ($p < 0.05$)

	Technical	Administrative	Service
Public	10	4	4
Private	3	9	4
Church	3	4	9

Since the same frequencies have been used for each, superficially, the data look the same, but the question to be answered has determined the nature of the sample and the choice of statistical instrument for providing an answer. Unfortunately, they all appear as contingency tables and since statistical packages have no idea from where the data were obtained, they will provide both χ^2 analysis and association analysis. Thus, the researcher has to have defined the question carefully if the appropriate analysis to support the answer to the research question is to be selected. Also, as we will see, Cramér's C is based upon the χ^2-ratio, which makes it potentially all the more confusing.

As a result of the question, data collected and subsequent analysis shown in Table 21.5(a), it could be concluded that there was a small *association* between the type of secondary school attended and subsequent career choice. From the question, data collected and analysis shown in Table 21.5(b), it could be concluded that there was a *difference* in career choice across groups (not individuals), dependent on which type of secondary school they attended. From the question asked, data collected and analysis shown in Table 21.5(c), it could be concluded that there was a *difference* across groups in the three career areas in the distribution across secondary schools. Three different questions result in three different samples and three different answers.

Calculating Cramér's C

The value of Cramér's C is dependent on the χ^2-ratio for the contingency table, the sample size and the smaller of the two category sets. It is given by:

$$C = \sqrt{\frac{x^2}{n(L-1)}} \tag{21.18}$$

where χ^2 is the chi-square ratio for the data, n is the total sample size, and L is the smaller of the number of rows and the number of columns. Due to the use of χ^2, its value can range only from 0 to 1.0, though this is quite reasonable when considering that neither variable has any direction or rank.

This statistic is easily implemented by starting with a two-dimensional χ^2 worksheet and adding the calculation for the coefficient, as described in Activity 21.7. This process automatically provides a check on the significance of any value of C, simply by inspecting the value of the χ^2-ratio, and provides an estimate of the power when using this test. In this activity, you will also see how Cramér's C is influenced by sample size.

Activity 21.7

1   The easiest way to set up Cramér's C is to start by copying the worksheet for the two-dimensional χ^2-test in Figure 20.1. Replace the row and column titles and the data with that in Table 21.5(a), as shown in Figure 21.7. Then add equation (21.18) as shown in cell **D13**. This also provides a significance test, since the χ^2-ratio is used for this purpose and already calculated. It also provides a way of estimating the power of the test, as shown.

> 2   To see the influence of sample size, simply double each of the frequencies in the nine cells. What happens to Cramér's C?
>
> **Answers:** 1 See Figure 21.5.
> 2 It stays the same, thus it does not appear to be sensitive to the sample size. What does change is the power of the test for significance, from 0.64 to 0.98. Thus the probability that we have correctly found a value for $C \neq 0$ has increased.

Siegel and Castellan (1988) note some limitations of Cramér's C that users should be aware of. First, the same limitation that exists for χ^2-tests applies to Cramér's C: only 20% of the cells can have an expected frequency less than 5. Otherwise the underlying assumptions of the sampling distribution are not likely to be met.

Second, Cramér's C is not comparable to Pearson's or Spearman's coefficients, since the latter describe relationships between ordered variables and not nominal data as used for C.

Finally, while the lack of any relationship will be easily identified when $C = 0.0$, the interpretation of a perfect relationship, $C = 1.00$, is clearest for square contingency tables – for example, 3×3 or 4×4. In such cases, the frequency in only one cell for each row and each column will be non-zero. Here each variable category is perfectly associated with one of the other variable's categories, as illustrated in Table 21.6(a). Rectangular contingency tables – for example, 3×4, 4×5 – are more difficult to interpret when $C = 1.00$, since one dimension – for example, columns – will have only one non-zero cell,

FIGURE 21.7
A copy of the worksheet in Figure 20.1, with data from Figure 21.6 inserted in shaded cells and equation (21.18) for Cramér's C added

	A	B	C	D	E	F	G	H	I	J
1		Public	Private	Church	Combined	Exp.prob.	Exp.Pub.	Exp.Priv.	Exp.Chur.	$(O{-}E)^2/E$
2	Technical	10					5.76			3.121
3			3					5.12		0.878
4				3	16	32.00%			5.12	0.878
5	Adminis-	4					6.12			0.734
6	trative		9					5.44		2.330
7				4	17	34.00%			5.44	0.381
8	Service	4					6.12			0.734
9			4					5.44		0.381
10				9	17	34.00%			5.44	2.330
11	Totals:	18	16	16	50	100.00%	18	16	16	11.767
12							$df =$	4	χ^2(4,0.05)=	9.488
13		Cramér's $C =$		0.34			$\alpha =$	0.05	$\lambda =$	8.77
14									$c =$	1.687
15		=SQRT(J11/(E11*(3–1)))							$df' =$	7.57
16									$hi\text{-}pow =$	0.689
17									$lo\text{-}pow =$	0.584
18									$power =$	0.64

while the rows may have more than one, as shown in Table 21.6(b). Thus it would not be a perfect correlation even though $C = 1.00$. Obviously the same difficulty applies when C approaches 1.00 when frequencies are very high in one cell per column and very low in others. To investigate the problems of interpretation of near 1.00 values of C, try Activity 21.8.

Activity 21.8

1 Insert the data from the 3×3 table in Table 21.6(a) into the worksheet in Figure 21.7. Now change some of the cells containing 0 into small frequencies of 1 or 2.
2 Make a copy of Figure 21.7 on a new worksheet and change it to a 3×4 sheet as follows: **Insert Column** for Expected at **H** and a corresponding column for the data at **C** (call it Charitable), and **Insert Rows** at **9**, **6** and **3**, in that order. At this stage, none of the values on the sheet should have changed.

   Add new raw data in column **C**: 2, 1 and 1. Change the three formulae under Combined to include these, **F5**, **F9** and **F13**. Copy sums formula to **I14** and **C14**. Copy diagonally formulae for the new Expected column to **I3**, **I7** and **I11**. Add the formulae under the $(O - E)^2/E$ column. Check that the sums under the two sets of four columns match and that the Combined Total matches the original total for the above data. Change df to $(3 - 1) * (4 - 1) = 6$. Would you interpret it the same as the 3×3 table with the C? Why or why not?
3 Change the values in the 3×4 sheet to obtain a Cramér's C approaching 1.0. What does it mean?

Other uses for Cramér's C: ordinal versus nominal tests

There will be situations where the question of a possible relationship involves one variable that is nominal and another that is ordinal (or even interval). It is possible to treat the ordinal variable as nominal and use Cramér's C, though the interpretation will have to reflect this. In other words, the relationship would be described as for two nominal variables. For example, is there any relationship between social class and career choice among final-year undergraduates? A random sample of undergraduate students in their last year would generate data pairs of social class (ordinal) and career choice (nominal).

TABLE 21.6
Two situations where Cramér's $C = 1.00$

(a)				(b)			
22	0	0		24	0	0	0
0	23	0		0	23	0	0
0	0	24		0	0	21	20

COEFFICIENT PHI, ϕ, FOR DICHOTOMOUS NOMINAL DATA

There is a special case involving nominal variables which is relatively easy to interpret: the situation where there are only two categories for each variable. These dichotomies result in a simple 2×2 contingency table. For example, Quercas Query wanted to know if there was any relationship between gender and attitudes towards nuclear power. At the time the nuclear power industry was privatized in Britain, he devised a simple (and I do mean *simple*) study where he surveyed 50 patrons of several local pubs. He asked each person (noting their gender): 'If you had £1000 that had to be spent on shares (and nothing else), would you buy shares in newly privatized nuclear power companies?' His results are shown in Table 21.7, which he found reasonably easy to interpret: men would tend to support the nuclear power industry more strongly than women. In other words, he maintained that there was a link between gender and attitude.

Now the results of this table can be summarized by the coefficient phi, ϕ, which can range from 0 to 1.0. In this case it has a value of 0.48, indicating a reasonable association between gender and response to the question. You might well ask why we cannot just use 2×2 chi-square as in Chapter 19? The answer is much the same as before. If the single sample has been a random one, then the phi coefficient of association described tells if any *relationship* exists between gender and attitude. On the other hand, had there been two random samples of male and female voters, then one would use χ^2-test to see if there was a *difference* in voting pattern.

Which question does the researcher want to answer: is there a tendency for male or females to have a positive attitude towards nuclear power *or* is there a significant difference in attitudes between male and female? Both studies would be ex post facto, but answering different questions.

The calculation of ϕ is a simple extension of that for Cramér's C (equation (21.18)), where the number of categories, $L = 2$:

$$\phi = \sqrt{\frac{\chi^2}{n}} \qquad \phi \text{ coefficient} \qquad (21.19)$$

where χ^2 is the chi-square ratio for the data and n is the total sample size. As this is based upon the χ^2-ratio, again it can easily be used to check the significance of the coefficient and its power.

Alternatively, the ϕ coefficient can be thought of as a variation of Pearson's product moment correlation and can be shown mathematically to be so (Guilford and Fruchter, 1973). Carry out Activity 21.9 to set up a worksheet for calculating ϕ.

TABLE 21.7
Results of a study to determine propensity to buy shares in nuclear power industry, $\phi = 0.48$

	Buy	Not buy
Male	15	5
Female	4	11

> ## Activity 21.9
>
> 1 Set up the data as shown in Figure 21.8 on a χ^2 worksheet to determine coefficient ϕ.
> 2 Comment on the design of this study.
>
> **Answers:** 2 Do the answers to the question constitute a valid indication of attitude towards nuclear power? There would be potential confounding from other factors, such as sample, and knowledge of share investment. Since the question put to respondents was so simple, there is no way to know why they responded as they did, making it difficult to report anything but contentious inferences as to why, like 'Women support nuclear power less than men!'. Also, even the single sample was neither random nor obviously representative of any larger population.

POINT BISERIAL, r_{pb}, FOR DICHOTOMOUS VERSUS INTERVAL/RATIO DATA

Finally, we will consider a rather special combination of variables, where one is interval/ratio and the other is dichotomous. This would apply to situations where naturally dichotomous variables are used: for example, gender, voted/did not vote, normal/schizophrenic, home owner/not home owner, and drinks/abstains. There are bimodal distributions that could result in dichotomous classifications, such as alcoholic/not alcoholic (based on a cut-off consumption rate). Alternatively, dichotomies such as pass/fail, older/younger, and well-groomed/not well-groomed are all the result of some determined

	A	B	C	D	E	F	G	H
1		Buy	Not buy	Combined	Exp. prob.	Exp. Buy	Exp. Not	$(O-E)^2/E$
2	Male	15				10.86		1.581
3			5	20	57.14%		9.14	1.877
4	Female	4				8.14		2.108
5			11	15	42.86%		6.86	2.503
6	Totals:	19	16	35	100.00%	19	16	8.069
7					$df =$	1	$\chi^2(1,0.05)=$	3.841
8			Coef $\phi =$	0.48	$\alpha =$	0.05	$\lambda =$	8.07
9							$c =$	1.890
10							$df' =$	4.80
11			=SQRT(H6/D6)				hi-$pow =$	0.845
12							lo-$pow =$	0.730
13							$power =$	0.82

FIGURE 21.8
Worksheet for coefficient ϕ, using data from Table 21.7.

criteria applied to continuous data. Some corresponding typical continuous variables could be income, age, IQ, anxiety, or body weight.

The formula for this coefficient is

$$r_{pb} = \frac{\bar{x}_p - \bar{x}_q}{S} \sqrt{pq} \qquad (21.20)$$

where $\bar{x}_p$ is the higher mean of continuous variable scores, group p; $\bar{x}_q$ the lower mean of continuous variable scores, group q; S the standard deviation of all scores, x_i, for both groups together; p the proportion of cases in the higher-mean group; and q the proportion of cases in the lower-mean group.

It is derived from the Pearson product moment correlation; the derivation can be found in Guilford and Fruchter (1973). The value of r_{pb} can range from 0.00 to 1.00, assuming the difference in the two means is positive. A negative value tells us nothing new in such cases since the correlation involves one dichotomous variable.

Let us consider the example of Sibyl Shrink, who wanted to know if there was any relationship between examination performance and a self-perceived sense of anxiety about taking tests. She took a random sample of undergraduate psychology students and asked them to complete a brief questionnaire before an examination, one question of which asked them if they perceived themselves as anxious about taking tests. The results of the question and examination are shown in Table 21.8. The overall standard deviation for the sample was $S = 9.0$, therefore

$$r_{pb} = \frac{63.4 - 55.6}{9.0} \sqrt{0.42 \times 0.58} = 0.43$$

Thus there appears to be some association between performance on *this* examination and perceived anxiety.

Now this situation does not answer all the possible questions. As has been noted for other coefficients determined on single samples, the corresponding experimental design would answer a different question. If random samples were taken from each of the two groups, then the question could be: 'Is there a *difference* in test performance between those who perceive themselves to be anxious and those who do not?' The question would be resolved by a *t*-test using the means of the two groups, assuming it was possible to identify the two groups ahead of time without introducing confounding by, for example, making subjects anxious by asking about it! As there is a mathematical link between the point biserial correlation and Pearson's product moment correlation, it is possible to test for significance in the same way, using the procedure in Figure 21.3. Carry out Activity 21.10 now to consider some examples.

TABLE 21.8
Contrived data for a study to investigate any link between self-perceived anxiety and examination performance, $r_{pb} = 0.43$

	Anxious	Not	Together
Mean =	55.6	63.4	
$n =$	33	24	57
$S =$	8.7	9.2	9.0
Proportion	0.58	0.42	1.00

Activity 21.10

1 (a) Was the value for r_{pb} found by Sibyl significant? What was the power?
  (b) How would you improve Sibyl Shrink's correlational study?
2 Terry Tippler suspected, from listening to conversations in his local pub that there was a tendency for older voters to choose more conservative candidates. He took a random sample of patrons one evening and asked them two questions: their age and who they voted for in the last local election. He then grouped them according to the candidates and their political tendencies. The results are shown in the following table:

	Liberal	Conservative	Together
Mean age	40.2	42.5	
n	22	20	42
S	5.2	4.9	5.1
Proportion	0.52	0.48	1.00

  (a) Find the point biserial correlation to see if there is a relationship between age and voting.
  (b) What does it tell you?
  (c) What could be done to improve this study?

Answers: 1(a) The *t*-ratio is 3.53, $p < 0.05$, power = 0.93. (b) Anxiety is not really a binary trait, particularly when it comes to examinations. To improve the study, design an instrument for measuring anxiety that would provide an interval or at least an ordinal score. Then administer it with respect to a variety of examinations, as anxiety may depend on the specific examination. This would allow generalization to all types of tests sampled.

2(a) $r_{pb} = 0.23$. (b) There is a weak relationship between age and voting, though it is not statistically significant. (c) Either increase the sample, randomly selecting a sample from a wider population, or try an ex post facto study to determine if there is a difference in mean age of Liberal and Conservative voters (two samples).

SOURCES OF MISLEADING RESULTS

Correlations, like most statistics, are prone to problems of interpretation and results that can be misleading, even when the research question has been carefully worded and the instruments have a high reliability and validity. No single study is likely to be afflicted with all the following sources, and not all apply to every one of the different coefficients encountered in this chapter. They are provided to help you be aware of common pitfalls, so that you can avoid them when possible.

Measuring instruments that are intended to provide interval data should aim to have a reasonable range of possible scores. Even when this has been achieved through trials, it is possible that during the actual study only a restricted range of scores is provided by subjects, possibly due to sampling error. For example, somehow you have only the children with higher reading scores, subjects who score in a low range of possible scores for schizophrenia, or even a narrow middle range of IQ scores. This tends to bunch up the scores on one of the axes. For example, consider the consequences of only having students with an IQ below 100 in the survey described at the beginning of this chapter. If we reproduce the scatter diagram of Figure 21.1(a) then visually block out those with IQ above 100 and calculate the Pearson product moment correlation, we obtain Figure 21.9, with $r_{xy} = 0.58$. Similarly, if we consider only those with IQ scores of at least 100, the correlation is also greatly reduced, $r_{xy} = 0.66$, from the correlation for the whole range of IQ, $r_{xy} = 0.85$.

Only a little of the reduced correlation can be attributed to the smaller sample. This can be shown by generating a new set of data, by ordering the original list provided in Figure 21.2 according to IQ score and choosing every other student across the full range of IQ scores. This smaller, but representative, sample has $r_{xy} = 0.82$. You should also note the less than linear nature of the two reduced scatter diagrams in Figure 21.9. Restricted ranges simply tend to

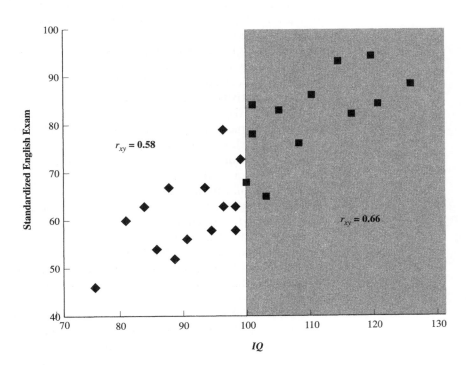

FIGURE 21.9
Scatter diagrams splitting Figure 21.1(a) in half, with one section for IQ scores below 100 and the other for IQ scores of at least 100

reduce the resulting correlation, and there would be similar consequences for any coefficient where one of the variables was continuous.

We have already encountered some examples of non-linear monotonic relationships where one variable increases (or decreases) with respect to the other, but not linearly (recall Activity 21.2, Question 3). In this case it appeared to violate the linearity assumption of Pearson's product moment correlation, and in Activity 21.4, Question 1, Spearman's *rho* was found to be not much different (which will not always be the case). The real difference will appear in the next chapter when trying to make predictions using regression lines. On the other hand, neither coefficient provided an intuitively satisfying correlation for the inverted U-distribution of Activity 21.2, Question 4 and Activity 21.4, Question 3, approaching zero in both cases. This is not surprising since it was neither linear (violating the assumption of Pearson's correlation) nor monotonic (violating the assumption of Spearman's rho). The shape of scatter diagrams is always worth inspecting.

Surveys often produce copious results, and there is the temptation to correlate all the possible pairs of variables on the respondents. While this may seem to be a valid way of searching for possible variables to pursue in subsequent studies, a large number of correlations on a sample can result in a chance finding of statistical significance. The possibility that the correlations between some of the pairs of variables might be meaningless should discourage the practice of correlating every possible pair. On the other hand, if the research questions suggest the possibility of a large number of meaningful correlations, then it may be reasonable to reduce α to 0.01.

Several authors (for example, Daly *et al.*, 1995; Grimm, 1993; Howell, 1997; Blalock, 1979) warn of the effects of a few extreme cases or extreme groups on correlations. Figure 21.10 provides you with a selection of nightmares: six contrived scatter diagrams that all produce the same correlation coefficient. These are most likely to occur when samples are small, but again are detectable by simply plotting a scatter diagram. You will have the opportunity to decide in what way the correlation might be influenced and the source of the peculiarities for each in Activity 21.11, along with some other cases.

There also exists the possibility of not choosing the best variables to support the research question. Glass and Hopkins (1996) suggest that correlations among units (classrooms, schools, cities) instead of individuals, described as *ecological correlations*, tend to be higher, but actually answer different questions. Thus a correlation between the mean scores by school on an examination and the location (urban, suburban, rural) would be higher than that for data pairs consisting of scores and the school the child attended, but the question being answered is different. In the first instance the correlation is between school type and their group performance. In the second, it is between the school attended and individual children's performances. Again, one must be sure that there is logical consistency between the question asked and the units and measures that are to be the operational definition of the variables (construct validity).

Related to this is the potential danger associated with using someone else's data. There is a large amount of raw data available, often from household surveys and censuses, which were originally collected with no obvious research questions in mind (or at least they are not obvious). Some very 'interesting' inferences have been made about populations based upon such data that verge on the amusing. What would you do with a high correlation between frequency of sunspots and tooth decay? Or between UFO sightings and increased number of pets per household (is your dog an alien)? Carry out Activity 21.11.

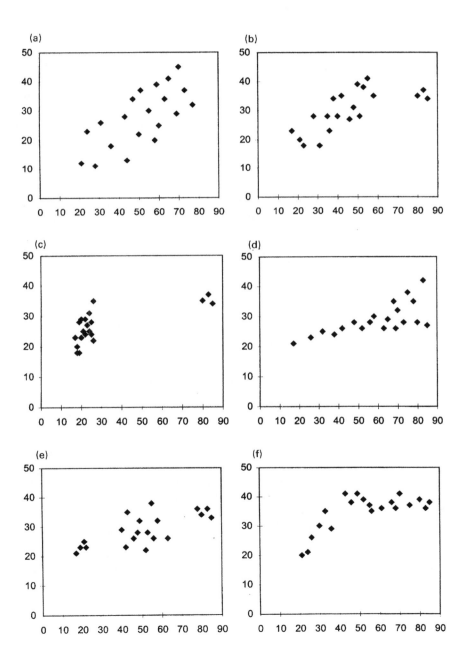

FIGURE 21.10
Six different scatter diagrams with $r_{xy} = 0.70$

Activity 21.11

1 For each of the scatter diagrams in Figure 21.10, suggest how the correlation coefficient might be distorted – for example, sampling, measuring instruments, etc. If another coefficient would be more appropriate, suggest which one and give reasons.

2 In each of the following (contrived) studies, identify what would be misleading about the results (if anything), and why:

(a) A random sample of 100 first-year university psychology students produced a correlation of 0.28 between IQ score and reading speed for an article from *Reader's Digest*. It was felt that the relationship between IQ and reading speed should have been considerably higher.

(b) A random sample of 20 young people aged 25–30 produced a correlation of 0.42 between their income and their father's maximum income when employed, but it was found not to be significant ($p > 0.05$).

(c) When considering a random sample of 1000 persons from Freedonia's national census data, a correlation of 0.83 was found between income and number of pets in the house. This was used to support the hypothesis that there was a strong relationship between security due to pets and success.

(d) A random sample of 100 undergraduates at Flatland University found a significant difference between male and female students in the amount of weekly spending money each had (t-ratio $=3.47$, $p < 0.05$).

(e) An international organization found that data from 15 developing countries showed a significant correlation of -0.43 between percentage of 20-year-olds having completed primary education and birth rate among that group. It was proposed that more aid money be spent on primary education for these countries to lower the birth rate.

Suggested answers

The nature of Activity 21.11 requires a bit more than just short answers. In one sense, it represents the most difficult part of analysing data, so what will be provided here are some suggested answers. You might not agree with all of them fully, but remember, analysing discrepant or unexpected outcomes requires some speculation and should at least influence the planning of future studies.

1 (a) This is the only one that looks like what one would expect, or at least wish to have, for which Pearson's product moment correlation would be appropriate.

(b) The three points off by themselves are sometimes referred to as *outliers,* and some authors would recommend they be dropped from the analysis (without them, $r_{xy} = 0.79$). I would suggest that one should look at the sample, data recording and measuring instruments first before taking such a step and removing data. If the sample is random and the data have been accurately recorded, then they do represent the population, they are just part of the random variation. When at least one of the variables is a score on a questionnaire, then it is worth looking to see if the respondent has simply marked every answer the same, for example, all 5s on a Likert scale, even for items where the scale values have been reversed. Then it might be justified to drop this subject. On the other hand, what you may have are two subpopulations that need to be investigated separately. If the sampling approach leaves something to be desired, then outliers may simply reflect this and the outliers may be a consequence of a gap along the axes in representative members of the group. In other words, you missed some. Picking and choosing data just to make the results look better is cheating, so removal of any subjects after data collection requires careful justification. There are any number of 'diagnostic' tools built into computer programs that will tell just how much of an influence such data points will have – see, for example, Howell (1997) – but they do not tell you why they are there.

(c) One possible cause could be sampling: there is more homogeneity for the x-axis trait than would be found naturally. Assuming a representative sample, this little horror would seem to reflect two subgroups and an instrument that has done an efficient job of separating them for the trait. It also has done a poor job of spreading out the values for the left-hand group.

(d) Such a scatter diagram might suggest that the horizontal variable is ordinal and that Spearman's rho might be a better indicator of a relationship.

(e) It appears that there might be three distinct groups here. Either the three groups could be surveyed separately if they exist, or the measuring instrument checked for bias, or the sampling procedure investigated.

(f) This is obviously non-linear, Spearman's rho might provide a higher correlation, but would also require a different interpretation.

2 (a) There was a restricted range of IQ scores due to sampling, since subjects would typically have higher IQ scores than the general population, and the range of their reading ability is likely to be only part of that of the general population's.

(b) This study suffers from a very small sample, no correlation less than 0.45 will be significant.

(c) The validity of the measure for this study is questionable since it used demographic data, which are usually collected with no hypotheses in mind. Correlating such numbers is potentially prone to the 'garbage in, garbage out' effect, since you are assigning operational definitions to variables because they are convenient. Do they really withstand the test of construct validity?

(d) The hypothesis describes a *difference* but the researcher used a single sample and should have looked for an association, describing findings using the point biserial correlation.

(e) A large correlation does not justify claiming a causal relationship. In fact, with a little bit of perverse logic, one could say that the cause of the drop in birth rate was due to the high expense of primary education compelling people to have fewer children. Thus lowering the cost of primary education through aid could *raise* the birth rate. This has no more support than the original conclusion, highlighting the weakness of using correlations as indicators of causality.

SUMMARY

This chapter has presented a variety of ways of describing relationships between pairs of variables that are not causal. Correlational studies have great potential and correlations are widely used to describe the outcomes of surveys, since they are based upon a single sample. The choice of statistical tool is, as always, dependent on the research question asked. The question also governs the nature of the instrument, the type of sample, and consequently whether the study is experimental, ex post facto, or correlational. Questions that ask about relationships tend to lead to correlational studies based upon a single sample that compares pairs of variables. Those enquiring about stronger links or causality result in single samples with random assignment to treatments or multiple samples based upon life-experience variables, and aim to resolve questions of difference in outcomes across groups. The choice of correlation or association coefficient is dependent on the combinations of scales of the data, as summarized in Table 21.2. Each of the coefficients shown there was described and spreadsheets were developed to facilitate calculations.

The next chapter explores regression equations and their role in making predictions and resolving hypotheses. Correlations form an important component of regression analysis, but as usual the appropriate application of these tools is dependent on the nature of the questions that underlie the research.

Regression

22

In the previous chapter, the distinction was made between correlation and regression: correlations indicated the strength of relationship between two variables while regression would allow predictions (extrapolation and interpolation) based upon a best-fit line. Also, while some would restrict regression studies to those that were experimental where both variables were interval/ratio, common usage results in the frequent extension of correlational relationships into regression lines for purposes of prediction. Regression is just a tool, therefore any decision about its use should be based upon the aim of the study and subsequent design, since ultimately these will influence the nature of the conclusions. Will they describe causal relationship or just predictions based upon correlations? Carefully planned experimental studies will aim to establish causality through the manipulation of one of the variables, having controlled all other possible extraneous variables. Ex post facto studies will describe correlational relationships that *might* be causal, but have possible extraneous variables that could be the cause of the outcomes. The distinction is an important one that should be kept in mind while exploring this valuable tool.

We will start with simple two-variable linear relationships and progress to explore ways of describing more complex situations involving three or more variables. In both cases, commonly available computer-based tools allow the determination of complex relationships that would be prohibitively arduous to establish by hand or pocket calculator. Finally, we will consider other types of predictions that may be of use in interpreting data, including those describing curvilinear relationships.

LINEAR REGRESSION EQUATIONS

As we saw in Chapter 21, few, if any, scatter diagrams produce data points that are perfect straight lines. Therefore, any straight line from which we make predictions is going to have to be a compromise for all the data and a mathematical procedure will have to be used to obtain an optimum line. The process is reasonably easy to carry out and only requires the correlation coefficient, since the equation of a straight line is very simple. In general, the equation of all straight lines can be written as

$$y = b_{yx}x + c \qquad (22.1)$$

where y is the value we want to know from the vertical axis; x is the value that we have, on the horizontal axis; b_{yx} is the slope or gradient of the line, the regression coefficient; and c is where the line crosses the vertical axis, called the y-intercept.

The *slope* or *gradient* of a line indicates the angle which the line makes with the x-axis and is simply the ratio of the vertical rise to the horizontal distance, as shown in Figure 22.1. It is like saying how steep a hill is. Taking two points on the graph, the slope is found simply by finding the ratio of the rise, 6.0, over the horizontal distance, 3.0, resulting in a slope of 2.0. We can also see from the graph that the y-intercept, where $x = 0$, is 3.0, completing the visualization of each of the components of the equation of a straight line, $y = 2x + 3$.

Since the regression line is a best-fit line for a set of data, the slope of a scatter diagram depends on the correlation coefficient (how strong the relationship is) as well as the two scales. The easiest way to find the slope of the line, b_{yx}, uses the correlation coefficient and the standard deviations of the two variables (the derivation of this can be found in Grimm, 1993). The equation is

$$b_{yx} = r_{xy}\frac{s_y}{s_x} \qquad (22.2)$$

where r_{xy} is the correlation coefficient, s_y is the standard deviation of the y variable and s_x is the standard deviation of the x variable.

The y-intercept, c, is found by taking the special case where $x = \bar{x}$ and $y = \bar{y}$, since the line will always go through the two means:

$$c = \bar{y} - b_{yx}\bar{x} \qquad (22.3)$$

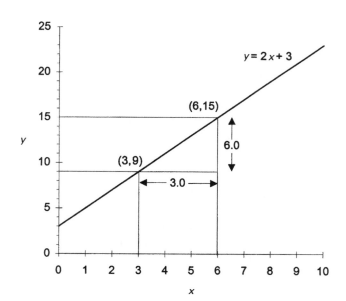

FIGURE 22.1
A straight line graph with its equation

For example, let us use the data that generated Figure 21.1(a), provided in Figure 21.2, to predict scores on the standardized English exam based upon IQ scores. It was stated that $r_{xy} = 0.85$, but more precisely, the value was $r_{xy} = 0.8485$ and from the raw data the following values can easily be found:

$$\bar{y} = 70.85 \quad s_y = 13.50$$
$$\bar{x} = 99.38 \quad s_x = 12.82$$

Then calculating the regression coefficient is a matter of substituting into equation (22.2):

$$b_{yx} = 0.8485 \frac{13.50}{12.82}$$
$$= 0.8935$$

Using equation (22.3), the y-intercept is found to be

$$c = 70.85 - 0.8935 \times 99.38$$
$$c = -17.95$$

Thus, the regression equation is

$$y = 0.8935x - 17.95$$

Looking at Figure 22.2, which shows the line corresponding to this equation overlaid on the scatter diagram, it is possible to see the y-intercept, where the line crosses the vertical axis. If we want to know what the likely score on the standardized English exam would be of someone who had an IQ of 119, then

$$y = 0.8935 \times 119 - 17.95$$
$$= 88.38$$

If we look at the data in Figure 21.2, we see that Martha had an IQ score of 119 and a test score of 94, fairly close to the prediction, but not exactly. Mary is just one of the data points in Figure 22.2, while the regression line represents a group tendency.

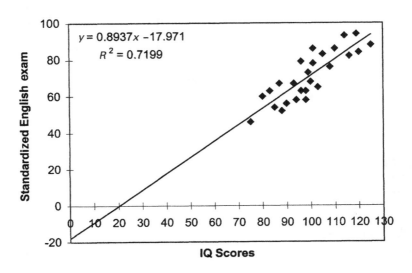

FIGURE 22.2
Regression line for
Figure 21.1(a), where
standardized
English exam scores
are predicted from
IQ Scores, $r_{xy} = 0.85$

Now that it has been established from where the regression equation comes, you will be relieved to know that it is not necessary to carry out the calculations by hand. Built into Excel are facilities not only for drawing the regression line, but also for providing the regression equation as shown in Figure 22.2 for the example just considered. You should notice that the coefficients in the equation for the line provided on the graph vary a little from those above in the far decimal places. The process used does not round off values as we tend to do with our calculators, so results will tend to differ slightly. We will see how to do this in the next activity, but first let us consider the reverse situation.

What if you wanted to predict the IQ score of someone based upon their standardized English exam score? In that case, a new equation is needed, since y is now the IQ score, and the standardized English exam score is x. The scatter diagrams would have to be plotted with the axes reversed, as shown in Figure 22.3. Looking at equation (22.2), the values in the second term are now reversed and the new regression coefficient becomes

$$b_{yx} = 0.8485 \frac{12.82}{13.50}$$
$$b_{yx} = 0.8058$$

and the y-intercept is

$$c = 99.38 - 0.8058 \times 70.85$$
$$= 42.29$$

This gives a new equation of

$$y = 0.8058x + 42.29$$

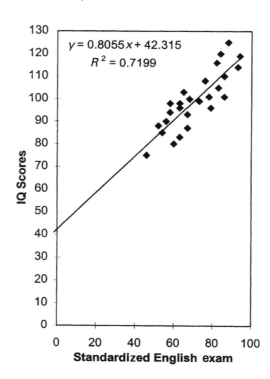

FIGURE 22.3
Regression line where IQ scores are predicted from standardized English exam scores, $r_{xy} = 0.85$

IQ Scores

$y = 0.8055x + 42.315$
$R^2 = 0.7199$

Standardized English exam

Again, these values are just slightly different from those in Figure 22.3 due to round-off error.

Looking once more at Figure 22.3, it is possible to see the y-intercept, where the line crosses the vertical axis. Doing the reverse of the above example and predicting what would be the IQ score of someone who had a score of 88.38 on the standardized English exam, we would find

$$y = 0.8058 \times 88.38 + 42.29$$
$$= 113.5$$

This is equal not to 119, the IQ score with which we started. Does this mean the scheme is flawed? No, it simply reflects the fact that the correlation is not 1.00. The observation that our cycle of predictions does not deviate too far from where we started suggests a high correlation. It is useful to consider both regression lines on the same graph, as shown in Figure 22.4. As you will find, Excel produces all of its equations for graphs in one format of $y = b_{yx} + c$, regardless of the order in which one wants to consider the relationship. Thus a conversion must be made to show the two equations in their proper format. The upper regression line in the figure allows the prediction of the standardized English exam score, y, from an IQ score, x. Since the lower regression line is now on the same graph, it now has an equation of the form

$$x = b_{xy}y + d \tag{22.4}$$

where b_{xy} is the regression coefficient for predicting x from y, and d is the x-intercept, where the line crosses the horizontal axis.

In our example above, both values of $R^2 = r_{xy}^2$ are the same. The point to keep in mind is that *there are two possible regression lines for every scatter diagram*. A consequence of this is that the higher the correlation, then the closer they will be to each other, and the smaller the correlation, the greater the difference between them. Figure 22.5 provides the regression lines for a scatter diagram with a very low correlation, $r_{xy} = 0.08$. Now you will see how to generate regression lines and equations in Activity 22.1.

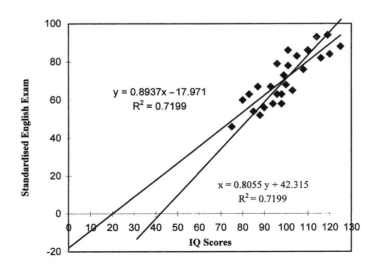

FIGURE 22.4
Both regression lines and equations for the example, $r_{xy} = 0.85$ score x. Since the lower regression line is on the same graph, it now has an equation of the form $x = b_{xy}y + d$

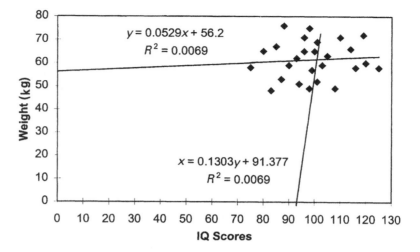

FIGURE 22.5
Both regression lines
for the scatter
diagrams in Figure
21.1(b), where
$r_{xy} = 0.08$

Activity 22.1

Carl Canvass was planning the election campaign of a conservative politician, but on a small budget. To target his audience for visits, he wanted to determine the relationship between house value and conservatism. He randomly selected 12 households in the constituency and succeeded in getting one member in each to complete the Canvass Measure of Conservatism (CMC). Estimating the value of each house, he assembled the following data:

House value ($000)	120	150	160	190	190	230	240	270	280	290	320	400
CMC score	19.4	13.7	10.6	14.6	16.7	12.3	28.7	17.5	31.1	25.9	23.1	25.6

(a) Plot a scatter diagram (see Activity 21.1) for the data.
(b) To obtain the regression equation, activate the chart and activate the data points. From the main menu, select **Insert, Trendline**, which will provide the following. Select the type of line, **Linear**, shown in black.

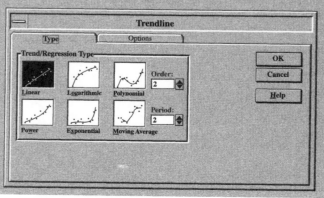

Click on the **Options** tab to obtain the following, and select the two options at the bottom to obtain the equation, by clicking in the boxes. Click on the | OK | button.

```
┌──────────────────────────────────────────────────────────────┐
│ ─                       Trendline                              │
│   ┌───────────────┐┌─────────────────────┐                     │
│   │     Type      ││       Options       │                     │
│ ┌─Trendline Name──────────────────────────────┐  ┌──────────┐  │
│ │ ◉ Automatic:   Linear (Series1)             │  │    OK    │  │
│ │ ○ Custom:      ┌──────────────────────────┐ │  └──────────┘  │
│ │                └──────────────────────────┘ │  ┌──────────┐  │
│ └─────────────────────────────────────────────┘  │  Cancel  │  │
│ ┌─Forecast──────────────────────────────┐        └──────────┘  │
│ │ Forward:    ┌──┐ ▲ Units              │        ┌──────────┐  │
│ │             │0 │ ▼                     │        │   Help   │  │
│ │ Backward:   ┌──┐ ▲ Units              │        └──────────┘  │
│ │             │0 │ ▼                     │                      │
│ └───────────────────────────────────────┘                      │
│ □ Set Intecept =      │0 │                                      │
│ ☒ Display Equation on Chart                                     │
│ ☒ Display R-squared Value on Chart                              │
└──────────────────────────────────────────────────────────────┘
```

This will generate a regression line, the corresponding equation and the correlation coefficient squared on the chart. Repeat the process, but with the order of the variables reversed, to obtain the second regression equation. This means the second graph, in **Step 1**, sweep the columns in reverse order, separating them with a comma.

(c)   Using the regression equations, do a circular prediction for Carl, starting with a house value of $200 000. While the first equation will be as Excel produces it, $y = b_{yx} + c$, rewrite the second one exchanging x and y so that it reads $x = b_{xy}y + d$. What does the prediction show? (The answer to this question is given in Activity 22.2)

If we were pedantic and followed the description of regression studies provided in the previous chapter, which said that these are based upon experimental studies where both variables are interval/ratio and the design controls extraneous variables, then only *one* regression line would be possible. We would have established a hypothesis that the dependent variable, y, would change as we changed the independent variable, x. The purpose of the study would be to determine the validity of the hypothesis describing a causal relationship. As noted then, regression equations are also used in correlational studies where causality is not the issue, but strength of relationship is, *and* one wishes to make predictions on the basis of any established relationship.

In the example provided above, being very literate (scoring high on the standardized English exam) does not *cause* one to be intelligent (score high on the IQ test), nor vice versa. The relationship between them is strong and one can be equally well predicted from the other.

Confidence intervals and accuracy of predictions

Now it is fairly obvious that most predictions will be at best estimates, and there will be a range in which we could reasonably expect the true value to be. Not surprisingly, this range can be expressed as a distribution of probabilities with the regression line as the set of most likely predictions. It is possible to visualize the regression line provided earlier (with scatter diagram points removed) as shown in Figure 22.6, with some of the distributions of probabilities of the y values being on either side of the most likely value.

Thus, in the example, the most likely value of y for an $x = 119$, was $y = 88.40$, a data point right on the regression line. From the mini-distribution, the likelihood of it being at either extreme is small, but finite. The standard deviation of this distribution is known as the *standard error of the estimate* and is found by

$$s_{yx} = s_y \sqrt{1 - r_{xy}^2} \tag{22.5}$$

when predicting values of y from values of x, using equation (22.1). If we were to predict values of x from values of y using the alternative regression line described by equation (22.4), then the standard error of the estimate would be

$$s_{xy} = s_x \sqrt{1 - r_{xy}^2} \tag{22.6}$$

Therefore, in the example of predicting standardized English exam scores from IQ,

$$s_{yx} = 13.50 \sqrt{1 - (0.85)^2}$$
$$= 7.11$$

Thus, one standard deviation for each of the distributions is 7.11 and there is a 95% probability that the score will be $\pm 1.96\, s_{yx} = \pm 13.94$ either side of a predicted score. So in the example above, where it was predicted that someone with an IQ score of 119 would attain a score of 88.40 on the standardized English exam, this would be better described as

$$y = 88.40 \pm 13.94$$

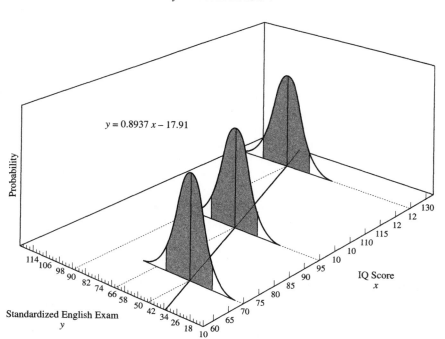

FIGURE 22.6
Regression line with three distributions for confidence intervals for values of y (standardized English exam score) predicted from values of x (IQ score)

Alternatively, this could be expressed as the interval in which there is a 95% probability that the score will be:

95% confidence interval: 74.46 to 102.34

One could express this as a 50% confidence interval, or any other for that matter, depending on the choice of interval and appropriate choice of z-score corresponding to the percentage. Now carry out Activity 22.2.

Activity 22.2

Using the equations derived from the data given in Activity 22.1,

$y = 0.0523x + 7.549$ (house to CMC)

$x = 7.2909y + 91.335$ (CMC to house)

the circular prediction was roughly \$200 000 → 18 → \$223 000. That is, if $x = \$200\,000$, then $y = 18$ from the first equation, and this substituted in the second equation results in $x = \$223\,000$ (all values rounded). Carl also found that everyone who scored 18 or over would vote for his candidate.

(a) Provide a 95% confidence interval for the initial prediction of CMC, y from house values, x.

(b) What would be the 99% confidence interval?

(c) What does this tell Carl?

Answers: (a) $s_{yx} = 5.12$, ±10.4. (b) ±11.93. (c) He is going to have a difficult time predicting conservatism from house prices, and consequently, who is likely to vote for his candidate.

Assumptions

As before, a distinction will be made between experimental (regression) and ex post facto (correlational) studies, since both use the same tool: a regression equation. In the first case, a true experimental regression study would involve determining a range of values for the proposed independent variable, x, therefore it would be considered to be a *fixed* variable (fixed by the experimenter). Consequently, there would be no assumption about a distribution of x values. In addition to the sample being representative of the population and the relationship being linear, there would be an additional assumption about the distribution of the dependent variable, y, so that the generation of linear regression equations would be valid. It is presumed that the distribution of y data for each x value (or range) around the regression line is normal, since it is a *random* variable, and has the same variance as all the others. This last characteristic is called *homoscedasticity*, from the Greek *homo* meaning 'same' and *scedastos* meaning 'capable of being scattered'.

To illustrate this, instead of a scatter diagram for a set of data, think of the data points as being piled up in groups, making a third dimension, as shown in Figure 22.7. Here the contrived data represent a sample of 108 subjects measured for anxiety (dependent random variable y) when presented with sets of examination questions. The number of questions (independent fixed variable x) to be answered on an exam paper was varied from 10 to 90. The data produce a correlation of about 0.80. The regression line lies on the floor under-neath the mountain range, having the equation shown, crossing the y-axis at 68.8 when $x = 0$. To demonstrate homoscedasticity, a series of x values is chosen, say at every 10 points, and a cross-sectional slice is taken of the moun-tain. These should produce a set of normal distributions all having roughly the same standard deviation. In the example, each y standard deviation is roughly between 8 and 13, even though the peaks drop at each end. It should be noted that for an experimental study with control over x, the ends would not be neces-sarily rounded, but could drop off abruptly. The assumption of homoscedasti-city pertains to our raw data, which should correspond to the constant normal distributions based upon the standard error of the estimate when making pre-dictions (Figure 22.6). For this example, the overall standard deviation for y is $s_y = 20.86$, and standard error of the estimate, $s_{yx} = 9.47$, within the range of standard deviations in the cross-sections of the raw data. This illustrates, though, the need for homoscedasticity if predictions are to be accurate even within the confidence intervals stated. The data on which we base the equations must support their use by having similar characteristics to the distributions of the predictions.

In contrast, correlational studies are a consequence of no control over either of the variables; *both* are considered random variables and would have normal distributions. In such cases, we should be able to slice the mountain parallel to either axis and find normal distributions, since the predictions conceivably could be made with either variable considered to be independent of the other in terms of a regression equation (as above). Such a mountain that shows normal distributions parallel to both axes is called a *bivariate* normal distribu-tion (two variables). Fortuitously, Figure 22.7 approximates this with standard deviations of x ranging from 10.3 to 12.7. Since there is a definite correlation, it is still a mountain ridge, being long and narrow. If there were no correlation, it would appear as a symmetrical, round hill.

FIGURE 22.7
Scatter diagram displayed as frequencies, showing reasonable homoscedasticity (roughly equal standard deviations of cross-sectional slices), with the corresponding regression line (dashed) provided on the 'floor' of the diagram

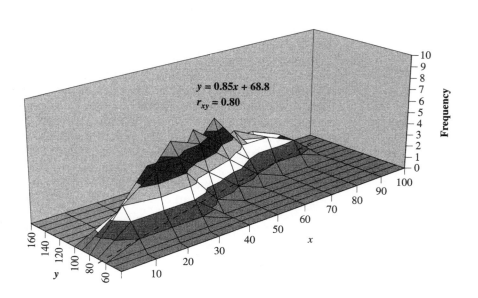

Now there has been a bit of a leap from the simple equation of a straight line to that of the regression equation. Calculating the slope (the regression coefficient) from the correlation coefficient and the standard deviations is a short-cut that hides a more complex process. Any straight line for a scatter diagram is going to be a 'best possible fit'. An optimum process would involve finding a line that had as many data points above as below, with the sum of the distances above equalling the sum of those below. In other words, the best line would be the one where the errors cancelled each other. The mathematical process is called the *least-squares method*, and involves finding the sum of all the differences of y data values and the y value on the line squared. The aim is to find the line for which the sum of these squares is as close to zero as possible. Obviously, to do this on a trial and error basis would take a long time, so we make some assumptions: the correlation coefficient is a good indicator of the overall spread of the points, and the standard deviations of x and y provide us with the scales. As with any mathematical short-cut, we must keep an eye on the assumptions if its use is to be valid.

Associated variances

Explaining the relationship between two correlated variables is not easy, particularly when trying to avoid statements that sound like expressions of causality. Yet, as we have seen, a relationship exists, one that at least allows predictions to be made. More can be said about the relationship between the two variables that is revealing, but this is based upon mathematics and shared variability and requires some mathematical derivations.

Starting with equation (22.5), which describes the standard error of the estimate for predicting y from x, and squaring both sides, we get

$$s_{yx}^2 = s_y^2(1 - r_{xy}^2)$$

Rearranging this gives the equality

$$1 = \frac{s_{yx}^2}{s_y^2} + r_{xy}^2 \qquad (22.7)$$

What this says is that 100% of the variance can be broken down into two parts: s_{yx}^2/s_y^2, that proportion which *cannot* be explained; and r_{xy}^2, that proportion which can be explained by the relationship between y and x. This becomes more apparent when considering that it is also possible to describe the overall observed total variance of the y-variable as

$$s_y^2 = s_{pred}^2 + s_{yx}^2 \qquad (22.8)$$

where s_{pred}^2 is the predictable variance from the relationship and s_{yx}^2 is the unexplained or error variance (the squared standard error of the estimate). Thus, if equation (22.7) is solved for r_{xy}^2, then

$$r_{xy}^2 = 1 - \frac{s_{yx}^2}{s_y^2} = \frac{s_y^2 - s_{yx}^2}{s_y^2}$$

$$r_{xy}^2 = \frac{s_{pred}^2}{s_y^2}$$

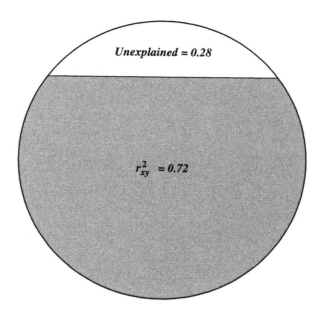

FIGURE 22.8
Shared variances for
$r_{xy} = 0.85$

This says mathematically that the correlation coefficient squared is equal to the *proportion* of the total variance that is predictable. Thus the higher the correlation coefficient, the greater the proportion of the variability in y that can be explained by variability in x, rather than unknown extraneous variables and/or error. The proportion of shared or common variance provides us with an explanation of the relationship between the two variables. In the example above, the proportion of the variance in standardized English exam scores that could be explained by variance in the IQ scores was $r_{xy}^2 = (0.85)^2 \cong 0.72$, or about 72%. The other 28% is unexplained and due to error or extraneous variables, which is why some texts refer to r_{xy}^2 as the *coefficient of determination*. The relationship can be shown as a proportion of a full circle, as shown in Figure 22.8, an approach we will return to later to explain multiple correlation.

Considering correlations in terms of associated variances also assists in understanding why low values can be considered of limited importance in some situations. A correlation of 0.20 will have only 4% of the variance in y explained by that in x, with 96% unexplained. Yet in some cases, this might provide a lead for further research.

MULTIPLE REGRESSION

There will be situations where we wish to determine the nature of the relationship between a dependent variable and more than one independent variable. We have already encountered one tool for resolving whether there are differences when the independent variables are nominal (different types or levels of different treatments), and the dependent variable is interval/ratio: factorial analysis of

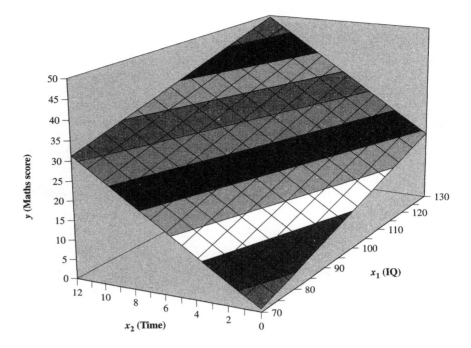

FIGURE 22.9
Multiple regression
plane for
$y = -20.09 + 0.30x_1$
$+ 2.51x_2$

variance (Chapter 17). Now we need a tool to contend with cases where *all* the variables are interval/ratio. While this becomes extremely complex mathematically for one dependent variable and three or more independent variables, it is quite straightforward for one dependent and two independent variables. Therefore, an example of this will be used to describe and understand the process and we will depend upon computer software for generating answers for the more complex cases.

For example, Figure 22.9 shows a contrived relationship of proficiency in a mathematical skill (making approximations), time spent learning, and intelligence of children. Here mathematical proficiency is the dependent variable, with learning time and intelligence the proposed independent variables. As this is a plane in three dimensions, it is possible to express the relationship in the form

$$y = c + b_1 x_1 + b_2 x_2 \qquad (22.9)$$

This is analogous to the equation (22.1) for the straight line in two dimensions for linear regression for two variables. This equation describes a plane using two regression coefficients, b_1 and b_2, with the y-intercept at c. Again, it is appropriate when all the relationships are linear. Such a graph could be used to predict values of scores on the test of ability to approximate (y) for pairs of values of IQ score (x_1) and hours of practice (x_2). The prediction would correspond to a point on the plane. For example, a student with an IQ score of 90 who spends 4 hours practicing could be expected to achieve a score of about 17 on the test. Try this in Activity 22.3.

Activity 22.3

(a) Find this point (4, 90, 17) on the diagram in Figure 22.9. The square grid on the plane shows the values of x_1 and x_2, where the diagonal bands correspond to the y-axis values.

(b) What score on the test would we expect from a student who

  (i) has an IQ score of 115 and spends 5 hours on the package?
  (ii) has an IQ score of 80 and spends 10 hours on the package?

(c) It is relatively easy to generate a plane from the equation using Excel.

  (i) Set up a worksheet as shown in Figure 22.10.
  (ii) Select ChartWizard and mark out a rough area. Then proceed as follows:

  Step 1 Enter the **Range: =A2:D5**.
  Step 2 Select **3-D Surface**.
  Step 3 Select **1**.
  Step 4 Make sure that you **Use First** [1] **Column(s)** and **Use First** [1] **Row(s)**.
  Step 5 You do not need a Legend, but enter axes titles.

  (iii) Double-click on the chart and find a corner point to double-click on so you can wrestle the chart around to the perspective you want.
  (iv) Select the lower left axis, double click to obtain **Format Axis** and under **Scale**, choose **Categories in Reverse Order**. Your plane should look like the one in Figure 22.9, though without the grid. To obtain a grid, you would need more than three values for x_1 and x_2, though this is not necessary just to see the plane. Simply change the values for c, b_1 and b_2 to see new planes in subsequent activities.

Answers: (b) (i) 27. (ii) 29.

Obviously, a multiple regression plane is a valuable way of visualizing the relationship among the three variables, but one's imagination must be pretty good to do the same for four or more variables, a problem not uncommon in mathematics. When such situations do arise, graphics must give way to the interpretation of equations. While the hard work of generating the coefficients and y-intercept will most often be done using computer programs, we need to understand from where they come. To begin the process we will use the above example. Similar to what was done with simple linear regression, we will start with the description of a hypothetical study that collects the raw data and, from these, determine values for b_1, b_2 and c.

	A	B	C	D	E	F
1	$c =$	-20.09	$b_1 =$	0.302	$b_2 =$	2.507
2	$x_1 \backslash x_2$	0	6	12		
3	70	1.1	16.1	31.1		
4	100	10.1	25.2	40.2		
5	130	19.2	34.2	49.3		

=$B$1+$D$1*$A3+$F$1*B$2 and
Copy to other eight cells

FIGURE 22.10
Worksheet for
Activity 22.4

Having observed her students over several years, Norma Number wanted to know what the effect might be of apparent inherent ability (as measured by IQ scores) and practice time on achievement in mathematics. She decided on the operational definitions of her variables as follows:

- *Achievement* would be the children's scores on a test of ability to make approximations, corresponding to variable y.
- *Intelligence* would be measured using IQ scores and represented by variable x_1.
- *time for learning* would be quantified by the number of hours of practice allowed on a computer-assisted learning package for the topic (approximating), and represented by variable x_2.

She randomly chose 25 fourteen-year-old students from the schools in her town and arranged to have the computer package available for them to use. She randomly assigned each student to a time period, after which he or she would take the achievement test on approximation. They were encouraged to continue after that time and take the test again later if they wished. By randomly selecting the students she was able to ensure she had a range of abilities that reflected the age group, with a mean IQ score of 100.6 and a standard deviation of 15.63. Through random assignment, the ability range would be equitably distributed across the times for measurement. The raw data that Norma collected are shown in Table 22.1.

First of all, the raw data will appear not as a scatter diagram in two dimensions, but a cloud of points, like a swarm of bees, in three dimensions, as shown in Figure 22.11. The higher the correlation, the flatter the cloud, the closer it approximates a plane, just as the higher a simple correlation for two variables the closer the scatter diagram would approximate a straight line. Let us now see how these data were used to generate the equation of the plane shown in Figure 22.9.

To obtain the values for the regression coefficients and y-intercept in equation (22.7) requires two steps (the detailed mathematics behind this can be found in Guilford and Fruchter, 1973; or Glass and Hopkins, 1996). This process

TABLE 22.1
Raw data (contrived)
for multiple
regression example

Subject	$y =$ Approx	$x_1 =$ IQ	$x_2 =$ Time
John	6.5	90	0
Henry	12	105	0
Jane	17	120	0
Fred	5	75	1
Mary	16	115	1
Albert	22	130	1
Sam	15	100	2
Ellen	13	90	2
Ted	20	105	3
Anne	17	100	3
Hilary	13	80	4
Barbara	20	95	5
Betty	28	115	5
Terry	17	70	6
Robert	25	100	6
Tom	24	85	7
James	28	105	7
Nancy	37	120	8
Peter	32	95	9
David	30	80	10
Melanie	38	110	10
Sonya	37	95	11
Jacob	46	125	11
Sean	39	100	12
Shirley	42	110	12

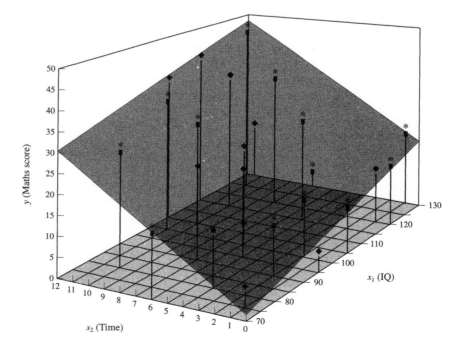

FIGURE 22.11
Three-dimensional
scatter diagram of
raw data in Table
22.1, used to
generate the
equation of the plane
in Figure 22.8 (∗ are
above the plane
while ◆ are below
the plane)

TABLE 22.2
Multiple correlation output from **Tools, Data Analysis, Correlation** in Excel for the three data columns in Table 22.1

	y = Approx	x_1 = IQ	x_2 = Time	Means	s
y = Approx	1			23.98	11.33
x_1 = IQ	0.4222826	1		100.6	15.63
x_2 = Time	0.9057274	0.0054827	1	5.44	4.08

requires the determination of coefficients β, for standardized regression equations, from

$$b_j = \beta_j \frac{s_y}{s_j} \qquad (22.10)$$

where j is either 1 or 2 in our case, corresponding to variables x_1 or x_2. One way to find the values for β_1 and β_2 requires one to solve two equations for two unknowns (Kerlinger, 1986):

$$r_{x_1 x_1}\beta_1 + r_{x_1 x_2}\beta_2 = r_{yx_1} \qquad (22.11)$$
$$r_{x_2 x_1}\beta_1 + r_{x_2 x_2}\beta_2 = r_{yx_2} \qquad (22.12)$$

From Table 22.2, generated by Excel as we will see in the next activity, the correlations (rounded off), were found to be: $r_{x_1 x_1} = 1.00$ between x_1 and itself; $r_{x_2 x_2} = 1.00$ between x_2 and itself; $r_{yx_1} = 0.422$ between y and x_1; $r_{yx_2} = 0.906$ between y and x_2; and $r_{x_1 x_2} = r_{x_2 x_1} = 0.0055$ between x_1 and x_2. First, solving equation (22.11) for β_1 and substituting in values, provides an expression for β_1 in terms of only β_2,

$$\beta_1 = \frac{r_{yx_1} - r_{x_1 x_2}\beta_2}{r_{x_1 x_1}}$$
$$= \frac{0.422 - 0.0055\beta_2}{1.00}$$
$$\beta_1 = 0.422 - 0.0055\beta_2$$

Substituting this into equation (22.12) gives

$$r_{x_2 x_1}(0.422 - 0.0055\beta_2) + r_{x_2 x_2}\beta_2 = r_{yx_2}$$

Finally, substituting in values for the correlations and solving for β_2 gives

$$0.0055(0.422 - 0.0055\beta_2) + 1.00\beta_2 = 0.906$$
$$\beta_2 \cong 0.906$$

Substituting this in the expression above gives

$$\beta_1 \cong 0.417$$

Now these values can be used to find b_1 and b_2 from equation (22.10)

$$b_1 = 0.417\frac{11.33}{15.63} = 0.302$$
$$b_2 = 0.906\frac{11.33}{4.08} = 2.516$$

The y-intercept, c, is found in the same way as it was for the equation of a line,

$$c = \bar{y} - b_1\bar{x}_1 - b_2\bar{x}_2 \tag{22.13}$$
$$= 23.98 - 0.302 \times 100.6 - 2.516 \times 5.44$$
$$c = -20.08$$

Thus, the equation for the plane in Figure 22.11 is

$$y = -20.08 + 0.30x_1 + 2.52x_2$$

This is virtually identical to that found using Excel as described in Figure 22.9, the small differences again being attributable to rounding error. Note that c does not actually appear in Figure 22.9 or 22.11. In this case, it is just a mathematical descriptor as it intercepts with the y-axis below the floor of the graph. The meaningful and functional range of the table is only for positive values of y, the test score, and x_1, the time spent learning, and mostly where the IQ score range is above 70, which includes over 97% of children. This drawn-out process is done for you by most statistical packages, as will be seen in the next Activity 22.4, to be carried out now.

Activity 22.4

(a) Using the equation of the plane above and that provided by Excel, find the expected values of a student who

    (i)   has an IQ score of 115 and spends 5 hours on the package.
    (ii) has an IQ score of 80 and spends 10 hours on the package.

(b) Enter the data in Table 22.1 into a new worksheet in columns **A** to **D**.

    (i)   From the main menu, select **Tools, Data Analysis, Correlation**. The input range includes the raw data. Leave column **E** blank and type the cell designation of the upper left-hand corner, **$F$1**, under **Output Range** as shown. Click on the [OK] button and you should get the analysis shown in the first four columns of Table 22.2.

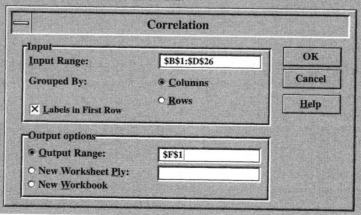

(ii)   From the main menu, select **Tools**, **Data Analysis**, **Regres-sion**. This time the input ranges for y and the two (or more) x variables are separate. Again leave the adjacent column blank and as long as there is nothing in the space to the right or below, you can just indicate the upper left-hand corner for the **Output Range**. Click on the | OK | button and you should get the analysis shown in Table 22.3, the contents of which are discussed below.

Regression

Input

Input Y Range: $B$1:$B$26

Input X Range: $C$1:$D$26

☒ Labels   ☐ Constant is Zero
☒ Confidence Level   95   %

OK

Cancel

Help

Output options

⦿ Output Range: $F$7

◯ New Worksheet Ply:

◯ New Workbook

Residuals

☐ Residuals   ☐ Residuals Plots
☐ Standardized Residuals   ☐ Line Fit Plots

Normal Probability

☐ Normal Probability Plots

Answers: (a) (i) 27.0. (ii) 29.1.

INTERPRETING REGRESSION INFORMATION

This unfortunately is not an easy task, but then anytime one is trying to determine the contributions of more than one variable, the problem ceases to be simple. We will consider the copious output from Excel (the content of which is not much different from other packages) from several perspectives, starting with the easiest case to interpret and progressing on to a more complex example. Our example above tends to have characteristics that make its interpretation relatively straightforward.

The lower left-hand corner of Table 22.3 gives values under 'coefficients' for c, b_1 and b_2, which you will notice are the ones used to generate the equation of the plane in Figure 22.9. The output also provides other useful information, which will be considered, starting at the top of the table. A second example will also be given shortly in order to provide a contrast.

TABLE 22.3
Output table for **Tools, Data Analysis, Regression** in Excel, for data in Table 22.1.

SUMMARY	OUTPUT

Regression	*Statistics*
Multiple *R*	0.997246528
R Square	0.994500638
Adjusted *R* Square	0.994000696
Standard error	0.877622165
Observations	25

ANOVA

	df	SS	MS	F	Significance F
Regression	2	3064.295145	1532.147573	1989.231974	1.39135E–25
Residual	22	16.94485461	0.770220664		
Total	24	3081.24			

	Coefficients	Standard error	t-stat	P-value	Lower 95%	Upper 95%
Intercept	− 20.0854534	1.188959097	− 16.893309	4.39232E–14	− 22.5512063	− 17.6197005
x_1 = IQ	0.302461926	0.011458904	26.39536258	3.77139E–18	0.278697588	0.326226264
x_2 = Time	2.506945521	0.043872994	57.14097191	2.03635E–25	2.415958403	2.59793264

Multiple R and R^2

The multiple correlation coefficient, R, describes the overall correlation between y and *all* the independent variables together. Expressed as R^2 it describes the proportion of the variance in y that is accounted for by all the independent variables. We will see how this is calculated, but all computer-based packages routinely generate a value for this, even when there is only one independent variable and the regression equation is a straight line in two dimensions. In such cases this is simply $R^2 = r_{xy}^2$. For situations like the example above where there are two independent variables, it is found from

$$R^2 = \frac{r_{yx_1}^2 + r_{yx_2}^2 - 2r_{yx_1}r_{yx_2}r_{x_1x_2}}{1 - r_{x_1x_2}^2} \tag{22.14}$$

Alternatively, if the values for the beta coefficients are known, we have

$$R^2 = \beta_1 r_{yx_1} + \beta_2 r_{yx_2} \tag{22.15}$$

which could also be written in terms of the regression coefficients, referring back to equation (22.10), as

$$R^2 = b_1 \frac{s_1}{s_y} r_{yx_1} + b_2 \frac{s_2}{s_y} r_{yx_2} \tag{22.16}$$

TABLE 22.4
Multiple correlations for changed data to illustrate impact of higher correlation between independent variables x_1 and x_2

	$y = $ Approx	$x_1 = $ IQ	$x_2 = $ Time	Mean	s
$y = $ Approx	1			21.82	14.22
$x_1 = $ IQ	0.4278956	1		99.00	13.46
$x_2 = $ Time	0.9033144	0.5047923	1	5.44	4.08

These equations also show the relationship between the multiple correlation coefficient and the individual correlation coefficients. This is not a simple one, unless the correlation between the two independent variables happens to be 0.00, which almost happens in our example above, where $r_{x_1 x_2}$ is only 0.0055. Thus it is not surprising to find that in this case

$$R^2 \cong 0.422^2 + 0.906^2 = 0.178 + 0.821 = 0.999$$

From the more accurate calculation in Table 22.3, $R^2 = 0.9945$, we still see that over 99% of the variance in the maths score is accounted for by the combination of the two variables. This also means that the values of b_1 and b_2 approximately describe the slope of the lines made by the plane intersecting the walls of the graph in Figure 22.8, which is *not* the usual case.

A word about this contrived example is necessary at this point, since this is not likely to happen often. In the example it could only happen under the following circumstances:

- If the learning package were perfectly suitable for all levels of children (as measured by IQ tests).
- If perseverance at learning had nothing to do with IQ. While having a 'perfect' package for all and absolute control over learner perseverance may be a developer's dream, the graph of the plane did allow the clear illustration of mathematical relationships.
- If the sample were representative of students and they were randomly assigned to time durations.

To see the consequences of there being a moderate relationship between the two independent variables, in other words, $r_{x_1 x_2} >> 0$, and a smaller R^2, the original data were massaged to produce the correlations in Table 22.4. The main difference is the correlation between x_1 and x_2 has increased from almost zero to over 0.50. This was achieved primarily by changing the data so that low-IQ students tended to have only low times and high-IQ students longer times. Such a situation might have been the consequence in a study of *not* randomly assigning students, or if low-IQ students did not persevere and tended to spend less time on the learning activity.

The regression equation and the plane

The new situation described in Table 22.4 results in the plane in Figure 22.12 which has rotated with respect to that in Figure 22.8. Taking the regression

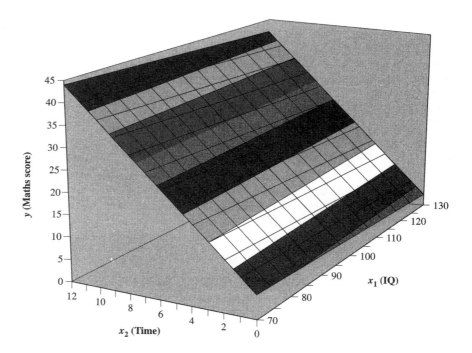

FIGURE 22.12
Multiple regression
plane for
$y = 8.29 - 0.04x_1$
$+ 3.21x_2$

coefficients and y-intercept from the Excel analysis, this equation can be written
as

$$y = 8.29 - 0.04x_1 + 3.21x_2$$

This time, finding a predicted achievement test score, y, on the plane results in
an interesting outcome. Choosing a time, we find that the difference in y depending on a value for the IQ is very small. For example, for a time of 7 hours, we
find that the achievement test scores will vary only a little, from about 23 for IQ
scores of 70, to 21 for IQ scores of 130. Basically, IQ appears to have little to do
with it, but this may be an artefact of the data collection: low-IQ children tend
to spend less time than high-IQ ones. Some caution must be exercised in interpreting the regression equation in this way. The magnitude of the regression
coefficients, b, is dependent upon the scale and standard deviation of the
measure, thus differences may be exaggerated. Part of the reason for the
small value of b_1 relative to b_2 above was due to x_1 being measured in tens
and its standard deviation was 13.46, whereas x_2 was measured in units and
its standard deviation was 4.08. Thus in terms of relative influence, the standardized regression coefficients, β, are a better indicator. Here they would be
$\beta_1 = -0.04$, $\beta_2 = 0.92$, and the relative contributions are still as suggested.

As Howell (1997) also notes, the relative influence of variables may change
radically with the sample. In other words, a replication with a new sample
may produce radically different regression coefficients, but with much the
same R^2. Before going off to make radical decisions based on a regression equation, it might be worthwhile seeing if it does survive the test of replication. As we
have seen with other designs, the quality of the sample and measuring instru-

ments will have an impact on replicatibility. With the temptation of making 'exact' predictions based upon a rather elegant-appearing mathematical model, the regression equation, some restraint may be in order until it becomes justified to do so.

Strength of relationships

Considering the outcome from a second perspective, the two results can be said to support different relationships, as shown in Figure 22.13. We will again start with the one that is potentially easiest to interpret. In the original situation (Figure 22.13(a)) there was almost zero correlation between the two independent variables, which simply meant that they were (virtually) independent of each other. The regression equation shows how both independent variables, IQ (moderate) and time learning (strong) influence the predicted value for achievement.

In the second situation (Figure 22.13(b)) with an inter-variable correlation of over 0.50, virtually all the predictive potential of the regression equation lies with the value of the time for learning (strong). It could be said here that the IQ score influenced the learning time which in turn influenced the achievement, but that there is less evidence for IQ influencing the achievement directly. Just how IQ influences achievement is not distinguishable from the influence of time to learn. This is more typical of regression results and why they can be very difficult to interpret.

Part correlations

A third way of interpreting the results is to return to R^2 and think about the contribution of the variances by each of the independent variables to the total variance in achievement, y. To resolve the apportionment of contributions requires some logic and a recognition of what is obtainable from our data. We can easily

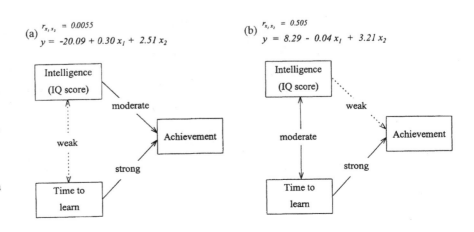

FIGURE 22.13
Strength of predictions based upon the two independent variables for the two hypothetical situations, and strength of relationship between independent variables

find the correlations between each of the three variables, r_{yx_1}, r_{yx_2}, $r_{x_1x_2}$, and the multiple correlation coefficient, R; the relationship among these shown in equation (22.14). While R^2 does provide a way of identifying the total amount of variance accounted for by all the independent variables, separating out the individual contributions is best illustrated by a general picture, such as Figure 22.14. This shows a circle that includes 100% of the variance in y, with the combined shaded areas equalling R^2. The segments marked off indicate contributions and, since they rarely sum to the full 100%, the residue will be the *unexplained* proportion of the final variance that would be accounted for by unknown variables and any error. To describe the contributions of the variables individually requires the use of *part correlations* (sometimes referred to as semi-partial correlations). These are correlations between y and one of the independent variables without the influence of the other. For example, the part correlation between y and x_1, designated as $r_{y(x_1)}$ would be the correlation of y with that part of x_1 that is independent of x_2. The diagram shows the relationships between the correlations, the part correlations and the indistinguishable shared contributions of variance.

Recognizing that the first three in the list on the right of Figure 22.14 are easily found from raw data, some simple relationships can be established to find the bottom four. Stating the area relationships mathematically:

$$R^2 = r_{y(x_1)}^2 + r_{y(x_2)}^2 + r_{(x_1x_2)}^2 \qquad \text{(the total shaded area)}$$
$$r_{yx_1}^2 = r_{y(x_1)}^2 + r_{(x_1x_2)}^2 \qquad \text{(the left two shaded areas)}$$
$$r_{yx_2}^2 = r_{y(x_2)}^2 + r_{(x_1x_2)}^2 \qquad \text{(the right two shaded areas)}$$

Now solving for the part correlations,

$$r_{y(x_1)}^2 = R^2 - r_{yx_2}^2 \qquad (22.17)$$
$$r_{y(x_2)}^2 = R^2 - r_{yx_1}^2 \qquad (22.18)$$

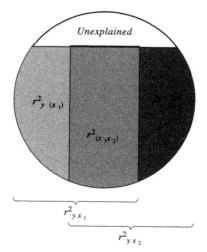

FIGURE 22.14
Diagrammatic representation of apportioned variances

R^2 = multiple correlation coefficient squared

$r_{yx_1}^2$ = correlation between y and x_1 squared

$r_{yx_2}^2$ = correlation between y and x_2 squared

Unexplained = variance due to unknown variables and any error

$r_{y(x_1)}^2$ = part correlation between y and x_1 squared

$r_{y(x_2)}^2$ = part correlation between y and x_2 squared

$r_{(x_1x_2)}^2$ = common variance between x_1 and x_2 attributable to y, squared

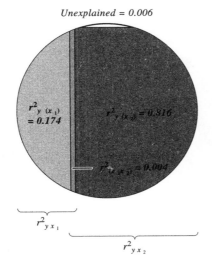

Unexplained = 0.006

$r^2_{y\,(x_1)} = 0.174$ $r^2_{y\,(x_2)} = 0.816$

$r^2_{(x_1 x_2)} = 0.004$

$\underbrace{\qquad\qquad}_{r^2_{y\,x_1}}$

$\underbrace{\qquad\qquad\qquad\qquad}_{r^2_{y\,x_2}}$

FIGURE 22.15
Diagrammatic representation of apportioned variances for the first of the two cases, where
$y = -20.09 + 0.30x_1 + 2.51x_2$

From the data,

$$R^2 = 0.9945$$

$$r^2_{y\,x_1} = 0.4222^2 = 0.1783$$

$$r^2_{yx_2} = 0.9057^2 = 0.8203$$

Substituting into equations (22.15 – 22.17)

$$r^2_{y\,(x_1)} = 0.9945 - 0.8203 \cong 0.174$$

$$r^2_{y\,(x_2)} = 0.9945 - 0.1783 \cong 0.816$$

$$r^2_{(x_1 x_2)} = 0.9945 - 0.174 - 0.817 \cong 0.004$$

Unexplained $= 1.0000 - 0.9945 \cong 0.006$

the indistinguishable variance contribution,

$$r^2_{(x_1 x_2)} = R^2 - r^2_{y(x_1)} - r^2_{y(x_2)} \qquad (22.19)$$

and finally the unexplained residue of variances,

$$unexplained = 1 - R^2$$

Using the three equations, it is possible to construct specific circles for the two examples. Figure 22.15 provides the results for the first example, where there was a random sample of children used (Tables 22.1 and 22.2, and Figure 22.11), the regression equation being provided. The contributions of the two proposed independent variables are quite distinct, with little unattributable variance. Carry out Activity 22.5.

Activity 22:5

Using the data in Table 22.4 for the second example ($R^2 = 0.817$), find part correlations and sketch a circle like Figures 22.14 and 22.15 for the squares of these values to show the attribution of variances for the second example. (The answer follows.)

In the second case, where there was a sizeable correlation between the two independent variables ($r_{x_1 x_2} = 0.505$) we see the consequences not only in the regression equation, but also when accounting for the total variance in y. Here, as seen in Figure 22.16, both the unexplained variance and the common indistinguishable variance contribution from the two independent variables are higher than for the first example. Only 63.4% of the variance can unequivocally be attributed to a single variable.

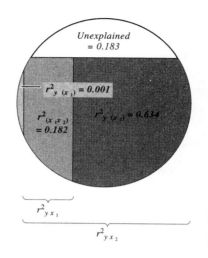

From the data,

$$R^2 = 0.8170$$

$$r^2_{yx_1} = 0.4279^2 = 0.1831$$

$$r^2_{yx_2} = 0.9033^2 = 0.8160$$

Substituting into equations (22.15 – 22.17)

$$r^2_{y\,(x_1)} = 0.817 - 0.816 \cong 0.001$$

$$r^2_{y\,(x_2)} = 0.817 - 0.183 \cong 0.634$$

$$r^2_{(x_1 x_2)} = 0.817 - 0.001 - 0.634 \cong 0.182$$

$$Unexplained = 1.0000 - 0.817 \cong 0.183$$

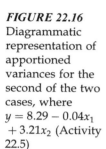

FIGURE 22.16 Diagrammatic representation of apportioned variances for the second of the two cases, where $y = 8.29 - 0.04x_1 + 3.21x_2$ (Activity 22.5)

Partial correlations

There is one other descriptor employed to describe the relationships, that of *partial correlations*, in the case of two independent variables the correlation between y and one of the variables while the other is held constant. Thus the partial correlation $r_{yx_1[x_2]}$ is the correlation between y and x_1 while x_2 is held constant. In the example we have been using, this would describe the correlation between the score on the maths approximation test and IQ score for any given time spent learning. This isolates the impact of IQ from that of time spent learning. This can be determined from the individual correlations,

$$r_{yx_1[x_2]} = \frac{r_{yx_1} - r_{yx_2}r_{x_1x_2}}{\sqrt{\left(1 - r^2_{yx_2}\right)\left(1 - r^2_{x_1x_2}\right)}} \tag{22.20}$$

If one already knows what the part correlations are, then the calculation is much simpler:

$$r^2_{yx_1[x_2]} = \frac{\text{part correlation } y \text{ and } x_1}{\text{remaining variance without } x_2}$$

$$r^2_{yx_1[x_2]} = \frac{r^2_{y(x_1)}}{1 - r^2_{yx_2}} \tag{22.21}$$

This is illustrated in Figure 22.17 as the ratio of the shaded portion to the whole of the upper left-hand part of the circle only, without the lower right-hand contribution by $r^2_{yx_2}$. In our first example, using data in Figure 22.15, this would mean that the partial correlation between y, the mathematics test of approximations, and x_1, IQ score, would be

$$r_{yx_1[x_2]} = \sqrt{\frac{0.174}{1 - 0.8203}} = \sqrt{0.968} = 0.984$$

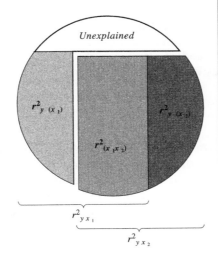

R^2 = multiple correlation coefficient squared

$r^2_{y x_1}$ = correlation between y and x_1 squared

$r^2_{yx_2}$ = correlation between y and x_2 squared

Unexplained = variance due to unknown variables and any error

$r^2_{y (x_1)}$ = part correlation between y and x_1 squared

$r^2_{y (x_2)}$ = part correlation between y and x_2 squared

$r^2_{(x_1 x_2)}$ = common variance between x_1 and x_2 attributable to y, squared

$r^2_{yx_1 [x_2]}$ = partial correlation between y and x_1, with x_2 kept constant

$$= \frac{r^2_{y (x_1)}}{r^2_{y (x_1)} + \text{unexplained}}$$

FIGURE 22.17
Partial correlation of y to x_1: shown as the ratio of the part correlation between y and x_1 squared to the variance excluding x_2

and the partial correlation between y and x_2, time spent learning, would be

$$r_{yx_2[x_1]} = \sqrt{\frac{0.816}{1 - 0.1783}}$$
$$= \sqrt{0.993}$$
$$= 0.996$$

Both of these numbers may seem very high, but remember that the correlation between the two independent variables is almost zero. Carry out Activity 22.6 to see what happens when this correlation is substantial.

Activity 22.6

Use the data for the example in Figure 22.16, where the correlation between the two independent variables is $r_{x_1 x_2} = 0.505$, find the two *partial* correlations and compare them to those for the example in Figure 22.15.

Answer: $r_{yx_1[x_2]} \cong 0.07$, $r_{yx_2[x_1]} \cong 0.88$. Thus when time spent is kept constant, there is little correlation with IQ, and when IQ score is kept constant, there is a high correlation with time spent. Compare these values to the original correlations, and we see that there is a weaker relationship than first implied in Table 22.4, again due to the correlation between independent variables.

As we have seen, interpreting multiple correlation and regression is not an easy task with just two independent variables. It becomes even more complex with three or more, thus such studies are not often seen, and when they are, the interpretation can be difficult. What has been observed is a case where having all variables carefully controlled, here through random selection, random assignment, and no attrition in the sample, seemed to make it possible to interpret complex results more precisely.

Adjusted R^2

Since the multiple correlation coefficient, R, is found from sample data, like other statistics it has the potential for being higher than it would be if the whole sample had been used. As we have seen before, the true variance is equal to the observed variance plus variance due to error, which could be made up of sampling, measurement and/or data-collection errors. Here that would be expressed as a relationship between population parameter, sample statistic and error,

$$R^2_{pop} = R^2_{sample} + \text{error variance}$$

It is possible to generate an estimate of the population value for the multiple correlation coefficient, sometimes referred to as *adjusted R*. Several equations have been used providing much the same answer, but from the following it is relatively easy to see how R^2_{adj} depends on sample size and number of variables:

$$R^2_{adj} = 1 - \frac{(1 - R^2)(n - 1)}{n - p - 1} \qquad (22.22)$$

where R^2 is the sample value, n is the sample size and p is the number of variables. In the example whose results are displayed in Table 22.3,

$$R^2_{adj} = 1 - \frac{(1 - 0.9945)(25 - 1)}{25 - 2 - 1} = 0.9940$$

If you try other numbers, you will find that the larger the sample and/or the fewer the number of variables, the closer R^2 is to R^2_{adj}.

Standard error

Recall that the standard error of the estimate allows us to set probabilistic limits on any prediction or outcome through the use of confidence intervals. Analogous to the set of distributions used in Figure 22.6, it is possible to imagine such distributions for any prediction of y based upon a point in the planes in Figures 22.9 and 22.11. Since it is the value of y that is being estimated based upon any combination of dependent variables, the standard error for y is found from equation (22.5) using the multiple correlation coefficient. It should be noted that Excel uses R^2_{adj}, presumably because this should be a more accurate estimation of the population parameter,

$$s_{yx} = s_y \sqrt{1 - R^2_{adj}} \qquad (22.23)$$

Therefore, from the data in Tables 22.2 and 22.3 for the first example,

$$s_{yx} = 11.33\sqrt{1 - 0.994}$$
$$= 0.8776$$

which corresponds to the value in Table 22.3. The 95% confidence interval for any predicted value of y is found again from $\pm 1.96 s_{yx} = \pm 1.72$. Thus the earlier prediction in Activity 22.4 of $y = 28.1$, based on values $x = 115$ and $x_2 = 5$, would be better expressed as

$$y = 28.1 \pm 1.72$$

This indicates that the prediction should be quite accurate, and considering the high value for R^2, this is not too surprising. Carry out Activity 22.7 to compare this result with that of the second example.

Activity 22.7

Take the second example above, where there was a considerable correlation between the two independent variables (Table 22.4), $R^2 = 0.8170$, $s_y = 14.22$, and the regression equation was $y = 8.292 - 0.04x_1 + 3.211x_2$.

(a) By calculator, find R^2_{adj}.
(b) Now find the standard error of the estimate, s_{yx}.
(c) Determine the 95% confidence interval and provide a predicted value for y.
(d) How does this compare with the first example (Table 22.2) and to what would you attribute the difference?

Answer: (a) 0.800. (b) 6.36. (c) $y = 19.7 \pm 12.4$. (d) Obviously, this is not nearly as accurate a prediction. s_{yx} has increased somewhat because s_y increased (you can check this) but primarily because R^2 has decreased due to the correlation between x_1 and x_2.

The results of Activity 22.7 point up an interesting consequence of what might at first seem a small decline in the multiple correlation coefficient, R, from 0.997 to 0.904. Unfortunately, the differences are exacerbated by the fact we are considering the variances and R^2, thus everything becomes magnified. While multiple regression is a powerful tool, the accuracy of predictions is just as strongly affected by reduced correlations as in simple two-variable cases. Thus, unless adding more variables actually increases R^2, this will not increase the accuracy of any predictions.

This is also not inconsistent with Figures 22.14 and 22.15, where the proportion of the variance that can be directly attributable to the separate variables declined from 0.996 to 0.863. In other words, the unexplained (error) variance increased from 0.6% to 18.3% of the total variance.

Significance test of regression

Chapter 21 provides a test of significance for a simple individual pair of correlations, but what of the multiple correlation coefficient, R^2? Could this have arisen by chance alone? The test for this is derived from analysis of variance principles (see Hays, 1994; Ferguson, 1976), but is easily calculated from the formula

$$F = \frac{R^2}{1 - R^2} \left(\frac{n - p - 1}{p} \right) \tag{22.24}$$

where R^2 is the multiple correlation coefficient, n is the sample size and p is the number of independent variables. Thus for the first example with data shown in Table 22.3,

$$F = \frac{0.9945}{1 - 0.9945} \left(\frac{25 - 2 - 1}{2} \right) \cong 1989$$

This is comparable to the value in the table. When checked against the appropriate F-table for $df_1 = 2$ and $df_2 = 24$, it is obvious that $p < 0.05$, and that due to the size, the power of the test is about 1.00. As we saw earlier, the larger the value of F, the higher the power, which from equation (22.4) can be seen to depend inversely on the number of independent variables and directly on the sample size. In other words, for a given value of R^2, the more variables the harder it will be to find significance, but the larger the sample the easier it will be. This supports the statement made earlier that it is not always worthwhile adding another variable, unless it is going to increase R^2 considerably.

Other possible inferences

As you might suspect from Table 22.3, it is also possible to test for the significance of each of the coefficients c, b_1 and b_2, and thus give confidence intervals in which one would expect to find the population values. The t-test is based upon the premise that the null hypothesis is there is no difference between a regression coefficient, b_j, and zero. Thus, the t-test is stated as

$$t = \frac{b_j - 0}{s_{b_j}}$$

or more simply,

$$t = \frac{b_j}{s_{b_j}} \tag{22.25}$$

where b_j is the jth regression coefficient and s_{b_j} is the standard error for b_j (whose calculation is beyond the scope of this text but can be found in Hays (1994), and is in any case done by most statistical packages).

The confidence interval for each b_j is found as before, using the critical value for the t-distribution which is dependent on sample size, n, and the number of variables, k, such that $df = n - k - 1$ (Hays, 1994). This can be expressed as

$$b_{\text{pop}\,j} = b_j \pm t_{\text{crit}}\, s_{b_j} \tag{22.26}$$

Thus there would be a 95% probability that the population value for b_j would fall within this range. In the first example whose data are shown in Table 22.3, the confidence interval for b_1 would be, since $t_{\text{crit}}(0.05,\ df = 22) = 2.074$,

$$b_{\text{pop } 1} = 0.302 \pm 2.074 \times 0.0115 = 0.302 \pm 0.024$$

Alternatively, it could be expressed as

$$0.278 \le b_{\text{pop } j} \le 0.326$$

This range is the same as that provided by Table 22.3, taking into account rounding error. Now try Activity 22.8 to put all of the multiple regression analysis and interpretation together using a new set of data.

Activity 22.8

Peter Personnel wanted to establish a way of modelling possible factors that influence successful employees in order to improve recruiting. He established from supervisors a rating of 15 employees in the technical department using a questionnaire on overall employee quality (ten Likert scale questions, response range 10–50). From records, he also acquired the following: qualifications achieved (number of years in education) and score on the company aptitude test (numeracy, interpreting technical drawings and literacy). The data set is as follows:

$y =$ Productivity	25	28	32	20	40	33	45	38	28	25	36	24	33	25	25
$x_1 =$ Education	10	14	16	11	18	13	19	11	15	11	16	12	14	17	13
$x_2 =$ Aptitude	30	55	48	33	45	40	48	49	55	51	43	39	47	44	34

(a) Find the correlation coefficients.
(b) Generate a table equivalent to Table 22.3. Find the regression coefficients and y-intercept, then write out the regression equation. Is the relationship significant?
(c) Partition the variances and sketch a circle for this as in Figure 22.14.
(d) What is the standard error for y and what does it tell you about predictions of y?
(e) What does this all tell you about the relationships among the variables?

Peter thought it might improve his scheme if he included some rating of letters of recommendation, so he devised a set of criteria and a scoring system for letters of reference. For the subjects involved, this gave the following data:

$x_3 =$ References	12	7	9	9	17	10	14	17	16	8	13	9	12	9	7

(f) Would adding this variable improve his predictions? If so, and why?
(g) What measurement problems will he face?

Answers

(a)

	y	x_1
y	1	
x_1	0.62	1
x_2	0.39	0.40

(b) $y = 0.15x_2 + 1.40x_1 + 4.17$; $F = 4.13$ ($p < 0.05$)

(c) $R^2 = 0.41$

$r^2_{yx_1} = 0.38$

$r^2_{yx_2} = 0.15$

$r^2_{y(x_1)} = 0.26$

$r^2_{y(x_2)} = 0.02$

$r^2_{(x_1 x_2)} = 0.13$

$unexplained = 0.59$

(d) $s_{yx} = 5.82$, thus predicted y values ± 11.4.

(e)   There is a strong relationship between education and productivity, but any relationship between productivity and aptitude is masked by the relationship between aptitude and education. Also, there is considerable unexplained variance, thus the overall accuracy of predictions is going to have a larger error, as seen from the standard error of the mean.

(f)   Yes, since R^2 would increase to 0.65. The new correlation table would be as follows:

	y	x_1	x_2
y	1		
x_1	0.62	1	
x_2	0.39	0.40	1
x_3	0.67	0.30	0.25

and the regression equation is $y = 1.06x_3 + 0.08x_2 + 1.09x_1 - 0.08$, with a standard error for y of 4.66, increasing the potential accuracy of predictions. Since the intercorrelation between independent variables is considerable, identifying individual contributions will be less definite.

(g)   Defining and quantifying 'productivity' and 'quality of references' will be difficult, possibly adding to the error variance.

Final comments on regression analysis

Regression analysis is like many topics covered in a chapter in this text: there are whole textbooks available for those interested in pursuing it deeper. The focus here has been on describing the appropriate use of this approach, showing from where the coefficients come, and demonstrating alternative ways to interpret regression equations and multiple, part and partial correlation coefficients. Having seen some of the difficulties in carrying out and interpreting the results of regression analysis for one dependent and two independent variables, the simplest situations, it seems only appropriate to review the important issues.

- The purpose of the study should be clear from the outset: is it experimental, where there is clear control over the proposed independent variables; or is it correlational (ex post facto) where control over independent variable(s) is lacking? Different assumptions about the data will apply (the nature of the sample or samples), as well as possible interpretations of the results: is there a causal relationship or a correlational one? In the former, the intent is to attempt to establish causality, while in the latter the aim is to make predictions without presuming causality. In many situations, the answer to the question will be ambiguous, since it may be possible to control some of the variables (as in the case of time to learn in one of our examples) but not others (for example, IQ). As a consequence, while the study may have the appearance of a true experimental design, the nature of the control (or lack of control) may preclude one establishing causality, while still allowing the hint of some sort of relationship. Some authors will completely avoid talking about causality, though there will be some situations in tightly controlled laboratory conditions where it can be established. The difficulty is that frequently field research, sometimes referred to as 'real life', is more interesting, even if control is lacking. As noted earlier, we are confronted with difficult choices when designing research, choices that ultimately influence the range of possible valid conclusions.
- Interpretation of results for multiple regression is greatly simplified when the correlations between pairs of proposed independent variables approach zero. When this is true, it is much easier to determine the nature of the relationships between individual independent variables and the dependent variable. When correlations between independent variables are considerable, relative contributions of individual variables are difficult to determine. This was illustrated for the situation of two independent variables by the angle of plane for the regression equation, the magnitude of confidence intervals and the circles showing shared variances.
- Increasing the number of variables in a multiple regression equation is of value in making predictions only if R^2 increases. This does not negate the value of testing for contributions of additional variables, but does mean that increasing the number of variables (easily done now with the aid of computer software) does not necessarily increase the accuracy of predictions.
- As with other statistical techniques, the question arises whether the results have occurred by chance alone. Again, significance testing is needed to determine whether correlations and regression coefficients are more than random events.

- As mentioned earlier, confidence intervals are particularly important when making predictions. They provide an indication of the range of possibilities, rather than considering any prediction to be a single value.
- When considering three or more independent variables, the difficulty of interpretation increases. While situations with two independent variables can be illustrated as a plane in three dimensions, three or more require a vivid imagination – realistically we must depend on interpreting the regression equations alone.

While it is recognized that relationships in the real world are rarely simple and usually involve more than two variables, designing, controlling, carrying out and interpreting the results of multivariate studies is a serious challenge. Not only are the situations increasingly complex, but so also are the tools required to interpret the outcomes. A first stop beyond this chapter might be Hays (1994) who devotes over 200 pages to the topic, a small text in its own right.

OTHER TYPES OF PREDICTIONS

Not all the relationships of interest that we will encounter will be linear and using linear regression equations will provide us with poor predictions. Remember that regression lines are an attempt to *model* reality, therefore it is necessary to consider the possibility that not all relationships will be linear. The tendency to overlay all data with straight lines simply because it is mathematically easiest is no longer justifiable. There are numerous curve-fitting programs that allow us to generate mathematical models of non-linear data as easily as linear data.

A brief survey of what is available in Excel will introduce you to some of the possibilities. Refer to Activity 22.1, which shows the dialogue boxes for **Trend-line** with thumbnail sketches of the curves. Basically, one would look at the scatter diagram and the sketches, then choose the closest one. While this provides the user with some guidance, it is necessary to recognize the limitations of the sketches, as they only show representative of families of curves. Table 22.5 provides the generalized equations for each, with some additional clues to their characteristics. For example, it is possible to find a match not with the sketches themselves, but with a mirror image. Sometimes these are the result of negative coefficients, as we saw with the case of linear equations: the lines can go uphill as well as downhill. Logarithmic curves are good for representing situations where there is saturation or diminishing returns. For example, as medical provision (number of doctors per 100 000 population) in countries increases (x), average life expectancy (y) first increases rapidly, but then starts to level off. Polynomial equations will fit an even wider range of wiggly scatter diagrams, depending on how many orders are chosen. These allow one to make predictions within the original data range, but often outside this range the curve can sometimes take bizarre turns and consequently predictions would be invalid.

Power and exponential curves can represent either growth or decay. If the constant b is a positive number, they will match a growth curve, y increasing as x increases, as in the thumbnail sketch. On the other hand, if b is negative, then they match a decay curve, the mirror image, where y starts high and

TABLE 22.5
Trendline possible
equations in Excel

Type	Equation	Comments
Linear	$y = bx + c$	Standard linear equation, with slope b and y-intercept c
Logarithmic	$y = a \ln x + b$	Natural logarithm of x; a and b are constants; when $x = 1$, then $y = b$. x must be greater than zero.
Polynomial	$y = a + bx + cx^2 + dx^3$ $+ ex^4 + fx^5 + gx^6$	Number of terms (degree or order $+1$) determined by choice of **Order**
Power	$y = ax^b$	a and b are constants; when $x = 0$ then $y = 0$
Exponential	$y = ae^{bx}$	e $= 2.718$, a and b are constants; when $x = 0$, then $y = e^b = $ const. If $b > 0$, growth curve; and if $b < 0$, then decay curve (mirror image)
Moving Average	each new point is the average of n points	$n = $ **Period**

falls as x increases. Which is most appropriate for a set of data will depend on any underlying relationships.

While the difference may seem small from the sketches, it may be a matter of trying several to see which fits best. For example, Figure 22.18 shows the same set of data with two different trendlines, showing best-fit exponential decay and best-fit power decay. It is quite obvious visually that the latter is the better of the two, but the values of R^2 confirm this.

Using the equations from any of these first five types of fit, as shown in the graphs, it is possible to make predictions. The final choice is moving average, which simply takes as many points as designated in the period box and averages their y values, using this as a new point. Since this does not generate an equation, it is not possible to make predictions for y based on values of x, though it is used to smooth time series data, where time is plotted along the x-axis.

SUMMARY

Regression equations describe the relationship between two (or more) continuous variables. This tool can be used in both experimental and ex post facto designs, thus the use of the tool should be rationalized if appropriate conclusions are to be drawn from a study. If the design is experimental and the aim is to determine a causal relationship, then one of the variables must be under the direct control of the researcher. Changing this independent variable while controlling all other possible extraneous variables through sampling, measurement procedures, and environmental situations, provides the conditions for observing corresponding changes in the dependent variable. As noted repeatedly, it is not the statistical test that provides proof of causality, it is the design and execution of the study in such a manner that no extraneous variable could possibly contribute to the outcome.

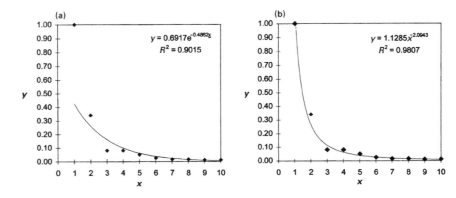

FIGURE 22.18
Two **Trendlines** for
the same set of data
showing relative
quality of fit. (a)
Exponential decay;
(b) Power decay

Other situations will arise, particularly for ex post facto situations, where control of the extraneous variable (due to time, other events, etc.) is not possible, yet strong relationships are evident. Scatter diagrams will show tight clustering, the regression lines will cross, forming with small angles, but whether x caused y, y caused x, they influenced each other or a third variable influenced both of them is not clear. This does not prevent the use of regression equations for making predictions, but their existence does not provide support for causality. As with all other tools provided in this text, they are not a substitute for well-designed, carefully executed studies. They are a decision support device and no more.

POSTSCRIPT

WHERE YOU HAVE BEEN

At the beginning of this book, it was suggested that one role of research was to test theories or parts of theories. Alternatively, there are more practical problems that are the source of inspiration for researchers. Due to the inherent complexity of quantitative research, either intent leads to the need to plan research in a systematic way if all the components are going to support the overall validity of the conclusions. To assist this process, several component validities were identified in order to isolate some of the complexities.

While we base research on theories, the models that are produced describe relationships among variables, sometimes mathematically with graphical illustrations. They are a way of expressing the interactions and relationships, both causal and associative. What must be kept in mind is that there is a difference between the model and reality: more than one model may be possible to explain reality and make accurate predictions. Researchers can become enamoured with their theories and models, sometimes confusing them with reality. We model reality in an endeavour to make sense of all the data and information impinging on us. Research can help us to test the veracity of existing models and whether they can be extended to other situations or populations. Early chapters provided a schema which used variable maps to describe relationships among variables and the impact of potential extraneous variables, to help us as researchers to find ways of 'controlling' them. Using the models highlighted the need to maintain the four validities:

- *internal* – ensuring that extraneous variables are controlled so that the relationship between independent and dependent variables is unequivocal;
- *external* – sampling both subjects and situations to ensure that the study is generalizable to a larger population and real situations;
- *construct* – ensuring that instruments measure what they are supposed to measure;
- *statistical* – selecting statistical tests that are consistent with the questions asked and the data collected.

Implicit in each of these are the procedures for carrying out each stage of planning and execution of the study. Internal validity can be reduced at numerous stages, through poor choice of variables, choice of subjects, extending the time over which the study is conducted, loss of subjects, and administration of measuring instruments.

While there are numerous techniques for obtaining sample groups of subjects, some will result in greater validity than others. Also, sampling must include consideration of the environment and conditions in which the study is conducted if generalization is to be extended not only to larger populations but also to real-world situations.

The discussion of construct validity drew attention to the use of concepts from a theory and possibly even the instruments used elsewhere in testing components of that theory. In some cases it has even been argued that there was a need to develop a better operational definition of the concept or concepts in the theory if this is to be enhanced or even preserved. The technology of instrument design is not trivial, and without care, the instruments themselves can reduce not only construct but also internal validity.

Finally, we considered the complex area of statistical validity. Most physical scientists can walk into the laboratory and choose their instruments off the shelf, and the results are self-evident from the measures. Unfortunately, our results are clouded by natural variability in traits and a certain amount of error introduced by less than perfect instruments. Therefore, we have a need for sophisticated analytic tools in the form of statistical tests. The appropriate choice here is dependent on the original question, the consequential nature of the variables, and the type of data generated. And then the answer is only 'probably'. This is not to underrate statistics, but to recall that tests only allow us to reject or not reject the null hypothesis of no difference. The view taken here has been that the hypothesis or question can be resolved, but never absolutely.

Statistical tools are just that: tools. They help us to make decisions, but cannot make them for us. What is statistically significant is determined by the level of α, which in turn is determined by our tolerances for the consequences of making Type I and Type II errors. We are always in control and cannot pass the buck. The tools are numerous, but the inferential tests still only tell us whether a difference exists or not. The interpretation of any differences (or lack thereof) is still ours and the control of extraneous variables through sampling, measurement, choice of design and choice of test will strengthen the validity of any conclusions. But, as noted in the Preface, much of this is technology and the quality of the research question may be a determining factor in the quality of the outcome, regardless of our technical proficiency.

While some projects focus on testing theories, others may focus on more practical problems. Here the generalizability may be limited to all personnel in one organization, but the results will be used for immediate decision-making. While this appears more 'practical' and less 'theoretical', such studies will still have a theoretical basis and often depend on variables derived from abstract concepts (such as motivation) as well as more concrete ones (such as number of widgets produced per hour.)

A major distinction was made between experimental (and quasi-experimental) designs where the researcher controls the variables, and ex post facto studies where some, if not all, the variables are life experiences. The latter tend to be linked more to so called 'real-life' problems, but generate more headaches because of the lack of control over variables. Ex post facto designs allow us to identify relationships in the real world, but establishing causality will not always be possible. Even though many of the same statistical tests that are used in experimental designs are employed, the researcher does not have the same control over the independent variable and possible extraneous variables. The challenges are greater but the outcomes can be very rewarding.

Throughout the book, attempts have been made to draw links between the various points at which a researcher must make decisions. While there are some rules, and more rules of thumb, about what to do and what not to do, in many cases there is more than one set of guidelines to consider. Just like our research, there are multiple variables that interact and potentially influence the outcomes of a study. Do we increase the reliability of an instrument to reduce the error variance in order to raise the power (our potential to reject H_0 correctly) or is it better to increase the sample size? Should we employ a non-parametric test, or stretch a point and take data that could be considered ordinal to be interval and use its parametric counterpart? How will the nature of our sample influence the overall validity of any conclusions? Often the answers to these depend on the resources available. This is why care, planning and foresight can enhance the quality of the outcomes: having considered such issues ahead of time, you will be less likely to be surprised or placed in the position of exceeding your 'budget' (which could be in units of time as well as money).

OTHER THINGS YOU COULD DO

As you will have noticed, many of the chapters presented here have counterparts in entire books. When you plan to employ any of the sampling, measurement or statistical techniques, do consult more advanced or extensive texts on the special technique you intend to use. The focus here has been on understanding basic concepts underlying practices and tests through examples. You now have the basis for consulting more complex references that will provide greater detail on applications, additional examples and, in some cases, more sophisticated rationale for the limitations. All of this will assist you in choosing and appropriately applying these techniques.

The chapters on the design of measuring instruments have focused on a logical or rational approach to instrument design. You may wish to consider factor-analytic or empirical approaches, in addition to consulting more specialized texts on instrument construction based upon a rational approach. Not all the possible inferential statistical tests have been presented. You may wish to consider three-dimensional ANOVA factorial designs. There are even more non-parametric tests than have been presented here. Other topics have only been introduced and whole texts are required to provide thorough coverage, such as multivariate analysis and path analysis. Statistical tools are numerous, but you should now have a sufficient background to pursue more complex topics if you wish.

Where to go next

Obviously one becomes more proficient as intellectual tools are used in a variety of situations. Those presented here, with their criteria, should be valuable in planning your own research as well as evaluating existing published research. Practice in decision-making throughout has allowed you to see the interaction of various components of a design, but greater diversity of applications will enhance your proficiency. Research goes much more smoothly if you simply apply one little dictum: plan ahead, don't let anything just happen!

Appendix A
An Introduction to Spreadsheets

Why use a spreadsheet?

With all the various statistical packages available for micro- and mainframe computers, you might ask, why bother to use a spreadsheet utility package? The simple answer is mainly that with such software it is relatively easy to enter your raw data into a worksheet, and that recent versions now allow you to carry out many common statistical operations. Some advanced statistical packages also allow you to import your raw data from a spreadsheet-generated worksheet rather than typing it in using their own (sometimes rather unfriendly) systems. For example, SPSS/PC+ (version 6.1) has a **File**, **Open**, **Data** menu sequence that allows you to import data listed in an Excel (version 4.0) worksheet and a **Save data** menu choice that allows you to save data as an Excel worksheet. Thus if you wish to use such a package later, it will not be necessary to retype your data.

A second advantage to using a spreadsheet is that you have control over which equations are used in carrying out calculations, since you enter them yourself. This means that you are not limited by the functionality of the statistical package itself. It does have the same requirement that you have to set up your data carefully and there is a little work involved in entering some of the equations yourself, but, as will be shown in various chapters, it is possible to build in checks to ensure that errors are identified if they occur. This will also allow you to explore mathematical relationships that would be difficult to consider on dedicated statistical packages.

Third, any basic operations can be carried out easily to generate visually pleasing graphs, a function that is often missing in some more specialized statistical packages. This makes it easier to transfer results to a written report, particularly if it is word-processed, or to print out the graphs directly for inclusion in a report. Some statistical packages still only plot graphs using alphanumeric characters – for example, strings of *x*s to make a crude histogram lying on its side.

Finally, almost everyone has a spreadsheet program on their computer. It is easier to learn about statistics this way and then later decide which statistical package is best for you. One of the greatest sins that can be committed in the world of statistics is to use a statistical package without understanding what it is doing. They often generate every possible statistic and carry out all operations for a set of numbers, leaving it to the user to decide which is most appropriate or even legitimate. This has led the uninitiated to use inappropriate statistical tests just because the package generated them. Computer software is incredibly powerful and immensely time-saving, but *you* must stay in control.

SPREADSHEETS: SOME BASICS

Most spreadsheet packages come with either paper-based or computer-based learning materials to acquaint you with their functionality. This book uses Excel, though there are many similarities with other packages. If you are new to the world of spreadsheets, just think of a *worksheet* as a huge sheet of paper with a grid of boxes called *cells* (see Figure A.1). In these cells, we can put words, numbers, or even formulae that will automatically calculate numbers. When you first call up a spreadsheet program, you are presented with a blank worksheet of cells, each of which has an address based upon a combination of its column (**A, B, C, . . .**) and its row (**1, 2, 3, . . .**), with one cell highlighted, the *active cell*, equivalent to the cursor in a word-processor (cell **D1** in Figure A.1). Usually, a new worksheet will begin with the cell pointer in cell **A1** in the upper left-hand corner. You could enter something in that cell by typing the words or numbers and pressing the ⟨Rtn⟩ key, sometimes marked with a ⏎, then move to another cell using the arrow keys on your keyboard or your mouse.

A spreadsheet program such as Excel will appear with a menu across the top, as illustrated in Figure A.1. One selects an operation either by using the mouse and clicking on an operation, or by calling up the menu choice by typing the underlined letter while pressing the < Alt > key.

In Windows-based systems, choosing a menu option will bring down a further menu, such as shown in Figure A.1 for Excel where the choices for **Edit** are shown. This tree-like structure can cause a bit of confusion, but there is usually a built-in help facility and there are usually books on how to use the package in addition to the reference manual issued by the software company.

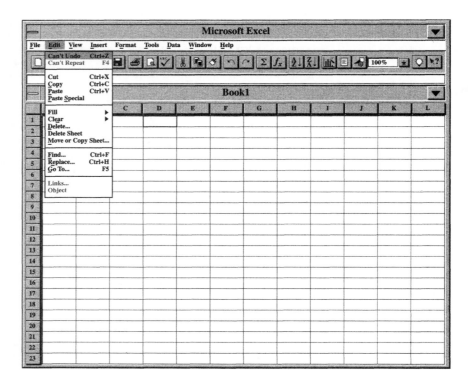

FIGURE A.1
An Excel worksheet with main menu and **Edit** submenu shown

FIGURE A.2
The menu page for
the Quick Preview
set of computer
based learning
sessions

Spreadsheets are very versatile and flexible utility packages, and for the purposes of the exercises here, you will only use a very limited range of commands and facilities. This book will refer to Excel, which will load a Lotus worksheet and convert it to an Excel worksheet.

If you are unfamiliar with Excel, Version 5.0 contains two packages to introduce new users to its structure and commands. Both of these are accessed through the **Help** menu choice, the first being under **Quick Preview**. The menu for this is shown in Figure A.2, with estimates of times needed for each session. These will provide a good starting-point for anyone either just beginning or changing from another spreadsheet program.

The second set provides more detailed actions, not all of which will be needed in the exercises in this text. These are in **Examples and Demos**; the choices are listed in Figure A.3, and can be accessed as needed by selecting **Help** on the main menu bar. Some of these will be referred to in the following sections on Wizards and editing. It is recommended that you go through the following ones before proceeding, to provide a general background in the basics of Excel:

❏ Working in Workbooks
❏ Selecting Cells, Choosing Commands
❏ Using Toolbars
❏ Entering Data
❏ Editing a Worksheet

Others will be referred to in following sections at appropriate times, and some cover more advanced topics. The latter can be consulted when you need them.

Summary of cell formats and symbols

Listed in Table A.1 are common symbols that appear in cells when entering calculations. Every cell that has an equation calculation or refers to another cell for its data begins with an equals sign. Therefore, if you want cell **B2** to contain the same number as **A1**, you would type in cell **B2** the following, **=A1**, and press ⟨Return⟩:

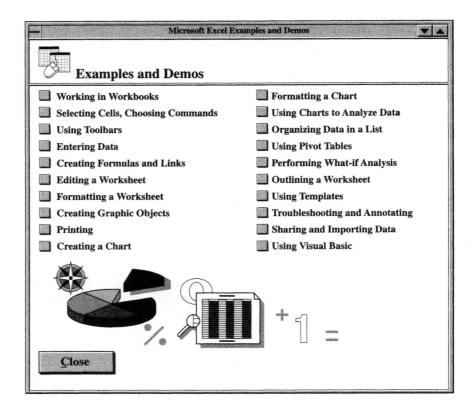

FIGURE A.3
The menu page for **Examples and Demos**, accessed through the **Help**

TABLE A.1
Symbols used in cell equations

Symbol	Meaning
=	Equals, precedes every equation, function or cell reference
:	Colon, used between cell designations to indicate a range, e.g. **B6:B9**
( )	Parentheses, to isolate parts of an equation
+	Plus, indicates addition
-	Minus, indicates subtraction or a negative number
*	Asterisk, indicates multiplication, e.g., **=3*B6**, 3 times the contents of **B6**
/	Oblique, indicates division, e.g., **=A5/12**, the contents of **A5** divided by 12
^	Hat, indicates exponential power, e.g., **=C5^2**, the contents of **C5** squared
$	Dollar, to make a cell designation *absolute* regardless where it is copied

	A	B	C
1	45		
2		45	
3			

$=A1$

There are a few simple rules one must follow when entering an equation in a cell, which if not followed may result in a message that there is an error in the cell, or you may just get a wrong answer. These rules are as follows:

- There must be an equal number of left and right parentheses, ( ), in a cell.
- Some operations need to be enclosed in parentheses – for example, to multiply the sum of the contents of **B2** and **C5** by 6 type $=6*(B2+C5)$. When in doubt, use parentheses.
- When you **Copy** a cell designation to another cell, it will change by the difference in the number of rows and columns unless it is *absolute*, i.e., it has **$**. For example, if the contents of **B2** ($=A1$) were **Copy**ed to **C3**, it would become $=B2$ (add one row and one column), if **Copy**ed to **C2**, then it would become $=B1$ (add one column). If the contents of **B2** had been $=\$A\$1$, then **Copy**ing it to **C3** would mean that **C3** or **C2** or any cell would also contain $=\$A\$1$. If the contents of **B2** had been $=A\$1$, then copying it to **C3** would result in **C3** containing $=C\$1$, the **A** would change to **C**, but **$1** would remain **$1**. *If you do not want cell designations to change when* **Copy***ing, use absolute designation.*

WIZARDS

Excel version 5.0 has several facilities that make specific tasks much easier, which are referred to as 'Wizards'. The two that will be commonly used here, with their icons as they appear on the menu bar at the top of a worksheet, are:

 Function Wizard, which takes you through the necessary steps to insert a function in a cell;

 ChartWizard, which takes you through five steps to generate a chart from a frequency table.

The steps within representative windows will be shown below for you to refer to when setting up charts or worksheets in the activities in the text.

Function Wizard

There are a very large number of built-in functions in Excel, which can carry out simple and complex actions on data. These are what make a spreadsheet powerful, providing functionality that saves an immense amount of time and makes it possible to model and illustrate graphically many statistical concepts. We will use a relatively small proportion of these, but the Function Wizard makes it unnecessary to type in everything, minimizing errors due to wayward fingers. It presents a series of windows that prompt you to fill in boxes, then deposits the resulting function in the chosen cell, complete with all the parameters. Before going through this section, look at the following short sequence under **Help**:

Examples and Demos,

❑ Creating Formulas and Links,
  Using the Function Wizard.

This will provide an overview and an example from the Financial category of functions.

Call up a new worksheet to experiment with. Type in the contents of cells **A2:I2** from Figure 11.1 in Chapter 11, to serve as data. To use the Function Wizard, first of all place the cursor in the cell where you want the outcome of a function to appear, in our case cell **J2**, then click on the Function Wizard icon. This brings up the following window:

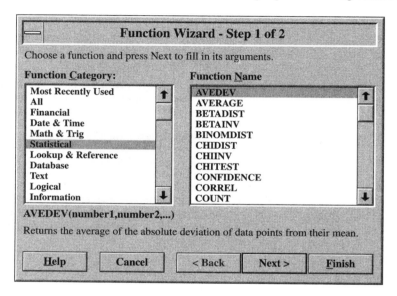

First you choose a category on the left (I have chosen Statistical), then the function on the right. There is a description of the function that is highlighted and if you click on the `Help` button, more information will be revealed. You can supplement the help information by annotating it with your own notes. Each function has a unique window, so it is not possible to show them all, but let us consider two to see how they work. First is a simple function for finding the mean of a set of numbers, **AVERAGE**, second from the top of the statistical function list. Using as an example the first time a function appears in the text, Figure 11.1, and having placed the cursor in cell **J2**, we select **AVERAGE** and click on the `Next >` button, which results in the following window:

Function Wizard - Step 2 of 2

AVERAGE   Value: | 25.625 |

Returns the average of its arguments.

Number1 (required)

Number1,number2,... are 1 to 30 numeric arguments for which you want the average.

number1 f_x | B2:I2 | | {27,26,29,23,21, |
number2 f_x | | | |

| Help | Cancel | < Back | Next > | Finish |

For this example, I clicked on cell **B2**, held the left button down and swept over to include all cells up to **I2** in the row. The result appears in the **Value** box, which will appear in cell **I2** when the ▮ **Finish** ▮ button is clicked. Note that in Figure 11.1 the answer has been rounded to one decimal place fewer, 25.63, since I formatted the cell to have only two decimal places.

A second example illustrates a novel, but not well-documented, type of function, one that produces a *set* of numbers (an array) instead of a single value. To show this, we will use the example in Figure 12.5. Here we want to generate a frequency table for the raw data in the first two columns and the designated real upper limits of the intervals in column **D**. Having placed the cursor in cell **F3,** this time in the **Statistical** function category of **Step 1 of 2** we choose the **FREQUENCY** function and click on the ▮ **Next >** ▮ button, which brings up the following window:

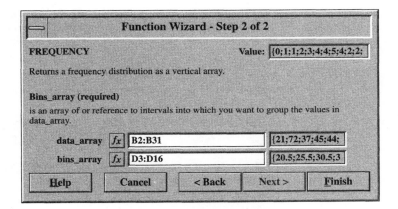

This time I have two entries. The first identifies the raw data in the second column, which is entered by clicking on **B2** and holding down the left button while sweeping down the column to **B31**. Placing the cursor in the **bins_array** box, you now identify the set of intervals for the frequency table. As you will find implied under **Help**, this set of numbers provide the upper real limits for the intervals into which the raw data will be grouped. These are in cells **D3:D16**. As a consequence, there will be one more interval than designated, for any data beyond the highest interval. If we click on the ▮ **Finish** ▮ button, the first number, 0, appears in the chosen cell **F3**. To expand the array down the page next to the intervals, highlight the cells **F3:F16** by clicking on **F3** and, with the left button held down, sweep to **F16,** leaving the boxes inverted in colour. Now with the cursor *before* the function statement in the data entry box at the top of the spreadsheet (*not* in the cell itself) as shown below:

F3	⬇ × ✓ *fx*	=FREQUENCY(B2:B31,D3:D16)

simultaneously press on the keyboard ⟨Ctrl⟩ + ⟨Shift⟩ + ⟨Return⟩ (or as on some keyboards ⟨Ctrl⟩ + ⟨⇑⟩ + ⟨⏎⟩). The array of frequencies will distribute itself in the highlighted cells. If you examine any cell, it will contain **{=FREQUENCY (B2:B31,D3:D16)}**, the surrounding curly brackets indicating an array. As an array function, it cannot be edited without repeating the entire process. The function actually produces one more frequency than the number of intervals, the last one being the frequency beyond the highest interval. If this is likely to include something besides 0, then it should be included when sweeping down the column with the mouse, otherwise it can be omitted by highlighting a number of cells equal to the number of real upper limits (bins array).

ChartWizard

This section provides greater detail on the process of using the ChartWizard than that described in Excel. Before going through this, a quick view can be had by viewing the following short sequence under **Help:**

Examples and Demos
❑ Creating a Chart,
Creating a Chart with the ChartWizard.

You should load Excel and start a new worksheet to try out the following activity. The sequence uses the frequency table in Figure 12.9, cells **D2:F6.** The five windows that appear in the ChartWizard are presented so that you can refer back to them as needed.

When you first click on the ChartWizard icon, you will need to mark out on the worksheet you are using, or on a new one, roughly where you want the chart to be. Place the mouse pointer in the upper left-hand corner and, while holding down the left button, move to the lower right-hand corner. Its actual size can be adjusted easily later, but you should make sure there is adequate room for it. You will be able to **Copy** the resulting chart to another document, like a Word file, for a report later. After the area is marked out, the following window will appear as you release the left button:

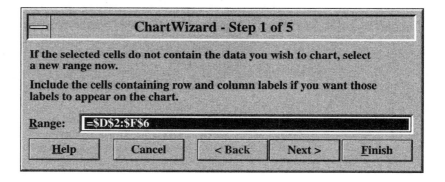

Again, use the mouse to identify the frequency table you wish to use, clicking on the upper left corner of the set and, with the left button pressed, sweeping down to the lower right. If the columns are not adjacent, then after sweeping one column, type a comma and sweep the second. Both will appear in the **Range** box above, separated by the comma. The ranges can include the column titles, which is particularly useful if you are plotting the results of more than one group and therefore will have more than one line or set of bars. A legend will be automatically generated using the column titles as will be seen in later steps. Click on the Next > button for the Step 2 window below:

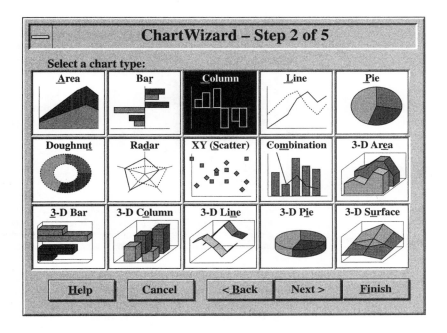

The ChartWizard will automatically select what it thinks is the most appropriate chart for the data, but it may not always be the best. To change it, simply place the mouse pointer in the cell for the chart type you want and click the left button. When you are satisfied with the choice (which you can change easily later), click on the | Next > | button to go to Step 3, shown below:

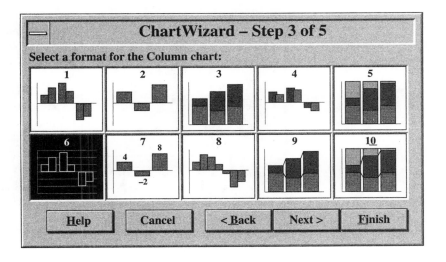

For each of the 15 types of chart in Step 2, there will be a selection of variations on that theme from which to choose. Again, the ChartWizard will select what is seen to be the most appropriate. In this case, I will choose format **4** instead of the one highlighted by placing the mouse pointer on that cell and clicking the left button. Clicking on the | Next > | button will take you to Step 4, shown below:

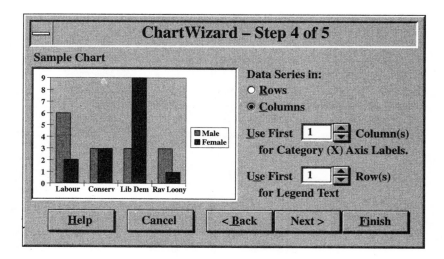

Note the two boxes to the right of the Sample Chart: if the **Use First □ Column(s)** box contains a **1**, the first column of data provides the horizontal axis labels, whether they are numbers or, as in this case, names, from the frequency table. If the **Use First □ Row(s)** box contains a **1**, then the column headings will appear in the Legend box on the right side of the chart. This can be edited later. If you only have one set of data on a graph, a legend is not essential, and can be removed in Step 5, which will appear when the Next > button is clicked:

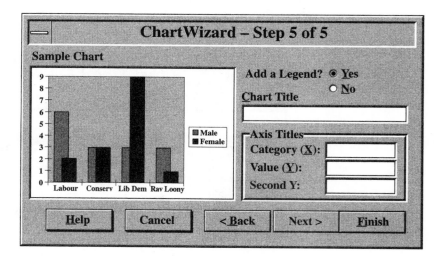

If you do not want a legend, just click the empty circle next to **No**. At this point, you can add a chart title and axis titles, such as those shown below:

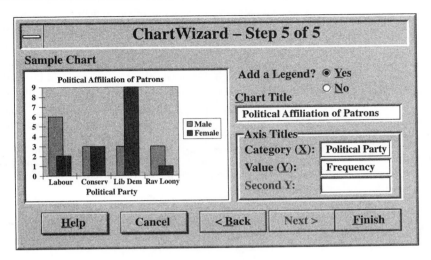

This is the limit to what you can do in the ChartWizard, and the final image is shown on the left of the dialogue box. You can go back to previous steps by clicking on the < Back button, or place the chart on the page by clicking on the Finish button. If along the way you decide you do not want to continue, then click on the Cancel button and start again later.

Editing a chart after the ChartWizard from the menu bar

The chart can be further edited by double-clicking on the chart to activate it, which changes the main menu bar contents as shown below (but note that you *cannot* get two menus down at the same time in the way shown):

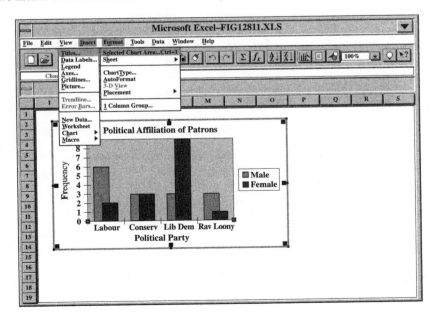

In these menus, the following are used for editing the chart, under **Insert**:

Titles	if you do not already have a title or want to remove it,
Data Labels	to display individual frequencies for each column or data point on the chart (see **Examples and Demos,** ❏ Creating a Chart, <u>Adding Data Labels</u>),
Legend	if you do not already have one, add it,
Axes	to add or remove number or category labels on axes,
Gridlines	if you want to add or remove grid lines on the chart,
New Data	if you want to add another variable to a chart (column of data).

Under **Format** there are three choices that provide windows to assist in editing the chart. The first is **Selected Chart Area. . .**, where you click on a chart part and come to this menu; since it is easier just to double-click on the parts, this facility is described below separately. The next is **Chart Type** which provides a window such as below for the type of chart in use. The choices of chart type are actually fewer than under **AutoFormat** below, but the **Options** provide some useful ways of adjusting the chart.

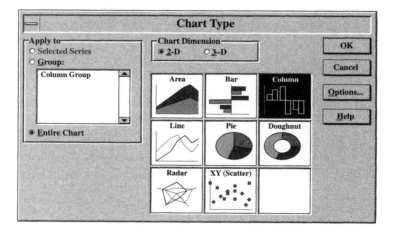

When **Options** is selected, a window with three or four 'tabs' appears, such as the one for the chart illustrated.

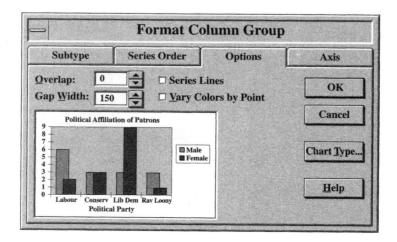

Of these tabs, the **Options** tab is the most useful to click on, providing the opportunity to change such characteristics as the width of the columns, by changing the **Overlap** and **Gap Width** values, watching the effect in the sketch below. What can be changed here will vary with the chart type.

The **AutoFormat** choice allows you to go back and change the type of chart you have, selecting the basic type from the list on the left under **Galleries**, for which there will be provided up to ten different **Formats** in the little boxes, providing 103 different formats in Excel 5.0. Click on one and your chart will change automatically. You can even design your own, but that is beyond this guide.

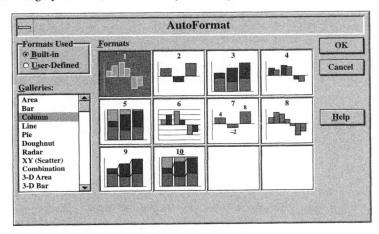

There is a fourth option that becomes active only if you have a 3-D chart, called **3-D View** which assists in getting the best perspective for such a chart. This requires some patience, as moving a three-dimensional shape about is not trivial.

Editing charts directly using the mouse

The most fundamental change that can be made in a chart is its size, which can be adjusted by clicking on the chart and dragging one of the selection handles (see **Examples and Demos,** ❑ Formatting a Chart, Arranging and Sizing Chart Items).

In addition to the menus above, you change specific aspects of the chart by using the mouse pointer. To select the part of the chart you want, click once on the item (such as an axis), at which point little squares will appear at either end or on the components shown in the case of the *x*-axis in the chart below.

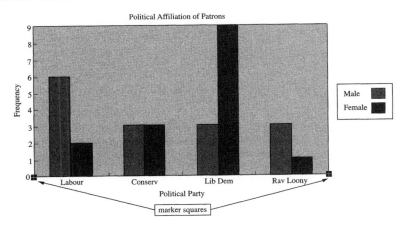

Then double-click on specific part of the chart to produce a window with menus and option 'tabs' for you to choose. Positioning the mouse pointer can be a bit tricky, since the mouse is very sensitive as to where it is when you click. If you are just a little bit off from where you should be, you may get a window other than the one you want. The ease of use may depend on the resolution of your monitor and the type of mouse, but with practice you can select parts of the chart, raising the following windows, with the number of 'tabs' to choose from in parentheses ( ), with those in *italics* being the most useful, in my opinion:

- **Format Chart Area** (2): Patterns (colour/shading around chart), Font (only if you want one font/size for whole chart).
- **Format Plot Area** (1): border (if any) and colour/shading inside.
- **Format Axis** (5): either *x*- or *y*-axis: Font (for numbers), Number (decimal places/style), Scale (max/min, categories, where axes cross), Patterns (of axis line), Alignment (of numbers/categories).
- **Format Data Series** (6): XY values, Data Labels, Y Error Bars, Name and Values, Axis (range, etc.), Patterns (to change line and bar shapes/colours).
- **Format Data Point** (2): only if you want to highlight a single data point, pie section, or column – Pattern, Data Labels.
- **Format Legend** (3): Patterns, Font, Placement.
- **Format Axis Title** (3): Patterns, Font, Alignment (vertical/horizontal).
- **Format Chart Title** (3): the same as Format Axis Title.

With all the combinations of tabs, it is not possible to show them all, but it will be fairly self-evident in what function they perform. You can also change the contents of the legend and titles by clicking on them and activating an outline box, after which you can place the cursor inside and type.

Finally, sometimes it is desirable to place a label somewhere specific on a chart that is not accessible by the above. On the main menu is the icon for the Text Box 📧 which allows you to mark out a rectangular area anywhere and type in it. To format it, double-click and you will get the window entitled:

- **Format Object** (5): Patterns (box outline, fill, etc.), Font, Properties (including whether it is printed), Alignment, Protection.

All of these choices and options can be a bit bewildering when you start, but with use, and using the **Help** facilities, it will become easier. It is worth making notes of commonly used procedures to save time later.

EXPANDING AND CONTRACTING WORKSHEETS

This section describes how you can take an existing basic worksheet and add rows, columns or cells to accommodate additional or less data than the original sheet, without ruining the functions and formulae. This will also describe how to copy cells when needed. The first time you might need this will be in Chapter 11. Therefore, an example from that chapter will be used to illustrate these processes, Figure 11.2, reproduced here as Figure A.4.

Inserting columns

In this example, we would want to add data for more examinees to the table. While there are a number of places one could insert more columns, doing it where it causes the least disruption to the whole table is best. Therefore, adding a column between **B** and **C**, **C** and **D**, **D** and **E** or **E** and **F** would be acceptable, but doing so between **A** and **B** or **F** and **G** would break up the worksheet. To add a column, first use the mouse pointer and click on the letter of a column, noting that the new column will appear on the left of it. For example, click on **E** and the whole column is highlighted; choose **Insert, Columns** from the main menu and a new empty column appears. All the formulae in the

FIGURE A.4
Scores for an
instrument with five
questions, maximum
of 10 points each,
(e.g., five essay
questions, five
equally weighted
parts of a single
essay or five
responses on a
questionnaire) taken
by 10 students,
presented on a
spreadsheet to
calculate Cronbach's
alpha and item-total
correlations

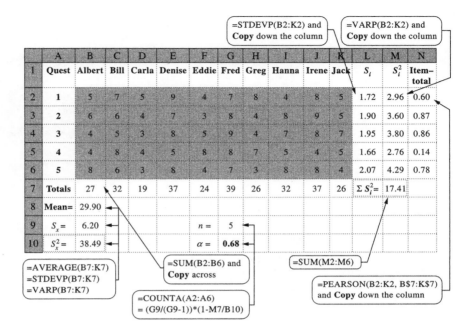

displaced columns have been automatically adjusted, so none of the values generated by equations should have changed. New data can be entered and formulae **Copy**ed to cells in the new column. Formulae that were in columns **L**, **M** and **N** have not only been moved over one, but they now *include* any data in the new column. Therefore, when new data are added to the new column, you will find that the values in **L**, **M** and **N** change accordingly. This will also be true of values in column **B**, once you have **Copy**ed the **SUM** function in row **7** to the new column. The process can be repeated as many times as necessary to add sufficient columns for new examinees.

Inserting rows

In the example, to add another question would require another row. A new row is inserted *above* the one you highlight, but you do not want to choose the row after the data, row **7**. Using this row would insert a new one, but all the **SUM** functions would have to be rewritten since they would not include the new row. Therefore, highlight row **6**, and select **Insert**, **Rows** from the main menu. None of the formula values should change. Then **Copy** all the data in what is now row **7** to row **6** and type in new raw data for the new question. As the new data are entered, the values calculated by the various functions will automatically change. In some cases, such as our example, you will need to insert new values like that for *n* in cell **H10**, as well as raw data. The process of adding rows can be repeated as many times as needed for more questions. If you had added one row and one column, your worksheet would look like the one in Figure A.5 with the new function ranges indicated.

Deleting columns

Some worksheets will have more columns than needed. In some cases, it will be possible simply to erase the data and leave the columns blank. In others, it may be desirable to remove some columns. This can be achieved without disrupting the rest of the worksheet if done carefully. Sometimes it will be necessary to recopy functions to cells.

=VARP(B2:L2)

=STDEVP(B2:L2)

	A	B	C	D	E	F	G	H	I	J	K	L	M	N	O
1	Quest	Albert	Bill		Carla	Denise	Eddie	Fred	Greg	Hanna	Irene	Jack	S_i	S_i^2	Item total
2	1	5	7		5	9	4	7	8	4	8	5	1.72	2.96	0.60
3	2	6	6		4	7	3	8	4	8	9	5	1.90	3.60	0.87
4	3	4	5		3	8	5	9	4	7	8	7	1.95	3.80	0.86
5	4	4	8		4	5	8	8	7	5	4	5	1.66	2.76	0.14
6															
7	5	8	6		3	8	4	7	3	8	8	4	2.07	4.29	0.78
8	Totals:	27	32		19	37	24	39	26	32	37	26	$\Sigma S_i^2 =$	17.41	
9	Mean	29.90													
10	$S_x =$	6.20					$n =$	5							
11	$S_x^2 =$	38.49					$\alpha =$	0.68							

FIGURE A.5
The worksheet with one row and one column added

=AVERAGE(B8:L8)
=STDEVP(B8:L8)
=VARP(B8:L8)

=SUM(B2:B7)

=COUNTA(A2:A7)
=(H10/(H10−1))*(1−N8/B11)

=SUM(N2:N7)

=PEARSON(B2:L2,B$8:L$8)

To illustrate the process, click on column **D** to highlight it and then select from the main menu **Edit**, **Delete**. The column disappears and all the others are shifted one to the left. All the function ranges are automatically adjusted, which should be obvious in this case since no data have been added. All the values for means, standard deviations, alpha, etc., will remain unchanged.

Deleting Rows

In a similar manner, unwanted rows can be removed. Highlight the row to be removed and select from the main menu **Edit**, **Delete**. The row disappears and all the others are shifted up by one. Again, since no new data have been added, all the results will be the same. Had there been data there, then the results would have changed.

Inserting selected cells

There will be times when it is not desirable to insert rows or columns, but a set of blank cells. Done carefully, this will also not disrupt a worksheet. To illustrate this, we will insert cells in such a way as to provide the same result as above. Starting with the original worksheet in Figure A.4, highlight just cells **F1:F8** (Eddie's data) and select from the main menu **Insert**, **Cells**. You will then get:

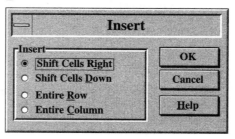

In this case, you do want to **Shift Cells Right**, but in others you may want to shift them some other way than designated by the default. Click on the ▭ OK ▭ button and the cells will be inserted. If you repeat the process for the cells containing numbers in row 6, this time using **Shift Cells Down**, you should achieve the same effect in this case as adding a row and a column as shown above.

Deleting selected cells

Selected cells on a worksheet can be removed altogether (not just the contents). To try this, block the new empty cells **F1:F7** and select **Edit, Delete**, which will result in:

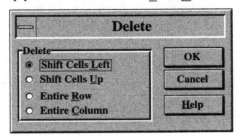

Again, not always will the default be correct, but in this case shifting left would be best. The same can be done for horizontal rows of cells. By now, if you have gone through the entire set of directions, you should be back to the original worksheet.

APPENDIX B
STATISTICAL TABLES

Some of the statistical tables that follow were generated using the Excel functions indicated for each. They have all been checked against commonly used tables and differences noted where they occur. One advantage to these tables is that if you wish to have a number that is not there, it is very easy to interpolate or extrapolate for the desired situation using the appropriate Excel functions.

TABLE B.1
Areas under the
normal distribution*

z	Area btwn $\bar{x}$ and z	Area beyond z	z	Area btwn $\bar{x}$ and z	Area beyond z	z	Area btwn $\bar{x}$ and z	Area beyond z
0.00	0.0000	0.5000	0.50	0.1915	0.3085	1.00	0.3413	0.1587
0.01	0.0040	0.4960	0.51	0.1950	0.3050	1.01	0.3438	0.1562
0.02	0.0080	0.4920	0.52	0.1985	0.3015	1.02	0.3461	0.1539
0.03	0.0120	0.4880	0.53	0.2019	0.2981	1.03	0.3485	0.1515
0.04	0.0160	0.4840	0.54	0.2054	0.2946	1.04	0.3508	0.1492
0.05	0.0199	0.4801	0.55	0.2088	0.2912	1.05	0.3531	0.1469
0.06	0.0239	0.4761	0.56	0.2123	0.2877	1.06	0.3554	0.1446
0.07	0.0279	0.4721	0.57	0.2157	0.2843	1.07	0.3577	0.1423
0.08	0.0319	0.4681	0.58	0.2190	0.2810	1.08	0.3599	0.1401
0.09	0.0359	0.4641	0.59	0.2224	0.2776	1.09	0.3621	0.1379
0.10	0.0398	0.4602	0.60	0.2257	0.2743	1.10	0.3643	0.1357
0.11	0.0438	0.4562	0.61	0.2291	0.2709	1.11	0.3665	0.1335
0.12	0.0478	0.4522	0.62	0.2324	0.2676	1.12	0.3686	0.1314
0.13	0.0517	0.4483	0.63	0.2357	0.2643	1.13	0.3708	0.1292
0.14	0.0557	0.4443	0.64	0.2389	0.2611	1.14	0.3729	0.1271
0.15	0.0596	0.4404	0.65	0.2422	0.2578	1.15	0.3749	0.1251
0.16	0.0636	0.4364	0.66	0.2454	0.2546	1.16	0.3770	0.1230
0.17	0.0675	0.4325	0.67	0.2486	0.2514	1.17	0.3790	0.1210
0.18	0.0714	0.4286	0.68	0.2517	0.2483	1.18	0.3810	0.1190
0.19	0.0753	0.4247	0.69	0.2549	0.2451	1.19	0.3830	0.1170
0.20	0.0793	0.4207	0.70	0.2580	0.2420	1.20	0.3849	0.1151
0.21	0.0832	0.4168	0.71	0.2611	0.2389	1.21	0.3869	0.1131
0.22	0.0871	0.4129	0.72	0.2642	0.2358	1.22	0.3888	0.1112
0.23	0.0910	0.4090	0.73	0.2673	0.2327	1.23	0.3907	0.1093
0.24	0.0948	0.4052	0.74	0.2704	0.2296	1.24	0.3925	0.1075
0.25	0.0987	0.4013	0.75	0.2734	0.2266	1.25	0.3944	0.1056
0.26	0.1026	0.3974	0.76	0.2764	0.2236	1.26	0.3962	0.1038
0.27	0.1064	0.3936	0.77	0.2794	0.2206	1.27	0.3980	0.1020
0.28	0.1103	0.3897	0.78	0.2823	0.2177	1.28	0.3997	0.1003
0.29	0.1141	0.3859	0.79	0.2852	0.2148	1.29	0.4015	0.0985
0.30	0.1179	0.3821	0.80	0.2881	0.2119	1.30	0.4032	0.0968
0.31	0.1217	0.3783	0.81	0.2910	0.2090	1.31	0.4049	0.0951
0.32	0.1255	0.3745	0.82	0.2939	0.2061	1.32	0.4066	0.0934
0.33	0.1293	0.3707	0.83	0.2967	0.2033	1.33	0.4082	0.0918
0.34	0.1331	0.3669	0.84	0.2995	0.2005	1.34	0.4099	0.0901
0.35	0.1368	0.3632	0.85	0.3023	0.1977	1.35	0.4115	0.0885
0.36	0.1406	0.3594	0.86	0.3051	0.1949	1.36	0.4131	0.0869
0.37	0.1443	0.3557	0.87	0.3078	0.1922	1.37	0.4147	0.0853
0.38	0.1480	0.3520	0.88	0.3106	0.1894	1.38	0.4162	0.0838
0.39	0.1517	0.3483	0.89	0.3133	0.1867	1.39	0.4177	0.0823
0.40	0.1554	0.3446	0.90	0.3159	0.1841	1.40	0.4192	0.0808
0.41	0.1591	0.3409	0.91	0.3186	0.1814	1.41	0.4207	0.0793
0.42	0.1628	0.3372	0.92	0.3212	0.1788	1.42	0.4222	0.0778
0.43	0.1664	0.3336	0.93	0.3238	0.1762	1.43	0.4236	0.0764
0.44	0.1700	0.3300	0.94	0.3264	0.1736	1.44	0.4251	0.0749
0.45	0.1736	0.3264	0.95	0.3289	0.1711	1.45	0.4265	0.0735
0.46	0.1772	0.3228	0.96	0.3315	0.1685	1.46	0.4279	0.0721
0.47	0.1808	0.3192	0.97	0.3340	0.1660	1.47	0.4292	0.0708
0.48	0.1844	0.3156	0.98	0.3365	0.1635	1.48	0.4306	0.0694
0.49	0.1879	0.3121	0.99	0.3389	0.1611	1.49	0.4319	0.0681
0.50	0.1915	0.3085	1.00	0.3413	0.1587	1.50	0.4332	0.0668

TABLE B.1
continued

z	Area btwn $\bar{x}$ and z	Area beyond z		z	Area btwn $\bar{x}$ and z	Area beyond z		z	Area btwn $\bar{x}$ and z	Area beyond z
1.50	0.4332	0.0668		2.00	0.4772	0.0228		2.50	0.4938	0.0062
1.51	0.4345	0.0655		2.01	0.4778	0.0222		2.51	0.4940	0.0060
1.52	0.4357	0.0643		2.02	0.4783	0.0217		2.52	0.4941	0.0059
1.53	0.4370	0.0630		2.03	0.4788	0.0212		2.53	0.4943	0.0057
1.54	0.4382	0.0618		2.04	0.4793	0.0207		2.54	0.4945	0.0055
1.55	0.4394	0.0606		2.05	0.4798	0.0202		2.55	0.4946	0.0054
1.56	0.4406	0.0594		2.06	0.4803	0.0197		2.56	0.4948	0.0052
1.57	0.4418	0.0582		2.07	0.4808	0.0192		2.57	0.4949	0.0051
1.58	0.4429	0.0571		2.08	0.4812	0.0188		2.58	0.4951	0.0049
1.59	0.4441	0.0559		2.09	0.4817	0.0183		2.59	0.4952	0.0048
1.60	0.4452	0.0548		2.10	0.4821	0.0179		2.60	0.4953	0.0047
1.61	0.4463	0.0537		2.11	0.4826	0.0174		2.61	0.4955	0.0045
1.62	0.4474	0.0526		2.12	0.4830	0.0170		2.62	0.4956	0.0044
1.63	0.4484	0.0516		2.13	0.4834	0.0166		2.63	0.4957	0.0043
1.64	0.4495	0.0505		2.14	0.4838	0.0162		2.64	0.4959	0.0041
1.65	0.4505	0.0495		2.15	0.4842	0.0158		2.65	0.4960	0.0040
1.66	0.4515	0.0485		2.16	0.4846	0.0154		2.66	0.4961	0.0039
1.67	0.4525	0.0475		2.17	0.4850	0.0150		2.67	0.4962	0.0038
1.68	0.4535	0.0465		2.18	0.4854	0.0146		2.68	0.4963	0.0037
1.69	0.4545	0.0455		2.19	0.4857	0.0143		2.69	0.4964	0.0036
1.70	0.4554	0.0446		2.20	0.4861	0.0139		2.70	0.4965	0.0035
1.71	0.4564	0.0436		2.21	0.4864	0.0136		2.71	0.4966	0.0034
1.72	0.4573	0.0427		2.22	0.4868	0.0132		2.72	0.4967	0.0033
1.73	0.4582	0.0418		2.23	0.4871	0.0129		2.73	0.4968	0.0032
1.74	0.4591	0.0409		2.24	0.4875	0.0125		2.74	0.4969	0.0031
1.75	0.4599	0.0401		2.25	0.4878	0.0122		2.75	0.4970	0.0030
1.76	0.4608	0.0392		2.26	0.4881	0.0119		2.76	0.4971	0.0029
1.77	0.4616	0.0384		2.27	0.4884	0.0116		2.77	0.4972	0.0028
1.78	0.4625	0.0375		2.28	0.4887	0.0113		2.78	0.4973	0.0027
1.79	0.4633	0.0367		2.29	0.4890	0.0110		2.79	0.4974	0.0026
1.80	0.4641	0.0359		2.30	0.4893	0.0107		2.80	0.4974	0.0026
1.81	0.4649	0.0351		2.31	0.4896	0.0104		2.81	0.4975	0.0025
1.82	0.4656	0.0344		2.32	0.4898	0.0102		2.82	0.4976	0.0024
1.83	0.4664	0.0336		2.33	0.4901	0.0099		2.83	0.4977	0.0023
1.84	0.4671	0.0329		2.34	0.4904	0.0096		2.84	0.4977	0.0023
1.85	0.4678	0.0322		2.35	0.4906	0.0094		2.85	0.4978	0.0022
1.86	0.4686	0.0314		2.36	0.4909	0.0091		2.90	0.4981	0.0019
1.87	0.4693	0.0307		2.37	0.4911	0.0089		2.95	0.4984	0.0016
1.88	0.4699	0.0301		2.38	0.4913	0.0087		3.00	0.4987	0.0013
1.89	0.4706	0.0294		2.39	0.4916	0.0084		3.05	0.4989	0.0011
1.90	0.4713	0.0287		2.40	0.4918	0.0082		3.10	0.4990	0.0010
1.91	0.4719	0.0281		2.41	0.4920	0.0080		3.15	0.4992	0.0008
1.92	0.4726	0.0274		2.42	0.4922	0.0078		3.20	0.4993	0.0007
1.93	0.4732	0.0268		2.43	0.4925	0.0075		3.25	0.4994	0.0006
1.94	0.4738	0.0262		2.44	0.4927	0.0073		3.30	0.4995	0.0005
1.95	0.4744	0.0256		2.45	0.4929	0.0071		3.35	0.4996	0.0004
1.96	0.4750	0.0250		2.46	0.4931	0.0069		3.40	0.4997	0.0003
1.97	0.4756	0.0244		2.47	0.4932	0.0068		3.50	0.4998	0.0002
1.98	0.4761	0.0239		2.48	0.4934	0.0066		3.60	0.4998	0.0002
1.99	0.4767	0.0233		2.49	0.4936	0.0064		3.70	0.4999	0.0001
2.00	0.4772	0.0228		2.50	0.4938	0.0062		3.80	0.4999	0.0001

*Generated in Excel using functions
=NORMSDIST(Z)-0.5
and
=1-NORMSDIST(Z),
respectively

TABLE B.2
Critical values for
levels of significance
and *df* for Student's
t-distributions*

	Level of significance for a one-tailed test					
	0.10	0.05	0.025	0.01	0.005	0.0005

	Level of significance for a two-tailed test					
df	0.20	0.10	0.05	0.02	0.01	0.001
1	3.078	6.314	12.706	31.821	*63.656*	*636.578*
2	1.886	2.920	4.303	6.965	9.925	*31.600*
3	1.638	2.353	3.182	4.541	5.841	12.924
4	1.533	2.132	2.776	3.747	4.604	8.610
5	1.476	2.015	2.571	3.365	4.032	6.869
6	1.440	1.943	2.447	3.143	3.707	5.959
7	1.415	1.895	2.365	2.998	3.499	5.408
8	1.397	1.860	2.306	2.896	3.355	5.041
9	1.383	1.833	2.262	2.821	3.250	4.781
10	1.372	1.812	2.228	2.764	3.169	4.587
11	1.363	1.796	2.201	2.718	3.106	4.437
12	1.356	1.782	2.179	2.681	3.055	4.318
13	1.350	1.771	2.160	2.650	3.012	4.221
14	1.345	1.761	2.145	2.624	2.977	4.140
15	1.341	1.753	2.131	2.602	2.947	4.073
16	1.337	1.746	2.120	2.583	2.921	4.015
17	1.333	1.740	2.110	2.567	2.898	3.965
18	1.330	1.734	2.101	2.552	2.878	3.922
19	1.328	1.729	2.093	2.539	2.861	3.883
20	1.325	1.725	2.086	2.528	2.845	3.850
21	1.323	1.721	2.080	2.518	2.831	3.819
22	1.321	1.717	2.074	2.508	2.819	3.792
23	1.319	1.714	2.069	2.500	2.807	3.768
24	1.318	1.711	2.064	2.492	2.797	3.745
25	1.316	1.708	2.060	2.485	2.787	3.725
26	1.315	1.706	2.056	2.479	2.779	3.707
27	1.314	1.703	2.052	2.473	2.771	3.689
28	1.313	1.701	2.048	2.467	2.763	3.674
29	1.311	1.699	2.045	2.462	2.756	3.660
30	1.310	1.697	2.042	2.457	2.750	3.646
40	1.303	1.684	2.021	2.423	2.704	3.551
50	1.299	1.676	2.009	2.403	2.678	3.496
60	1.296	1.671	2.000	2.390	2.660	3.460
80	1.292	1.664	1.990	2.374	2.639	3.416
100	1.290	1.660	1.984	2.364	2.626	3.390
120	1.289	1.658	1.980	2.358	2.617	3.373
$\infty(= z)$	1.282	1.645	1.960	2.326	2.576	3.290

*Generated in Excel using functions **=TINV(p,df)** and **=-NORMSINV(p)**. The three values in italics in the upper right-hand corner differ slightly from published tables commonly used in other texts (c.f. Howell, 1997), but only in the fifth significant figure.

TABLE B.3
Critical values for
the *F*-distribution

| | (a) $\alpha = 0.05$* | | | | | | | | | |

Degrees of freedom for numerator

	1	2	3	4	5	6	7	8	9	10
1	161.4	199.5	215.7	224.6	230.2	234.0	236.8	238.9	240.5	241.9
2	18.51	19.00	19.16	19.25	19.30	19.33	19.35	19.37	19.38	19.40
3	10.13	9.55	9.28	9.12	9.01	8.94	8.89	8.85	8.81	8.79
4	7.71	6.94	6.59	6.39	6.26	6.16	6.09	6.04	6.00	5.96
5	6.61	5.79	5.41	5.19	5.05	4.95	4.88	4.82	4.77	4.74
6	5.99	5.14	4.76	4.53	4.39	4.28	4.21	4.15	4.10	4.06
7	5.59	4.74	4.35	4.12	3.97	3.87	3.79	3.73	3.68	3.64
8	5.32	4.46	4.07	3.84	3.69	3.58	3.50	3.44	3.39	3.35
9	5.12	4.26	3.86	3.63	3.48	3.37	3.29	3.23	3.18	3.14
10	4.96	4.10	3.71	3.48	3.33	3.22	3.14	3.07	3.02	2.98
11	4.84	3.98	3.59	3.36	3.20	3.09	3.01	2.95	2.90	2.85
12	4.75	3.89	3.49	3.26	3.11	3.00	2.91	2.85	2.80	2.75
13	4.67	3.81	3.41	3.18	3.03	2.92	2.83	2.77	2.71	2.67
14	4.60	3.74	3.34	3.11	2.96	2.85	2.76	2.70	2.65	2.60
15	4.54	3.68	3.29	3.06	2.90	2.79	2.71	2.64	2.59	2.54
16	4.49	3.63	3.24	3.01	2.85	2.74	2.66	2.59	2.54	2.49
17	4.45	3.59	3.20	2.96	2.81	2.70	2.61	2.55	2.49	2.45
18	4.41	3.55	3.16	2.93	2.77	2.66	2.58	2.51	2.46	2.41
19	4.38	3.52	3.13	2.90	2.74	2.63	2.54	2.48	2.42	2.38
20	4.35	3.49	3.10	2.87	2.71	2.60	2.51	2.45	2.39	2.35
22	4.30	3.44	3.05	2.82	2.66	2.55	2.46	2.40	2.34	2.30
24	4.26	3.40	3.01	2.78	2.62	2.51	2.42	2.36	2.30	2.25
26	4.23	3.37	2.98	2.74	2.59	2.47	2.39	2.32	2.27	2.22
28	4.20	3.34	2.95	2.71	2.56	2.45	2.36	2.29	2.24	2.19
30	4.17	3.32	2.92	2.69	2.53	2.42	2.33	2.27	2.21	2.16
40	4.08	3.23	2.84	2.61	2.45	2.34	2.25	2.18	2.12	2.08
50	4.03	3.18	2.79	2.56	2.40	2.29	2.20	2.13	2.07	2.03
60	4.00	3.15	2.76	2.53	2.37	2.25	2.17	2.10	2.04	1.99
100	3.94	3.09	2.70	2.46	2.31	2.19	2.10	2.03	1.97	1.93
200	3.89	3.04	2.65	2.42	2.26	2.14	2.06	1.98	1.93	1.88
500	3.86	3.01	2.62	2.39	2.23	2.12	2.03	1.96	1.90	1.85
1000	3.85	3.00	2.61	2.38	2.22	2.11	2.02	1.95	1.89	1.84

Degrees of freedom for denominator

*Table generated using Excel: **= FINV(.05, df_{num}, df_{den})**.

TABLE B.3
Critical values for
the *F*-distribution

		(b) $\alpha = 0.01$[†]								

Degrees of freedom for numerator

	1	2	3	4	5	6	7	8	9	10
1	4052.2	4999.3	5403.5	5624.3	5764.0	5859.0	5928.3	5981.0	6022.4	6055.9
2	98.50	99.00	99.16	99.25	99.30	99.33	99.36	99.38	99.39	99.40
3	34.12	30.82	29.46	28.71	28.24	27.91	27.67	27.49	27.34	27.23
4	21.20	18.00	16.69	15.98	15.52	15.21	14.98	14.80	14.66	14.55
5	16.26	13.27	12.06	11.39	10.97	10.67	10.46	10.29	10.16	10.05
6	13.75	10.92	9.78	9.15	8.75	8.47	8.26	8.10	7.98	7.87
7	12.25	9.55	8.45	7.85	7.46	7.19	6.99	6.84	6.72	6.62
8	11.26	8.65	7.59	7.01	6.63	6.37	6.18	6.03	5.91	5.81
9	10.56	8.02	6.99	6.42	6.06	5.80	5.61	5.47	5.35	5.26
10	10.04	7.56	6.55	5.99	5.64	5.39	5.20	5.06	4.94	4.85
11	9.65	7.21	6.22	5.67	5.32	5.07	4.89	4.74	4.63	4.54
12	9.33	6.93	5.95	5.41	5.06	4.82	4.64	4.50	4.39	4.30
13	9.07	6.70	5.74	5.21	4.86	4.62	4.44	4.30	4.19	4.10
14	8.86	6.51	5.56	5.04	4.69	4.46	4.28	4.14	4.03	3.94
15	8.68	6.36	5.42	4.89	4.56	4.32	4.14	4.00	3.89	3.80
16	8.53	6.23	5.29	4.77	4.44	4.20	4.03	3.89	3.78	3.69
17	8.40	6.11	5.19	4.67	4.34	4.10	3.93	3.79	3.68	3.59
18	8.29	6.01	5.09	4.58	4.25	4.01	3.84	3.71	3.60	3.51
19	8.18	5.93	5.01	4.50	4.17	3.94	3.77	3.63	3.52	3.43
20	8.10	5.85	4.94	4.43	4.10	3.87	3.70	3.56	3.46	3.37
22	7.95	5.72	4.82	4.31	3.99	3.76	3.59	3.45	3.35	3.26
24	7.82	5.61	4.72	4.22	3.90	3.67	3.50	3.36	3.26	3.17
26	7.72	5.53	4.64	4.14	3.82	3.59	3.42	3.29	3.18	3.09
28	7.64	5.45	4.57	4.07	3.75	3.53	3.36	3.23	3.12	3.03
30	7.56	5.39	4.51	4.02	3.70	3.47	3.30	3.17	3.07	2.98
40	7.31	5.18	4.31	3.83	3.51	3.29	3.12	2.99	2.89	2.80
50	7.17	5.06	4.20	3.72	3.41	3.19	3.02	2.89	2.78	2.70
60	7.08	4.98	4.13	3.65	3.34	3.12	2.95	2.82	2.72	2.63
100	6.90	4.82	3.98	3.51	3.21	2.99	2.82	2.69	2.59	2.50
200	6.76	4.71	3.88	3.41	3.11	2.89	2.73	2.60	2.50	2.41
500	6.69	4.65	3.82	3.36	3.05	2.84	2.68	2.55	2.44	2.36
1000	6.66	4.63	3.80	3.34	3.04	2.82	2.66	2.53	2.43	2.34

Degrees of freedom for denominator

[†]Table generated using Excel: **=FINV(.01, df_{num}, df_{den})**.

TABLE B.4
Hartley's test for homogeneity of variance, S_{max}^2/S_{min}^2

$n-1$	$k=2$	3	4	5	6	7	8	9	10	11	12
					UPPER 0.05 POINTS						
2	39.0	87.5	142	202	266	333	403	475	550	626	704
3	15.4	27.8	39.2	50.7	62.0	72.9	83.5	93.9	104	114	124
4	9.60	15.5	20.6	25.2	29.5	33.6	37.5	41.1	44.6	48.0	51.4
5	7.15	10.8	13.7	16.3	18.7	20.8	22.9	24.7	26.5	28.2	29.9
6	5.82	8.38	10.4	12.1	13.7	15.0	16.3	17.5	18.6	19.7	20.7
7	4.99	6.94	8.44	9.70	10.8	11.8	12.7	13.5	14.3	15.1	15.8
8	4.43	6.00	7.18	8.12	9.03	9.78	10.5	11.1	11.7	12.2	12.7
9	4.03	5.34	6.31	7.11	7.80	8.41	8.95	9.45	9.91	10.3	10.7
10	3.72	4.85	5.67	6.34	6.92	7.42	7.87	8.28	8.66	9.01	9.34
12	3.28	4.16	4.79	5.30	5.72	6.09	6.42	6.72	7.00	7.25	7.48
15	2.86	3.54	4.01	4.37	4.68	4.95	5.19	5.40	5.59	5.77	5.93
20	2.46	2.95	3.29	3.54	3.76	3.94	4.10	4.24	4.37	4.49	4.59
30	2.07	2.40	2.61	2.78	2.91	3.02	3.12	3.21	3.29	3.36	3.39
60	1.67	1.85	1.96	2.04	2.11	2.17	2.22	2.26	2.30	2.33	2.36
∞	1.00	1.00	1.00	1.00	1.00	1.00	1.00	1.00	1.00	1.00	1.00

$n-1$	$k=2$	3	4	5	6	7	8	9	10	11	12
					UPPER 0.01 POINTS						
2	199	448	729	1036	1362	1705	2063	2432	2813	3204	3605
3	47.5	85	120	151	184	21(6)	24(9)	28(1)	31(0)	33(7)	36(1)
4	23.2	37	49	59	69	79	89	97	106	113	120
5	14.9	22	28	33	38	42	46	50	54	57	60
6	11.1	15.5	19.1	22	25	27	30	32	34	36	37
7	8.89	12.1	14.5	16.5	18.4	20	22	23	24	26	27
8	7.50	9.9	11.7	13.2	14.5	15.8	16.9	17.9	18.9	19.8	21
9	6.54	8.5	9.9	11.1	12.1	13.1	13.9	14.7	15.3	16.0	16.6
10	5.85	7.4	8.6	9.6	10.4	11.1	11.8	12.4	12.9	13.4	13.9
12	4.91	6.1	6.9	7.6	8.2	8.7	9.1	9.5	9.9	10.2	10.6
15	4.07	4.9	5.5	6.0	6.4	6.7	7.1	7.3	7.5	7.8	8.0
20	3.32	3.8	4.3	4.6	4.9	5.1	5.3	5.5	5.6	5.8	5.9
30	2.63	3.0	3.3	3.4	3.6	3.7	3.8	3.9	4.0	4.1	4.2
60	1.96	2.2	2.3	2.4	2.4	2.5	2.5	2.6	2.6	2.7	2.7
∞	1.00	1.0	1.0	1.0	1.0	1.0	1.0	1.0	1.0	1.0	1.0

Note: Values in the column $k = 2$ and in the rows $n - 1 = 2$ and ∞ are exact. Elsewhere the third digit may be in error by a few units for the 0.05 points and several units for the 0.01 points. The third-digit figures in brackets for $n - 1 = 3$ are the most uncertain.

Source: Pearson and Hartley (1970), by permission of Biometrika Trustees.

TABLE B.5
Critical values for
Dunn's test
(Bonferonni t), t'

(a) $\alpha = 0.05$*

Comparisons

$df_{w/in}$	2	3	4	5	6	7	8	9	10	15	20	30	40	50
5	3.16	3.53	3.81	4.03	4.22	4.38	4.53	4.66	4.77	5.25	5.60	6.14	6.54	6.87
6	2.97	3.29	3.52	3.71	3.86	4.00	4.12	4.22	4.32	4.70	4.98	5.40	5.71	5.96
7	2.84	3.13	3.34	3.50	3.64	3.75	3.86	3.95	4.03	4.36	4.59	4.94	5.20	5.41
8	2.75	3.02	3.21	3.36	3.48	3.58	3.68	3.76	3.83	4.12	4.33	4.64	4.86	5.04
9	2.69	2.93	3.11	3.25	3.36	3.46	3.55	3.62	3.69	3.95	4.15	4.42	4.62	4.78
10	2.63	2.87	3.04	3.17	3.28	3.37	3.45	3.52	3.58	3.83	4.00	4.26	4.44	4.59
11	2.59	2.82	2.98	3.11	3.21	3.29	3.37	3.44	3.50	3.73	3.89	4.13	4.30	4.44
12	2.56	2.78	2.93	3.05	3.15	3.24	3.31	3.37	3.43	3.65	3.81	4.03	4.19	4.32
13	2.53	2.75	2.90	3.01	3.11	3.19	3.26	3.32	3.37	3.58	3.73	3.95	4.10	4.22
14	2.51	2.72	2.86	2.98	3.07	3.15	3.21	3.27	3.33	3.53	3.67	3.88	4.03	4.14
15	2.49	2.69	2.84	2.95	3.04	3.11	3.18	3.23	3.29	3.48	3.62	3.82	3.96	4.07
16	2.47	2.67	2.81	2.92	3.01	3.08	3.15	3.20	3.25	3.44	3.58	3.77	3.91	4.01
17	2.46	2.65	2.79	2.90	2.98	3.06	3.12	3.17	3.22	3.41	3.54	3.73	3.86	3.97
18	2.45	2.64	2.77	2.88	2.96	3.03	3.09	3.15	3.20	3.38	3.51	3.69	3.82	3.92
19	2.43	2.63	2.76	2.86	2.94	3.01	3.07	3.13	3.17	3.35	3.48	3.66	3.79	3.88
20	2.42	2.61	2.74	2.85	2.93	3.00	3.06	3.11	3.15	3.33	3.46	3.63	3.75	3.85
25	2.38	2.57	2.69	2.79	2.86	2.93	2.99	3.03	3.08	3.24	3.36	3.52	3.64	3.73
30	2.36	2.54	2.66	2.75	2.82	2.89	2.94	2.99	3.03	3.19	3.30	3.45	3.56	3.65
35	2.34	2.51	2.63	2.72	2.80	2.86	2.91	2.96	3.00	3.15	3.26	3.41	3.51	3.59
40	2.33	2.50	2.62	2.70	2.78	2.84	2.89	2.93	2.97	3.12	3.23	3.37	3.47	3.55
45	2.32	2.49	2.60	2.69	2.76	2.82	2.87	2.91	2.95	3.10	3.20	3.35	3.44	3.52
50	2.31	2.48	2.59	2.68	2.75	2.81	2.85	2.90	2.94	3.08	3.18	3.32	3.42	3.50
100	2.28	2.43	2.54	2.63	2.69	2.75	2.79	2.83	2.87	3.01	3.10	3.23	3.32	3.39
∞	2.24	2.39	2.50	2.58	2.64	2.69	2.73	2.77	2.81	2.94	3.02	3.14	3.23	3.29

*Table generated using Excel: **=TINV(.05/no. of comparisons, *df*)**

(b) $\alpha = 0.01$[†]

Comparisons

$df_{w/in}$	2	3	4	5	6	7	8	9	10	15	20	30	40	50
5	4.77	5.25	5.60	5.89	6.14	6.35	6.54	6.71	6.87	7.50	7.98	8.69	9.23	9.68
6	4.32	4.70	4.98	5.21	5.40	5.56	5.71	5.84	5.96	6.43	6.79	7.32	7.71	8.02
7	4.03	4.36	4.59	4.79	4.94	5.08	5.20	5.31	5.41	5.80	6.08	6.50	6.81	7.06
8	3.83	4.12	4.33	4.50	4.64	4.76	4.86	4.96	5.04	5.37	5.62	5.97	6.23	6.44
9	3.69	3.95	4.15	4.30	4.42	4.53	4.62	4.71	4.78	5.08	5.29	5.60	5.83	6.01
10	3.58	3.83	4.00	4.14	4.26	4.36	4.44	4.52	4.59	4.85	5.05	5.33	5.53	5.69
11	3.50	3.73	3.89	4.02	4.13	4.22	4.30	4.37	4.44	4.68	4.86	5.12	5.31	5.45
12	3.43	3.65	3.81	3.93	4.03	4.12	4.19	4.26	4.32	4.55	4.72	4.96	5.13	5.26
13	3.37	3.58	3.73	3.85	3.95	4.03	4.10	4.16	4.22	4.44	4.60	4.82	4.98	5.11
14	3.33	3.53	3.67	3.79	3.88	3.96	4.03	4.09	4.14	4.35	4.50	4.71	4.86	4.98
15	3.29	3.48	3.62	3.73	3.82	3.90	3.96	4.02	4.07	4.27	4.42	4.62	4.77	4.88
16	3.25	3.44	3.58	3.69	3.77	3.85	3.91	3.96	4.01	4.21	4.35	4.54	4.68	4.79
17	3.22	3.41	3.54	3.65	3.73	3.80	3.86	3.92	3.97	4.15	4.29	4.48	4.61	4.71
18	3.20	3.38	3.51	3.61	3.69	3.76	3.82	3.87	3.92	4.10	4.23	4.42	4.55	4.65
19	3.17	3.35	3.48	3.58	3.66	3.73	3.79	3.84	3.88	4.06	4.19	4.36	4.49	4.59
20	3.15	3.33	3.46	3.55	3.63	3.70	3.75	3.80	3.85	4.02	4.15	4.32	4.44	4.54
25	3.08	3.24	3.36	3.45	3.52	3.58	3.64	3.68	3.73	3.88	4.00	4.15	4.27	4.35
30	3.03	3.19	3.30	3.39	3.45	3.51	3.56	3.61	3.65	3.80	3.90	4.05	4.15	4.23
35	3.00	3.15	3.26	3.34	3.41	3.46	3.51	3.55	3.59	3.74	3.84	3.98	4.08	4.15
40	2.97	3.12	3.23	3.31	3.37	3.43	3.47	3.51	3.55	3.69	3.79	3.92	4.02	4.09
45	2.95	3.10	3.20	3.28	3.35	3.40	3.44	3.48	3.52	3.66	3.75	3.88	3.98	4.05
50	2.94	3.08	3.18	3.26	3.32	3.38	3.42	3.46	3.50	3.63	3.72	3.85	3.94	4.01
100	2.87	3.01	3.10	3.17	3.23	3.28	3.32	3.36	3.39	3.51	3.60	3.72	3.80	3.86
∞	2.81	2.94	3.02	3.09	3.14	3.19	3.23	3.26	3.29	3.40	3.48	3.59	3.66	3.72

[†]Table generated using Excel: **=TINV(.01/no. of comparisons, *df*)**.

TABLE B.6(a)   Critical values for Studentized range statistic

(a) Upper 0.05 points

df_{within}	r = 2	3	4	5	6	7	8	9	10	11	12	13	14	15	16	17	18	19	20
1	17.97	26.98	32.82	37.08	40.41	43.12	45.40	47.36	49.07	50.59	51.96	53.20	54.33	55.36	56.32	57.22	58.04	58.83	59.56
2	6.08	8.33	9.80	10.88	11.74	12.44	13.03	13.54	13.99	14.39	14.75	15.08	15.38	15.65	15.91	16.14	16.37	16.57	16.77
3	4.50	5.91	6.82	7.50	8.04	8.48	8.85	9.18	9.46	9.72	9.95	10.15	10.35	10.52	10.69	10.84	10.98	11.11	11.24
4	3.93	5.04	5.76	6.29	6.71	7.05	7.35	7.60	7.83	8.03	8.21	8.37	8.52	8.66	8.79	8.91	9.03	9.13	9.23
5	3.64	4.60	5.22	5.67	6.03	6.33	6.58	6.80	6.99	7.17	7.32	7.47	7.60	7.72	7.83	7.93	8.03	8.12	8.21
6	3.46	4.34	4.90	5.30	5.63	5.90	6.12	6.32	6.49	6.65	6.79	6.92	7.03	7.14	7.24	7.34	7.43	7.51	7.59
7	3.34	4.16	4.68	5.06	5.36	5.61	5.82	6.00	6.16	6.30	6.43	6.55	6.66	6.76	6.85	6.94	7.02	7.10	7.17
8	3.26	4.04	4.53	4.89	5.17	5.40	5.60	5.77	5.92	6.05	6.18	6.29	6.39	6.48	6.57	6.65	6.73	6.80	6.87
9	3.20	3.95	4.41	4.76	5.02	5.24	5.43	5.59	5.74	5.87	5.98	6.09	6.19	6.28	6.36	6.44	6.51	6.58	6.64
10	3.15	3.88	4.33	4.65	4.91	5.12	5.30	5.46	5.60	5.72	5.83	5.93	6.03	6.11	6.19	6.27	6.34	6.40	6.47
11	3.11	3.82	4.26	4.57	4.82	5.03	5.20	5.35	5.49	5.61	5.71	5.81	5.90	5.98	6.06	6.13	6.20	6.27	6.33
12	3.08	3.77	4.20	4.51	4.75	4.95	5.12	5.27	5.39	5.51	5.61	5.71	5.80	5.88	5.95	6.02	6.09	6.15	6.21
13	3.06	3.73	4.15	4.45	4.69	4.88	5.05	5.19	5.32	5.43	5.53	5.63	5.71	5.79	5.86	5.93	5.99	6.05	6.11
14	3.03	3.70	4.11	4.41	4.64	4.83	4.99	5.13	5.25	5.36	5.46	5.55	5.64	5.71	5.79	5.85	5.91	5.97	6.03
15	3.01	3.67	4.08	4.37	4.59	4.78	4.94	5.08	5.20	5.31	5.40	5.49	5.57	5.65	5.72	5.78	5.85	5.90	5.96
16	3.00	3.65	4.05	4.33	4.56	4.74	4.90	5.03	5.15	5.26	5.35	5.44	5.52	5.59	5.66	5.73	5.79	5.84	5.90
17	2.98	3.63	4.02	4.30	4.52	4.70	4.86	4.99	5.11	5.21	5.31	5.39	5.47	5.54	5.61	5.67	5.73	5.79	5.84
18	2.97	3.61	4.00	4.28	4.49	4.67	4.82	4.96	5.07	5.17	5.27	5.35	5.43	5.50	5.57	5.63	5.69	5.74	5.79
19	2.96	3.59	3.98	4.25	4.47	4.65	4.79	4.92	5.04	5.14	5.23	5.31	5.39	5.46	5.53	5.59	5.65	5.70	5.75
20	2.95	3.58	3.96	4.23	4.45	4.62	4.77	4.90	5.01	5.11	5.20	5.28	5.36	5.43	5.49	5.55	5.61	5.66	5.71
24	2.92	3.53	3.90	4.17	4.37	4.54	4.68	4.81	4.92	5.01	5.10	5.18	5.25	5.32	5.38	5.44	5.49	5.55	5.59
30	2.89	3.49	3.85	4.10	4.30	4.46	4.60	4.72	4.82	4.92	5.00	5.08	5.15	5.21	5.27	5.33	5.38	5.43	5.47
40	2.86	3.44	3.79	4.04	4.23	4.39	4.52	4.63	4.73	4.82	4.90	4.98	5.04	5.11	5.16	5.22	5.27	5.31	5.36
60	2.83	3.40	3.74	3.98	4.16	4.31	4.44	4.55	4.65	4.73	4.81	4.88	4.94	5.00	5.06	5.11	5.15	5.20	5.24
120	2.80	3.36	3.68	3.92	4.10	4.24	4.36	4.47	4.56	4.64	4.71	4.78	4.84	4.90	4.95	5.00	5.04	5.09	5.13
∞	2.77	3.31	3.63	3.86	4.03	4.17	4.29	4.39	4.47	4.55	4.62	4.68	4.74	4.80	4.85	4.89	4.93	4.97	5.01

Source: Pearson and Hartley (1970), by permission of Biometrika Trustees.

TABLE B.6(b) Critical values for Studentized range statistic

(b) Upper 0.01 points

df_{within}	r = 2	3	4	5	6	7	8	9	10	11	12	13	14	15	16	17	18	19	20
1	90.03	135.0	164.3	185.6	202.2	215.8	227.2	237.0	245.6	253.2	260.0	266.2	271.8	277.0	281.8	286.3	290.4	294.3	298.0
2	14.04	19.02	22.29	24.72	26.63	28.20	29.53	30.68	31.69	32.59	33.40	34.13	34.81	35.43	36.00	36.53	37.03	37.50	37.95
3	8.26	10.62	12.17	13.33	14.24	15.00	15.64	16.20	16.69	17.13	17.53	17.89	18.22	18.52	18.81	19.07	19.32	19.55	19.77
4	6.51	8.12	9.17	9.96	10.58	11.10	11.55	11.93	12.27	12.57	12.84	13.09	13.32	13.53	13.73	13.91	14.08	14.24	14.40
5	5.70	6.98	7.80	8.42	8.91	9.32	9.67	9.97	10.24	10.48	10.70	10.89	11.08	11.24	11.40	11.55	11.68	11.81	11.93
6	5.24	6.33	7.03	7.56	7.97	8.32	8.61	8.87	9.10	9.30	9.48	9.65	9.81	9.95	10.08	10.21	10.32	10.43	10.54
7	4.95	5.92	6.54	7.01	7.37	7.68	7.94	8.17	8.37	8.55	8.71	8.86	9.00	9.12	9.24	9.35	9.46	9.55	9.65
8	4.75	5.64	6.20	6.62	6.96	7.24	7.47	7.68	7.86	8.03	8.18	8.31	8.44	8.55	8.66	8.76	8.85	8.94	9.03
9	4.60	5.43	5.96	6.35	6.66	6.91	7.13	7.33	7.49	7.65	7.78	7.91	8.03	8.13	8.23	8.33	8.41	8.49	8.57
10	4.48	5.27	5.77	6.14	6.43	6.67	6.87	7.05	7.21	7.36	7.49	7.60	7.71	7.81	7.91	7.99	8.08	8.15	8.23
11	4.39	5.15	5.62	5.97	6.25	6.48	6.67	6.84	6.99	7.13	7.25	7.36	7.46	7.56	7.65	7.73	7.81	7.88	7.95
12	4.32	5.05	5.50	5.84	6.10	6.32	6.51	6.67	6.81	6.94	7.06	7.17	7.26	7.36	7.44	7.52	7.59	7.66	7.73
13	4.26	4.96	5.40	5.73	5.98	6.19	6.37	6.53	6.67	6.79	6.90	7.01	7.10	7.19	7.27	7.35	7.42	7.48	7.55
14	4.21	4.89	5.32	5.63	5.88	6.08	6.26	6.41	6.54	6.66	6.77	6.87	6.96	7.05	7.13	7.20	7.27	7.33	7.39
15	4.17	4.84	5.25	5.56	5.80	5.99	6.16	6.31	6.44	6.55	6.66	6.76	6.84	6.93	7.00	7.07	7.14	7.20	7.26
16	4.13	4.79	5.19	5.49	5.72	5.92	6.08	6.22	6.35	6.46	6.56	6.66	6.74	6.82	6.90	6.97	7.03	7.09	7.15
17	4.10	4.74	5.14	5.43	5.66	5.85	6.01	6.15	6.27	6.38	6.48	6.57	6.66	6.73	6.81	6.87	6.94	7.00	7.05
18	4.07	4.70	5.09	5.38	5.60	5.79	5.94	6.08	6.20	6.31	6.41	6.50	6.58	6.65	6.73	6.79	6.85	6.91	6.97
19	4.05	4.67	5.05	5.33	5.55	5.73	5.89	6.02	6.14	6.25	6.34	6.43	6.51	6.58	6.65	6.72	6.78	6.84	6.89
20	4.02	4.64	5.02	5.29	5.51	5.69	5.84	5.97	6.09	6.19	6.28	6.37	6.45	6.52	6.59	6.65	6.71	6.77	6.82
24	3.96	4.55	4.91	5.17	5.37	5.54	5.69	5.81	5.92	6.02	6.11	6.19	6.26	6.33	6.39	6.45	6.51	6.56	6.61
30	3.89	4.45	4.80	5.05	5.24	5.40	5.54	5.65	5.76	5.85	5.93	6.01	6.08	6.14	6.20	6.26	6.31	6.36	6.41
40	3.82	4.37	4.70	4.93	5.11	5.26	5.39	5.50	5.60	5.69	5.76	5.83	5.90	5.96	6.02	6.07	6.12	6.16	6.21
60	3.76	4.28	4.59	4.82	4.99	5.13	5.25	5.36	5.45	5.53	5.60	5.67	5.73	5.78	5.84	5.89	5.93	5.97	6.01
120	3.70	4.20	4.50	4.71	4.87	5.01	5.12	5.21	5.30	5.37	5.44	5.50	5.56	5.61	5.66	5.71	5.75	5.79	5.83
∞	3.64	4.12	4.40	4.60	4.76	4.88	4.99	5.08	5.16	5.23	5.29	5.35	5.40	5.45	5.49	5.54	5.57	5.61	5.65

Source: Pearson and Hartley (1970), by permission of Biometrika Trustees.

TABLE B.7(a) Critical values for Duncan's test

(a) Number of groups spanned ($\alpha = 0.05$)

df_{within}	$r = 2$	3	4	5	6	7	8	9	10	12	14	16	18	20	50	100
1	18.0	18.0	18.0	18.0	18.0	18.0	18.0	18.0	18.0	18.0	18.0	18.0	18.0	18.0	18.0	18.0
2	6.09	6.09	6.09	6.09	6.09	6.09	6.09	6.09	6.09	6.09	6.09	6.09	6.09	6.09	6.09	6.09
3	4.50	4.50	4.50	4.50	4.50	4.50	4.50	4.50	4.50	4.50	4.50	4.50	4.50	4.50	4.50	4.5
4	3.93	4.01	4.02	4.02	4.02	4.02	4.02	4.02	4.02	4.02	4.02	4.02	4.02	4.02	4.02	4.02
5	3.64	3.74	3.79	3.83	3.83	3.83	3.83	3.83	3.83	3.83	3.83	3.83	3.83	3.83	3.83	3.83
6	3.46	3.58	3.64	3.68	3.68	3.68	3.68	3.68	3.68	3.68	3.68	3.68	3.68	3.68	3.68	3.68
7	3.35	3.47	3.54	3.58	3.60	3.61	3.61	3.61	3.61	3.61	3.61	3.61	3.61	3.61	3.61	3.61
8	3.26	3.39	3.47	3.52	3.55	3.56	3.56	3.56	3.56	3.56	3.56	3.56	3.56	3.56	3.56	3.56
9	3.20	3.34	3.41	3.47	3.50	3.52	3.52	3.52	3.52	3.52	3.52	3.52	3.52	3.52	3.52	3.52
10	3.15	3.30	3.37	3.43	3.46	3.47	3.47	3.47	3.47	3.47	3.47	3.47	3.47	3.48	3.48	3.48
11	3.11	3.27	3.35	3.39	3.43	3.44	3.45	3.46	3.46	3.46	3.46	3.46	3.47	3.48	3.48	3.48
12	3.08	3.23	3.33	3.36	3.40	3.42	3.44	3.44	3.46	3.46	3.46	3.46	3.47	3.48	3.48	3.48
13	3.06	3.21	3.30	3.35	3.38	3.41	3.42	3.44	3.45	3.45	3.46	3.46	3.47	3.47	3.47	3.47
14	3.03	3.18	3.27	3.33	3.37	3.39	3.41	3.42	3.44	3.45	3.46	3.46	3.47	3.47	3.47	3.47
15	3.01	3.16	3.25	3.31	3.36	3.38	3.40	3.42	3.43	3.44	3.45	3.46	3.47	3.47	3.47	3.47
16	3.00	3.15	3.23	3.30	3.34	3.37	3.39	3.41	3.43	3.44	3.45	3.46	3.47	3.47	3.47	3.47
17	2.98	3.13	3.22	3.28	3.33	3.36	3.38	3.40	3.42	3.44	3.45	3.46	3.47	3.47	3.47	3.47
18	2.97	3.12	3.21	3.27	3.32	3.35	3.37	3.39	3.41	3.43	3.45	3.46	3.47	3.47	3.47	3.47
19	2.96	3.11	3.19	3.26	3.31	3.35	3.37	3.39	3.41	3.43	3.44	3.46	3.47	3.47	3.47	3.47
20	2.95	3.10	3.18	3.25	3.30	3.34	3.36	3.38	3.40	3.43	3.44	3.46	3.47	3.47	3.47	3.47
22	2.93	3.08	3.17	3.24	3.29	3.32	3.35	3.37	3.39	3.42	3.44	3.45	3.47	3.47	3.47	3.47
24	2.92	3.07	3.15	3.22	3.28	3.31	3.34	3.37	3.38	3.41	3.44	3.45	3.47	3.47	3.47	3.47
26	2.91	3.06	3.14	3.21	3.27	3.30	3.34	3.36	3.38	3.41	3.43	3.45	3.46	3.47	3.47	3.47
28	2.90	3.04	3.13	3.20	3.26	3.30	3.33	3.35	3.37	3.40	3.43	3.45	3.46	3.47	3.47	3.47
30	2.89	3.04	3.12	3.20	3.25	3.29	3.32	3.35	3.37	3.40	3.42	3.44	3.46	3.47	3.47	3.47
40	2.86	3.01	3.10	3.17	3.22	3.27	3.30	3.33	3.35	3.39	3.40	3.44	3.46	3.47	3.47	3.47
60	2.83	2.98	3.08	3.14	3.20	3.24	3.28	3.31	3.33	3.37	3.40	3.43	3.45	3.47	3.48	3.48
100	2.80	2.95	3.05	3.12	3.18	3.22	3.26	3.29	3.32	3.36	3.40	3.42	3.45	3.47	3.53	3.53
∞	2.77	2.92	3.02	3.09	3.15	3.19	3.23	3.26	3.29	3.34	3.38	3.41	3.44	3.47	3.61	3.67

TABLE B.7(b) Critical values for Duncan's test

(b) $\alpha = 0.01$

df_{within}	$r = 2$	3	4	5	6	7	8	9	10	12	14	16	18	20	50	100
1	90.0	90.0	90.0	90.0	90.0	90.0	90.0	90.0	90.0	90.0	90.0	90.0	90.0	90.0	90.0	90.0
2	14.0	14.0	14.0	14.0	14.0	14.0	14.0	14.0	14.0	14.0	14.0	14.0	14.0	14.0	14.0	14.0
3	8.26	8.5	8.6	8.7	8.8	8.9	8.9	9.0	9.0	9.0	9.1	9.2	9.3	9.3	9.3	9.3
4	6.51	6.8	6.9	7.0	7.1	7.1	7.2	7.2	7.3	7.3	7.4	7.4	7.5	7.5	7.5	7.5
5	5.70	5.96	6.11	6.18	6.26	6.33	6.40	6.44	6.5	6.6	6.6	6.7	6.7	6.8	6.8	6.8
6	5.24	5.51	5.65	5.73	5.81	5.88	5.95	6.00	6.0	6.1	6.2	6.2	6.3	6.3	6.3	6.3
7	4.95	5.22	5.37	5.45	5.53	5.61	5.69	5.73	5.8	5.8	5.9	5.9	6.0	6.0	6.0	6.0
8	4.74	5.00	5.14	5.23	5.32	5.40	5.47	5.51	5.5	5.6	5.7	5.7	5.8	5.8	5.8	5.8
9	4.60	4.86	4.99	5.08	5.17	5.25	5.32	5.36	5.4	5.5	5.5	5.6	5.7	5.7	5.7	5.7
10	4.48	4.73	4.88	4.94	5.06	5.13	5.20	5.24	5.28	5.36	5.42	5.48	5.54	5.55	5.55	5.55
11	4.39	4.63	4.77	4.86	4.96	5.01	5.06	5.12	5.15	5.24	5.28	5.34	5.38	5.39	5.39	5.39
12	4.32	4.55	4.68	4.76	4.84	4.92	4.96	5.02	5.07	5.13	5.17	5.22	5.24	5.26	5.26	5.26
13	4.26	4.48	4.62	4.69	4.74	4.84	4.88	4.94	4.98	5.04	5.08	5.13	5.14	5.15	5.15	5.15
14	4.21	4.42	4.55	4.63	4.70	4.78	4.83	4.87	4.91	4.96	5.00	5.04	5.06	5.07	5.07	5.07
15	4.17	4.37	4.50	4.58	4.64	4.72	4.77	4.81	4.84	4.90	4.94	4.97	4.99	5.00	5.00	5.00
16	4.13	4.34	4.45	4.54	4.60	4.67	4.72	4.76	4.79	4.84	4.88	4.91	4.93	4.94	4.94	4.94
17	4.10	4.30	4.41	4.50	4.56	4.63	4.68	4.72	4.75	4.80	4.83	4.86	4.88	4.89	4.89	4.89
18	4.07	4.27	4.38	4.46	4.53	4.59	4.64	4.68	4.71	4.76	4.79	4.82	4.84	4.85	4.85	4.85
19	4.05	4.24	4.35	4.43	4.50	4.56	4.61	4.64	4.67	4.72	4.76	4.79	4.81	4.82	4.82	4.82
20	4.02	4.22	4.33	4.40	4.47	4.53	4.58	4.61	4.65	4.69	4.73	4.76	4.78	4.79	4.79	4.79
22	3.99	4.17	4.28	4.36	4.42	4.48	4.53	4.57	4.60	4.65	4.68	4.71	4.74	4.75	4.75	4.75
24	3.96	4.14	4.24	4.33	4.39	4.44	4.49	4.53	4.57	4.62	4.64	4.67	4.70	4.72	4.74	4.74
26	3.93	4.11	4.21	4.30	4.36	4.41	4.46	4.50	4.53	4.58	4.60	4.65	4.67	4.69	4.73	4.73
28	3.91	4.08	4.18	4.28	4.34	4.39	4.43	4.47	4.51	4.56	4.60	4.62	4.65	4.67	4.72	4.72
30	3.89	4.06	4.16	4.22	4.32	4.36	4.41	4.45	4.48	4.54	4.58	4.61	4.63	4.65	4.71	4.71
40	3.82	3.99	4.10	4.17	4.24	4.30	4.34	4.37	4.41	4.46	4.51	4.54	4.57	4.59	4.69	4.69
60	3.76	3.92	4.03	4.12	4.17	4.23	4.27	4.31	4.34	4.39	4.44	4.47	4.50	4.53	4.66	4.66
100	3.71	3.86	3.98	4.06	4.11	4.17	4.21	4.25	4.29	4.35	4.38	4.42	4.45	4.48	4.64	4.65
∞	3.64	3.80	3.90	3.98	4.04	4.09	4.14	4.17	4.20	4.26	4.31	4.34	4.38	4.41	4.60	4.68

Source: Reproduced from Duncan (1955), with permission from the International Biometric Society.

TABLE B.8

Critical values for Dunnett's test, $c =$ number of treatments excluding the control

df_{within}	$c = 1$	2	3	4	5	6	7	8	9
5	3.37	3.90	4.21	4.43	4.60	4.73	4.85	4.94	5.03
6	3.14	3.61	3.88	4.07	4.21	4.33	4.43	4.51	4.59
7	3.00	3.42	3.66	3.83	3.96	4.07	4.15	4.23	4.30
8	2.90	3.29	3.51	3.67	3.79	3.88	3.96	4.03	4.09
9	2.82	3.19	3.40	3.55	3.66	3.75	3.82	3.89	3.94
10	2.76	3.11	3.31	3.45	3.56	3.64	3.71	3.78	3.83
11	2.72	3.06	3.25	3.38	3.48	3.56	3.63	3.69	3.74
12	2.68	3.01	3.19	3.32	3.42	3.50	2.56	3.62	3.67
13	2.65	2.97	3.15	3.27	3.37	3.44	3.51	3.56	3.61
14	2.62	2.94	3.11	3.23	3.32	3.40	3.46	3.51	3.56
15	2.60	2.91	3.08	3.20	3.29	3.36	3.42	3.47	3.52
16	2.58	2.88	3.05	3.17	3.26	3.33	3.39	3.44	3.48
17	2.57	2.86	3.03	3.14	3.23	3.30	3.36	3.41	3.45
18	2.55	2.84	3.01	3.12	3.21	3.27	3.33	3.38	3.42
19	2.54	2.83	2.99	3.10	3.18	3.25	3.31	3.36	3.40
20	2.53	2.81	2.97	3.08	3.17	3.23	3.29	3.34	3.38
24	2.49	2.77	2.92	3.03	3.11	3.17	3.22	3.27	3.31
30	2.46	2.72	2.87	2.97	3.05	3.11	3.16	3.21	3.24
40	2.42	2.68	2.82	2.92	2.99	3.05	3.10	3.14	3.18
60	2.39	2.64	2.78	2.87	2.94	3.00	3.04	3.08	3.12
120	2.36	2.60	2.73	2.82	2.89	2.94	2.99	3.03	3.06
∞	2.33	2.56	5.68	2.77	2.84	2.89	2.93	2.97	3.00

$\alpha = 0.01$, one-tailed test

df_{within}	$c = 1$	2	3	4	5	6	7	8	9
5	2.02	2.44	2.68	2.85	2.98	3.08	3.16	3.24	3.30
6	1.94	2.34	2.56	2.71	2.83	2.92	3.00	3.07	3.12
7	1.89	2.27	2.48	2.62	2.73	2.82	2.89	2.95	3.01
8	1.86	2.22	2.42	2.55	2.66	2.74	2.81	2.87	2.92
9	1.83	2.18	2.37	2.50	2.60	2.68	2.75	2.81	2.86
10	1.81	2.15	2.34	2.47	2.56	2.64	2.70	2.76	2.81
11	1.80	2.13	2.31	2.44	2.53	2.60	2.67	2.72	2.77
12	1.78	2.11	2.29	2.41	2.50	2.58	2.64	2.69	2.74
13	1.77	2.09	2.27	2.39	2.48	2.55	2.61	2.66	2.71
14	1.76	2.08	2.25	2.37	2.46	2.53	2.59	2.64	2.69
15	1.75	2.07	2.24	2.36	2.44	2.51	2.57	2.62	2.67
16	1.75	2.06	2.23	2.34	2.43	2.50	2.56	2.61	2.65
17	1.74	2.05	2.22	2.33	2.42	2.49	2.54	2.59	2.64
18	1.73	2.04	2.21	2.32	2.41	2.48	2.53	2.58	2.62
19	1.73	2.03	2.20	2.31	2.40	2.47	2.52	2.57	2.61
20	1.72	2.03	2.19	2.30	2.39	2.46	2.51	2.56	2.60
24	1.71	2.01	2.17	2.28	2.36	2.43	2.48	2.53	2.57
30	1.70	1.99	2.15	2.25	2.33	2.40	2.45	2.50	2.54
40	1.68	1.97	2.13	2.23	2.31	2.37	2.42	2.47	2.51
60	1.67	1.95	2.10	2.21	2.28	2.35	2.39	2.44	2.48
120	1.66	1.93	2.08	2.18	2.26	2.32	2.37	2.41	2.45
∞	1.64	1.92	2.06	2.16	2.23	2.29	2.34	2.38	2.42

$\alpha = 0.05$, one-tailed test

TABLE B.9
Critical values for chi square test*

df	α					
	0.10	0.05	0.025	0.01	0.005	0.001
1	2.71	3.84	5.02	6.63	7.88	10.83
2	4.61	5.99	7.38	9.21	10.60	13.82
3	6.25	7.81	9.35	11.34	12.84	16.27
4	7.78	9.49	11.14	13.28	14.86	18.47
5	9.24	11.07	12.83	15.09	16.75	20.51
6	10.64	12.59	14.45	16.81	18.55	22.46
7	12.02	14.07	16.01	18.48	20.28	24.32
8	13.36	15.51	17.53	20.09	21.95	26.12
9	14.68	16.92	19.02	21.67	23.59	27.88
10	15.99	18.31	20.48	23.21	25.19	29.59
11	17.28	19.68	21.92	24.73	26.76	31.26
12	18.55	21.03	23.34	26.22	28.30	32.91
13	19.81	22.36	24.74	27.69	29.82	34.53
14	21.06	23.68	26.12	29.14	31.32	36.12
15	22.31	25.00	27.49	30.58	32.80	37.70
16	23.54	26.30	28.85	32.00	34.27	39.25
17	24.77	27.59	30.19	33.41	35.72	40.79
18	25.99	28.87	31.53	34.81	37.16	42.31
19	27.20	30.14	32.85	36.19	38.58	43.82
20	28.41	31.41	34.17	37.57	40.00	45.31
21	29.62	32.67	35.48	38.93	41.40	46.80
22	30.81	33.92	36.78	40.29	42.80	48.27
23	32.01	35.17	38.08	41.64	44.18	49.73
24	33.20	36.42	39.36	42.98	45.56	51.18
25	34.38	37.65	40.65	44.31	46.93	52.62
26	35.56	38.89	41.92	45.64	48.29	54.05
27	36.74	40.11	43.19	46.96	49.65	55.48
28	37.92	41.34	44.46	48.28	50.99	56.89
29	39.09	42.56	45.72	49.59	52.34	58.30
30	40.26	43.77	46.98	50.89	53.67	59.70
40	51.81	55.76	59.34	63.69	66.77	73.40
50	63.17	67.50	71.42	76.15	79.49	86.66
60	74.40	79.08	83.30	88.38	91.95	99.61
70	85.53	90.53	95.02	100.43	104.21	112.32
80	96.58	101.88	106.63	112.33	116.32	124.84
90	107.57	113.15	118.14	124.12	128.30	137.21
100	118.50	124.34	129.56	135.81	140.17	149.45

*Table generated in Excel using **=CHIINV(alpha, *df*)**.

TABLE B.10
Random digits*

34	83	40	41	02	32	74	16	19	06	63	32	36	40	31	88	27	56	01	58
19	17	17	64	09	92	78	72	57	59	04	38	77	40	45	93	41	36	21	16
93	50	44	94	47	98	64	72	94	91	54	05	24	16	94	40	40	83	04	65
05	23	65	83	40	41	95	92	75	89	16	58	24	06	72	91	86	46	82	90
50	37	84	54	65	17	11	36	57	23	75	09	11	98	61	48	25	48	88	80
74	95	43	17	94	03	83	66	78	44	39	36	67	55	08	40	02	31	14	04
06	21	72	68	62	69	46	07	45	22	81	75	04	60	19	33	23	69	33	73
55	25	89	59	40	82	60	02	67	79	29	81	94	39	51	66	85	15	58	06
47	87	72	84	09	36	72	28	05	11	25	85	71	89	51	64	07	67	50	78
10	50	53	57	17	64	87	71	49	17	12	11	81	39	91	10	86	23	10	89
17	75	47	58	84	27	96	79	07	16	17	93	42	07	41	73	11	27	31	20
01	88	27	94	98	23	73	45	19	08	15	48	15	91	35	30	41	57	02	33
48	68	38	04	95	20	26	02	75	07	71	44	90	81	57	33	23	05	22	16
79	70	75	79	15	68	47	05	55	71	74	69	12	59	93	87	94	34	02	46
73	34	40	74	25	83	76	25	81	67	26	57	03	54	61	99	26	25	59	50
65	95	19	57	66	37	75	91	90	94	46	09	64	51	30	44	70	85	74	80
91	87	34	91	09	21	93	66	93	35	10	78	86	86	81	68	93	83	92	41
60	53	40	59	11	65	75	84	53	68	91	43	93	30	40	48	55	62	82	47
36	99	88	54	62	02	80	21	27	87	98	66	40	76	17	10	88	19	29	36
51	62	79	57	56	59	12	09	28	33	61	27	57	55	92	70	56	15	89	38
81	32	22	95	21	65	33	43	60	64	78	98	43	44	21	48	83	76	37	12
04	73	30	79	87	51	92	50	58	10	25	86	87	72	94	87	09	86	99	99
85	11	46	25	58	42	98	66	61	68	73	62	51	53	39	53	31	82	44	07
03	64	59	70	14	17	65	61	55	91	08	88	36	92	97	81	75	19	25	66
91	20	46	98	69	47	89	47	72	25	66	74	38	33	38	94	38	47	52	43
44	64	92	68	69	65	56	79	44	28	61	94	92	10	99	57	44	23	28	96
31	52	43	64	84	12	72	69	25	12	57	18	55	29	96	94	90	28	32	57
65	02	73	83	79	44	22	94	74	95	19	21	76	97	26	52	36	80	30	30
54	01	83	60	42	73	08	01	61	30	94	73	67	84	17	16	89	36	88	06
26	63	70	70	46	56	33	86	11	07	37	01	48	61	35	40	25	49	12	74
63	18	53	45	13	54	65	88	97	09	81	09	60	57	16	59	81	01	04	48
51	61	58	69	85	63	77	37	46	69	31	49	14	60	43	42	98	88	19	36
81	50	33	47	51	08	66	29	74	07	46	56	15	11	61	29	80	49	92	90
99	81	51	50	09	70	18	49	56	50	58	92	63	48	98	95	29	40	83	10
91	85	14	01	57	73	16	15	89	11	79	07	52	16	63	09	15	45	80	26
02	79	59	09	72	22	98	59	36	33	76	50	64	01	78	75	99	67	58	15
65	81	93	55	75	45	92	50	95	82	55	50	87	09	75	58	03	88	35	58
93	73	35	10	52	16	81	93	36	27	37	67	44	96	56	37	27	68	67	02
91	54	98	36	15	87	19	55	01	46	45	38	08	74	06	26	91	94	49	70
06	13	75	51	10	36	12	27	88	18	72	35	46	47	07	97	77	18	92	72

* Use in any combination of sets of digits. Generated in Excel using
RANDBETWEEN.

GLOSSARY OF MATHEMATICAL SYMBOLS, EQUATIONS AND EXCEL FUNCTIONS

Symbol	Definition, description	Representative mathematical equation or graphical illustration or Table	Excel function/equation/worksheet	Discussion and explanation
α	Greek letter alpha: (a) Critical level for significance testing. (b) Probability of a Type I error.	(a) Figure 13.9 (sampling distribution with α) (b) Figure 14.8 (sampling distribution with α, with alternative distributions for H_0 false)		(a) Chapter 13 (b) Chapter 14
α	Cronbach's reliability coefficient: (a) internal consistency (average of all split-half coefficients for a set of N questions); (b) inter-scorer reliability (among N judges).	$$\alpha = \frac{N}{N-1}\left[1 - \frac{\sum\limits_{i=1}^{N} S_i^2}{S_x^2}\right]$$	(a) Figures 11.2, 11.5 (b) Figure 11.6	Chapter 11, equation (11.6)
β	Greek letter beta: the probability of a Type II error, i.e. the probability of accepting H_0 when in reality it is false.	Figure 14.9 (sampling distributions for z-test) Figure 15.9 (sampling distributions for t-test) Figure 16.11 (sampling distributions for ANOVA)	Figure 14.9 (z-test worksheet) Figure 15.10 (t-test worksheet) Figure 16.12 (ANOVA worksheet) Figure 17.12 (factorial worksheet) Figure 18.3 (randomized block worksheet)	Chapter 14 (z-test) Chapter 15 (t-test) Chapter 16 (ANOVA)
β_j	Multiple regression coefficients	$b_j = \beta_j \dfrac{s_y}{s_j}$ where $y = c + b_1 x_1 + b_2 x_2$ Figures 22.9, 22.10	Activities 22.3 and 22.4, Tables 22.2, 22.3	Chapter 22, equations (22.9) and (22.10)
b_{yx}, b_{xy}	Linear regression coefficients	$y = b_{yx} x + c$ where $b_{yx} = r_{xy}\dfrac{s_y}{s_x}$ Figures 22.1–22.7	Table 22.3, Activity 22.1	Chapter 22, equations (22.1), (22.2), (22.4)
C	Cramér's C	$C = \sqrt{\dfrac{\chi^2}{n(L-1)}}$ and Tables 21.5 and 21.6	Figure 21.7 (Cramér's C worksheet)	Chapter 21, equation (21.18)
cov_{AB}	Covariance	$$\text{cov}_{AB} = \frac{\sum\limits_{i=1}^{n}(x_{Ai} - \bar{x}_A)(x_{Bi} - \bar{x}_B)}{n-1}$$	Figure 18.4 (worksheet for variance and covariance matrix)	Chapter 18, equation (18.3)

D	Discrimination index for achievement test items (scores with a normal distribution). U = no. in upper group answering correct L = no. in lower group answering correct n = number in each group	$D = \dfrac{U - L}{n}$ Table 11.2	Chapter 11, equation (11.8)
df	Degrees of freedom, the number of observations free to vary at one time without affecting the result. Used when evaluating the results of inferential statistical tests.	See specific tests for appropriate calculations, e.g., χ^2, F-test, t-test.	Chapters 13–20
E	Discrimination index for achievement test items, scores not distribution dependent. (See D above.) n_1 = no. in upper group. n_2 = no. in lower group. U = no. in upper group answering correctly. L = no. in lower group answering correctly.	$E = \dfrac{2U - 2L - n_1 + n_2}{n_1 + n_2}$ Table 11.2	Figure 11.8 (worksheet for item analysis for criterion-referenced tests) Chapter 11, equation (11.12)
F	F-ratio for analysis of variance (ANOVA) s_{between}^2 = estimate of population variance based on variance between sample means. s_{within}^2 = estimate of population variance based on average of sample means.	$F = \dfrac{s_{\text{between}}^2}{s_{\text{within}}^2} = \dfrac{MS_{\text{between}}}{MS_{\text{within}}}$	Figures 16.2, 16.5, 16.6, 16.7, 16.10, 16.12 (worksheets for one-way ANOVA) Chapter 16, equation (16.5)
F_{crit}	Critical value for F-test, dependent on α, df_{between}, and df_{within}, for one way ANOVA: $df_{\text{between}} = k - 1$, k = no. of groups $df_{\text{within}} = N - k$, N = no. of subjects	Figure 16.3 (exemplar sampling F-distributions for variety of sample sizes and number of treatment groups) See Appendix B, Table B.3, for values.	**=FINV(alpha, df_{between}, df_{within})** Chapter 16
H_0	Null hypothesis		Chapter 13

Symbol	Definition, description	Representative mathematical equation or graphical illustration or Table	Excel function/ equation/ worksheet	Discussion and explanation
i	As a subscript, it is a counter and varies from 1 to n; often used to indicate members of a sample of size n.			
j	As a subscript, it is a counter and varies from 1 to k; often used to indicate different groups.			
λ	Greek letter lambda: the non-centrality parameter, a value used when determining the alternative sampling distribution associated with H_0 being false. Used in calculating estimates of power.	$\lambda = (k-1)\left(\dfrac{F}{cf}-1\right)$ (F-test) where $cf = \dfrac{k}{k+0.4}$ for k treatments. $\chi' = \chi^2 - df + 1$ (chi square)		Chapter 16, equations (16.33) and (16.34) Chapter 19, equation (19.9)
μ	Greek letter mu: the population mean for a trait, a parameter.			Chapter 12, equation (12.1)
n	Number in the sample group.			
n_j	Number in sample group j.			
$\tilde{n}$	Harmonic mean, estimate of sample size when unequal cell sizes in ANOVA for k groups.	$\tilde{n} = \dfrac{k}{\dfrac{1}{n_1}+\dfrac{1}{n_2}+\dfrac{1}{n_3}+\ldots+\dfrac{1}{n_k}}$		Chapter 16, Activity 16.7
N	Usually the number of questions on a test. Can be total subjects.			Chapter 11
p	Probability of an event (e.g., $p < 0.05$ says that the probability of the null hypothesis being true is less than 5%).			Chapter 13
power	The probability of correctly rejecting H_0 when in reality it is false.	power $= 1 - \beta$ Figure 14.8 (z-test) Figure 15.9 (t-test) Figure 16.11 (ANOVA) Figure 19.6 (chi square)	Figure 14.9 (z-test) Figure 15.10 (t-test) Figure 16.13 (one-way ANOVA) Figure 17.12 (factorial ANOVA) Figure 18.3 (randomized block)	Chapter 14 (z-test) Chapter 15 (t-test) Chapter 16 (ANOVA) Chapters 19 and 20 (chi square) Chapter 21 (correlation)

power *continued*

Symbol	Definition	Formula	Reference
			Figure 19.7 (one/two-sample χ^2) Figure 20.1 (three or more sample χ^2) Figure 21.3 (test of significance of Pearson's r_{xy})
p_i	Difficulty of item i, proportion of group answering an item, i, correctly, and $q_i = 1 - p_i$.	$p_i = \dfrac{\text{number answering correctly}}{\text{total number of examinees}}$	Chapter 11, equation (11.9)
q_i	Proportion of group answering an item, i, incorrectly.	$q_i = 1 - p_i$	Chapter 11
r_{AB}	Pearson product moment correlation coefficient between tests A and B (interval/ratio data).	=**PEARSON**(range_a, range_b) $$r_{AB} = \frac{\sum_{i=1}^{n}[(x_{Ai} - \bar{x}_A)(x_{Bi} - \bar{x}_B)]}{nS_A S_B}$$	Chapter 11, equation (11.4)
r_{xy}	Pearson product moment correlation coefficient between two variables, x and y.	=**PEARSON**(range_x, range_y) $$r_{xy} = \frac{\sum_{i=1}^{n}(x_i - \bar{x})(y_i - \bar{y})}{(n - 1)s_x s_y}$$ $$r_{xy} = \frac{\text{cov}_{xy}}{s_x s_y}$$	Chapter 21, equations (21.5) and (21.6)
r_{pb}	Point biserial coefficient for nominal versus interval/ratio data.	$$r_{pb} = \frac{\bar{x}_p - \bar{x}_q}{S}\sqrt{pq}$$ where $\bar{x}_p$ = higher mean of continuous variable scores, group p $\bar{x}_q$ = lower mean of continuous variable scores, group q S = standard deviation of all scores, x_i, for both groups together p = proportion of cases in higher-mean group q = proportion of cases in lower-mean group	Chapter 21, equation (21.20)
r_{xx}	Reliability coefficient (definition) for measuring instruments, based on definition, where: S_t^2 true score variance; S_x^2 observed score variance; S_e^2 error variance.	$$r_{xx} = \frac{S_t^2}{S_x^2} = 1 - \frac{S_e^2}{S_x^2}$$	Chapter 11, equation (11.1)

Symbol	Definition, description	Representative mathematical equation or graphical illustration or Table	Excel function/ equation/ worksheet	Discussion and explanation
r_{xy}^2	Square of Pearson's, proportion of variance which can be explained by relationship between x and y.		Reported as R square in Excel under **Tools, Data Analysis, Regression**	Chapter 21, equation (22.7)
r_S	Spearman's rho, correlation coefficient for ordinal data.	$$r_S = \frac{\sum_{i=1}^n (x_i - \bar{x})(y_i - \bar{y})}{\sqrt{\sum_{i=1}^n (x_i - \bar{x})^2 \sum_{i=1}^n (y_i - \bar{y})^2}}$$	Figures 21.5 and 21.6 (worksheets for Spearman's rho)	Chapter 21, equations (21.16) and (21.7)
R^2	Multiple correlation coefficient squared, proportion of variance which can be explained by relationship between y and x_1 and x_2.	$$R^2 = \frac{r_{yx_1}^2 + r_{yx_2}^2 - 2r_{yx_1} r_{yx_2} r_{x_1 x_2}}{1 - r_{x_1 x_2}^2}$$ $$R^2 = b_1 \frac{s_1}{s_y} r_{yx_1} + b_2 \frac{s_2}{s_y} r_{yx_2}$$	Reported as R square in Excel under **Tools, Data Analysis, Regression**	Chapter 22, equations (22.14), (22.15) and (22.16)
$\sum_{i=1}^n (\ )$	Greek capital letter sigma: it says add up all in the ( ) counting i from 1 to n. If adding a row or column of data on a spreadsheet, then use the Excel function.		**=SUM(range)**	
S^2	Variance of data for a sample.	$$S^2 = \frac{\sum_{i=1}^n (x_i - \bar{x})^2}{n}$$	**=VARP(range)**	Chapter 12, equation (12.6)
S	Standard deviation for a set of sample data.	$$S = \sqrt{\frac{\sum_{i=1}^n (x_i - \bar{x})^2}{n}}$$	**=STDEVP(range)**	Chapter 12, equation (12.3)
s^2	Unbiased estimate of population variance based on a set of sample data.	$$s^2 = \frac{\sum_{i=1}^n (x_i - \bar{x})^2}{n-1}$$	**=VAR(range)**	Chapter 12, equation (12.7)
s	Unbiased estimate of population standard deviation based on a set of sample data.	$$s = \sqrt{\frac{\sum_{i=1}^n (x_i - \bar{x})^2}{n-1}}$$	**=STDEV(range)**	Chapter 12, equation (12.4)

Symbol	Description	Formula / Excel	Reference
σ^2	Greek lower-case letter sigma: the variance of a population trait, a parameter.	=VARP(range)	Chapter 12, equation (12.5)
σ	Standard deviation of a population trait.	=STDEVP(range)	Chapter 12, equation (12.2)
$\sigma_{\bar{x}}$	Standard error of the mean for a sampling distribution where the population standard deviation, σ, is known.	$\sigma_{\bar{x}} = \dfrac{\sigma}{\sqrt{n}}$	Chapter 13, equation (13.2)
$s^2_{between}$	Estimate of population variance based upon the variance of the sample means (also $MS_{between}$). $s^2_{treatment}$ = variance attributable to treatment effects. $s^2_{ind\,diff}$ = variance attributable to individual differences. s^2_{error} = variance attributable to measurement error. $\bar{X}$ = grand mean.	$s^2_{within} = s^2_{treatment} + s^2_{ind\,diff} + s^2_{error}$ $$s^2_{between} = \frac{\sum_{j=1}^{k} n_j(\bar{x}_j - \bar{X})^2}{k - 1} \quad \text{(unequal } n)$$	Figure 16.5 (worksheet for one-way ANOVA, unequal n) Chapter 16, equation (16.12) Chapter 16, equation (16.6)
s^2_{within}	Estimate of population variance based upon the average of all the sample variances (also MS_{within}).	$s^2_{within} = s^2_{ind\,diff} + s^2_{error}$ $$s^2_{within} = \frac{\sum_{j=1}^{k} n_j s^2_j}{\sum_{j=1}^{k} n_j} \quad \text{(unequal } n)$$	Figure 16.5 (worksheet for one-way ANOVA, unequal n) Chapter 16, equation (16.10) Chapter 16, equation (16.9)
S^2_x	Observed score variance, the variance in the set of scores. S^2_t = true score variance. S^2_e = error variance.	$S^2_x = S^2_t + S^2_e$	Chapter 11, equation (11.2)
s_{diff}	Standard error of the difference, denominator in t-statistic, for small samples instead of standard error of mean. Which depends on nature of sample: (a) Unpooled variance, for samples of 30 or more. (b) Pooled variance, for samples less than 30.	(a) $s_{diff\,unpooled} = \sqrt{\dfrac{s^2_A}{n_A} + \dfrac{s^2_B}{n_B}}$ (b) $s_{diff\,pooled} = \sqrt{\dfrac{(n_A - 1)s^2_A + (n_B - 1)s^2_B}{n_A + n_B}\left(\dfrac{1}{n_A} + \dfrac{1}{n_B}\right)}$	Chapter 15, equation (15.6) Chapter 15, equation (15.13)

Symbol	Definition, description	Representative mathematical equation or graphical illustration or Table	Excel function/ equation/ worksheet	Discussion and explanation
s_{diff} *continued*	(c) For related/matched samples where s_D is the standard deviation of the differences.	(c) $s_{D_{\text{diff}}} = \dfrac{s_D}{\sqrt{n}}$		Chapter 15, equation (15.16)
$s_{\bar{x}}$	Standard error of the mean: standard deviation of distribution of sampling means, based upon sample group or data (see z-test).	$s_{\bar{x}} = \dfrac{s_A}{\sqrt{n_A}}$		Chapter 5, equations (5.1) and (5.2) and Chapter 13, equations (13.2) and (13.4)
t	Student t-statistic for testing differences between means of two groups. Three possible variations on this equation, depending on conditions (see s_{diff} above for the variations).	$t = \dfrac{\bar{x}_1 - \bar{x}_2}{s_{\text{diff}}}$ Figure 15.14 provides a decision chart.	Figure 15.10 (worksheet for carrying out the four t-tests)	Chapter 15, equation (15.4)
t_{crit}	Critical value for t-test, based upon degrees of freedom, $df = n_A + n_B - 2$, where n_A and n_B are sample sizes, and α the critical level.	Figure 15.4 and 15.5, t-distributions dependent on df See Appendix B, Table B.2, for critical values.	$=$**TINV(alpha, *df*)**	Chapter 15
t_D	Critical adjusted t for Dunnett's post hoc test between groups and a control.			Appendix B, Table B.8
t_r	Test for significance of a Pearson's product moment correlation coefficient.	$t_r = \dfrac{r_{xy}\sqrt{n-2}}{\sqrt{1-r_{xy}^2}}$	Figure 21.3 (worksheet for testing significance of r_{xy})	Chapter 21, equation (21.9)
ϕ	Greek letter phi: association between nominal variables. $n =$ total sample size.	$\phi = \sqrt{\dfrac{\chi^2}{n}}$	Figure 21.8 (worksheet for coefficient ϕ)	Chapter 21, equation (21.19)
χ^2	Chi-square test, two groups or one group and population, m categories:	$\chi^2 = \displaystyle\sum_{i=1}^{m} \dfrac{(O_i - E_i)^2}{E_i}$	$=$**CHIDIST(value, *df*)** (to check the significance of the χ^2 statistic)	Chapter 19, equation (19.5)

Symbol	Definition	Equation	Reference
χ^2 *continued*	O_i = frequency of occurrence observed E_i = frequency of occurrence expected i = number of category, 1 to m.		=**CHITEST(obs_range, exp_range)** (to check the significance for a set of observed and expected scores, but does *not* provide χ^2-ratio) Figure 19.5 (worksheet for χ^2)	Chapter 20, equation (20.1)
χ^2	Chi-square test, three or more (k) groups, m categories: O_{ij} = frequency of occurrence observed E_{ij} = frequency of occurrence expected i = number of category, 1 to m j = number of group, 1 to k.	$$\chi^2 = \sum_{i=1}^{m}\sum_{j=1}^{k}\frac{(O_{ij}-E_{ij})^2}{E_{ij}}$$	=**CHIDIST(value, df)** (to check the significance of the χ^2 statistic) =**CHITEST(obs_range, exp_range)** (to check the significance for a set of observed and expected scores, but does not provide χ^2-ratio) Figure 20.1 (worksheet for χ^2)	
$\chi^2(df,\alpha)$	Critical value for chi-square test, where: df = degrees of freedom $= m-1$ (two groups, m categories) $= (m-1)(k-1)$ (k groups) α = critical level.	Figure 19.4 Examples of χ^2-distributions.	=**CHIINV(df, alpha)**	Chapters 19 and 20 See Appendix B, Table B.9, for critical values.
x_i	Individual measurement for each member of a sample.			
$\bar{x}$	Sample mean for a trait or measurement, a statistic.	$$\bar{x} = \frac{\sum_{i=1}^{n}x_i}{n}$$	=**AVERAGE (range)**	Chapter 12, equation (12.1)
$\bar{X}$	Grand mean, mean of all data in ANOVA designs.	$$\bar{X} = \frac{\sum_{j=1}^{k}\sum_{i=1}^{n_j}x_{ij}}{\sum_{j=1}^{k}n_j}$$		Chapter 16
z	z-score, tells how many standard deviations, S, from the mean an individual score is.	$$z = \frac{x_i - \bar{x}}{S}$$		Chapter 13, equation (13.1)

Symbol	Definition, description	Representative mathematical equation or graphical illustration or Table	Excel function/ equation/ worksheet	Discussion and explanation
z	z-test to determine how many standard deviations (standard error of the mean, $\sigma_{\bar{x}}$ or $s_{\bar{x}}$) from the population mean a sample mean is. Significance is tested against a z-distribution, unless $n < 30$, when a t-distribution is used. $df = n - 1$	$z = \dfrac{\bar{x} - \mu}{\sigma_{\bar{x}}}$		Chapter 13, equation (13.3)

BIBLIOGRAPHY

Anastasi, A. (1990) *Psychological Testing* (6th edn). New York: Macmillan.

Andersen, H.A. and Koutnik, P.G. (1972) *Toward More Effective Science Instruction in Secondary Education*. New York: Macmillan.

Anderson, D.R., Sweeney, D.J. and Williams, T.A. (1993) *Statistics for Business and Economics*. St Paul, MN: West Publishing.

Atkinson, R.L., Atkinson, R.C., Smith, E.E., Bem, D.J. and Hilgard, E.R. (1990) *Introduction to Psychology* (10th edn). San Diego, CA: Harcourt Brace Jovanovich.

Berk, R.A. (1978) A consumers' guide to criterion-referenced test item statistics. *NCME: Measurement in Education*, 9, 1.

Black, T.R. (1987) A discrimination index for criterion-referenced test items, *British Journal of Educational Psychology*, 57: 380–8.

Black, T.R. (1993) *Evaluating Social Science Research: An Introduction*. London: Sage.

Black, T.R. (1997a) Calculating power of chi square tests. Internal paper, University of Surrey.

Black, T.R. (1997b) Calculating power of *F*-tests. Internal paper, University of Surrey.

Black, T.R., Atwaru-Okello, D., Kiwanuka, J., Serwadda, D., Birabi, O., Malinga, F., Biumigishu, A. and Rodd, A. (1998) Science Education in Uganda: Progress and possibilities. *International Journal of Science Education*, 20(2): 239–52.

Blalock, H.M. (ed.) (1975) *Measurement in the Social Sciences: Theories and Strategies*. London: Macmillan.

Blalock, H.M. (1979) *Social Statistics* (rev. 2nd edn). Tokyo: McGraw-Hill International Student Edition.

Bloom, B.S. (ed.) (1956) *Taxonomy of Educational Objectives: The Classification of Educational Goals. Handbook I: Cognitive Domain*. New York: David McKay.

Blum, M.L. and Foos, P.W. (1986) *Data Gathering: Experimental Methods Plus*. New York: Harper & Row.

Bourner, T. and Hamed, M. (1987) *Entry qualifications and degree performance*. London: Council for National Academic Awards.

Breakwell, G.M., Hammond, S. and Fife-Schaw, C. (eds) (1995) *Research Methods in Psychology*. London: Sage.

Brewer, M.B. and Collins, B.E. (eds) (1981) *Scientific Enquiry and the Social Sciences*. San Francisco: Jossey-Bass.

British Psychological Society (1993) Ethical principles for conducting research with human participants, in C. Robson, *Real World Research: A Resource for Social Scientists and Practitioner-Researchers*. Oxford: Blackwell.

Bynner, J. and Stribley, K.M. (eds) (1979) *Social Research: Principles and Practices*. London: Longman Group.

Callender, J.T. and Jackson, R. (1995) *Exploring Probability and Statistics with Spreadsheets*. London: Prentice Hall.

Campbell, D.T. and Stanley, J.C. (1963) Experimental and quasi-experimental designs for research on teaching, in N.L. Gage (ed.), *Handbook of Research on Teaching*. Chicago: Rand McNally. Also published in 1966 as a separate book, *Experimental and Quasi-Experimental Designs for Research*. Chicago: Rand McNally.

Canter, D. (1994) *Criminal Shadows: Inside the Mind of the Serial Killer*. London: HarperCollins.

Carley, M. (1981) *Social Measures and Social Indicators*. London: George Allen & Unwin.

Carlisle, E. (1972) The conceptual structure of social indicators, in A. Shonfield and S. Shaw (eds), *Social Indicators and Social Policy*. London: Heinemann.

Cazes, B. (1972) The development of social indicators: a survey, in A. Shonfield and S. Shaw (eds), *Social Indicators and Social Policy*. London: Heinemann.

Chase, C.I. (1985) *Elementary Statistical Procedures* (3rd edn). New York: McGraw-Hill.

Chopin, B. (1972) *After A-Level? A Study of the Transition from School to Higher Education*. Slough: National Foundation for Educational Research.

Cohen, J. (1988) *Statistical Power Analysis for the Behavioral Sciences* (2nd edn). Hillsdale, NJ: Lawrence Erlbaum.

Cohen, L. and Manion, L. (1989) *Research Methods in Education* (3rd edn). London: Routledge.

Coolican, H. (1994) *Research Methods and Statistics in Psychology* (2nd edn). London: Hodder and Stoughton.

Cook, T.D. and Campbell, D.T. (1979) *Quasi-Experimentation: Design and Analysis Issues for Field Settings*. Boston: Houghton Mifflin.

Cook, T.D., Campbell, D.T. and Peracchio, L. (1990) Quasi experimentation, in M.D. Dunnette and L.M. Hough (eds), *Handbook of Industrial and Organizational Psychology: Volume 1* (2nd edn). Palo Alto, CA: Consulting Psychologists Press.

Crick, F. (1994) *The Astonishing Hypothesis*. London: Simon and Schuster.

Crocker, L. and Algina, J. (1986) *Introduction to Classical and Modern Test Theory*. New York: Holt, Rinehart and Winston.

Cronbach, L.J. (1990) *Essentials of Psychological Testing*. (5th edn). New York: Harper Row.

Cureton, E.E. (1957) The upper and lower twenty-seven percent rule. *Psychometrika*, 22: 293–6.

Daly, F., Hand, D.J., Jones, M.C., Lunn, A.D. and McConway, K.J. (1995) *Elements of Statistics*. Wokingham: Addison-Wesley.

Davis, J.A. (1985) *The Logic of Causal Order*. London: Sage.

Dixon, B.R., Bouma, G.D. and Atkinson, G.B.J. (1987) *A Handbook of Social Science Research*. Oxford: Oxford University Press.

Duncan, D.B. (1955) Multiple range and multiple *F* tests. *Biometrics*, 11: 1–42.

Dunnett, C.W. (1955) A multiple comparison procedure for comparing several treatments with a control. *Journal of the American Statistical Association*, 50: 1096–121.

Ebel, R.L. (1979) *Essentials of Educational Measurement* (3rd edn). Englewood Cliffs, NJ: Prentice Hall.

Edwards, A.L. (1972) *Experimental Design in Psychological Research* (4th edn). New York: Holt, Rinehart and Winston.

Everitt, B.S. (1977) *The Analysis of Contingency Tables*. London: Chapman & Hall.

Ferguson, G.A. (1976) *Statistical Analysis in Psychology and Education* (4th edn). New York: McGraw-Hill.

Fisher, R.A. (1966) *The Design of Experiments* (8th edn). Edinburgh: Oliver & Boyd.

Fitz-Gibbon, C.T. (ed.) (1990) *Performance Indicators*. Clevedon, Avon: Multilingual Matters.

Fowler, F.J. (1993) *Survey Research Methods* (2nd edn). London: Sage.

Frankfort-Nachmias, C. and Nachmias, D. (1992) *Research Methods in the Social Sciences* (4th edn). London: Edward Arnold.

Fuller, M. (1984) Black girls in a London comprehensive school, in M. Hammersley and P. Woods (eds), *Life in School: the Sociology of Pupil Culture*. Milton Keynes: Open University Press.

Gagné, R.M. (1985) *The Conditions of Learning* (4th edn). New York: Holt, Rinehart and Winston.

Gagné, R.M., Briggs, L.J. and Wager, W.W. (1992) *Principles of Instructional Design* (4th edn). Fort Worth, TX: Harcourt Brace Jovanovich.

Gardner, P. (1975) Scales and statistics, *Review of Educational Research*, 45: 43–57.

Gibbons, J.D. and Chakraborti, S. (1992) *Nonparametric Statistical Inference*. (3rd edn) Marcel Dekker.

Gilbert, N. (1993) Research, theory and method, in N. Gilbert (ed.), *Researching Social Life*. London: Sage.

Glass, G.V. and Hopkins, K.D. (1996) *Statistical Methods in Education and Psychology* (3rd edn). Boston: Allyn and Bacon.

Grimm, L.G. (1993) *Statistical Applications for the Behavioral Sciences*. New York: Wiley.

Gronlund, N.E. (1970) *Stating Behavioral Objectives for Classroom Instruction*. New York: Macmillan.

Guilford, J.P. (1956) The structure of the intellect, *Psychological Bulletin,* 53: 267–93.

Guilford, J.P. and Fruchter, B. (1973) *Fundamental Statistics in Psychology and Education* (5th edn). Tokyo: McGraw-Hill Kogakusha.

Guilford, J.P. and Fruchter, B. (1981) *Fundamental Statistics in Psychology and Education* (6th edn). Tokyo: McGraw-Hill Kogakusha.

Hair, J.F., Anderson, R.E., Tatham, R.L. and Black, W.C. (1992) *Multivariate Data Analysis* (3rd edn). New York: Macmillan.

Haralambos, M. and Holborn, M. (1991) *Sociology: Themes and Perspectives* (3rd edn). London: Collins Educational.

Haviland, M.G. (1990) Yates' correction for continuity and the analysis of 2×2 contingency tables. *Statistics in Medicine*, 9: 363–7.

Hays, W.L. (1994) *Statistics* (5th edn). Fort Worth, TX: Harcourt Brace College.

Hedrick, T.E., Bickman, L. and Rog, D.J. (1993) *Applied Research Design: A Practical Guide*. London: Sage.

Hempel, C.G. (1966) *Philosophy of Natural Science*. Englewood Cliffs, NJ: Prentice Hall.

Horn, R.V. (1993) *Statistical Indicators for the Economic and Social Sciences*. Cambridge: Cambridge University Press.

Hornsby-Smith, M. (1993) Gaining access, in N. Gilbert (ed.), *Researching Social Life*. London: Sage.

Howell, D.C. (1997) *Statistical Methods for Psychology* (4th edn). Belmont, CA: Duxbury Press.

Huff, D. (1954) *How to Lie with Statistics*. Penguin.

Huitema, B.E. (1980) *The Analysis of Covariance and Alternatives*. New York: Wiley.

Jaeger, R.M. (1984) *Sampling in Education and the Social Sciences*. New York: Longmans.

Jolliffe, F.R. (1986) *Survey Design and Analysis*. Chichester: Ellis Horwood.

Kalton, G. (1983) *Survey Methods in Social Investigations* (2nd edn). New York: Basic Books.

Katz, J., Aspden, P. and Reich, W.A. (1997) Public attitudes towards voice-based messaging technologies in the United States: A national survey of opinions about voice response units and telephone answering machines. *Behaviour & Information Technology*, 16(3): 125–44.

Kaufman, R. and Thiagarajan, S. (1987) Identifying and specifying requirements for instruction, in R.M. Gagné (ed.), *Instructional Technology: Foundations*. Hillsdale, NJ: Lawrence Erlbaum Associates.

Keppel, G. (1973) *Design and Analysis: A Researcher's Handbook*. Englewood Cliffs, NJ: Prentice Hall.

Kerlinger, F.N. (1973) *Foundations of Behavioral Research* (2nd edn). London: Holt, Rinehart and Winston.

Kerlinger, F.N. (1986) *Foundations of Behavioral Research* (3rd edn). Fort Worth, TX: Holt, Rinehart and Winston International Edition.

Kibler, R.J., Barker, L.L. and Miles, D.T. (1970) *Behavioral Objectives and Instruction*. Boston: Allyn and Bacon.

Kish, L. (1965) *Survey Sampling*. New York: Wiley.

Kline, P. (1991) *Intelligence: The Psychometric View*. London: Routledge.

Knapp, T.R. (1971) *Statistics for Educational Measurement*. Scranton, PA: Intext Educational Publishers.

Kraft, C.H. and van Eeden, C. (1968) *A Nonparametric Introduction to Statistics*. New York: Macmillan.

Krathwohl, D.R., Bloom, B.S. and Masia, B.B. (1964) *Taxonomy of Educational Objectives: The Classification of Educational Goals. Handbook II: Affective Domain*. New York: David McKay.

Lehmann, I.J. and Mehrens, W.A. (1984) *Educational Research: Readings in Focus*. New York: Holt, Rinehart and Winston.

Levine, R.A. (1966) *Dreams and Deeds: Achievement Motivation in Nigeria*. Chicago: University of Chicago Press.

Lipsey, M.V. (1990) *Design Sensitivity: Statistical Power for Experimental Research*. Newbury Park, CA: Sage.

Livingston, S.A. (1972) Criterion-referenced applications of classical test theory, *Journal of Educational Measurement*, 9(1): 13–26.

Mager, R.F. (1962) *Preparing Instructional Objectives*. Belmont, CA: Fearon.

McBurney, D.H. (1994) *Research Methods*. Pacific Grove, CA: Brooks/Cole.

McCain, L.J. and McCleary, R. (1979) The statistical analysis of the simple interrupted time-series quasi-experiment, in T.D. Cook and D.T. Campbell (eds), *Quasi-Experimentation: Design and Analysis Issues for Field Settings*. Boston: Houghton Mifflin.

McKennell, A. (1979) Attitude measurement: Use of coefficient alpha with cluster or factor analysis, in J. Bynner and K.M. Stribley (eds), *Social Research: Principles and Procedures*. London: Longmans Group.

Mehrens, W.A. and Lehmann, I.J. (1984) *Measurement and Evaluation in Education and Psychology* (3rd edn). New York: Holt, Rinehart and Winston.

Ministry of Education and Sports (1994a) *Draft Educational Statistical Abstracts: 1993*. Kampala: Planning Unit, Statistics Division.

Ministry of Education and Sports (1994b) *Statistical Abstract 1989–1992 (Secondary Schools)*. Kampala: Planning Unit, Statistics Division.

Minium, E.W., King, B.M. and Bear, G. (1993) *Statistical Reasoning in Psychology and Education* (3rd edn). New York: Wiley.

Mitchell, M. and Jolley, J. (1988) *Research Design Explained*. New York: Holt, Rinehart and Winston.

Montgomery, D.C. (1991) *Design and Analysis of Experiments* (3rd edn). New York: John Wiley.

Moore, D.S. (1991) *Statistics: Concepts and Controversies* (3rd edn). New York: W.H. Freeman.

Muijs, R.D. (1997) Predictors of academic achievement and academic self-concept: A longitudinal perspective. *British Journal of Educational Psychology*, 67: 263–77.

Murphy, R.J.L. (1981) O-level grades and teachers' estimates as predictors of the A-level results of UCCA applicants, *British Journal of Educational Psychology*, 51: 1–9.

Murphy, K.R. and Davidshofer, C.O. (1991) *Psychological Testing: Principles and Applications* (2nd edn). Englewood Cliffs, NJ: Prentice Hall.

Novak, J.D. and Gowin, D.B. (1984) *Learning How to Learn*. Cambridge: Cambridge University Press.

Nunnally, J. and Bernstein, I.H. (1994) *Psychometric Theory* (3rd edn). New York: McGraw-Hill.

Oppenheim, A.N. (1992) *Questionnaire Design, Interviewing and Attitude Measurement* (2nd edn). London: Pinter.

Patnaik, P.B. (1949) The non-central χ^2- and F-distributions and their applications. *Biometrika*, 36: 202–32.

Pearson, E.S. and Hartley, H.O. (1970) *Biometrika Tables for Statisticians: Volume I*. Cambridge: Cambridge University Press.

Polit, D.F. and Hungler, B.P. (1991) *Nursing Research: Principles and Methods* (4th edn). Philadelphia: J.B. Lippincott.

Popham, W.J. (1973) *The Uses of Instructional Objectives*. Belmont, CA: Fearon.

Popper, K.R. (1972) *The Logic of Scientific Discovery* (3rd edn). London: Hutchinson.

Reichardt, C.S. (1979) The statistical analysis of data from nonequivalent group designs, in T.D. Cook and D.T. Campbell (eds), *Quasi-Experimentation: Design and Analysis Issues for Field Settings.* Boston: Houghton Mifflin.

Robson, C. (1993) *Real World Research: A Resource for Social Scientists and Practitioner-Researchers.* Oxford: Blackwell.

Rose, S. (1993) No way to treat the mind, *New Scientist*, no. 1869 (17 April).

Rosenthal, R. and Jacobson, L. (1968) *Pygmalion in the Classroom.* New York: Holt, Rinehart and Winston.

Rowntree, D. (1981) *Statistics without Tears.* London: Penguin.

Sear, K. (1983) The correlation between A level grades and degree results in England and Wales, *Higher Education*, 12: 609–19.

Shonfield, A. and Shaw, S. (1972) *Social Indicators and Social Policy.* London: Heinemann.

Siegel, S. and Castellan, N.J. (1988) *Nonparametric Statistics for the Behavioral Sciences* (2nd edn). New York: McGraw-Hill.

Singer, H. and Donlan, D. (1980) *Reading and Learning from Text.* Boston: Little Brown.

Sirkin, R.M. (1995) *Statistics for the Social Sciences.* Thousand Oaks, CA: Sage.

Solomon, R.L. (1949) An extension of control group design. *Psychological Bulletin*, 46: 137–50.

Southern Examining Group (1988) *GCSE Science (Single Certification) and Science (Double Certification): 1990 Examination.* Guildford: Southern Examining Group.

Thorndike, R.L. and Hagen, E.P. (1977) *Measurement and Evaluation in Psychology and Education* (4th edn). New York: Wiley.

Traub, R.E. (1994) *Reliability for the Social Sciences: Theory and Applications.* London: Sage.

Vargas, J.S. (1972) *Writing Worthwhile Behavioral Objectives.* New York: Harper & Row.

Weick, K.E. (1985) Systematic observational methods, in G. Lindsay and E. Aronson (eds), *The Handbook of Social Psychology.* New York: Random House.

Welkowitz, J., Ewen, R.B. and Cohen, J. (1991) *Introductory Statistics for the Behavioral Sciences* (4th edn). New York: Academic Press.

Wiersma, W. and Jurs, S.G. (1990) *Educational Measurement and Testing* (2nd edn). Boston: Allyn and Bacon.

Winer, B.J., Brown, D.R. and Michels, K.M. (1991) *Statistical Principles in Experimental Design* (3rd edn). New York: McGraw-Hill.

Wright, D.B. (1997) *Understanding Statistics: An Introduction for the Social Sciences.* London: Sage.

INDEX

a posteriori contrasts, 466–473
a priori contrasts, 464–466
  Dunn's test, 465–466
achievement tests, 242–271
adjusted R^2, 678, 686
alpha (α)
  Cronbach's, 279–281, 286–290
  level of significance and choice of, 362–400
  and Type I error, 380–400
analysis of covariance (ANCOVA), 519–520, 527–532
  assumptions, 531
  SPSS example, 529–530
analysis of variance (ANOVA)
  application example, 99–102
  assumptions, 449
  degrees of freedom, 445, 452–453
  F ratio, 451–453
  factorial, 497–503
    worksheet, 504, 508
  heterogeneity of variance, 458–463
  influences of sources of invalidity, 454–457
  one-way, 441–483
    worksheet, 479, 483
  paired comparisons *see* planned comparisons *and* post hoc analysis
  partitioning variances, 454, 456–457, 499, 520–521
  power, 473–482
    worksheet, 478–479
  randomised block, 520–527
    worksheet, 524
  unequal cell sizes, 451–454
apparent limits, 313
association, 627
attitude measurement, 215–241

Barlett's test for homogeneity of variance, 458–460
beta (β)
  regression coefficient, 675
  and Type II error, 382–400

between subjects variance, 444, 451
Bloom's taxonomy, 246–248, 251–256
Bonferroni t test *see* Dunn's test

case studies, 47–48
categorical variables, 550
causality, 7, 12–16, 19, 35, 39–44, 102, 141–142, 168–169
ceiling effect, 534–535
central distribution, 382–393, 473–476
central tendency, 329–330
  mean, 330
  median, 330
  mode, 330
charts *see* graphs
checklists, 235–236
chi-square
  application examples, 83–86, 131–132
  assumptions, 558, 577–578
  Cramér's C and, 645–646
  degrees of freedom, 556, 577, 586
  distribution, 556–557
  goodness of fit, 551–564
    example, 131–132
    worksheet, 558, 564
  phi (ϕ) coefficient and, 649–650
  power, 560–564, 579–581, 586
  small expected frequencies, 558, 578, 580
  three or more samples, m × k tables, 585–591
    worksheet, 586
  two-samples, k × 2 tables, 576–581
    worksheet, 578, 581
  z and link with, 551–555
cleaning data, 199
Cochran Q test, 602–604
coding responses
  errors, 199
  frame, 199, 234
cognitive domain, 245–249

common knowledge, 4–6
concepts, 35–38
confidence intervals, 129–130, 363–364, 636–638, 667
confounding *see also* invalidity
 sources of, 72–78, 141–148, 456–457
 variables, 61–63
consistency
 internal (reliability), 195–199
 logical (designs) *see* validity, internal
constructs, 35–38, 219–222
contingency tables, 644–648
control
 extraneous variables, 25, 44, 60–63
 group in experimental designs, 44
 in ex post facto designs *see* sampling
correlation and association, 625–627
 coefficients
  adjusted Pearson, 630
  Cramér's *C*, 644–648
  Kendall's *tau*, 641
  Pearson product moment, 627–638
  phi, 649–650
  point biserial, 650–652
  Spearman's *rho*, 639–642
  squared, 632–633, 678
 confidence intervals, 636–638
 designs, 42–42, 46, 71–72, 169–171, 621–623
 examples of, 102–105
 interpretation of, 54, 618–627, 681
 misleading results, 652–655
 multiple, 678–679, 681–686
 non-linear, 692–693
 part, 681–683
 partial, 684–685
 scatter diagrams, 623, 653, 655
 shared variance, 632–633
 significance of
  academic, 632–633
  power, 635–636
  statistical, 633–635
covariance
 analysis of, 519–520, 527–532
 matrix, 525–527
Cramér's *C*, 644–648
Cronbach's alpha, 279–281, 286–290
criterion-referenced tests, 291–296

data
 collection problems, 213–214
 interval, 52–54, 188–190, 305, 312–317, 343–353
 nominal, 52–54, 189, 305, 317–321, 341–342
 ordinal, 52–54, 189, 305, 307–312, 342–343
 ratio, 52–54, 189, 305, 312–317, 343–353
decision support, 2, 696
deduction, 8–9
definition, operational, 24–25, 35–41, 45
degrees of freedom *see specific tests*
dependent variable, 32, 37, 39–44

descriptive statistics
 central tendency, 329–331
 graphical, 304–330
  implementing on a spreadsheet, 307–330
 variability, 330–335
designs
 correlational, 42–43, 46, 64, 71–72, 102–105, 618–658
 ex post facto, 47–48, 64, 69–71, 99–102, 165–167, 541
 experimental, 64, 68–69
  pre- and post- tests, 69, 71, 87–90, 155–158, 535–539
  post-test only, 69, 71, 90–92, 160–162
 interrelated groups, 420–424, 516–518, 527–528, 552, 595–608
 matched sample, 516–517
 multivariate, 179, 182–183
 normative, 46, 54, 126–132
 notation defined, 65
 pre-experimental, 64–68
  one-sample group, 67–68, 78–83, 148–152
  two available groups, 68, 83–86, 152–153
 quasi-experimental, 47, 64, 69–71, 95–99, 164–167, 539–540
 randomized block, 518–527
 repeated treatments and measures, 517–518, 523–527
 Solomon four design, 173–175, 544–546
 time series, 173–178, 518, 541–542
dice, probabilities for, 341–347
difficulty index, 284–285
discrimination indices
 criterion-referenced, 292–295
 item-total correlation, 280–281, 287
 norm-referenced, 282–285, 293–295
distribution shapes
 bi-modal, 331
 normal, 354–355
 sampling means, 357–361
 skewed, 331, 366–371
distributions, sampling
 chi square, 556–557
 Fisher's *F*, 446–449
 normal (*z*), 357–361
 Student's *t*, 407–412
Duncan's test, 467
 tables, Appendix B.7
Dunnett's test, 468–470
Dunn's test, 465–466
 tables, Appendix B.5

effect size
 for ANOVA, 475
 for *t*-test, 413
 for *z*-test, 394–395
empirical approaches, 3–6
errors
 measurement, 196, 273–274
 non-sampling, 132

errors (*cont.*)
    sampling, 126–132
    Type I, 380–400
    Type II, 380–400
ethical issues, 137–138
experimental designs
    two groups, post-test only, 64, 66, 90–93
    two groups, pre- and post-test, 64, 66, 87–90, 93
    Solomon four, 173–175, 544–546
    time series with control group
ex post facto design
    post-test only, 47–48, 69–71, 99–102, 167–169, 541
extraneous variables
    control of, 25, 44, 60–63, 75, 116–123, 201
    sources of, 72–78, 141–148

factor analysis, 220
factorial designs, 484–512
    advantages of, 487
    analysis of variance, 497–513
    interactions, 488–496
    worksheet, 504, 508, 511
F-distribution, 446–449
free response questions, 202, 233–234, 265–270
Friedman two-way ANOVA (ranks), 604–608
frequency
    polygon, 316–317, 321–324
    tables, 307–326
F-test *see* analysis of variance

gain scores, 69, 532–534
generalise, desirability, 49–51
graphs
    bar chart, 307–310
    frequency polygon, 316–317, 321–324
    histograms, 312–316, 321–330
    pie charts, 311–312
    regression lines (trendlines), 664–665, 692–693
    scatter diagram, 43, 623, 653, 655
    smoothed frequency polygon, 367

halo effect, 237
Hartley's test for homogeneity of variance, 458
    tables, Appendix B.4
Hawthorn effect, 143
homogeneity of variance, 371
    Bartlett's test (for ANOVA), 458–459
    F-test (for *t*-tests), 419
    Hartley's test (for ANOVA), 458
homoscedasticity, 667
histogram, 312–316, 321–330
hypotheses
    criteria, 51
    development of, 19–20, 24–25, 34, 45–51
    null, 53–56
    testing of, 5, 25
    transforming into a design, 60–68

independent variables, 39–42
indicators, social, 207–212
induction, 8
inferences, 17, 24, 33–37, 53
inferential statistics, 48, 355–361
interactions, 62, 114–115, 488–513
interest scales, 240
inter-rater (scorer) reliability, 289–290
interrelated samples, 420–424, 516–518, 527–528, 552, 595–608
interval data, 52–54, 189, 305, 312–317, 343–353
intervening variables, 16, 34, 38–42, 104
interview schedules
    design, 238–239
    quantifying results, 238–240
intra-scorer reliability, 291
invalidity, sources of, 72–78, 141–148, 457
    causality, uncertainty of direction, 141–142
    Hawthorn effect, 143
    instrument reliability, 144–145
    instrument validity, 143–144
    interactions between sources, 77, 146–147
    learning from instrument, 145–146
    measurement, 143–147
    regression to the mean, 76
    sampling, 75–77
    time, 74–75, 77
    unnatural experiment/treatment, 142–143
item analysis, 272–302
item–total correlation, 280–281, 287

Kolmogorov-Smirnov, 565–570
    application example, 97–99
Kruskal-Wallis one-way ANOVA, 590–595
Kuder-Richardson reliability coefficients
    KR 20, 282–286
    KR 21, 286

latent variables, 13, 40
Likert scales, 227–230
limits, apparent and real, 313

macrovariables, 13–16, 19, 34, 40, 64, 102, 104, 141
main effects, 486
Mann-Whitney *U*-test, 570
matching questions, 261
maturation, 74–75
McNemar change test, 596–598
mean, 330
    distribution of sampling means, 126–130
measurement
    error, 196, 273–274
    levels, 52–54, 307–317
    operational definition, 24–25, 35–41, 45
median, 330, 590
microvariables, 13–15, 40, 141
mode, 330
molar level, 13–14

multiple choice items, 262–263
multiple comparisons *see* planned comparisons *and*
    post hoc analysis
multivariate designs *see also* factorial designs, 115,
    179–183
multiple regression, 670–686
multiple *t*-tests, 464

Newmann-Keuls test, 467
    tables, Appendix B.6
nominal measures, 52–54, 189, 305, 307–310, 317–321,
    341–342
non-causal relationships, 15–16, 42–44, 618–621
non-central distribution, 382–393, 424–425, 473–476,
    561
non-centrality parameter (λ), 473–479, 561–563
non-empirical approaches, 4–5
normal distribution, 354–355
    table of areas under, Appendix B.1
normative research/tests, 46, 54
null hypotheses
    accepting versus failing to reject, 396
    stating, 53–56, 356
nuisance variables, 516

objective test questions, 257–265
objectives, behavioural/performance, 248–253
objectivity, 20, 198–199, 235–237, 257
observation schedules, 234–238
    piloting, 238
one-tailed tests, 394–396, 418
operational definitions, 24–25, 35–41, 45, 210, 239–240,
    245
ordinal level of measurement, 52–54, 189, 305,
    307–312, 342–343
outliers, 657

pairwise comparisons, 464–473, 588–591, 594–595,
    606–608
parameters, 48
part correlations, 681–683
partial correlations, 684–685
participation chart, 236–237
partitioning variance, 454, 456, 520–521
Pearson product moment correlation, 627–638
percentile group, 354–355
perceptions, 26, 36–37, 221, 237
performance objectives, 249–253
personality measures, 240–241
phi (f) coefficient, 649–650
planned comparisons (ANOVA), 465–466
    Bonferroni *t* (Dunn's), 465–466
    Dunnett's, 468–469
point biserial, 650–652
populations
    definition of, 111–116
    parameters, 48
    sampling frames for, 119

post hoc analysis
    ANOVA, 466–473
        Duncan, 467–468
        Newmann-Keuls, 467
        Tukey, 468
        Scheffé, 468
        worksheet, 474, 478–479
    chi square, 588–591
    Friedman, 606–608
    Kruskal-Wallis, 594–595
power *see also individual statistical tests*, 382–400
    enhancing, 393–395
    and reliability, 429–431
    and sample size, 388–392, 433–434, 480–483,
        579–581, 634–636
    worksheet, 389
pre- and post-test designs, 66–71
pre-experimental designs
    one sample post test only, 66–67, 78–81
    one sample pre- and post-test, 66–67, 82–83
    two-sample non-equivalent groups, 66, 68, 83–86
probability
    general, 339–355
    sampling, 117–123
    and statistical inference, 355–364
process skills, 22–26

quasi-experimental design
    non-equivalent groups, 47, 69–71, 92, 95–99,
        164–167, 539–540
    time series without control group
quantifying variables, 241
questionnaires
    design guidelines, 215–241
    enhancing response rate, 195, 201, 213–214
    as operational definitions, 37
questions
    closed, 202, 226–232
    criteria for wording of, 201–207
    factual, 200–201
    free response,
        open, 202, 233–234, 265–270
    Likert, 227–230
    matching, 261
    multiple choice, 262–264
    objective, 257–265
    rating, 226–227, 236–238
    research, 30–33, 40
    short answer, 260–261
    true-false, 262
    wording of, 201–207

random
    assignment, 63, 137
    numbers table, Appendix B.10
    sampling, 63, 116–123
randomized block design, 518–527
    worksheet, 524, 526

rank order, 565–575
rating scales, 226–227, 236–238
ratio data, 52–54
real limits, 313
reductionist view, 14, 21
regression
    assumptions, 659, 667–669
    confidence intervals, 686–689
    design, 659
    linear equations, 659–665
    non-linear, 692–693
    significance test, 688
    to the mean, 76
    trendlines, 664–665, 692–693
reliability, 144–145, 195–198, 272–302
    criterion-referenced tests, 291–292
    definition, 273–274
    equivalence, 195, 277
    inter-judge (-scorer), 195, 237, 268, 289–290
    internal consistency, 195, 197, 229–230, 235, 278–289
        Cronbach's alpha, 279–281, 286–290
        Kuder-Richardson, 282–286
        split-half, 195, 278–279, 286–289
    intra-judge (-scorer), 195, 268, 291
    stability, 195, 197
    test-retest, 275–277
repeated measures design, 523–527, 602–608
    worksheet, 524, 526, 603, 607–608
replication, 20, 398
research
    errors, 380–384
    process of designing, 20–22
    questions, 30–33, 40
    scientific, 19–25
    skills, 22–26
response (reply) rates, 132–136
response sets, 223–224

samples
    representativeness, 49–51
    size of, 136–137
        attrition, 76
        planning for optimal, 388–392, 433–434, 480–483, 579–581, 634–636
    test of representativeness of population, 46, 54, 126–132
sampling
    accidental, 125
    cluster, 121–122
    convenience, 125
    errors, 126–132
    frame, 119
    loss, 132–136
    means, distribution of, 126
    non-random (non-probability), 124–125
    overregistration, 120

purposive, 124
quota, 124
random, 116–123
simple random, 119–120
snowball, 125
stage, 122–123
stratified random, 120–121
underregistration, 120
volunteers, 125
with replacement, 120
scales
    interval, 52–54, 189, 305, 312–317, 343–353
    nominal, 52–54, 189, 305, 307–312, 317–321, 341–342
    ordinal, 52–54, 189, 305, 307–312, 342–343
    ratio, 52–54, 189, 305, 312–317, 343–353
scatter diagram, 43, 623, 653, 655
scientific approach, 19–22
scores
    gain, 69, 532–534
    observed, 76, 196
    true, 76, 196
significance
    academic versus statistical, 434
    statistical, 124–128, 362–400
skewness, 368–370, 571–572
slope of regression line, 660–661
social indicators, 207–212
Solomon four design, 171–173, 544–545
Spearman's *rho*, 639–642
spreadsheets, how to use, Appendix A
standard deviation
    from the mean, 332–335
    of distribution of sampling means, 126, 358–359
standard error
    of the difference, 404
    of the estimate, 666–667, 686–687
    of the mean, 126, 358–359
    of the measurement, 297–298
standardized measures, 217, 240–241
statistical inferences, 355–361
statistical power *see* power
statistical tests
    one-tailed, 394–396, 418
    two-tailed, 359–361
statistical vs academic significance, 632–635
Student's *t* distribution, 406–412
    table of critical values, Appendix B.2
studentized-range statistic, 467–468
    table of critical values, Appendix B.6
systematic planning, 5, 20–22
    questions to ask, 27–30

t-test, 402–440
    application examples (acceptable), 87–92
    application examples (weak), 82–83, 86

heterogeneity of variance, 419–420
interrelated/correlated groups, 420–424
large (> 30) and/or equal groups, 413–416
one group with population data, 362–363
power, 424–434
small (< 30) and/or unequal groups, 416–418
worksheet, 428
table of constructs (concept definition), 221–222, 230–233
table of specifications (achievement tests), 253–259
tests
    criterion-referenced, 391–396
    norm-referenced, 394–396
    standardized, 217, 240–241
theory building, 6–10, 16–18, 20–22
time sequence of events, 15
time series designs, 175–180, 518, 541–542
transformations
    arcsine, 459–460
    logarithmic, 461–462
    reciprocal, 461
    square root, 460, 462
trendlines, 664–665, 692–693
two-tailed tests, 359–361
Type I error and alpha (α), 380–400
Type II error and beta (β), 382–400

validity, instrument
    construct, 192, 194, 219–222, 298–300
    content, 193–194, 243–256, 300
    criterion-related, 192, 299–300
        concurrent, 192, 194, 222–223, 300
        predictive, 103, 193–194, 300
    face, 195, 225, 231–232
    general, 191–195, 222–224
validity, research design
    construct, 35–38, 99, 102, 105, 141–142, 219–222
    external, 49–51, 58, 75–77, 99, 102
    internal, 44–45, 57–58, 74–77, 99, 102
    statistical, 57–58, 76, 99, 102, 552

variability
    between groups, 444
    standard deviation, 334–335
    within groups, 445
variable maps, 62, 80, 83, 85, 89, 91, 95, 98, 101, 104, 149, 151, 153, 158, 161, 165, 166, 168, 485
variables
    classifying, 38–42, 54
    confounding, 61–63
    continuous, 52
    controlling, 25, 44, 60–63
    dependent, 32, 37, 39–44
    extraneous, 25, 44, 60–63, 75, 104
    independent, 39–42
    intervening, 16, 34, 38–42, 104
    measurable, 52–53
    nuisance, 518
    observed, 37, 54
    specifying, 33–44
    unanticipated, 61–63
variance, 332–333
    apportioned in regression, 681–686
    error, 196–197, 273–274, 297–299
    homogeneity/heterogeneity of, 371
    observed score, 196–197, 273–274, 297–299
    partitioning of (ANOVA), 454, 456–457, 498–499
    pooled, 416–418
    shared, 632–633, 669–670
    true score, 196–197, 273–274, 297–299
    unpooled, 404, 412–413
variation, explaining using correlations, 632–633, 669–670, 681

Wilcoxon-Mann-Whitney test, 570–575
Wilcoxon rank sum test, 570
Wilcoxon signed-rank test, 598–601

z-scores, 125
z-test, 125–127, 361–362, 378–380
    compared with χ^2, 563–564
    worksheet, 377

MACHINE

By Elizabeth Bear from Gollancz

White Space Novels
Ancestral Night
Machine

Jacob's Ladder Sequence
Pinion
Sanction
Cleave

Jenny Casey Series
Hammered
Scardown
Worldwired